W9-AGI-414

Table of Contents

Part I

The Art and Science of Investing in Stocks
Is This the Right Investment Book for You?

The last time I stopped by the investment section of my local bookstore, there was no shortage of books about investing in the stock market. Fortunately, several copies of the latest edition of *The 100 Best Stocks You Can Buy* were prominently displayed.

However, I saw only one lonely soul trying to find a book to his liking. I was tempted to suggest that mine was the best one on the shelf. But I refrained. I recalled that on my previous trip to the bookstore I had made a similar suggestion and was totally ignored. He didn't even look up to see who was offering him this sage advice. I was tempted to report the recalcitrant cad to the manager but thought better of it.

Since you have the book in your hands and are wondering whether this is the one for you, let me give you a song and dance that will convince you that your search has ended; you don't need to look any further.

To begin, let me congratulate you on making the decision to educate yourself on the intricacies of the stock market. Many people totally ignore the importance of saving money for the future. It could be that they believe their company 401(k), along with Social Security, will do the job. The odds are that you will need more, particularly if you work for a firm that insists your 401(k) should be stuffed with your employer's company stock.

If you want to build a solid portfolio, it makes better sense to buy stocks on a regular basis—at least once a year. I suggest setting aside at least 10 percent of your gross income every year for stock purchases. And don't skip a year because you don't like the antics of the stock market at that particular time. Forecasting the market is a no-no. You can't do it—nor can anyone else.

Why People Don't Read about Investing

One reason that people don't read about investing is because they are overwhelmed by the complexity of the financial scene. I heartily concur—it *is* overwhelming. That's because there are thousands of mutual funds, common stocks, preferred stocks, certificates of deposit, options, bonds, annuities, and assorted investment products.

Even if you simply confined your search to the stocks listed on the New York Stock Exchange, the task would be daunting, since some 3,000 stocks are traded there. Or you might decide to "Let George do it," by investing in mutual funds. There, too, you will encounter infinite decisions, since there are over 14,000 mutual funds—most of which underperform such market indexes as the Dow Jones Industrial Average (called the Dow, Dow Jones, or DJIA) or the Standard & Poor's 500 (S&P 500).

If you are like many buyers of my books, you are not a sophisticated investor. You have a good job, have an income that is well above average, and you are serious about your career. That means that you spend time improving yourself by reading trade journals and taking courses at a local college.

Why Not Burn the Midnight Oil?

In other words, your day is already taken up with reading. How can you possibly start poring over annual reports, Standard & Poor's reports, *Fortune*, *Value Line Investment Survey*, the *Wall Street Journal*, *Forbes*, *BusinessWeek*, *Barron's*, and a half-dozen books on the stock market? Easy. Drink lots of coffee and stay up until two in the morning.

If you object to this routine, you will be better off with my book, since I try to make investing a lot simpler than you thought it would be. For one thing, my style of writing is easy to understand. At least that's what people tell me.

Incidentally, I am one of the few authors who take calls from readers. My address and phone number are on page 343. I assume you will confine your calls to regular business hours, based on Eastern Time, since I live in Vermont.

Whenever I buy a book, I always check to see if the writer has good credentials. For my part, I have been on the investment scene for a good forty years. I started as a plain vanilla stockbroker, and then became editor of a publication devoted to mutual funds, followed by several years as a securities analyst for a brokerage firm. I spent a few years as a portfolio manager and started operating my own firm, managing portfolios on a fee basis for investors with assets of $100,000 or more.

During these years, I did a lot of writing, first for *Barron's Financial Weekly*, and later for such publications as *Physician's Management* and *Better Investing*. During the same period, I wrote tons of reports on stocks for the brokerage firms that paid my salary. In recent years, I have written nine books: *Safe Investing*, *Straight Talk About Stock Investing*, and seven editions of *The 100 Best Stocks You Can Buy*.

I also wrote two great novels, but no publisher seems to agree that they are great, so I am not currently getting royalties on them.

As I mentioned previously, the number of stocks and mutual funds out there is infinite. Besides the 3,000 stocks on the New York Stock Exchange, plus the thousands of mutual funds, there are also thousands of stocks listed on the NASDAQ and thousands more traded on markets in Europe, Asia, Latin America, and Canada.

The beauty of my book is that I whittle the number of stocks you need to know about down to 100. Among that 100 are four types of stocks, depending on your particular temperament. The types are stocks for Income, Growth and Income, Conservative Growth, and Aggressive Growth.

Diversification, the First Rule of Investing

Of course, there is no need to confine your investing exclusively to one category. A well-diversified portfolio could have half a dozen from each sector. Incidentally, diversity is the key to investing. Whenever you concentrate on one type of stock, such as technology, energy, banks, utilities, or pharmaceuticals, you expose yourself to extra risk. Don't do it. Let me emphasize that again—don't do it.

When I was a portfolio strategist in Cleveland a few years ago, I examined portfolios submitted to our firm for analysis. About 100 percent of them were not diversified. They were typically concentrated in only three industries: public utilities, banks, and oil.

Before you make up your mind which stocks to buy, you will want to collect some information. If you have access to a brokerage house, you can easily get a copy of a report prepared by *Value Line Investment Survey*. You can also subscribe yourself, but be prepared to spend over $500 a year for this service, which covers about 1,700 well-known stocks. A less-expensive alternative is the same service limited to 600 stocks. Still another good source is

Standard & Poor's tear sheets, which can be obtained from a broker or library. Finally, most brokerage houses have a staff of analysts that turns out reports on a multitude of stocks.

My Sources of Information

A final source of information is this book, which is updated every year. I believe that my write-ups are valuable in ways that the other sources are not. When I first began writing this series of books, I obtained my information from each company's annual report, as well as from the two services mentioned. Now, I go much further afield. On a daily basis, I collect information on these companies from such sources as *Barron's*, *Forbes*, *Better Investing*, *BusinessWeek*, and other monthly investment publications. In addition, I consult well-known newspapers across the country, including the *Boston Globe*, the *New York Times*, as well as papers in Chicago, Philadelphia, Atlanta, Denver, St. Louis, Houston, Milwaukee, Los Angeles, Detroit, San Francisco, Miami, and Dallas.

Whenever I see an article on one of my companies, I clip it out and file it for future reference and examine it again when I sit at my computer to prepare a report. Using this vast collection, I sift through the facts to find reasons why this stock is attractive. I also look for factors that have a negative tone. In other words, I don't want to give you a purely one-sided view of this stock. By contrast, if you read the company's annual report, you will only hear about the attributes of the company and not about its problems and deficiencies.

Similarly, if you read a report from a brokerage house, it is rarely negative. The analyst normally tells you to buy—rarely to sell. One reason for this is the tie brokerage houses have to these companies that can lead to underwriting and corporate finance deals that are extremely lucrative. If the analyst tells investors to avoid the stock, the company may decide to avoid the brokerage house and give its business to someone else.

Obviously, I have no reason to be anything but unbiased.

Forty Years of Experience Is the Key

Finally, the 100 stocks have to be selected. The publisher is not the one who picks the stocks. I do. My forty years of varied experience on the investment scene give me an edge in this regard. And, of course, I am intimately involved in stock selection from a personal perspective. I have a large portfolio of stocks, over fifty at present, which have made my wife and me millionaires.

If you would like to reach the same comfortable plateau, why not invest $14.95 and start reading?

Oh, and here's one more thing. If you read the rest of these introductory chapters, you will see that I have provided a helpful glossary that explains all the terms you will need to know to understand the fundamentals of investing.

I also have a chapter on asset allocation that will tell you what percentage of your holdings should be in stocks and how much in such fixed-income vehicles as bonds and money-market funds. Finally, there also are chapters on how I select my stocks, an intriguing way to reduce risk, the possible benefits of dollar cost averaging, and still another on how to analyze stocks. There is also a short chapter that focuses on the four essentials of successful investing. You'll be surprised at how simple investing can be if you read this chapter.

Why Invest in Stocks?

Investing is a complex business. But, then, so is medicine, engineering, chemistry, geology, law, philosophy, photography, history, accounting—you name it. In fact, investing is so intimidating that many intelligent individuals avoid it. Instead, they stash their money in certificates of deposit (CDs), annuities, bonds, or mutual funds. Apparently, they can't face buying common stocks. This is too bad, because that's precisely where the money is made. You don't make money every day, every week, or even every year. But over the long term, you will make the most out of your investment dollars.

Look at the Facts

One persuasive study contends that common stocks will make money for you in most years. This study, done by the brokerage firm Smith Barney, looked at the thirty-five one-year periods between 1960 and 1995.

The study computed total return, which adds capital gains and dividends. Over that span, stocks (as represented by the Standard & Poor's 500 index) performed unsatisfactorily in only eight of those thirty-five years. In other words, you would have been better off in money-market funds during those eight years. Common stocks would have been more successful in twenty-seven of those thirty-five years.

Investing for the Long Term

Investing, however, is not a one-year endeavor. Most investors start their programs in their forties and fifties, which means they could be investing over a twenty-, thirty-, or forty-year period.

If we look at the relative returns of different investments over five-year periods—rather than one-year periods—the results are even more encouraging. During the years from 1960 through 1994, there were thirty-one such periods. In only two of those five-year periods did the total return of the Standard & Poor's–based portfolio become negative.

Let's move ahead to all ten-year holding periods. There were twenty-six in that span. Exactly 100 percent worked out profitably. Equally important, the returns to the investor were impressive in all of these one-, five-, and ten-year periods. The one-year periods, for instance, gave you an average annual total return of 11.1 percent; for five-year periods, it was 10.5 percent, and for ten-year periods, it was 10.2 percent.

Based on this study, we can say with confidence that over a lifetime of investing, an investor will reap a total annual return of 10 percent or more. If you compare this with the amount you could earn by owning CDs, annuities, government bonds, or any other conservative investment, the difference is considerable.

Some Profitable Comparisons

Let's see how that difference adds up. Suppose you invested $25,000 in a list of common stocks at the age of forty, and your portfolio built up at a 10 percent compound annual rate. By the time you reached sixty-five, your common stock nest egg would be worth $270,868.

Now, let's say you had invested your money in government bonds, yielding 6 percent. The same $25,000 would be worth only $107,297, which is a difference of $163,571. Neither of these calculations has accounted for income taxes or brokerage commissions.

Now, let's look at the timid soul who invested $25,000 in CDs at age forty and averaged a return of 4 percent. By age sixty-five, that investment would be worth a paltry $66,646.

Why Doesn't Everyone Buy Common Stocks?

That's a good question, and I'm not sure I can provide you with a satisfactory answer. Part of the reason may be ignorance. Not everyone is willing to investigate the field of common stocks. These noninvestors may be too preoccupied with their jobs, sports, reading, gardening, travel, or whatever. Then, there are those who are heavily influenced by family members who have told them that stocks are too speculative and better left to millionaires. (Of course, that's how many of these millionaires became millionaires.)

Even if you are convinced that I may be right about the potential of stocks, you are probably wondering how anyone can possibly figure out which stocks to buy, since there are tens of thousands to choose from. That, in essence, is the purpose of this book.

A Real-Life Example

If you are a newcomer to investing, you may still doubt that you are capable of building a portfolio of stocks that will make you rich. Not all stocks are going to live up to their early promise, no matter how much time you devote to making a selection. On the other hand, even if you pick your stocks blindfolded, you will have some winners. Let's suppose that you want to invest $100,000 in twenty stocks, or $5,000 in each. Some will work out and some won't.

Hypothetically, it does not seem unreasonable to project that ten of these stocks will just plug along, making you neither rich nor poor. Suppose we assume that these ten stocks will appreciate (rise in value) an average of only 7 percent per year over the next ten or twenty years. Toss in a 2 percent annual dividend and the total return adds up to 9 percent per year. That is not exactly

riches, since stocks over the last seventy-five years have averaged about 11 percent.

At any rate, here is what your $50,000 will be worth at the end of ten years and twenty years:

$118,368 $280,221

Next, let's look at the three stocks that performed above your wildest dreams. They appreciated an average of 15 percent per year. Add in a modest annual dividend of only 1 percent, and you have a total return of 16 percent.

Assuming you invest $5,000 in each of these three stocks, that $15,000 will be worth over the next ten- and twenty-year periods:

$66,172 $291,911

So far, so good. Now, for the bad news. Two of your stocks hit the skids and never recovered. Total results for the $10,000 invested in these losers is: zero.

$00,000 $00,000

Finally, five of your twenty stocks do about average. They appreciate an average of 9 percent per year and have an average yearly dividend of 2 percent. That's a total return of 11 percent. Since you have five stocks in this category, your total investment is $25,000. Here is what you end up with ten and twenty years from now:

$70,986 $201,558

If we add up these various results, the final figures make you look reasonably rich:

$255,525 $773,690

By contrast, had you acted in a cowardly manner and invested exclusively in CDs, you would have only the following at the end of the two periods:

$162,889 $265,330

One final note. If you figure in taxes, you look even better, since the capital gains (on your stocks) are taxed at a much lower rate than ordinary income (which applies to CDs). And, you wouldn't even have to worry about capital gains on your stocks if you elected not to sell them.

How My 100 Stocks Were Selected

Although I talk on the telephone with investors from all over the country, I rarely hear from people overseas. It was early on a Thursday morning when my phone rang, and a voice said, "Mr. Slatter, I'm calling from London, England. My name is Thorpe. Is this an opportune time to ask you a few questions?"

"That name sounds familiar," I said. "Can you believe that I just finished reading a book by one of your compatriots, one K. Burnham Thorpe. I assume he's not one of your kinfolk."

"As a matter of fact," he said, "*my name is K. Burnham Thorpe. My latest book is The Age of Caesar and Cicero. Is that the one you're referring to?"

"It's a masterpiece, Mr. Thorpe," I told him.

"I know you Yanks like to address people by their first names, so why don't you call me Burnham, old fellow," he replied.

"Fine," I said, "and everyone calls me Slats."

"The reason I'm calling," he continued, "is to ask you how you pick your 100 stocks. It must be a bit of a sticky wicket when the world has thousands of companies."

"Before I give you the answer," I said, "I wanted to ask you about one of your earlier books, the one called *100 Ancient Lives*. You did a spectacular job of describing the lives of such notables as Hannibal, Cleopatra, Cato, Sappho, and Archimedes. I tracked down a copy in an out-of-state library, but I haven't been able to get a hold of a copy for myself."

"You're in luck, old fellow. I have a an entire shelf of copies right here. If you give me some good answers, I'll send you an autographed copy. Fair enough?"

"You've got a deal. Okay, let's get started. I assume this phone call will set you back big bucks—or should I say *pounds*—so I'll try not to ramble on. First off, there are at least a dozen factors I look for when I examine a stock. For one thing, I want a company that's growing, so I get out my *Value Line* and check the history of earnings per share over the past ten or fifteen years. Ideally, I would hope earnings are expanding at 15 or 20 percent a year, but that's rare, since such stocks typically sell for a huge premium over the market, like forty, fifty, or seventy-five times earnings. That's too rich for me. I'll settle for 10 or 12 percent growth, and hope the P/E ratio is not too far above the market. Okay so far, Burnham?"

"In other words, old fellow, you're looking for a solid company, not a spectacular one. Correct?"

"Right, Burnham. I am a conservative cuss, not a wild man or gambler. I guess I'm too much of a coward. I don't want to risk everything on one roll of the dice. Next, I examine the company's dividend record. Basically, I want the dividends to be growing in line with the earnings. Companies that raise their dividends every year are my favorites. But I don't want them to raise the dividends in the face of flat or declining earnings. That's not a healthy situation."

"Sounds good so far, Slats. What's next?"

"One important factor is the payout ratio. I avoid companies that pay out a big percentage of their earnings, such as 60 or 70 percent. The best companies are those that pay out less than 50 percent of earnings. Except for utilities. Most utilities pay out 70 percent or more. But even here, I prefer those that pay out less than average, such as 60 percent or less."

"I suppose the reason you like a low payout ratio is because those companies are plowing back cash into research, marketing, and new facilities."

"I can see you're been reading my book, Burnham. Research *is* another factor I look for. You will note that many of my 100 stocks are pharmaceuticals. That's partly because they spend a heap of money on research. They won't survive unless they find new drugs, and that means hiring an army of scientists. Not all companies need to spend money on research, of course. I doubt that Wal-Mart or SBC Communications worries too much about new products. But 3M and Microsoft certainly do."

"I think you're earning your copy of *100 Ancient Lives*, old fellow. Keep up the good work."

"Great. I need a good book to read before I doze off at night. Next, you should be sure your company has a good marketing arm. Take Procter & Gamble, for instance. They spend a ton of money on advertising. In the drug area, companies like Merck and Pfizer employ thousands of salespeople—they sometimes call them 'detail men, or detail persons'—who haunt doctors' offices, doling out samples and literature and extolling the virtues of their latest nostrums. They even advertise their wares to the general public, hoping that ailing readers will suggest that their doctors prescribe certain drugs. It seems to work, although I'm not sure that the medical profession is thrilled to have patients telling them how to practice medicine."

"I'm getting a copy of *100 Ancient Lives* off the shelf, Slats. Do you want to try for two?"

"Why not? I'll have one for my bedside and one for the office. Back to my rules. Since I'm of a conservative stripe, I prefer to avoid stocks that bounce around a lot. That means they should not have a high beta coefficient. *Value Line* gives this information. A beta coefficient of 1.0 means the stock tends to rise and fall in tandem with the market. But if it has a high beta, such as 1.4, 1.5, or even 2, it means the stock is volatile or speculative. Many NASDAQ stocks have high betas. You can get rich quick with high-beta stocks—but you can also get poor fast."

"My feeling exactly, old fellow. Let somebody else do the gambling."

"I guess we're on the same wavelength, Burnham. Another thing to consider is debt. Most companies have some, but too much is an indication that the stock may be speculative. My rule of thumb is to limit debt to 25 percent of capitalization. Except for public utilities. They generally have far more debt. But even here, I would select those with the least debt."

"Does that mean I have to pay off my mortgage, Slats?"

"Debt makes me nervous, Burnham. But not everyone has enough cash around to pay off their mortgage. Now, on to another topic before British Telecom finds out you're talking to a Yank. Another factor I insist on is a company with products that are not commodities. In other words, they are proprietary, and they are dominant in their field. Most of GE's products, for instance, are number one or two in their category. A company with a large market share is in a position to control its own destiny. Along this same vein, I would prefer that the company is increasing its market share. In order to do that, the company needs a superior product that is priced competitively."

"So far, old fellow, you have come up with a lot of features to look for. I'm just wondering how many companies would have all these features?"

"Good point. You're right, very few companies score 100 percent on all my criteria. Companies—like people—are never perfect. The trick is to find those that come closest to perfection."

"Sounds reasonable. You've almost qualified for the second copy of *100 Ancient Lives*—but not quite."

"Guess I better knuckle down. One thing you shouldn't forget is labor relations. You've got to keep your people happy if you expect them to stay with you and do a good job. That means paying a decent wage, promoting from within, and providing solid fringe benefits. If the company has a union, friction may be difficult to deal with. In the automotive sector, however, Ford Motor Company seems to know how to cope. However, General Motors appears to prefer confronting labor and often has to put up with strikes. An even better way to deal with the problem is to do such a good job that your people reject the idea of having a union represent them."

"I'm glad I called you, old fellow. I'm getting a liberal education. I assume you are about to run out of factors."

"Not really. I tend to be a bit long-winded—especially when someone else is paying for the phone call. Next, let's look at stock splits. Most people love stock splits. They seem to think it makes them richer. Actually, a stock split is like cutting an apple pie in half. You have two pieces, but you don't have any more pie. On the other hand, a company with a history of stock splits is often one that is doing well, since stock splits are generally granted because the price of the stock is up toward $100. After a two-for-one split, the two pieces are down to $50.

"Another thing that might be worth examining," I continued, "is the percentage of outstanding stock owned by managers and board members. This is not too important when you look at huge com-panies like 3M, Philip Morris (now known at Altria Group), or International Paper. But when you look at medium-sized companies or smaller ones, there is often ownership by management of 10, 15, or 20 percent. Then you know they are paying attention to their knitting."

"You never seem to run dry, Slats. It's a good thing I can afford a humongous phone bill. What's next on the agenda?"

"Just a couple more things. If you can get a copy of *Value Line* or the company's annual report, find out what it is earning on common equity. Ideally, the company should earn at least 15 percent. Twenty percent is better still.

"Finally, forget about new companies that aren't dry behind the ears. Most of them are still spewing out red ink and are a long way from paying a dividend. Let someone else buy those turkeys. You should stick to seasoned companies that have at least a ten-year history. They should be profitable and paying a modest dividend. Can you believe it—I'm running out of juice."

"Great. How would you like three copies of *100 Ancient Lives*? You deserve them, old fellow. You've given me a lot of good information. I'll recommend your book to some blokes at the club."

"Wow! Now I'll have a copy for my coffee table, too. When people see it, I can tell them one of my good buddies is the distinguished author K. Burnham Thorpe. I can't wait to get the books."

"You'll get my autograph as well. And the next time you're in London, I'll treat you to some fish and chips at Maxwell's."

"Now, you're talking, Burnham. My wife and I love Maxwell's—as I recall, it's right across the street from the Belsize Park tube station—just so long as we don't have to put up with a game of cricket. It's about time you people gave up cricket and switched to baseball."

The phone went dead.

Some Thoughts on Analyzing Stocks

Ideally, a stock you plan to purchase should have all of the following characteristics:

- A rising trend of earnings, dividends, and book value per share.
- A balance sheet with less debt than other companies in its particular industry.
- An S&P rating of B+ or better.
- A P/E ratio no higher than average.
- A dividend yield that suits your particular needs.
- A stock that insiders are not selling in significant quantities.
- A below-average dividend payout ratio.
- A history of earnings and dividends not pockmarked by erratic ups and downs.
- Companies whose return on equity is 15 or better.
- A ratio of price to cash flow that is not too high when compared to other stocks in the same industry.

Where to Get Information

If you are going to concentrate your efforts on the thirty Dow stocks, you must do some reading. Most people don't want to own all thirty stocks. In addition, you will probably find some stocks not to your liking. Let's say you are opposed to tobacco—then you may want to omit Altria Group from your portfolio. Or, you may think that traditional retailers, such as Sears, Roebuck, are not going to do well against such companies as Wal-Mart; Bed, Bath & Beyond; or Home Depot. Similarly, a cyclical company like International Paper might appear too stodgy for an aggressive investor.

Because the Dow stocks are large and prominent, there is no shortage of information about them. In any given day, the *Wall Street Journal* will have a story about one or two Dow stocks. The same might be said for the *New York Times*. If you are serious about doing your homework, it would be wise to clip out these articles and file them away for future reference. You will also see articles on these companies in such publications as *Barron's*, *Better Investing*, *Forbes*, *BusinessWeek*, and *Fortune*.

There are two well-known advisory services that you won't want to ignore: Standard & Poor's publishes "tear sheets" on thousands of companies. Of course, your only interest will be in the thirty Dow stocks. These tear sheets are available in public libraries and brokerage houses.

And don't forget to check *Value Line Survey*. It reviews 1,700 companies on a regular basis. Every thirteen weeks, your Dow Stocks are updated. This service costs over $500 a year, but is readily available in brokerage offices and libraries.

In this modern age, you may also be tempted to seek out information on the Internet. Here is a sampling of what you can check:

- *www.briefing.com* reports upgrades and downgrades on stocks by full-service brokers and gives a detailed report on the market three times daily. It also offers in-depth comments on several stocks during the day.
- *www.hoovers.com* provides profiles of thousands of companies, as well as financial data and links to company home pages.
- *www.investorama.com* provides more than 8,000 links to other investment Web sites.
- *www.zacks.com* provides consensus earnings predictions for the coming quarter, current year, and next year. It also shows whether company insiders are buying or selling.

The Four Essentials of Successful Investing

If you want to be rich at sixty-five, here are the factors to bear in mind.

First, start young. Many people wait until age fifty before they realize what has happened. Let's assume you want to have $1 million by age sixty-five. That may not be enough, but it's a lot more than most people have when they decide to retire from the world of commerce and frustration.

If you start at age thirty-five and can realize an annual return of 10 percent compounded, you will have to put aside $6,079 each year. If you delay until you are forty-five, it will mean you have to set aside $17,460 each year. If you start at age fifty-five, the amount gets a little steep—$62,746!

Invest Mostly in Stocks, Not Bonds

It takes commitment, even if you start early, to save for the future. But if you buy bonds, CDs, or a money market fund, the task is even tougher. Let's try the different ages again, but this time assuming a compound annual return of 6, instead of 10, percent.

If you start at thirty-five and want to have a million bucks at sixty-five, it will mean plunking $12,649 into a CD each year—that's a lot more than the first illustration, which required an annual payment of $6,079. If you start at age forty-five, the annual contribution will have to be $27,185. Finally, those who start their programs at age fifty-five and pick fixed-income vehicles will be forced to set aside $75,868 each year.

Don't Be a Spendthrift

An important ingredient of successful investing is discipline. Of course, it pays to earn an above-average salary. If you make $30,000 a year and have four children, you are not likely to end up rich. Sorry about that.

On the other hand, there are plenty of people who make great incomes and still don't own any stocks. The reason: They can always find things to buy.

Successful investors not only make a good income, but they are thrifty shoppers. For instance, do you *need* a new car every two years? I happen to be rich, and I buy used cars. Not rusted-out jalopies—normally, I buy Buicks that are three years old.

If you want to find out how people get rich, you should get *The Millionaire Next Door* by Thomas J. Stanley and William D. Danko. Typically, millionaires are extremely careful how they spend their money, and they invest in good-quality common stocks with very infrequent trading.

Picking the Right Investments

The final factor is picking the right stocks or mutual funds. Surprisingly, this is the *least* important factor. That's because no one knows how to do it consistently. There are mutual funds with good records, but those managers are rarely able to duplicate their performance year after year. However, that shouldn't deter you from trying. You will pick your share of winners if you do your homework and exercise patience. Finally, make sure you don't make any big bets. I prefer to own twenty or more stocks, with no more than 10 percent in any one industry.

In brief, here are the four rules:

- Start early in life to invest.
- Invest in common stocks.
- Invest enough to make it worthwhile, such as 10 percent of your income. You can only do this if you are thrifty.
- Study this book and do enough reading to ensure you pick stocks that have the potential to make you rich.

One Way to Reduce Risk:
Watch Out for the Summer Slump

I wouldn't want you to tell anyone, but I am addicted to garage sales. My only regret is that people don't tend to have them during the winter or early spring. If you decide to take up this pastime, it is important to be selective: The best items are found in good neighborhoods. For a crack at the choice items, moreover, you have to be on hand when the garage door goes up, usually at 8 A.M.—before the "early birds" and dealers scoop up all the good stuff.

But if you are looking for a rowing machine, a treadmill, or some other piece of equipment that will make you hale and hearty, don't hurry. For some reason, these muscle benders don't sell very fast, no matter how cut-rate the prices.

One balmy morning in June, I had the good fortune to find a stationary bike at a garage sale on Upper Constantine Terrace, where you see lots of three-car garages stuffed with Buicks, Cadillacs, Lincoln Town Cars, and Mercedes.

Although I had several other "torture machines," I didn't have a good exercise bike. This one looked brand new. I tried it out and was delighted. Wondering what the price would be, I said, "Who's in charge here?"

A husky middle-age man, dressed in tan corduroy slacks, came forward. "I'm Turner T. Peridson," he said, as he tugged at his belt, trying to pull his trousers up over his girth. "I see you like my bike. It cost me $899 a couple of years ago. How would $50 sound—that's delivered."

"Well, I don't know, Mr. Peridson. Last Saturday, I bought a rowing machine for $5. I like the bike, but maybe we could come to a better agreement. I'm just a poor, struggling writer. My budget is a bit bent out of shape at the moment. I'm waiting for a royalty check."

Without hesitation, he said, "I think we can make an adjustment. By the way, most people call me Turner. How does $25 sound? What kind of books do you write?"

I gave him the money and handed him one of my business cards. I have these printed up with some propaganda on the reverse side, including the names of my books and a brief mention of my advisory business.

"It looks like you are in the investment business, Mr. Slatter. I used to be gung-ho on stocks, but I'm afraid I'm stuck with a few losers. I've had Goodyear Tire and Rubber for a dozen years, and it's still under water. My IRA ain't what it used to be. No doubt your portfolio is in the same shape. I can see why you are having trouble coming up with the cash for this bike."

I didn't tell him that my wife and I own fifty-five stocks or that I am not as poor as I made out. "Things have been tough on investors the past two or three years, Turner, but I have some ideas that you might find interesting. Take your Goodyear, for instance. If you used a new strategy I developed, your Goodyear would not be under water. I'd be glad to explain it to you if you stop at my office."

"I assume you are not giving your services away free."

"For a good garage sale buddy, I think I can help you without draining your resources any further. I make my money by managing portfolios. I don't charge for a brief chat. Give me a call when you want to stop in. I'll even show you my exercise room. With this fine bike, I now have seven torture machines."

A few days later, Turner and I sat down in my office to discuss an idea that is not well known to investors but that is nonetheless an effective strategy for reducing risk and increasing the performance of your portfolio. Here's how I explained it to him.

"As I recall, Turner, you said your Goodyear shares were a big disappointment. According to my calculations, Goodyear was selling for just under $26 a share at the end of October 1988. As of April 30, 2002, it was down to $18.63. I can see why you are not happy. However, if you had held these same shares during the cold months of the year and dumped them during the warm months, you would be ahead of the game."

"Are you suggesting that I become a trader?"

"Most people prefer to hold their stocks for several years, but as it appears, that may not be the best strategy. To help you see what I'm getting at, here's a table showing what would happen if you sold your shares on April 30 of each year and then bought them back at the end of October. As of the end April, 2002, the thirteen previous summer periods suffered an average loss of 2.28 percent, while the fourteen preceding cold periods showed a tidy gain that averaged 11.02 percent." He peered at the table below:

GOODYEAR TIRE & RUBBER FROM OCT. 31, 1988 TO APRIL 30, 2002

Date	Price	% Change (Warm)	Date	Price	% Change (Cold)
10/31/88	$25.937	(start)	4/30/89	25.25	−2.65%
10/31/89	22.187	−12.13%	4/30/90	17.687	−20.28
10/31/90	7.625	−56.89	4/30/91	10.625	+39.34
10/31/91	25.00	+135.29	4/30/92	36.312	+45.25
10/31/92	34.5	−4.99	4/30/93	37.312	+8.15
10/31/93	44.75	+19.93	4/30/94	39.00	−12.85
10/31/94	35.125	−9.94	4/30/95	38.00	+8.19
10/31/95	38.00	0.00	4/30/96	52.125	+37.17
10/31/96	45.875	−11.99	4/30/97	52.625	+14.71
10/31/97	62.625	+19.00	4/30/98	70.00	+11.78
10/31/98	53.875	−23.04	4/30/99	57.187	+6.15
10/31/99	41.312	−27.76	4/30/00	27.625	−33.13
10/31/00	18.5	−33.03	4/30/01	24.62	+33.08
10/31/01	18.63	−24.33	4/30/02	22.25	+19.43

Average changes for all six-month periods:
Warm periods (from 4/30–10/31)   −2.28%
Cold periods (from 10/31–4/30)   +11.02%

Turner examined the table and said, "It looks like I would have missed a huge gain in the summer of 1991 of 135.29 percent. I'm not so sure you've convinced me, Mr. Slatter."

"Nothing in the investment realm is perfect," I said. "You will also note that you avoided a loss of 56.89 percent the prior year, not to mention big losses in 1998, 1999, 2000, and 2001. Overall, the average annual loss was 2.28 percent, compared with an annual gain of more than 11 percent during the cold months. What's more, I have not included the interest you would have obtained during these summer months by investing your proceeds in a money-market fund, bank CD, or a six-month treasury bill."

"Do you have any other evidence for your theory?" he asked.

"Plenty. This concept has been working for decades. It's been checked back to 1950 by Yale Hirsch, founder of the *Stock Market Traders Almanac*.

Between 1950 and 2000, $10,000 invested in the Dow Jones Industrial Average would have produced a profit of $415,890. By contrast, the same $10,000 invested in the warmer months would have given you a trivial gain of $1,743."

"I am beginning to see the light," Turner said. "Tell me more."

"I've been checking this strategy since the publication of my 2002 edition. It seems to work at least 80 percent of the time. In order to check it out, I went on the Internet, using a Web site called Wall Street City (www.wallstreetcity.com). All you do is type in the ticker symbol and then click on the "Historical Quotes" link. Then you type in the beginning and ending dates, plus whether you want daily, weekly, monthly, or quarterly numbers. It's all very simple. The only disadvantage is that you can't go back any further than 1988."

"You seem to have come up with a very interesting idea. I'm curious how you discovered it," Turner said.

"I came across the idea when I read an article by Mark Hulbert, editor of the Hulbert Financial Digest. He is also a freelance writer. His column—which I never fail to read—appears every other Sunday in the New York Times.

"The idea was originally created by Sven Bouman, a portfolio manager at Aegon, an insurer based in the Netherlands, and Ben Jacobsen, an associate professor of finance at Erasmus University, in Rotterdam. These two researchers found that the pattern existed between 1970 and 1998 in thirty-six of thirty-seven developed and emerging market countries. In the British stock market, moreover, the strategy worked all the way back to 1694."

"Did you just say 1694?" Turner asked in amazement.

"That's right," I said. "According to Mark Hulbert, the reason this idea works is because investors tend to reduce their equity holdings before their summer vacations, which in turn lowers the stock market's returns.

"Looking around the world, here is how investors have fared in the six cold-weather months (between January 1970 through August of 1998), versus the six warm-weather months. For instance, in Hong Kong, stocks advanced 11.0 percent during the cold months, compared with 5.9 percent in warm months. In other countries, the pattern was similar. Look at these numbers."

Denmark: 7.6 vs. 5.6
United States: 8.5 vs. 3.0
Canada: 8.4 vs. 1.6
United Kingdom: 13.1 vs. 0.9
Spain: 12.0 vs. 0.7
Germany: 8.8 vs. 0.5
Japan: 8.8 vs. −0.3
France: 13.1 vs. −0.8
Italy: 13.6 vs. −2.6

"I think I'm getting my money's worth, Mr. Slatter. Anything else?"

"Plenty. I've been using Wall Street City (www.wallstreetcity.com) for months, trying to find a flaw in this strategy. So far, no luck. It works more than 80 percent of the time. Here are some stocks that I looked at from October 31, 1988, to April 30, 2002. In most instances, the stocks performed better during the winter months than during the summer. The times when this was not the case are indicated with italics."

NAME OF STOCK	ACTION IN WARM MONTHS	ACTION IN COLD MONTHS
Advanced Micro Devices	−20.89	+65.10
Alcoa	−1.00	+15.20
American Express	+1.72	+16.09
Archer Daniels	+9.34	−0.12
Boeing	+3.95	+9.01
Coca-Cola	+12.47	+9.18
Computer Associates	+7.96	+13.26
ConAgra	+12.03	−0.31
Dana Corp.	−11.66	+19.39
Danaher Corp.	+2.64	+23.85
Deere and Co.	−3.63%	+14.61%

NAME OF STOCK	ACTION IN WARM MONTHS	ACTION IN COLD MONTHS	NAME OF STOCK	ACTION IN WARM MONTHS	ACTION IN COLD MONTHS
Dell Computer	+27.64	+31.23	PPG Industries	−3.86	+11.74
Delta Air Lines	−8.44	+11.81	Parker-Hannifin	−1.00	+17.66
Deluxe Corp.	−0.58	+6.62	Pitney Bowes	−0.42	+13.78
Devon Energy	+12.91	+13.07	Safeway Inc.	+7.62	+21.29
Walt Disney	−4.59	+20.31	*Schering-Plough*	*+17.44*	*+1.96*
Dollar General	+7.74	+18.33	Snap-On Tools	−5.07	+7.32
Dow Chemical	−4.03	+9.09	Sun Trust Banks	+6.24	+10.43
DuPont	−2.70	+13.48	Tribune Company	+0.63	+14.60
Eastman Kodak	−1.70	+3.36	Vulcan Materials	+0.79	+9.96
Eaton Corp.	−6.07	+17.28	Washington REIT	−0.13	+7.72
ExxonMobil	+2.48	+7.79	Wells Fargo	+0.11	+19.23
General Electric	+5.72	+12.78	Winn-Dixie	+2.09	+8.80
General Motors	−10.02	+18.92	Standard & Poor's 500	+2.88	+8.05
Gillette	+8.51	+9.74	Dow Jones Ind. Average	+1.74	+10.41
Robert Half	+11.09	+19.93	**AVERAGE OF 51 READINGS**	**+2.74%**	**+13.59%**
Humana	+5.33	+9.39			
IBM	+2.02	+8.53			
Illinois Tool Works	+1.46	+16.35			
Interpublic	+3.50	+15.31			
Lincoln National	+4.86	+8.98			
Manor Care	+5.13	+14.66			
Marathon Oil	+1.01	+3.05			
May Dept. Stores	+1.70	+8.54			
Omnicom	+7.47	+17.40			
Orthodontic Centers	+19.49	+26.40			

Turner examined the table, and I could see that he was puzzled. He said, "Your numbers are convincing, Mr. Slatter—all except Advanced Micro Devices. Do you have that table handy?"

After a few minutes of leafing through my pile of printouts, I found it. "Here it is," I said.

WARM AND COLD PERIODS: ADVANCED MICRO DEVICES (OCT. 1988–APRIL 2002)

DATE	PRICE	% CHANGE (WARM)	DATE	PRICE	% CHANGE (COLD)
10/31/88	$4.50	(start)	4/30/89	4.437	−1.40%
10/31/89	3.937	−11.27%	4/30/90	4.375	+11.13
10/31/90	1.937	−55.73	4/30/91	6.125	+216.21
10/31/91	6.375	+4.08	4/30/92	8.937	+40.19
10/31/92	8.25	−7.69	4/30/93	14.062	+70.45
10/31/93	9.875	−29.78	4/30/94	13.187	+33.54
10/31/94	13.187	0.00	4/30/95	18.00	+36.50
10/31/95	11.75	−34.72	4/30/96	9.312	−20.75
10/31/96	8.875	−4.69	4/30/97	21.25	+139.44
10/31/97	11.5	−45.88	4/30/98	13.875	+20.65
10/31/98	11.281	−18.7	4/30/99	8.25	−26.87
10/31/99	9.906	+20.07	4/30/00	43.75	+341.65
10/31/00	22.625	−48.29	4/30/01	31.00	+37.02
10/31/01	9.84	−68.26	4/30/02	11.18	+13.62

Average changes for all six-month periods:
Warm periods (from 4/30–10/31) −20.89%
Cold periods (from 10/31–4/30) +65.10%

All he said was, "Simply amazing. Amazing."

"As you can see, Turner, this strategy has a lot going for it. In very few instances does it fail. What it amounts to is this. For six months of the year, you are out of the market, thus reducing your risk dramatically. What's more, this money does not lie fallow. It can be invested in a money-market fund, a bank CD, or a six-month treasury bill."

In my opinion, my presentation seemed very convincing. Of the fifty-one observations, only four failed to sustain my thesis. In other words, it worked 90 percent of the time. The average gain for a six-month holding period was 13.59 percent, far better than the alternative of 2.74 percent. I was sure that Turner would eagerly hand over his portfolio, so that I could manage it for him. His only comment was this.

"Let's look at your exercise room, Mr. Slatter. Maybe I could offer you an incentive to sell me back the stationary bike. I think a little exercise would do me good. My waistline is getting out of control."

Twenty-One More Ways to Reduce Investment Risk

No matter where you invest your money, there is always risk. Even bonds are not safe from inflation and rising interest rates. CDs also suffer from inflation. Stocks, as everyone knows, are regarded as the riskiest investments. However, they are also the most profitable—at least in the long run. In the short run, who knows what they will do.

Based on my long experience in the stock market, I have figured out twenty-one ways you can reduce this risk. Since I use most of them myself and for my clients, I have emerged from the recent bear market relatively intact. Since more bear markets are not out of the question, here are my thoughts on ways to mitigate your discomfort.

You will find some of these same ideas discussed in greater detail in other chapters of this book. This may seem repetitive, but sometimes repetition is one of the best ways to cram new knowledge into your gray matter. Here are the twenty-one ways to reduce your risk, presented for the first time:

1. The first rule of investing is *diversification*. Although most investors are aware of this concept, most do not know how to implement it. Of course, the most grievous blunder is to invest your whole portfolio in one stock. I have seen what this can do.

A few years ago, I met an architect after delivering a lecture. He had more than a million dollars invested in an obscure stock called Comdisco, which was selling around $30 a share. I convinced him to sell $300,000 worth and have me manage that portfolio, which is now worth about $500,000. Meanwhile, Comdisco climbed to $57 a share, which made the architect happy. However, by the end of 2001 it was worth only fifty-two cents a share, and my client had failed to sell it.

Still another investor came to me with all his money invested in WorldCom. He had bought the shares much lower and was well ahead of the game. He agreed to sell it all and have me manage his portfolio by buying twenty-five stocks. It's no secret what has happened to WorldCom.

When I was in Cleveland, I had the task of evaluating portfolios for the firm's clients. Almost without exception, these customers had some diversification. They often had twenty, thirty, or forty stocks, which is considered adequate. But most of these stocks were in three industries: oil, utilities, and banks. That's certainly a far cry from prudent diversification.

2. Not to be forgotten is asset allocation. This concept is similar to diversification, but it goes one step further. Instead of investing all your money in stocks, you should spread it around in such assets as bonds, foreign stocks, and mutual funds. No one knows what the market is going to do, so it makes sense to hedge your bets with prudent asset allocation. In the past three years, bonds have far outperformed stocks. That doesn't mean you should sell all your stocks and concentrate in bonds. Who knows? Now may be the time to be in stocks. Still, it pays to have some money in fixed-income assets, even if you think a new bull market is just ahead.

3. One way to measure whether a stock is overpriced is to calculate its price-earnings ratio (known as the P/E ratio). Simply divide the stock price by the com-

pany's most recent twelve-month earnings per share. P/E ratios can vary all the way from 10 to 100 or more. In most instances, a high ratio indicates a company with good prospects for the future. A low P/E ratio often means the company has a lackluster future. Although I am not suggesting that you stuff your portfolio with low P/E stocks, I am suggesting that you avoid stocks that are selling at very high P/E ratios. I would avoid any stock with a ratio of 40 or higher. In the long run, they don't do well. Many studies prove this point.

(4.) Many investors ignore real estate investment trusts, usually known as REITs. They look stodgy and dull and typically have a dividend yield of 5 percent or higher. In the past two years, REITs have not only avoided the debacle that has engulfed most other stocks, but they have actually risen in value. That's because REITs act counter to the market. In a rising market, for instance, they would not do as well as growth stocks.

For my own part, I own several of them, such as Washington Real Estate Investment Trust, Kimco Realty, Equity Office Properties, and New Plan Excel Realty. REITs are not all alike. Some invest in apartment buildings, some in office buildings, and some in shopping malls. And there are others, as well. Most REITs are well diversified geographically.

5.   In recent years, dividends have largely been ignored. Historically, however, dividends have played a prominent role in investing. Approximately half of the 11 or 12 percent annual return that investors enjoy can be attributed to dividends. Lately this has not been the case, as companies have tended to buy back their own shares, rather than pay out profits to shareholders. Even so, when I pick stocks, I look for a dividend and a history of regular increases. Stocks that pay a dividend are less likely to plunge in value than those that prefer to reinvest their profits in growth.

6.   A strong balance sheet is an essential for a company that you want to consider. It's simply a relationship between the amount of debt as a percentage of capitalization. My preference is for 75 percent in equity (the book value of the common stock). A strong balance sheet makes it easier for the company to finance an acquisition. If you have access to *Value Line Investment Survey*, it's easy to find out this percentage.

7.   If you elect to buy bonds, don't look for the highest yield. For one thing, a high yield is often characteristic of a weak company. When the yield gets too large, the bonds are referred to as "junk bonds." The safest bonds are those issued by the federal government. In today's market, you can't get much more than 4 percent, and that's for bonds that mature in twenty or thirty years. Shorter maturities are as low as 3 percent or less. It's best to stick to maturities of five years or less. The reason is that the bond will sink like a stone if interest rates start climbing. This does not happen for bonds due in less than five years, since all you have to do is wait and you'll get the face value of the bond. A bond due in thirty years, by contrast, will drop, and you may not live long enough to get the face value.

8.   In an effort to avoid the risk of owning stocks, some people think it pays to buy preferred stocks, convertible bonds, annuities, commodities or by selling short. None of these vehicles are recommended—at least not by me. Here's why:

• **Preferred stocks sound safe and sound?** Not necessarily. A preferred stock is somewhat like a bond, in that the dividend is paid regularly and never changes. But a preferred stock—unlike a bond— never matures. In other words, you can't get your money back by waiting for the maturity date. Unlike a common stock, the dividend will never be increased. But if the company has problems, the dividend can be cut. If interest rates go up, the value of a preferred stock will decline. Avoid them at all cost.

- **Convertible bonds** appeal to some investors because they have a higher yield than the same company's common stock. They can also be converted into the company's common stock. On the other hand, unless you really know what you are doing, you may find that the company calls in the convertible when it suits their purposes. If you are bound and determined to buy convertibles, I advise you to do it by investing in a mutual fund that is managed by professionals. Even so, I'm not so sure you will be a happy camper.

- **Annuities** are issued by insurance companies. There are two main types. The more conservative is invested in such things as bonds and mortgages. When you are ready to retire, the insurance company will set up a monthly payment plan that will assure you of the same amount each month until you die. Assuming you leave behind a husband or wife, the income will not continue to that survivor. However, if you are willing to take a smaller monthly payment, the company will continue paying that amount to your survivor until his or her death, too. In any event, the amount you receive will not be much more than a basketful of dividend-paying stocks. Finally, insurance companies charge a pretty penny for their products, since they have to pay the agent for talking you into it.

- **Variable annuities** are another version of annuity, called "variable" since it is invested in common stocks and other assets of your choosing. Here again, the cost of these products is high. You would be better off buying a conventional mutual fund. The costs are usually about 1.5 percent a year.

- **If you are a speculator, you may find an interest in options, such as puts and calls, and many variations.** A call enables you to buy a particular common stock some weeks or months in the future at today's price. If the stock goes up substantially, this works out fine. But if it drops or advances only modestly, you lose the price of the option. "Puts" work for stocks that are expected to decline. But if they don't decline, you lose. In short, options are best avoided.

- **Commodities** have to do with speculating in such agricultural items as corn, wheat, soybeans, and pork bellies. It is possible to make a lot of money quickly in commodities. But very few people actually do because Mother Nature has a hand in your results. If you think a drought will help the price of your commodity, you might get rich—unless it starts raining, which can lead to a surplus and too much of that commodity, thus reducing prices drastically. This is no game for amateurs.

- **Selling short is similar to calls and puts.** If you think a stock is likely to decline in price, you can make money by selling short. You simply instruct your broker to borrow the shares from one of the firm's accounts. You then sell those shares at today's price. Let's say the stock is selling for $50 a share. Then, when the price drops to $30, you buy shares in the market and give them back to the investor who loaned them to you. Thus, you make a tidy profit of $20 a share. The catch is that the price may very well shoot up to $75, and what do you do then. If you buy back at this level, you lose $25 a share. There is no limit to the amount you can lose when you sell short. If you wait until the price goes to $150, you lose $100 a share. This is not my idea of having fun.

9.   The biggest problem with investing is its vast scope. There are thousands of mutual funds and tens of thousands of stocks, both domestic and foreign. A simple way to get rid of the clutter is to

concentrate your investing on a small universe, the thirty stocks that make up the Dow Jones Industrial Average. They include such blue chips as General Electric, Johnson & Johnson, Procter & Gamble, ExxonMobil, and Coca-Cola. Over the years, the Dow has performed well, so why not buy all thirty stocks, rather than hunt under every rock looking for the stock that will make you a millionaire? Another advantage is knowing when to sell. My strategy is sell only when a stock is removed from the Index, about one stock a year. This cuts down on your capital gains taxes, since most of the stocks you remove from your portfolio are losers, not winners.

10. Some investors can't stand inaction. Instead of buying and holding, they insist on selling winners and holding losers. All you do that way is end up with a portfolio of losers. It's better to let your winners run. The more you buy and sell, the more taxes you will have to pay.

11. Be careful in selecting a stock-broker. Most people start with a traditional full-service firm, since their salespeople are aggressively seeking new clients. Brokerage firms can supply you with research material, but these firms rely heavily for their profits on investment banking and their analysts may not be impartial. For their part, the salespeople make their money from commissions, which are much higher than such discount firms as Schwab or Waterhouse. Even worse, they tend to recommend products that have a high commission and limited prospects.

12. If you invest in stocks, avoid companies that are losing money. Instead, look for companies that have a long history of profitable operation, with a rising trend in earnings per share. If you buy stocks that are losing money, you are a speculator, not an investor.

13. Stocks are traded on the New York Stock Exchange, the American Stock Exchange, and NASDAQ. The leading companies are usually listed on the New York Stock Exchange. Those traded elsewhere are less mature and often of lower quality.

14. If you buy mutual funds, make sure you examine the "expense ratio." Even no-load funds are not free. To pay the salary of analysts and other employees, along with expenses like advertising, rent, and travel, mutual funds subtract these costs from your profits. The average expense ratio is about 1.5 percent per year. Studies show that funds with the highest expense ratios perform worst, while those with the lowest perform the best.

15. Although I am not a fan of mutual funds, I would avoid those with new management. Before you invest, call the company and ask the age of the manager and how long he has been in charge. I would prefer a manager at least forty years of age and a tenure of at least five years.

16. Avoid stocks with excessively high yields, at least in relation to other companies in that industry. Those with high yields are often in trouble and are likely to cut their dividend.

17. Seek companies that are financially strong. This can be determined in two ways. Standard & Poor's rates stocks by letter. The highest rating is A+. An average rating is B+. Avoid those with a rating below B+. *Value Line* uses a similar rating, but its highest rating is A++, and an average one is B++. Again, don't go below B++.

18. Examine the dividend payout ratio. It's calculated by dividing the annual dividend by the annual earnings per share for the past twelve months. If the dividend is $1, and the earnings per share are $4, the payout ratio would be 25 percent. That signifies a company that is plowing back earnings into research, new products, stock repurchase, debt reduction, or acquisitions. However, if the payout ratio is high, let's say 75 percent, it is indicative of a company that has limited growth potential.

19. The economy has an impact on most companies, but there are some industries that are considered cyclical, such as chemicals, autos, appliances, machinery, metals and mining, paper, and railroads. Most of these have limited long-term growth. The only way to make money is by buying them when they are in trouble and selling them when money is rolling in. It's not that easy to be able to jump in and out with any consistency. Instead of cyclical stocks, concentrate on industries that are more stable, such as food processors, banks, REITs, utilities, food supermarkets, life insurance, medical supplies, and household products.

20. When a major company buys another major company, avoid the buyer. A good case in point is the purchase of Compaq by Hewlett-Packard. Rarely is there an exception to this rule.

21. Most investors are busy people, such as doctors, accountants, executives, and business owners. That means their time is limited. Even so, some time must be allotted for reading annual reports, the *Wall Street Journal, BusinessWeek*, and *Value Line*. To be a successful investor, you have to know how the game is played. This should also include reading at least one book on investing every year.

Basic Terminology

If you are new to the investment arena, you may have difficulty understanding parts of this book. To get you over the rough spots, I have listed some common expressions that appear frequently in books on investing. You will also encounter them in the *Wall Street Journal*, *Forbes*, *BusinessWeek*, *Barron's*, and other periodicals devoted to investing.

This is not a glossary but merely a brief list of terms that are essential for understanding this book. If you would like a more complete glossary, refer to either of my previous books: *Safe Investing* (Simon & Schuster, 1991) or *Straight Talk About Stock Investing* (McGraw-Hill, 1995).

Analyst

In nearly every one of the 100 articles, you will note that I refer to "analysts" and what they think about the prospects for a particular stock. Analysts are individuals who have special training in analyzing stocks. Typically, they have such advanced degrees as M.B.A.s or C.F.A.s. Many of them work for brokerage houses, but they may also be employed by banks, insurance companies, mutual funds, pension plans, or other institutions. Most analysts specialize in one or two industries. A good analyst can tell you nearly everything there is to know about a particular stock or the industry it's part of.

However, analysts can be dead wrong about the future action of a stock. The reason is surprises. Companies are constantly changing, which means they are acquiring, divesting, developing new products, restructuring, buying back their shares, and so forth. When they make a change and announce this change to Wall Street, the surprise can change the course of the stock. In short, analysts can be helpful, but don't bet the store on what they tell you.

As you can see, analysts are usually intelligent, hardworking, and conscientious. Even so, they don't always succeed in guiding you to riches. Perhaps the biggest beef most people have is the tie that analysts have to the companies they follow. They know these people well and may be reluctant to say anything negative.

One reason for this is economic. Most brokerage firms make a ton of money from their investment banking division. If the analyst antagonizes the company, that company may give its investment banking business to a firm that says nice things rather than pointing out warts and all.

This reluctance to see no evil and speak no evil can be seen when you examine the number of times that analysts advise investors to sell. According to the research firm First Call, more than 70 percent of the 27,000 recommendations outstanding in November 2000 were strong buys or buys. Fewer than 1 percent were sells or strong sells. To recap: Of the 27,000 recommendations, 26.6 percent were holds, 36.8 percent were buys, 35.7 percent were strong buys, and a mere 0.9 percent were sells or strong sells. I rest my case.

Annual Report

If you own a common stock, you can be certain that you will receive a fancy annual report a couple of months after the close of the year. If the year ends December 31, look for your annual report in March or April. If the fiscal year ends some other time of the year, such as September 30, the annual report will appear in your mailbox two or three months later.

Not all investors read annual reports, but they might be better off if they did. Although most companies will not list their problems, you can usually get a pretty good idea how things are going. In particular, read the report by the president or CEO. It's usually one, two, or three pages long and is written in language you can understand.

If you want detailed information on the company's various businesses, the annual report will often overwhelm you with details that may be difficult to fathom. If you are really curious about what they are trying to say, feel free to call the investor contact. I have provided the phone number of this person in all 100 stocks listed. Have a list of questions ready, and call during the person's lunch hour, leaving your name and phone number. This sneaky little strategy means the cost of the call back will be paid by the company, not you. By the way, don't assume you will be intimidated by the investor contact. Investor contacts are usually quite personable and helpful.

Asset Allocation

This is not the same as diversification. Rather, it refers to the strategy of allocating your investment funds among different types of investments, such as stocks, bonds, or money-market funds. In the long run, you will be better off with all of your assets concentrated in common stocks. In the short run, this may not be true, since the market occasionally has a sinking spell. A severe one, such as that of 2000–2002, can cause your holdings to decline in value 20 percent or more. To protect against this, most investors spread their money around. They may, for instance, allocate 50 percent to stocks, 40 percent to bonds, and 10 percent to a money-market fund. A more realistic breakdown might be 70 percent in stocks, 25 percent in bonds, and 5 percent in a money-market fund.

Balance Sheet

All corporations issue at least two financial statements: the balance sheet and the income statement. Both are important. The balance sheet is a financial picture of the company on a specific date, such as December 31 or at the end of a quarter.

On the left side of the balance sheet are the company's assets, such as cash, current assets, inventories, accounts receivable, and buildings. On the right side are its liabilities, including accounts payable and long-term debt. Also on the right side is shareholders' equity. The right side of the balance sheet adds up to the same value as the left side, which is why it is called a balance sheet.

In most instances, corporations give you figures for the current year and the prior year. By examining the changes, you can get an idea of whether the company's finances are improving or deteriorating.

Bonds

Entire books have been written on the various kinds of bonds. A bond, unlike a stock, is not a form of ownership. A bond is a contractual agreement that means you have loaned money to some entity, and that entity has agreed to pay you a certain sum of money (interest) every six months until that bond matures. At that time, you will also get back the money you originally invested—no more, no less. Most bonds are issued in $1,000 denominations. The safest bonds are those issued by the U.S. government. Not since the War of 1812 has there been a default on government bonds. The two advantages of bonds are safety and income. If you wait until the maturity date, you will be assured of getting the face value of the bond. In the meantime, however, the bond will fluctuate, because of changes in interest rates or the creditworthiness of the corporation. Long-term bonds, moreover, fluctuate far more than short-term bonds. But enough about bonds. This book is about stocks.

Capital Gains

When you buy common stocks, you expect to make money in two ways: capital gains and dividends. Over an extended period of time, about half of your total return will come from each sector. If the stock rises in value and you sell it above your cost, you are enjoying a capital gain. The tax on long-term capital gains is a maximum of 15 percent if the stock is held for twelve months.

Chief Executive Officer (CEO)

The executive of a company who reports to the board of directors. That corporate body can terminate the CEO if he or she fails to do an effective job of managing the company. In some instances, the CEO may also have the title of either president or chairman of the board, or both.

Closed-End Investment Company

A managed investment portfolio, similar to a mutual fund, which is generally traded on a stock exchange. The price fluctuates with supply and demand, not because of changes in the assets within the trust. An open-end investment trust, or mutual fund, changes in size as investors buy new shares or surrender their shares for cash. A closed-end trust, by contrast, does not permit new money to be invested, nor can shares be redeemed by the company. Thus, the number of shares remains the same once the trust begins trading. One feature of the closed-end trust is worth mentioning: they often sell at a discount to their asset value. An open-end trust always sells at precisely its asset value.

Common Stocks

We might as well define what a common stock is, since this whole book is devoted to them. All publicly owned companies—those that trade their shares outside of a small group of executives or the founding family—are based on common stocks. A common stock is evidence of partial ownership in a corporation. Most of the stocks described in this book have millions of shares of their stock outstanding, and the really large ones may have in excess of 100 million shares. When you own common stock, there are no guarantees. If the company is successful, it will probably pay a dividend four times a year. These dividends may be raised periodically, perhaps once a year. If, however, the company has problems, it may cut or eliminate its dividend. This can happen even to a major company, such as IBM, Goodyear, or General Motors. As I said, there are no guarantees.

Investors who own common stock can sell their shares at any time. All you do is call your broker, and the trade is executed a few minutes later at the prevailing price—which fluctuates nearly every day, sometimes by a few cents or sometimes two or three points.

Current Ratio

The current ratio is calculated by dividing current assets by current liabilities. Current assets include any assets that will become cash within one year, including cash itself. Current liabilities are those that will be paid off within a year. A current ratio of 2 is considered ideal. Most companies these days have a current ratio of less than 2.

Diversification

Since investments are inherently risky, it pays to spread the risk by diversifying. If you don't, you may be too heavily invested in a stock or bond that turns sour. Even well-known stocks such as Alcoa, International Paper, Eastman Kodak, and American Express can experience occasional sinking spells.

To be on the safe side, don't invest more than 5 percent of your portfolio in any one stock. In addition, don't invest too heavily in any one sector of the economy. A good strategy is to divide stocks among twelve sectors: industrials, information technology, capital goods, consumer discretion, consumer staples, drugs/health, financial, materials, transportation, utilities, and consumer growth.

Here's a rule of thumb that will keep you out of trouble: Invest at least 4 percent in each sector but not more than 12 percent. That means that you should own at least twelve stocks so that you have representation in all twelve sectors.

Dividends

Unlike bonds, common stocks may pay a dividend. Bonds pay interest. Most dividends are paid quarterly, but there is no set date that all corporations use. Some, for instance, may pay January 1, March 1, July 1, and September 1. Another company may pay February 10, May 10, August 10, and November 10. If you want to receive checks every month, you will have to make sure you buy stocks that pay dividends at different times of the year. The Standard & Poor's *Stock Guide* is a source for this information, as is the *Value Line Survey*. Most companies like to pay the same dividend every quarter until they can afford to increase it. Above all, they don't like to cut their dividends, since investors who depend on this income will sell their shares, and the stock will decline in price. If you use good judgment in selecting your stocks, you can expect that your companies will increase their dividends nearly every year.

Dividend Payout

If a company earns $4 a share in a twelve-month period and pays out $3 to shareholders in the form of dividends, it has a payout ratio of 75 percent. However, if it pays only $1, the payout ratio is 25 per-

cent. In the past, many investors looked favorably on a low payout ratio. The thinking was that such a company was plowing back its earnings into such projects as research, new facilities, acquisitions, and new equipment. It sounds logical.

Now, there is evidence that you are better off buying a company with a higher payout ratio. Mark Hulbert, who writes frequently for the Sunday *New York Times*, has discovered some studies that focus on this concept. According to work done by Michael C. Jensen, currently a professor emeritus of business administration at Harvard Business School, "the more cash that companies have now (beyond what is needed for current projects), the less efficient they will be in the future."

Two other scholars concur that a higher payout ratio serves investors better than a low one. They are Robert D. Arnott of First Quadrant and Clifford S. Asness of AQR Capital Management. For one thing, they found that "For the overall stock market between 1871 and 2001, corporate profits grew fastest in the ten years following the calendar year in which companies had the highest average dividend payout ratio." What's more, their study showed that in the period from 1946 to 1991, there was solid evidence for a strong correlation demonstrating conclusively that companies with a high payout ratio performed far better than those that were stingy with their dividend distributions.

Mr. Hulbert concludes, "The common theme that emerges from these various studies is a very unflattering portrait of corporate management: Give executives lots of rope and they too often end up hanging themselves. It would appear that a high dividend payout ratio is an effective way to reduce the length of that rope."

The Dividend Reinvestment Plan

Unless you are retired, you might like to reinvest your dividends in more shares.

Many companies have a dividend reinvestment plan (also known as a DRIP) that will allow you to do this, and the charge for this service is often minimal. Most of these companies also allow you to mail in additional cash, which will be used to purchase new shares, again at minimal cost.

In recent years, a few companies have created "direct" dividend reinvestment plans. Unlike most plans, direct plans enable you to buy your initial shares directly from the company. To alert you to which companies have direct plans, I have inserted the word *direct*. Companies having such plans include ExxonMobil, McDonald's, Procter & Gamble, Merck, and Lilly. Incidentally, you can rarely buy just one share. Many companies have a minimum amount, such as $500.

This may sound like a good way to avoid paying brokerage commissions, but there are some drawbacks to bear in mind. For one thing, you can't time your purchases, since it may be a week or more before your purchase is made.

Even worse is calculating your cost basis for tax purposes. By the time you sell, you may have made scores of small investments in the same stock, each with a different cost basis. Make sure you keep a file for each company so that you can make these calculations when the time comes. Or, better still, don't sell.

Dollar Cost Averaging

Dollar cost averaging is a systematic way to invest money over a long period, such as ten, fifteen, or twenty years. It entails investing the same amount of money regularly, such as each month or each quarter. If you do this faithfully, you will be buying more stock when the price is lower, and less stock when the price is higher. This tends to smooth out the gyrations of the market. Dollar cost averaging is often used with a mutual fund,

but it can just as easily be done with a company that has a dividend reinvestment plan (DRIP).

Income Statement

Most investors are more interested in the income statement than they are in the balance sheet. They are particularly interested in the progress (or lack of it) in earnings per share (EPS). The income statement lists such items as net sales, cost of sales, interest expense, and gross profit. As with the balance sheet, it makes sense to compare this year's numbers with those of the prior year.

Inflation-Indexed Treasury Bonds

Conventional bonds—those that pay a fixed rate of return, such as 5 percent—have one big drawback: They are vulnerable to rising interest rates. For example, if you buy a bond that promises to pay you 5 percent for the next fifteen or twenty years, you will lose principal if interest rates climb to 7 percent. The reason is that new bonds being issued give investors a much better return. Thus, those that pay only 5 percent will sag in price until they hit a level that equates them to the new bonds that pay 7 percent. The loss of principal, moreover, is much greater with long-term bonds, such as those due in fifteen, twenty, or thirty years.

By contrast, short-term bonds, those coming due in three or four years, are much less volatile because you can often hold the bonds until the maturity date. Thus, you are certain to receive the full face value. Of course, you can do the same thing with a twenty-year bond, but twenty years is a long time.

The way to beat this disadvantage is to buy the relatively new bonds being issued by the U.S. government, since they are indexed to inflation. For this reason, you are unlikely to lose principal. To be sure, they pay less initially, currently 3.8 percent. But the ultimate return may be much better if inflation continues to impact the economy.

Suppose you invested $1,000 in inflation bonds at the current yield of 3.8 percent. If consumer prices rose 2.5 percent over the next year, your principal would climb to $1,025, and you would earn interest equal to 3.8 percent on this growing sum. Thus, if you spent the interest but didn't cash in any bonds, you would enjoy a rising stream of income while keeping your principal's spending power intact.

One thing to bear in mind: With inflation-indexed Treasury bonds, you have to pay federal income taxes each year on both the interest you earn and also the increase in the bonds' principal value. One way to take the sting out of this tax is to use these bonds in a tax-deferred account, such as an IRA.

Despite the tax implications, inflation bonds may be useful outside an IRA. Because these bonds don't perform as erratically as conventional bonds, they can be a good place to park money you may need if something unexpected comes along, such as a medical bill not fully covered by insurance. If inflation-indexed bonds ring a bell, ask the teller at your bank to get you started. She won't charge you a fee, and there is no red tape.

Investment Advisor

Investors who do not have the time or inclination to manage their own portfolios may elect to employ an investment advisor. Most advisors charge 1 percent a year. Thus, if you own stocks worth $300,000, your annual fee would be $3,000. Advisors differ from brokers, since they do not profit from changes. Brokers, by contrast, charge a commission on each transaction, which means they profit from changes in your portfolio. Advisors profit only when the value of your holdings increases. For instance, if

the value of your portfolio increases to $500,000, the annual fee will be $5,000. You, of course, will be $200,000 richer.

Moving Average

Some investors use the moving average to time the market. The strategy is to buy a stock when it is selling above its moving average and sell when it falls below. A popular moving average is the 200-day version. A dotted line is drawn, taking the average price of the stock over the previous 200 days. The actual price of the stock is plotted on the same graph. Studies show that this method of timing the market does not work on a consistent basis.

PEG Ratio

The PEG ratio is supposed to be helpful in determining if a stock is too expensive. It is calculated by dividing the price-earnings ratio by the expected earnings growth rate. Let's say the P/E ratio of American International Group is 34.39, which is calculated by dividing the price ($98) by the expected EPS in 2001 of $2.85. Meanwhile, the earnings per share in the 1989–1999 period expanded from $0.67 to $2.18, a compound annual growth rate of 12.52 percent. When you divide 34.39 by 12.52, the PEG ratio is 2.75. According to Michael Sivy, a writer for *Money* magazine, "Stocks with a PEG ratio of 1.5 or less are often the best buys."

By that rule, you would avoid American International Group. Curiously, Mr. Sivy includes AIG on his list of "100 Stocks for Long-Term Investors," published in January 2001. By his calculation, AIG had a PEG ratio at that time of 2.5.

Once again, I am a doubting Thomas. Who is to say what a company's future growth rate will be? You can easily determine what it has been in the past. And that may give you some indication of the future, but it is far from reliable. The P/E ratio is also a slippery number, since you are expected to base it on the EPS for the year ahead. I prefer to base it on the most recent twelve months, since that is a figure that does not depend on a crystal ball.

Preferred Stock

The name sounds impressive. In actual practice, owning preferred stocks is about as exciting as watching your cat take a bath. A preferred stock is much like a bond. It pays the same dividend year in and year out. The yield is usually higher than a common stock. If the company issuing the preferred stock does well, you do not benefit. If it does poorly, however, you may suffer, since the dividend could be cut or eliminated. My advice is: Never, never buy a preferred stock.

Price–Earnings Ratio (P/E)

This is a term that is extremely important. Don't make the mistake of overlooking it. Whole books have been written on the importance of the P/E ratio, which is sometimes referred to as "the P/E" or "the multiple."

The P/E ratio tells you whether a stock is cheap or expensive. It is calculated by dividing the price of the stock by the company's earnings per share over the most recent twelve months. For instance, if you refer to the *Stock Guide*, you will see that Leggett and Platt had earnings of $2.23. At the time, the stock was selling for $52. Divide that figure by $2.23 and you get a P/E of 23.32.

In most instances, a low P/E indicates a stock that Wall Street is not too excited about. If they like a stock, they will bid it up to the point where its P/E is quite high, let's say twenty-five or thirty. Coca-Cola is such a stock. In this same *Stock Guide*, Coca-Cola had annual earnings per share of $1.59. Based on the price of the stock at that time (it was $75), that works out to a P/E ratio of 47.17. Of course, Coca-Cola is

extremely well regarded by investors and is expected to do well in the future—but is it really worth forty-seven times earnings?

Reverse Stock Split

Stock splits are normally a happy occasion. If you have 100 shares of a stock selling for $80 a share, the company may announced a two-for-one stock split. In due course, you will have 200 shares, each worth $40. You are no richer, but you may be happier.

A reverse stock split, however, is *not* good news. If you have 200 shares of a stock selling for $1.25, the company may be contemplating upgrading your shares by announcing a reverse stock split. They will issue new shares worth, say, ten times as much. Now you have only twenty shares, each one worth $12.50. Again, you are no richer. But you may be unhappy. You should be. Studies show that a reverse stock split is a bad omen.

In July 1997, the *Journal of Business* measured all reverse stock splits from 1926 to 1991. The authors were two professors of accounting, Hemang A. Desai of Southern Methodist University and Prem C. Jain of Georgetown. According to an article in the *New York Times* by Mark Hulbert (dated November 3, 2002), "They found that, over the year after the announcement, the average stock undergoing a reverse stock split performed 8.5 percent worse than the stock market."

Mr. Hulbert explained why some companies resort to this device. "David L. Ikenberry, a finance professor at the University of Illinois at Urbana-Champaign, and Sundaresh Ramnath, an accounting professor at Georgetown, have developed a theory that does explain it. They believe that when management lacks confidence in its company's stock, it is more likely to use a reverse split. By contrast, they say, if management believes that the low price is just temporary, it will be more likely to leave the stock alone."

Stock Split

Corporations know that investors like to invest in lower-priced stocks. Thus, when the price of the stock gets to a certain level, which varies with the company, they will split the stock. For instance, if the stock is $75, they might split it three-for-one. Your original 100 shares now become 300 shares. Unfortunately, your 300 shares are worth exactly the same as your original 100 shares. What it amounts to is this: Splits please small investors, but they don't make them any richer. One company, Berkshire Hathaway, has never been split. It is now worth a huge amount per share: over $70,000. It also pays no dividend. The company is run by the legendary Warren Buffett. He has made a lot of people very wealthy without a stock split or dividend.

Technician

There are two basic ways to analyze stocks. One is *fundamental*; the other is *technical*.

Fundamental analysts examine a stock's management, sales and earnings potential, research capabilities, new products, competitive strength, balance sheet strength, dividend growth, political developments, and industry conditions.

Technicians, by contrast, rarely consider any of these fundamental factors. They rely on charts and graphs and a host of other arcane statistical factors, such as point-and-figure charts, breadth indicators, head-and-shoulders formations, relative strength ratings, and the 200-day-moving average. This technical jargon is often difficult to fathom for the average investor. Among professional portfolio managers, the fundamental approach predominates, although some institutions may also employ a technician.

The question is: Do technicians have the key to stock picking or predicting the trend of the market? Frankly, I am a skeptic, as are most academic analysts. Among the nonbelievers is Kenneth L. Fisher, the longtime columnist for *Forbes* magazine who I mentioned earlier. His columns are among my favorites. Here is what Mr. Fisher says about technicians. "One of the questions I hear most often is, 'Can charts really predict stock prices?' Naturally, there is only one answer: a flat 'No.'"

Mr. Fisher goes on to say: "There is virtually nothing in theory or empiricism to indicated anyone can predict stock prices based solely on prior stock price action. Nevertheless, a big world of chartists continues to exist, amplified by recent Internet day trading. Yet the world of investors with long-lasting success is devoid of them."

Such eminently successful portfolio managers as Peter Lynch and Warren Buffett, for instance, don't resort to charts and other technical mumbo jumbo.

Yield

If your company pays a dividend, you can relate this dividend to the price of the stock in order to calculate the yield. A $50 stock that pays a $2 annual dividend (which amounts to 50 cents per quarter) will have a yield of 4 percent. You arrive at this figure by dividing $2 by $50. Actually, you don't have to make this calculation, since the yield is given to you in the stock tables of the *Wall Street Journal*. Here are some typical yields: Coca-Cola, 1.5 percent; ExxonMobil, 2.0 percent; General Electric, 1.3 percent; Illinois Tool Works, 1.2 percent; Kimberly-Clark, 1.8 percent; and Minnesota Mining and Manufacturing, 2.0 percent. Although the yield is of some importance, you should not judge a stock by its yield without looking at many other factors.

The Pros and Cons of Dollar Cost Averaging

If you are relatively new to the investment scene, a good way to get started is through a dollar cost averaging program. The chances are that you don't have a big enough nest egg to buy 100 shares of ExxonMobil, GE, Merck, International Paper, Procter & Gamble, American Express, Becton, Dickinson, Air Products & Chemicals, or Caterpillar.

Fortunately, all of these companies make it easy for you to launch your program. Each has a "direct" dividend reinvestment program. These programs enable you to buy your initial shares directly from the company. However, most have a minimum investment level to start out as well as a minimum amount that you can invest at any given time. A good source of this information is the June issue of the *AAII Journal*, a publication of the American Association of Individual Investors.

Minimum Initial Investment	Minimum Payments	Thereafter
Air Products	$500	$100
American Express	$1,000	$50
Becton, Dickinson	$250	$50
Caterpillar	$500	$50
ExxonMobil	$250	$50
General Electric	$250	$10
International Paper	$500	$50
Merck	$350	$50
Procter & Gamble	$250	$100

Even so, the minimum is a lot less than the cost of buying 100 shares. Incidentally, there is no rule that says you must buy 100 shares. You can buy eighteen shares, fifty-two shares, fourteen shares, or any number of shares that strike your fancy. However, bear in mind that most

brokerage houses have a minimum commission, often $50 or more.

Now, back to dollar cost averaging. If you have never invested before, you can start a program by calling one of the companies that has a "direct" program. You will find their telephone numbers is in this book, at the beginning of the listing for each company.

Your first decision is to make up your mind which stock you want to begin with. Of course, there is no reason why you have to restrict yourself to one. Let's say you have $500 to invest each month. You could begin your program by calling ExxonMobil and GE, since each has a $250 minimum. The following month you could call Merck, and so forth. Once you have five stocks, you can mail in $100 a month to each one until you reach a certain goal, such as $5,000.

Since five stocks don't constitute a well-diversified portfolio, you could then pick out a few new candidates, once you reach your goals in the initial five stocks.

The Advantages of Dollar Cost Averaging

You don't have to worry about *when* to buy a stock. You are buying shares every month over a period of several years. On balance, you will be paying a fairly average price—sometimes when it's too high, sometimes at a bargain level. Assuming the stock has a generally rising trend, your results will be satisfactory. Here are a few features and advantages to investing using the dollar cost averaging method:

• Most companies don't charge a commission. If they do, it's modest.

• Dividends are automatically reinvested with no fee.

• You will receive quarterly and annual reports, enabling you to determine if you want to continue your program. However, you should not limit your reading to information provided by the company. Read about your stocks in such publications as the *New York Times*, the *Wall Street Journal*, *Forbes*, *BusinessWeek*, or *Better Investing*. You want to be an informed investor.

Don't Forget the Shortcomings

According to most articles on dollar-cost averaging, you are likely to have good results because you are buying a constant dollar amount worth of stock each month or quarter. For instance, if you invest $500 a month over a period of twenty or thirty years, the rising trend of the stock market is likely to be kind to you, and you will end up wealthy. To be sure, if you actually invested $500 a month for twenty years, you should be happy with the value of your shares.

On the other hand, life is not that simple. Your situation is likely to change, depending on your job, your health, or your marital situation. What happens to your program if you lose your job? You might spend six months looking for a new one. Meanwhile, you will probably not be investing $500 a month. What's more, the new job may not pay as well as the old one. Marriages have a habit of falling apart, which may mean someone has to pay alimony—another blow to your investment plan.

Or, on a happier note, you might get a better job and suddenly be able to invest $1,000 a month. That would also change your program, since it could happen at a time when the stock market is very high, which would mean you may be investing a much larger amount during a period when you are also paying too much for your favorite stocks.

If you want to sell some of your shares to pay off the mortgage or scrape up cash for a down payment on a house, you may have to wait for your money a week or two. By contrast, if you have shares at a brokerage house, you can sell in a few minutes and have your cash a few days later. In addition, you will know exactly what you are getting for your shares when they are held by a broker. But if you have a dividend reinvestment program, the price you receive may not be exactly the same as they are the day you direct the company to liquidate some of your shares.

When you sell your shares sometime in the future, let's say twenty years from now, you will have to furnish the IRS with a cost basis. That will not make you happy, particularly if you don't have a complete file on the stock being sold. Make sure you have a file folder for each stock, and also make sure you keep it up to date as dividend statements and quarterly reports come in.

In order to determine your cost basis, you have to find out exactly how much was invested in that stock, including the initial purchase of $500, all the monthly payments you mailed in, and each quarterly dividend. If you have owned the stock for twenty years, that means eighty separate dividends, each with a different price and each for a different amount. It may take you several hours to make this tabulation. In despair, you may let your CPA do it, and you can be sure the fee will be substantial.

Summary

I speak from experience when I discuss dollar cost averaging and the dividend reinvestment plan. Several of the stocks my wife and I own were obtained in this way. I recently sold some of my Eli Lilly, and I found out that determining the cost basis was not something I want to do again very soon.

On a more positive note, my investments have enabled me to become financially secure (translation: rich). My wife and I own fifty-five stocks, and they are worth many hundreds of thousands of dollars.

Whether you buy your stocks from a broker or through a plan is not the key issue. The key issue is initiating your investment program early in life and investing a substantial amount, such as 10 percent of your income each year. If you do that for thirty years or more, you won't have to rely entirely on Social Security.

Some Simple Formulas for Asset Allocation

Serious investors spend a lot of time deciding which stocks or mutual funds to buy. I can't quarrel with that. If you are going to invest $10,000 in Merck, Illinois Tool Works, Praxair, Leggett & Platt, or United Technologies, you shouldn't do it without some research and thought.

On the other hand, some financial gurus maintain that it is far more important to make an effort to achieve an effective approach to asset allocation. They believe that you should place your emphasis on how much of your portfolio is invested in such sectors as:

Government bonds
Corporate bonds
Municipal bonds
Convertible bonds
Preferred stocks
Large-capitalization domestic stocks
Small-capitalization domestic stocks
Foreign stocks
Foreign bonds
Certificates of deposit
Annuities
Money-market funds

There are probably a few other categories you could include in your portfolio, but I think that examining this list gives you an idea of what is meant by asset allocation.

To illustrate the importance of asset allocation, look at 1998. You may recall that the long bull market temporarily aborted in mid-July of that year. Prior to that time, the big blue chip stocks had been making heady progress. Beneath the surface, however, the small and medium-size stocks were already in their own bear

market. Thus, if you had avoided these smaller companies in the first six months of 1998, you would have sidestepped the devastation that was taking place in this sector.

After mid-July, however, the big stocks—particularly the financial stocks such as J. P. Morgan, Travelers (now Citigroup), and American Express—took a real tumble. The best place to be during this period was in U.S. government bonds. Once again, we are talking about asset allocation and how it can help or hurt you.

My Approach to Asset Allocation

From the comments made so far, you can see that asset allocation, like everything else in the world of finance, can get rather complex and confusing. It is no wonder that many people don't delve into this arcane realm. That's where John Slatter comes to the rescue. My idea of investing is to make it simple. After all, there are just so many hours in the day. If you are still gainfully employed, you probably work eight hours a day making a living. In the evenings, you may spend a few hours a week reading journals and other material so that you don't get fired. Obviously, that doesn't leave much time for studying the stock market.

For my part, I don't invest in many small-cap stocks, foreign stocks, bonds, convertibles, preferred stocks, or most of the other stuff on my list. I prefer to invest mostly in big-cap stocks (such as ExxonMobil, GE, Merck, IBM, Procter & Gamble, and Johnson & Johnson) and money-market funds (a safe alternative to cash).

This reduces my categories to two, not a dozen. All you have to do is decide what percentage of your portfolio is in stocks. The rest is in a money-market fund. Of course, the *percentage* is vitally important.

A Few Alternatives to Consider

Some people may be shocked that I am not concerned about foreign stocks. One firm I once worked for insisted that we strive to invest 20 percent of each investor's portfolio in foreign stocks, such as Schlumberger, Repsol, Royal Dutch Petroleum, British Telecommunications, or Elf Aquitaine.

I have no objection to such stocks, but I see no urgency to adhere to a rigid percentage. For one thing, foreign stocks are more difficult to research. Their annual reports are far less revealing than those put out by corporations here at home. They also have different and less informative accounting.

In any event, the United States has hundreds of great companies. We are the envy of the world when it comes to business. The Japanese—at least for a decade or two—tried to convince people otherwise. But they have spent that last several years wallowing in a serious recession.

As far as bonds are concerned, they don't have a particularly impressive record. Except for a year here or there, common stocks have always been a better place to be. What's more, the return on bonds today is not much better than the rate you can get on a money-market fund.

One more thing: Bonds, even U.S. Treasuries, have an element of risk; they decline in value when interest rates go up. Long-term bonds, moreover, slide precipitously when rates shoot up.

I don't want to spend too much time discussing the shortcomings of the rest of the list. I would prefer to point out the virtues of major stocks, such as McDonald's, Wal-Mart, Hewlett-Packard, Caterpillar, Boeing, Alcoa, Eli Lilly, 3M Company, and Walt Disney.

Blue chip companies are not likely to go bankrupt. To be sure, they have their troubles, but they are big enough to hire a CEO who can bring them back to life. Among the thirty companies in the Dow Jones Industrial Average, for instance, such companies as IBM, Eastman Kodak, AT&T, Sears, United Technologies, and AlliedSignal were restructured in recent years by a few dynamic executives.

Major corporations are also found in most institutional portfolios such as mutual funds, pension plans, bank trust departments, and insurance companies. One reason they like these big-capitalization stocks is liquidity. Since institutions have huge amounts of cash to invest, they feel comfortable with these stocks. The reason: The number of shares outstanding is huge, which means they won't disturb the market when they buy or sell. By contrast, if a major institution tries to invest a million dollars in a tiny NASDAQ company, the stock will shoot up several points before they complete their investing. It could be just as disruptive when they try to get out. As a consequence, major companies are in demand and are not left to drift. On the other hand, there are thousands of small companies that no one ever heard of. The only investors who can push them up are individuals—not institutions.

Another reason I like big companies is because they can afford to hire top-notch executives and they have the resources to allocate to research and marketing. In addition, their new products, acquisitions, management changes, and strategies are discussed frequently in such publications as the *Wall Street Journal*, the *New York Times*, *Barron's*, *Fortune*, *Forbes*, and *BusinessWeek*, all of which I subscribe to.

How Much Should You Invest in Stocks?

When it comes to deciding on the percentage you should devote to common stocks, there are several alternatives that should be considered. All have some merit, and none are perfect.

In fact, there is no such thing as a perfect formula for asset allocation. It depends on such factors as your age and your temperament. It might also depend on what you think the market is going to do. If it's about to soar, you would want to be fully invested. But if you think stocks are poised to fall off a cliff, you might prefer to seek the safety of a money-market fund.

Forget about Everything Else and Buy Only Stocks

Believe it or not, there are some investors who are convinced that common stocks—and common stocks alone—are the royal road to riches. A good friend of mine has never bought anything but stocks, and he's been doing it for many years. He even went through the severe bear market of 1973–1974, when stocks plunged over 40 percent. He wasn't exactly happy to see his stocks being ground to a pulp, but he hung on. Today, he is a millionaire many times over. His name is David A. Seidenfeld, a businessman in Cleveland.

Dave (who died in June of 2003) got his start by listening to the late S. Allen Nathanson, a savvy investor who wrote a series of magazine articles on why common stocks are the best way to achieve great wealth. Dave Seidenfeld recently collected these essays and published them as a hardcover book, *Bullishly Speaking*, which is available in Borders bookstores.

If you start investing early, such as in your forties, this method can work. If you systematically invest, setting aside 10 or 15 percent of your earnings each year and doing it through thick and thin, you won't need any bonds, money-market funds, or any of the other alternatives that financial magazines seem to think you must have. You will arrive at retirement with a large portfolio that will enable you to live off the dividends.

However, if you arrived late to the investment party—let's say in your late fifties or early sixties—you may not be able to sleep too well if you rely entirely on common stocks. After all, stocks have their shortcomings, too. They tend to bounce around a lot, and they can cut their dividends when things turn bleak.

Some Options to Consider

If you are an ultraconservative investor, I suggest you invest only 55 percent of your portfolio in common stocks. To be sure, when the stock market is marching ahead, as it has in recent years, you won't be able to keep pace. But if it falters and heads south for a year or two, your cautious approach will keep you out of the clutches of insomnia. Frankly, I don't think such a timid approach is the best way to approach asset allocation. However, I worked for a firm a few years ago that used this formula on nearly everyone. As far as I know, there weren't too many people complaining.

A better way to handle the uncertainty is to invest 70 percent in stocks, with the rest in a money-market fund. Once you decide on a particular percentage, stick with it. Don't change it every time someone makes a market forecast. These market forecasts don't work often enough to pay any attention to them. To my knowledge, no professional investor has a consistent record in forecasting. Every once in a while, one of these pundits makes a correct call at a crucial turning point, and from that day on, everyone listens intently to the pronouncements of this person—until the day the pronouncement is totally wrong. That day always comes.

My Favorite Formula for Asset Allocation

I think age is the key to asset allocation. The older you are, the less you should have in common stocks. If you are age sixty-five, you should have 65 percent in common stocks, with the rest in a money-market fund. If you are younger than sixty-five, add 1 percent per year to your common stock sector. As an example, if you are sixty years old, you will have 70 percent in stocks.

If you are older than sixty-five, deduct 1 percent a year. Thus, if you are age seventy, you will have only 60 percent in stock. When you reach eighty, you will be 50–50. And if you are much younger than sixty-five, let's say forty-five, you will have 85 percent in stocks.

If you are not sure what this all means, here is a table breaking down the two percentages by age:

AGE	STOCKS	MONEY-MARKET FUNDS
40	90%	10%
45	85	15
50	80	20
55	75	25
60	70	30
65	65	35
70	60	40
75	55	45
80	50	50
85	45	55

Part II

100 Best Stocks You Can Buy

The following table lists the 100 stocks discussed in this book, with a brief description of each.

The ticker symbol is given so that you can easily look up the stock on the Internet or use the quote machine in your broker's office. This also makes it easier to get a quote over the phone from your broker, since brokers don't know every ticker symbol.

In the table, "Industry" refers to one of the company's main businesses. This is not always easy to express in one or two words.

For instance, United Technologies is involved in such industries as aircraft engines, elevators, and air-conditioning equipment. To describe the company succinctly, I arbitrarily picked the designation "aircraft engines."

General Electric presents an even more daunting problem since it owns NBC and makes appliances, aircraft engines, medical devices, and a host of other things.

"Sector" indicates the broad economic industry group that the company operates in. In this book, I specify the following ten sectors: Energy, Financial, Drug & Health Care, Consumer Staples, Consumer Discretion, Information Technology, Industrials, Materials, Telecommunications, and Utilities. A properly diversified portfolio should include at least one stock from each of the ten sectors.

"Category" refers to the type of investment the stock represents, as follows: "Income" for income stocks; "Gro Inc" for growth and income; "Con Grow" for conservative growth; and "Aggr Gro" for aggressive growth. As with the sectors your stocks represent, it might make sense to have some stocks from each category, even if you have a strong preference for only one.

I have not included the page numbers because of space limitations. In any event, it is easy enough to find a particular stock, since they appear alphabetically in the book.

COMPANY	SYMBOL	INDUSTRY	SECTOR	CATEGORY
3M Company	MMM	Diversified	Industrials	Gro Inc
–A–				
Abbott Laboratories	ABT	Med Supplies	Drugs/Health	Con Grow
Air Products	APD	Gases	Materials	Con Grow
Alberto-Culver	ACV	Cosmetics	Cons Staples	Con Grow
Alcoa	AA	Aluminum	Materials	Aggr Gro
Anheuser-Busch	BUD	Beer	Cons Staples	Con Grow
Automatic Data *	ADP	Data Proc	Industrials	Aggr Gro
AutoZone *	AZO	Auto Parts	Cons Discret	Aggr Gro
Avery Dennison	AVY	Adhesives	Industrials	Con Grow
–B–				
Banta	BN	Printing	Industrials	Gro Inc
Bard, C.R. *	BCR	Med Supplies	Drugs/Health	Con Grow
Baxter Int'l	BAX	Med Supplies	Drugs/Health	Aggr Gro
Becton, Dickinson	BDX	Med Supplies	Drugs/Health	Con Grow
Bemis Company	BMS	Packaging	Materials	Con Grow
Biomet, Inc. *	BMET	Orthopedic	Drugs/Health	Aggr Gro
Block, H&R	HRB	Income Tax	Industrials	Con Grow
Boeing	BA	Aerospace	Industrials	Aggr Gro
Boston Properties	BXP	REIT	Financial	Income
Brinker Internat'l *	EAT	Restaurants	Cons Discret	Aggr Gro
Brown-Forman *	BRO	Liquors	Cons Staples	Con Grow

α dropped in 2005 edition

-C-

Cardinal Health ✓	CAH	Health Care	Drugs/Health	Aggr Gro
Caterpillar *	CAT	Machinery	Industrials	Gro Inc
Cedar Fair	FUN	Entertainm't	Cons Discret	Income
Cintas ✓	CTAS	Uniforms	Industrials	Aggr Gro
Clorox	CLX	Household Pd	Cons Staples	Gro Inc
Coca-Cola	KO	Beverages	Cons Staples	Con Grow
Colgate-Palmolive	CL	Household Pd	Cons Staples	Con Grow
ConAgra	CAG	Food	Cons Staples	Income
Costco Wholesale	COST	Wholesale	Cons Discret	Aggr Gro
Craftmade *	CRFT	Elect Fixt	Cons Discret	Aggr Gro

-D-

Darden Restaurants *	DRI	Restaurants	Cons Discret	Con Grow
DeVry	DV	Schools	Industrials	Aggr Gro
Dominion Resources	D	G&E Utility	Utilities	Income
Donaldson	DCI	Filtration	Industrials	Con Grow

-E-

Ecolab	ECL	Cleaning	Materials	Aggr Gro
Emerson Electric	EMR	Elect Equip	Industrials	Gro Inc
Equity Office Prop.	EOP	REIT	Financial	Income
Ethan Allen	ETH	Furniture	Cons Discret	Aggr Gro

-F-

Family Dollar Stores *	FDO	Retail	Cons Discret	Aggr Gro
FedEx Corporation	FDX	Air Freight	Industrials	Aggr Gro
Fortune Brands	FO	Consumer Prod	Cons Discret	Gro Inc

-G-

Gannett	GCI	Media	Cons Discret	Con Grow
General Electric	GE	Elect Equip	Industrials	Gro Inc
General Motors	GM	Automobile	Cons Discret	Gro Inc
Genuine Parts *	GPC	Automotive	Industrials	Income
Gillette *	G	Razor Blades	Cons Staples	Aggr Gro
Grainger, W. W. *	GWW	Maintenance	Industrials	Con Grow

-H-

Harman International *	HAR	Audio Prod	Cons Discret	Aggr Gro
Health Mgt. Assoc. *	HMA	Hospitals	Drugs/Health	Aggr Gro
Hormel Foods	HRL	Food	Cons Staples	Con Grow

-I-

Illinois Tool Works	ITW	Machinery	Industrials	Con Grow
Intel	INTC	Computers	Inform Tech	Aggr Gro
Int'l Business Mach	IBM	Computer	Inform Tech	Aggr Gro

-J-

Johnson & Johnson	JNJ	Med Supplies	Drugs/Health	Con Grow
Johnson Controls	JCI	Elect Equip	Cons Discret	Con Grow

-K-

Kimco Realty	KIM	REIT	Financial	Income

-L-

Lancaster Colony *	LANC	Food	Cons Staples	Gro Inc
La-Z-Boy *	LZB	Furniture	Cons Discret	Gro Inc
Leggett & Platt *	LEG	Furn Comp	Industrials	Con Grow
Lennar Corporation *	LEN	Housing	Cons Discret	Aggr Gro
Lilly, Eli	LLY	Drugs	Drugs/Health	Aggr Gro
Lockheed Martin	LMT	Aerospace	Industrials	Aggr Gro
Lowe's Companies	LOW	Retail	Cons Discret	Con Grow

–M–

McCormick & Co.	MKC	Spices	Cons Staples	Con Grow
McGraw-Hill	MHP	Publishing	Cons Discret	Con Grow
MDU Resources	MDU	G&E Utility	Utilities	Gro Inc
Medtronic	MDT	Med Devices	Drugs/Health	Aggr Gro
Merck	MRK	Drugs	Drugs/Health	Gro Inc
Meredith *	MDP	Publishing	Cons Discret	Con Grow
Microsoft	MSFT	Comp Softw	Inform Tech	Aggr Gro

–N–

National City	NCC	Bank	Financial	Gro Inc
The New York Times *	NYT	Media	Cons Discret	Con Grow
Newell Rubbermaid *	NWL	Household Pd	Cons Discret	Aggr Gro

–O–

Oshkosh Truck *	OSK	Trucks	Industrials	Aggr Gro

–P–

Patterson Dental *	PDCO	Dental	Drugs/Health	Aggr Gro
PepsiCo	PEP	Beverages	Cons Staples	Con Grow
Pfizer	PFE	Drugs	Drugs/Health	Aggr Gro
Piedmont Nat'l Gas	PNY	Nat'l Gas	Utilities	Income
Pitney Bowes	PBI	Postage Mtrs	Industrials	Gro Inc
Praxair	PX	Indust Gases	Materials	Con Grow
Procter & Gamble	PG	Household Pd	Cons Staples	Con Grow

–R–

Reynolds & Reynolds *	REY	Mgt Info	Inform Tech	Con Grow
RPM International *	RPM	Coatings	Cons Discret	Gro Inc
Ruby Tuesday *	RI	Restaurants	Cons Discret	Con Grow

–S–

Scholastic Corp. *	SCHL	Publishing	Cons Discret	Aggr Gro
Scripps, E. W. *	SSP	Media	Cons Discret	Aggr Gro
Staples *	SPLS	Office Prod	Cons Discret	Aggr Gro
Stryker	SYK	Medical Sup	Drugs/Health	Aggr Gro
Sysco Corporation	SYY	Food Distrib	Cons Staples	Con Grow

–T–

Target	TGT	Retail	Cons Discret	Aggr Gro
Toll Brothers *	TOL	Home Builder	Cons Discret	Aggr Gro
Tractor Supply *	TSCO	Retail	Cons Discret	Con Grow

–U–

UnitedHealth	UNH	Health Care	Drugs/Health	Con Grow
United Parcel *	UPS	Expr Carrier	Industrials	Aggr Gro
United Technologies	UTX	Aircraft Eng	Industrials	Con Grow

–V–

Varian Medical	VAR	Med Devices	Drugs/Health	Aggr Gro

–W–

Walgreen	WAG	Drug Stores	Cons Staples	Aggr Gro
Wal-Mart	WMT	Retail	Cons Discret	Aggr Gro
Washington Real Est.	WRE	REIT	Financial	Income
Weingarten Realty	WRI	REIT	Financial	Income

* New in this edition.

3M Company

(Formerly Minnesota Mining & Manufacturing Company)

3M Center, Building 225-1S-15 □ St. Paul, Minnesota 55144-1000 □ (651) 733-8206 □ Web site: www.3M.com □ Listed: NYSE □ Dividend reinvestment plan available: (800) 401-1952 □ Ticker symbol: MMM □ S&P rating: A- □ Value Line financial strength rating: A++

When GE selected a new chief executive to replace the legendary Jack Welch, the two runners-up for the post were immediately courted by companies looking for their own CEO replacements.

Among the companies was 3M (Minnesota Mining & Manufacturing), since its chairman, Livio D. DeSimone was slated to retire on January 1, 2001. W. James McNerney, Jr., who headed GE's aircraft-engines division, was fifty-one years old when he took the reins of 3M in December of 2000.

Mr. McNerney said that a notably bright spot is 3M's technology business, which he described as "far broader and deeper than most people understand." One of the company's strongest performers in the technology realm is the electro and communications segment, maker of fiber-optic cabling systems and tiny, flexible circuits used in inkjet printers.

Within the first three weeks on the job, Mr. McNerney outlined a cost-cutting strategy that focused on four key factors, one of which was the implementation of Six Sigma—an efficiency and quality assurance strategy he brought with him from General Electric. To be sure, 3M is relatively inexperienced when dealing with these new programs and strategies. However, "there can be no doubt regarding their effectiveness," said an analyst with Argus Research Corporation.

According to James R. Sanders, in a report issued by *Standard & Poor's Stock Reports* in November of 2002: "Over the past ten years, EPS [earnings per share] and retained earnings (a good proxy for net asset performance) grew at low average annual rates of 4.3 percent and 5.3 percent, respectively.

"Despite these historical issues, Mr. McNerney has much to work with. 3M possesses excellent brand names and maintains dominant positions in most of its markets. In addition, it has strong global reach, as shown by international sales contributions (more than 50 percent of revenues, and more than 60 percent of operating profits). The company is highly profitable: three of its six business units boast profit margins of 20 percent or more; return on equity over the last ten years averaged 23 percent."

Company Profile

Minnesota Mining & Manufacturing—now known as 3M Company—is a $16-billion diversified technology company with leading positions in industrial, consumer and office, health care, safety, electronics, telecommunications, and other markets. The company has operations in more than 60 countries and serves customers in nearly 200 countries.

3M has a vast array of products (more than 50,000), including such items as tapes, adhesives, electronic components, sealants, coatings, fasteners, floor coverings, cleaning agents, roofing granules, firefighting agents, graphic arts, dental products, medical products, specialty chemicals, and reflective sheeting.

The company's Industrial and Consumer Sector is the world's largest supplier of tapes, producing more than 900 varieties. It is also a leader in coated abrasives, specialty chemicals, repositionable notes, home cleaning sponges and pads, electronic circuits, and other important products.

The Life Sciences Sector is a global leader in reflective materials for transportation safety, respirators for worker safety, closures for disposable diapers, and high-quality graphics for indoor and outdoor use. This sector also holds leading positions in medical and surgical supplies, drug-delivery systems, and dental products.

3M has a decentralized organization with a large number of relatively small profit centers, aimed at creating an entrepreneurial atmosphere.

Shortcomings to Bear in Mind

- 3M was one of the few good performers among the Dow 30 in 2002. Consequently, its P/E ratio is a bit higher than normal. It may make sense to hold off your purchase until a brokerage firm downgrades the stock and makes it more affordable.

Reasons to Buy

3M has many strengths:

- 3M is a leader in most of its businesses, often number one or number two in market share. In fact, this company has created many markets, frequently by developing products that people didn't even realize they needed.
- The company draws on more than thirty core technologies—from adhesives and non-wovens to specialty chemicals and microreplication.
- 3M serves an extremely broad array of markets—from automotive and health care to office supply and telecommunications. This diversity gives the company many avenues for growth while also cushioning the company from disruption in any single market.
- 3M's success in developing a steady stream of new products and entering new markets stems from its deep-rooted

corporate structure. It's an environment in which 3M people listen to customers, act on their own initiative, and share technologies and other expertise widely and freely.

- 3M has companies in more than 60 countries around the world. It sells its products in nearly 200 countries.
- 3M is a low-cost supplier in many of its product lines. This is increasingly important in today's value-conscious and competitive world.
- 3M is one of a small number of domestic companies whose debt carries the highest rating for credit quality.
- To sustain a strong flow of new products, 3M continues to make substantial investments—about $1 billion a year—in research and development.
- 3M is a global leader in industrial, consumer, office, health care, safety, and other markets. The company draws on many strengths, including a rich pool of technology, innovative products, strong customer service, and efficient manufacturing.
- The company's unrelenting drive toward smaller, lighter, more powerful, and more economical electronic products creates strong demand for leading-edge offerings like 3M microflex circuits. 3M is the world's number one supplier of adhesiveless flexible circuitry. 3M microflex circuits connect components in many of the world's inkjet printers. They also link integrated circuits to printed circuit boards efficiently and reliably, making it possible to develop even smaller cellular phones, portable computers, pagers, and other electronic devices.
- 3M supplies a wide variety of products to the automotive market, including high-performance tape attachment systems; structural adhesives; catalytic converter mounts; decorative, functional, and protective films; and trim and identification products.

- The Life Sciences Sector produces innovative products that improve health and safety for people around the world. In consumer and professional health care, 3M has captured a significant share of the first-aid market with a superior line of bandages. 3M Active Strips flexible foam bandages adhere better to skin—even when wet—and 3M Comfort Strips ultracomfortable bandages set new standards for wearing comfort. Under development are tapes, specialty dressings, and skin treatments that will reinforce and broaden the company's leading market positions and accelerate sales growth.

- In pharmaceuticals, 3M is a global leader in technologies for delivering medications that are inhaled or absorbed through the skin, and the company is expanding its horizons in new molecule discovery.

- Hostile conditions lie under any vehicle's hood, but 3M's Dyneon fluoropolymers withstand the heat. Found in seals, gaskets, O-rings, and hoses in automotive and airplane engines, the company's fluoropolymers outperform the competition when high temperatures and chemicals cross paths. And 3M technology isn't merely under the hood. The company also makes products for the vehicle's body and cabin that identify, insulate, protect, and bond—such as dimensional graphics, Thinsulate acoustic insulation, cabin filters, and superstrong adhesives and tapes that replace screws and rivets. The company is also developing window films that help keep the cabin cool by absorbing ultraviolet light and reflecting infrared light.

- Post-It Notes were named one of the twentieth century's best products by *Fortune* magazine, and Scotch tape was listed among the century's 100 best innovations by *BusinessWeek* magazine. Also, 3M ranked as the world's most respected consumer-goods company and fifteenth overall in a survey published by the *Financial Times* of London. Finally, 3M received Achieved Vendor of the Year status from four leaders in the office-supply industry.

- On February 20, 2003, Karen L. Reidy, a portfolio manager for two of the Janus funds, had this to say about 3M, "I'd point to 3M, which I've owned for two and a half years. I bought it just prior to W. James McNerney Jr. taking the role of CEO.

  "Obviously, I think a great deal of McNerney. Most people don't appreciate that this manufacturing, industrial conglomerate has had only one year in the last ten where returns on equity were below 20 percent. It consistently operates at about a 20 percent operating margin. It has returns on invested capital north of 30 percent, and has shown the ability to grow the top line somewhere between 1.5 and 2 times GDP (gross domestic product).

  "Now why is that? Because what might appear at the outside as a sleepy manufacturing company is actually a number of technologies where the company has defensible positions, whether that's in adhesives, abrasive, or optical displays. Or even in a dental products franchise, which is a market that's quietly growing behind the scenes. McNerney has been working to expose the company to markets or product niches where they can accelerate top-line growth."

  This interview was conducted by Ian McDonald for the *Wall Street Journal*.

Total assets: $14,606 million
Current ratio: 1.45
Common shares outstanding: 390 million
Return on 2002 shareholder's equity: 30.5%

	2002	2001	2000	1999	1998	1997	1996	1995
Revenues (millions)	16,332	16,079	16,724	15,659	15,021	15,070	14,236	13,460
Net income (millions)	2,082	1,430	1,782	1,711	1,526	1,626	1,516	1,359
Earnings per share	5.26	4.36	4.45	4.21	3.74	3.88	3.63	3.23
Dividends per share	2.48	2.40	2.32	2.24	2.20	2.12	1.92	1.88
Price High	131.6	127.0	122.9	103.4	97.9	105.5	85.9	69.9
Low	100.0	85.9	78.2	69.3	65.6	80.0	61.3	50.8

CONSERVATIVE GROWTH

Abbott Laboratories

100 Abbott Park Road □ Abbott Park, Illinois 60064-6400 □ (847) 937-8945 □ Dividend reinvestment plan available: (847) 937-7300 □ Web site: www.abbott.com □ Ticker symbol: ABT □ Listed: NYSE □ S&P rating: A □ Value Line financial strength rating: A++

In early 2003, Abbott received approval from the FDA for Humira, a drug that Abbott believes will "be the next huge-selling rheumatoid arthritis drug," according to an article written by Naomi Aoki for the *Boston Globe*. "This drug has been called liquid gold," said Kevin O'Sullivan, vice president of development at Massachusetts Biomedical Initiatives, a Worcester economic development organization.

"It could provide a huge economic and psychological lift for the region."

Ms. Aoki went on to say, "Humira's introduction is also arguably the most important commercial launch in Abbott's 115-year history. It has the potential to be the company's most lucrative drug, generating more than a billion dollars in annual sales within the next three to four years and perhaps, one day, reaching $2 billion a year."

"Abbott has not been known in recent years as a pharmaceutical powerhouse," said Bruce Cranna, an analyst with Leerink Swann & Company in Boston. "Its drug business has been sluggish. It has an aging portfolio. But in Humira, you have a drug that has the potential to single-handedly rejuvenate its business."

"But the competition for the $3-billion rheumatoid arthritis market in the United States promises to be fierce. The chief rivals, Enbrel and Remicade, are both huge-selling drugs considered highly effective in treating the debilitating autoimmune disease, easing the pain, swelling, and stiffness in patients' joints that often strikes in their twenties or thirties and gradually robs them of their ability to walk, climb stairs, and perform other rudimentary tasks."

Enbrel is marketed by Amgen and Wyeth, while Remicade was developed by Johnson & Johnson. Abbott acquired the rights to Humira when it bought the Knoll Pharmaceutical unit of Germany's BASF AG.

Remicade, administered intravenously, is approved for payment by Medicare and thus tends to be the drug of choice for the elderly. Enbrel and Humira are taken as shots, but not intravenously, so they don't qualify for Medicare reimbursement.

According to a January 2003 article in the *Wall Street Journal*, "All three drugs are expensive, underscoring the potential need for a broad prescription-drug benefit for senior citizens in the federal Medicare insurance program. The American College of Rheumatology estimates that, depending on dosage and frequency, Remicade costs between $13,940 and $36,694 a year. The rheumatology group estimates the cost of Enbrel at $15,436 annually, and Abbott has said the cost of Humira will be identical to Enbrel."

Company Profile

Abbott Laboratories is one of the largest diversified health care manufacturers in the world. The company's products are sold in more than 130 countries, with about 40 percent of sales derived from international operations. Abbott has paid consecutive quarterly dividends since 1924.

Abbott's major business segments include Pharmaceuticals & Nutritionals (prescription drugs, medical nutritionals, and infant formulas) and Hospital & Laboratory Products (intravenous solutions, administrative sets, drug-delivery devices, and diagnostic equipment and reagents).

The company's leading brands are the following:

- AxSym systems and reagents (immunodiagnostics)
- Biaxin/Biaxin XL/Klalcid/Klaricid (macrolide antibiotic)
- Depakote (bipolar disorder; epilepsy; migraine prevention)
- Depakote ER (migraine prevention)
- Ensure (adult nutritionals)
- Isomil (soy-based infant formula)
- MediSense glucose-monitoring products
- Similac (infant formula)
- Ultane/Sevorane (anesthetic)

Although revenue growth in Abbott's infant formula and diagnostics businesses has slowed in recent years, new drugs (such as the antibiotic clarithromycin), new indications (including the BPH claim for Hytrin), the launch of disease-specific medical nutritionals, and cost-cutting (diagnostics and hospital supplies) continue to boost the company's profits.

In its biggest acquisition to date, Abbott Laboratories bought the drug business of the German chemical giant BASF AG for $6.9 billion in 2001. BASF's Knoll Pharmaceuticals has developed a promising rheumatoid arthritis treatment, a drug referred to as D2E7. Analysts believe it could be a blockbuster, with annual sales of $1 billion or more. The drug is expected to be commercially available in 2003.

Before its purchase of Knoll, Abbott had come under fire from analysts for not having a major blockbuster drug, either in the works or on the market. Its top-selling drug has been Depakote, which treats bipolar disorder and generates $700 million a year in annual sales. Abbott's joint venture with Takeda Chemical Industries benefits from more than $2 billion in annual sales of Prevacid, but Abbott splits those profits with its Japanese partner.

Shortcomings to Bear in Mind

- In late 2002, H. B. Saftlas, an analyst with *Standard & Poor's Stock Reports*, said, "The company continues to struggle with manufacturing problems. In mid-May, the FDA found that Abbott's Lake County diagnostic plant was not in conformity with quality systems regulations. A lengthy plant closing could cause a loss of market share in diagnostics and hold up approval of new diagnostic products."
- In another article on the same topic, written for the *Wall Street Journal* by Thomas M. Burton, the author said, "Certainly, Abbott has been uniquely hamstrung by its dealings with federal authorities. Only this month (October of 2002), it relaunched the clot-dissolving drug Abbokinase, which has been off the market for more than three years because of the FDA concerns about its manufacturing process."

- George Rho, an analyst with *Value Line Investment Survey*, had some negative thoughts in December of 2002: "These top-quality shares don't look particularly attractive to us. They haven't been favorably ranked for years, reflecting muted earnings and share-price momentum. The manufacturing issue is certainly a concern, having hovered around for so long. Last, despite our expectations that earnings growth will accelerate over the next three to five years, our long-term projections suggest below-average capital appreciation potential."

Reasons to Buy

- Abbott is the leader in rapid testing, in both hospitals and doctor's offices, with tests for strep, pregnancy, and a microbe that causes ulcers. The company's Determine line of tests are self-contained, low in cost, and easy to use. Since its acquisition of MediSense, Inc., in 1996, the company's blood glucose monitoring systems have been well received by diabetic patients. In a move to enhance its drug-discovery capabilities, Abbott Laboratories purchased a biotech firm in 2002. BioDisplay Technologies was founded by researchers from the University of Illinois at Urbana-Champaign. BioDisplay has technology that enables Abbott to shorten the time it takes to discover new drugs. This technology enables scientists to express vast numbers of antibodies on the surface of a single yeast cell. Researchers can create a library of a million different mutated antibodies in days and then select the most promising ones. "The whole idea is to develop a way to pick a needle out of a haystack," said David Kranz, a biochemistry professor at the University of Illinois. "What we are trying to do is pull out the needle, or the best antibody, in the haystack. The haystack is all sorts of different antibodies."

- Like all pharmaceutical companies, Abbott has a host of drugs under investigation. Several of the promising cancer drugs are "non-cytotoxic" agents with relatively benign side effects—unlike most chemotherapy drugs that cause adverse reactions as hair loss and nausea. A number of these new experimental drugs are designed to create "the ability to live with cancer, not die from it and to stabilize the disease," said Perry Nisen, Abbott's divisional vice president of oncology development.

  For instance, several Abbott oncology drugs target the process of angiogenesis, the tendency of a tumor to develop new blood vessels and a new blood supply. One promising drug, called ABT-510, appears to inhibit growth of bladder-cancer tumors. "It's the only angiogenesis inhibitor that I know of that shrinks tumors," Dr. Nisen said.

- In a 2002 move to bolster its line of genetic tests for detecting various types of cancers, Abbott acquired Vysis Inc., a biotech company that produces tests that detect genetic changes in cells. Prior to the acquisition, Abbott's existing molecular diagnostic tests had been largely used for infectious diseases. "Not only does this help in the diagnosis of cancer, but also in selecting therapy," said Ed Michael, Abbott's vice president of diagnostic assays and systems. "There are not a lot of real world examples where you have a diagnostic that is linked to the therapeutic."

- "The real reason to buy Abbott is that it is in the early stages of a growth spurt," according to an article in *Money* magazine in February 2003. "The company will spend heavily this year to launch its much-anticipated arthritis drug, Humira, but by 2004 the drug is expected to boost earnings per share by a hefty 15 percent. Abbott should also have its manufacturing problems behind it by then, and its recent job cuts are expected to generate up to $100 million in annual cost savings for the company." The article was signed "L. G."

Total assets: $24,259 million
Current ratio: 1.26
Common shares outstanding: 1,563 million
Return on 2002 shareholders' equity: 28.3%

	2002	2001	2000	1999	1998	1997	1996	1995
Revenues (millions)	17,685	16,285	13,746	13,178	12,513	11,889	11,018	10,012
Net income (millions)	3,243	1,550	2,786	2,446	2,334	2,079	1,874	1,689
Earnings per share	2.06	.99	1.78	1.57	1.50	1.32	1.18	1.06
Dividends per share	.94	.82	.76	.68	.60	.54	.48	.42
Price High	58.0	57.2	56.2	53.3	50.1	34.9	28.7	22.4
Low	29.8	42.0	29.4	27.9	32.5	24.9	19.1	15.4

CONSERVATIVE GROWTH

Air Products and Chemicals, Inc.

7201 Hamilton Boulevard □ Allentown, PA 18195-1501 □ (610) 481-7461 □ Direct dividend reinvestment plan available: (877) 322-4941 □ Web site: www.airproducts.com □ Listed: NYSE □ Fiscal years end September 30 □ Ticker symbol: APD □ S&P rating: A- □ Value Line financial strength rating: B++

Through joint-venture partnerships with established manufacturers, Air Products has become an accepted local supplier of gases and chemicals in Asia. According to CEO John J. Jones, III, "Our technical strength, operational excellence programs, and safety programs complement our partners' infrastructure and knowledge of local markets. Today, we operate in ten Asian countries, and sales to the region total $1 billion, including equity affiliates.

"Air Products and Chemicals Korea President Matt Cho oversees our gases and chemicals businesses in South Korea, which for years has been one of Asia's fastest-growing economies. At our Ulsan facility, we manufacture vinyl acetate emulsions for adhesives manufacturers throughout Asia. Customers value the quality and consistency of our emulsions, the breadth of our product line, and the local technical support we provide."

Company Profile

Air Products and Chemicals, Inc., is a leading supplier of industrial gases and related equipment, specialty and intermediate chemicals, as well as environmental and energy systems. It has operations in thirty countries.

Air Products' industrial gas and chemical products are used by a diverse base of customers in manufacturing, process, and service industries.

In the environmental and energy businesses, Air Products and its affiliates own and operate facilities to reduce air and water pollution, dispose of solid waste, and generate electric power.

Industrial Gases

- APD is a world leader.
- Its products are essential in many manufacturing processes.
- Gases are produced by cryogenic, adsorption, and membrane technologies.
- They are supplied by tankers, on-site plants, pipelines, and cylinders.
- International sales, including the company's share of joint ventures, represent more than half of Air Products' gas revenues.

The markets served by Industrial Gases include chemical processing, metals, oil and gas production, electronics, research, food, glass, health care, and pulp and paper. Principal products are industrial gases, such as nitrogen, oxygen, hydrogen, argon, and helium, and various specialty, cutting, and welding gases.

Chemicals

• APD has a leadership position in more than 80 percent of the markets served.

• Markets include a wide range of attractive, diversified end uses that reduce overall exposure to economic cycles.

• World-scale, state-of-the-art production facilities and process technology skills ensure consistent, low-cost products while enhancing long-term customer relationships.

• International sales, including exports to more than 100 countries, represent about 40 percent of Air Products' business.

The markets served by the Chemicals operation include adhesives, agriculture, furniture, automotive products, paints and coatings, textiles, paper, and building products. Its principal products are emulsions, polyvinyl alcohol, polyurethane and epoxy additives, surfactants, amines, and polyurethane intermediaries.

Environmental and Energy Systems

• Facilities, owned and operated with partners, dispose of solid waste, reduce air pollution, and generate electrical power.

• Strong positions are built by extending core skills developed in the industrial gas business.

• Forces driving this market are environmental regulations, demand for efficient sources of electrical power, utility deregulation, and privatization. Principal products are waste-to-energy plants, electric power services, and air pollution-control systems.

The markets served by Environmental and Energy Systems include solid waste disposal, electrical power generation, and air pollution reduction.

Equipment and Services

• Cryogenic and noncryogenic equipment is designed and manufactured for various gas-processing applications.

• Equipment is sold worldwide or manufactured for Air Products' industrial gas business and its international network of joint ventures.

The markets served by Equipment and Services include chemicals, steel, oil and gas recovery and power generation.

Shortcomings to Bear in Mind

■ Air Products has a somewhat leveraged balance sheet. Its common stock represents only 64 percent of capitalization. My preference is for common stock to represent 75 percent of capitalization.

■ In the 1992–2002 period, earnings per share grew from $1.19 to $2.33, a compound annual growth rate of only 6.95 percent. In the same ten-year span, moreover, dividends increased from $.42 to $.82, a similar growth rate of 6.92 percent.

Reasons to Buy

■ Early in fiscal 2003, Air Products bought American Homecare Supply for $165 million. Based in Pennsylvania, American Homecare Supply is among the top ten providers of home respiratory therapy and equipment. With this move, Air Products will serve more than 275,000 patients in fourteen countries. Industry analysts expect that the gases segment of the home health care market, which includes oxygen and nitrogen systems, will expand between 7 and 10 percent a year. Robert E. Gadomski, executive vice president of Air Products' Gases and Equipment

Group, said that the company expects to buy more companies as the industry consolidates. "We'll be making acquisitions fairly routinely in this business," he said. "There are thousands of small firms that can be acquired in this sector."

- In the fourth quarter of 2002, according to Mr. Jones, "We took a major step forward in building our leading Asian electronics position by acquiring a controlling interest in San Fu Chemical Company, Ltd., our Taiwanese affiliate. We also signed new business in the Gulf Coast with Murphy Oil USA, Inc., expanding our leading market position in the supply of refinery hydrogen for clean fuels. And we introduced Airflex EF811, a new, environmentally friendly emulsion polymer, which we believe will be a breakthrough for the coatings industry."

- In fiscal 2002, Air Products' sales declined 8 percent. However, net income was about flat with the prior year. Commenting on the year, Mr. Jones, said, "We outperformed the S&P 500 for a second year in a row, a testament to our portfolio-management actions, commitment to improving return on capital, and our focused business execution.

  "On the portfolio front, in addition to the acquisition of San Fu, we improved our business mix by divesting our U.S. packaged gases business. And on October 1st, we completed the acquisition of American Homecare Supply, marking our entry into the U.S. respiratory homecare market."

- Air Products' CPI division is the world's leading supplier of HyCO products (hydrogen, carbon monoxide, and syngas, a mix of hydrogen and carbon monoxide). The company has increased its capacity tenfold in the last ten years, and about 75 percent of its volume is delivered to major global refining and chemical centers via the company's pipelines.

  Air Products' technical leadership, operational expertise, and established franchises make the company the first choice of customers in the petrochemical, refining, specialty chemical, and life sciences industries. Air Products is also NASA's sole supplier of liquid hydrogen for space shuttle launches.

- Air Products got its start in helium in the 1950s, when the federal government hired the company to extract this "noble gas" from natural gas deposits in the Midwestern United States—currently the world's main source of helium. Nearly fifty years later, Air Products is the world's leading helium producer.

  Helium has the lowest melting and boiling point of any element. It is colorless, odorless, and noninflammable. Helium is used in light-air balloons to make artificial "air" (with oxygen) for deep-sea divers. It is also used in welding, semiconductors, and lasers. In addition, liquid helium is used in cryogenics, a branch of physics that studies materials and effects at temperatures approaching absolute zero.

  The helium market is expected to expand by at least 6 percent per year. At this rate, it seems that another expansion in the Air Products Kansas complex will be needed about every two years. And by supplying helium to high-growth markets such as laser welding, semiconductor manufacturing, and fiber optics manufacturing, Air Products is growing faster than the market. The company's KeepCOLD cryogen fill services program supplies more than 4,500 MRI customer sites around the world. Finally, Air Products owns Gardner Cryogenics, a world leader in manufacturing liquid helium and liquid hydrogen distribution and storage equipment.

Total assets: $8,495 million
Current ratio: 1.52
Common shares outstanding: 218 million
Return on 2002 shareholders' equity: 16%

		2002	2001	2000	1999	1998	1997	1996	1995
Revenues (millions)		5,401	5,858	5,467	5,020	4,919	4,638	4,008	3,865
Net income (millions)		525	466	533	451	489	429	416	368
Earnings per share		2.33	2.12	2.46	2.09	2.22	1.95	1.69	1.62
Dividends per share		.82	.78	.74	.70	.64	.58	.54	.51
Price	High	53.5	49.0	42.2	49.3	45.3	44.8	35.3	29.8
	Low	40.0	32.2	23.0	25.7	33.2	25.2	21.9	19.4

CONSERVATIVE GROWTH

Alberto-Culver Company

2525 Armitage Avenue □ Melrose Park, Illinois 60160 □ (708) 450-3145 □ Web site: www.alberto.com □ Dividend reinvestment plan not available □ Fiscal years end September 30 □ Listed: NYSE □ Ticker symbol: ACV □ Standard & Poor's rating: A+ □ Value Line financial strength rating: B++

"In the early 1950s, entrepreneur and beauty-supply distributor, Blaine Culver, found a chemist named Alberto to formulate a hair treatment that helped motion picture starlets contend with the drying effects of harsh film studio Klieg lights," says a brokerage-house report prepared by UBS Warburg in 2002.

The report goes on: "The product, a combination of five vital oils, was labeled Alberto VO5. In 1955, the year Leonard Lavin purchased Alberto-Culver, the company reported sales of $500,000. From such improbable niche beginnings and through more than forty years of brand and trade consolidation, Alberto-Culver has somehow managed to navigate a global personal care landscape dominated by the likes of Procter & Gamble, Unilever, and L'Oreal."

In fiscal 2002, Alberto-Culver saw its revenues climb to $2.65 billion. The company has seen its sales and earnings increase during good times and bad, including the recession and turmoil that have affected the country during the past three years.

Company Profile

Alberto-Culver Company, a pioneer on the global package-goods stage, has carried the flag from country to country, continent to continent. Today, the company sells its products, such as Alberto VO5 and St. Ives Swiss Formula, in 120 countries, with manufacturing facilities in Sweden, the United Kingdom, Australia, Argentina, Mexico, Puerto Rico, and Canada, as well as here at home.

Alberto-Culver is a leading developer and manufacturer of personal-care products, primarily for hair care, retail food products, household items, and health and hygiene products.

Alberto-Culver is comprised of three strong businesses built around potent brands and trademarks:

• Alberto-Culver USA develops innovative brand name products for the retail, professional beauty, and institutional markets. Personal-use products span a wide range: hair fixatives, shampoos, hair dressings, and conditioners sold under such trademarks as Alberto VO5, Bold Hold, Alberto, Alberto Balsam, Consort, TRESemmé, and FDS (feminine deodorant spray).

Retail food product labels include SugarTwin, Mrs. Dash, Molly McButter, Baker's Joy, and Village Saucerie.

Household products include Static Guard (anti-static spray) and Kleen Guard (furniture polish).

• Alberto-Culver International has carried the Alberto VO5 flag into more than 120 countries, and from that solid base has built products, new brands, and businesses focused on the needs of each market.

• Sally Beauty Company is the engine that drives Alberto-Culver. With more than 2,700 outlets in the United States, the United Kingdom, Canada, Puerto Rico, Japan, and Germany, Sally Beauty is the largest cash-and-carry supplier of professional beauty products in the world.

The typical Sally Beauty store averages 1,800 square feet and is situated in a strip shopping center. It carries more than 3,000 items. About three-quarters of Sally Beauty's sales are to small beauty salons and barber shops, with the rest to retail customers.

Sally Beauty is the only national player in the United States in cash-and-carry beauty supplies sold primarily to professionals. It is the market leader by a wide margin. The store capitalizes on its dominance in that niche, which provides beauty professionals the opportunity to purchase products from a wide selection of vendors at wholesale prices without having to manage and carry inventory in their stores.

The company's products do not have a common origin. They have come to Alberto-Culver in diverse ways. For instance, the original Alberto VO5 Hairdressing was a small regional brand that the company acquired because it felt it had national sales potential.

In another instance, the FDS products and its mousse products had counterparts in the marketplace in Europe. Conse-quently, Alberto-Culver brought the ideas to the United States and introduced its products to an American audience.

In another realm, Mrs. Dash, Static Guard, and Consort were all developed internally by the company's research and development team because its customers identified a specific need for these products to meet.

In yet another instance, SugarTwin and TRESemmé were acquired by the company as tiny brands and have grown to the strong positions they hold today.

Perhaps the company's most important acquisition—after the original purchase of Alberto VO5 Conditioning Hairdressing—was the purchase of the Sally Beauty Company, originally a chain of twelve stores, many of which were franchised.

Today, the chain has more than 2,700 company-owned stores, including units in Great Britain, Germany, and Japan. Sally Beauty is the largest distributor of professional beauty supplies in the world.

The primary customer for Sally Beauty is the salon and barber professional who can find there an unmatched selection of professional beauty supplies available at discount prices. In addition to the supplies they need, these professionals find a valuable source of information about trends and products that they can take back to their customers.

One of the keys to Sally Beauty's success is its ability to quickly get product from warehouse to shelf. This process starts with proprietary point-of-sale registers in each store that record and report each sale. Sally Beauty is now investing millions of dollars to add a second POS register to each store to enhance its ability to serve customers.

Shortcomings to Bear in Mind

■ At the end of fiscal 2002, CEO Howard B. Bernick said, "We believe that we have the brands, the plans, the people, and the focus that can carry us to our twelfth consecutive record sales and record earnings year in fiscal 2003." However, he cautioned it would not be an easy year. "Given the recent slow-down in consumer spending, the financial markets' volatility, the pressures on some of our trade partners, and an uncertain international situation, fiscal 2003—like the one we just completed—may very well be another year of substantial challenge for all companies. Albert-Culver has shown over its entire history that it can and does produce in good times and bad times, and we are working hard and investing to grow our business and our shareholder value over the long term."

- Sally Beauty Company experiences domestic and international competition from a wide range of retail outlets, including mass merchandisers, drug stores, and supermarkets, many of which carry a full line of health and beauty products. In addition, Sally Beauty competes with thousands of local and regional beauty supply stores and full-service dealers selling directly to salons through both professional and distributor sales consultants as well as cash-and-carry outlets open only to salon professionals. Sally Beauty also faces competition from certain manufacturers that employ their own sales forces to distribute professional beauty products directly to salons.

Reasons to Buy

- In fiscal 2002, Alberto-Culver had another record year, as sales increased 11.4 percent to $2.65 billion. Even better, net earnings climbed 24.7 percent, to $137.7 million. Diluted earnings per share advanced 21.5 percent, to $2.32. Mr. Bernick said that the company was particularly proud of the 2002 results because they had come at a time

"when the marketplace was under severe pressure from the effects following the events of September 11, weaker foreign currencies in certain markets, the bankruptcy filing of a key customer, and an uncertain global financial situation."

- Alberto-Culver's success has not gone unnoticed. Barron's, the leading weekly financial newspaper, said in 2002, "Alberto-Culver's growth is all the more remarkable because of its many large and small rivals in the personal-care business. The big competitors include Avon Products, Procter & Gamble, and Gillette." Barron's went on to say, "As things now stand in the industry, the distribution end of the business is clearly dominated by Alberto-Culver. Most other distributors have fallen short of the success of Sally Beauty and Beauty Systems, frequently giving up by selling out to Alberto-Culver."

- Alberto VO5 Conditioning Hairdressing remains by far the number one brand in its category and the bestselling hairdressing in the world. VO5 is among the market leaders in the United States, Great Britain, Scandinavia, Canada, Mexico, Australia, and Japan.

- In more than 120 countries, Alberto-Culver International markets or manufactures many of the consumer brands that it markets in the United States, including Alberto VO5 and St. Ives Swiss Formula brands.

In addition, some of the company's international units offer products unique to their markets. In the Scandinavian countries, Alberto-Culver is the market leader in a wide range of toiletries and household products. In the United Kingdom, the company is a market leader in hair-styling products. What's more, it has introduced several items in the hair-coloring segment. Finally, in Canada, Alberto-Culver produces the top-selling Alberto-European styling line, and its SugarTwin artificial sweetener is number one in its category.

- In the 1992–2002 period, earnings per share advanced impressively, from $0.68 to $2.32, for a compound annual growth rate of 13.1 percent. What's more, there were no declines along the way. In the same ten-year stretch, dividends per share climbed from $.12 to $.36, a growth rate of 11.6 percent. Despite this fine record, the stock normally sells at or below the market P/E multiple.

Total assets: $1,729 million
Current ratio: 2.13
Common shares outstanding: 58 million
Return on 2002 shareholders' equity: 17.2%

		2002	2001	2000	1999	1998	1997	1996	1995
Revenues (millions)		2,651	2,494	2,247	1,976	1,835	1,775	1,590	1,358
Net income (millions)		137.7	110.4	97.2	86.3	83.1	75.6	62.7	52.7
Earnings per share		2.32	1.91	1.83	1.51	1.37	1.25	1.06	.94
Dividends per share		.35	.32	.29	.26	.24	.20	.18	.16
Price	High	57.9	46.3	43.5	27.9	32.4	32.6	25.0	18.3
	Low	41.6	36.9	19.4	21.6	19.8	23.6	16.3	12.9

AGGRESSIVE GROWTH

Alcoa, Inc.

201 Isabella Street at 7th Street Bridge □ Pittsburgh, PA 15212-5858 □ (212) 836-2674 □ Dividend reinvestment plan available: (800) 317-4445 □ Web site: www.alcoa.com □ Listed: NYSE □ Ticker symbol: AA □ S&P rating: B+ □ Value Line financial strength rating: A

"In aerospace, we strengthened our position with the acquisition of Fairchild Fasteners," said CEO Alain Belda on February 20, 2003. "Fairchild's product line complements the fastening products from Huck, which we supply to aircraft manufacturers, and gives Alcoa the broadest product line in this part of the aerospace industry. The new Alcoa Fastening System, combining Huck and Fairchild, will be the premier supplier in this niche.

"And we added to our already strong position in the packaging market with the acquisition of Ivex Packaging, which has broadened our food and foodservice packaging offerings. Our packaging business—ranging from closures, to Reynolds consumer products, to the design, prepress, and imaging business of Southern Graphic Systems—continued their stellar performance this year (2002), and with the combination of Ivex this should continue."

Company Profile

Alcoa (formerly Aluminum Company of America), founded in 1888, is the world's leading integrated producer of aluminum products. The company is active in all major aspects of the industry—technology, mining, refining, smelting, fabricating, and recycling.

Alcoa's aluminum products and components are used worldwide in aircraft, automobiles, beverage cans, buildings, chemicals, sports and recreation, and a wide variety of industrial and consumer applications. These include such Alcoa consumer brands as Alcoa wheels, Reynolds Wrap aluminum foil, and Baco household wraps.

Related businesses include packaging machinery, precision castings, vinyl siding, plastic bottles and closures, fiber optic cables, and electrical distribution systems for cars and trucks.

Since aluminum is expensive and has difficulty competing against steel—even though it has some admirable qualities—it might appear to be a rare element. Not so.

Aluminum is an abundant metal; in fact, it is the most abundant metal in the earth's crust. Of all the elements, only oxygen and silicon are more plentiful. Aluminum makes up 8 percent of the crust. It is found in the minerals of bauxite, mica, and cryolite, as well as in clay.

Until about 100 years ago, aluminum was virtually a precious metal. Despite its abundance, it was very rare as a pure metal. The reason is that aluminum was very difficult to extract from its ore. This is because aluminum is a reactive metal, and it cannot be extracted by smelting with carbon.

To solve the enigma, displacement reactions were tried, but metals such as sodium or potassium had to be used, making the cost prohibitive.

Electrolysis of the molten ore was tried, but the most plentiful ore, bauxite, contains aluminum oxide, which does not melt until it reaches 2050 degrees centigrade.

The solution to the problem of extracting aluminum from its ore was discovered by Charles Hall in the United States and by Paul Heroult in France—both working independently. The method now used to extract aluminum from its ore is called the Hall-Heroult process.

I won't bore you with the steps taken to effect this process. The important fact to remember is that it is far from cheap. Even so, it can be done economically enough to make aluminum the second most widely used metal. However, it is not likely to replace iron and steel anytime

soon. Iron makes up more than 90 percent of the metal used in the world.

The main cost in the Hall-Heroult process is electricity. So much energy is required that aluminum smelters have to be situated near a cheap source of power, normally hydroelectric.

The price of entry into the business is so high that it discourages most upstarts from taking the plunge.

On the other hand, this frustrating effort to produce commercial aluminum is worth the cost, since the white metal has a number of valuable attributes. It has a low density. It doesn't rust and is highly resistant to corrosion. It is lightweight—one-third the weight of steel. It is an excellent reflector of heat and light, nonmagnetic, easy to assemble, and nontoxic.

Aluminum can be made strong with alloys and can easily be rolled into thin sheets. It has good electrical and thermal conductivity.

Shortcomings to Bear in Mind

- Alcoa's balance sheet is not especially strong, with only 54 percent in shareholders' equity, compared against my preferred 75 percent. Coverage of bond interest is borderline, at best, at 5.6 times.

- Over the years, earnings have been volatile, with many ups and downs, with four down years in the past ten. CEO Alain Belda commented on what went wrong in 2002. "At Alcoa, we have a steady focus on the bottom line and always measure ourselves against the best. That is why I can only describe our financial performance in 2002 as disappointing. We did make strides to strengthen the company for the future, solidify relationships with customers, and lay a path for profitable growth.

  "However, the extended weakness in the general manufacturing environment and specific markets—particularly aerospace, telecommunications, and industrial gas turbines—overshadowed some outstanding work and reinforced the need to increase the scope of our cost savings and restructuring initiatives."

Reasons to Buy

- "In 2002, we conducted a portfolio review of our businesses and the markets they serve," said Mr. Belda in February 2003. "As part of the review, we established ongoing criteria for aluminum and non-aluminum businesses, including:
  - The ability to grow in excess of GDP, or
  - The ability to deliver superior returns in sectors where Alcoa has a sustainable competitive advantage.

  "As a result of this review, we are in the process of divesting businesses that do not meet these criteria. Those businesses range from specialty chemicals and specialty packaging equipment to architectural products in North America and commodity automotive fasteners. Many of these are good, solid operations with strong management, customer focus, and excellent workforces; they just do not meet our ongoing criteria.

  "The businesses being divested generated approximately $1.3 billion in total revenues in 2002, and proceeds from the sales are expected to be as much as $1 billion. Those proceeds will be deployed primarily to reduce debt, increasing the company's flexibility for future growth opportunities in core businesses."

- During periods when the aluminum industry suffers through a protracted slump in aluminum prices, Alcoa has seen its profits rise. Part of that is due to the effects of recent acquisitions. But much of the improvement can be traced to a new corporate philosophy, called the Alcoa Business System. Essentially, it calls for plants to produce more, produce it faster, and not let it sit on the docks for too long. The new production processes are "deceptively simple and seemingly obvious," says one analyst. But, on top of other cost-cutting efforts already in the works, they are helping Alcoa weather what otherwise might be a dismal year. As aluminum prices recover—either because of growing demand or because excess capacity is shuttered—Alcoa stands to see earnings jump dramatically. Analysts say that each penny's worth of increase in the LME price of aluminum boosts Alcoa's per-share earnings by about 12 cents. LME refers to the spot price of aluminum ingots on the London Metals Exchange. Normally, the prevailing world price of aluminum is an important determinant of aluminum companies' profits. From 1982 through 1995, Alcoa's earnings and the LME price moved in lockstep. Since then, however, the LME price has dropped while Alcoa's earnings have held steady or drifted up. According to the company's chief financial officer, Richard Kelson, "We are breaking away from the LME pricing."

- Automakers Nissan and Daimler-Chrysler and truck maker Freightliner are featuring components made of Alcoa's enhanced 6022 alloy in their 2002 cars and trucks. The new alloy provides improved strength, formability, and corrosion-resistance.

  Nissan is using it for hoods and deck lids in its 2002 Altima, named Car of the Year at the North American International Auto Show. DaimlerChrysler employs it for hoods in both the 2001 and 2002 Concorde and LHS vehicles. Freightliner also used Alcoa sheet in 2002 for the newest member of its heavy-duty truck line. Ford's redesigned Explorer and 2002 models of the Dodge Ram 4x2 and 4x4 pickup trucks feature an Alcoa aluminum steering knuckle, the component that attaches the wheel to the vehicle's steering and suspension system.

- In its January 24, 2003 issue, *Value Line Investment Survey* gave the stock a below-average "4" rating for "timeliness." However, the analyst Stuart Plesser had this favorable comment: "Alcoa's long-term plans probably entail shifting its smelting capacity to lower-cost regions. For example, it recently approved a new 322,000-metric-ton smelter in Eastern Iceland (costing about $1.1 billion) with production likely to commence in 2007. Such moves, we believe, are imperative to the long-term profitability of the company, especially considering the high cost of its U.S. production."

- Leo Larkin, writing for *Standard & Poor's Stock Reports* on January 14, 2003, was even more upbeat. "We are very positive on industry fundamentals. AA, and the sector in general, should benefit from an eventual decline in Russian and Chinese exports of the metal, and from further industry consolidation.

"The market glut in 2002 was partly the result of higher production and exports from China. However, an increase in internal consumption and the eventual shutdown of smaller, less efficient smelters is seen reducing China's negative impact."

Total assets: $29,810 million
Current ratio: 1.42
Common shares outstanding: 844 million
Return on 2002 shareholders' equity: 7.8%

	2002	2001	2000	1999	1998	1997	1996	1995
Revenues (millions)	20,263	22,859	22,936	16,323	15,340	13,319	13,061	12,500
Net income (millions)	498	908	1,484	1,054	859	759	555	796
Earnings per share	.58	1.05	1.80	1.41	1.22	1.09	.79	1.11
Dividends per share	.60	.60	.50	.40	.38	.25	.33	.23
Price High	39.8	45.7	43.6	41.7	20.3	22.4	16.6	15.1
Low	17.6	27.4	23.1	18.0	14.5	16.1	12.3	9.2

CONSERVATIVE GROWTH

Anheuser-Busch Companies, Inc.

One Busch Place □ St. Louis, Missouri 63118 □ (314) 577-2000 □ Dividend reinvestment plan available: (888) 213-0964 □ Web site: www.budweiser.com □ Listed: NYSE □ Ticker symbol: BUD □ S&P rating: A+ □ Value Line financial strength rating: A++

Unless you are an investor who is averse to investing in "evil" companies, such as those that make cigarettes, smokeless tobacco, or alcoholic beverages, or those who manage gambling casinos and racetracks, you might like to consider a beer company with a steady history of sales and earnings. What's more, the company has a history of increasing its dividend every year. In the past ten years, the payout increased at a 9.1 percent compound annual rate.

Anheuser-Busch, Inc., the company's U.S. brewing subsidiary, began its tradition of quality in 1852 and has led the U.S. brewing industry since 1957.

Among those who like the company is *Standard & Poor's Stock Reports*. In early 2003, Howard Choe, the S&P analyst, had this comment: "We recently upgraded the shares to buy, from accumulate, reflecting better volume trends for the beer category and a positive earnings growth outlook.

"Despite taking price increases, BUD's beer volume growth has remained steady on a normalized basis. We attribute this to the strength of the company's brands and price increases that are amenable to consumers. BUD should continue to benefit from a favorable demographic shift over the next decade, with strong growth in the twenty-one- to twenty-seven-year-old population."

Company Profile

Dating back to 1875, Anheuser-Busch Companies is the parent of the largest domestic brewer. In recent years, the company has increased its emphasis on its brewing operations. Meanwhile, it has divested a number of non-beer businesses, including its baseball franchise, the St. Louis Cardinals; spun off its food operations to shareholders as the Earthgrains Company; and divested Eagle Snacks, Inc.

Anheuser-Busch's remaining operations and resources are now focused on beer, adventure park entertainment, and packaging. BUD also has interests in aluminum beverage container recycling, malt production, rice milling, real-estate development, turf farming, creative services, metalized paper label printing, and transportation services. Here are some comments on a few of the most important operations.

Bacardi Silver

Bacardi Silver leverages the heritage, resources, and commitment to quality of two industry leaders, Anheuser-Busch, the world's largest brewer, and Bacardi U.S.A., importer of the world's number one distilled spirit. Each brings more than 130 years of experience to this alliance.

Produced, marketed, and exclusively distributed by Anheuser-Busch, Bacardi Silver is a clear malt beverage made with

the flavors of Bacardi rum and citrus that features a crisp, refreshing taste. Bacardi rum is a component in the flavor of Bacardi Silver.

Anheuser-Busch Companies, Inc.

Anheuser-Busch is the world's largest brewer, operating fourteen breweries, twelve in the United States and two overseas. The company currently brews about thirty beers for sale in the United States. Overseas, BUD sells beer in more than eighty countries. What's more, it is the world's leading brewer, with a 11.3 percent market share, well ahead of Belgium's Interbrew, with 5.8 percent.

In the United States, Anheuser-Busch has a 48.8 percent share of the market, far above the second-place brewer, Miller, which has a 19.3 percent share. Anheuser-Busch, moreover, has been the domestic industry leader for forty-six consecutive years. Here is a brief description of its various brewing operations.

Budweiser Family

Budweiser—Brewed and sold since 1876, "The King of Beers" is the biggest-selling beer in the world. Budweiser has been the world's bestselling beer since 1957. It is distributed in more than seventy countries. Budweiser leads the U.S. premium beer category, outselling all other domestic premium beers combined.

Bud Light—Introduced nationally in 1982, Bud Light is brewed with a malt and hops ratio different from Budweiser for a distinctly crisp taste with fewer calories. It became the country's number one light beer in 1994 and has grown at a double-digit pace for the past eight years.

Bud Ice—Introduced in 1994, Bud Ice is a smooth-tasting ice beer. Combined with Bud Ice Light, Bud Ice is one of the country's top-selling ice beers.

Bud Ice Light—Introduced in 1994, Bud Ice Light has fewer calories (only 112 calories per 12-ounce serving) than Bud Ice.

Michelob Family

Michelob—Super-premium Michelob was developed in 1996 as a "draught beer for connoisseurs."

Michelob Golden Draft—Introduced in 1991 and distributed in select U.S. markets.

Michelob Golden Draft Light—Also made its debut in 1991.

The above beers are the most important, but by no means do they represent the entire list. The company also has a stake in light beers, nonalcohol brews, and a line sold under the Busch label, as well as malt liquors, among others.

Anheuser-Busch Entertainment Operations

Busch Entertainment Corporation, the company's family entertainment subsidiary, is one of the largest adventure park operators in the United States. Its parks are situated throughout the country. They include SeaWorld Orlando, Busch Gardens Tampa Bay, Adventure Island, SeaWorld San Diego, Busch Gardens Williamsburg, Water Country USA, SeaWorld San Antonio, and Discovery Cove.

Anheuser-Busch Packaging

Anheuser-Busch is one of the largest U.S. manufacturers of aluminum beverage containers and the world's largest recycler of aluminum beverage containers.

Shortcomings to Bear in Mind

- For the past century and a half, the CEO of Anheuser-Busch has borne the name of Busch. Most recently, the family CEO was August A. Busch III, who, "perhaps the shrewdest, sternest Busch to emerge since Adolphus Busch took control of the St. Louis brewery in the mid-1880s, has begun a succession process as tightly orchestrated as any in

the House of Windsor," according to an article that appeared in *BusinessWeek* on November 11, 2002.

- As of July 1, 2003, the new CEO of BUD is a long-time company executive, Patrick T. Stokes. However, Mr. Busch remains the chairman. Mr. Stokes is sixty and is expected to retire in five years. But which Busch family member will take the reins at that time? That's what worries some investors. The two candidates are both sons of the chairman. August Busch IV, age thirty-eight, (referred to as "the Fourth") has worked for the company for two decades, "showing an instinctive understanding of the kind of advertisements that stir young men. The Budweiser bullfrogs came to life under his watch, as did such tropes as 'Wassup,'" said *BusinessWeek*.

On the other hand, the Fourth's credentials for becoming CEO five years from now are open to question. According to the article, "Even rivals acknowledge that the company in recent years has produced the most consistently inventive beer advertising in the U.S. But the Fourth hasn't yet made a name for himself in any other way. He has never operated the company's network of a dozen U.S. breweries, managed its complex relations with independent wholesalers, or run its international and theme park units."

The other candidate is a half-brother of the Fourth. In the words of the *BusinessWeek* article, "His twenty-five-year-old half-brother, Steven Busch, is emerging as a potential rival. Steven is known to be smart, hardworking, and serious. He's considered a long shot, but A-B has a long history of sibling warfare for the top spot. For now, few are willing to hazard a firm prediction on how the Fourth would fare in the bigger role."

Reasons to Buy

- *Value Line's* analyst, Kenneth A. Nugent, commented in a report issued at the end of 2002, "The company continues to make additional inroads into lucrative foreign markets. Early in the December quarter, Anheuser-Busch inked a $182 million agreement with Tsingtao that will ultimately increase Anheuser-Busch ownership in the Chinese brewer to 27 percent. The transaction has received Chinese governmental approval, and we look for it to be completed in early 2003. The deal seems to be a good strategic move, as China is the second-largest beer market in the world, and Tsingtao is the country's largest brewer, with a 12.8 percent market share."

- In a report issued by Prudential Financial Research in 2002, the analyst said, "BUD boasts solid projected growth and strong financials. We think the beauty of BUD's earnings model is its operating leverage. Size matters in the beer business, and with a simple 1 percent volume and price increase, $0.02 and $0.08 per share earnings, respectively, drops to BUD's bottom line. With pricing expected to be up more than 2 percent this year (2002), and volume projected to increase around 2 percent, it doesn't take much to generate sizable earnings, particularly with costs relatively benign. Add to that its exclusive wholesale network, and BUD has competitive advantages that we think no other domestic brewer can match."

- In 2002, the company announced the rollout of its premium-flavored malt beverage, Bacardi Silver. "It is with great anticipation and excitement that we unveil Bacardi Silver, an innovative product that we believe will appeal to contemporary adult consumers," said August A. Busch IV, group vice president, marketing and wholesale operation.

  Bacardi Silver is being supported by a marketing budget of nearly $60 million. It includes advertising and media, sales promotion items and merchandising. Media support includes national television, print, radio, outdoor, and Internet advertising.

Total assets: $14,119 million
Current ratio: 0.84
Common shares outstanding: 869 million
Return on 2002 shareholders' equity: 54.5%

	2002	2001	2000	1999	1998	1997	1996	1995
Revenues (millions)	13,566	12,912	12,262	11,704	11,246	11,066	10,884	10,341
Net income (millions)	1,934	1,705	1,552	1,402	1,233	1,179	1,123	986
Earnings per share	2.20	1.89	1.69	1.47	1.27	1.18	1.11	.95
Dividends per share	.78	.69	.64	.58	.54	.50	.46	.42
Price High	55.0	46.9	49.9	42.0	34.1	24.1	22.5	17.0
Low	43.7	36.8	27.3	32.2	21.5	19.3	16.2	12.7

AGGRESSIVE GROWTH

Automatic Data Processing, Inc.

One ADP Boulevard □ Roseland, New Jersey 07068-1728 □ (973) 974-5000 □ Dividend reinvestment plan not available □ Web site: www.adp.com □ Listed: NYSE □ Fiscal years end June 30 □ Ticker symbol: ADP □ S&P rating: A+ □ Value Line financial strength rating: A++

"After posting forty-one consecutive years of 10 percent-plus earnings gains, the nation's leading payroll processor said in July 2002 that earnings would rise only about 5 percent in 2003. Naturally, investors slammed the stock, dragging it down 24 percent the next day."

These remarks were written by David Landis for *Kiplinger's* magazine in October of 2002. Mr. Landis went on to say, "Some analysts think the company was overly conservative. Perhaps it could have kept the streak alive through cost-cutting (beyond $250 million in cuts in the past two years), buying back more shares (which juices earnings per share without necessarily improving performance) or including gains from it $2.8-billion investment portfolio as income. But CEO Arthur Weinbach said he wouldn't jeopardize the company's long-term prospects for the sake of keeping the streak alive.

"What did in the streak was rising unemployment and the bum stock market. The rise in joblessness hit ADP's employer-services division (60 percent of revenues), while falling share prices hampered the division that processes transactions for brokerages (25 percent of revenues). To make matters worse, falling interest rates cut into the float ADP earns on some $12 billion in funds held for clients.

"Next year's shortfall doesn't seem to indicate any long-term problems. ADP is still one of just nine companies with triple-A credit ratings from both *Standard & Poor's* and Moody's."

Company Profile

Automatic Data Processing, with over $7 billion in annual revenues and 500,000 clients, is one of the largest independent computing-services firms in the world. ADP's four largest businesses represent more than 95 percent of the company's total revenues. Each is a market leader "and a key strategic element of our future growth," said a company spokesman. These four segments are the following.

Brokerage Services

As the premier provider of transaction-related services to the financial industry, ADP has the capacity and technological expertise to assist its clients in differentiating themselves in the marketplace. ADP brings to financial intermediaries advanced, integrated systems for securities processing, desktop productivity, and investor communications services, "all focused on providing unique solutions for straight-through processing and world class service."

Claims Services

ADP Claims Services Group, a wholly owned subsidiary of Automatic Data Services, Inc., is the leading provider of integrated business solutions for clients in the property and casualty, general health, collision repair, and automotive recycling industries.

Dealer Services

ADP Dealer Services provides integrated computing solutions to more than 16,000 automotive and truck dealers in the United States, Canada, and Europe. ADP Dealer Services is ADP's third-largest business unit.

Employer Services

ADP's Employer Services Division is a leading provider of integrated business administrative solutions that help its more than 450,000 clients efficiently manage their internal processes, allowing them to focus on core competencies. ADP's Employer Services include both traditional and Internet-based outsourcing products and services, giving clients the ability to select from ADP's comprehensive range of world-class service solutions.

Shortcomings to Bear in Mind

- In the August 30, 2002, issue of *Value Line Investment Survey*, insiders (such as executives and board members) were selling shares of Automatic Data Processing heavily over the previous nine months, with thirty-seven sales and no purchases. In this instance, they guessed right, as the stock plunged from a high of $69.9 in late 2000 to $31.2 in mid-2002.
- In the same issue, the *Value Line* analyst, John Koller, said, "Automatic Data Processing appears to have entered the mature stage of its life cycle. The company has posted forty-one consecutive years of double-digit share-net gains. Given its size and penetration in the marketplace, and the current economic environment, we think that this string is probably over."

  Mr. Koller continued his negative thoughts, "In sum, we think the company is entering a stage where redeployment of its capital is probably necessary, either in the form of higher dividends, more stock repurchases, or acquisitions."

Reasons to Buy

- To be sure, Automatic Data Processing took a few lumps in 2002, as did most of corporate America. However, the company had some notable accomplishments:
  - Consolidated revenues grew 2 percent, reaching $7 billion.
  - Pre-tax earnings increased 7 percent.
  - Earnings per share advanced 10 percent.
  - Cash flow from operations was very strong, at $1.5 billion.
  - Cash and marketable securities balances were over $2.7 billion at year-end, and long-term debt was down to about $91 million. Thus, common equity as a percentage of total capitalization was a solid 98 percent.
  - Return on common equity exceeded 22 percent. Most companies would be happy with 15 percent.
  - The board of directors increased the dividend for the twenty-eighth consecutive year, in this instance by 12 percent.
- Over the past ten years (1992–2002), earnings per share climbed from $.46 to $1.75, with no dips along the way, for a compound annual growth rate of 14.3 percent.
- The slump in economic activity made it easier for the company to make acquisitions at reasonable prices. Among the more important were the following:
  - In August, ADP acquired Avert, Inc., a leading pre-employment background verification and human resource help-desk company.
  - In October, the company acquired IBM's Output Services business, which, according to management, "expands our statement printing capacity and strengthens our position as a market leader in statement production and distribution to the financial services industry."
  - In April, the company acquired Digital Motorworks to provide the integration of key automotive data across multiple dealer management systems used by automotive manufacturers and the dealer consolidators.
- ADP launched more new products and services in 2002 than in any other year in its history. Here are just a few from a long list of these developments:
  - Employer Services broadened the scope and depth of its product offerings that help employers in every segment of the market. "These offerings are aimed at helping employers staff, manage, pay, and retain their employees more efficiently," according to the 2002 annual report.

- Pay-by-Pay Workers Compensation lets small businesses manage their cash more effectively by enabling them to pay their workers' compensation insurance premiums, based upon actual payroll data, via electronic deduction each pay period. This new offering eliminates significant upfront deposits and subsequent audits customarily required by traditional insurance practices.
- HR Help Desk enables small business owners to get answers to questions related to human resources (HR). It also alows them to download important forms over the Internet and receive access to compliance and pre-employment screening services that improve hiring practices.
- "For the long term, we are maintaining our BUY rating on the ADP shares," said an analyst with Argus Research Corporation in late 2002. "This company has a very long track record of operating success, and the prosperity should continue under the guidance of a talented management team."

Total assets: $18,277 million
Current ratio: 2.19
Common shares outstanding: 620 million
Return on 2002 shareholders' equity: 22.4%

	2002	2001	2000	1999	1998	1997	1996	1995
Revenues (millions)	7,004	7,018	6,288	5,540	4,798	4,112	3,567	2,894
Net income (millions)	1,101	976	841	697	605	524	455	395
Earnings per share	1.75	1.52	1.31	1.10	.99	.90	.79	.69
Dividends per share	.45	.40	.34	.30	.26	.22	.20	.12
Price High	58.8	63.6	69.9	54.8	42.2	31.3	22.9	20.6
Low	31.2	41.0	40.0	36.3	28.8	19.8	17.8	14.4

AGGRESSIVE GROWTH

AutoZone, Inc.

123 South Front Street □ Memphis, Tennessee 38103 □ (901) 495-7185 □ □ Dividend reinvestment plan not available □ Fiscal years end last Saturday in August □ Listed: NYSE □ Web site: www.autozone.com □ Ticker symbol: AZO □ S&P rating: B+ □ Value Line financial strength rating: B++

"This is an exciting industry with incredible growth potential," said Steve Odland, CEO of AutoZone, Inc., the nation's largest retailer of auto parts and accessories in the United States.

"According to the Federal Highway Administration, Americans are driving over 2.5 trillion miles per year. The number of older vehicles on the road is increasing. SUVs, mini-vans and light trucks are aging and becoming 'our-kind-of-vehicles,' or OKVs. The number of people engaged in do-it-yourself (DIY) automotive activities is growing. Today, almost half of all U.S. households engage in DIY automotive maintenance and repairs.

"An estimated $60 billion in automotive maintenance goes unperformed each year, and an estimated 25 million cars are driven with the check-engine lights on. Tapping these opportunities has the potential to significantly increase the size of our industry."

Company Profile

Founded in 1979, AutoZone sells auto and light truck replacement parts, from additives to motor oil, from accessories to detailing kits. The stores are, according to the company, "designed to inspire the do-it-yourselfer." However, the company also provides "state-of-the-art diagnostics, technical advice, and easy on-line ordering," as well as "reaching out to the professional technician, through our commercial business."

AutoZone sells auto and light truck parts, chemicals and accessories through 3,068 AutoZone stores in forty-four states and the District of Columbia, thirty-nine AutoZone stores in Mexico and online at *www.autoZone.com*. AutoZone also sells automotive diagnostic and repair software through ALLDATA, and *www.alldatadiy.com*. The company's stores are highly concentrated in such states as California (about 400 stores), Texas (about 350), Ohio, Florida, Illinois, Tennessee, Michigan, Indiana, Georgia, and North Carolina, with at least 100 outlets in each. Some 1,300 stores are spread out over the other thirty-three states.

During fiscal 2002, the company opened 102 auto parts stores in the United States, replaced fifteen and closed fifty-three, bringing the year-end total to 3,068. In addition, twelve new auto parts stores were opened in Mexico in the fourth quarter, for a total of eighteen new stores in Mexico for the year.

The company's stores are generally in high-visibility locations. They range in size from 4,000 square feet to just over 8,000, with newer stores tending toward the larger size. AutoZone offers low everyday prices and endeavors to be the price leader in hard parts. Stores typically carry between 19,000 and 22,000 stock-keeping units.

Shortcomings to Bear in Mind

- The company has a very leveraged balance sheet, with almost as much debt as common equity. At the end of fiscal 2002, common equity was only 54 percent of total capitalization. On a more positive note, that was a major improvement over the prior year, when common equity was only 41 percent of the total.

- In a recent nine-month period, there was considerable selling of the company's stock by insiders, such as executives and board members. In that span, there were twelve sales and only one purchase.

- In its August 16, 2002, issue, *Value Line Investment Survey* was somewhat ambivalent. Its analyst, Damon Churchwell, gave AutoZone a Timeliness rating of 1 (its best rating). The analyst said, "This stock is timely. However, its three- to five-year appreciation prospects are unexciting. Macro economic factors now working in the company's favor, may not be as helpful in the 2005–2007 time frame."

Reasons to Buy

- AutoZone enjoyed a banner year in 2002. In the words of Mr. Odland, "Sales reached a record $5.3 billion. Market share increased. Gross profit margins expanded. Net income grew 58 percent, and earnings per share rose 68 percent, excluding the fiscal 2001 nonrecurring charges. Cash flow from operations strengthened to $739 million and exceeded our capital needs, allowing us to repurchase almost $700 million of our stock. And, with concerted efforts to be disciplined with our investment of capital and to control our costs, return on invested capital reached an outstanding 19.8 percent."

- In the past ten years (1992–2002), AutoZone carved out an impressive record of growth. During that span, earnings per share mushroomed from $.44 to $4.00, for a compound annual growth rate of 24.7 percent.

- Despite the problems suffered by the economy in 2002, AutoZone achieved impressive results, as sales expanded by 10.5 percent, to $5.3 billion. Earnings per share climbed 68 percent to a record $4 per share; cash flow from operations strengthened to $739 million; return on invested capital reached a record 19.8 percent; and the company delivered a 52 percent annual return to shareholders.

- Good news also emanated from other sectors of the company, according to Mr. Odland. "In our $532 million AZ Commercial business, we grew an outstanding 20 percent. We expanded our selection of hard parts and the number of AutoZone stores equipped to handle commercial orders. The company dedicated a sales force to reach out to national customers, regional chains, and independent automotive repair shops. ALLDATA—our premier professional diagnostic and repair software—also delivered record sales.

"The beauty of our emerging commercial business is that within a short time, it has grown to over a half billion dollars in sales, requiring little new investment. It capitalizes on our existing retail stores, our supply chain, our broad inventories, our ALLDATA relationships, and our extensive geographic reach to drive incremental sales, profit, and return on invested capital."

- AutoZone is active in promoting its assets. "Our upbeat ads communicate—in English and in Spanish—the importance of automotive safety and reliability," said Mr. Odland. "Owning a car is a significant investment. We explain the role that routine maintenance, cleaning, waxing, and tuning play in preserving vehicle longevity and value.

"Inside our stores, we create attention-getting product displays—'Zones'—that encourage maintenance and enhancement.

Zones feature filters, waxes, and polishes, as well as products that upgrade aging vehicles, such as car mats and seat covers. Our stores also offer products that personalize vehicles and that improve the driving experience, such as hands-free phones and other driving accessories."

- In a report written by Efraim Levy in late 2002, *Standard & Poor's Stock Reports* had some kind comments: "Revenues should grow in the mid- to upper-single digits for the next several years, driven by sales increases at existing units and new store openings. Low to mid-single-digit same-store sales increases should be driven primarily by additional commercial sales and new product offerings, and by an expanding do-it-yourself segment; the number of cars older than seven years, the point after which vehicles tend to require more post-warranty repairs, is rising."

- One key to the success of AutoZone is its well-trained sales people. The company says, "We're trouble-shooters simplifying repairs, demystifying technology, enhancing reliability, and providing solutions.

"We keep making it easier to diagnose automotive problems. Online, at *www.autozone.com*, we help troubleshoot problems through a series of questions about vehicles' symptoms. In-store and curbside, we have ASE certified parts professionals, diagnostic specialists, and equipment to decode the on-board computer systems in cars today.

"Through our Loan-a-Tool program, we take the cost and complexity out of repairs by putting specialty tools in the hands of the do-it-yourselfer. Ultimately, our goal is to help folks keep their vehicles in good repair, making them safer, longer lasting, and reliable."

- To be sure, the do-it-yourself market is not the whole story. Many motorists prefer to have a professional patch up their ailing vehicles. With millions of vehicles on the road today and more than 400,000 professional technicians to serve them, the need for one-stop parts ordering and delivery is clear. Yet the market supplying repair and replacement parts is highly fragmented. Company-owned and operated, full-assortment, national suppliers are virtually nonexistent, leaving most commercial technicians reliant on a myriad of supply sources to fulfill parts orders.

Sensing a unique opportunity, says the company, "We began establishing a commercial delivery business. Today, we are a leading national player and full-assortment provider to professional technicians. With the full-assortment inventories and extensive reach of our AutoZone stores, we put brand name parts in the hands of 'do-it-for-me' technicians faster and more cost effectively than ever before."

Total assets: $3,478 million
Current ratio: 0.95
Common shares outstanding: 92 million
Return on 2002 shareholders' equity: 27.5%

	2002	2001	2000	1999	1998	1997	1996	1995
Revenues (millions)	5,326	4,818	4,483	4,116	3,243	2,691	2,243	1,808
Net income (millions)	428	271	268	245	228	195	167	139
Earnings per share	4.00	2.38	2.00	1.63	1.48	1.48	1.11	.93
Dividends per share	Nil	—	—	—	—	—	—	—
Price High	89.3	80.0	31.6	37.3	38.0	32.8	37.6	30.1
Low	59.2	24.4	21.0	22.6	20.5	19.5	22.1	22.0

CONSERVATIVE GROWTH

Avery Dennison Corporation

150 North Orange Grove Boulevard □ Pasadena, California 91103-3596 □ (626) 304-2204 □ Direct dividend reinvestment plan available: (800) 649-2291 □ Web site: www.averydennison.com □ Listed: NYSE □ Ticker symbol: AVY □ S&P rating: A+ □ Value Line Financial Rating: A

Unlike many other corporations, Avery Dennison fared well in 2002. Earnings per share, on a diluted basis, advanced to $2.59, compared with $2.47 a year earlier. Excluding the impact of restructuring and asset-impairment charges, annual earnings reached $2.81 per share in 2002, an increase of 14 percent over 2001.

Reported sales grew 11 percent to $4.2 billion. Excluding the impact of currency exchange rates, acquisitions, and divestitures, revenues increased by about 5 percent compared with the prior year.

Unit volume, moreover, improved by 7 or 8 percent over 2001, excluding the impact of acquisitions and divestitures.

Operating margin was 11.4 percent, excluding non-recurring items. This was an improvement of 40 basis points over 2001. (There are 100 basis points in 1 percentage point.)

Cash flow from operations in 2002 increased by an impressive 39 percent to $523 million.

Return on shareholders' equity was 25.7 percent in 2002, down slightly from the prior year's 27.4 percent. Similarly, return on total capital slipped modestly to 15.8 percent, compared with 16.2 in 2001.

Company Profile

Avery Dennison is a global company whose specialty is chemical, industrial, and consumer products. Its pioneering pressure-sensitive technology is an integral part of products found in virtually every major industry. The company was formed in 1990 with the merger of Avery International Corporation and Dennison Manufacturing Corporation.

The company's primary businesses are organized into two sectors under a decentralized management structure.

The Pressure-Sensitive Adhesives and Materials Sector manufactures adhesives and base materials for industrial and commercial applications.

The Consumer and Converted Products Sector manufactures self-adhesive products for the office and home—including desktop printer labels and cards, markers and organization and presentation products—and a variety of self-adhesive industrial labels, fastening devices, self-adhesive postage stamps, battery tester labels, and other specialized label products for global markets. The company employs more than 17,400 people in 200 manufacturing and sales facilities that produce and sell Avery Dennison products in eighty-nine countries.

The company is best known for its Avery-brand office products, Fasson-brand self-adhesive base materials, peel-and-stick postage stamps, industrial and security labels, retail tag and labeling systems, self-adhesive tapes, and specialty chemicals. Well-known products include the United States Postal Service's self-adhesive stamps and Duracell's battery-testing labels.

Under the Avery Dennison and Fasson brands, the company makes papers, films, and foils coated with adhesive and sold in rolls to printers. The company also makes school and office products (under familiar brands like Avery, Marks-A-Lot, or Hi-LITER), such as notebooks, three-ring binders, markers, fasteners, business forms, tickets, tags, and imprinting equipment.

Shortcomings to Bear in Mind

- The balance sheet is on the weak side, with only 57 percent of capitalization in shareholders' equity. I prefer at least 75 percent.

Reasons to Buy

- The dividend has been increased for twenty-seven consecutive years. In the last ten years (1992–2002), dividends advanced from $.41 to $1.35, a compound annual growth rate of 12.7 percent. In the same period, earnings per share expanded from $.67 to $2.81, a growth rate of 15.4 percent.
- Self-adhesive labels imprinted with bar codes have greatly increased the speed and accuracy of baggage sorting—as well as a multitude of other tasks. For instance, they're used for inventory control, product tracking, distribution, and logistics management. What's more, you'll find them everywhere, from airports to hospitals, to warehouses, to retail stores, to packages ordered on the Internet.
- The company's Fasson-brand materials sets the industry standard for variable information printing applications. They ensure superior bar-coding, which translates into accurate scanning. Also, they stay stuck to a wide variety of surfaces, even in harsh environments.
- In another sector, Avery Dennison automotive products decorate, seal, identify, and secure items throughout millions of automobiles. The automotive industry uses the company's specialty self-adhesive tapes instead of nuts, bolts, and other fasteners. What's more, that industry uses Avery's labels to carry all kinds of important information—from part numbers to safety warnings—on components like air bags and radiator covers.

These products can also enhance a car's appearance, inside and out, with attractive exterior graphics, including decorative striping, and interior laminates such as wood-grain films.

In addition, Avery Dennison Avloy Dry Paint film is changing the way the automotive industry thinks about finishing plastic-based car parts. Major manufacturers are using the company's performance films more and more as an alternative to spray-painting—on everything from side moldings to spoilers. And with good reason. Avery Dennison Avloy film looks great and is durable, cost-effective, and friendly to the environment.

- Although Avery Dennison is well known for its office products, the company is now expanding beyond the office, with useful, creative, and fun products for making personalized items right at home. These include greeting cards, banners, posters, flyers, and T-shirts.
- Even the wine industry is being attracted to Avery products.

For wine label designers, the possibilities are endless. According to management, "Wineries love the production efficiencies—hundreds of domestic wineries are using pressure-sensitive labels already—and Avery Dennison is leading the way worldwide."

Avery Dennison's Decorating Technologies Division worked with E&J Gallo Winery to create a new Avery Dennison Clear ADvantage heat-transfer label for a new line of wines known as Wild Vines. Gallo selected the Avery Dennison labeling process because of its unique capability in achieving a frosted-bottle look.

- Nor has the company ignored the Internet. The Avery Web site enhanced consumer awareness and demand for Avery-brand products. The site, which got several million hits in 2002, provides free Avery Wizard and Avery LabelPro software. These can be downloaded to create an instant base of new customers.

- The company now has a European Films Center in Gotha, Germany, the largest label film facility outside North America, to meet rapidly growing demand for Fasson pressure-sensitive label materials throughout Europe.
- The company's Fasson Roll Specialty business has achieved double-digit growth, creating innovative, customized solutions—such as dissolvable labels, holographic films, and unique wall-covering materials—that incorporate pressure-sensitive adhesive technology.
- South of the border, Avery has been aggressively pursuing its Latin American growth strategy—including the acquisition of a prominent pressure-sensitive materials business in Colombia and substantial majority ownership in its label materials operation in Argentina—significantly strengthening the company's market presence of its roll materials business in this expanding region.
- Across the Pacific, despite economic turmoil in some Asian nations, the company's label materials operation in Asia Pacific continues to grow, reflecting the rapid growth of consumer products markets in the region. Sales of the company's pressure-sensitive materials have been growing in China at a double-digit pace.
- In 2001, Polaroid Corporation and Avery Dennison introduced an instant photo-identification badge kit that contains everything needed to produce cut-and-paste photo ID badges. Included in the kit is a Polaroid Pocket ID instant camera as well as name badges that are easy to print and format, produced by Avery.
- Avery Dennison Corporation announced in 2001 that it had established Avery Dennison Medical, a new business unit in the company's Worldwide Specialty Tape Division.

Avery Dennison Medical operates as a full-line supplier, building on its core competencies in manufacturing, converting, and research and development to create specialized adhesives and proprietary technologies for the wound-care, surgical, ostomy, electro-medical, and diagnostic markets.

"Our specialty tapes are already used by some of the largest medical product innovators in the industry," said Philip M. Neal, CEO of Avery Dennison. "The health care industry is constantly looking for new products that will reduce costs and improve patient outcomes."

"Highly specialized wound-care products that reduce the time required for care or improve the quality of patient comfort will win," added Mr. Neal. "Advances in medical technology have resulted in new, minimally invasive surgical procedures that have created increased demand for advanced, over-the-counter health-care products as patient care shifts from the hospital to the home environment."

The demand for advanced health care management products is projected to expand annually at double-digit rates. Key factors driving growth include longer life spans and new medical technologies that reduce mortality and morbidity as well as enhance quality of life.

Total assets: $3,302 million
Current ratio: 1.02
Common shares outstanding: 98 million
Return on 2002 shareholders' equity: 25.7%

	2002	2001	2000	1999	1998	1997	1996	1995
Revenues (millions)	4,207	3,803	3,894	3,768	3,460	3,346	3,222	3,114
Net income (millions)	257	243	284	215	223	205	174	143
Earnings per share	2.59	2.47	2.85	2.55	2.15	1.94	1.61	1.34
Dividends per share	1.35	1.23	1.11	1.13	.87	.72	.62	.56
Price High	69.7	60.5	78.5	73.0	62.1	45.8	36.5	25.1
Low	52.1	43.3	41.1	39.4	39.4	33.4	23.8	16.6

GROWTH AND INCOME

Banta Corporation

225 Main Street ▢ Post Office Box 8003 ▢ Menasha, Wisconsin 54952-8003 ▢ (920) 751-7713 ▢ Dividend reinvestment program not available ▢ Web site: www.banta.com ▢ Listed: NYSE ▢ Ticker symbol: BN ▢ S&P rating: B+ ▢ Value Line financial strength rating: B+

In 2002, *Fortune* magazine named Banta Corporation as one of its "Most Admired Companies" in America. The list was compiled following extensive research and analysis.

A select group of 10,000 executives, directors, and analysts used eight attributes to rate the ten largest companies in each of the fifty-eight industries. In the printing industry, Banta ranked first in the employee talent attribute and second in use of corporate assets, social responsibility, financial soundness, long-term investment value, and quality of products and services.

"We are honored to be included in this prestigious list for the second consecutive year," said Donald Belcher, chairman and former CEO of Banta. "It's especially gratifying to receive this recognition, since the input that prompts the rankings come from our peers, industry analysts and others outside of Banta. For more than 100 years, we have focused our energies on advancing the eight attributes on which the list is based."

Company Profile

Banta is much more than a leading provider of printing and digital imaging services. The supply-chain management business, the fastest-growing segment of Banta's operations, offers important value-added products and services to support the growth of Banta's core printing businesses.

Although you probably never gave it much thought, the last time you opened a carton containing a new computer, VCR, or other piece of electronic gear, there was a good chance that Banta printed the instruction booklet, installation guide, warranty cards, and other printed matter inside; provided how-to video- or audio-tape; supplied the software kit, including diskettes; and provided all of the packaging, whether plastic, cardboard, or paper.

Banta Corporation is a market leader in two primary businesses: printing and supply-chain management. The company has more than thirty-five operations in North America, Europe, and the Far East. Founded in 1901, Banta became a public company in 1971.

Business, trade, and special-interest magazine publishers turn to Banta for the production of nearly 800 titles. Three modern facilities provide a focused production environment for printing and mailing short- to medium-run publications.

Its publishing market products include the following:

• Educational, trade, juvenile, professional, and religious books
• Business, trade, association, and consumer special-interest magazines
  • Journals and newsletters
  • Technical manuals
  • Calendars
  • Directories
  • Multimedia kits
  • Instructional games
  • CD-ROMs
  • Video and audio cassettes
  • Web sites

Banta provides a full spectrum of direct-marketing materials and personalization technologies that maximize the effectiveness of direct-response print. The company is the leader in the production and distribution of specialty and retail catalogues.

Finally, Banta holds a leadership position in each of its market segments.

Banta Healthcare products extends the company's reach beyond the traditional printing and digital-imagine segments. Three manufacturing facilities produce sterile and non-sterile products used in hospitals, outpatient clinics, and dental offices. These specialized products are composed of paper, non-woven materials, and polyethylene film. The product line also extends to related applications in the foodservice industry, such as disposable bibs, tablecloths, and gloves.

Shortcomings to Bear in Mind

■ In the past ten years (1992–2002), earnings per share advanced from $1.19 to $2.35, a compound annual growth rate of only 7.0 percent. What's more, earnings per share declined three times during this period.

Reasons to Buy

■ Stephanie A. Streeter, Banta's new president and CEO, said the company recorded strong operating performance in 2002, despite a very difficult economic environment. "Reduced advertising and promotional spending negatively impacted many of our businesses, especially direct marketing and publications. Yet, before the asset impairment charge, we were able to deliver an all-time high in net earnings and match our record for diluted EPS established during an exceptionally strong 2000. We also produced record free cash flow during the year, lowering our debt levels and interest expense.

"Financially, Banta has never been stronger," said Ms. Streeter. "Our balance sheet is in excellent condition, with strong borrowing capacity. We are well positioned to continue investing in the latest technologies and capabilities, and to aggressively pursue acquisition opportunities."

■ In an interview conducted by the *Wall Street Transcript* in 2001, Mr. Belcher answered this question: "How do you perceive your standing as far as your competition goes?"

Mr. Belcher said, "We're certainly among the top rank of printers in this country. We're very much a niche player. We focus on two segments: one is the publishing segment where we print softcover books and special-interest magazines. Our books include educational materials and trade books, and our specialty magazines are short- to medium-run publications that focus on hobbies, professions, and other special interests.

"Our second print sector is direct marketing, where we produce catalogs and direct mail. So, we're very much a niche player, and we are a leader in each of those categories. We don't try to compete across the board. And in terms of industry prominence, we certainly place ourselves among the top echelon of printers in North America.

"In supply-chain management, we're operating on a global basis now, with the blue chip companies of the technology world. Among our larger clients are Compaq, Microsoft, Cisco, Dell, Oracle, IBM, and Sun Microsystems. Again, we rank in the top echelon of those competitors that are providing outsourcing services to the technology sector."

■ Mr. Belcher explained why his company favors working with special-interest magazines. "These magazines are attractive to advertisers because the specialized readerships allows them to target their messages to their best prospects. As a result, special-interest magazines are less prone to advertising cycles. This has been one of our fastest-growing print markets, and we see that growth continuing for us through both market growth and by taking market share, which we have effectively done over the years. Our customers realize that we really specialize in producing short- to medium-run monthly magazines and, as a result, provide the value-added services and print schedule fidelity that are essential to their businesses."

■ He went on to explain why Banta does well in direct marketing. "Direct marketing is the fastest-growing print category. The material that shows up in your mailbox seems to increase instead of reduce, and that's an area which is projected to continue growing in the 6 percent to 7 percent annual range over the next several years."

■ Supply-chain management has been a key factor in Banta's growth. Commenting on this business, Mr. Belcher said, "Supply-chain management is our global growth engine. This is a business where the underlying trends for outsourcing services, which are really what we provide in supply-chain management, are very strong. More and more companies, particularly in technology—but other industries as well, are looking for companies to help take over all or part of their manufacturing and distribution processes, so that they can concentrate on their own core competencies. Industry forecasts indicate that the demand for these services will expand at a more than 30 percent compound annual growth rate over the next several years."

■ Mr. Belcher went on to say, "In the supply-chain management area, I would say we are extremely well positioned with technology companies. One of the things that we are working on very hard right now is looking to find other related industries where we can bring this same outsourcing solution to capitalize on our particular strengths.

"One very good product example is medical devices. A company we are working with right now manufactures diabetic testing kits. We source the various materials for the kit, assemble and test the devices, and then provide the packaging, distribution, and fulfillment requirements for our customer. Those are the same type of services that we are providing for companies like Compaq, Microsoft, Dell, Cisco, IBM, and several other key players in the technology arena."

Total assets: $805 million
Current ratio: 2.48
Common shares outstanding: 25 million
Return on 2002 shareholders' equity: 10.8%

	2002	2001	2000	1999	1998	1997	1996	1995
Revenues (millions)	1,366	1,453	1,538	1,278	1,336	1,202	1,084	1,023
Net income (millions)	44	50	59	54	53	52	51	54
Earnings per share	2.35	2.31	2.35	2.02	1.80	1.73	1.63	1.75
Dividends per share	.64	.62	.60	.52	.51	.47	.44	.37
Price High	39.1	31.0	25.7	27.4	35.3	29.9	30.7	30.1
Low	29.0	22.5	17.2	16.8	21.8	21.6	20.5	19.0

CONSERVATIVE GROWTH

C. R. Bard, Inc.

730 Central Avenue □ Murray Hill, New Jersey 07974 □ (908) 277-8139 □ Direct dividend reinvestment plan available: (800) 828-1639 □ Web site: www.crbard.com □ Listed: NYSE □ Ticker symbol: BCR □ S&P rating: B+ □ Value Line Financial Rating: A

"Our results are not only steady, they reflect genuine improvement," said CEO William H. Longfield on March 3, 2003. "We operate under the premise that every day we should perform better than the day before. We approach 2003 with good momentum in many of our major businesses.

"Within our Davol division, the soft tissue repair business attained more than 20 percent growth in 2002 for the third consecutive year. This year looks to be just as good, driven by our move into the ventral hernia market with a variety of products to meet specific hernia repair needs.

"In our specialty access business, we continue to increase global market share in both Europe and Japan, and we have experienced exceptional growth in our PICC catheter and port products lines.

"At our medical division, we are expanding our market leadership position in urinary drainage products by converting an increasing percentage of the market to our Bardex I.C. Foley catheter. This product offering not only presents an economic benefit to the hospital, but more importantly, it provides quality-of-life benefits to patients we serve.

"In our urological business, we continue to enhance market share with our brachytherapy treatment for prostate cancer—and are now the number-two market share leader."

Company Profile

Founded in 1907 by Charles Russell Bard, C. R. Bard initially sold urethral catheters and other urinary products.

One of its first medical products was the silk urethral catheter imported from France.

Today, C. R. Bard markets a wide range of medical, surgical, diagnostic, and patient-care devices. It does business worldwide to hospitals, individual health care professionals, extended care facilities, and alternate site facilities. In general, Bard's products are intended to be used once and then discarded.

The company offers a complete line of urological diagnosis and intervention products (33 percent of sales in 2002), including the well-known Foley catheters, procedure kits, trays, and related urine monitoring and collection systems; urethral stents; and specialty devices for incontinence.

Urology

The Foley catheter, introduced by Bard in 1934, remains one of the most important products in the urological field. Foley catheters are marketed in individual sterile packages, but, more importantly, they are included in sterile procedural kits and trays, a concept pioneered by Bard. The company is the market leader in Foley catheters, which currently are Bard's largest-selling urological product.

Newer products include the infection control Foley catheter, which reduces the rate of urinary tract infections; an innovative collagen implant and sling materials used to treat urinary incontinence; and brachytherapy services, devices, and radioactive seeds to treat prostate cancer.

Oncology

In the realm of oncology (24 percent), C. R. Bard's products are designed for the detection and treatment of various types of cancer. Products include specialty access catheters and ports; gastroenterological products (endoscopic accessories, percutaneous feeding devices and stents);

biopsy devices; and a suturing system for gastroesophageal reflux disease. The company's chemotherapy products serve a well-established market in which Bard holds a major market position.

Vascular Products

The company's line of vascular diagnosis and intervention products (20 percent) includes peripheral angioplasty stents, catheters, guide wires, introducers and accessories, vena cava filters, and biopsy devices; electrophysiology products, such as cardiac mapping and laboratory systems, and diagnostic and temporary pacing electrode catheters; fabrics and meshes; and implantable blood vessel replacements.

Bard's memotherm nitinol stent technology from the company's Angiomed subsidiary established the company as a major player in this peripheral growth market. With the acquisition of Impra, Inc., in 1996, Bard has the broadest line available of vascular grafts.

Surgical Products

Surgical specialties products (18 percent of 2002 revenues) include meshes for vessel and hernia repair; irrigation devices for orthopedic and laparoscopic procedures; and topical hemostatic devices.

The innovation of Bard's PerFix plug and Composix sheet has significantly improved the way hernias are repaired and has reduced the time needed for repair from hours to minutes. Hernia operations can now be done in an outpatient setting in about twenty minutes. What's more, the patient generally can return to normal activity with little or no recovery time.

The balance of sales (5 percent) fall into the "other" category.

International

Bard markets its products through twenty-two subsidiaries and a joint venture in ninety-two countries outside the United States. Principal markets are Japan, Canada, the United Kingdom, and continental Europe.

Shortcomings to Bear in Mind

- Although profits have advanced at a good clip in recent years, revenues have been lackluster. In the 1993–2002 period, sales inched ahead from $971 million to $1,274 million, a compound growth rate of only 3.1 percent. In the same period, however, earnings per share climbed from $1.60 to $3.35, a compound growth rate of 8.6 percent.

Reasons to Buy

Although 2002 was a difficult year for many businesses, C. R. Bard fared well:

- Revenue growth—8 percent
- Net income—$176.7 million (up 14 percent), excluding non-recurring items
- Earnings per share—$3.35 (up 12 percent), excluding non-recurring items
- Cash generated from operations— $272.3 million
- Cash and short-term investments at year-end—$383.2 million, while debt decreased to $153.1 million
- Debt-to-total-capital ratio—14.8 percent

- C. R. Bard has an acquisition strategy that targets small research or developing companies as well as larger established companies with market leadership positions. In addition to acquiring companies, Bard has expanded its business in the medical field by acquiring product lines, entering into licensing agreements and joint ventures, and making equity investments in companies with emerging technologies.

In 2002, Bard invested $25.3 million for the acquisition of businesses, patents, trademarks, purchase rights, and other related items to augment its existing product lines. In the two prior years, however, the company allocated even more: $44.7 million in 2001 and $68.6 million in 2000.

- "Perhaps one of the most practical methods of assessing our operations is to compare Bard's performance to others in the medical technology industry," said Mr. Longfield. "Our inventory days at 90.9 days—down 38.1 days from 2001— and our receivable days of 49.8 days—an improvement of 2.7 days from 2001—are benchmarks for our industry peer group. Bard's continued focus on shortening the operating cycle—from the ordering of raw materials through to customer collections—has had a dramatic effect on our cash flow, while maintaining and even improving our historical commitment to exceptional service. As a consequence, our balance sheet continues to represent a powerful strategic asset.

"Looking ahead, we will use the strength of our balance sheet and the benefits from our 2002 restructuring to significantly increase funding for our future. In total, we currently expect our efficiency efforts to provide more than $23 million in annual savings, most of which will be used to expand and accelerate our research and development programs. This effort is currently tracking ahead of schedule—as evidenced by the 34 percent increase in research and development spending in the fourth quarter of 2002 and our financial guidance forecasting a similar increase in 2003."

- In 2002, C. R. Bard's research and development outlays totaled $61.7 million, or 4.8 percent of sales, including $3.5 million associated with the agreement to purchase Genyx Medical, a privately held company that develops, manufactures, and markets Uryx, a proprietary injectable bulking agent for the treatment of stress urinary incontinence.

■ George Rho, an analyst with *Value Line Investment Survey*, had this comment in a report issued March 7, 2003, "Bard sells a broad range of products in diverse geographic markets. Important, too, it's not reliant on any single product or market for a significant portion of its sales or profits. As such, the company's growth prospects are reasonably well defined, as illustrated by the fact that 2002's December period marked the sixteenth successive quarter of 7 percent to 10 percent constant-currency sales growth. This visibility is also underscored by Bard's high Earnings Predictability, which stands at 90 (out of 100)."

Total assets: $1,417 million
Current ratio: 2.39
Common shares outstanding: 52 million
Return on 2002 equity: 18.6%

		2002	2001	2000	1999	1998	1997	1996	1995
Revenues (millions)		1,274	1,181	1,099	1,037	1,165	1,214	1,194	1,138
Net income (millions)		155	143	125	118	96	96	104	100
Earnings per share		3.35	2.75	2.45	2.27	1.72	1.66	1.82	1.77
Dividends per share		.86	.84	.82	.78	.74	.70	.66	.62
Price	High	63.9	64.9	54.9	59.9	50.3	39.0	37.4	32.3
	Low	44.1	40.9	35.0	41.7	28.5	26.4	25.9	25.5

AGGRESSIVE GROWTH

Baxter International, Inc.

One Baxter Parkway □ Deerfield, Illinois 60015 □ (847) 948-2875 □ Dividend reinvestment program available: (201) 324-0498 □ Web site: www.baxter.com □ Listed: NYSE □ Ticker symbol: BAX □ S&P rating: B □ Value Line financial strength rating: A+

Early in 2003, Baxter and Alpha Therapeutic Corporation announced that Alpha had received FDA authorization for Aralast alpha-1 proteinase inhibitor (human) as augmentation therapy for patients with congenital deficiency of alpha-1 proteinase inhibitor and clinically evident emphysema. Baxter was appointed the exclusive distributor of Aralast.

If left untreated, A1PI deficiency can result in emphysema and premature death. It is often misdiagnosed as asthma or chronic obstructive pulmonary disease. "Less than 10 percent of the estimated 100,000 Americans with A1PI deficiency are accurately diagnosed and even fewer are receiving augmentation therapy," said Edward J. Campbell, M.D., professor of medicine, University of Utah. "The availability of Aralast will allow more patients to be treated."

"As a company dedicated to meeting the needs of people with chronic, life-threatening diseases, we are pleased to have successfully brought this product from the clinic and through the approval process," said Edward Colton, president and CEO of Alpha. "We're very pleased to be working closely with Baxter to address the needs of an under-served patient population."

Company Profile

Baxter dates back to 1931, when it was the first producer of commercially prepared intravenous solutions. The company is now a leading producer of medical products and equipment, with an emphasis on products and technologies associated with the blood and circulatory system. Sales abroad account for about half of annual revenues.

In 2000, the company spun off its cardiovascular business as a separate publicly traded company. As now constituted, Baxter operates three divisions:

Medication Delivery

2002 Sales: $3.32 billion

The Medication Delivery division manufactures a range of products used to deliver fluids and drugs to patients. These products provide fluid replacement, nutrition therapy, pain management, antibiotic therapy, chemotherapy, and other therapies.

The company provides intravenous (IV) and irrigating solutions in flexible, plastic containers; premixed liquid and frozen drugs for IV delivery; IV access systems and tubing sets; electronic IV infusion pumps; solutions, containers, and automated compounding systems for IV nutrition; IV anesthesia devices and inhalation agents; and ambulatory infusion systems.

BioScience

2002 Sales: $3.10 billion

This segment produces therapeutic proteins from plasma and through recombinant methods to treat hemophilia, immune deficiencies, and other blood-related disorders. These include coagulation factors, immune globulins, albumin, wound-management products, and vaccines. Baxter also has a stake in blood-collection containers and automated blood-cell separation and collection systems. These products are used by hospitals, blood banks, and plasma-collection centers to collect and process blood components for therapeutic use, or for processing into therapeutic products, such as albumin. Therapeutic blood components are used to treat patients undergoing surgery, cancer therapy, and other critical therapies.

Renal

2002 Sales: $1.70 billion

The Renal division provides a range of renal dialysis products and services to support people with kidney failure. The company is the world's leading manufacturer of products for peritoneal dialysis (PD), a home dialysis therapy. These products include PD solutions, container systems, and automated machines that cleanse patients' blood overnight while they sleep. Baxter also manufactures dialyzers and instrumentation for hemodialysis (HD). Baxter's Renal Therapy Services (RTS) operates dialysis clinics in twelve countries outside the United States, while Renal Management Strategies, Inc. (RMS), works with U.S. nephrologists to provide a kidney-disease management program to health care payers.

Baxter continues to develop new PD solutions to better manage specific patient needs. One example is Extraneal, which improves the removal of excess fluids and toxins from patients with end-stage renal disease. Introduced in Europe in 1997, and approved in twenty-eight countries, Extraneal today is being used by more than 6,000 European patients—more than a third of Baxter's European PD population—and is currently under regulatory review in the United States.

Shortcomings to Bear in Mind

■ At the end of 2002, Baxter announced that it would sell most of its ailing dialysis services unit to focus on higher-margin medical products and drugs used to treat patients with kidney disease. The services unit has fallen on hard times of late, especially in Latin America, where Baxter's operations have been hit by currency devaluation in Argentina and Brazil. Dialysis service operations accounted for about 13 percent of the renal division's total $1.7 billion in 2002. The services unit woes came on top of already weak sales of renal products since 2001, when the company's dialysis filters were linked to the deaths of more than fifty patients in seven countries, including the United States.

- In a report issued October 18, 2002, Robert M. Gold, an analyst with *Standard & Poor's Stock Reports*, said, "We are concerned about volume and price erosion in the plasma business, declining growth in renal, and prospects of rising SG&A costs, all of which could put into question our revenue and EPS assumptions. In addition, there could be some exposure to patient liability if it were shown that BAX dialysis machines played a role in recent patient deaths in the U.S."

Reasons to Buy

- In 2002, Baxter purchased Wyeth's ESI Lederle generic injectable pharmaceuticals business, a $305 million acquisition that Baxter predicted will make "a strategic fit." With this move, Baxter expanded its injected-drug portfolio and its drug-manufacturing capacity.
- In 2002, Baxter once again led the industry in production of recombinant treatment for hemophilia, and in 2002 submitted filings with Canadian, European, and United States regulatory authorities for the company's new anti-hemophilic factor (recombinant), plasma/albumin-free method (rAHF-PFM). Baxter's rAHF-PFM is the first Factor VIII recombinant therapy to be clinically developed and prepared without the addition of any human- or animal-derived raw materials in the cell culture process, purification, or final formulation.
- Also in 2002, Baxter grew its vaccines business with licensure of its NeisVac-C vaccine in several additional countries and completed bulk shipments of smallpox vaccine to partner Acambis, Inc., on behalf of the U.S. government.

The company also received licensure for its InfluJect vaccine in the Nether-

lands, and it began construction of two state-of-the-art vaccine production facilities in Krems, Austria, and Bohumile, Czech Republic.

- As we enter the twenty-first century, the growing, aging population is creating unprecedented, explosive growth in medical conditions that occur more frequently and grow more acute with age. Baxter manufactures and markets products and services that are used to treat patients with many of these conditions, including cancer, trauma, hemophilia, immune deficiencies, infectious diseases, kidney disease, and other disorders.

The company also makes products that are used in the treatment of patients undergoing most surgical procedures. All of these conditions can cause severe physical, emotional, and financial burdens to patients and their families. Baxter's role is to help alleviate these burdens by developing innovative technologies that improve the patient's quality of life and medical outcome, and lower the overall cost of patient care. The majority of Baxter's businesses are pioneers in their field, with more than 70 percent of sales coming from products with leading market positions.

- Injury or trauma is the leading cause of death for people under age forty-four. Many trauma victims receive Baxter products—IV solutions, plasma-volume expanders, blood-transfusion products, and other products for fluid replenishment and blood-volume stabilization.
- In 2002, Baxter bought Fusion Medical Technologies, Inc., a company that develops products used to control bleeding during surgery. "The acquisition of Fusion expands and enhances our strong portfolio of bio-therapeutic solutions for surgery and tissue repair," said Thomas Glanzmann, president of Baxter BioScience. "Fusion's expertise in collagen and gelatin-based products

complements Baxter's strength in fibrin-based technologies. With the combination, we will be able to offer surgeons an array of solutions to seal tissue, enhance wound healing, and manage hemostasis—now including bleeding."

■ According to Christopher Helman, writing for *Forbes* magazine (April 2002), "John Schroer, president of hedge fund Itros Capital Management, is particularly jazzed about Baxter's booming hemophilia drug. Factor VIII provides a blood component absent in hemophiliacs that allows blood to clot normally. The drug is in great demand by the nation's 40,000 hemophiliacs. Many take Factor VIII prophylactically before participating in risky activities like sports. Baxter sold $750 million of the drug last year (2001) and is on target to sell $1.3 billion in 2003. The drug's operating margins are 50 percent, double those of the company's total product line."

Total assets: $9,663 million
Current ratio: 1.33
Common shares outstanding: 593 million
Return on 2002 shareholders' equity: 27.5%

	2002	2001	2000	1999	1998	1997	1996	1995
Revenues (millions)	8,110	7,356	6,896	6,380	6,599	6,138	5,438	5,048
Net income (millions)	778	612	740	779	731	652	575	485
Earnings per share	1.26	1.00	1.24	1.34	0.55	0.53	1.06	0.67
Dividends per share	0.58	0.58	0.58	0.58	0.58	0.57	0.59	0.56
Price High	59.9	55.9	45.1	38.0	33.0	30.1	24.1	22.4
Low	24.1	40.1	25.9	28.4	24.3	19.9	19.9	13.4

CONSERVATIVE GROWTH

Becton, Dickinson and Company

1 Becton Drive □ Franklin Lakes, New Jersey 07417-1880 □ (201) 847-7102 □ Direct dividend reinvestment plan available: (800) 955-4743 □ Web site: www.bd.com □ Listed: NYSE □ Fiscal years end September 30 □ Ticker symbol: BDX □ S&P rating: A □ Value Line financial strength rating: A+

Becton, Dickinson (known as BD), a leader in the manufacture of a broad range of medical supplies, devices, and diagnostic products, announced the launch of the BD Ultra-Fine III Mini Pen Needle in 2002, a significant advance in insulin injection technology.

It is the shortest pen needle available in the United States and is safe and effective for a wide range of patients. The new 5-millimeter mini pen needle is 38 percent shorter than the "short" 8-millimeter needle, and 60 percent shorter than the "original" 12.7-millimeter needle.

"The 5-millimeter mini pen needle may help adults and children who are fearful of injections maintain better control of their blood glucose levels by reducing needle phobia and increase compliance with insulin treatment," said Carol J. Levy, M.D., C.D.E., Assistant Professor of Medicine, Division of Endocrinology, Diabetes, and Metabolism at Cornell University Medical Center in New York. In a recent survey, 92 percent of diabetes patients surveyed found the 5-millimeter mini pen needle more comfortable than the needle they currently use.

According to American Diabetes Association records, 10.3 million people in the United States have been diagnosed with diabetes. Among them, 3.5 million (almost 34 percent) must take daily insulin injections to maintain their blood glucose levels. While the insulin injection device of choice in the United States remains the syringe, the demand for insulin pens and needles is growing rapidly.

Company Profile

BD is a medical technology company that manufactures a broad range of supplies, devices, and systems for use by health care professionals, medical research institutions, industry, and the general public.

The company focuses strategically on achieving growth in three worldwide business segments:

- BD Medical Systems, with 2002 worldwide revenues of just over $2 billion, an increase of 7.3 percent from the prior year. It includes hypodermic products specifically designed for diabetes care, prefilled drug-delivery systems, and infusion therapy products. The segment also includes specialty blades and cannulas for ophthalmic surgery procedures, anesthetic needles, critical care systems, elastic support products, and thermometers.

- BD Biosciences, with 2002 sales of $590 million, an increase of 9.4 percent. The segment sells clinical and industrial microbiology products, flow cytometry systems for cellular analysis, tissue culture labware, hematology instruments, and other diagnostic systems, including immuno-diagnostic test kits.

- BD Clinical Laboratory Solutions had its 2002 worldwide revenues advance 7.4 percent to $1.15 billion. This segment sells clinical and industrial microbiology products, sample collection products, specimen management systems, hematology instruments, and other diagnostic systems, including immuno-diagnostic test kits. Finally, this part of BD has a stake in consulting services and customized, automated bar-code systems for patient identification and point-of-care data capture.

The company's products are marketed here at home through independent distribution channels and directly to end-users. Outside the United States, products are sold through independent distribution channels, sales representatives, and, in some markets, directly to end-users.

BD generates close to 50 percent of its revenues outside the United States. Demand for health care products and services continues to be strong worldwide, despite the ongoing focus on health care cost containment around the world. The health care environment favors good continued growth in medical delivery systems due to new products and opportunities.

In particular, the domestic market is poised for broad scale conversion to advanced protection devices due to the growing awareness of benefits of protecting health care workers against accidental needle-sticks and a high level of current legislative and regulatory activity favoring conversion.

Shortcomings to Bear in Mind

- Nearly half of the company's sales come from abroad. This exposes it to the risks associated with foreign currency rates that could create increased volatility in reported earnings. On the other hand, BD has done a good job of managing foreign currency exposure, and the impact on earnings has typically been limited to only 1 or 2 percent.

- Keith A. Markey, an analyst with *Value Line Investment Survey*, had a few negative words about BD. "We're not enthused with Becton, Dickinson shares. The medical supplies sector has fallen out of investors' favor, and underlying business trends have not been very strong."

Reasons to Buy

- According to a company spokesman, "We are a leader in a number of platforms in the Biosciences segment. In the last few years, we made key acquisitions in the areas of immunology, cell biology, and molecular biology. Growth in research products is driven by the expansion in genomic research and increased pharmaceutical and government spending in this area.

"In the Clinical Laboratory Solutions's segment, we have strong marketing positions. We also have opportunities for further growth in this segment. For example, nearly half of the world's population lives in medical markets that do not currently use evacuated blood collection systems, one of our principal products in this segment."

- "Looking further into the future," said CEO E. J. Ludwig, "we have a range of genuinely exciting technologies and product platforms under development, particularly in the area of advanced drug delivery. This opportunity is especially compelling because these drug delivery systems are coming of age at the dawn of the biotechnology era. Large-molecule biotechnology-based drugs today most often must be injected, as opposed to ingested. Early tests indicate that the delivery systems we have under development could significantly increase the effectiveness of such drugs. When added to the drug discovery role played by BD Biosciences and the diagnostics performed by BD Clinical Laboratory Solutions, BD is poised to participate in every phase of the biotechnology revolution, from drug discovery through diagnostics to drug delivery."

- Becton, Dickinson has been growing at a solid pace. In the 1992–2002 period, earnings per share climbed from $.64 to $1.79, a compound annual growth rate of 10.8 percent—nor did earnings dip in any of those years. In the same ten-year span, dividends per share expanded from $.15 to $.39, a growth rate of 10.0 percent.

- The company has been repositioning the newly formed Bioscience/Diagnostics business toward faster-growing markets through new technologies. In the past, BD has been strong in two markets: clinical microbiology, and flow cytometry for clinical and research applications.

In the microbiology market, the company is trying to leverage its strong market position by introducing new technology platforms. These include a new automated microbiology system as well as the new Probetec DNA analyzer.

In flow cytometry, BD is trying to compete more broadly (both in research and clinical diagnostics), relying partly on acquisitions. For instance, the acquisition of Biometric Imaging (BMI) broadened the company's technology platform in cellular analysis. In addition, the purchase of Clontech Laboratories, a rapidly growing maker of reagents and tools used in the study of molecular biology (such as genomics), added research products for gene expression analysis.

- Domestic sales of insulin needles and syringes are expected to increase in the high-single digits during the next few years, fueled by the estimated 5 percent annual growth in the number of Americans suffering from diabetes, plus the trend toward multiple insulin injections. Recent scientific studies have shown that the use of multiple daily injections of insulin reduces the severity of the disease's longer-term deleterious effects. BD accounts for about 90 percent of the domestic insulin syringe market. The company has entered into an arrangement with Eli Lilly, the largest domestic producer of insulin products, and Boehringer Mannheim, a major manufacturer of glucose-monitoring devices, to provide information to diabetics regarding the best manner in which to control their disease. Over time, this program should accelerate the trend toward multiple daily insulin injections. The company is also reviewing a number of noninvasive techniques to monitor glucose levels in diabetics. This device could reach the market before the end of the decade and further enhance the company's overall position in the diabetic sector.

- The company's use of computer-aided design and manufacturing technology enables Becton to bring quality products to market faster and at a lower cost. One such technology is stereo lithography, which uses a laser system to quickly create a three-dimensional physical object from a computer-aided design model. Engineers can use this extremely accurate model as a prototype, improving

both the quality of the product design and the speed of the product development process.

BD has the technology to help reduce the medical errors that have received attention of late. A U.S. government scientific panel found that about 75,000 hospital patients die each year from medical mistakes. Yet only 9 percent of the facilities have invested in equipment to address the problem.

For its part, BD is offering two handheld devices, based on 3Com's Palm computing technology. One tracks drugs from the initial order through their administration. The other serves a similar purpose for specimen collection, testing, and patient file management.

Total assets: $4,802 million
Current ratio: 1.43
Common shares outstanding: 257 million
Return on 2002 shareholders' equity: 18.5%

	2002	2001	2000	1999	1998	1997	1996	1995
Revenues (millions)	4,033	3,746	3,618	3,418	3,117	2,810	2,770	2,712
Net income (millions)	480	402	393	386	360	315	283	252
Earnings per share	1.79	1.63	1.49	1.46	1.37	1.21	1.06	.90
Dividends per share	.39	.38	.37	.34	.29	.26	.23	.21
Price High	38.6	39.3	35.3	44.2	49.6	27.8	22.8	19.0
Low	24.7	30.0	21.8	22.4	24.4	20.9	17.7	12.0

CONSERVATIVE GROWTH

Bemis Company, Inc.

222 South Ninth Street, Suite 2300 ▫ Minneapolis, Minnesota 55402-4099 ▫ (612) 376-3030 ▫ Dividend reinvestment plan is available: (800)468-9716 ▫ Listed: NYSE ▫ Web site: www.bemis.com ▫ Ticker symbol: BMS ▫ S&P rating: A+ ▫ Value Line financial strength rating: A+

The key to market leadership is cutting-edge technology and innovation, based primarily upon material science. At Bemis's Flexible Packaging operations, differing grades of polymers, such as polyethylene, polystyrene, polypropylene, nylon, and polyester, are combined in a variety of ways to create films that are stronger, shinier, clearer, abuse-resistant, peelable, easier to print, sterilizable, and easier to process on machinery.

What's more, the company's recent acquisition of a shrink-packaging business introduced a patented technology that was not previously available to Bemis. The combination of this shrink film technology and "our material science expertise creates sizable opportunities for a variety of new innovations for our Flexible Packaging operations," said a company spokesman.

"Our research and development efforts go beyond the laboratory to the manufacturing floor, designing films that work better on even the newest high-speed machinery. We go into customer plants to design innovative solutions for their packaging and marketing needs. Bemis consistently devotes a significant effort to the development of new products and processes that will keep us at the forefront of the industry and keep our customers anticipating the next generation of packing innovation."

Company Profile

Dating back to 1858, Bemis is a leading manufacturer of flexible packaging and pressure-sensitive materials. More than 75 percent of the company's sales are packaging related.

Flexible packaging refers to product packaging that can be easily bent, twisted, or folded. The opposite is rigid packaging, which includes things like glass and plastic bottles, metal cans, and cardboard boxes. Examples of flexible packaging include candy bar wrappers, pouches for shredded cheese, bread bags, and dog food bags.

Flexible packaging is an attractive means of packaging a wide variety of products because of its light weight, strength, and the ability it offers to use small amounts of material in most applications. That results in lower costs for the package itself and less material to be disposed of after the package is used.

The primary market for the company's products is the food industry. It accounts for more than 65 percent of sales. Other markets include medical, pharmaceutical, chemical, agribusiness, printing, and graphic arts, as well as a variety of other industrial end uses. Bemis holds a strong position in many of its markets and actively seeks new market segments where its technical skill and other capabilities provide a competitive advantage.

Bemis has a strong technical base in polymer chemistry, film extrusion coating and laminating, printing and converting, and pressure-sensitive adhesive technologies. These capabilities are being integrated to provide greater innovation and accelerated growth in the company's core businesses.

Flexible Packaging

Bemis is the leading manufacturer of flexible packaging in North America. The company provides multinational and North American food and consumer products companies with packaging solutions that protect contents during shipment, extend shelf life, and offer attractive, consumer-friendly designs. More than 60 percent of Flexible Packaging sales are printed film materials. The balance is sold as plain film for retail and institutional food as well as a variety of other markets.

This segment breaks down into three smaller pieces:

• High Barrier Products (42 percent of sales) includes controlled and modified atmosphere packaging for food, medical, personal care, and non-food applications consisting of complex barrier, multilayer polymer film structures, and laminates. Primary markets are processed and fresh meat, liquids, snacks, cheese, coffee, condiments, candy, pet food, personal care, and medical packaging.

• Polyethylene Products (26 percent of sales) include monolayer and coextruded polymer films that have been converted to bags, roll stock, or shrink wrap. Primary markets are bakery products, seed, retail, lawn and garden, ice, fresh produce, frozen vegetables, shrink wrap, tissue, and sanitary products.

• Paper Products (9 percent of sales) include multiwall and single-ply paper bags, balers, printed paper roll stock, and bag-closing materials. Primary markets are pet products, seed, chemicals, dairy products, fertilizers, feed, minerals, flour, rice, and sugar.

Pressure-Sensitive Materials

Bemis is a major worldwide manufacturer of pressure-sensitive adhesive coated materials for a variety of markets. Under the brand name of MACtac, Bemis delivers advanced product performance to the pressure-sensitive industry. Examples include labeling for cold-temperature food packaging, harsh environment conditions, wet manufacturing processes, miniature electronic components, tamper evident packaging, and technologically advanced fastener applications.

This segment is divided up as follows:

● Roll Label Products (11 percent of sales) include unprinted rolls of pressure-sensitive adhesive-coated papers and film. These products are sold to converters who print labels for bar coding, product decoration, identification, safety marking, and product instructions. Primary markets are food packaging, personal-care product packaging, inventory control labeling, and laser/inkjet printed labels.

● Graphics and Distribution Products include unprinted rolls or sheets of pressure-sensitive adhesive-coated papers and films. Offset printers, sign makers, and photo labs use these products on short-run and/or digital printing technology to create labels, sign, or vehicle graphics. Primary markets are sheet printers, shipping labels, indoor and outdoor signs, photograph and digital print overlaminates, and vehicle graphics.

● Technical and Industrial Products include pressure-sensitive adhesive-coated tapes used for mounting, bonding, and fastening. Tapes sold to medical markets feature medical-grade adhesives suitable for direct skin contact. Primary markets are batteries, electronics, medical, and pharmaceuticals.

In August 2002, Bemis agreed to sell its global pressure-sensitive business (MACtac) to UPM-Kymmene for $420 million. The Pressure Sensitive Materials segment, which makes sheet printing products, roll labels, technical products, and graphic films, had 2001 sales of $491 million.

Shortcomings to Bear in Mind

■ According to CEO Jeff Curler, "The most significant challenge in 2002 was the polyethylene product line, which experienced weak economic activity and highly competitive pricing in the industrial markets. Capacity limitations also hampered efficiency in the higher margin printed products earlier in the year. Strong emphasis is being placed on improving efficiency throughout this product category, and we are expecting improved performance in 2003."

■ In a report issued in October of 2002, *Value Line Investment Survey* said, "These timely shares hold little long-term investment interest. It appear that many of the positives, including the pending deals, associated with this stock have already been discounted." The analyst was Joseph A. Beyrouty.

Reasons to Buy

■ Bemis has a solid record of growth. In the 1992–2002 period, earnings per share expanded from $1.11 to $3.08, a compound annual growth rate of 10.7 percent. What's more, there were no dips along the way. That's particularly noteworthy in view of the recession that took place in 2001 and 2002. The dividend in the same ten-year span advance from $0.46 to $1.04, and it was raised every year during that period.

■ Bemis has been active on the acquisition front. In late 2001, the company acquired Duralam, Inc., a maker of films for packaging meat, cheese, candy, and other foods, for $69 million. A year earlier, Bemis purchased the specialty plastic films business (with sales of about $150 million per year) of Viskase Companies, Inc. It paid $228 million in cash. The Viskase line gave Bemis immediate access to important fresh-meat markets and was a natural extension of its position in processed meat, cheese, and poultry. Finally, the company also purchased the flexible packaging business of Arrow Industries (with annual sales of about $33 million) during 2000.

In July of 2002, Bemis purchased the global Clysar shrink film business of E. I. Du Pont de Nemours and Company for a cash price of $142 million. The acquired business is a global supplier of premium polyolefin shrink film used primarily in total overwrap applications for the display, protective packaging, and food markets.

In the fall of 2002, Bemis completed the purchase of the Walki Films business of UPM-Kymmene (NYSE: UPM) for a cash price of about $68.5 million. The acquired business became the largest component of Bemis's European packaging operations. It specializes in high-barrier vacuum and modified atmosphere packaging used primarily for packaging meat, cheese, and other fresh foods. The acquisition includes manu-

facturing plants in Valkeakoski, Finland, and Epernon, France. The acquisition of Walki should double the company's sales to the European market.

- "Our attention to maintaining a world-class manufacturing organization has rewarded our customers with competitive edge and flexibility in packaging options," said a company spokesman. "Over the past five years, Bemis has devoted substantial resources to improving capacity and expanding world-class operating facilities to meet the increasing demand for sophisticated barrier films.

"Since the majority of the packages we sell in the Flexible Packaging business are printed, graphics capabilities are a significant source of expertise and competitive edge for Bemis. We are vertically integrated, offering customers our graphic design and color separation expertise. Bemis manufacturing operators work directly with graphic designers to create the highest quality printed package. Our state-of-the-art printing presses significantly improve our manufacturing efficiencies with robotics to reduce press idle-time during change over to new colors."

Total assets: $2,257 million
Current ratio: 2.21
Common shares outstanding: 53 million
Return on 2002 shareholders' equity: 16.5%

	2002	2001	2000	1999	1998	1997	1996	1995
Revenues (millions)	2,369	2,293	2,165	1,918	1,848	1,877	1,655	1,523
Net income (millions)	166	140	131	115	111	108	101	85
Earnings per share	3.08	2.64	2.44	2.18	2.09	2.00	1.90	1.63
Dividends per share	1.04	1.00	.96	.92	.88	.80	.72	.64
Price　High	58.2	52.5	39.3	40.4	46.9	47.9	37.6	30.0
Low	39.4	28.7	22.9	30.2	33.5	33.6	25.6	23.0

AGGRESSIVE GROWTH

Biomet, Inc.

56 East Bell Drive □ Warsaw, Indiana 46582 □ (574) 372-1514 □ Dividend reinvestment plan not available □ Fiscal years end May 31 □ Listed: NASDAQ □ Web site: www.biomet.com □ Ticker symbol: BMET □ S&P rating: A- □ Value Line financial strength rating: A+

In its first year of operation (1977), Biomet recorded sales of $17,000—and a net loss of $63,000. Today, the company is a leader in the musculoskeletal marketplace, with sales approaching $1.2 billion. Its products include the design and manufacture of four major product groups: reconstructive devices, fixation products, spinal products, and other products.

Favorable demographics and a shift to technologically advanced products are fueling the estimated 12 percent growth in the $7.62 billion domestic musculoskeletal market. The demand for musculoskeletal products continues to grow with the aging of the baby boomer generation. According to the U.S. Census Bureau projections, the 55- to 75-year-old population group is expected to grow about 70 percent in the next 20 years, to 74.7 million people. What's more, the traditional 55- to 75-year-old orthopedic implant population continues to expand below age 55 and above age 75.

Procedures are now being recommended for patients at younger ages, as skilled engineering of new products and increasingly effective technology directly contribute to the greater probability of successful implant performance and longevity. In addition, the elderly are leading more active lifestyles than past generations, resulting in stronger, healthier individuals who are excellent candidates for reconstructive implant procedures, creating a greater need for products and services to treat musculoskeletal disorders.

Company Profile

Biomet ranks among the world's largest orthopedic manufacturers. The company offers a wide variety of products that are used primarily by orthopedic medical specialists in the surgical replacement of hip and knee joints and in fracture fixation procedures as an aid in healing. They include reconstructive implants, electrical bone stimulators, and related products.

Reconstructive devices, which accounted for 60 percent of sales in fiscal 2002, are employed to replace joints that have deteriorated because of such diseases as osteoarthritis or injury. These include implants for replacement of hips, knees, shoulders, ankles, and elbows.

Fixation products accounted for 18 percent of revenues in 2002. These devices are used to treat stubborn bone fractures that have not healed with conventional surgical or nonsurgical therapy. In addition, some external fixation devices are used for complicated trauma, limb-lengthening, and deformity correction uses and fracture repair. Internal fixation devices include nails, plates, screws, pins, and wires to stabilize bone injuries.

Spinal products made up 11 percent of sales in 2002. These include implantable, direct-current electrical-stimulation devices that provide an adjunct to surgical intervention in the treatment of nonunions and spinal fusions.

Other products (11 percent of 2002 revenues) include orthopedic support devices, arthroscopy products, operating-room supplies, casting materials, general surgical instruments, and related items.

Biomet now operates more than fifty facilities, including eighteen manufacturing centers, with a marketing arm of about 1,850 sales representatives. The company's products are distributed in more than 100 countries.

Shortcomings to Bear in Mind

- Because of its outstanding record, Biomet is rarely on the bargain table. Its P/E ratio is usually above the market.
- In a recent nine-month period, ending in June of 2002, there were a number of sales of company shares by such insiders as executives and board members. In this stretch, there were thirteen sales and only one purchase. During those months, the stock sagged from a high of $34.4 to a low of $21.8.

Reasons to Buy

- In the most recent ten years (1992–2002), earnings per share climbed without interruption for a compound annual growth rate of 16.4 percent.
- In order to be competitive, Biomet spends a large percentage of its revenues on research and development, generally about 4.2 percent. In fiscal 2002, for example, the company allocated $50.8 million to R&D. During this period, research focused on reconstruction devices, electrical stimulation, spinal fixation and revision products, dental reconstructive implants, arthroscopy products, resorbable technology, biomaterials, gene therapy technologies, and image-guided software in the musculoskeletal products realm.
- In a report issued in the fall of 2002, Robert M. Gold, an analyst with *Standard & Poor's Stock Reports*, said, "Biomet has historically been one of the more consistent revenue, cash flow, and EPS generators in our medical device universe, participating in one of the most fundamentally sound segments of the device industry. BMET is capturing market share in several areas, most notably in the knee and hip implant and spine segments, and the dental implant business is a steady contributor."
- Biomet's growth has been augmented by timely acquisitions, beginning in 1984 with the acquisition of Orthopedic Equipment Company (OEC). With this move, Biomet obtained manufacturing facilities in Swindon, England, and Bridgend, South Wales, as well as an established sales network in Europe. OEC also contributed a strong product line of internal fixation devices and operating room supplies.

The 1988 acquisition of Electro-Biology, Inc. (EBI), provided Biomet with market-leading positions in the electrical bone growth stimulation and external fixation device markets. Since the acquisition, spinal products and softgoods and bracing products have been added to EBI's product mix.

In 1990, Biomet entered the arthroscopy market with its Arthrotek, Inc., subsidiary, which focuses on procedure-specific arthroscopy products and associated instruments, including its line of resorbable products.

Biomet acquired Walter Lorenz Surgical, Inc., in 1992, affording the company access to the craniomaxillofacial market. Lorenz Surgical was already an established leader in the domestic market. However, Biomet's vast distribution network abroad enabled Lorenz Surgical to spread its wings overseas.

In 1994, Biomet acquired Kirschner Medical Corporation, which gave the company complementary reconstructive and softgoods and bracing products. This move also gave Biomet a manufacturing plant in Spain, giving the company additional manufacturing capabilities and resources in Europe.

In 1999, Biomet acquired Implant Innovations, Inc. (3I), a worldwide leader in the dental reconstructive implant market. Biomet and 3I are working together to develop new products and technologies such as bone substitute materials and autologous growth factors.

In 2000, the company acquired Biolectron, Inc. The products obtained through this merger were external bone growth stimulation devices for the spine and long-bone fracture, as well as a bone-tunneling product used for reattachment of soft tissue to bone in arthroscopy procedures.

- Biomet and Merck KGaA formed a joint venture in January 1998. Merck KGaA is a chemical, pharmaceutical laboratory company situated in Darmstadt, Germany. The joint venture offered additional opportunities for Biomet in Europe, particularly in France and Germany. Biomet also benefited by gaining exclusive rights to Merck's vast collection of biomaterials products, in addition to future developments in biomaterials research.

While 72 percent of Biomet's revenues are now generated here at home, the company continues to expand its market share in the estimated $14 billion worldwide musculoskeletal products market. In fewer than five years of operation, Biomet Merck has become the fourth-largest musculoskeletal market participant in Europe.

- Biomet was one of the first companies to use and promote the use of titanium alloy for its orthopedic implants. Titanium alloy is now the material of choice because of its high biocompatibility as well as its strength, durability, and elasticity, which is more similar to that of natural bone than other metals. Biomet also pioneered the use of a proprietary titanium porous coating, known as plasma spray, to encourage bone growth onto the implant for stability.
- Another Biomet advance was the development of hip stems with a tapered stem design, which offloads stress to the femur in a uniform manner and reduces stress shielding of the bone.
- In October of 2002, Biomet announced the FDA clearance of its RingLoc constrained hip liners, which are used in revision hip procedures. The RingLoc constrained liners, are polyethylene liners used in conjunction with metal-backed acetabular shells. These liners are intended for use in primary or revision procedures in patients with a high risk of hip dislocation. Dane A. Miller, Ph.D., CEO of Biomet, said, "We are pleased to receive FDA clearance on the RingLoc constrained hip liner, which should improve Biomet's performance in the domestic market for revision hip products estimated to be in excess of $200 million per year."
- Biomet's balance sheet remains strong, with $386 million in cash and investments, no long-term debt, and a working capital ratio of four-to-one. "Biomet's solid balance sheet and positive cash flow from operations continue to offer opportunities for external growth through investments in, and acquisitions of, new product lines, technologies and companies," said Dr. Miller.

Total assets: $1,522 million
Current ratio: 4.27
Common shares outstanding: 258 million
Return on 2002 shareholders' equity: 20.6%

	2002	2001	2000	1999	1998	1997	1996	1995
Revenues (millions)	1,192	1,031	921	757	651	580	535	452
Net income (millions)	240	198	174	116	125	106	94	79
Earnings per share	.88	.79	.65	.59	.49	.42	.36	.31
Dividends per share	.09	.07	.06	.05	.05	.04	Nil	—
Price High	33.3	34.4	27.8	20.3	18.3	12.0	9.2	8.8
Low	21.8	20.5	12.1	10.9	10.5	6.3	5.6	5.8

CONSERVATIVE GROWTH

H&R Block, Inc.

4410 Main Street □ Kansas City, Missouri 64111 □ (816) 701-4443 □ Dividend reinvestment plan available: (888) 224-2741 □ Web site: www.hrblock.com □ Listed: NYSE □ Fiscal years end April 30 □ Ticker symbol: HRB □ S&P rating: A- □ Value Line financial strength rating: A

Tax changes keep H&R Block's business humming. In the spring of 2002, another flood of tax changes prompted H&R Block to join forces with EarthLink to offer a comprehensive range of Internet-based tax tools available on the taxpayer's home computer.

EarthLink, one of the nation's leading Internet services providers, is helping to mitigate the guesswork and frustration that comes with the tax-preparation process. It now does this by providing its subscribers with direct access to H&R Block's latest online tax services. Under this arrangement, EarthLink subscribers can now access H&R Block's vast array of online tax solutions.

"By teaming up with H&R Block, we combine the reliable source of financial services and information with the convenience of a fast, stable Internet connection," said Jon Irwin, EarthLink's executive vice president of customer experience. "EarthLink subscribers can simply log on to their Personal Start Page, and in seconds they can access information regarding the latest tax laws. They also can receive tax advice, and confidently prepare, review, and file their taxes—right from their home or office computer."

Company Profile

Founded in 1955, H&R Block provides a wide range of financial services through more than 10,400 offices situated in the United States, Canada, Australia, and the United Kingdom. Operations fall under five headings.

U.S. Tax Operations

This segment consists of the company's traditional tax business, which serves 16.9 million taxpayers—more than any other company. Tax-related service revenues include fees from company-owned tax offices and royalties from franchised offices. As of April 15, 2002, there were 9,072 H&R Block offices located in the United States.

In addition to its regular offices, the company offers tax return preparation services at 484 H&R Block Premium offices for taxpayers with more complicated returns.

This segment also participates in the refund-anticipation loan products offered by a third-party lending institution to tax clients. This segment includes the company's tax preparation software Kiplinger TaxCut from H&R Block, other personal productivity software, online tax preparation through a tax preparer (whereby the client fills out an online tax organizer and sends it to a tax preparer for preparation), online do-it-yourself-tax preparation, online professional tax review, and online tax advice through the *www.hrblock.com* Web site.

International Tax Operations

This segment has a stake in providing local tax return preparation and filing. It consists of 1,378 company-owned and franchised offices in Canada, Australia, and the United Kingdom.

In addition, there are franchise offices in nine countries that prepare U.S. tax returns for U.S. citizens living abroad. Tax-related service revenues include fees from company-owned tax offices and royalties from franchised offices.

Mortgage Operations

This operation is engaged in the origination, servicing, and sale of nonconforming and conforming mortgage loans. Through a network of mortgage brokers, it offers a flexible product line to borrowers who are creditworthy but do not meet traditional underwriting criteria. Conforming mortgage loan products, as well as the same flexible product line available through brokers, are offered through H&R Block Financial Centers and H&R Block Mortgage Corporation retail offices.

Investment Services

This segment has a stake in offering full-service investment advice through H&R Block Financial Advisors, Inc., a full-service discount securities broker. Financial planning and investment advice are offered through H&R Block Financial Centers, H&R Block Financial Advisors offices, and tax offices. Stocks, bonds, mutual funds, and other products and securities are offered through a nationwide network of registered representatives at the same locations.

Business Services

The Business Services operation provides accounting, tax, and consulting services to business clients, as well as tax, estate planning, financial planning, wealth management, and insurance services to individuals.

The business services operation consists essentially of RSM McGladrey, Inc. (RSM). In fiscal 2002, RSM purchased and integrated assets of regional firms Messina, Ceci, Archer & Company and Fisk & Robinson. An investment-banking firm, EquiCo, was acquired in November of 2001.

Shortcomings to Bear in Mind

- During 2002, several insiders—such as corporate executives and board members—sold part of their holdings in the company. Very few were buyers during this same period.
- In mid-2002, Michael W. Jaffe, an analyst with *Standard & Poor's Stock Reports*, had this comment: "We expect HRB's business to remain quite solid in fiscal 2003, as new tax laws and the company's strong marketing efforts should continue to stimulate good demand for its services. Despite that positive outlook, the general expectation of an economic rebound in the U.S. might drive some investors toward companies with more cyclical businesses than those of HRB."

Reasons to Buy

- A key element in the recent success of H&R Block is the company's CEO, Mark A. Ernst. Ever since the forty-three-year-old former American Express executive joined the company in 1998, he has been hell-bent on diversifying into other financial services. What's more, he is undeterred by the failure of his predecessors' moves into legal services or the ill-timed sale in 1998 of Internet service provider CompuServe Corporation for $1.3 billion, when critics said its was worth twice that.

  Investors quickly voted their confidence in Mr. Ernst's actions. After languishing for years, the stock climbed 117 percent in 2001, while the *Standard & Poor's* 500 average sagged nearly 12 percent.

- An analyst with *Value Line Investment Survey*, Charles Clark, wrote these comments in 2002: "Block's tax operations are of primary interest to investors. First of all, Tax Services is by far the largest contributor to operating income—despite the recent strength of Mortgage Services. And although some seasons may be better than others, the tax business is likely to continue expanding at a moderate pace in coming years, while mortgage operations are tied to the housing cycle. Digging a little deeper, the return on assets at Tax has been at least five times higher than at Mortgage over the last three years."

- In the past ten years (1992–2002), earnings per share advanced from $0.75 to $2.31, a compound annual growth rate of 11.9 percent. Earnings dipped only once in that span. Dividends per share in this same period did not perform as well, rising from $0.43 to $0.63, a growth rate of only 3.9 percent.

■ In a recent financial report to share-holders, CEO Mark A. Ernst said, "In fiscal 2002, H&R Block served nearly 21 million tax clients around the world, helping them navigate the intricacies of increasingly complex tax laws. As tax law changes continue, coupled with uncer-tainty in financial markets, our ability to meet clients' needs through financial advice and personalized tax service is more relevant than ever. This strategy is a long-term campaign to build client sat-isfaction and improve client loyalty, which will further enhance the strength and value of the H&R Block brand."

Mr. Ernst went on to say, "Consumer research shows that H&R Block enjoys better brand recognition than many of the largest financial services companies. And our client satisfaction consistently ranks higher than that of other financial services companies. This brand strength is a competitive advantage that we are carefully cultivating for future growth."

■ The personal data contained in a typical tax return represents a marketing gold mine for H&R Block. The company obtains a customer's permission before tapping that data, and Block reports that a majority of its clients sign the waiver. Employees can then steer tax customers toward the company's proprietary finan-cial products and services.

H&R Block has about 2,000 employees trained to serve as financial advisers. Its goal is to have ten times that number qualified to cross-sell within the next three or four years. Finally, Block is targeting low- and middle-income households, the 90 per-cent of the population ignored by its competitors.

Total assets: $4,231 million
Current ratio: 1.19
Common shares outstanding: 181 million
Return on 2002 shareholders' equity: 34.2%

		2002	2001	2000	1999	1998	1997	1996	1995
Revenues (millions)		3,318	3,002	2,452	1,645	1,307	1,916	861	1,326
Net income (millions)		434	277	252	238	174	48	125	107
Earnings per share		2.31	1.52	1.28	1.18	.81	.23	.59	.51
Dividends per share		.59	.54	.51	.43	.40	.52	.64	.61
Price	High	53.5	46.4	24.8	29.8	24.5	22.9	21.1	24.4
	Low	29.0	18.3	13.5	19.0	17.7	14.0	11.8	16.7

AGGRESSIVE GROWTH

The Boeing Company

100 North Riverside Plaza □ Chicago, Illinois 60606-1596 □ Listed: NYSE □ (312) 544-2140 □ Dividend reinvestment plan available: (888) 777-0923 □ Web site: www.boeing.com □ Ticker symbol: BA □ S&P rating: B □ Value Line financial strength rating: A

The Boeing 777-300ER completed its maiden flight February 24, 2003, begin-ning a 1,600-hour flight-test program that's expected to bring U.S. government certifi-cation by early 2004.

"The Boeing 777 is an incredible flying machine," said chief test pilot Frank Santoni. "It's no wonder pilots call it the 'World's Greatest Airplane.'"

During the February flight, test pilots Santoni and John Cashman took the 777-300ER to an altitude of 15,000 feet and an air speed of .50 Mach, or about 370 miles per hour. Typically, the 777's cruise altitude is 35,000 feet, and its cruise speed is .84 Mach, or about 484 miles per hour.

Touted as the world's most technologically advanced airplane, the 777-300ER will have updated avionic, electrical, flight, and environmental control systems. GE Aircraft Engines manufactures the engines for the 777-200LR and the 777-300ER airplanes. The new engines have been recognized as the world's most powerful commercial jet engines, and they currently hold a Guinness World Record for thrust.

Both the 777-300ER and the 777-200LR were launched in February 2002 by Boeing and GE Aircraft Engines at the request of customers who asked for an airplane with additional flexibility to serve the nonstop routes that passengers demand.

The 777 family has captured nearly 70 percent of the market since the airplane's October 1990 launch. Thirty-nine customers and operators worldwide have ordered a total of 619 of the 777s, including sixty-one longer-range 777s ordered by seven customers: Air France, All Nippon Airways, EVA Airways, GE Capital Aviation Services, ILFC, Japan Airlines, and Pakistan International Airlines.

Company Profile

Founded eighty-seven years ago by William E. Boeing, The Boeing Company is the leading aerospace company in the world, as measured by total revenues. The holder of more than 5,000 patents, Boeing is the world's largest manufacturer of commercial jetliners and military aircraft and provides related services worldwide.

Boeing is also NASA's largest contractor. The company's capabilities and related services include helicopters, electronic and defense systems, missiles, rocket engines, launch systems, and advanced information and communications systems. Boeing has customers in 145 countries.

Boeing's military aircraft include the F/A-18 Hornet strike fighter, the F-15E Eagle fighter-bomber, the C-17 Globemaster III transport, and the AH-64D Apache Longbow helicopter.

Boeing's space operations include communications satellites, Delta rockets, and the space shuttle (with Lockheed Martin). Finally, the company is also the prime contractor for the International Space Station.

Boeing's defense and space operations primarily makes the F-18 fighter jet for the U.S. Navy, the E-3 Airborne Warning and Control System (AWACS), the 767-based AWACS, and CH-47 helicopter. The company also has development programs: the Joint Strike Fighter, the Airborne Laser, the F-22 fighter, and the expendable launch vehicle. The unit makes Delta rockets, used to carry satellites.

Shortcomings to Bear in Mind

■ "Boeing is the largest contractor for NASA's manned space program," said Jonathan R. Laing, writing for *Barron's* on February 10, 2003. "It and Lockheed Martin are fifty/fifty partners in the United Space Alliance, the venture to which NASA outsources management of the shuttle program. Among other things, the alliance trains astronauts and ground controllers, prepares the shuttle for launch, makes all necessary repairs, and services all engines and communications equipment. Likewise, Boeing is the lead integrator for the International Space Station, whose future has been called into question as a result of the cost overruns, mission shrink, and the Columbia catastrophe."

Mr. Laing also said, "Boeing now sees no recovery in its aircraft deliveries until 2005. It estimates deliveries at 280 in 2003 and 275 to 300 in 2004. In contrast, in 1999, Boeing delivered a record 620 planes."

On the other hand, *Barron's* is not entirely negative on Boeing's prospects. For instance, the publication spoke highly of the company in an article published in April of 2002. At that time, it liked Boeing's "well-timed diversification into the defense industry with military procurement spending rising sharply, increasing production efficiencies that Boeing was realizing on its plant floors, plus its pre-eminence in fast-growing areas such as missile defense, spy satellites, and electronic integration of battlefield systems. The thesis is still valid, but will take time to work out."

Reasons to Buy

- Boeing's chief competitor, Airbus Industrie, is developing a superjumbo jet. For its part, Boeing says it will focus on a new, near-supersonic jet that the company says will be able to fly 20 percent faster than today's conventional planes without boosting operating costs. This move allows Boeing, the world's largest manufacturer of commercial jets, to stake out a fundamentally different view of the future of commercial aviation than that of Europe's Airbus. While Airbus is betting more than $12 billion that airlines want superjumbo jets that can carry more than 600 passengers on long trips to a given destination, Boeing is convinced there is much larger demand for smaller, faster planes that take people directly to their destination.
- The airline industry has not fared well since the terrorist attacks on September 11, 2001. On the other hand, the defense industry stands to benefit. Boeing is particularly well positioned to gain, according to one defense analyst. He contends that Boeing's F-15 Eagle, F/A-18E and F Super Hornet, and AV-8B Harrier production lines are still up and running.

- Boeing won a major contract in March of 2002 to develop an entire network of new weapons, communications systems, and intelligence-gathering sensors. The Pentagon hopes they will one day revolutionize the way the army fights wars.

  The overall value of these contracts could top $10 billion as elements of future combat systems are deployed over the next decade. For the first time, the U.S. Army is asking a single contractor to oversee development of a range of new technologies and weapons the would bring the service into the digital age.
- Boeing may not admit it, but its new finance unit (created early in 2001), aspires to be a GE Capital clone. Boeing Capital is moving aggressively to help its parent not only sell more aircraft and expand into aerospace, but also move into financing such big-ticket items as oil rigs, barges, and cargo ships. Boeing Capital was created as part of the company's diversification strategy.

  "Clearly we believe in the concept of a financial-service company," says Boeing Capital president, James F. Palmer. "One doesn't have to look any further than GE to see what they have been able to do. The key question is: 'How do you grow at a profitable rate?'" The crux of BA's growth plan is to stick to financing airplanes and heavy equipment. Mr. Palmer also sees new opportunities in commercial satellite financing—particularly now that Boeing owns Hughes Satellite Company.
- About 85 percent of the world's jetliners are built by Boeing, and an estimated $74 billion a year is spent to keep them flying. However, up until recently, Boeing was giving away its engineering drawings to third-party service providers. No longer. It is now making an across-the-board push into maintenance, modifications, financing, air-traffic control, even pilot training.

"This could be big stuff," said Cai von Rumohr, an aerospace analyst with SG Cowen. Already, more than 20 percent of Boeing's military revenues emanate from activities such as maintaining air force bases, and its Web site for spare parts have generated revenues of $400 million a year. In a sign of how far the services push might go, Boeing agreed to buy thirty-four used 757s from British Airways, convert them into freighters, and lease them to carrier DHL with a fixed hourly maintenance fee.

■ Boeing began installing new landing aids in the cockpits of thousands of its jet-liners in 2002. The additional feature is designed to give pilots earlier and more clear-cut warnings if an aircraft is fol-lowing a wrong trajectory approaching an airport, or if the airplane is likely to land too short or too far down a runway to safely slow down and turn off at an appropriate spot. Boeing crash studies indicate that in the past ten years, 51 per-cent of all major accidents involving Western-built jetliners occurred during the final approach and landing. "It is the single most important thing we can do in the short term to improve safety," said Bob Myers, the Boeing manager in charge of the project. The goal is to give cockpit crews extra time to gauge the momentum of aircraft during the hectic last few minutes of the flight so they can adjust the rate of descent or abort a landing if necessary.

■ Boeing has been gradually adopting "lean" manufacturing strategies since the early 1990s. However, the company was not the first to emulate the Japanese approach. Domestic car companies made similar moves a decade earlier. The basic philosophy of the strategy is to make it easier for workers to boost output using less space and fewer movements.

Since late 1998, when Boeing began applying lean activities to its newest model, the 777, the time it takes to assemble the major components into a finished aircraft has dropped to thirty-seven days from seventy-one. The impact can be seen in the operating margins of the commercial airplane divi-sion—Boeing's largest, and the source of 61 percent of it revenue.

In 1998, the unit's profit margin was a puny 1 percent. In 2002, it surpassed 10 percent. Although some of the gain emanates from the company's increasing unwillingness to get into a price war with Airbus, executives also say that lean manufacturing has made a big impact.

"The whole concept is to look for quantum leaps in efficiency, to the tune of 50 percent," says David Swain, presi-dent of the Phantom Works division. "We are looking for whole new ways to build airplanes."

Total assets: $52,269 million
Current ratio: .85
Common shares outstanding: 799 million
Return on 2002 shareholders' equity: NM*

	2002	2001	2000	1999	1998	1997	1996	1995
Revenues (millions)	54,069	58,198	51,321	57,993	56,154	45,800	22,681	19,515
Net income (millions)	2,319	2,721	2,513	2,309	1,120	632	976	393
Earnings per share	2.87	3.41	2.44	2.49	1.15	.63	1.42	.58
Dividends per share	.68	.68	.59	.56	.56	.56	.55	.50
Price High	51.1	69.8	70.9	48.5	56.3	60.5	53.8	40.0
Low	28.5	27.6	32.0	31.6	29.0	43.0	37.1	22.2

* Not meaningful

Boston Properties, Inc.

111 Huntington Avenue □ Boston, Massachusetts 02199 □ Listed: NYSE □ (617) 236-3400 □ Dividend reinvestment plan available: (888) 485-2389 □ □ Web site: www.bostonproperties.com □ Ticker symbol: BXP □ S&P rating: Not rated □ Value Line financial strength rating: Not rated

Boston Properties is one of the premier office real-estate companies. Its Class A office buildings are situated in markets that are difficult to enter, such as Boston, New York, Washington, and San Francisco. Erecting new office buildings is difficult because of the physical constraints of these particular cities, coupled with stringent approval processes and the complexity of the building process. Yet the demand for office space continues unabated, causing rents to climb.

Company Profile

Founded in 1970 by Mortimer B. Zuckerman and Edward H. Linde, Boston Properties completed its initial public offering in June 1997. Boston Properties is a fully integrated, self-administered, and self-managed real estate investment trust (REIT) that develops, redevelops, acquires, manages, operates, and owns a diverse portfolio of Class A office properties in the United States, concentrated in four core markets—Boston, Washington, D.C., Midtown Manhattan, and San Francisco. As of year-end 2002, Boston properties owned 142 properties totaling 42.4 million square feet. In addition, the company had six properties under construction at the end of 2002, totaling about 2.8 million square feet.

Among the company's largest properties are the following: Embarcadero Center in San Francisco, with 3,931,381 net rentable square feet; The Prudential Center in Boston, with 2,140,832 square feet; and Carnegie Center in Princeton, New Jersey, with 1,856,018 square feet.

At the other extreme are such smaller properties as Three Cambridge Center in Cambridge, Massachusetts, with 107,484 net rentable square feet; the Arboretum in Reston, Virginia, with 95,584 square feet; 17 Hartwell Avenue in Lexington, Massachusetts, with 30,000 square feet; and 560 Forbes Boulevard in San Francisco, California, with 40,000 square feet.

Class A office buildings are generally considered those that have excellent locations and access, attract high-quality tenants, are well-maintained, and professionally managed.

The company is one of the largest owners, acquirers, and developers of Class A office properties in the United States. The company's primary focus is office space. However, its property portfolio also includes hotels and industrial buildings.

Since becoming a public company in June 1997, Boston Properties has experienced rapid growth by acquisitions in excess of $4 billion of office properties in existing and complementary markets. To support continued growth, Boston Properties raised over $800 million in equity through a secondary stock offering in January 1998, $140 million in May 1999, and $634 million in October 2000.

What Is an Equity REIT?

Equity REITs make their money by owning properties, as opposed to mortgage REITs, which lend money to property owners. Equity REITs allow you to invest in a diversified collection of apartment buildings, hospitals, shopping centers, hotels, warehouses, and office buildings.

Like mutual funds, REITs are not taxed themselves, providing they pay out at least 90 percent of their taxable income. That translates into fat dividends for shareholders, as REITs pass along the rents and other income they collect. Dividend yields are typically 6 percent or more. "Put it all together, and you are looking at a double-digit total return. Over the long haul, the return should be lower than traditional stocks, but higher than bonds," says Chris Mayer, a real-estate professor at the University of Pennsylvania's Wharton School.

Kevin Bernzott, an investment adviser in Camarillo, California, views REITs as a stock-bond hybrid. "If you select quality REITs, they kick off a highly predictable stream of income, and eventually you may get some price appreciation. We plug them into the bond portion of the portfolio. They're almost like a bond with an equity kicker."

Shortcomings to Bear in Mind

- Some investors might be concerned that Boston Properties is not well diversified, since most of its properties are situated in only four cities. Also, the company's holdings are essentially concentrated in office buildings, to the exclusion of such sectors as retail shopping centers, apartment buildings, and industrial parks.
- At the end of 2002, the occupancy rate slipped modestly to 93.9 percent, compared with 95.3 percent a year earlier.

Reasons to Buy

- "Management believes prospects for internal growth are strong, in light of the REIT's high-quality portfolio and the fact that its properties are located in desirable locations in markets that are experiencing low vacancy rates," said Raymond Mathis, an analyst with *Standard & Poor's Stock Reports*, in the fall of 2002. "Internal growth prospects are also bolstered by the fact that BXP's properties are in general located in markets in which supply is limited by lack of available sites, and by difficulty in obtaining needed approvals to develop vacant land. These high barriers to entry argue for the trust's ability to obtain strong increases in rental revenue in coming periods."

- As noted previously, Boston Properties is not well diversified geographically. Instead, it concentrates on four cities:

  San Francisco is the nation's West Coast financial center. It is home to leading financial institutions, investment management firms, venture capitalists, law firms, consultants, and other business services.

  A combination of factors including a talented, highly educated labor pool and exceptional "quality of life" continue to draw and to keep the most successful businesses in San Francisco.

  In San Francisco, new supply is projected to be limited by several factors, including legislated growth restrictions and lack of sites that can be developed in the core financial district.

  New York City is the nation's leader in financial services and international business and the worldwide center of commerce, finance, and culture. The city's extensive infrastructure includes the largest mass-transit system in the nation. The media and financial services sectors, particularly financial, legal, communications, and other specialty businesses, are the economic engines that drive demand for office space, most markedly in midtown Manhattan.

  Northern Virginia and suburban Maryland, in addition to the District of Columbia, is the nation's fifth-largest metropolitan area and third-largest office market after New York and Chicago. The economy of the entire region benefits enormously from the presence, stability, and funding of the federal government. It is home to one of the most highly educated work forces, the highest concentration of scientists and engineers, and the second-largest concentration of high technology firms in the country.

Business service and government consulting industries have been the driving engines of growth, particularly knowledge-based enterprises such as information technology management and data communications firms. Fairfax County, Virginia, has become the technology center of the region, while Montgomery County, Maryland, is experiencing the emergence of specialized research companies, reflecting proximity to and increased funding from the National Institutes of Health and U.S. Food and Drug Administration and strengthening the overall economic growth and diversity of the area.

The greater Boston area centers around both stable and established companies and the emergence of a large number of small to mid-sized firms in four industry groups: financial services, health care, high technology, and knowledge creation, including research and development, consulting, and education.

Economic growth in this seventh-largest metropolitan area reflects the diverse mix of companies, the presence of leading universities and medical research institutions, the availability of local venture and growth capital, the vitality of the city of Boston as a business, cultural and residential center, and major improvements in the transportation infrastructure that are currently underway.

■ The company's management believes prospects for internal growth are strong.

This is in light of the REIT's high-quality portfolio and the fact that its properties are situated in desirable locations in markets that are experiencing rising rents, low vacancy rates, and increasing demand for office and industrial space.

Internal growth prospects are also bolstered by two facts: that the company's properties are usually in markets where supply is limited by the lack of available sites, and that it is difficult to obtain the necessary approvals for developing vacant land. These high barriers to entry argue for the trust's ability to obtain strong increases in rental revenue in the years ahead.

■ Boston Properties has always followed a conservative strategy of entering into long-term leases with tenants of strong financial standing. In any given year, therefore, the turnover with its existing portfolio is moderate. More specifically, leases on only 7.5 percent of the space in existing buildings terminated in 2001, and only 8.3 percent in 2002.

■ Boston Properties has long been recognized for its ability to create value through the development of its own properties, as opposed to purchase. While notable acquisitions have been an important part of its impressive growth, the company has also demonstrated that high returns can be achieved by employing its team of skilled professionals to create projects from the ground up. Boston Properties has fully staffed development and construction operations in each of its markets. The company, moreover, has more development project in the works today than at any other office REIT.

Total assets: $ 8,427 million
Current ratio: NA
Return on 2002 equity: 20.4%
Common shares outstanding: 93 million

	2002	2001	2000	1999	1998	1997*
Revenues (millions)	1,235	1,047	879	787	514	140
Net income (millions)	441	201	146	114	93	35.2
Earnings per share	4.66	2.19	2.05	1.72	1.53	.70
Funds from operations	3.75	3.57	3.31	2.89	2.50	1.96
Dividends per share	2.44	2.27	1.96	1.75	1.66	1.62
Price High	41.6	43.9	44.9	40.8	41.6	36.2
Low	33.0	34.0	29.0	30.9	33.4	30.3

* Statistical information only available since the company went public in 1997.

CONSERVATIVE GROWTH

Brinker International, Inc.

6820 LBJ Freeway □ Dallas, Texas 75240 □ (972) 770-7228 □ Dividend reinvestment plan not available □ Web site: www.brinker.com □ Listed: NYSE □ Fiscal years end last Wednesday in June □ Ticker symbol: EAT □ S&P rating: B+ □ Value Line financial strength rating: B+

Brinker International, a leader in the casual dining industry, continued its winning ways in fiscal 2002 as earnings per share advanced once again, despite such obstacles as a slow economy, world turmoil, and the threat of terrorism.

Over the past ten years, earnings per share advanced from $.34 to $1.56, an impressive compound annual growth rate of 16.5 percent. The success of the company has not gone unnoticed:

• For the past three years (2000–2002), *Forbes* has listed Brinker in its annual list of the "400 Best Companies in America."

• For the past four years (1999–2002), Romano's Macaroni Grill has won the Dinner House category in the *Restaurant & Institutions's* annual Choice in Chains Award.

• *Fortune* lists Brinker as number five in the Food Service category in "2002 Largest American Companies."

• *Fortune* lists Brinker as number four in the Food Service category in "America's Most Admired Companies."

What's more, *Value Line Investment Survey* speaks highly of Brinker Interna-

tional: "New-restaurant openings (company-owned) are slated to accelerate over the next several years, from just over 100 units in the current year (2002) to upwards of 160 by 2005. Notably, management still sees ample room to expand its flagship concept (Chili's), with plans to ultimately double the size of the current store base."

The *Value Line* analyst, Robert M. Greene, CFA, goes on to say, "the company's strong cash flow should allow it to fund its capital program without the need for external financing."

Company Profile

In little more than two decades, Brinker International (formerly Chili's) has grown from a single restaurant in Dallas to multiple casual dining concepts. The company provides dining experiences for nearly 500,000 people every day. Its strategy is, on the one hand, to aggressively expand concepts that exceed its high expectations for return on invested capital and, on the other hand, to reposition or divest those concepts that fail to measure up. As a result, the company continues to develop new concepts. What's more, over the years, Brinker International has acquired restaurant concepts, using shares of its own stock in payment.

Among the company's concept restaurant chains are Chili's Grill & Bar (820 units), Romano's Macaroni Grill (183), On the Border's (129), Maggiano's Little Italy (20), the Corner Bakery Café (76), Cozymel's Coastal Grill (16), Big Bowl Asian Kitchen (12), and Rockfish Seafood Grill (12).

Chili's is committed to "providing our guests with new and exciting menu items," said management, "while keeping the sizzle of our "Famous and Favorites," such as Big Mouth Burgers, Baby Back Ribs, Fajitas, and the Presidente Margarita."

Romano's Macaroni Grill has a "distinctive chef-driven menu," according to the company's 2002 annual report. It features imported Italian ingredients such as olive oil, sun-dried tomatoes, balsamic vinegar, prosciutto and Parmesan, and buffalo mozzarella cheese. "A newly redesigned menu showcases favorites like the Mama's Trio and Spaghettini and Meatballs, while featuring signature dishes like Chicken Portobello and Filet Firenza."

The company's On the Border Mexican Grill & Cantina has a menu that features such items as quesadillas, enchiladas, fajitas, and "our famous Border Sampler." These dishes have been augmented recently by such items as Salmon Mexicano, Blackened Chicken Salad, and Carnitas.

Cozymel's Coastal Grill, according to the company, "celebrates the rich culture, cuisine, and family traditions of the Latin and Caribbean coasts in a lush, tropical ambiance. Distinctive sauces, flavorful spices, grilled beef and chicken, slow-roasted pork, and fresh seafood recall the resonant tastes and textures of tropical islands."

At the Big Bowl Asian Kitchen, "distinctive and flavorful noodle and rice dishes, prepared in our open display kitchens, blend centuries-old Asian cuisine with contemporary, lighthearted food," said management. "We've brought together the best Asian culinary traditions in our menu favorites such as Kung Pao and Lemon Chicken, Pad Thai, the Ultimate Combo appetizer, and our 'You Choose' interactive stir-fry bar."

The company's Rockfish Seafood Grill features such menu items as "our generous shrimp Basket, Fish Tacos, Stuffed Fish, Rock-a-Rita Margarita, eighteen-ounce beer schooner, and award-winning Mexican Shrimp Martini."

Highlights of 2002

- Brinker added 129 new restaurants, bringing the system-wide total to 1,268 units.
- System-wide sales surpassed $3.4 billion.
- The company acquired thirty-nine Chili's and future development rights in eleven states from a franchise partner.
- Restaurants were opened in three new countries: Taiwan, Qatar, and Oman, giving the company presence in twenty-two countries.
- Romano's Macaroni Grill won *Restaurants & Institutions's* "Platinum Choice in Chains" Award for the fourth straight year.
- Opened a new Chili's in Anchorage, Alaska, expanding the company's presence in forty-nine states.
- The stock of Brinker International hit a new all-time high, despite the grinding bear market.

Shortcomings to Bear in Mind

- In a report issued by *Standard & Poor's Stock Reports* in the fall of 2002, Dennis P. Milton said, "Recent same-store sales growth at Chili's restaurants has been mostly offset by same-store declines at Macaroni Grill restaurants.

We expect restaurant margins to remain flat, with higher insurance costs, but lower commodity pricing over the first six months of the fiscal year (2003)."

- During fiscal 2002 (which ended the last Wednesday in June of 2002), insiders, such as executives and board members, were selling shares in the company. During the same period, there were no purchases by these knowledgeable investors.

Reasons to Buy

- According to the *Standard & Poor's* tear sheet in 2002, "We believe that the restaurant industry stands poised to benefit from a long-term trend toward dining out, and that EAT should continue to benefit from its expansion plans." The S&P analyst goes on to say, "The company's growth strategy includes entering smaller markets, including airports and regional malls, with its Chili's concept."
- In 2002, Chili's expansion continued with more restaurant openings than ever before and over five consecutive years of same-store sales increases. With its Anchorage, Alaska, store, Chili's entered its forty-ninth state with record-breaking sales. At the same time, Chili's international representation increased to twenty-two countries with the addition of Qatar, Oman, and Taiwan. What's more, the operation's new prototypes are also succeeding in untapped, smaller markets and high-traffic spots such as airports and regional malls, thus expanding the potential size of the Chili's universe.
- In 2002, Romano's Macaroni Grill added such new selections as the Chicken Florentine Salad, Sole Parmi-

giano, Tuscan Lunch, and the popular Create Your Own Pasta.

- According to the 2002 annual report, the popularity of the company's Maggiano's Little Italy chain "continues to grow with five new restaurants opening in the year ahead. Most of our locations offer carry-out meals for an authentic Italian-American feast anywhere."
- In 2002, Brinker's Corner Bakery Café was honored with People Report's "Top Achiever" Award for management retention and diversity. During the year, the company added thirteen new outlets and plans to add a dozen more in 2003. The company said that "our menu is always being refined, with additions like Pesto Cavatappi Pasta, Chicken Santa Fe Salad, and the Uptown Turkey Sandwich joining our signature Panini and favorites like the Corner Combo and Trio Salad."
- A recent "Hot Concept of the Year" Award winner, Big Bowl has also been recognized for its child-friendly menu atmosphere.

    According to management, "The kids' menu comes tucked inside a Chinese carry-out carton containing a fortune cookie, toy, and children's chopsticks, designed for young fingers."
- In 2002, Rockfish Seafood Grill opened its twelfth restaurant in Texas. The chain recently opened its first store outside of Texas, near Phoenix in Chandler, Arizona. According to the latest annual report, "Our management formula continues to prove its success with the recruitment of passionate and entrepreneurial Chef Partners for nine more openings in the coming year. We're also expanding our To Go service and introducing party platters at all locations to make the Rockfish experience one our guests can share anywhere."

Total assets: $1,783 million
Current ratio: 0.50
Common shares outstanding: 98 million
Return on 2002 shareholders' equity: 15.6%

	2002	2001	2000	1999	1998	1997	1996	1995
Revenues (millions)	2,887	2,474	2,160	1,871	1,574	1,335	1,163	1,042
Net income (millions)	166	145	118	90	69	60	61	73
Earnings per share	1.56	1.46	1.20	0.80	0.70	0.54	0.52	0.65
Dividends per share	Nil	1.42	1.17	.88	.68	—	—	—
Price High	36.0	31.3	28.9	20.4	19.5	11.9	12.7	13.9
Low	24.1	21.3	13.8	13.3	10.0	7.1	8.5	7.9

CONSERVATIVE GROWTH

Brown-Forman Corporation

850 Dixie Highway □ Louisville, Kentucky 40210 □ (502) 774-7074 □ □ Dividend reinvestment plan available: (502) 774-7074 □ Web site: www.brown-forman.com □ Listed: NYSE □ Fiscal years end April 30 □ Ticker symbol: BF.B □ S&P rating: A □ Value Line financial strength rating: A+

In the words of an analyst writing for Deutsche Bank, "The most valuable asset in the group is Jack Daniel's, which has one of the most impressive records in the spirits industry. It is the fifth-largest premium spirits brand in the world, with one of the highest growth rates.

"This has been driven by steady progress in its domestic market (where overall spirits sales have been in decline) and explosive growth internationally. Export volume sales have increased by 700 percent over the past twelve years. At a time when brown spirits sales have been in decline throughout the developed world, Jack Daniel's has bucked the trend through some outstanding marketing.

"The consistency of support behind the brand, in terms of both message and investment, have been the key to its success. By focusing on the heritage and quality of the brand, Jack Daniel's has become an American icon throughout the world, successfully appealing to young consumers in a way that few brown spirits have managed to emulate.

"We believe the growth rates of the brand are likely to accelerate due to the increasing share of sales coming from international, which is growing at a faster pace than sales in the U.S. In addition, we believe it will also benefit from the breakup of the old Seagram business, which was one of its major competitors in bourbon."

Company Profile

Dating back to 1870, Brown-Forman is the world's fourth-largest producer of distilled spirits. Although the company has a host of well-known brands, it is best known for its Jack Daniel's Tennessee Whiskey. It is the company's leading brand and is responsible for a good deal of its profits.

Brown-Forman also has a stake in such consumer durable products as Lenox china, crystal, and glassware, as well as Hartmann luggage. These items account for about 28 percent of sales and 13 percent of earnings. These consumer durables, sold under the Lenox and Gorham trademarks, are sold through retail outlets and company-operated stores. The segment also includes Dansk, a producer of tableware and giftware.

While many other companies in the alcoholic beverage industry have made an effort to diversify away from this business, which is deemed quite mature, Brown-

Forman has steadfastly refused to follow their lead. Its line includes such whiskeys and bourbons as Jack Daniel's, Canadian Mist, Southern Comfort, and Early Times. According to case sales, Jack Daniel's is the largest-selling Tennessee whiskey in the United States; Canadian Mist is the largest-selling Canadian domestic whiskey; and Southern Comfort is the leading domestic proprietary liqueur.

Finally, the company's other alcoholic beverages include such brands as Fetzer and Bolla wines and Korbel champagnes.

Most of these brands are doing well, like the following:

- With sales in more than 130 countries around the world, Jack Daniel's is by far the largest and most important brand to Brown-Forman. Worldwide sales grew 2.5 percent in fiscal 2002, reaching a record 6.5 million cases. Of the top twenty markets in the world for Jack Daniel's, seventeen gained volume in 2002.

- Southern Comfort has experienced a resurgence in the United States, with double-digit gross profit growth in each of the last two years. The brand derives 40 percent of its volume from countries outside the United States. According to the company's 2002 annual report, "An exciting new package has been introduced globally over the past twelve months."

- Finlandia is the number-three superpremium vodka globally, with over 1.7 million cases sold in 2002. It is available in more than 100 countries. The superpremium vodka segment is one of the fastest growing and "exciting segments in the worldwide spirits market," according to the company.

- Canadian Mist is the second-largest imported whiskey in the United States, selling nearly 2.4 million cases in 2002. The brand's "Easy Pour" package, introduced in spring 2000, has proven to be popular with consumers and retailers.

- Fetzer is the largest-selling California wine in the $7–$10 price seg-

ment. Fetzer is the best-selling U.S. premium wine brand in the United Kingdom. In 2002, the company introduced a superpremium line extension, Five Rivers Ranch, into the domestic market.

- Bolla is the number one selling premium Italian wine in the United States. This brand currently sells 1.7 million cases worldwide, up 8 percent over the previous year. In the United States, the Italian category has shown "vibrant growth, growing faster than the Australian and French categories over the past twelve months," according to Brown-Forman.

- As the sales and marketing agent for Korbel since 1965, Brown-Forman "takes great pride in representing America's number-one selling premium champagne," according to the company's 2002 annual report. With a market share of more than 17 percent, Korbel has the strongest brand recognition in the category.

Shortcomings to Bear in Mind

- A trend toward informal dining has hurt sales of Dansk, Gorham, and Lenox china and silverware. What's more, the slowdown in travel following the September 2001 terrorist attacks has dampened sales for Hartmann luggage. Some analysts look for Brown-Forman to sell these operations in the years ahead.

- According to a report issued by Deutsche Bank, "Brown-Forman's greatest failure, in our opinion, has been its inability to participate in the consolidation of the spirits industry. Given its strong brand marketing skills and the scope to strengthen its distribution operations, the company could have added significant value to its business through expanding the portfolio."

Reasons to Buy

- Brown-Forman has been aggressive in launching new products, such as Jack

Daniel's Country Cocktails, a line of low-alcohol beverages, and Tropical Freezes, low-alcohol, preblended frozen cocktails.

- In the words of Steven T. Goldberg, writing for *Kiplinger's* magazine, "Jack Daniel's whiskey accounts for more than half of Brown-Forman's earnings. The brand's consumers tend to be incredibly loyal. Indeed, some 250,000 people make the pilgrimage to Jack Daniel's distillery in Lynchburg, Tennessee, every year. And overseas sales of Jack Daniel's—already 45 percent of the total—are rising rapidly.

  "Like Coca-Cola syrup (the main product of one of Berkshire's biggest holdings), Jack Daniel's costs little to produce. That explains why Brown-Forman generates such high (20 percent-plus) operating margins."

- The company has an impressive balance sheet with 97 percent of capitalization is in shareholders' equity. What's more, its accounting is conservative.

- For the tenth consecutive year, Jack Daniel's continued to grow around the world. The brand grew 6 percent in markets outside the United States, led by strong growth in the United Kingdom, Spain, Italy, and Korea. At home, however, sales were essentially flat in 2002

- According to CEO Owsley Brown II, "For many years, our beverage divisions have chosen their international distributors on a country-by-country basis. We have always felt that it made the most sense to select the best distributor for each market and let that distributor use its local expertise to sell our brands.

  "Employing this philosophy, we renewed our distribution contact with Suntory in Japan during fiscal 2002. In addition to joint ownership of our Australian distributor, we recently expanded our relationship with Allied-Domecq in much of Central and Eastern Europe. We have also made other constructive changes in countries such as South Africa, Russia, and Taiwan."

- *Standard & Poor's Stock Reports* made favorable comments on the company in a mid-2002 report. The analyst, Richard Joy, said, "We view the shares as a worthwhile holding, reflecting Brown-Forman's solid balance sheet and consistent earnings and dividend growth. The company's alcoholic beverage business generates relatively steady cash flow, which can be applied toward strategic acquisitions and the expansion of its international market presence.

  "Although U.S. spirits markets are quite mature, Brown-Forman has shown that it can expand its sales base through product line extensions and overseas expansion. A new distribution alliance with Bacardi in the U.K. will boost profitability and improve the company's competitive position."

Total assets: $2,016 million
Current ratio: 2.08
Common shares outstanding: 68 million
Return on 2002 shareholders' equity: 18.5%

	2002	2001	2000	1999	1998	1997	1996	1995
Revenues (millions)	1,958	1,924	1,877	1,776	1,669	1,584	1,544	1,420
Net income (millions)	228	233	218	202	185	169	160	149
Earnings per share	3.33	3.40	3.18	2.93	2.67	2.45	2.31	2.15
Dividends per share	1.28	1.21	1.18	1.12	1.10	1.06	1.02	.97
Price High	80.5	72.0	69.3	77.3	76.9	55.4	47.5	40.8
Low	58.7	57.7	41.9	54.9	51.8	42.0	35.3	29.4

Cardinal Health, Inc.

7000 Cardinal Place □ Dublin, Ohio 43017 □ (614) 757-7067 □ Dividend reinvestment plan not available □ Web site: www.cardinal.com □ Listed: NYSE □ Fiscal years end June 30 □ Ticker symbol: CAH □ S&P rating: A+ □ Value Line financial strength rating: B++

"Cardinal Health had another outstanding year" in fiscal 2002, according to CEO Robert D. Walter. "We set records in virtually every key financial metric, including total sales, total earnings per share. We achieved record return on sales and capital, and cash flow approached $1 billion.

"Return on equity exceeded 20 percent for the first time, while year-end net debt-to-capital reached an historic low of 12 percent. We accomplished all this without compromising future performance. In fact, we invested aggressively, pouring upwards of $285 million in capital expenditures into expansion and modernization of our facilities, redirected almost $100 million of current earnings into research, development and new initiatives, and spent a total of $384 million on eight strategic acquisitions that further expand our capabilities and offerings to customers." The company's accomplishments for fiscal year 2002 include:

- Earnings per share up 22 percent
- Revenues of $44 billion, up 15 percent
- Return on sales, up for all segments of the company
- Investment spending, about $100 million, up 20 percent
- Return on committed capital reached 32.5 percent, up from 30 percent the prior year
- Return on equity reached 20.5 percent, up from 19.3 percent
- Operating cash flows climbed to $984 million
- 12 percent net debt to capital

Company Profile

Cardinal Health provides innovative products and services to tens of thousands of customers in the health care industry. The company maintains market-leading positions in pharmaceutical formulation, manufacturing, packaging, and distribution; medical-surgical product manufacturing and distribution; and automation and information services by working with its customers to address challenges they face in the fast-changing health care environment. Cardinal operates a family of businesses, offering many complementary products and services to its health care manufacturer and provider customers. The company segregates its operations into four primary business segments, as follows, that reflect the products they provide and the customers they serve.

Pharmaceutical Distribution and Provider Services (82 percent of fiscal 2002 operating revenue) offers pharmaceutical and specialty product distribution, repackaging, retail pharmacy franchising, hospital pharmacy management, and other services to health care providers.

Medical-Surgical Products and Services (14 percent of operating revenue) manufactures and distributes a comprehensive array of medical-surgical and lab products used by hospitals, surgery centers, physicians' offices, and long-term care facilities.

Pharmaceutical Technologies and Services (3 percent of operating revenue) provides comprehensive services to pharmaceutical manufacturers and biotechnology companies, including proprietary drug delivery technologies and contract manufacturing processes, integrated packaging services, as well as sales and marketing.

Automation and Information Services (1 percent of operating revenue) develops automated systems for dispensing pharmaceuticals and medical-surgical supplies and a variety of information systems used by health care providers and manufacturers.

Shortcomings to Bear in Mind

- The health care industry is subject to constant change as a result of product innovation, cost pressures, competitive pressures, and new legislation.
- Because Cardinal has been so consistently successful, it is a difficult stock to buy at a reasonable price. Typically, it sells at a P/E of 30 or more.
- Cardinal Health acquired Syncor International in June of 2002. A major product is Cardiolite, which it distributes for Bristol-Myers Squibb, but the contract is something of a question mark, since it expires December 31, 2003.

Reasons to Buy

- In the fall of 2002, Phillip M. Seligman, an analyst with *Standard & Poor's Stock Reports*, said, "Cardinal Health remains one of the best-managed companies in our health care universe, with a broad array of distribution, specialized, and pharmaceutical packaging services for the health care industry. The company is also among the most consistent generators of cash flow and earnings in the sector."
- *Value Line*'s analyst, Kenneth A. Nugent, also had good things to say about Cardinal in the fall of 2002. "Cardinal Health seems poised to continue its streak of 20 percent-plus earnings comparisons. The company recently reported strong double-digit sales and earnings comparisons for fiscal 2002 (ended June 30), thanks, in large part, to impressive performances by all four of CAH's business segments. And we look for more good news during fiscal 2003."
- Health care providers can meet more than 80 percent of their medical-surgical and laboratory supply needs through Cardinal Health. As the largest distributor of such products in the world, the company can maintain an inventory of 500,000 different products from as many as 2,200 leading manufacturers. In the words of a company spokesman, "We can deliver over 1 million boxes of products to 6,000 health care customers each day. In 2002, even more providers looked to us to cover their patient supply needs, including the prestigious Mayo Foundation for Medical Education and Research."
- In addition to its excellent distribution, Cardinal Health is a leader in the manufacture of respected medical-surgical products. Each day, the company produces more than 3 million products in twenty-eight plants around the world. These products include surgical drapes, gowns, gloves, preparation and skin care products, respiratory care and suction devices, and the finest in surgical instruments.
- To keep pace with the expanding pharmacy industry, the reach of its distribution capabilities is extensive. According to the company, "We keep over 75,000 different pharmaceutical products in our inventory and make 24,000 customer deliveries daily throughout the U.S. To accomplish this, Cardinal Health maintains one of the most sophisticated distribution systems in the world. We have recently invested more than $500 million to upgrade our facilities, taking us well beyond traditional distribution. In 2002, more than 90 percent of all pharmaceutical order transactions were performed electronically, and all orders—even those processed manually—may be easily accessed and tracked via the Internet."
- People over fifty make up the fastest-growing demographic category of the population. Today they represent 27 percent of the U.S. population, and in just five years their numbers will increase 13

percent, to a total of 85 million. This category of consumers spends $610 billion on health care, uses 74 percent of all pharmaceuticals, represents 65 percent of hospital bed days, and accounts for 42 percent of physician visits.

- Health care is an enormous industry, representing about 14 percent of the gross domestic product. With an aging population, there is a solid long-term demand for everything that Cardinal does. For example, during the next five years, more than $34 billion of branded pharmaceuticals face patent expiration. Cardinal's Pharmaceutical Distribution and Provider Services businesses should benefit from this trend because sales of generic products tend to be more profitable for the company than sales of equivalent branded products.

At the other end of the spectrum, Cardinal's Pharmaceutical Technologies and Services businesses are well-positioned to assist branded manufacturers in the development of new or reformulated pharmaceutical products to help replace sales of products losing patent protection. In addition, the government appears poised to pass some form of Medicare drug benefit for seniors that should encourage greater consumption of pharmaceuticals, especially generics.

- Cardinal Health provides manufacturers with highly efficient and economical distribution services, essential for its products. Cardinal handles all of the logistics, inventory, and receivables management,

and the company also handles the administrative activities involved in delivering pharmaceutical products to more than 26,000 pharmacy locations every day.

For its pharmacy customers, Cardinal consolidates orders for products, potentially from hundreds of manufacturers, into pharmacy-specific deliveries of the right products to the right place at the right time.

- In mid-2002, Cardinal Health moved into the nuclear-medicine business in a big way with an $867 million agreement to acquire Syncor International Corporation, the number one company in that business. Syncor operates 130 "nuclear pharmacies" in the United States. These pharmacies can, in a matter of minutes, prepare radioactive compounds used in hospital diagnostic work, as well for therapy. In 2001, Syncor had sales of $774.7 million, up 23 percent over the prior year.

Syncor's major product, which it distributes for Bristol-Myers Squibb, is Cardiolite. This compound is used in studies known as cardiac perfusion imaging, which uses radiation to measure levels of blood flow in and around the heart. In 2001, Cardiolite represented about 58 percent of all domestic imaging and was 42 percent of Syncor's revenues.

Syncor also distributes products such as FDG, the compound used in PET imaging (positron emission tomography), a sophisticated form of imaging used in evaluating heart disease as well as many types of cancer.

Total assets: 16,438 million
Current ratio: 1.83
Common shares outstanding: 452 million
Return on 2002 shareholders' equity: 20.5%

	2002	2001	2000	1999	1998	1997	1996	1995
Revenues (millions)	44,394	38,660	25,247	21,481	12,927	10,968	8,862	7,806
Net income (millions)	1,126	943	730	574	283	221	160	85
Earnings per share	2.64	2.07	1.71	1.37	1.13	.90	.73	.60
Dividends per share	.10	.09	.07	.06	.05	.04	.04	.04
Price High	73.7	77.3	70.0	55.5	50.9	35.0	26.0	17.2
Low	46.6	56.7	24.7	24.7	31.0	22.9	15.5	12.3

Caterpillar, Inc.

100 N. E. Adams Street □ Peoria, Illinois 61629-7310 □ (309) 675-1000 □ Direct dividend reinvestment plan is available: (800)842-7629 □ Web site: www.cat.com □ Listed: NYSE □ Ticker symbol: CAT □ S&P rating: B+ □ Value Line financial strength rating: B+

"Caterpillar's famous yellow-and-black bulldozers, backhoes, and tractors move mountains of earth around the world, yet its stock rarely stirs investors," says Jeff Nash, writing for *Money* magazine in February 2003. "Over the past five years, its shares returned just 12 percent and have mostly traded in the $40s and $50s. But lately this Dow Jones industrial average component has generated the kind of buzz usually reserved for the next hot stock."

Mr. Nash goes on to ask, "Why all the fuss? A new diesel engine that some on Wall Street say will put Cat years ahead of rivals like Cummins and Navistar. Cat's competitors use a well-known technology (exhaust-gas recirculation) to get emissions of smog-producing nitrogen below the Environmental Protection Agency's new requirements for on-road vehicles. Cat says it has developed a cleaner and more cost-effective process that can also be easily modified to meet the next round of EPA requirements in 2007.

"The engine, to be unveiled later this year, will be used in Cat's electric power generation systems, on-road vehicles, and heavy machinery, and sold to other manufacturers. Sanford Bernstein analyst Ann Duignan recently called the engine a 'huge strategic win' for Caterpillar, labeling the stock a buy.

"Duignan and others see Cat's heavy-machinery business gaining ground with an economic recovery. Wall Street predicts that profits at Cat will rise 20 percent in 2003 and 66 percent in 2004. 'It's the perfect time in the cycle to own Cat,' says Carl Domino, co-manager of Northern Large Cap fund."

Company Profile

Caterpillar's distinctive yellow machines are in service in nearly every country in the world, and about 49 percent of the company's revenues are derived from outside North America. What's more, about 71 percent of Cat's 220 independent dealers are based outside the United States.

In 2002, global revenue contributions by geographic region were as follows: North America, 51 percent; Europe/Africa/Middle East, 28 percent; Asia/Pacific, 13 percent; and Latin America, 8.5 percent.

Headquartered in Peoria, Illinois, Caterpillar is the world's largest manufacturer of construction and mining equipment, diesel and natural gas engines, and industrial gas turbines. It is a *Fortune* 50 industrial company with nearly $33 billion in assets.

Caterpillar's broad product line ranges from the company's new line of compact construction equipment to hydraulic excavators, backhoe loaders, track-type tractors, forest products, off-highway trucks, agricultural tractors, diesel and natural gas engines, and industrial gas turbines. Cat products are used in the construction, road-building, mining, forestry, energy, transportation, and material-handling industries.

Over the years, Caterpillar has earned a reputation for rugged machines that typically set industry standards for performance, durability, quality, and value. The company's goal is to remain the technological leader in its product lines. Today, thanks to accelerated design and testing, computer-based diagnostics and operations, and greatly improved materials, the company can deliver new and better products to its customers sooner.

Caterpillar products are sold in more than 200 countries, and rental services are offered through more than 1,200 outlets worldwide. The company delivers superior service through its extensive worldwide network of 220 dealers. Many of these dealers have relationships with their customers that have spanned at least two generations. More than 80 percent of Cat's sales are to repeat customers.

Caterpillar products and components are manufactured in forty-one plants in the United States and forty-three plants in Australia, Brazil, Canada, England, France, Germany, Hungary, India, Indonesia, Italy, Japan, Mexico, the Netherlands, Northern Ireland, China, Poland, Russia, South Africa, and Sweden.

Caterpillar's commitment to customer service is demonstrated by the fastest parts delivery system in its industry. Caterpillar's customers can obtain replacement parts from their dealers usually upon request. If not, Caterpillar ships them anywhere in the world within twelve hours, often much sooner.

Caterpillar offers its customers an easy means of buying Cat equipment through its financial products subsidiary, Caterpillar Financial Services Corporation, a global enterprise with an $11.6 billion managed portfolio.

Shortcomings to Bear in Mind

- Caterpillar has an extremely leveraged balance sheet—only 32 percent of its capitalization is in common equity. I prefer 75 percent. What's more, coverage of bond interest is a low 2.5 times. I prefer 6 times.
- There's no assurance that Caterpillar's new engine will be a breakthrough. "If this is as good as Cat says it is, few will be able to match it, but we just don't

know that for sure yet," said Michael Braig, an analyst with A. G. Edwards.
- According to Mr. Nash, Caterpillar "needs an increase in construction activity worldwide to drive its machinery unit, which makes construction, mining, and agricultural equipment, and accounts for 60 percent of the company's total revenue. The past five years have been tough for Cat and its industry peers as a weak global economy dampened heavy-machinery sales."
- Kevin P. Tynan, an analyst with *Argus Company Report*, was less than enthusiastic about the company on January 31, 2003: "We are maintaining our HOLD rating on CAT shares, as we expect a 4 percent drop in revenues and a 4.7 percent drop in earnings for 2003."

Reasons to Buy

- "We've learned from the recessions of the past," said CEO Glen A. Barton in late January 2003. "Simply put, Caterpillar is not the same company we were ten years ago. We've made some hard choices to diversify our business so we're not only the 'tractor company' we used to be known as. We're also a more nimble, diverse business that in 2002 achieved strong profits in tough times—including three years of global economic downturn in most of our major markets, political turmoil and the continued threat of war.

"While our machinery business has a broad product line and continues to gain market share, our engine business now represents 36 percent of sales—by 2007, it may grow to 45 percent. Caterpillar Financial Services Corporation manages an $18 billion portfolio that makes a substantial contribution to our bottom line. Caterpillar Logistics, which provides services to more than forty third-party clients, is growing rapidly—due in part to an agreement with Ford Motor

Company that provides the opportunity to double the size of our logistics business. We are no longer a victim of the same business cycles we experienced in the past."

- Mr. Barton went on to say, "In fact, we've substantially outperformed the market despite weakening industry fundamentals. When the second half forecasted economic recovery did not occur, we took steps to reduce spending of all types, including capital expenditures. As a result, even with sales and revenues down from 2001, our machinery and engines net free cash flow increased $645 million—even after making contributions to our pension funds of $179 million."

- Of course, the recession and sluggishness of 2000 through early 2003 may not continue. After all, bear markets do eventually end—usually when it's not apparent to the average investor. Mr. Barton is convinced that Caterpillar is poised to take advantage of an upturn: "We're well-positioned to participate in and benefit from economic growth. Many of our products are tied directly to the economy. Our machines build the infrastructure all people and economies need to grow and prosper—and help harvest the energy, minerals, products required by a growing populace.

"Our clean diesel engines help transport these goods on the world's highways, railways, and waterways. And our power-generation products deliver power for businesses and homes all over the world. In short, we have all the ingredients for a strong future—quality products, diverse services, a proven business model and a dealer organization long recognized as one of the world's best. No matter where on the globe our customers are working, Cat dealers are there to support them—with the machines, parts, service, support and expertise customers need to run their businesses more effectively."

- In a competitive world, it's necessary to invest for the future. This is what Mr. Barton has to say on that subject: "We're investing $4 million each working day in technology. Best products and solutions have always been at the root of our success, and our continued investments in technology have produced breakthroughs in emissions reduction, increased product and component life, and improved safety and fuel economy—enabling us to better serve customers' needs."

- In January of 2003, *Value Line's* analyst, David M. Reimer, had this to say about the company's long-term prospects: "True, the stock is ranked to underperform the year-ahead market, but patient investors stand to gain. An eventual global economic rebound would allow CAT to leverage its good diversity and tight cost structure. The stock's total-return potential to 2005–2007 is attractive."

Total assets: $32,851 million
Current ratio: 1.29
Common shares outstanding: 344 million
Return on 2002 shareholders' equity: 14.6%

	2002	2001	2000	1999	1998	1997	1996	1995
Revenues (millions)	20,152	20,450	20,175	19,702	20,977	18,925	16,522	16,072
Net income (millions)	798	805	1,051	946	1,513	1,665	1,361	1,136
Earnings per share	2.30	2.32	3.02	2.63	4.11	4.37	3.54	2.86
Dividends per share	1.40	1.39	1.33	1.25	1.15	.95	.78	.60
Price High	60.0	56.8	55.1	66.4	60.8	61.6	40.5	37.6
Low	33.8	39.8	29.6	42.0	39.1	36.3	27.0	24.1

Cedar Fair, L.P.

One Cedar Point Drive □ Sandusky, Ohio 44870-5259 □ (419) 627-2173 □ Dividend reinvestment plan available: (800) 278-4353 □ Web site: www.cedarfair.com □ Listed: NYSE □ Ticker symbol: FUN □ S&P rating: Not rated □ Value Line financial strength rating: B+

"We are very pleased with the record results achieved in 2002," said Cedar Fair's CEO, Dick Kinzel, in February 2003. "For the year, combined attendance at our eleven properties increased 4 percent from last year (2001), to a record 12.4 million guests, boosted by the successful capital programs a both Cedar Point and Knott's Berry Farm, and another record year at Dorney Park. Meanwhile, average in-park guest per capita spending increased to $34.50, from $34.41 a year ago."

Looking ahead to the 2003 season, Mr. Kinzel reported that the partnership is investing $48 million in capital improvements at its eleven properties. The major projects include the introduction of Cedar Point's 420-foot-tall Top Thrill Dragster, which will be the world's tallest and fastest roller coaster, and the addition of a double-impulse roller coaster, called Steel Venom, at Valleyfair. "Our capital projects are all proceeding on schedule and on budget and should be ready for the 2003 season," he said.

Company Profile

Cedar Fair, L.P., owns and operates six amusement parks, five major water parks, three resort hotels, several year-round restaurants, a marina, and an RV campground. The company's parks attract more than 10 million visitors a year.

Cedar Point, first developed as a recreational area in 1870, is believed to be the largest seasonal amusement park in the United States, based on number of rides and attractions and capacity per hour. It is situated on a 365-acre peninsula in Sandusky, Ohio.

Cedar Point offers more than sixty-five rides and attractions, including fifteen roller coasters, live entertainment shows, Camp Snoopy, a family play land whose theme is based upon the Peanuts comic strip characters, a 950-seat IMAX movie theater, bathing beach facilities, and a miniature golf course. The park also owns and operates four hotel facilities, a marina, and the Cedar Point Causeway, which serves as a major access route to the park.

Cedar Fair prides itself on the growth of its roller coasters. Cedar Point alone boasts fifteen—more than any other park in the world. All told, Cedar Fair parks have thirty-eight roller coasters, including some of the tallest, steepest, and highest-rated coasters ever built.

Cedar Fair's Six Parks

Cedar Point, which is located on Lake Erie between Cleveland and Toledo, is one of the largest amusement parks in the United States. It serves a total market area of 26 million people. Cedar Point serves a six-state region in the midwestern United States, which includes nearly all of Ohio and Michigan, as well as western Pennsylvania, New York, northern West Virginia, Indiana, and southwestern Ontario, Canada.

Valleyfair, located near Minneapolis-St. Paul, draws from a total population of 8 million people in a multistate market area. Opened in 1976, Valleyfair was acquired by Cedar Fair in 1978. Situated on some 125 acres, Valleyfair offers guests more than thirty-five rides and attractions, including Power Tower, a 275-foot-tall thrill ride; Wild Thing, one of the tallest and fastest roller coasters in the world;

Mad Mouse, a family-style roller coaster; and four additional roller coasters. The park also features a whitewater raft ride, a nostalgic train ride, a giant Ferris wheel, and the Pepsi-Cola IMAX Movie Theater, with its sixty-foot-tall screen.

Dorney Park & Wildwater Kingdom is located near Allentown, Pennsylvania. It serves a total market area of 35 million people in the Northeast. First developed as a summer resort area in 1884, it was acquired by Cedar Fair in 1992. Situated on about 200 acres, Dorney Park features more than fifty rides and attractions. New for the 2002 season was Meteor, a ride that takes riders sixty-five feet up into the air to be inverted with nothing between their feet and the sky. Dorney Park also hosts Talon, one of the tallest and fastest inverted coasters in the world.

Worlds of Fun/Oceans of Fun, in Kansas City, Missouri, draws from a total market area of 7 million people. This park opened in 1973 and was acquired by Cedar Fair in 1995. Worlds of Fun is a traditional amusement park themed around Jules Verne's adventure book, *Around the World in Eighty Days*. The park offers its guests fifty rides and attractions, including (new in 2002) Thunderhawk, a six-story-tall spinning thrill ride; Boomerang, a twelve-story-tall steel roller coaster; Mamba, one of the tallest and fastest coasters in the world; the 200-foot-tall Detonator; and Timber Wolf, a world-class wooden roller coaster.

Knott's Berry Farm, near Los Angeles, is one of several major year-round theme parks in southern California. First opened as a tea room and berry market in 1920, it was acquired in late 1997. It serves a total market area of 20 million people and a large national and international tourist population.

New to Knott's Berry Farm in 2002 is Xcelerator, the single largest investment in Knott's Berry Farm's history, launching riders from zero to eighty-two miles per hour in only 2.3 seconds and reaching heights of 205 feet. In addition to Xcelerator, Knott's Berry Farm also hosts Supreme Scream, one of the world's tallest thrill rides; and Ghost Rider, one of the longest wooden coasters in the West.

Michigan's Adventure and **Oasis Water Park**, the company's newest parks, were acquired in 2001. Michigan Adventure is the largest amusement park in Michigan. Situated on 250 acres, it offers guests more than forty rides and attractions, including Shivering Timbers, one of the longest, tallest, and fastest wooden roller coasters in the world. The park also features the Giant Gondola Wheel, an eight-story-tall Ferris wheel, and the Adventure Falls water ride. Seven new attractions were added to Michigan's Adventure for the 2002 season. For no additional charge, guests can enjoy Wild Water Adventure, Michigan's largest and most modern water park.

How They Operate

The parks are family-oriented, providing clean and attractive environments with exciting rides and entertainment. Except for Knott's Berry Farm (which is open all year), the operating season is generally from May through September.

The parks charge a basic daily admission price that provides unlimited use of virtually all rides and attractions. Admissions accounting for 50 percent of revenues, with food, merchandise and games contributing 41 percent and accommodations the other 9 percent.

Shortcomings to Bear in Mind

- About two-thirds of the company's revenue is derived from the Midwest and Mid-Atlantic regions. Adverse economic conditions in these regions could hurt attendance at Cedar Fair parks. On the other hand, the acquisition of Knott's Berry Farm lessens this risk somewhat.

- When you file your income tax, you may find that Cedar Fair has failed to send you the usual paperwork for an owner of its stock. In 2002, I didn't get paperwork from them until March 16. I had already given my CPA the rest, and he had completed my return before I realized my blunder. Unfortunately, it was back to square one—at my expense.

Reasons to Buy

- Both Cedar Fair and Knott's Berry Farm are recent recipients of the Applause Award, the industry's highest honor for "foresight, originality and sound business development." And for the third consecutive year, Cedar Fair received the prestigious Golden Ticket Award for being named the Best Amusement Park in the World, in an international survey conducted by *Amusement Today*, a newspaper that ranks the "best of the best" in the amusement industry.

  The company's parks also placed four coasters in the Top Roller Coaster ranking: Magnum, at number one; Millennium Force, at number two; and Raptor, at number five. Dorney Park's Wildwater Kingdom, moreover, ranked as the number-three theme water park in the *Amusement Today* survey.

- Cedar Fair's parks are well-run and boast profit margins that are the highest in the industry.

- At Cedar Point, more than a third of the park's visitors, the highest ever, spent the night as part of their visit to the park. To build this momentum, said Mr. Kinzel, "We are adding an upscale camping complex, called Lighthouse Point, to our popular Camper Village RV campground. Lighthouse Point will feature upscale cabins, cottages and RV campsites, as well as a swimming pool, fishing pier, and other amenities."

- According to one analyst, Cedar Fair's management team "exhibits both strength and depth." The general managers at the five parks have an average tenure of nearly twenty-five years with the company.

- Cedar Fair operates in an industry with high barriers to entry, with scant likelihood of new competition. The absence of direct competition gives the parks pricing power in their regions, bolstering profit margins.

- In November 2002, Alan G. House, an analyst with *Value Line Investment Survey*, said, "The partnership looks to be well-positioned for the long ride. Cedar has done a good job of allocating its capital expenditures proportionally among its existing six theme parks and five water parks over the past few years."

  Mr. House also said, "These shares offer worthwhile long-term total-return potential. The company increased the cash distribution rate for the fifteenth consecutive year during the current quarter, and we look for this trend to continue."

Total assets: $822 million
Current ratio: 0.51
Partnership units: 51 million
Return on 2002 partners' capital: 24.5%

	2002	2001	2000	1999	1998	1997	1996	1995
Revenues (millions)	503	477	473	438	420	264	250	218
Net income (millions)	71	58	78	86	84	68	74	66
Earnings per share	1.39	1.13	1.50	1.63	1.58	1.47	1.59	1.45
Dividends per share	1.65	1.58	1.50	1.40	1.29	1.26	1.20	1.14
Price High	24.8	25.0	20.9	26.1	30.1	28.3	19.5	18.6
Low	19.6	17.8	17.4	18.4	21.8	17.7	16.1	14.1

Cintas Corporation

Post Office Box 625737 □ Cincinnati, Ohio 45262-5737 □ (513) 573-4915 □ Dividend reinvestment plan not available □ Web site: www.cintas.com □ Fiscal years end May 31 □ Listed: NASDAQ □ Ticker symbol: CTAS □ S&P rating: A+ □ Value Line financial strength rating: B++

According to the company's latest annual report, "Some of the biggest names in the hospitality, transportation, and entertainment industries turn to Cintas for our award-winning designs that capture the essence of their businesses. Our design team blends fashion with function, developing garments with just the right cut, just the right style, just the right image.

"That is why Chicago's Peninsula Hotel, Ritz-Carlton's Reynolds Plantation, Alamo, Culver's, and The Inn at Spanish Bay hired Cintas. The uniform industry's highest honors were recently bestowed on Cintas's designs for these prestigious clients in 2002 Image of the Year Awards."

A recent survey by an independent firm sponsored by the Uniform and Textile Service Association found that the vast majority of people have far more confidence and trust when they buy from, or deal with, people wearing corporate identity uniforms.

Company Profile

Cintas is North America's leading provider of corporate identity uniforms through rental and sales programs, as well as related business services, including entrance mats, hygiene products, clean-room services, and first-aid and safety supplies.

Cintas serves businesses of all sizes, from small shops to large national companies employing thousands of people. Today, more than 5 million people go to work wearing a Cintas uniform every day. That is well over 3 percent of the non-farm, civilian work force in the United States and Canada.

Cintas provides its award-winning design capability and top-quality craftsmanship to the high end of the market—hotels, airlines, cruise ships, and the like. The company delivers the proper uniform to anyone in any job classification, from the doorman to the cocktail waitress in a hotel; from the mechanic to the pilot at the airlines; and even people working in the retail sector.

According to a Cintas spokesman, "Companies like Albertson's use Cintas uniforms to identify their employees to their customers. An employee who wears a clean, crisp, and attractive uniform is always viewed as more professional than someone in ordinary work clothes. Uniforms also complement a company's esprit de corps by building camaraderie and loyalty. Bottom line—we don't just sell uniforms—we sell image, identification, teamwork, morale, pride, and professionalism." Put another way, Cintas believes that when people look good, they feel good. And when they feel good, they work better. What's more, their improved attitude results in a decline in absenteeism and turnover.

Shortcomings to Bear in Mind

■ Fiscal 2002 (ended May 31, 2002) was a difficult year for Cintas. According to Scott D. Farmer, the company's president and chief operating officer, "The recession and the tragic events of September 11 combined to significantly impact the economy. As a result, while we continued our track record of uninterrupted growth in sales and profits for a thirty-third consecutive year, our results fell short of our goals and short of our historical standard."

Mr. Farmer went on to say, "These results reflect the challenges facing our customers. Many have cut the size of their work force, closed plants, and eliminated shifts. As a consequence, millions of workers have lost their jobs in North America, and many of them wore Cintas uniforms. While this has cut into our business with current customers, it has not affected Cintas's ability to add new customers. In fact, we wrote more new business and added more new customers in fiscal 2002 than in any previous year. New business was up 16 percent over the previous fiscal year, and we increased spending to continue our growth by adding to our sales force, expanding our advertising programs and offering new products and services to our customers. At the same time, we continued aggressively managing costs to maintain our profit margins."

Reasons to Buy

- Despite a slack economy and concern over war and terrorism, Cintas continued its winning ways in 2002:
  - The company achieved thirty-three consecutive years of uninterrupted growth in sales and profits.
  - Revenue hit a record $2.27 billion, up 5 percent.
  - Profits hit another peak, up 5 percent, to $234 million.
  - Dividends climbed an impressive 14 percent, continuing a long record of uninterrupted increases.
  - The company added 1,000 new rental routes.
  - Cintas expanded its uniform rental presence into nine new cities.
  - The company opened seven new state-of-the-art uniform rental plants in 2002.
  - Cintas donated industrial workwear and medical supplies to rescue workers at the World Trade Center.
  - For the fourth consecutive year, the company was ranked among best-performing big corporations in the *Forbes* Platinum 400 list.
  - In 2002, Cintas was recognized as one of the world's most valuable companies in *BusinessWeek's* Global 1000.
  - The company was ranked as a top outsourcing business in *Fortune* magazine's 2002 survey on "America's Most Admired Companies."
  - In 2002, Cintas was recognized as the Preferred Uniform and the Preferred First Aid Supplier of NASCAR.
  - Cintas received top honors in the 2002 Image of the Year Awards—the uniform industry's highest honor for uniform design.
  - The company was ranked as having the number one Web site in America within the professional services category by a leading business-to-business magazine.

- In the past ten years (1992–2002), earnings per share advanced from $0.26 to $1.36, a compound annual growth rate of 18 percent. In the same span, dividends per share climbed at an impressive clip, from $0.04 to $0.25, a growth rate of 20.1 percent. Few companies can match such a consistent and unbroken record of growth.

- According to an analytical report issued by Robert W. Baird & Co. (a brokerage firm, with offices in the United States, France, Spain, Germany, and the United Kingdom), "In addition to the current market served, there are another roughly 25 million employees (according to American Apparel Manufacturer) that currently purchase work apparel specific for their occupation through retail outlets, which we believe could potentially be served by the industry.

  "Furthermore, we believe that there are another 20–25 million employees in occupations that could be conducive to a uniform program, but that do not currently utilize one. If the industry penetrated these two potential markets, we estimate that the direct sales market could potentially reach $11 billion."

- Many large corporations are re-engineering all aspects of their business, and they are consolidating their source of supply of products and services. They prefer to deal with fewer suppliers to reduce purchasing and administrative costs. They often prefer to do business with Cintas because the company is a complete uniform service, whether the customer wants to rent, lease, or buy their uniforms. In addition, Cintas also provides online ordering, inventory control and paperless systems.

- In the spring of 2002, Cintas announced that it had acquired Omni Services, Inc., a wholly owned subsidiary of Filuxel SA. With annual revenues of about $320 million, Omni Services is one of the leading uniform rental companies in the United States, serving more than 90,000 customers throughout thirty-one states.

Robert J. Kohlhepp, chief executive of Cintas, said, "We have always had a great deal of respect for the Omni organization, and we are delighted to join forces with them. Each year, the majority of Cintas and Omni's new business comes from companies that have never used our services before. We estimate there are over 85 million people who need our uniforms, and there are more than 5 million businesses that can use our ancillary services.

"The combined sales and marketing teams of Cintas and Omni will continue their focus on developing that potential market. The combination of our two great companies will also benefit our existing customers with an enhanced product and service offering making us an even more valuable resource."

Upon completion of the acquisition, Cintas had the following:

- Annual revenues exceeding $2.5 billion.
- Uniform rental locations covering thirty-nine states and four Canadian provinces.
- In excess of 500,000 customers being served on a regular basis, usually weekly.
- More than 5 million individuals wearing Cintas uniforms.
- Significant synergies from combining the operations.
- Additional products and services to offer customers.

This acquisition is not a new strategy for Cintas. In past years, a key part of the company's growth strategy has been through acquisitions.

- According to Robert M. Greene, CFA, an analyst with *Value Line Investment Survey*, "The company has solid long-term growth prospects. Cintas gets a majority of its new rental accounts from no-programmers (businesses without an existing uniform program), which suggests a sizable untapped market for uniform services still exists.

"Meanwhile, efforts to cross-sell ancillary products, including entrance mats and first-aid supplies, are still in their early stages."

- According to the company, "When on-the-job injuries occur, business need to handle them. Cintas can help by delivering our Xpect line of first aid and safety products and services.

"Cintas regularly and reliably stocks first aid cabinets, provides safety and emergency products, and conducts training to ensure that workplaces are safer and more prepared. Our products and services run the gamut—everything from pain relievers to defibrillators, from back injury prevention to emergency oxygen, from ergonomics to OSHA compliance."

Total assets: $2,519 million
Current ratio: 2.73
Common shares outstanding: 170 million
Return on 2002 shareholders' equity: 17.6%

	2002	2001	2000	1999	1998	1997	1996	1995
Revenues (millions)	2,271	2,161	1,902	1,752	1,198	840	730	615
Net income (millions)	234	222	193	139	123	91	75	63
Earnings per share	1.36	1.30	1.14	.82	.79	.64	.53	.45
Dividends per share	.25	.22	.19	.15	.10	.08	.07	.06
Price High	56.2	53.3	54.0	52.3	47.5	28.3	21.2	16.0
Low	39.2	33.8	23.2	26.0	26.0	17.0	13.9	11.2

GROWTH AND INCOME

The Clorox Company

1221 Broadway □ Oakland, California 94612 □ (510) 271-7000 □ Dividend reinvestment plan available: (888) 259-6973 □ Web site: www.clorox.com □ Fiscal years end June 30 □ Listed: NYSE □ Ticker symbol: CLX □ Standard & Poor's rating: A □ Value Line financial strength rating: A+

What's the secret to successfully executing a major new-product launch with the fastest speed-to-retail distribution—in six weeks—in the company's history? According to the Clorox ReadyMop teams, "It's all about working together." The Clorox ReadyMop is a self-contained mopping system introduced in January of 2002.

"It sounds simple, but, from day one, all of the key stakeholders were at the table together," said Christine Vickers, director of marketing for Clorox ReadyMop. "From Research and Development to Product Supply to Sales and Marketing, everybody realized the magnitude of this launch and knew that no single group could take it on alone."

According to David Chu, consumer insights manager for the product, "Clorox ReadyMop was one of the company's biggest product introductions ever, and we wanted to make sure we got it right out of the gate. We talked to consumers every step of the way and used their feedback to continually refine and enhance the product right up to the launch."

This feedback is reflected in everything from Clorox ReadyMop's overall ergonomic design to details such as how the liquid-dispenser nozzle attaches to the mop head.

Within ten weeks of launch, Clorox ReadyMop was on display in more than half of the United States food, drug, and mass-merchandising retail outlets, as measured by an independent service. By the end of fiscal 2002, moreover, it was outselling its closest competitor by two to one.

Company Profile

In 1913, a group of Oakland businessmen founded the Electro-Alkaline Company, a forerunner of The Clorox Company. The company originally produced an industrial-strength liquid bleach. It was sold in five-gallon crockery jugs to industrial customers in the San Francisco Bay area.

A household version of Clorox liquid bleach was developed in 1916 and subsequently was distributed in sample pint bottles. Demand for the product grew, and its distribution was gradually expanded nationally until it became the country's best-selling liquid bleach.

Clorox was a one-product company for its first fifty-six years, including the eleven years from 1957 through 1968, when it was operated as a division of the

Procter & Gamble Company. Following its divestiture by Procter & Gamble in 1969, the company has broadened and diversified its product line and expanded geographically. Today, Clorox manufactures a wide range of products that are marketed to consumers in the United States and internationally. It is also a supplier of products to food service and institutional customers and the janitorial trades. Although the company's growth in the first few years after divestiture came largely through the acquisition of other companies and products, strong emphasis is now being given to the internal development of new products.

The company's line of domestic retail products includes many of the country's best-known brands of laundry additives, home cleaning products, cat litters, insecticides, charcoal briquettes, salad dressings, sauces, and water-filtration systems. The great majority of the company's brands are either number one or number two in their categories.

Included in Clorox products are such well-known names as Formula 409, Liquid-Plumr, Pine-Sol, Soft Scrub, S.O.S., Tilex, Armor All, Kingsford charcoal, Match Light, Black Flag insecticides, Fresh Step cat litter, Hidden Valley salad dressing, and Kitchen Bouquet.

Clorox's Professional Products unit is focused on extending many of the company's successful retail equities in cleaning and food products to new channels of distribution, such as institutional and professional markets and the foodservice industry.

Internationally, Clorox markets laundry additives, home cleaning products, and insecticides, primarily in developing countries. What's more, Clorox is investing heavily to expand this part of its business. Overall, Clorox products are sold in more than seventy countries and are manufactured in thirty-five plants at locations in the United States, Puerto Rico, and abroad.

Shortcomings to Bear in Mind

- In fiscal 2002, shipments of the Brita business declined 4 percent, as volume gains for faucet-mount systems and filters were more than offset by distribution losses for Brita Fill & Go sports bottles, plus a decline in shipments of pour-through systems and filters and the impact of lower shipments to Kmart.

- In the past ten years (1992–2002), earnings per share advanced from $.66 to $1.37, a compound annual rate of only 7.6 percent. In the same span, dividends expanded from $.40 to $.84, a growth rate of 7.7 percent. Neither record is particularly impressive.

Reasons to Buy

- Although the company's growth rate is not impressive, its performance in fiscal 2002 was far better than most of corporate America. Both revenues and earnings per share advanced mostly.

    This indicates a company that is not subject to the ups and downs of the economy and is thus a good stock for a conservative investor.

- Clorox is sound financially. *Standard & Poor's* rates the stock A, while *Value Line Investment Survey* gives the company a similar rating of A+.

- In fiscal 2001, Clorox introduced its response to the needs of the modern driver with the launch of STP 6,000-Mile Oil Extender, a new premium oil additive that enables users to drive up to 6,000 miles between oil changes. The introduction of the new additive comes on the heels of extensive qualitative research showing the number one undelivered benefit consumers seek from an oil additive is extending their oil change interval. In addition, a recent survey shows that nearly 55 percent of Americans worry more about changing their oil on a regular basis than other routine car maintenance tasks.

STP 6,000-Mile Oil Extender became available in stores nationwide late in 2000; it carries a price tag of $6.99 for the 15-ounce bottle. According to the company, "The major benefit that this product brings to users is that Oil Extender maintains the viscosity of the motor oil while boosting the level of the oil's performance additives. By boosting these ingredients, STP 6,000-Mile Oil Extender provides an extra level of protection in your motor oil."

- In fiscal 2001, the company announced an agreement with Brita GmbH of Germany to acquire full control of Brita water-filtration products in North and South America, including the exclusive use of the Brita trademark, full rights to develop and market new products under the Brita name, and all business assets in the region.

"The buyout of the joint venture will enhance the ability of Brita Products to pursue new business opportunities, and improve its operating efficiency in the Americas," according to Scott Weiss, Clorox's general manager for Brita Products. He added that the two Brita entities will continue to share marketing, research, and development information.

- Clorox continues to expand where the company sees an opportunity to enter a market with a competitive advantage. Once Clorox acquires a business, it expands it by modernizing plants. What's more, the company builds mass through line extensions and strategic acquisitions.

Clorox also upgrades packaging and leverage marketing expertise gained in the United States by putting it to use in a new country with the company's just-acquired brands. In sum, that's how Clorox built leadership positions in the majority of its worldwide markets.

- In fiscal 2002, the company's Glad business was a key focus of management's efforts to restore growth, following a lackluster 2001. These efforts paid off, and Glad's business expanded by 5 percent in 2002, enhanced by new products in the GladWare disposable containers line, coupled with an improved price-value relationship for trash bags and increased advertising. What's more, profits increased, and Glad achieved its highest gross margin in five years.

- In fiscal 2002, the company's Specialty Products segment had a volume increase of 3 percent and a sales increase of 7 percent. Results were helped by a double-digit increase in Kingsford charcoal shipments, with an overall gain of 11 percent.

Also strongly contributing to the segment's good showing were increased shipments of Armor All wipes and tire protectant products—including the recently launched Armor All leather spray and wipes.

The company also benefited from volume gains from Fresh Step and Scoop Away cat litters, helped by product improvements, increased marketing support for Fresh Step, and line extensions such as Fresh Step Cedar cat litter.

Finally, successfully addressing ongoing competitive pressure, the food products business turned around in 2002 to record solid volume growth, reflecting higher shipments of Hidden Valley dressings and KC Masterpiece marinades.

Total assets: $3,630 million
Current ratio: 0.98
Common shares outstanding: 230 million
Return on 2002 shareholders' equity: 19.8%

	2002	2001	2000	1999	1998	1997	1996	1995
Revenues (millions)	4,061	3,903	4,083	4,003	2,741	2,533	2,218	1,984
Net income (millions)	322	325	394	246	298	249	222	201
Earnings per share	1.37	1.35	1.64	1.03	1.41	1.21	1.07	.95
Dividends per share	.84	.84	.80	.72	.64	.58	.53	.48
Price High	48.0	40.85	56.4	66.5	58.8	40.2	27.6	19.8
Low	31.9	29.95	28.4	37.5	37.2	24.3	17.5	13.8

CONSERVATIVE GROWTH

The Coca-Cola Company

One Coca-Cola Plaza □ Atlanta, Georgia 30311 □ (404) 676-8054 □ Dividend reinvestment plan available: (888) 265-3747 □ Web site: www.coca-cola.com □ Listed: NYSE □ Ticker symbol: KO □ S&P rating: A- □ Value Line financial strength rating: A++

The CEO of Coca-Cola, Douglas Daft, has drawn on the lessons he learned in his previous post as head of the company's Asian operations. His mantra is, "Think local, act local." Daft wants to sell more products suited to local tastes, whether under existing U.S. brands (Minute Maid juices, Powerade sports drinks, Dasani water) or new ones tailored to local markets (such as a drink in Japan called Tea Water Leafs).

This strategy is based on two facts about the global market. One is that while Coke already controls half of carbonated drink sales around the world, it only accounts for 18 percent of the total nonalcoholic beverage market. On that basis alone, there's simply much more room for Coke to expand in noncarbonated drinks. Second, outside the United States, noncola drinks are far more popular than colas.

As an example of how Mr. Daft has changed things at Coke, let's take a look at some tiny countries in the Baltic region, such as Estonia. A couple of years ago, Coke decided it had to act fast to counter the surging popularity of kvass, a beverage made from stale bread, sugar, and yeast—not exactly a concoction that might appeal to someone in Boston, Denver, Mil-

waukee, or Atlanta. To deal with the problem, Coke bought the Baltic producers of this ancient Russian thirst-quencher.

The local Coke producer struck a deal with Tallinn-based AS Osel Foods and acquired the rights to the Estonian kvass brand name, Linnuse Kali, and the Latvian brand name, Pilskalna. With kvass threatening to surpass cola in the Baltic region, Coca-Cola concluded that it couldn't fight Estonians' and Latvians' rediscovered taste for the brownish, cider-like drink Russians have quaffed for more than 300 years. The beverage gets its name from the Slavic word for "ferment."

"This is the essence of our 'think local' strategy," said Aki Hirvonen, the marketing manager for Coca-Cola Baltic Beverage, Ltd. After Osel Foods started selling kvass in 1998, its market share expanded eightfold, to 32 percent in Latvia. Coke and kvass now have a fifth each of the Baltic soft-drink market.

Company Profile

The Coca-Cola Company is the world's largest producer and distributor of soft-drink syrups and concentrates. Company products are sold through bottlers, fountain wholesalers, and distributors in nearly 200 countries. The company's products represent about 48 percent of total soft-drink unit-case volume consumer world-wide. (A unit-case is equal to twenty-four 8-ounce servings.)

Trademark Coca-Cola accounts for about 68 percent of the company's world-wide gallon shipments of beverage products (excluding those distributed by the Minute Maid Company).

The company's allied brands account for the remaining 32 percent of gallon sales. These brands are: Sprite, Diet Sprite, TAB, Fanta, Fresca, Mr Pibb, Hi-C, Mello Yello, Barq's, Powerade, Fruitopia, and specialty overseas brands.

The company's operations are managed in five operating groups and the Minute Maid Company. Excluding those products distributed by the Minute Maid Company, the company's unit case volume by region is as follows: North America Group, 31 percent; Latin America Group, 25 percent; Greater Europe Group, 21 percent; Middle and Far East Group, 19 percent; and Africa Group, 4 percent.

The Minute Maid Company, headquartered in Houston, Texas, is the world's largest marketer of juice and juice-drink products.

Major products of the Minute Maid Company include the following:
- Minute Maid chilled ready-to-serve and frozen concentrated citrus and variety juices, lemonades, and fruit punches
- Hi-C brand ready-to-serve fruit drinks
- Bright & Early breakfast beverages
- Bacardi tropical fruit mixes

Shortcomings to Bear in Mind

■ An analyst with Argus Research Corporation had these negative comments in late 2002: "Investors should recognize the persistent risk facing Coca-Cola as it tries to expand its business simultaneously in over 200 countries. Under cur-rent and much-maligned CEO Douglas Daft, the company is much more flexible than it has been in the past. National chiefs determine marketing and product development locally, for instance. The company is justifiably proud of many marketing initiatives coming out of local offices. But no amount of ingenuity can protect Coke from the stark limitations on consumers' purchasing power around most of the globe. Recent performance in Latin America is sufficient illustration of this fact. With most of the world caught in the current economic slow-down, we sense more volume and revenue setbacks lie ahead for Coke."

■ Coke is the ultimate global company, selling $20 billion worth of beverages in nearly 200 countries. Its mission seems simple—sell more drinks to more people in more countries. But the execution can be difficult. The soda market here at home, by far the company's largest, is stagnant. Overseas markets, and especially the developing ones that Coke depends on for growth, are volatile.

And the theory that everyone, everywhere, will someday be drinking as much of the company's sodas as Americans do now—425 cups per person per year—doesn't seem to hold water. Coke also has been slow to recognize consumers' shift away from soda and toward an array of juices, sports drinks, teas, coffees, and bottled waters. Of late, however, it has been making some bold moves to catch up.

Reasons to Buy

■ In mid-2002, Coca-Cola teamed up with Groupe Danone for the production, marketing, and distribution of Danone's retail bottled spring and source water business in the United States. In addition to a $128 million cash payment for a 51 percent interest in the partnership, Coke will provide marketing, distribution, and management expertise.

- At the end of 2002, Richard Joy, an analyst with *Standard & Poor's Stock Reports*, had some favorable comments: "Revenues in 2003 should rise 5 percent to 6 percent, reflecting 5 percent higher worldwide volumes and modestly higher concentrate prices. Volumes should benefit from new products targeting high-growth beverage categories, contributions from a water partnership venture with Groupe Danone, continued expansion of Dasani water availability, and growth of Powerade. Operating profits should benefit from operating efficiencies, restructuring activities, lower media rates, and the absence of one-time marketing investments from the prior year."

  The S&P report went on to say, "The company's decentralized operating structure and aggressive new product development activity have improved its ability to operate more effectively at the local market level. This improved operational effectiveness should allow the company to achieve its annual worldwide volume growth target of 5 percent to 6 percent. We expect strong free cash flow growth over the next several years, which is expected to fund acquisitions and substantial share repurchase activity."

- In December of 2002, *Money* magazine had these comments on Coke: "Coca-Cola still has some growth prospects, as soft-drink consumption is still rising. It has been successfully raising prices and increasing shipment, and is expecting greater earnings. And it's not just a cola company. Coke is a leading player in the bottled-water business with its Dasani brand, plus it has a sizable fruit-juice business known as Minute Maid. Some argue that Coke may be the most focused and efficient company in the world.

  "More important, Coke is a very safe company. It has raised its dividend every year for more than a decade. Only twice during that time has it had to use more than half of its reported earnings to pay the dividend."

- Mr. Daft has decentralized management. To get closer to local markets, he has been reassigning hundreds of headquarters people to far-flung outposts. And, rolling back the overambitious expansion plans of Mr. Ivester, he is biting the bullet on poorly performing ventures in the Baltics and Japan—which cost $813 million in writedowns.

  The speed at which Coke's CEO is moving to bring change to Coke is winning him plaudits from observers, analysts, and influential investors in the company. The changes, those around him say, have been needed for years and are only the beginning. "I'm very impressed thus far not only with the quality of the management shifts, but the implications they have for the organization and the message it sends," said one analyst.

- Coke is not content merely to sell its flagship beverage. It is well aware that noncarbonated beverage consumption is expanding at a heady clip. In 2001, the company bought Odwalla, Inc., a small beverage company based in California that sells its juices in more than thirty states. Now a part of the Minute Maid Company, Odwalla markets flash-pasteurized juices and blends such as C Monster, Mo' Beta, Rooty Fruity, and Viva Las Veggies.

  At the time of the transaction, Don Short, president and CEO of the Minute Maid Company, said, "Under the leadership of Stephen Williamson and his team, Odwalla's talented and proven people have built unique brands with loyal followings. Odwalla, as the North American leader in the super premium juice category, is a key component of Coca-Cola's strategy for building category leaders and profitable growth in new beverage categories."

Superpremium juices are one of the fastest-growing beverage categories. Odwalla offers an appealing range of juices, vegetable drinks, fortified beverages, smoothies, shakes, soy and lactic beverages; impressive chilled direct store distribution capabilities—and a culture of innovation.

For Coca-Cola, the deal means a bigger slice of the "good-for-you beverage area," said John Sicher, editor of *Beverage Digest*, an industry publication. "It's a smart deal for Coke," he said. "It's easier to take a small brand that already has some real consumer following and make it into a bigger brand than to start from scratch."

The Odwalla deal was not an isolated event. In recent months, Coke has acquired Planet Java, a maker of coffee drinks, and Mad River Traders, Inc., which distributes New Age teas, juices, lemonades, and sodas.

■ Coke gained 0.6 percentage points to reach a 44.3 percent share of the domestic soft-drink market in 2002, after slipping to 43.7 percent the prior year. The U.S. soft-drink market in 2002 was $62.9 billion. The company's unit-case volume, a measure of sales and financial health in the soft-drink industry, rose 2.1 percent. By contrast, PepsiCo's unit-case volume gained only 0.2 percent in 2002. And its market share fell 0.2 percentage point, to 31.4 percent.

Total assets: $24,501 million
Current ratio: 1.00
Common shares outstanding: 2,480 million
Return on 2002 shareholders' equity: 36.5%

	2002	2001	2000	1999	1998	1997	1996	1995
Revenues (millions)	19,564	20,092	19,889	19,805	18,813	18,868	18,546	18,018
Net income (millions)	3,976	3,969	2,177	2,431	3,533	4,130	3,492	2,986
Earnings per share	1.60	1.60	.88	.98	1.42	1.64	1.40	1.19
Dividends per share	.80	.72	.68	.64	.60	.56	.50	.44
Price High	57.9	62.2	66.9	70.9	88.9	72.6	54.3	40.2
Low	42.9	42.4	42.9	47.3	53.6	50.0	36.1	24.4

CONSERVATIVE GROWTH

Colgate-Palmolive Company

❏ 300 Park Avenue ❏ New York, New York 10022-7499 ❏ Listed: NYSE ❏ (212) 310-3072 ❏ Dividend reinvestment plan available: (800) 756-8700 ❏ Web site: www.colgate.com ❏ Ticker symbol: CL ❏ S&P rating: A ❏ Value Line financial strength rating: A++

Reuben Mark, Colgate's chief executive officer, "has an MBA from Harvard Business School. Other than that, he shares little with the popular conception of a CEO," said the author of an article in *BusinessWeek* in September 2002.

"He's not a strapping former athlete. He sometimes pulls his hair back in a ponytail. When he travels overseas, which is often, since Colgate operates in 218 countries and gets 75 percent of its sales from outside the

U.S., it's not on a corporate jet. He likes to curse, hates publicity, and doesn't play golf.

"The way he runs Colgate is different, too. Although he assiduously courts institutional investors—Colgate's five biggest shareholders control 20 percent of its stock—he holds in great disdain many of the things Wall Street loves most. His record of meeting or beating quarterly earnings estimates is near perfect, but he doesn't go in for radical business moves."

The *BusinessWeek* writer also said, "Since Mark took over eighteen years ago, Colgate has made only two large acquisitions and has exited numerous businesses where it was not a leader. The company relies heavily on new products, but Mark deliberately does not stray out of four core areas of expertise: oral care, personal care, household cleaners, and pet food."

Importantly, Reuben Mark is "obsessed with profitability and has increased Colgate's gross profit margin to 55.1 percent in 2001, a steady climb from 47.9 percent in 1995. His goal is to reach 60 percent by 2008. That kind of control over costs has helped Colgate record higher profits without increasing the price of a tube of toothpaste in the U.S. in the past decade."

Company Profile

Colgate-Palmolive is a leading global consumer products company, marketing its products in more than 200 countries and territories under such internationally recognized brand names as Colgate toothpaste and brushes, Palmolive, Mennen Speed Stick deodorants, Ajax, Murphy Oil Soap, Fab, and Soupline/Suavitel, as well as Hill's Science Diet and Hill's Prescription Diet.

With 75 percent of its sales and earnings coming from abroad, Colgate is making its greatest gains in overseas markets.

Travelers, for instance, can find Colgate brands in a host of countries:

• They'll find Total toothpaste, with its proprietary antibacterial formula that fights plaque, tartar, and cavities, in more than seventy countries.

• The Care brand of baby products is popular in Asia.

• Colgate Plax makes Colgate number one in mouth rinses outside the United States.

• The Colgate Zig Zag toothbrush, popular in all major world regions outside the United States, helps make Colgate the number one toothbrush company in the world.

• Axion is an economical dishwashing paste popular in Asia, Africa, and Latin America.

Shortcomings to Bear in Mind

■ The company's balance sheet is quite leveraged. Long-term debt exceeds common equity by a wide margin.

■ In December of 2002, *Standard & Poor's Stock Reports* had some reservations concerning Colgate-Palmolive. Howard Choe said, "We have a hold opinion on the shares, reflecting our belief that CL's valuation is high; however, management continues to execute flawlessly. Based on P/E valuation, CL is the most expensive household products stock in our analytical universe. The shares recently traded at twenty-one times our 2003 estimate, a sizable premium to the S&P 500 and the company's peers. This premium can be attributed to continued market share gains in several key businesses, as well as the company's ongoing cost savings program."

Reasons to Buy

■ "The company's most important product launch this year (2002) is in oral care," said Alex Hudson, an analyst with *Value Line Investment Survey*, in October 2002. "In late August, Colgate's Simply White was introduced in commercial markets. The gel, which promises to whiten teeth in two weeks, is in direct competition with Procter & Gamble's White Strips, which have been in stores since May 2001.

"The market for whitening systems appears to have a substantial upside. Less than 4 percent of U.S. households use whitening systems, which is currently about a $200-million business. Retailers expect whitening system revenue to double in a year, as aging baby boomers become more concerned with maintaining a youthful appearance. Simply White's competitive advantage, barring consumer acceptance, is its $15 price-point, which is about half as much as White Strips."

- Technology-based new products and veterinary endorsements are driving growth at Hill's, the world's leader in specialty pet food. Hill's markets pet foods mainly under two trademarks: Science Diet, which is sold through pet supply retailers, breeders and veterinarians; and Prescription Diet for dogs and cats with disease conditions. Hill's sells its products in eighty-five countries.

   Recent introductions gaining wide acceptance are Science Diet Canine and Feline Oral Care, Science Diet Canine Light Small Bites, and new Prescription Diet Canine b/d, a clinically proven product that reduces the effect of canine aging.

- Colgate has a solid and consistent growth record. In the 1992–2002 period, earnings per share advanced from $0.73 to $2.19, a compound annual growth rate of 11.6 percent. In the same ten-year stretch, dividends climbed from $0.29 to $0.72, a compound growth rate of 9.5 percent, or far above the inflation rate.

- Colgate concentrates research expenditures on priority segments that have been identified for maximum growth and profitability. For example, the fast-growing liquid body-cleansing category has benefited from continuous innovation. As a result, European sales of Palmolive shower gel have nearly tripled during the past four years. The latest innovation, Palmolive Vitamins, uses unique technology to deliver two types of Vitamin E to the skin, thus providing both immediate and long-lasting protection.

   In another sector, focused R&D at Colgate's Hills subsidiary has resulted in a superior antioxidant formula that helps protect pets from oxidative damage,

including to the immune system. This discovery led to a significant nutritional advance of Hill's Science Diet dry pet foods, introduced in the United States in 2000. The product has gained excellent reception from vets, retailers, and their customers, aided by national media advertising. Hill's scientists have also developed a new Prescription Diet brand formulation that nutritionally helps avoid food-related allergies.

- Adding to region-specific initiatives is the company's vast consumer intelligence. Colgate interviews more than 500,000 consumers in more than thirty countries annually to learn more about their habits and usage of the company's product.

- Colgate's global reach lets the company conduct consumer research in countries with diverse economies and cultures to create product ideas with global appeal. The new product development process begins with the company's Global Technology and Business Development groups analyzing consumer insights from various countries to create products that can be sold in the greatest possible number of countries. Creating "universal" products saves time and money by maximizing the return on R&D, manufacturing and purchasing. To assure wide global appeal, potential new products are test-marketed in lead countries that represent both developing and mature economies.

- To best serve its geographic markets, Colgate has set up regional new product innovation centers. From these centers, in-market insight from thousands of consumer contacts is married with R&D, technology, and marketing expertise to capitalize on the best opportunities. Early on, the consumer appeal, size, and profitability of each opportunity are assessed. Once a new product concept is identified, it is simultaneously tested in different countries to assure acceptance across areas. Then, commercialization on a global scale takes place rapidly.

A prime example is Colgate Fresh Confidence, a translucent gel toothpaste aimed at young people seeking the social benefits of fresh breath and oral health reassurance. The process from product concept to product introduction in Venezuela took only one year. Within another six months, Colgate Fresh Confidence had been expanded throughout Latin America and began entering Asia and Europe. Today, less than a year after its first sale, Colgate Fresh Confidence is available in thirty-nine countries and is gaining new Colgate users among the targeted age group. Colgate Fresh Confidence, moreover, has expanded even faster than Colgate Total, the most successful toothpaste introduction ever.

The U.S. Surgeon General recently cited oral disease as a "silent epidemic,"

of which the primary victims are inner-city children. Initially designed to improve the oral health of urban youngsters in the United States, Colgate's "Bright Smiles, Bright Futures" program has expanded to address oral care needs in eighty countries.

In the midst of expanding the company's reach, Colgate dental vans are stopping in cities across the country. New York, Houston, Atlanta, Chicago, and Los Angeles are examples of the many cities where children benefit from the expertise of volunteer dental professionals. In partnership with retail giants such as Wal-Mart and Kmart, Colgate's program reaches children and their families outside those stores across the United States. Each year, this campaign reaches 5 million children in the United States as well as another 49 million around the world.

Total assets: $ 6,928 million
Current ratio: 0.97
Common shares outstanding: 543 million
Return on 2002 shareholders' equity: NMF*

	2002	2001	2000	1999	1998	1997	1996	1995
Revenues (millions)	9,294	9,084	9,358	9,118	8,972	9,057	8,749	8,358
Net income (millions)	1,288	1,147	1,064	937	849	740	635	541
Earnings per share	2.19	1.89	1.70	1.47	1.31	1.14	1.05	.90
Dividends per share	.72	.68	.63	.59	.55	.53	.47	.44
Price High	58.9	64.8	66.8	58.9	49.4	39.3	24.1	19.3
Low	44.1	48.5	40.5	36.6	32.5	22.5	17.2	14.5

* NMF: No meaningful figure.

INCOME

ConAgra Foods, Inc.

One ConAgra Drive □ Omaha, Nebraska 68102-5001 □ (402) 595-4154 □ Dividend reinvestment plan available: (800) 214-0349 □ Web site: www.conagra.com □ Listed: NYSE □ Fiscal years end last Sunday in May □ Ticker symbol: CAG □ S&P rating: A □ Value Line financial strength rating: A

Unlike many other companies, ConAgra had a solid year in fiscal 2002. In the words of CEO Bruce Rohde, "One of our recently introduced products, Banquet

Homestyle Bakes, became one of the industry's best-performing new items, registering consumer sales of more than $125 million in fiscal 2002. We also made new product news with other new items, including Chocolate Reddi-wip, ACT II Kettle Corn, Orville Redenbacher's Sweet 'n Buttery flavored popcorn, Hunt's Perfect Squeeze Ketchup, Wolfgang Puck wood-fired pizzas, Healthy Choice Mixed Grills, Fleischmann's Premium Blend with Olive Oil, and several other items. New products are key to improving our product mix."

Finally, the company's CEO said, "We won outstanding supplier awards from Wal-Mart, Wendy's, and Sysco, and other significant companies. Also, a number of our manufacturing facilities received awards for quality and workplace safety."

Company Profile

ConAgra Foods, Inc., is one of the world's most successful food companies. As North America's largest foodservice manufacturer and second-largest retail food supplier, ConAgra is a leader in several segments of the food business.

ConAgra has uniquely positioned its assets to take advantage of meals prepared at home as well as in such foodservice institutions as schools, hospitals, and restaurants. As a result of a constantly improving business mix, more than 75 percent of the company's profits are generated from sales of branded and value-added products. Less than 25 percent of the company's food profits come from commodity operations.

ConAgra's operations broke down as follows in fiscal 2002 (in millions of dollars):

	SALES	OPERATING PROFIT
Packaged Foods	$12,364	$1,610
Food Ingredients	1,669	160
Agricultural Products	3,573	19
Meat Processing	10,024	269
Total	**$27,630**	**$2,058**

Packaged Foods

In this segment, shelf-stable foods include a host of major brands, including Hunt's, Healthy Choice, Wesson, Orville Redenbacher's, Slim Jim, Act II, Peter Pan, Van Camp's Beanee Weenee, Manwich, Hunt's Snack Pack, Swiss Miss, Knott's Berry Farm, Chun King, La Choy, Rosarita, Gebhardt, Wolf Brand, Pemmican, Penrose, and Andy Capp's.

Also falling into the foodservice product category are such major brands as Lamb Weston, Fernando's, Casa de Oro, Holly Ridge, and Rosarita.

In the frozen food sector are such major brands as Healthy Choice, Banquet, Marie Callender's, Kid Cuisine, MaMa Rosa's, Papa G's, Gilardi's, The Max, Morton, Patio, Chun King, and La Choy.

Finally, Packaged Foods also has a substantial stake in dairy case products such as Parkay, Blue Bonnet, Fleischmann's, Move Over Butter, Egg Beaters, Healthy Choice, County Line, Reddi-wip, and Treasure Cave.

Meat Processing

ConAgra's meat-processing segment includes the fresh beef, pork, and poultry operations. This segment's principal activities include the production and marketing of fresh beef, pork, and poultry products for retail, foodservice, and further processing. Major brands include Armour, Butterball, ConAgra Beef, Country Pride, Flavorland Beef, Miller's Blue Ribbon Beef, Monfort, Swift, and To-Ricos.

Food Ingredients

This includes the company's non-grain-based ingredients, such as processed seasonings, blends and flavorings, as well as grain-based items that are processed for ingredient use.

Principal activities include manufacturing and distribution of a variety of ingredients to food and beverage processors.

This segment's products and services include flour milling, specialty food ingredients, vegetable processing, savory flavors manufacturing, oat and corn milling, and barley malting.

Agricultural Products

This part of the company focuses on basic grain processing, food ingredients, and the value-added business of crop inputs and yield-enhancement services. Major businesses include flour milling, specialty food ingredients manufacturing, oat and corn milling, dry edible bean processing and merchandising, and barley malting.

In the United Agri Products segment, principal activities include the distribution of crop input (seeds, fertilizer products, crop protection chemicals, and information systems), in the United States, Argentina, Bolivia, Canada, Chile, Ecuador, France, Mexico, Peru, South Africa, Taiwan, the United Kingdom, and Zimbabwe.

In the Trade Group segment, the company's principal activities are marketing bulk agricultural commodities throughout the world. Major businesses are grain procurement and merchandising, food-related commodity trading, and commodity services.

Shortcomings to Bear in Mind

■ According to a report written by Constance Napoli for Prudential Financial, "Commodity operations, such as agricultural chemicals, fertilizers, and beef and chicken processing, remain a significant component of CAG's daily business, but a drain on operating profits. Burdened by slow demand for fertilizers and farming chemicals, the agricultural division sustained an operating loss of $37.9 million in the third quarter (of 2002), a 10.5 percent drop from the $34.3 million loss posted in the prior year."

■ *Standard & Poor's Stock Reports* had some negative comments in a report issued in mid-2002. Richard Joy said, "We continue our 'hold' recommendation on the shares, as we are encouraged by moves by CAG to become more of a branded food company, but see only modest earnings gains for the next several quarters."

■ In recent years, ConAgra has pursued an aggressive acquisition policy. To be sure, this strategy has helped the company to enhance its profit margins. However, it has left it highly leveraged. At the end of 2002, common equity represented only 43 percent of ConAgra's balance sheet.

Reasons to Buy

■ ConAgra Foods acquired International Home Foods Corporation in fiscal 2001 for about $2.9 billion, including $1.3 billion in debt. This move enhanced the company's diversification by adding such products as Chef Boyardee pasta products, PAM cooking spray, Gulden's mustard, Bumble Bee Tuna, and other well-known shelf-stable products. International Home Foods' product portfolio is a good fit for ConAgra and should create immediate value for the company.

Twenty years ago, ConAgra had minimal presence in value-added foods and a limited number of recognizable brands. Today, ConAgra is known for household branded foods such as Healthy Choice, Butterball, Banquet, Hunt's, Orville Redenbacher's, Reddi-wip, Slim Jim, and Armour. ConAgra has twenty-seven brands with retail sales in excess of $100 million each.

■ ConAgra is the most diversified food company in the world, with more than seventy brands, along with meat processing, grain milling, and trading operations across major sectors.

■ One way to judge a company is to examine its return on shareholders' equity. In this regard, ConAgra gets high marks. In fiscal 2002, return on equity was an impressive 22.4 percent.

- At the end of 2001, ConAgra Foods merged its Australian grain business with rival Grainco Australia, Ltd., giving ConAgra greater access to supplies from the world's third-largest wheat exporter.

  "This joint venture allows CTG (ConAgra Trade Group) and Grainco Australia to participate in a larger grain marketing business within Australia," said Greg Heckman, ConAgra Trade Group's president.

  Australia ships about 16 percent of world trade in wheat and is also the biggest exporter of barley used to make beer and the second-biggest for canola.

- In fiscal 2001, ConAgra Foods introduced a host of new products, including Homestyle Bakes from Banquet, Jolly Rancher Gels, Orville Redenbacher's Chocolate Sensations, Act II Corn-on-the-Cob Popcorn, new Healthy Choice items, new Marie Callender's items, Hunt's Family Favorites, Butterball gravy, broth, and stuffing, Armour Guaranteed Tender Pork, Treasure Cave Gorgonzola Cheese Crumbles, and Reddi-wip Light, among others.

- In recent years, income stocks have been difficult to find. For its part, ConAgra is an ideal dividend stock, with a generous yield and a dividend that has been boosted on a regular basis, with annual increases dating back before 1985. In the past ten years (1992–2002), the per-share dividend climbed from $0.26 to $0.92, an impressive compound annual growth rate of 13.5 percent.

- In May of 2002, the company entered into an agreement to transfer its fresh beef and pork processing business to a new venture led by Hicks, Muse, Tate & Furst. Under terms of the agreement, ConAgra now owns a minority stake and substantially reduces its equity in the business, from $1 billion to $150 million. The divestiture netted ConAgra $800 million in cash and a 46 percent equity stake in the joint venture, which allows the company to maintain strong access to a large supply of top-quality meat products.

  According to William G. Ferguson, an analyst with *Value Line Investment Survey*, "The deal is a step in the right direction for ConAgra Foods. It should help the company enhance long-term shareholder value. More importantly, it rids the company of underperforming assets (meat processing sales declined 4 percent year over year in fiscal 2002, ended May 26). ConAgra Foods can now focus more attention on its Packaged Foods business, which posted sales growth of 6 percent in fiscal 2002. The company plans to concentrate its capital on branded and value-added food products, which tend to carry higher margins."

Total assets: $15,496 million
Current ratio: 1.50
Common shares outstanding: 524 million
Return on 2002 shareholders' equity: 22.4%

	2002	2001	2000	1999	1998	1997	1996	1995
Revenues (millions)	27,630	27,194	25,386	24,594	23,841	24,002	24,822	24,109
Net income (millions)	783	683	801	696	628	615	545	496
Earnings per share	1.47	1.33	1.67	1.46	1.36	1.34	1.17	1.03
Dividends per share	.92	.88	.79	.69	.61	.53	.46	.42
Price High	27.6	26.2	24.4	34.4	33.6	38.8	27.4	20.9
Low	20.9	17.5	15.1	20.6	22.6	24.5	18.8	14.9

Costco Wholesale Corporation

999 Lake Drive □ Issaquah, WA 98027 □ (425) 313-8203 □ No Dividend reinvestment plan available □ Web site: www.costco.com □ Listed: NASDAQ □ Fiscal years end Sunday nearest August 31 □ Ticker symbol: COST □ S&P rating: B □ Value Line financial strength rating: B++

The CEO of Costco is sixty-six-year-old James D. Sinegal. "A lifelong retailer, Sinegal opened the first Costco warehouse in 1983 in Seattle, with Jeffrey H. Brotman, who is chairman," according to an article in *BusinessWeek* in the fall of 2002. "Their strategy was to offer lower prices and better value by stripping away everything they deemed unnecessary, including deluxe store fixtures, salespeople, even delivery and backup inventory. And it works. Over the past five years, sales have grown 11.7 percent annually, as earnings climbed 13.2 percent a year.

"Their original concept has led to some revolutionary behavior. One of Sinegal's rules, for example, is to strictly limit markups to 12 percent on national brand items and 14 percent for private-label, Kirkland Signature goods."

Costco's strategy of retailing has grown in popularity among consumers and small business owners in recent years. As a consequence, it has taken market share from such traditional retailers as supermarkets and drugstores. As the leader in its field, Costco should be able to strengthen its position further by broadening its line of products and services and also by further penetrating into new markets, both at home and abroad.

A reputation for merchandising excellence and quality is a hallmark of Costco operations. These attributes have not gone unnoticed. The American Customer Satisfaction Index survey conducted by the University of Michigan Business School showed that Costco had the highest customer satisfaction rating of any domestic traditional national retailer.

Company Profile

Costco is the largest wholesale club operator in the United States (ahead of Wal-Mart's Sam's Club). Costco operates a chain of membership warehouses that sell high-quality merchandise, both nationally branded and selected private label goods, at low prices.

Costco is open only to members. It offers three types of membership: Business, Gold Star (individual), and Executive membership. Business members qualify by owning or operating a business, and pay an annual fee ($45 in the United States) to shop for resale, business, or personal use. This fee includes a spouse card. Business members may purchase up to six additional membership cards ($35 each) for partners or associates in the business. Gold Star members pay a $45 fee (in the United States), and this membership is available to individuals who do not own a business. This fee includes a spouse membership. Finally, the company has a third membership level, called the Executive Membership. In addition to offering all the usual membership benefits, it enables members to purchase a wide variety of discounted consumer services.

Costco's business is based on achieving high sales volumes and rapid inventory turnover by offering a limited assortment of merchandise in a wide variety of product categories at very competitive prices.

As of December 31, 2002, the company operated a chain of 412 warehouses in thirty-six states (304 locations), nine Canadian provinces (sixty-one locations), the United Kingdom (fifteen locations, through an 80 percent–owned subsidiary), Korea (five locations), Taiwan (three locations, through a 55 percent–owned subsidiary), and Japan (three locations). The company also operates fifty-one warehouses in Mexico through a 50 percent joint venture partner.

Costco units offer discount prices on nearly 4,000 products, ranging from alcoholic beverages and computer software to pharmaceuticals, meat, vegetables, books, clothing, and tires. Food and sundries account for 60 percent of sales. Certain club memberships also offer products and services, such as car and home insurance, mortgage services, and small business loans.

A typical warehouse format averages about 132,000 square feet. Floor plans are designed for economy and efficiency in the use of selling space, in the handling of merchandise, and in the control of inventory.

Merchandise is generally stored on racks above the sales floor and is displayed on pallets containing large quantities of each item, reducing labor required for handling and stocking.

Specific items in each product line are limited to fast-selling models, sizes, and colors. Costco carries only an average of about 3,500 to 4,500 stock keeping units (SKUs) per warehouse. Typically, a discount retailer or supermarket stocks 40,000 to 60,000 SKUs. Many products are offered for sale in case, carton, or multiple-pack quantities only.

Low prices on a limited selection of national brand merchandise and selected private-label products in a wide range of merchandise categories produce high sales volume and rapid inventory turnover. Rapid inventory turnover, combined with operating efficiencies achieved by volume purchasing in a no-frills self-service warehouse facility, enables the company to operate profitably at significantly lower gross margins than traditional retailers, discounters, or supermarkets.

The company buys virtually all of its merchandise from manufacturers for shipment either directly to the warehouse clubs or to a consolidation point (depot) where shipments are combined so as to minimize freight and handling costs.

Additionally, Costco Wholesale Industries, a division of the company, operates manufacturing businesses, including special food packaging, optical laboratories, meat processing, and jewelry distribution.

Shortcomings to Bear in Mind

- The *Standard & Poor's* financial strength rating is below average, at B. However, *Value Line* gives the company an average B++ rating.
- The wholesale club industry proved to be vulnerable to an economic slowdown, even though it sells basics, because of its business-membership exposure. What's more, the company's competition has stepped up its presence and is modeling itself more closely to the Costco strategy.
- Insiders, such as officer and board members, have been selling shares of Costco for the past year or so.

Reasons to Buy

- In fiscal 2002 (ended September 1, 2002), sales advanced 11 percent, to $37.99 billion. Comparable warehouse sales (thus excluding new units) increased 6 percent during this period. In view of the recession that gripped the country during these months, this was a good showing. What's more, the uptrend continued into 2003. In the first nine weeks, the company reported net sales of $6.6 billion, an increase of 8 percent.
- Costco warehouses generally operate on a seven-day, sixty-eight-hour week, and are open somewhat longer during the holiday season. Generally, warehouses are open between 10 A.M. and 8:30 P.M., with earlier closing hours on the weekend. Because

these hours of operation are shorter than those of traditional discount grocery stores and supermarkets, labor costs are lower relative to the volume of sales.

- The health of Costco's business can be measured not only by the record of sales and profit, but also by the record number of new members and membership renewal rates that remain at the highest level in the company's history. Further, Costco can point to the cleanest inventory levels and best inventory turn rates in its history. In addition, Costco has experienced strong expense control at every level of the company, as well as strong financial and procedural controls that enable the company to achieve the lowest inventory shrinkage (a polite way of saying "theft") numbers of any major retailer in the world. Finally, the company boasts a strong balance sheet.

- Costco has a major alliance with American Express Company, whereby Costco accepts American Express cards in all domestic Costco locations. The company says that American Express "has similar customer philosophies to Costco; a great degree of member/customer loyalty; and overall, an upscale consumer and small business focus. We believe that the card acceptance and co-branded card issuance are the first of many unique and strategic business opportunities that will benefit both Costco and American Express, along with the millions of members and cardholders of our two companies."

- Costco's policy generally is to limit advertising and promotional expenses to new warehouse openings and occasional direct-mail marketing to prospective new members. These practices result in lower marketing expenses as compared to typical discount retailers and supermarkets.

  In connection with new warehouse openings, Costco's marketing teams personally contact businesses in the region that are potential wholesale members. These contacts are supported by direct mailings during the period immediately prior to opening.

- Costco knows when a deal is too good to pass up. That's why the company is buying merchandise from Internet retailers. According to Richard Galanti, the firm's chief financial officer, "So many of these e-commerce companies, quite frankly, are using incredible valuations to sell stuff at ridiculous prices. We actually buy some things below cost from some of them."

- Deborah Y. Fung, an analyst with *Value Line Investment Survey*, had this to say about Costco in the fall of 2002: "Costco's style of retailing has grown in popularity among consumers and small-business owners over the past decade, as it has taken market share from drugstores and supermarkets. Being the leader in the field, the company should be able to strengthen its position further by broadening its product and service offerings, and expanding into new regions."

Total assets: $10,090 million
Current ratio: 1.00
Common shares outstanding: 455 million
Return on 2002 shareholders' equity: 13.6%

		2002	2001	2000	1999	1998	1997	1996	1995
Revenues (millions)		37,993	34,797	32,164	27,456	24,269	21,874	19,566	18,247
Net income (millions)		700.0	602.1	631.4	545.3	459.8	350.9	248.8	217.2
Earnings per share		1.48	1.29	1.35	1.18	1.02	.82	.61	.53
Dividends per share		Nil	—	—	—	—	—	—	—
Price	High	46.9	46.4	60.5	46.9	38.1	22.6	13.0	9.8
	Low	27.1	29.8	25.9	32.7	20.7	11.9	7.3	6.0

AGGRESSIVE GROWTH

Craftmade International, Inc.

650 South Royal Lane, Suite 100 □ Post Office Box 1037 □ Coppell, Texas 75019-1037 □ (972) 393-3800 Ext. 166 □ Dividend reinvestment program is not available □ Web site: www.craftmade.com □ Fiscal years end June 30 □ Listed: NASDAQ □ Ticker symbol: CRFT □ S&P rating: B+ □ Value Line financial strength rating: None

Craftmade International, a leader in the distribution of ceiling fans and lighting fixtures, is committed to energy conservation. To this end, the company introduced the national "Energy Star" program for its fans and compact fluorescent lights for outdoor lanterns. Using the latest technology in lighting, these lanterns will burn ten times as long as regular incandescent bulbs—yet they consume substantially less energy. According to the company, "Our goal is to design fans and lanterns that are as beautiful for their aesthetic appeal as they are for their savings."

Nor does that end the list of features provided by these innovative lighting products and services. "By introducing a state-of-the-art electronic commerce system, we have enabled both our showroom customers and our high-volume mass merchants to place orders, monitor inventory, track shipments, and check invoices on line. This essential technology not only increases the efficiency of Craftmade orders and deliveries, it has allowed us to maintain the same number of customer service personnel, even though the volume of orders has increased."

Company Profile

Founded in 1985, Craftmade International, Inc., is a market leader in the design, distribution, and marketing of superior quality ceiling fans, light kits, and related accessories for the lighting showroom market. The company is also an international wholesale distributor of table lamps and outdoor lanterns for mass-market retailers.

The company's extensive ceiling fan product line includes over two dozen fan designs, nearly eighty light fixture options, and more than 100 interchangeable glass and crystal accents, all sold under its Craftmade brand. In addition, Craftmade markets nearly a dozen styles of bathstrip lighting and over forty designs of outdoor lighting under its Accolade trade name.

These products are sold through a network of more than 1,600 premier lighting showrooms and electrical wholesalers, which specialize in the home construction, remodeling, and upscale commercial building markets. The distribution network relies on a national sales organization of about sixty-five independent sales representatives to provide immediate response and personal attention. To ensure quality control and exclusivity of proprietary designs, Craftmade's fan and bathstrip lighting products are manufactured through a strategic alliance with a single supplier, whose sole customer is Craftmade.

A wholly owned Craftmade subsidiary, Trade Source International, Inc., (TSI) is an international wholesale distributor of outdoor lighting fixtures, bath lighting, and ceiling fans to mass merchandisers. These products are sold under private labels as well as under TSI's brand name. In 2001, Trade Source International joined with lighting designer Pat Dolan to form Design Trends, a joint venture to design, manufacture, and distribute portable lighting to mass-merchandise retailers. The initial rollout was to Lowe's Home Improvement Centers. What's more, Lowe's—a household name in home improvement—was so impressed with Design Trends's table lamps, presented in a revolutionary space-saving display, that it picked up the products for all locations.

Shortcomings to Bear in Mind

- Craftmade is not for the faint of heart. The price of the stock seems to bounce around. For instance, in 2001, it was as high as $16.89 and as low as $6.20. The previous year, it climbed as high as $9.68 and fell as low as $4. In 1999, it shot up as high as $17.50 and plunged as low as $5.75. That's what I call "volatility."

- The company has benefited from low interest rates and a strong housing market. According to CEO Jimmy Ridings, "We look forward to a measurably strong performance again in fiscal 2003, especially if mortgage rates remain low, housing starts and move-up markets continue to be strong, and the mass-merchant retailers continue to thrive." But what if they don't?

Reasons to Buy

- Craftmade's ceiling fan product line has one of the lowest return rates in the industry. This is because the design features of a Craftmade fan make the line one of the most reliable, durable, and energy-efficient in the industry. The company has been steadily expanding this segment through new product introductions as well as by adding to its 1,600 premier showroom distribution channel.

- Craftmade has received many distinctions from both financial and consumer publications. Since 1990, Craftmade has been selected six times, most recently in the October issue, by *Forbes* magazine as one of the "200 Best Small Companies in America." And, according to *Consumer Digest*, "Craftmade has earned a reputation as one of the most reliable makers of ceiling fans."

- One way to judge a company's management is to examine "return on equity." A good return is 15 percent or above. For its part, Craftmade had an exceptional return of more than 30 percent in

fiscal 2002. In the past four years, moreover, the return has never been below 21 percent.

- In the 1993–2002 period, earnings per share increased from $.21 to $1.03, a compound annual growth rate of 19.3 percent. During that span, however, EPS from the prior year dropped twice (in 1995 and 2000).

- Craftmade continues to aggressively sell ceiling fans to independently owned showrooms and recently added Carpets of Dalton, the largest showroom in the United States, to its 1,600-showroom distribution network.

- In the fiscal year ended June 30, 2002, Craftmade had sales of $73.5 million, up from $71.1 million the previous year. Gross profit advanced as well, rising to $23.3 million, compared with $22.4 million in 2001. Best of all, earnings per share climbed more than 30 percent. Diluted earnings per share totaled $1.03, or well above the prior year's $.79. Finally, said Mr. Ridings, "Thanks to our excellent cash flow, we were able to pay down our revolving line of credit, to $9 million, from $19 million. Additionally, we reduced our long-term debt to $5.7 million, from $8.1 million."

- Through its joint venture with Design Trends, the company has developed a patented merchandising display system for portable lamps and shades. This gives consumers the flexibility to mix and match a lamp base and shade combination. It also reduces the amount of display space needed by about 35 percent and improves the marketability of the product. Craftmade has been marketing this revolutionary display system to other major retailers, and the program is currently in 1,300 retail outlets across the country. Management believes that it will increase the number of outlets by at least 50 percent by the end of fiscal 2003.

Total assets: $44.5 million
Current ratio: 1.71
Common shares outstanding: 5.6 million
Return on 2002 shareholders' equity: 30.5%

	2002	2001	2000	1999	1998	1997	1996	1995
Revenues (millions)	73.5	93.5	85.5	85.0	40.9	39.0	36.3	34.4
Net income (millions)	6.2	4.7	4.3	5.7	3.0	2.1	1.8	1.9
Earnings per share	1.03	.79	.63	.76	.47	.31	.25	.24
Dividends per share	.28	.25	.08	.08	.04	.03	.01	.01
Price High	19.0	16.9	8.7	17.5	17.0	8.5	3.7	4.6
Low	11.6	6.2	4.0	5.8	6.7	2.7	3.9	3.0

CONSERVATIVE GROWTH

Darden Restaurants, Inc.

5900 Lake Ellenor Drive □ Orlando, Florida 32809 □ (407) 245-5144 □ Dividend reinvestment plan available: (800) 829-8432 □ Web site: www.darden.com □ Fiscal years end last Sunday in May □ Listed: NYSE □ Ticker symbol: DRI □ Standard & Poor's rating: Not rated □ Value Line financial strength rating: A

In the heart of Tuscany is Riserva di Fizzano, a captivating, restored eleventh-century village, complete with a winery and restaurant. This faraway Italian town is a key reason why Olive Garden—one of Darden's restaurant chains—dominates the fiercely competitive segment of the casual dining market.

Each year, culinary managers from more than 100 different Olive Garden restaurants travel to this Tuscan village to immerse themselves in Italian cuisine and culture at the Olive Garden Riserva di Fizzano restaurant and adjoining Culinary Institute of Tuscany. Here they take courses from Executive Chef Romana Neri on Italian cooking essentials, such as the importance of the freshest of ingredients, the art of cooking pasta, the layering of flavors, and the marriage of Italian food and wine.

This represents an unprecedented partnership that Olive Garden has established with the Zingarelli family, owners of the property and of the Rocca della Macie winery. It has helped Olive Garden's talented culinary development team create award-winning dishes, such as Pork Filettino, Mixed Grill, Tortelloni di Fizzano, Spaghetti delle Rocca, and Lobster Spaghetti.

What's more, in recent years, according to the company, "We have focused on making wine an integral part of the Olive Garden dining experience. We created the Olive Garden Wine Institute of Napa Valley to train managers on how to make wine approachable and enjoyable for their guests, and expanded our offerings to include thirty-eight award-winning wines. *The Wall Street Journal* took notice and honored Olive Garden for having the best wine program in casual dining, as did the Monterey Wine Festival."

Company Profile

Darden Restaurants dates back to 1968, when William Darden launched the first Red Lobster restaurant in Lakeland, Florida. In 1970, the company was sold to General Mills. In May of 1995, the company became independent when General Mills distributed all Darden shares to its shareholders.

Darden Restaurants, Inc., is the largest publicly traded casual dining company in the world, serving more than 300 million meals a year at 1,211 restaurants in forty-nine states across the United States and Canada. The company, which operates four distinct restaurant concepts, had sales in 2002 of $4.4 billion.

The flagship brands, Red Lobster and Olive Garden, are the market leaders in their segments of casual dining, making Darden the only company in the industry to operate more than one restaurant company with sales exceeding $1.8 billion.

Bahama Breeze and Smokey Bones BBQ Sports Bar are Darden's two newest concepts, and both were developed internally.

Red Lobster

Founded in 1968, Red Lobster is America's most successful casual dining seafood restaurant company. It has led this segment of the industry since its inception. It had sales of $2.34 billion in fiscal year 2002. Its average restaurant sales were $3.5 million. Its market share of casual dining seafood was 49 percent in 2002.

Olive Garden

Founded twenty years ago, Olive Garden, a family of local restaurants, is the leader in the highly competitive Italian segment of casual dining. As of the end of fiscal 2002, Olive Garden could boast a record of consecutive thirty-one quarters of same-restaurant sales growth. Total sales in 2002 for Olive Garden were $1.86 billion, with average unit sales of $3.9 million. This represented a market share of 30 percent in casual dining Italian.

Bahama Breeze

After six years of operation, Bahama Breeze, according to management, "has built an exciting brand based on its promise of memorable island vacation experience, with delicious Caribbean cuisine, hand-crafted drinks, live music, and a relaxed atmosphere." In fiscal year 2002, this concept had total sales of $125.5 million.

Smokey Bones

Darden's newest concept, Smokey Bones BBQ Sports Bar, was introduced in September 1999 and began a national

expansion in fiscal 2002. The company says, "The restaurant mixes great-tasting barbecue with mountain lodge comfort and exciting sports action." It had sales of $42.4 million in 2002.

Shortcomings to Bear in Mind

- In fiscal 2003, the company announced that its second quarter was not going to meet analysts' expectations. Analysts thought the company would earn $.23 for that quarter, but the company said its own estimate was a penny or two below this. The company's CEO, Joe R. Lee, said, "The environment was more challenging than expected this month. Both Red Lobster and Olive Garden had value-oriented promotions, but as we began the month, it became clear that the advertising supporting Red Lobster's offer had a less compelling 'call to action' than circumstances warranted. We then made changes that were not fully in place until late in the month. Red Lobster began offering thirty shrimp for $9.99 in early September (2002)."
- The company pays a modest dividend of $.05 a share—and has paid the same dividend since 1996. Not exactly the sign of a growing company.

Reasons to Buy

- In 1995–2002, earnings per share climbed from $.45 to $1.29, a compound annual growth rate of 16.2 percent.
- While much of corporate America suffered through a prolonged period of stagnation, Darden Restaurants performed admirably in fiscal 2002:
  - Revenues increased 9 percent, to $4.37 billion, enhanced by continued same-restaurant sales growth at Red Lobster and Olive Garden.
  - Excluding unusual nonoperating gains, fiscal 2002's after-tax earnings increased 20 percent, to $236.2 million, the company's best showing yet.

- Earnings per share on a diluted basis rose 22 percent, to $1.29, excluding unusual nonoperating gains.
- Red Lobster's total sales were a record $2.34 billion, a 7.1 percent increase from the prior year. Red Lobster's same-restaurant sales growth for the year was 6.2 percent, with over half of it coming from guest-count increases (as opposed to price increases).
- Olive Garden grew even faster and achieved new sales records, with total sales increasing 9.5 percent, to $1.86 billion. Olive Garden's same-restaurant sales grew 6.3 percent, with over half of that gain emanating from guest-count growth.
- Bahama Breeze's award-winning culinary and beverage offerings and "outstanding service continued to provide a solid platform for expansion," said Mr. Lee. Bahama Breeze opened eight new restaurants, ending the year with twenty-nine units operating in twenty different markets. Mr. Lee said, "While we experienced softened sales in some markets, which we attribute to reduced air travel from the combined effects of the recession and terrorism-related safety concerns, Bahama Breeze continued to generate annualized sales per restaurant in excess of $5 million—among the highest in casual dining."
- Smokey Bones BBC Sports Bar more than doubled in size, opening ten new restaurants to end the year with nineteen in operation. Mr. Lee said, "Smokey Bones' combination of terrific smoked and barbecued foods in a relaxed sports bar atmosphere remains broadly appealing, and expansion will ramp up in 2003."

- Mr. Lee is confident that more of the same is on tap. He said, "Our industry, casual dining, is large and growing. With compound annual growth of nearly 7 percent since 1990, total sales reached $56 billion in calendar 2001. And we believe casual dining sales will continue to grow between 6 percent and 8 percent a year over the next ten years because of strong growth in the number of people entering their fifties and sixties, the peak years of casual dining usage, as well as continued increases in the number of working women, per capita incomes, and payroll employment levels.

"All of these developments support lifestyle changes we've witnessed for some time now, which place a premium on the time-saving and social connection benefits of dining out. The power of these factors was clearly demonstrated in 2002 when, despite the recession and other factors that put downward pressure on consumer confidence, casual dining sales grew 5.5 percent for the calendar year."

- Mr. Lee looks for the company's two newest segments to grow at a healthy clip in the years ahead. He said, "We also continue to expand our emerging companies, and their ultimate business potential is meaningful. We believe Bahama Breeze can reach at least $500 million in total sales in the first phase of our national expansion, and Smokey Bones is capable of becoming at least a $1.5 billion business.

"These two businesses also reflect our proven ability to create winning new concepts that are responsive to lasting consumer demand. The New Business team that developed Olive Garden, Bahama Breeze, and Smokey Bones continues to work on new opportunities with powerful market potential."

Total assets: $2,530 million
Current ratio: 0.75
Common shares outstanding: 171 million
Return on 2002 shareholders' equity: 22.0%

		2002	2001	2000	1999	1998	1997	1996	1995
Revenues (millions)		4,369	4,021	3,701	3,458	3,287	3,172	3,192	3,168
Net income (millions)		236	197	173	135	102	54	119	108
Earnings per share		1.29	1.06	.87	.64	.46	.23	.50	.45
Dividends per share		.05	.05	.05	.05	.05	.05	.05	Nil
Price	High	29.8	25.0	18.0	15.6	12.6	8.3	9.3	8.1
	Low	18.0	12.7	8.3	10.4	7.8	4.5	5.0	6.2

AGGRESSIVE GROWTH

DeVry, Inc.

One Tower Lane, Suite 1000 ◻ Oakbrook Terrace, Illinois 60181 ◻ (630) 574-1931 ◻ Dividend reinvestment plan not available ◻ Web site: www.dvry.com ◻ Listed: NYSE ◻ Fiscal years end June 30 ◻ Ticker symbol: DV ◻ S&P rating: B+ ◻ Value Line financial strength rating: B++

When DeVry University announced that it was building a new campus at Westminster—near Denver—in 2002, the Westminster City Manager, Brent McFall said, "We hear consistently from local employers that one of their greatest challenges is filling skilled positions. Having DeVry here will be a great benefit both to Westminster and other regional businesses who are seeking a well-educated technology workforce."

DeVry will offer courses in higher education opportunities in business and technology in the Denver metro area. "The new campus will offer classrooms with networked multimedia equipment, specialized technology laboratories, and a technical library complete with computer workstations and will be capable of supporting a student body of nearly 3,000 students," said Timothy Campagna, the president of DeVry University's Colorado campuses.

The New Economy Index by Milken Institute ranks Colorado number three in the nation among high-tech growth. The index criteria include percentage of advanced degrees in the state.

Company Profile

DeVry is one of the largest publicly held, international, higher-education companies in North America. It is the holding company for DeVry University and Becker Conviser Professional Review.

DeVry University is composed of an undergraduate division (DeVry Institutes) and a graduate school division (Keller Graduate School of Management). These operations provide rigorous academic preparation for careers in technology, business, and management. They deliver undergraduate, graduate, and lifelong learning programs that combine proven educational technologies with employer input and workplace applications. The DeVry University system emphasizes teaching and service to a diverse and geographically dispersed student population.

Founded in 1931, DeVry Institutes have provided career-oriented, technology-based bachelor and associate degree programs to high school graduates in the United States and Canada for more than seventy years. The institutes are situated at twenty-five campuses (three of which are in Canada), with more than 57,000 full- and part-time students.

The Keller Graduate School, founded in 1973, provides practitioner-oriented, graduate management degree programs leading to a master's degree. It awards master's degrees in business administration, accounting and financial management, information systems management, human resource management, project management, and telecommunications management. At the end of fiscal 2001, Keller classes were offered to more than 6,683 students at forty-two locations in the United States, including the Online Education Center.

Shortcomings to Bear in Mind

- DeVry is not without competition. The country has thousands of colleges, universities, and business schools eagerly looking for students.
- Nils C. Van Liew, an analyst with *Value Line Investment Survey*, had a few negative thoughts in his report issued in the fall of 2002: "We've lowered our fiscal 2003 earnings estimate. New undergraduate student enrollment at DeVry's flagship institutes has declined for the past two semesters and may very well remain weak until the technology sector rights itself. In general, weakening labor markets prompt workers to upgrade their skills through enrollment in educational programs. However, it appears people are hesitant to commit to tech training (DeVry's sweet spot), given widespread industry layoffs, particularly within the telecommunications and Internet sectors."

Reasons to Buy

- Since the company's initial public offering in June of 1991, DeVry's success has included a record of more than 20 percent growth in net income from operations annually, an accomplishment achieved during that decade by less than a dozen public companies.
- As the economy slowed and the technology sector weakened in fiscal 2002,

DeVry demonstrated its ability to maintain consistent financial results. Revenues for the year ended June 30, 2002 were $648.1 million, up 14.1 percent from the prior year. Net income for the year was $67.1 million, up 16.1 percent from 2001. Earnings per share advanced to a record $.95, compared with $.82 in 2001.

What's more, the company's balance sheet remains strong, with no debt and cash of $59.7 million, despite continued investment in geographic expansion throughout fiscal 2002. Capital expenditures totaled $85.9 million as the company opened two undergraduate campuses and six adult learner centers and purchased two previously leased undergraduate campuses.

Despite weakness in the technology sector, total DeVry University enrollments continued to increase in fiscal 2002, reaching a peak of nearly 57,000 in the fall term, with 48,032 undergraduate students and 8,893 course-takers at the graduate level.

- DeVry became the first private, for-profit institution in Canada to be provincially accredited to grant baccalaureate degrees. In February of 2001, the province of Alberta authorized DeVry/Calgary to offer bachelor of technology degree programs in electronics engineering technology and computer information systems, as well as a bachelor of business operations degree program.
- In the company's graduate and professional operations, Keller Graduate School received approval in Missouri for its seventh graduate degree program, the master of public administration. KGSM also receive approval in eight states for a certificate in entrepreneurship within its MBA program. Two new graduate certificates in educational management, approved in the state of Illinois, were launched in September 2001.

- In January of 2001, Becker Conviser Professional Review acquired Stalla Seminars business, a leading provider of CFA review courses and materials. Stalla Seminars, acquired for $8.6 million in cash, develops and markets exam preparation materials for the Chartered Financial Analyst professional certification, as administered by the Association for Investment Management and Research.

  To become a CFA, an analyst or portfolio manager must take a series of three all-day examinations that are very rigorous and difficult to pass without help from teachers such as those provided by Stalla Seminars. The exams, which have a high failure rate, are spaced a year apart, and successive tests cannot be taken until each is passed in its proper order.

  Like all of the acquisitions DeVry seeks, Stalla Seminars meets the company's high standards for quality and is expected to bolster earnings of the Becker Conviser operation.

- DeVry University Online now offers three undergraduate and seven graduate degree programs. According to CEO Dennis J. Keller, "By offering both online and onsite delivery options, we provide students with the opportunity to select an educational experience that best suits their needs. Whether addressing the needs of community college graduates, bachelor's degree holders seeking to advance their careers by obtaining a master's degree, or those wishing to reenter college to complete an unfinished undergraduate degree, DeVry is helping a growing number of adult learners achieve greater educational and career success."

- On another topic, Mr. Keller said in early fiscal 2003, "One of the mainstays of DeVry's growth strategy is continued geographic expansion. This year, two new undergraduate campuses were opened in the Seattle and Washington, D.C., areas. Development also began for campuses to open in fiscal 2003 in the Philadelphia and Miami areas. In addition, land was purchased for campus development in Houston, and ground was broken for a new facility in the Denver area to house existing operations next spring. Our graduate school operations were expanded into six new locations in the Columbus, San Francisco, Houston, Charlotte, Seattle, and Philadelphia metropolitan areas."

Total assets: $468 million
Current ratio: 1.05
Common shares outstanding: 70 million
Return on 2002 shareholders' equity: 21.0%

	2002	2001	2000	1999	1998	1997	1996	1995
Revenues (millions)	648	567	505	419	352	307	259	227
Net income (millions)	67.1	57.8	47.8	38.8	30.7	24.2	19.2	14.9
Earnings per share	.95	.82	.68	.55	.44	.36	.29	.22
Dividends per share	Nil	—	—	—	—	—	—	—
Price High	34.8	40.2	41.5	31.9	30.6	16.5	12.7	7.0
Low	12.1	22.8	16.1	15.6	14.0	9.5	6.4	3.8

INCOME

Dominion Resources, Inc.

Post Office Box 26532 □ Richmond, Virginia 23261-6532 □ Listed: NYSE □ (804) 819-2150 □ Direct Dividend reinvestment plan available: (800) 552-4034 □ Web site: www.dom.com □ Ticker symbol: D □ S&P rating: B □ Value Line financial strength rating: B++

Dominion Resources, a large gas and electric utility holding company, has a diversified and integrated portfolio consisting of nearly 24,000 megawatts of generation, 5.7 trillion cubic feet equivalent of natural gas reserves, 7,600 miles of natural gas transmission pipeline, and the nation's largest underground natural gas storage system, with more than 950 billion cubic feet of storage capacity.

Dominion also serves 3.8 million franchise natural gas and electric customers in five states and nearly 1 million unregulated retail customers in eight states. In addition, Dominion owns a managing equity interest in Dominion Fiber Ventures, LLC, owner of Dominion Telecom.

Company Profile

Headquartered in Richmond, Virginia, Dominion's principal subsidiaries are the following:

• Virginia Electric and Power Company, a regulated public utility engaged in the generation, transmission, distribution, and sale of electric energy with a 30,000-square-mile region in Virginia and northeastern North Carolina.

The company sells electric power to about 2.1 million retail customers (including government agencies) and to wholesale customers such as rural electric cooperatives, municipalities, power marketers, and other utilities.

• Consolidated Natural Gas Company (CNG), which was acquired January 28, 2000. CNG operates in all phases of the natural gas industry in the United States, including exploration for and production of oil and natural gas and natural gas transmission, storage, and distribution.

Its regulated retail gas distribution subsidiaries serve about 1.7 million residential, commercial, and industrial gas sales and transportation customers in Ohio, Pennsylvania, and West Virginia.

Its interstate gas transmission pipeline systems services each of its distribution subsidiaries, nonaffiliated utilities and end-use customers in the Midwest, the Mid-Atlantic and Northeast states.

CNG's exploration and production operations are conducted in several of the major gas and oil producing basins in the United States, both onshore and offshore, and in Canada.

• Dominion Energy (DEI) is engaged in the independent power production and the acquisition and production of natural gas and oil reserves. In Canada, DEI has a stake in natural gas exploration, production, and storage.

• Dominion Capital, Inc. (DCI), is Dominion's financial services subsidiary. DCI's primary business is financial services, which includes commercial lending and residential mortgage lending.

Shortcomings to Bear in Mind

■ In the fall of 2002, the company announced that it reduced its outlook for 2003. Dominion said that "because of unforeseen developments, it expects 2003 earnings to be [between] flat to up 4 percent more than 2002 earnings.

"Reasons for the reduced outlook include plans to further strengthen the company's balance sheet and debt coverage ratios as a result of changes in ratings agency requirements, which is expected to reduce 2003 earnings by as much as seventeen cents per share; increased security costs at our six nuclear units; a higher expected level of pension expense; expenses associated with new accounting for asset retirement obligations as a result of a new accounting standard, FAS 143; lengthening nuclear outages as a result of a recent NRC directive related to vessel head inspections; and flat trading and marketing earnings over the expected level in 2002. These impacts are partially offset by certain positive factors, including higher oil and gas prices and the State Line and Cove Point acquisitions."

Reasons to Buy

- On a more positive note, CEO Thomas E. Capps said, "While we are disappointed that we are modestly reducing the earnings outlook for 2003, we are pleased that Dominion's integrated business model has enabled it to withstand the temporary cyclical downturn in market conditions and other factors that have more severely affected most of our peers.

  "Much of the reduction in the outlook is due to non-cash items, such as accounting for asset retirement obligations. Cash flow remains strong, and we expect to generate about $2.5 billion in net cash flow from operating activities in 2002 and from $2.8 to $3.0 billion in 2003."

- Dominion is the largest producer of BTUs in the Midwest, Northeast, and Mid-Atlantic regions of the United States, home to 40 percent of the nation's demand for energy. The company built an even larger position in this region when it completed its $1.3-billion acquisition (2001) of the 1,954-megawatt Millstone Nuclear Power Station, situated in Connecticut on Long Island Sound.

  Adding Millstone of the company's growing generation fleet boosted its combined utility and non-utility capacity by 10 percent. According to Thomas Capps, Dominion's CEO, "We should see at least an extra five cents in earnings per share each year in the first two years of ownership—and even greater annual contributions beyond that. In 2001, we brought on line nearly 700 megawatts of additional gas-fired generation in Virginia and at our Elwood facility in Illinois, expanding what long-timers call 'iron in the ground.'

  "In the years immediately following this, Dominion's power generation team has nearly 3,850 megawatts of new capacity either under construction or on the drawing boards. We've secured turbines and identified site possibilities for another 2,400 megawatts. In total, we hope to have nearly 9,000 new megawatts in service by 2005, most of it gas-fired. Gas from our own production company delivered by our own pipeline will fire four of these facilities in Ohio, Pennsylvania, and West Virginia."

- The Consolidated Natural Gas acquisition made Dominion Resources the fourth-largest domestic electric and natural gas utility, with over $9 billion in annual revenues. The merger could realize cost savings gains of $150 million to $200 million by 2002.

- Dominion Resources is committed to continuing its $2.58 annual dividend. In the view of management, dividends are an important, if neglected, component of total return. Maintaining the dividend is important to many shareholders who depend on dividends for income.

  Some Wall Street pundits say a company intent on share-price growth can't afford to reward its investors with cash. Mr. Capps does not agree. "Unless the laws of gravity change, our share price should rise with rising earnings. And the percentage of earnings we pay as dividends will go down—something Wall Street will view favorably. At the end of 2001, our payout was about 72 percent of total earnings. Over time, we'll work to have earnings growth move that in the neighborhood of 50 to 55 percent."

- In the telecommunications and technology realm, the company is fortunate to have in-house expertise at Dominion Telecom that opens new opportunities. Dominion Telecom plans to invest about $700 million over the next two to three years to expand its fiber-optic network. The company will use this expanded network—planned to span more than 9,000 route miles—to provide Internet, video conferencing, and other broadband services. In the words of Mr. Capps, "Yes, we're looking to be a niche player. We aren't interested in going toe-to-toe with the national telecoms. But we see a real opportunity in offering telecom capacity to Cleveland, Buffalo, Toledo, and other underserved cities in our core energy markets."

- Investors are sometimes critical of company officials who don't own many shares of their own company. They ask the disturbing question: "How can they expect me to invest in their company when they don't have enough confidence to buy stock themselves?"

If you own Dominion Resources, you won't have this concern. Under voluntary guidelines adopted by the board of directors, Dominion's officers are expected to own company shares in amounts totaling from three to eight times their base salaries. This is a major obligation and has required most officers to borrow money.

According to Mr. Capps, "Loans to purchase these shares come due in five years, and our dividends help pay the interest. We're all personally on the hook if, in the interim, we have not made sound business decisions and grown the company profitably."

Total assets: $ 37.9 billion
Current ratio: .64
Common shares outstanding: 307 million
Return on 2002 equity: 12.5%

	2002	2001	2000	1999	1998	1997	1996	1995
Revenues (millions)	10,218	10,968	9,260	5,520	6,086	7,678	4,842	4,652
Net income (millions)	1,362	544	436	639	400	604	515	469
Earnings per share	4.83	2.15	2.50	2.99	1.72	3.00	2.65	2.45
Dividends per share	2.58	2.58	2.58	2.58	2.58	2.58	2.58	2.58
Price High	67.1	70.0	67.9	49.4	48.9	42.9	44.4	41.6
Low	35.4	55.1	34.8	36.6	37.8	33.3	36.9	34.9

CONSERVATIVE GROWTH

Donaldson Company, Inc.

Post Office Box 1299 ▫ Minneapolis, Minnesota 55440 ▫ (952) 887-3753 ▫ Dividend reinvestment plan available: (800) 468-9716 ▫ Web site: www.donaldson.com ▫ Fiscal years end July 31 ▫ Listed: NYSE ▫ Ticker symbol: DCI ▫ S&P rating: A+ ▫ Value Line financial strength rating: B++

You could expect to see Donaldson Company's filtration products on the heavy-duty truck traveling the interstate highway or on the construction equipment on the side of the road. "After all, that's where our company began," said CEO William G. Van Dyke.

"But you aren't as likely to expect our filters in the camera that captures memories of your daughter's birthday party. Or in the backup generator providing electricity to your computer center or office."

"Donaldson filters and related products are in many unexpected places—in products you see, touch, and use every day. Our long-term, focused investment in filtration technology has created the leverage to carry us into new product lines, new markets, and new geography. This diversification in end markets, linked by a common technology base, has enabled us to smooth out the ups and downs of the various market segments and to achieve our twelfth consecutive year of double-digit earnings growth—no small feat in these turbulent economic times.

"We're proud of our progress so far. Our industrial businesses are approaching our goal of 50 percent of total revenues, and our international businesses make up almost 38 percent of total revenues, with operations in nineteen countries. Donaldson holds more than 370 U.S. patents and related patents filed around the world, and our employees are constantly developing new ways to utilize superior filtration and acoustic technology for products that are still years away from market."

Company Profile

Donaldson Company is a leading worldwide provider of filtration systems and replacement parts. Founded in 1915, Donaldson is a technology-driven company committed to satisfying customers needs for filtration solutions through innovative research and development.

The company's product mix includes air and liquid filters, as well as exhaust and emission-control products for mobile equipment; in-plant air-cleaning systems; air intake systems for industrial gas turbines; and specialized filters for such diverse applications as computer disk drives, aircraft passenger cabins, and semiconductor processing.

The company has two reporting segments engaged in the design, manufacture, and sale of systems to filter air and liquid and other complementary products.

The **Engine Products** segment makes air intake systems, exhaust systems, and liquid filtration systems. The company sells to original-equipment manufacturers (OEMs) in the construction, industrial, mining, agriculture, and transportation markets, independent distributors, OEM dealer networks, private-label accounts, and large private fleets.

The **Industrial Products** segment consists of dust, fume, and mist collectors,

static and pulse-clean air filter systems of industrial gas turbines, computer disk drive filter products, and other specialized air-filtration systems. Donaldson sells to various industrial end-users, OEMs of gas-fired turbines, and OEMs and users requiring highly purified air.

The company operates plants throughout the world. Of these, fourteen facilities are in the United States, three in the United Kingdom, and there are two each in German, Japan, China, South Africa, and Mexico. Finally, the company has one plant in each of the following countries: Australia, France, Hong Kong, Italy, Belgium, and India.

Shortcomings to Bear in Mind

- Robert E. Du Boff, an analyst with *Value Line Investment Survey*, had a negative comment in a report issued in August of 2002. "The truck market has come on strong recently, as manufacturers have ramped up orders ahead of diesel emission regulations set to take effect in the U.S. in October 2002. But this trend may come to an end by the second quarter of 2003. Once the new emission standards take effect, the truck market should slip back to single-digit levels of growth.

  "Also, turbine manufacturers have indicated that the recent demand bubble may well burst by the end of calendar 2002, and we anticipate sales here will decline by roughly $50 million next year (2003)."

  On a brighter note, the *Value Line* analyst went on to say, "The aftermarket should pick up some of the slack, as turbines that went online at the start of the current cycle will soon require replacement filters. Donaldson's other product lines should also start to recover by then."

- Mr. Van Dyke had this to say concerning the turbine situation: "To fill the gas turbine hole, the Engine business appears to be turning up. Incoming orders have trended up strongly since the second quarter of 2002—especially overseas. New equipment orders in the fourth quarter were up 5 percent domestically and 24 percent overseas from last year (2001). Coupling higher volume with ongoing improvements in Engine profitability gives us important leverage for the coming year (2003)."

Reasons to Buy

- Donaldson has an enviable record of growth. In the past ten years (1992–2002), earnings per share advanced from $0.46 to $1.90, (with no dips along the way), a compound annual growth rate of 15.2 percent. In the same span, dividends climbed from $0.10 to $0.31, a compound annual growth rate of 12.0 percent.

  Despite this fine record of growth, the stock sells at a very reasonable P/E multiple.

- More than 21 million U.S. workers are exposed to poor indoor air quality, not to mention many millions more around the world. "We're doing our part to clean the air with dust-collection systems that filter harmful particles and fumes, enhancing conditions for employees, products, and manufacturing proceeds," said Mr. Van Dyke.

  "In 2001, we introduced the Torit Downflo Oval (DFO) dust-collection system, which offers a revolutionary oval cartridge filter, redesigned cabinet, and an enhanced cleaning system applicable to thousands of businesses in the powder, metal, woodworking, and processing industries worldwide.

  "For our customers, this patented system means more effective and efficient filtration, while requiring less floor space. One metalworking customer, using the new DFO, was able to more than double production capacity. Their 'old' dust collector was extremely undersized because of restricted floor space, and thus several of their steel cutting tables could run at only 40 percent capacity. Our new, smaller DFO fit into the available space and enabled them to ramp up to full production. Customer acceptance has been excellent, with over 300 DFO units already sold."

- Long before NAFTA, Donaldson realized the geographic and market advantages of working in Mexico. From a relatively modest start twenty years ago, "our presence has grown to include three manufacturing plants," said Mr. Van Dyke. "Our new 200,000-square-foot facility in Monterrey will enable us to bring more gas turbine filter production in-house and expand our capacity to meet increasing customer demands. The facility, our fourth plant worldwide devoted to gas turbines, will produce filter housings, inlet ducting, and silencing products.

  "We're also expanding our Aguascalientes facility, where 200 employees manufacture 5 million air, liquid, and oil filters a year.

  "In addition to producing large volumes of filters for shipment to the United States and Mexico, our Mexican facilities also serve our European and South American customers."

- In fiscal 2002, the company announced a major development contract with a leading Japanese automobile manufacturer to apply fuel cell–filtration science to fuel cell–powered automobiles, helping accelerate their commercialization. The first commercialized fuel cell vehicles will begin appearing in 2003. Donaldson FC3 products filter intake air and mitigate acoustics in fuel cells, helping a wide range of products—from cell phones to automobiles—make the leap from the laboratory to the marketplace.

The Donaldson FC3 business has more than twenty-five nondisclosure agreements with fuel cell manufacturers in Europe, North America, and Japan.

"Fuel cell developers, including automobile manufacturers, are recognizing the need for intake air—or cathode-side—filtration to ensure fuel cell reliability and performance," said Richard Canepa, director of the Donaldson FC3 business unit. "In all corners of the world, ambient air contains contaminants that can compromise the fuel cell

system durability, life, and performance. By incorporating current, state-of-the-art, proprietary FC3 technologies, we are making fuel cell-specific products that are cost effective and available today."

- In the 2002 annual report, Mr. Van Dyke said, "After thirty years here, I'm still sometimes surprised, impressed—and delighted—with what a good company this is. I am pleased to be writing to you about our thirteenth consecutive year of double-digit earnings growth—our best ever."

Total assets: $850 million
Current ratio: 2.11
Common shares outstanding: 44 million
Return on 2002 shareholders' equity: 24.8%

		2002	2001	2000	1999	1998	1997	1996	1995
Revenues (millions)		1,126	1,137	1,092	944	940	833	759	704
Net income (millions)		86.9	75.5	70.2	62.4	57.1	50.6	43.4	38.5
Earnings per share		1.90	1.66	1.51	1.31	1.14	.99	.84	.73
Dividends per share		.31	.30	.28	.24	.20	.18	.15	.14
Price	High	45.0	40.3	28.9	25.9	26.8	27.7	17.0	14.0
	Low	29.9	24.5	18.8	17.1	13.5	15.3	12.0	11.3

AGGRESSIVE GROWTH

Ecolab, Inc.

Ecolab Center □ 370 Wabasha Street North □ St. Paul, Minnesota 55102 □ □ (651) 293-2809 □ Dividend reinvestment program available: (201) 324-0313 □ Web site: www.ecolab.com □ Listed: NYSE □ Ticker symbol: ECL □ S&P rating: A □ Value Line financial strength rating: B++

Ecolab has a highly skilled research and development team that continues to turn out innovative new products. According to a company spokesman, "Never content with the status quo, we strive for constant improvement, so far earning nearly 2,600 patents worldwide. And we boast the industry's most sophisticated R&D facilities—where breakthroughs happen every day."

In 2002, for example, Ecolab launched a revolutionary foaming hand soap system for the janitorial and building service contractor markets. The EpiSoft foaming Lotion Soap System combines exceptional quality soap in a sleek dispenser.

Cutting-edge technology is the key to EpiSoft's success. Its patented anti-drip dispenser prevents wasteful spills with an auto-retraction device that keeps unused soap inside the dispenser. The unique reservoir system holds up to seventy additional washes, which allows the soap container to drain completely before being replaced, lessening waste while ensuring a continuous supply of foaming soap.

"Ecolab's ongoing focus on research and development gives us a great competitive advantage," said Tim Mulhere, the company's vice president and general manager of the Professional Products Division.

"EpiSoft combines superior foam and cleansing ingredients with innovative dispensing technology, which the janitorial segment hasn't been exposed to in the past."

The silky EpiSoft foam lathers faster and rinses more easily than conventional liquid soaps. Additionally, the superior quality and fresh scent of the foam encourages more frequent hand washing, which is the number one way to help reduce cross-infection and resulting illness and absenteeism.

According to the company's CEO, Allan Schuman, "When it comes to delivering premium commercial cleaning and sanitizing solutions on a truly global basis, Ecolab is the one. No other company comes close to rivaling our worldwide reach or the extraordinary breadth of products, systems, and services we offer.

"We meet the varied and specialized needs of thousands of diverse businesses and institutions in North America, Europe, Asia, Latin America, Africa, the Middle East—the list of countries in which we do business reads like an atlas. In 2001, we took decisive actions to ensure that Ecolab remains number one in the world for many years to come."

Company Profile

Founded in 1923, Ecolab is the leading global developer and marketer of premium cleaning, sanitizing, pest elimination, maintenance, and repair products as well as services for the world's hospitality, institutional, and industrial markets.

In the early years, Ecolab served the restaurant and lodging industries and has since broadened its scope to include hospitals, laundries, schools, and retail and commercial property, among others.

The company conducts its domestic business in three segments.

The **Institutional Division** is the leading provider of cleaners and sanitizers

for washing, laundry, kitchen cleaning, and general housecleaning, as well as product-dispensing equipment, dishwashing racks, and related kitchen sundries to the food-service, lodging, and health care industries. It also provides products and services for pool and spa treatment.

The **Food & Beverage Division** offers cleaning and sanitizing products and services to farms, dairy plants, food and beverage processors, and pharmaceutical plants.

The **Kay Division** is the largest supplier of cleaning and sanitizing products for the quick-service restaurant, convenience store, and flood retail markets.

Ecolab also sells janitorial and health care products, including detergents, floor care, disinfectants, odor control, and hand care under the Airkem and Huntington brand names; textile care products for large institutional and commercial laundries; vehicle care products for rental, fleet, and retail car washes; and water-treatment products for commercial, institutional, and industrial markets.

Other domestic services include institutional and commercial pest elimination and prevention and the GCS commercial kitchen equipment repair services.

Around the world, the company operates directly in nearly seventy countries. International sales account for 22 percent of sales. In addition, the company reaches customers in more than 100 countries through distributors, licensees, and export operations. To meet the global demands for its products, Ecolab operates more than fifty state-of-the-art manufacturing and distribution facilities worldwide.

Shortcomings to Bear in Mind

- Wall Street seems well aware that Ecolab has a bright future, since it has tagged it with a lofty multiple, close to 30 times earnings.

Reasons to Buy

- Over the past ten years (1992–2002) earnings per share advanced from $.26 to $.80, a compound annual growth rate of 11.9 percent. During that stretch, EPS declined only once, and then only modestly, from $.75 in 2000 to $.73 in 2001. In the same ten-year period, dividends climbed from $.09 to $.27, a growth rate of 11.6 percent. What's more, the dividend was boosted every year except 1992.

- In November of 2002, Ecolab announced the purchase of the Adams Healthcare business of Medical Solutions PLC. Adams Healthcare is a leading supplier of hospital hygiene products in the United Kingdom. Ecolab's CEO, Allan L. Schuman, said, "This acquisition not only brings us an excellent growth vehicle to serve the expanding U.K. health-care market, it also provides a base with which we can bolster our existing Hospital Hygiene activities in the European health-care market. Further, it represents our third acquisition this year in Europe, reflecting our commitment to expanding Ecolab's service offerings—and our growth opportunities—in that region."

- In September of 2002, Ecolab announced that it had expanded its industry-leading pest-elimination business to Europe through the purchase of Terminix Limited, a London-based provider of commercial pest elimination and property services throughout the United Kingdom and the Republic of Ireland. Mr. Schuman said, "By acquiring a leading commercial pest-elimination business in the U.K., we have started the process of bringing our proven Pest Elimination programs to our customers in Europe and capitalizing on that lucrative market with a strong franchise."

- "The company looks well-positioned to generate strong results in the coming three- to five-year period," said analyst Frederick L. Harris III in a report issued by *Value Line Investment Survey* in December 2002. "Ecolab's strategy of aggressively cross-selling its various divisions' complementary products and services has been quite successful in the past, and it seems that this trend will persist."

- In 2001, the company's GCS Service Division acquired Commercial Parts & Service, a provider of kitchen equipment repair services and parts with branches in Indiana, Kentucky, Tennessee, and Mississippi. GCS now covers nearly every major domestic restaurant market, with the broadest national independent service capability in the country.

- Mr. Schuman said, "The largest and best-trained sales-and-service organization only got better in 2001. In addition to more than 2,500 European associates added through the Henkel-Ecolab acquisition, we added more than 300 new associates to our field organization, which now totals more than 10,000 members. Simply put, our global service coverage is unmatched by anyone, anywhere."

- In 2002, the company acquired Chicago-based Audits International, a provider of food safety services since 1982, and launched a new service: EcoSure Food Safety Management. According to Mr. Schuman, "A natural extension of our growing service offerings, EcoSure evaluates food safety procedures of restaurants, hotels, supermarkets, and other foodservice and hospitality establishments."

Total assets: $2,878 million
Current ratio: 1.17
Common shares outstanding: 260 million
Return on 2002 shareholders' equity: 21.2%

	2002	2001	2000	1999	1998	1997	1996	1995
Revenues (millions)	3,404	2,321	2,264	2,080	1,888	1,640	1,490	1,341
Net income (millions)	210	188	209	176	155	134	113	99
Earnings per share	.80	.73	.79	.66	.58	.50	.44	.38
Dividends per share	27	.27	.25	.21	.19	.17	.15	.13
Price High	25.2	22.1	22.8	22.2	19.0	14.0	9.9	8.0
Low	18.2	14.2	14.0	15.8	13.0	9.1	7.3	5.0

GROWTH AND INCOME

Emerson Electric Company

8000 W. Florissant Avenue ▢ Post Office Box 4100 ▢ St. Louis, Missouri 63136-8506 ▢ (314) 553-2197 ▢ Dividend reinvestment plan available: (888) 213-0970 ▢ Web site: www.gotoemerson.com ▢ Listed: NYSE ▢ Ticker symbol: EMR ▢ Fiscal years end September 30 ▢ S&P rating: A+ ▢ Value Line financial strength rating: A++

"Emerson's long-time focus on technology leadership continues to be a key differentiator across our businesses," said CEO David N. Farr in 2002. "We lead the industries we serve with breakthrough innovation and technology such as PlantWeb digital architecture for the process industries; Copeland Scroll compressors for air-conditioning and refrigeration markets; reliable power systems for computing and communications; and variable-speed motors used in applications ranging from home appliances to industrial manufacturing equipment.

"In 2002, Emerson again strengthened its technology, global reach, and solutions and service capabilities. Nowhere is this more apparent than in our Climate Technology business, where Scroll compressor sales reached nearly $900 million. With the introduction of high-volume Scroll technology in the early 1990s, Emerson perfected a better way to compress gas and changed the game in the air-conditioning and refrigeration industries through increased energy efficiency and reliability, and quieter, more environmentally friendly operation.

"We are the leader in this business, and in 2002 we again led the market by introducing digital Scroll technology in Asian residential and U.S. commercial air-conditioning and refrigeration markets. The new technology offer infinite capacity modulation and increased efficiency and comfort, from high-rise apartments to computer rooms and telecommunication facilities.

"Emerson Climate Technology is also at the forefront in developing remote refrigeration and air-conditioning monitoring systems, which are improving energy efficiency and reducing costs for the world's top supermarket, convenience, and drug-store chains. Capabilities like this enabled us to sign major contracts with domestic and international supermarket chains in 2002 and helped extend our position in services and solutions in the commercial refrigeration market."

Company Profile

Emerson is a leading manufacturer of a broad list of intermediate products such as electrical motors and drives, appliance components, and process-control devices. The company also produces hand and power tools as well as accessories.

Founded 109 years ago, Emerson is not a typical high-tech capital goods producer. Rather, the company makes such prosaic things as refrigerator compressors, pressure gauges, and In-Sink Erator garbage disposals—basic products that are essential to industry.

The following are the company's five segments.

Emerson Industrial Automation provides integral horsepower motors, alternators, electronic and mechanical drives, industrial valves, electrical equipment, specialty heating, lighting, testing, and ultrasonic welding and cleaning products for industrial applications. Key growth drivers for the segment include the embedding of electronics into motors and other equipment to enable self-diagnosis and preventative maintenance functionality; also, Emerson makes alternators for diesel and natural gas generator sets to create reliable distributed power solutions. The Industrial Automation segment is the company's second largest, with revenues of $2.5 billion in fiscal 2002.

Emerson Process Control offers control systems and software; analytical instrumentation; measurement devices; and valves and other control equipment for customers in the oil and gas, chemical, power, water and wastewater, food and beverage, pharmaceutical, and other industries. Key growth drivers include Emerson's innovative PlantWeb technology, which redefines plant architecture, and new solution-and-service opportunities created by Emerson's unique ability to apply its technology to specific customer needs. In 2002, this segment, the company's largest, had revenues of $3.5 billion.

Emerson Heating, Ventilating, and Air Conditioning (HVAC) offers compressors, thermostats, temperature controls, hermetic terminals, and valves for HVAC and refrigeration systems. A key driver of this business is the Copeland Scroll compressor, a revolutionary technology that is more energy efficient, reliable, and quiet than competing traditional technologies. Scroll also has created entirely new compression markets outside of HVAC, such as microturbine gas boosters for distributed power generation. HVAC is the smallest segment of Emerson. In 2002, this segment had sales of $2.4 billion.

Electronics and Telecommunications, through Emerson Network Power, delivers comprehensive solutions for highly reliable power. Offerings include alternating current (AC) UPS Systems, direct current (DC) power systems, precision air-conditioning systems, embedded and power supplies, transfer switches, and site monitoring systems and services for the fast-growing communications and Internet infrastructure markets. Additionally, fiber-optic conduit and connectivity products support the global expansion of broadband communications. Key drivers include the rapid build-out of wireless, broadband, and other data and voice services, as well as the increasing need for dependable backup power to support the utility grid. In 2002, Electronics and Telecommunications had revenues of $2.9 billion.

Appliance and Tools includes the Emerson Storage Solutions, Emerson Tools, Emerson Appliance Solutions, and Emerson Motors brand platforms. Customer offerings feature an extensive range of consumer, commercial, and industrial storage products; market-leading tools; electrical components and systems for appliances; and the world's largest offering of fractional horsepower motors. Key growth drivers include professional-grade tools serving the fast-growing home center market, as well as advanced electrical motors, which create entirely new market opportunities for Emerson. This part of the company had sales in 2002 of $2.4 billion.

Shortcomings to Bear in Mind

- Edward Plank, an analyst with *Value Line Investment Survey*, had a negative thought in his report of October 18,

2002. "Emerson stock's three- to five-year appreciation potential is below average. Though the issue appears to be trading at a discount when compared to its average P/E ratio over the last ten years, the sluggish industrial recovery will likely crimp earnings growth in 2003, which could well continue to hold the share-price advance at bay."

- The *Standard & Poor's Stock Reports* wasn't too enthusiastic about Emerson in its report of November 2, 2002. James R. Sanders said, "We are maintaining our hold opinion, based upon our belief that most of EMR's end-markets will continue to struggle in the near term. Our discounted cash flow model (which values EMR by adding the sum of cash earnings growing at a projected 8 percent to 10 percent over the next ten years, and 3.5 percent thereafter) indicates that the shares are trading slightly above their fair value estimate of $44–$50."

Reasons to Buy

- In the process business, Emerson is the only company with a scalable, intelligent process automation architecture that is commercially available. According to Mr. Farr, "We call our technology PlantWeb, and since its launch in 1998, it has been selected over legacy process automation systems on more than 2,000 occasions. Virtually all major customers in the oil and gas, refinery, chemical, pharmaceutical, and other process industries have embraced PlantWeb."
- Technology is fundamental to Emerson's sales growth. As a consequence, the company has been increasing its investment in Engineering & Development, notably in such sectors as communications, software, and electronics. E&D investment, moreover, has risen every year since 1973.
- In 2002, Baxter Healthcare Corporation selected Emerson's digital process automation platform to improve quality and efficiency at multiple sites for critical pharmaceutical production.
- Tesco, United Kingdom's largest supermarket chain, called on Emerson's retail-monitoring services in 2002 to help ensure food quality and improve energy efficiency in its stores.
- Emerson's reliable power technology now protects a new high-tech thirty-two-story office building—and Lehman Brothers European office—in London's prestigious Canary Wharf business district.
- In Asia, Emerson's growing design, engineering, and manufacturing resources, combined with its best-in-class appliance technology, are meeting the needs of large customers such as Whirlpool, Maytag, and Haier.
- Emerson is now supplying the world's leading windmill manufacturer with more than 3,000 wind turbine generators, helping deliver electricity to the national grid for twenty-eight different countries.
- Despite the recession and a dip in sales and earnings in 2002, operating cash flow for the year increased 6 percent, to $1.8 billion, and free cash flow increased 24 percent, to a record $1.4 billion, representing more than 135 percent of earnings. That was the second consecutive year that free cash flow exceeded earnings, demonstrating the company's focus on improving working capital performance and conservative capital spending.
- "Throughout 2002, we continued to reposition Emerson into the mix of businesses that will provide maximum, long-term shareholder value," said Mr. Farr. "This process includes divesting companies that are no longer core or strategic, as well as acquiring companies with good growth potential. Over the past three years, we have sold companies with about $1.2 billion in revenues, including divestitures of approximately $300 million in 2002."

Total assets: $14,545 million
Current ratio: 1.03
Common shares outstanding: 421 million
Return on 2002 shareholders' equity: 17.9%

		2002	2001	2000	1999	1998	1997	1996	1995
Revenues (millions)		13,824	15,480	15,545	14,270	13,447	12,299	11,150	10,013
Net income (millions)		1,060	1,032	1,422	1,314	1,229	1,122	1,018	908
Earnings per share		2.52	2.50	3.30	3.00	2.77	2.52	2.28	2.03
Dividends per share		1.55	1.53	1.43	1.31	1.18	1.08	.98	.89
Price	High	66.1	79.6	79.8	71.4	67.4	60.4	51.8	40.8
	Low	41.7	44.0	40.5	51.4	54.5	45.0	38.8	30.8

INCOME

Equity Office Properties Trust

Two North Riverside Plaza □ Suite 2100 □ Chicago, Illinois 60606 □ Listed: NYSE □ (312) 466-3286 □ Direct dividend reinvestment plan available: (312) 466-4336 □ Web site: www.equityoffice.com □ Ticker symbol: EOP □ S&P rating: Not rated □ Value Line financial strength rating: B+

"In 2002, we were pleased to have executed roughly 23.2 million square feet in gross leasing activity, despite a very challenging year for the overall economy and for the real estate industry, in particular," said Richard D. Kincaid, president of Equity Office Properties Trust.

"In addition, we prudently added liquidity. We predict a slow recovery in 2003, but remain optimistic that office job growth will continue to accelerate, particularly in the latter half of the year."

Mr. Kincaid, then age forty, was named CEO of Equity Office Properties in November 2002, after a seven-month search. He had spent the bulk of his career working for Sam Zell's entities. Mr. Zell, a leader in the industry, is the trust's founder. In 1990, Mr. Kincaid joined the Chicago mogul's closely held Equity Group Investments, Inc., the predecessor to Equity Office, which went public in 1997. He was named the Equity Office chief financial officer (CFO) at age thirty-three.

Company Profile

Equity Office Properties Trust is the nation's largest publicly held owner and manager of office properties. The company owns and manages 125.6 million square feet of primary Class A office space in 731 buildings in thirty-two major metropolitan areas across the country. Equity Office Properties serves more than 6,800 businesses, including many of the most recognized companies in America. The company's buildings are situated in such cities as Boston (fifty-five buildings), Chicago (thirty), San Francisco (twenty-eight), New York (six), Seattle (twenty-one), Washington, D.C. (twenty-five), Atlanta (forty-five), San Jose/Silicon Valley (thirty-seven), Los Angeles (thirteen), and Denver (fifteen). All told, these top-ten markets are responsible for 77.6 percent of the company's operating income.

The company's origins date back to 1976, when an integrated real-estate management and acquisition organization was founded by Samuel Zell, now chairman of Equity Office Properties. The company's portfolio was consolidated and taken public in July 1997. Since its initial public offering (IPO), the company has nearly quadrupled in size, growing from 32.2 million square feet to more than 125 million square feet. This growth has come about through strategic acquisitions, including the $4.3 billion Beacon Properties, Inc., merger in December 1997 and the $4.5 billion Cornerstone Properties merger in June 2000.

Office buildings are structures used primarily for the conducting of business, such as administration, clerical services, and consultation with clients and associates. Class A office buildings are generally considered those that have excellent locations and access, attract high-quality tenants, are well maintained and professionally managed. They also achieve the highest rent, occupancy, and tenant retention rates within their markets.

Acquisitions

Acquisitions have played an integral part in the company's growth. Equity Office Properties Trust significantly expanded its operations in late 1997 with the acquisition of Beacon Properties for $4.3 billion, adding 130 properties and 21 million square feet to its holdings. In 1999, the Trust completed six acquisitions, investing $393 million and acquiring ten office properties that contained 589 spaces. In 2000, it completed the acquisition of Cornerstone Properties for $2.7 billion. Cornerstone is an office REIT that owns eighty-six office properties in the United States that total more than 18.5 million square feet. Finally, Equity's largest acquisition, as noted in the following, was Spieker Properties.

What Is an Equity REIT?

Equity REITs make their money by owning properties, as opposed to mortgage REITs, which lend money to property owners. Equity REITs allow you to invest in a diversified collection of apartment buildings, hospitals, shopping centers, hotels, warehouses, and office buildings.

Like mutual funds, REITs are not taxed themselves, providing they pay out at least 90 percent of their taxable income. That translates into fat dividends for share-holders, as REITs pass along the rents and other income they collect. Dividend yields are typically 6 percent or more. "Put it all together, and you are looking at a double-digit total return. Over the long haul, the return should be lower than traditional stocks, but higher than bonds," says Chris Mayer, a real-estate professor at the University of Pennsylvania's Wharton School.

Kevin Bernzott, an investment adviser in Camarillo, California, views REITs as a stock/bond hybrid. "If you select quality REITs, they kick off a highly predictable stream of income, and eventually you may get some price appreciation. We plug them into the bond portion of the portfolio. They're almost like a bond with an equity kicker."

Shortcomings to Bear in Mind

- The leasing of real estate is highly competitive. Equity Office's properties compete for tenants with similar properties situated in its markets, primarily on the basis of location, rent charged, services provided, and the design and condition of improvements.

  The company also experiences competition when attempting to acquire interests in desirable real estate, including competition from domestic and foreign financial institutions, other REITs, life insurance companies, pension trusts, trust funds, partnerships, and individual investors.

- In 2002, Equity's office occupancy declined to 88.6 percent, from 91.8 percent a year earlier. Similarly, the industry's occupancy declined to 89.3 percent in 2002, compared with 92.8 percent at the end of 2001.

  According to Raymond Mathis, an analyst with *Standard & Poor's Stock Reports*, this decline in occupancy reflects "deteriorating fundamentals in EOP's major markets. Weak employment numbers and tenant bankruptcies have caused the outlook for internal rent growth to turn negative. Average rentals on new and renewed leases are now lower than those of both expiring and terminated leases."

Reasons to Buy

- Equity Office Properties is well-positioned to sustain its growth, according to the company's President. "We believe that on average, our existing rents are more than 30 percent below current market rents. We expect to realize this embedded growth as new leases are signed at current market-level rents. Over the next five years, approximately 11 percent to 13 percent of our leases expire annually, giving us strong growth potential. The nature of this primary revenue stream—long-term leases with over 9,000 businesses across all industries—helps insulate Equity Office from economic downturns. Finally, our geographic diversity also mitigates our exposure to regional downturns."

- As the first real-estate company to be named to the S&P 500 and the only real estate company on the *Fortune* 500 list, Equity Office attracts top talent from across diverse industries. According to management, "The high caliber of the employee base and its drive to be a low-cost manager that provides high-quality service define EOP as a superior operating company."

- In an article appearing in the *Wall Street Journal* in November of 2001, Tom Lauricella said, "Real-estate investment trusts, the securities most widely owned by real-estate funds, have an extremely low correlation to broad stock market gauges and to bonds, meaning that REITs may zig when others zag, or vice versa.

   "In fact, researchers at Chicago-based Ibbotson Associates recently published a study showing that the correlation between REITs and other stocks is roughly half the correlation between stocks and bonds. 'As an asset class, REITs have some unique characteristics,' said Peng Chen, Ibbotson's director of research."

- Equity's clients are mostly *Fortune* 500 corporations that sign long-term leases, guaranteeing that revenues will flow even during an economic downturn. "Equity Office has the nameplate properties in big cities," said Bill Schaff, manager of Berger Large Cap Value Fund. "The nameplate properties are always filled."

- Michael Arndt, writing for *BusinessWeek* on December 31, 2001, said, "Today's best bets, say the pros, are industry leaders such as Equity Office Properties Trust. They have top-notch management teams, strong balance sheets, and such geographically diverse portfolios that they can weather downturns handily, whether it's the burst dotcom bubble in San Francisco or the blow from terrorism in Manhattan.

   "Although new-lease rents are down from 2000's peak across the U.S., Equity Office Properties, for instance, was still raising rents by an average of $4.50 per square foot in late 2001. How's that possible? Tenants whose leases are up for renewal typically have been paying rates set ten years ago. Even today's lower rents are higher than they were back then."

- Equity Office Properties bought Spieker Properties, Inc., in the summer of 2001. Spieker is the largest commercial real-estate owner on the West Coast. It added 25 million square feet to EOP's 124 million square feet across the country. At $7.2 billion, the purchase—for cash, stock, and assumed debt—was the biggest domestic transaction in real-estate history.

   According to Credit Suisse First Boston Corporation, "the Spieker merger improves EOP's all-important return on invested capital." What's more, said the Credit Suisse analyst, the merger will "increase the amount of free cash flow and improve overall balance sheet ratios." In this same report, the analyst also pointed out that Equity Office Properties can now "lay claim to being the number-one office player in Boston, Chicago, San Francisco, Silicon Valley, Seattle, Portland, and Atlanta."

Total assets: $ 25,247 million
Current ratio: NA
Return on 2002 equity: 10%
Common shares outstanding: 418 million

		2002	2001	2000	1999	1998	1997*
Revenues (millions)		3,506	3,081	2,264	1,942	1,680	752
Net income (millions)		770	618	473	442	357	282
Earnings per share		1.70	1.55	1.53	1.52	1.24	1.11
Funds from operations		3.21	2.86	2.86	2.57	2.33	0.89
Dividends per share		2.00	1.90	1.74	1.58	1.38	0.56
Price	High	31.4	33.2	33.5	29.4	32.0	34.7
	Low	22.8	26.2	22.9	20.8	20.2	21.0

* Statistical information only available since the company went public in 1997.

AGGRESSIVE GROWTH

Ethan Allen Interiors, Inc.

Ethan Allen Drive ◻ Danbury, Connecticut 06811 ◻ (203) 743-8234 ◻ Dividend reinvestment plan not available ◻ Web site: www.ethanallen.com ◻ Fiscal years end June 30 ◻ Listed: NYSE ◻ Ticker symbol: ETH ◻ S&P rating: B+ ◻ Value Line financial strength rating: B+

"Ethan Allen's return on equity, a measure of profitability, often exceeds 20 percent, far above that of most other publicly traded furniture retailers," said Jeffrey R. Kosnett, writing for *Kiplinger's* magazine. "The company generates healthy free cash flow (the money that's left after capital expenditures for dividends, share buy-backs, expansion, and other good stuff), and has big profit margins, little debt, and a reputation for customer service."

In his October 2002 comment, Mr. Kosnett went on to say, "Farooq Kathwari, Ethan Allen's CEO for seventeen years, knows furniture cold and talks manufacturing and marketing equally well. For example, just as he senses that the luxury-home business may be slowing, here comes Ethan Allen with a hot new product line aimed at condos and townhouses. Next year, he says, 'We're going to get more young people in our store' with a new collection for kids and teens. Business has been a little soft since summer, but Ethan Allen has closed plants, started to import more, and cut costs faster than sales are easing."

Company Profile

Ethan Allen, one of the ten largest manufacturers of household furniture in the United States, sells a full range of furniture products and decorative accessories through a network of 316 retail stores, of which 103 are company-owned. The rest are owned and operated by independent dealers. However, all stores sell Ethan Allen products exclusively. Retail stores are located in the United States, Canada, and Mexico, with more than eighteen located overseas. The company has eighteen manufacturing facilities, including three sawmills, located throughout the United States. In addition, Ethan Allen has six regional distribution centers situated throughout the United States.

The company's stores—it prefers the term "galleries"—are scattered across the country, with outlets in nearly every state. However, there are more than a dozen outlets in such states as California, Texas, and Florida. There is a also a concentrated cluster of Ethan Allen stores along the Eastern Seaboard in such states as New Jersey, Connecticut, and Massachusetts.

Within this fragmented industry, the company has the largest domestic furniture retail network that uses the gallery concept. Comparable-store sales have benefited from a repositioning of the product mix to appeal to a broader consumer base, a program to renovate or relocate existing stores, coupled with more frequent advertising and promotional campaigns.

Ethan Allen is pursuing an aggressive growth strategy, including investments in technology, employee training, and new stores. Margins have been enhanced by manufacturing efficiencies, lower interest expense, and a strengthening of the upholstery and accessory lines.

With an efficient and flexible vertically integrated structure, a strong, dedicated retail network, an impressive 95 percent brand name recognition and a seventy-year reputation for exceptional quality and service, Ethan Allen is uniquely positioned as a dominant force in the home furnishings industry.

As Ethan Allen enters the new millennium, the company's philosophy of design remains the same as it was when it was founded seventy years ago. Styles may have changed from colonial to eclectic, but the company's commitment to exceptional quality, classical design elements, innovative style, and functionality will continue to position Ethan Allen as a preferred brand for years to come.

In keeping with the way consumers live today, the company has organized its product programs into two broad style categories. "Classic" encompasses more historically inspired styles, from early European and French influences to designs from the eighteenth- and nineteenth-century masters. "Casual," on the other hand, captures a clean, contemporary line and an updated country aesthetic.

Shortcomings to Bear in Mind

- Even though Ethan Allen is the nation's leading retailer of furniture, as well as the number-six maker of furnishings, the company has more than a thousand competitors and controls a mere 1 or 2 percent of the $178-billion home furnishings market. What's more, furniture executives are painfully aware that gross profit margins of 50 percent are whittled down to a slender 3 percent after taking into account freight, retail displays, warehousing, handling, and assorted other costs.

- In an article written by Sue Robinson for the *Burlington Free Press*, Jerry Epperson, an analyst, said, "It's a tough business to be in because we are seeing prices of furniture decline as more imports—leather and wooden furniture—come in, and that is forcing everyone to adapt significantly." Mr. Epperson is a furnishings industry analyst at Mann, Armistead & Epperson in Virginia.

Reasons to Buy

- According to Mr. Kathwari, "The long-term demographics favor us. We are right now benefiting from the wave of the baby boom generation. Spending by baby boomers is not expected to peak for at least another five years. Focus on home and cocooning is very, very important. The economic trends, the industry trends and the positioning of Ethan Allen enables us to continue to grow the business."

Mr. Kathwari went on to say, "Also very important, we have the advantage of having designs that stay around for a longer time. It takes about a year or so at least for our craftspeople to get used to making a product. In our industry, most people do not keep their products for more than a year or a year and a half. We tend to keep our products from eight to twelve years, and that gives us the ability to be more efficient. The consumer does not get tired of our designs; it is generally the store buyers that get tired."

- The company employs a showcase gallery concept. Products are displayed in complete room ensembles, including furnishings, wall decor, window treatments, floor coverings, accents, and accessories. Ethan Allen believes the gallery concept leads to higher sales, as it encourages customers to buy a complete home collection, including case goods (furniture made of wood, rather than upholstered), upholstery, and accessories, as well as offering designers the opportunity to offer additional services.

- Ethan Allen benefits from vertical integration. Because the company controls many aspects of its operations, it is self-sufficient, efficient, and cost-effective. Business decisions regarding everything from sales events to manufacturing locations are made by Ethan Allen management. That way, the company can position its strategies based on what works best. In other words, the company has eliminated the middleman and the waste, and it is able to avoid bottlenecks. This translates into productivity, increased efficiency, satisfied customers, and steadily climbing profits.

- The company's new stores are situated in high-traffic shopping areas for customer convenience. Many existing stores have been relocated to better-traveled retail routes.

- Furniture is a fragile commodity. It's expensive to transport and can be damaged very easily. According to Mr. Kathwari, "About twelve years ago, we decided to take control of the logistics and deliver our products at one cost

nationally. This was a major decision and a major risk, both in terms of servicing the consumer more effectively, while reducing our inventories on a national level. But we have been able to improve our profitability.

"We have five national distribution warehouses, about 100 retail warehouses, and a trucking fleet to service our business. Technology has helped us become more efficient. We have state-of-the-art computer systems, and warehousing systems that receive the product and prepare it for delivery to the customer."

- Operating a store in today's environment is a complicated business if management doesn't have the right structure in place. Ethan Allen is convinced that "You need to be able to keep the store beautiful and inspiring, help customers select the right products, train and motivate the sales staff, grow a complicated custom business, make accessory house calls, and anticipate customer service requests—all at the same time."

To respond to these demands, Ethan Allen began testing new ways to staff its stores. For example, at its corporate headquarters in Danbury, Connecticut, management looked at its needs—especially on high-traffic weekends—and created an environment to better support the designers who were working on the front lines.

First, the company established the right sales management structure, so that designers were able to obtain the training and direction they needed to build their businesses. Then, Ethan Allen added specialists in the soft goods and accessories areas to help designers sell more of the complicated product programs. In addition, the company also added a merchandise manager to keep the store beautiful and a customer service specialist to address delivery and service issues.

Since this structure has been in place, traffic in the Danbury store increased about 19 percent. During that same period, the store's written business jumped up 35 percent.

■ Ethan Allan is now selling its wares over the Internet. In an effort to extend its reach and supplement traditional marketing efforts, the company has expanded and redesigned its Web site to allow for the direct sale of more than 5,000 home-furnishing products.

Analysts believe the company is uniquely positioned to leverage its widely recognized brand name and

favorable reputation to swiftly develop a valuable e-commerce endeavor. What's more, Ethan Allen's extensive distribution network and integrated retail structure provides it with a competitive advantage in servicing online customers.

Most other furniture producers have been reluctant to establish an Internet retail presence, as such a move might alienate its retail and wholesale customers. For its part, Ethan Allen has no such fears, since its furniture is marketed exclusively through its own network of stores.

Total assets: $689 million
Current ratio: 2.47
Common shares outstanding: 37.9 million
Return on 2002 shareholders' equity: 16.9%

		2002	2001	2000	1999	1998	1997	1996	1995
Revenues (millions)		892	904	856	762	693	572	510	476
Net income (millions)		82	80	91	81	72	49	28	23
Earnings per share		2.06	1.98	2.20	1.92	1.63	1.11	.65	.52
Dividends per share		.16	.16	.16	.12	.09	.06	.01	Nil
Price	High	42.2	42.3	33.8	37.8	44.4	28.6	13.0	8.3
	Low	27.2	26.5	20.5	24.7	15.7	12.3	6.5	5.7

AGGRESSIVE GROWTH

Family Dollar Stores, Inc.

10401 Old Monroe Road □ Post Office Box 1017 □ Charlotte, North Carolina 28201-1017 □ □ (704) 814-3252 □ Dividend reinvestment program is not available □ Fiscal years end last Saturday in August □ Web site: www.familydollar.com □ Listed: NYSE □ Ticker symbol: FDO □ S&P rating: A □ Value Line financial strength rating: A

The typical Family Dollar customer is a female who shops for a family with a median annual income under $35,000 and, in many instances, under $20,000. These families depend on Family Dollar to provide them with the good values they must have to stretch their limited disposable income.

U.S. Census statistics and demographic trends support the fact that Family Dollar's targeted low-to-middle-income customer base is large and growing. More than 40 percent of households in the United States have incomes below $35,000. Hispanic shoppers, the nation's fastest-growing demographic segment, like the company's

small-store format. Retirees, another expanding sector of the population, view these smaller stores located in their neighborhoods as a convenient and more enjoyable alternative to the "big box" discounters. As more baby boomers approach retirement with the prospect of reduced and fixed incomes, they particularly appreciate Family Dollar's everyday low prices.

The company does not try to meet all merchandising needs of all people. However, most merchandise is priced under $10, and the assortment covers basic products, such as health and beauty aids, household chemicals, paper products, and food. Shoppers can also select from an assortment of giftware and seasonal items, apparel for the entire family, and domestic furnishings such as towels, sheets, and pillows.

In recent years, in response to customer feedback, the mix of merchandise has shifted to more hardline consumables, including nationally advertised brand names. To make room for the expanded assortment of consumables and other hardline categories, the company completed a major space reallocation program in its stores in fiscal 2001. Hanging apparel space was reduced, and aisles were widened to make shopping easier.

Company Profile

Family Dollar Stores, Inc., is one of the fastest-growing discount store chains in the United States. During the last ten years, more than 2,300 new stores have been added to the chain, to which more than 1,500 locations have been added in the last five fiscal years. As of November 7, 2002, the company had 4,640 outlets in forty-one states, plus the District of Columbia.

The merchandising concept responsible for this growth provides customers with good values at low cost. The merchandise is sold at everyday low prices in a no-frills, low-overhead, self-service environment. Most merchandise is priced under $10.

Stores are situated in a contiguous forty-one-state area that ranges northeast to Maine, southeast to Florida, as far northwest as South Dakota, and southwest to Arizona. They generally range in size from 6,000 to 8,000 square feet, and most are operated under leases. The relatively small size permits the company to open new stores in rural areas and small towns, as well as in large urban centers. Within these markets, the stores are situated in shopping centers or as freestanding buildings convenient to the company's value-conscious customer base.

Since the opening of the first Family Dollar store in 1959, the store's expansion program has been financed entirely with internally generated funds. The company has no long-term debt.

Family Dollar's headquarters is based in Matthews, North Carolina, just outside Charlotte. The company operates automated, full-service distribution centers in Matthews, as well in West Memphis, Arkansas; Front Royal, Virginia; Duncan, Oklahoma; and Morehead, Kentucky. A sixth distribution center was opened in Maquoketa, Iowa, in the spring of 2002.

The proliferation of distribution centers has been rapid. Prior to 1994, the entire chain of Family Dollar stores was served by just one distribution center. As the pace of new store openings accelerated, a second facility opened in 1994. With the addition of three more facilities in the last four years, the new total is up to six.

The company purchases its merchandise from about 1,800 suppliers. About 57 percent of merchandise is manufactured in the United States, with substantially all such goods obtained directly from the manufacturer, rather than through wholesalers. Imported products, however, are purchased directly from the manufacturer or from importers.

Shortcomings to Bear in Mind

- In a recent nine-month period, insiders, such as executives and board members, sold some of their stock. In that span, there were fourteen sales and no purchases.
- Retail businesses rarely lack for competitors. New ideas in merchandising come along periodically and give fits to companies that are unable to adjust to a new environment. The "big boxes," for instance (such as Wal-Mart, Staples, Bed Bath & Beyond, Home Depot, and Lowe's) have punched holes in such companies as Montgomery Ward, Sears, J. C. Penney, and the thousands of mom-and-pop operations.

- Family Dollar shares tend to fluctuate more than the market. According to *Value Line Investment Survey*, the beta coefficient is 1.15. This means it fluctuates 15 percent more than the market. Thus, I have labeled the stock "aggressive growth."

- Although the company has an exceptional record of growth, it experienced a slight interruption to that trend in the summer of 2002. According to George R. Mahoney, Jr., the company's executive vice president, sales in the July reporting period "were adversely impacted by the elimination of an advertising circular that was distributed at the end of the July reporting period last year." As a result, "sales in existing stores decreased approximately 5.4 percent below sales for the fourth week in the prior fiscal year when the advertising circular was distributed."

Reasons to Buy

- Family Dollar Stores is the rare company with no long-term debt.

- In the 1992–2002 period, earnings per share advanced from $.33 to $1.25, with only one minor dip along the way. That amounts to a compound annual growth rate of 14.2 percent. During the same ten-year period, dividends per share climbed from $.08 to $.26, a growth rate of 12.5 percent.

- The company is expanding at a fast clip. In fiscal 2001, for instance, it added 502 new outlets, including 76 in Texas, 33

in New York, 27 in Michigan, 23 in Georgia, and 20 in both Florida and Louisiana. Similarly, in fiscal 2002, the company added 515 new stores, representing the largest number added in any given year. Nor will the pace slow in 2003, with another 575 stores slated to be added to the chain.

- Despite the recession that gripped the nation during the first two years of the decade, the company has continued to surge ahead, with twenty-six consecutive quarterly earnings increases as of the end of fiscal 2002. What's more, there was no slowdown in 2003. For the nine-week period ended November 2, 2002, sales were about $742.7 million, or 15.8 percent above the same period the prior year.

- The company is implementing a fully integrated system to improve inventory management from the time the purchase order is placed with the supplier to the time the customer purchases the goods at the cash register. According to management, "In the initial phases of this project, we have upgraded all point-of-sale equipment; formed an inventory control department; shifted to by-item inventory counts at all stores; and implemented a new inventory management system and a new demand forecasting system for replenishment of our distribution systems. These investments provide our merchants and supply chain specialists with a clear view of our inventory position and what our customers are buying."

Total assets: $1,755 million
Current ratio: 1.99
Common shares outstanding: 173 million
Return on 2002 shareholders' equity: 18.8%

		2002	2001	2000	1999	1998	1997	1996	1995
Revenues (millions)		4,163	3,665	3,133	2,751	2,362	1,995	1,715	1,547
Net income (millions)		217	190	172	140	103	75	61	58
Earnings per share		1.25	1.10	1.00	.81	.60	.44	.36	.34
Dividends per share		.26	.24	.22	.20	.18	.16	.14	.13
Price	High	37.2	31.3	24.5	26.8	22.4	15.1	7.0	6.6
	Low	23.8	18.4	14.3	14.0	11.5	6.3	3.7	3.6

FedEx Corporation

942 South Shady Grove Road □ Memphis, Tennessee 38120 □ (901) 818-7200 □ Web site: www.fedex.com □ Direct dividend reinvestment plan is available: (800) 446-2617 □ Fiscal years end May 31 □ Listed: NYSE □ Ticker symbol: FDX □ S&P rating: B □ Value Line financial strength rating: B++

The U.S. Postal Service struck a seven-year, $6.3-billion alliance with FedEx for air delivery of its priority, express, and first-class mail. The service began in August of 2001.

With the Postal Service expected to lose more than $1 billion in 2001, Postmaster General William J. Henderson said, tapping FedEx's fleet of more than 600 planes will give consumers better service at lower cost.

The U.S. Postal Service had been searching for a company to handle its express and priority mail. That job had previously been handled primarily by Emery Worldwide Airlines. But postal officials said that the deal with Emery had been too costly and inefficient.

Under the new pact, FedEx carries up to 3.5 million pounds of Postal Service mail a day, or the capacity of about thirty wide-body DC-10 airplanes. To meet the demand, FedEx had to hire some 500 new pilots and about 1,000 new mechanics and cargo handlers.

Company Profile

FedEx Corporation (formerly FDX Corp.) is the world's leading provider of guaranteed express delivery services. Using a $4 million inheritance as seed money, Frederick W. Smith founded FedEx in 1971 when he was only twenty-seven.

The company offers a wide range of express delivery services for the time-definite transportation of documents, packages, and freight. Commercial and military charter services are also offered by FedEx. The company operates in the United States, France, England, Canada, and Japan.

FedEx provides same-day service, overnight, and deferred delivery services for documents, packages, and freight, using a network of 50,000 ground vehicles, 647 aircraft, and 55,500 drop-off boxes. In fiscal 2002 (ended May 31, 2002), FedEx Express accounted for 74 percent of the company's revenues. FedEx Express is the company's original business; it is the leading provider of guaranteed, express delivery. The company has several other divisions, such as FedEx Ground and FedEx Freight. About 72 percent of FedEx Express's revenues are from domestic services, with about 71 percent express delivery and 29 percent lower-yielding deferred delivery.

International business (28 percent of FedEx Express revenues) provides packages and document delivery to 212 countries. FedEx has a strong position in Asian markets and is one of only four U.S. air carriers with rights to serve China. In 2002, FedEx Express revamped its international express network to reduce transit times, provide later customer pick-ups, and earlier deliveries in key global markets.

FedEx Ground (13 percent of 2002 total revenue) is North America's second-largest ground package delivery company. FedEx Ground operations are conducted with 13,500 owner-operated vehicles and 13,600 company-owned trailers.

FedEx reported sales of $20.6 billion in the fiscal year ended May 31, 2002. This represented an increase of 5 percent over the previous year.

Shortcomings to Bear in Mind

- According to management, "We are a very capital-intensive business. To do what we do takes big wide-bodied planes—and lots of them. It takes trucks and vans and large, costly operating hubs, both across America and abroad. It takes a lot of information and telecommunications devices, whether it be scanners and radios in the trucks or what-have-you."

On the other hand, FedEx's global network is now more or less complete, and that will make a big difference, not least because investors can expect the pace of capital spending to decline sharply.

- Over the years, the relationship between FedEx managers and some of its 4,000 pilots has been strained, in part because of CEO Fred Smith's opposition to unions.

"We had started with the dream that if the company rose to Fred's vision, we'd be at the top as well," said Don Wilson, a twenty-eight-year company veteran who helped organize the FedEx Pilots Union in 1992. "The company has exceeded beyond what anyone expected, but our pay and benefits have not," Mr. Wilson said.

On the other hand, the company has had a reputation as a great place to work, with employees claiming they "bleed purple and orange"—the company's colors—and living by Smith's mantra: "people, service, profit." FedEx has repeatedly been on *Fortune* magazine's list of the "100 Best Companies to Work For" and its lists of best places for minorities and women to work.

Reasons to Buy

- FedEx became the Official Worldwide Delivery Service Sponsor of the National Football League, beginning in the fall of 2000. The three-year agreement gave FedEx NFL marketing rights domestically and worldwide. FedEx also is now an official sponsor of the thirty-two NFL teams, Super Bowl, and Pro Bowl.

The company also sponsors:
- FedEx Field, the home of the NFL's Washington Redskins
- The FedEx St. Jude Classic, which raises money for the St. Jude's Children's Research Hospital
- The FedEx Championship Series, the country's premier open-wheel racing circuit (CART)
- USA Basketball, America's men's and women's Olympic teams
- The Ferrari Formula One racing team in Europe

- FedEx is more sensitive to shifts in the economy than such cyclical companies as paper and chemicals. As sales pick up for retailers, they order more goods, which flow back to companies that supply such things as boxes and bags. As a consequence, FedEx quickly feels the benefits of an economic recovery. That's because a shipping company obtains more business as soon as retailers order more goods.

- Increasingly, businesses are seeking strategic, cost-effective ways to manage their supply chains—the series of transportation and information exchanges required to convert parts and raw materials into finished, delivered products. According the management: "Experience tells us that customers prefer one supplier to meet all of their distribution and logistics needs. And FedEx has what it takes: Our unique global network, operational expertise, and air route authorities cannot be replicated by the competition. With FedEx, our customers have a strategic competitive weapon to squeeze time, mass, and cost from the supply chain."

- When a large corporation decentralizes shipping, it's like a computer's circuitry firing at random: interesting pyrotechnics, but not very productive. That's why Unisys chose to harness the buying power of hundreds of sales offices, service locations, and manufacturing sites by using FedEx's transportation management services. Unisys employees simply call a toll-free number staffed by Caliber Logistics. Caliber distribution experts rely on FedEx to ship everything from critical replacement parts to Unisys enterprise servers directly to the customer site. Each shipping decision reflects the most appropriate and cost-effective delivery solution.

- FedEx has invested heavily in recent years to develop an international infrastructure. It presently can reach locations accounting for 90 percent of world gross domestic product (GDP) with twenty-four- or forty-eight-hour service. International delivery services for documents and freight have been growing faster than domestic business in recent years.

- According to CEO Frederick W. Smith, "The new strategy we have put in place over the past several years has made us a full-service transportation company, offering the broadest array of services. With FedEx Express, FedEx Ground, FedEx Freight, FedEx Custom Critical, and FedEx Trade Networks, we can offer our customers an unprecedented array of shipping and supply chain services quickly and conveniently across the globe."

- In 2002, FedEx Ground experienced outstanding growth, growing year over year by double digits. FedEx Ground reached 2 million packages a day. This was due

mainly to an expanded network, improved service levels, improved sales capabilities—especially for small and medium-size customers—and the power of the FedEx brand. In the words of Mr. Smith, "Our new FedEx Home Delivery expanded to serve 90 percent of the U.S. residential market and will reach virtually 100 percent in September 2002."

- Despite a challenging economy in 2002, FedEx received a record number of accolades—ten in all, including *Fortune* magazine's Top 10 World's Most Admired companies, and Harris Interactive & Reputation Institute Top 10.

- In the fall of 2002, FedEx said that the company would invest $1.8 billion over the next six years to expand its fast-growing, ground-based service in Canada and the United States. This action will nearly double the rate of package deliveries. According to management, this move is designed to capture new business, such as small and medium-size customers. Some analysts, however, wonder whether FedEx has plans to pare back its air-delivery network, since the announcement came at a time when some customers, seeking cost savings in a slack economy, were switching from the more expensive air freight to ground-based service. A company spokesman said that no major changes are planned for the air network. "It isn't a tradeoff from one to the other."

Total assets: $13,812 million
Current ratio: 1.14
Common shares outstanding: 298 million
Return on 2002 shareholders' equity: 10.9%

		2002	2001	2000	1999	1998	1997	1996	1995
Revenues (millions)		20,607	19,629	18,257	16,773	15,703	11,520	10,274	9,392
Net income (millions)		710	663	688	531	526	348	308	282
Earnings per share		2.39	2.26	2.32	2.10	1.75	1.51	1.35	1.25
Dividends per share		.20	Nil	—	—	—	—	—	—
Price	High	61.4	53.5	49.8	61.9	46.6	42.3	22.5	21.5
	Low	42.8	33.2	30.6	34.9	21.8	21.0	16.7	14.7

Fortune Brands, Inc.

300 Tower Parkway □ Lincolnshire, Illinois 60069 □ (847) 484-4410 □ Dividend reinvestment plan available: (800) 225-2719 □ Web site: www.fortunebrands.com □ Listed: NYSE □ Ticker symbol: FO □ S&P rating: B- □ Value Line financial strength rating: A

Fortune Brands didn't let the sluggish economy slow it down in 2002. Here's how it fared:

- Net income was $525.6 million, or $3.41 per share, up 37 percent from the prior year.

- Reported sales were $5.68 billion, up 2 percent from 2001.

- Operating income shot up 48 percent, to $786.6 million.

- Free cash flow expanded to $420 million, even after dividends and restructuring spending.

- Return on equity increased to 22.7 percent (15 percent is considered good by most companies).

"We continued to win in the marketplace by building our powerful consumer brands," said CEO Norm Wesley. "We developed innovative new products and gained market share, especially with our home and golf brands. We strengthened our businesses with high-impact strategic initiatives to accelerate growth, most notably our extremely successful Omega cabinets acquisition and our turnaround in office products. We generated huge cash flow that we can use to make acquisitions, repurchase shares, and pay dividends."

Company Profile

Fortune Brands owns companies with leading consumer brands in home products, office products, golf equipment, and spirits and wine. These brands include familiar names like Moen, Titleist, Jim Beam, Master Lock, Swingline, Day-Timer, FootJoy, Cobra, Kensington, ACCO, Wilson Jones, and Geyser Peak.

Named Fortune Brands only since 1997, the company was formerly known as American Brands. It was incorporated in Delaware in 1985 as a holding company with subsidiaries in the previously mentioned businesses, as well as others in which it no longer has holdings.

Fortune Brands' roots were planted decades ago. In 1966, a former New Jersey-incorporated subsidiary changed its name to American Brands and began a diversification program with the acquisition of Sunshine Biscuits. The diversification extended to the distilled spirits business in 1967, with the acquisition of the company now known as Jim Beam Brands Worldwide. The first home and office brands— including Swingline, Master Lock, and Wilson Jones—were acquired in 1970. The 1976 acquisition of Acushnet, with its premier Titleist brand, led the charge into the golf business. In the ensuing years, a wide range of businesses and brands were both acquired and divested to promote the goal of enhanced shareholder value.

In 1994, American Brands, by then a wide collection of businesses with annual net sales totaling more than $15 billion, began a fundamental transformation. The new focus was solely on growing categories in which the company was a leader— home, office, golf, and distilled spirits. The company made significant divestitures in 1994, and, in 1997, the company spun off its remaining non-core subsidiary. With its fundamental transformation complete, the company changed its name to Fortune Brands in June of 1997.

Today, fifteen brands have annual sales exceeding $100 million each. Moen,

Titleist, and Jim Beam, the three largest brands, account for more than a quarter of Fortune Brands sales. More than 80 percent of sales come from brands that are number one or two in their markets, and more than 25 percent of sales come from new products. For two successive years, the company has been recognized by *Fortune* magazine's prestigious annual survey of executives, directors, and securities analysts as the most admired company in the world in its category. The 1999 survey proclaimed Fortune Brands as one of the top five U.S. "National Champions" and as one of the top three companies in the world in innovativeness.

Shortcomings to Bear in Mind

- At the end of 2002, Howard Choe, an analyst with *Standard & Poor's Stock Reports*, had this negative comment: "We recently lowered our opinion on the stock to accumulate, from buy, reflecting modest concerns regarding asbestos litigation, and potential for weaker sales growth at the home products division. In the company's 10Q filing, FO disclosed that it had been named as a codefendant in eighty-five asbestos litigation cases. Although the company did not expect this to have a material impact if the outcome is negative, we believe it is difficult to quantify an outcome, and are cautious as a result."

Reasons to Buy

- Lars L. Bainbridge, an analyst with *Value Line Investment Survey*, had this comment at the end of 2002: "Notably, about one-fourth of consolidated sales come from products introduced within the past three years. Management also remains on the hunt for suitable acquisition candidates and potential partners for joint ventures, especially in the highly fragmented home products market. Given the strong cash flows we

anticipate, the company should have ample resources at its disposal to fund all of these growth strategies and still return wealth directly to stockholders through dividend disbursements and share repurchases. All told, we project Fortune profits will rise, on average, at a double-digit pace to 2005–2007."

- In 2003, the company introduced the new King Cobra SS-i iron line and the new King Cobra SS 380 model driver. These innovative new golf clubs build on strong momentum for the Cobra brand, which doubled its sales and market share in 2002 and became the fastest-growing club brand in the marketplace.

  The new King Cobra SS-i irons deliver a variety of key enhancements to the original King Cobra SS design. The King Cobra SS-i iron line features an even larger "sweet spot," softer feel and custom fitting options as the relevant points of difference, as compared with competitive products in the game-improvement strategy, while strengthening the performance goals of longer distance and greater accuracy.

- In February of 2002, Home Depot selected Fortune Brands to supply its entire line of kitchen and bath cabinets for its 1,200 home improvement stores. "We are delighted to expand our relationship with the Home Depot and to combine our strength in semi-custom cabinetry with the well-known Thomasville brand name," said Rich Forbes, president of MasterBrand Cabinets, Fortune Brands' cabinet unit. "Under the Thomasville name, we'll offer Home Depot customers high-quality semi-custom cabinetry in a wide array of finishes and door styles that can meet virtually any kitchen design need."

- In 2002, Kolorfusion International, Inc., announced that a license agreement had been negotiated with Moen, Inc., a wholly owned subsidiary of Fortune

Brands. Kolorfusion is the owner of process patents for three-dimensional product decoration invented in France by Jean-Noel Claveau. The company's technology is considered a major breakthrough for product finishing, as the process actually transfers any design with any colors into a product's coating or directly into the plastic or aluminum itself, no matter what the shape. The result is a fully decorated product as durable as the coating or part.

"The license allows Moen to install and utilize Kolorfusion's patented process for us on their faucet and bath products. "Having licensed this process, we can now truly provide unique designs and customization to our customers," said David Lingafelter, vice president of marketing for Moen.

- In 2001, Fortune Brands announced that its Jim Beam Brands Worldwide unit had sold its U.K.–based Scotch whiskey business. The sale of the business, consisting of the Invergordon private-label and bulk Scotch operations and several regional brands in the United Kingdom, further sharpens Jim Beam Brands' global strategic focus on fast-growing, high-return premium and superpremium spirits and wine brands.

The selling price for the U.K.–based Scotch business was about $290 million in cash. The sale had no effect on the U.S. or international distribution of the Jim Beam Brands portfolio of premium and superpremium brands that includes Jim Beam bourbon, Knob Creek small batch bourbon, DeKuyper cordials, Vox vodka, and Geyser Peak wines. Jim Beam Brands will retain global ownership of After Shock, a fast-growing premium liqueur brand marketed in the United Kingdom, and will also hold a perpetual license in the United States to The Dal-

more, recently named the world's finest single-malt Scotch at the International Wine & Spirit Competition.

"This sale is another very positive strategic development for our Jim Beam Brands spirits and wine business," said Mr. Wesley. "On the heels of our creative distribution partnership with ABSOLUT vodka, this move will enable Jim Beam Brands to intensify its strategic focus on the premium and super-premium spirits and wine market, the fastest-growing segment in the industry. The U.K. Scotch business, while successful, offered lower returns and lower growth than our core spirits and wine business, and simply didn't fit with our strategic focus.

"This transaction will also further enhance Fortune Brands' financial flexibility to drive shareholder value higher. We'll evaluate our highest return opportunities for the use of the proceeds, including strategic acquisitions and attractive share repurchases," Wesley added.

- Jim Beam Brands moved aggressively in 2001 to strengthen its clout in the premium and superpremium market and reduce its distribution costs by teaming up with the maker of Absolut vodka for joint distribution of the two companies' spirits and wine brands. "Just four months after beginning operations, the Jim Beam-ABSOLUT partnership is already a distribution powerhouse," said Jim Beam Brands President & CEO Rich Reese. The partners now distribute the second-highest volume portfolio in the United States through their Future Brands LLC joint venture. They are also partners for distribution in key markets outside the United States through the Maxxium joint venture. Invergordon's private-label and bulk products are not distributed by Maxxium.

Total assets: $5,822 million
Current ratio: 3.77
Common shares outstanding: 150 million
Return on 2002 shareholders' equity: 22.7%

	2002	2001	2000	1999	1998	1997	1996	1995
Revenues (millions)	5,678	5,674	5,844	5,525	5,241	4,844	4,712	4,928
Net income (millions)	526	336	366	340	294	242	182	186
Earnings per share	3.41	2.49	2.29	1.99	1.67	1.41	1.04	.99
Dividends per share	1.08	.97	.93	.89	.85	.41	NA	NA
Price High	57.9	40.5	33.3	45.9	42.3	38.0	NA	NA
Low	36.8	28.4	19.2	29.4	25.3	30.4	NA	NA

NA: Not available because the company was restructured, and its tobacco business was eliminated.

CONSERVATIVE GROWTH

Gannett Company, Inc.

7950 Jones Branch Drive ▫ McLean, Virginia 22107 ▫ (703) 284-6918 ▫ Dividend reinvestment plan available: (800) 778-3299 ▫ Web site: www.gannett.com ▫ Listed: NYSE ▫ Ticker symbol: GCI ▫ S&P rating: A ▫ Value Line financial strength rating: A++

"Gannett has historically traded at a premium to its peer group, and based upon its strong management and top-tier margins, we think this premium is warranted," said Steven Barlow in July 2002, in a report issued by Prudential Financial, a major brokerage firm. "Gannett's intense focus on cost control has generated high operating margins in good years or in bad, in newspapers and in television.

"The company's markets have been fairly resilient to the downturn and are recovering more quickly than larger markets. Gannett's community newspapers, located in small and mid-sized cities, have held up better than their larger-market peers in terms of advertising. Community newspapers rely primarily on local retail advertising, which experienced modest (low- to mid-single-digit) declines in 2001 and started to recover to positive territory in May (2002). These newspapers are less dependent than larger-market newspapers on more-volatile national advertising and help-wanted advertising, which have been punished in the advertising downturn. As a result, Gannett's revenue performance continues to be near the top of its peer group.

"At the same time, the company is leveraged to an upturn in national advertising through its ownership of USA Today, which comprises about 10 percent of total revenues. We believe USA Today provides a potential upside opportunity for investors if national advertising returns to higher levels, especially from advertisers in the top four categories of travel, technology, entertainment, and automotive."

Company Profile

Founded in 1906 by Frank E. Gannett and associates, Gannett was incorporated in 1923 and listed on the New York Stock Exchange in 1967. Gannett is an international news and information company that publishes ninety-four daily newspapers in the United States. The combined paid daily circulation is 7.7 million. This includes USA Today, the nation's largest-selling daily newspaper, with a circulation of 2.3 million, available in sixty countries.

The company also owns a variety of non-daily publications in the United States as well as USA Weekend, a weekly newspaper magazine. In the United Kingdom, Gannett subsidiary Newsquest plc publishes nearly 300 titles, including fifteen daily newspapers. Gannett also operates twenty-two television stations in the United States.

Operations Worldwide

Gannett is an international company with headquarters in Arlington, Virginia, and operations in forty-three states as well as the District of Columbia, Guam, the United Kingdom, Germany, and Hong Kong.

Newspapers

Gannett is the largest domestic newspaper group, in terms of circulation. The company's ninety-four daily newspapers in the United States have a combined daily paid circulation of 7.7 million. They include USA Today, with a circulation of about 2.3 million. USA Today is available in sixty countries.

In addition, Gannett owns a variety of non-daily publications and USA Weekend, a weekly newspaper magazine with a circulation of 23.6 million. USA Weekend is delivered on Sundays in 591 Gannett and non-Gannett newspapers.

Newsquest plc, a wholly owned Gannett subsidiary acquired in mid-1999, is one of the largest regional newspaper publishers in England, with a portfolio of more than 300 titles. Its publications include fifteen daily newspapers with a combined circulation of about 600,000. Newsquest also publishes a variety of non-daily publications, including Berrow's Worcester Journal, the oldest continuously published newspaper in the world.

Broadcasting

The company owns and operates twenty-two television stations covering 17.7 percent of the United States.

On the Internet

Gannett has more than 100 Web sites in the United States and the United Kingdom, including www.usatoday.com, one of the leading newspaper sites on the Internet.

Other Ventures

Other company operations include Gannett News Service; Gannett Retail Advertising Group; Gannett TeleMarketing, Inc.; Gannett New Business and Product Development; Gannett Direct Marketing Services; Gannett Offset, a commercial printing operation; Gannett Media Technologies International; and Telematch, a database marketing company.

Shortcomings to Bear in Mind

- Some people consider newspapers a dying medium. In 1990, for instance, 113 million Americans read dailies; today, only 76.6 million do. Classifieds, which account for 27 percent of Gannett's annual revenues, seem destined to move to the Web.

- In a recent nine-month period, there was considerable selling of company shares by insiders, such as officers and board members. In that span, there were twenty-eight sales and only two purchases. It would appear that these major stockholders were convinced that it was an opportune time to lighten up their positions. As it turned out, however, the stock actually advanced.

- The price of newsprint (the paper that newspapers are published on) declined in 2002. Some analysts believe that newsprint may "increase markedly" in 2003.

Reasons to Buy

- Commenting on the company's performance, Douglas H. McCorkindale, president and CEO, said, "We are very pleased to report another quarter of strong year-over-year earnings growth, led by robust television results and another solid performance by our newspaper operations. Our television properties achieved strong year-over-year gains, propelled by record political advertising spending and a continued favorable advertising environment for our highly rated television stations. Our newspaper operations reported their best quarter of revenue and operating cash flow gains all year. Newsprint expense declined 13 percent for the quarter. In the U.K., our Newsquest properties achieved their strongest advertising revenue gains all year in the fourth quarter and made a strong contribution to earnings."

- Gannett Broadcasting's television stations are local market leaders. In the November 2001 ratings, three Gannett stations were top in the nation for late local news in the key sales demographic of adults aged twenty-five to fifty-four: KARE-TV, in Minneapolis-St. Paul, Minnesota; KSDK-TV, in St. Louis, Missouri; and KUSA-TV in Denver, Colorado.

  KPNX-TV in Phoenix, Arizona, joins those three in the top ten in the country. Tops among the nation's medium-sized or smaller markets are WBIR-TV, in Knoxville, Tennessee; WCSH-TV, in Portland, Maine; and WMAZ-TV, in Macon, Georgia.

  Three other stations purchased in the 1990s, all with a history of underperformance, made great strides in 2001: WGRZ-TV, in Buffalo, New York; KTHV-TV in Little Rock, Arkansas; and WLTX-TV, in Columbia, South Carolina. WGRZ went from third to first place in late news for the first time in the station's history. KTHV ranked number two in all news time periods with adults aged twenty-five to fifty-four.

- Although earnings declined modestly in 2001, the company has a solid record, and 2001 was the only year in the past ten that earnings dipped. In the 1992–2002 period, earnings per share advanced from $1.20 to $4.31, a compound annual growth rate of 13.6 percent. In the same period, however, dividends did not do nearly as well, rising from $.63 to $.94, a growth rate of only 4.1 percent.

- Most of the company's newspapers are the only daily publication in their respective cities. To be sure, that doesn't mean they have a monopoly on advertising; there are other ways to advertise, such as television, radio, and direct mail. Still, newspapers have always been an important advertising medium, and if you are the only game in town, it helps.

- As the Internet continues to be a growing part of people's lives, more Gannett newspapers are jumping into the World Wide Web. What's more, the online pioneers continue to enhance content and add new products, including those stemming from Gannett's participation in Classified Ventures and *www.careerpath.com*.

  As leading information providers for their communities, the company's newspapers are aware that fresh information is essential to success online. *Florida Today's* Space Online (*www.space.com*), for instance, covers launches of the space shuttle literally as it blasts off. Reporters with laptop computers file stories from the beach at Cape Canaveral, supplying live news online within moments of a launch.

- "Our opinion of the newspaper group in general, and of GCI in particular, remains positive for the near term," according to a report issued in January 2003 by *Standard & Poor's Stock Reports*. The analyst, William H. Donald, said, "The stock should remain at the forefront of the market recovery, as newspapers benefit from a strengthening of the economy and improving demand for advertising.

"The company's long-term operating prospects are bolstered by an attractive mix of print, broadcast, and Internet media properties, as well as geographic diversity across U.S. markets and expansion in the U.K."

- During the closing days of 2002, the company announced that Gannett U.K. Limited, the parent company of Newsquest, had entered into an agreement with SMG plc to acquire SMG's publishing business for $346 million. SMG Publishing consists of three

Scottish regional newspapers: *The Herald, Sunday Herald*, and *Evening Times*; eleven specialist consumer and business-to-business magazine titles; and an online advertising and content business.

In announcing the agreement, Mr. McCorkindale said, "We are delighted that SMG Publishing will become part of Gannett. These publications extend our portfolio to Scotland for the first time and offer enhanced opportunities for growth."

Total assets: $13,111 million
Current ratio: 0.88
Common shares outstanding: 267 million
Return on 2002 shareholders' equity: 17.8%

		2002	2001	2000	1999	1998	1997	1996	1995
Revenues (millions)		6,422	6,300	6,222	5,260	5,121	4,730	4,421	4,007
Net income (millions)		1,160	831	972	919	816	713	531	477
Earnings per share		4.31	3.12	3.63	3.26	2.86	2.50	1.89	1.71
Dividends per share		.94	.89	.86	.82	.78	.74	.71	.68
Price	High	79.9	71.1	81.6	83.6	75.1	61.8	39.4	32.4
	Low	62.8	53.0	48.4	60.6	47.6	35.7	29.5	24.8

GROWTH AND INCOME

General Electric Company

3135 Easton Turnpike □ Fairfield, Connecticut 06431 □ (203) 373-2468 □ Direct dividend reinvestment plan available: (800) 786-2543 □ Web site: www.ge.com □ Listed: NYSE □ Ticker symbol: GE □ S&P rating: A+ □ Value Line financial strength rating: A++

Some companies manufacture locomotives, and some engineer thermoplastics for a living.

Others design high-end cooktops; still others operate national TV networks.

Not many, though, offer a full range of economy-fueling financial services on a global scale.

Fewer still make jet engines.

Or sophisticated medical scanners.

Or multi-megawatt gas-fired power turbines.

And only one company delivers on all these things.

Only GE.

Company Profile

General Electric, a superbly managed company, provides a broad range of industrial products and services. Under the stewardship of CEO Jack Welch, GE has transformed itself from operating as a maker of diverse industrial equipment to being a provider of a broad range of commercial and consumer services.

In 1980, manufacturing operations generated about 85 percent of operating profits; currently, services operations generate 70 percent of total operating profits. GE Capital (the company's enormous financing arm, and the world's largest nonbank financial operation) alone generates nearly 30 percent of operating profits.

General Electric is one of the world's largest corporations, with 2002 revenues of more than $132 billion. Although GE can trace its origins back to Thomas Edison, who invented the light bulb in 1879, the company was actually founded in 1892.

The company's broad diversification is clearly evident if you examine its components. Operations are divided into two groups: product, service, and media businesses; and GE Capital Services (GECS).

The product, service, and media group includes eleven businesses: aircraft engines, appliances, lighting, medical systems, the NBC television network, plastics, power systems, electrical distribution and control, information services, motors and industrial systems, and transportation systems.

In 2002, the company—often criticized for the complexity of its structure and the resulting opacity of its numbers—said it would break up GE Capital, by far its largest business, into four businesses. The new businesses are GE Commercial Finance, GE Insurance, GE Consumer Finance, and GE Equipment Management.

Shortcomings to Bear in Mind

- *Standard & Poor's Stock Reports* analyst Robert E. Friedman, CFA, had a few negative comments on GE at the end of 2002. "We forecast that over the next decade, average annual EPS growth may slow to 9 percent, with debt-adjusted return on equity (ROE) remaining at middling 7 percent to 10 percent levels. We believe that the sheer size of GE may make it very difficult for the company to match historical revenue and EPS growth rates, and ROE. Ironically, increasing sales contributions from GE's enormous financing and leasing segment (50 percent of revenues) may hamper long-term profitability, which would, in turn, justifiably compress GE's lofty P/E ratio. With profit margins of 8 percent-plus, GE Capital is one of the least profitable of the company's eight enormous operating segments."

Reasons to Buy

- When legendary CEO Jack Welch retired a couple of years ago, a number of exceptional executives were poised to take the reins. However, there could be only one winner. Two that didn't get the nod, resigned and took CEO positions elsewhere.

The winner was Jeffrey R. Immelt, then forty-four, president and chief executive of GE Medical Systems, a $7-billion segment of General Electric. The division, based in Waukesha, Wisconsin, is a world leader in medical diagnostic technology and information systems. Mr. Immelt took over that division in 1997 and had increased profits by 20 percent a year.

Effective at the end of November 2000, Mr. Immelt became president and chairman-elect. In announcing the GE board's decision, Mr. Welch described Immelt as "a natural leader, and ideally suited to lead GE for many years."

Immelt joined GE in 1982, and after a brief stint in corporate marketing, held a series of jobs in the company's plastics division. He moved to appliances in 1989 before becoming vice president of consumer service in 1991, and he was then made vice president of marketing and product management.

The transition to the top spot was enhanced by Robert Wright and Dennis Dammerman, two GE vice chairmen with extensive experience in the company's broadcasting and finance operations. They assured investors that Mr. Immelt would have qualified tutors to indoctrinate the new CEO in the GE operations he knows least.

- Over the years, General Electric has been honored on many occasions:
  - Global Most Admired Company— *Fortune* (1998, 1999, 2000, 2001, 2002)
  - World's Most Respected Company— *Financial Times* (1998, 1999, 2000, 2001)
  - America's Most Admired Company—*Fortune* (1998, 1999, 2000, 2001, 2002)
  - America's Greatest Wealth Creator—*Fortune* (1998, 1999, 2000)
  - Number One—*Forbes* 100 (1998, 1999, 2000)
  - Number One—*BusinessWeek* 1000 (1999)
  - Number One—*BusinessWeek*'s 25 Best Boards of Directors (2000)
  - Number Five—*Fortune* 500. If ranked independently, thirteen GE businesses would appear on the *Fortune* 500.
- GE paid $5.3 billion to acquire Heller Financial, a big domestic specialty lender, in 2001. Denis Nayden, chairman and CEO of GE Capital, said the takeover would lead to a "significant increase" in GE Capital's corporate finance business by adding Heller's international factoring operations, which are based in France. "The deal gives us a real chance to be a player in that game across Europe," said Mr. Nayden. In addition, he said that the acquisition gives GE a niche business in health care finance and strengthens GE Capital's presence in the market for small and medium-size corporate borrowers. Of the three specialty finance groups that changed hands in the first half of 2001, Heller was the most profitable.
- The key to GE's business plan is the requirement that businesses be first or second in market share in their industries. Those that fail to achieve this status are divested.
- Jack Welch, the previous CEO, developed a defect-reduction program called Six Sigma. Six Sigma contributes mightily to GE's earning growth. Think of sigma as a mark on a bell curve that measures standard deviation. Most companies have between 35,000 and 50,000 defects per million operations, or about 3 sigma. For GE, a defect could be anything from the misbilling of an NBC advertiser to faulty wiring in locomotives. Four years ago, engineers determined that the company was averaging 35,000 defects per million operations— or about 3.5 sigma. (The higher the sigma, the fewer the errors.) That was a better-than-average showing, but not enough for Welch's restless mind. He became maniacal about hitting his goal of reducing defects to the point where errors would be almost nonexistent; the goal he strove to achieve was 3.4 defects per million, or 6 sigma.
- Despite its huge size, the company continues to demonstrate growth. In the 1992–2002 period, earnings per share climbed from $0.42 to $1.51, a compound annual growth rate of 13.6 percent. (The company, moreover, has had twenty-six consecutive annual earnings increases.) In the same ten-year span, dividends per share advanced from $0.19 a share to $0.72, a growth rate of 14.2 percent.
- NBC, one of the nation's four major television networks and a GE business, is number one in virtually every segment of the schedule—morning, news, prime time, and late night—in terms of total viewers and the coveted adults-under-fifty audience. But NBC executives are most proud of something nobody paid much attention to until just a few years ago: their lead in the "75K-plus" demographic, which enables them to charge more for advertising air time. NBC's richer audience means it can make more

money. For instance, amid one of the worst advertising recessions in years, NBC is the most profitable of the four major networks.

- At the end of 2002, GE said it had developed a mobile mammogram unit that makes it easier for women to receive breast exams using digital technology. The unit, a mobile version of digital mammography equipment used in hospitals, is housed in a 30-foot van. It is a significant development in women's health care, said Lori Strachowski, a radiologist at San Francisco General Hospital, where the GE equipment was introduced. The van is especially useful in rural areas where women often lack access to mammography. With digital imaging, doctors and technicians can check breast images seconds after the images appear on a computer monitor. Digital mammography results in fewer recalls of women for a second mammogram when initial tests are inconclusive, said a GE spokesman.

- In an interview with Ron Insana, a leading financial commentator, late in 2002, Mr. Immelt said, "We're one of the few companies with AAA credit ratings; we have in excess of $15 billion of cash flow each year. We have numerous levers for growth—we've got technology, a strong sales forces, we're going to China—and acquisitions are just a relatively small part of how we look at things. I think this is a company that'll continue to grow between 5 percent and 10 percent each year from an organic standpoint, and then do acquisitions when we see strategic opportunity."

- "Chalk up another victory for GE Aircraft Engines (GEAE), based in Evendale, Ohio, near Cincinnati," said Stanley Holmes in an article in *BusinessWeek* in January 2003. "GE already controls 64 percent of the world market for commercial-jet engines, largely on the strength of its popular CFM56, which is used on narrow-body planes such as the Airbus A320 or Boeing Co.'s 737, and the GE-90, which carries Boeing's big 777 aloft. Yet GEAE executives believe the explosive growth in regional jets—those with up to 100 seats and ranges of up to 1,500 miles—will be the division's future."

Total assets: $575 billion
Current ratio: 0.62
Common shares outstanding: 9,950 million
Return on 2002 shareholders' equity: 22.7%

		2002	2001	2000	1999	1998	1997	1996	1995
Revenues (millions)		131,698	125,913	129,853	111,630	100,469	54,515	46,119	43,013
Net income (millions)		14,118	13,684	12,735	10,717	9,296	8,203	7,280	6,573
Earnings per share		1.51	1.41	1.27	1.07	0.93	0.83	0.73	0.65
Dividends/share		0.73	0.64	0.57	0.48	0.42	0.36	0.32	0.28
Price	High	41.8	53.6	60.5	53.2	34.6	25.5	17.7	12.2
	Low	21.4	28.5	41.6	31.4	23.0	16.0	11.6	8.3

GROWTH AND INCOME

General Motors Corporation

300 Renaissance Center □ Detroit, Michigan 48265 □ (313) 667-1500 □ Dividend reinvestment plan is available: (800) 331-9922 □ Web site: www.gm.com □ Listed: NYSE □ Ticker symbol: GM □ S&P rating: B □ Value Line financial strength rating: A

"A paramount factor contributing to GM's momentum is its success in the marketplace," said John Devine, vice chairman and chief financial officer of General Motors, in September of 2002. "GM increased its market share in 2001 in North America, Asia Pacific, and Latin America. GM's continued market success in North America in 2002 has been largely based on the success of new products such as the Cadillac CTS, the Pontiac Vibe, and the Chevrolet Trail-Blazer and GMC Envoy mid-utilities. Driving shareholder value at GM begins with the design, engineering, manufacturing, and sale of exciting new vehicles.

"Further evidence of momentum at GM was the recently announced positive results from the J. D. Power and Associates 2002 Initial Quality Survey and The Harbour Report North America 2002. In the J. D. Power report, which measures the number of problems consumers experience during the first ninety days of vehicle ownership, GM was recognized as the best-performing domestic manufacturer in initial quality, and three GM assembly plants were named best in initial quality for North America.

"Additionally, according to the Harbour report, which measures manufacturing productivity, GM outpaced all manufacturers with an overall productivity improvement of 4.5 percent. These kinds of operating results are key factors in driving employee, dealer, and stockholder enthusiasm—as well as financial results."

Mr. Devine went on to say, "It is not enough to deliver strong financial results for a year or two. Sustained strong financial performance over the long term must be the focus of our efforts. In that regard, GM management recently announced that the company's goal is to deliver earnings per share of $10 by mid-decade. GM earnings of $10 per share are expected to go a long way to driving both stockholder value and stock price."

Company Profile

General Motors Corporation, founded in 1908, is the world's largest vehicle manufacturer. GM designs, manufactures, and markets cars, trucks, automotive systems, heavy-duty transmissions, and locomotives worldwide.

Other substantial business interests include Hughes Electronics Corporation and General Motors Acceptance Corporation (GMAC).

GM cars and trucks are sold in close to 190 countries, and the company has manufacturing, assembly, or component operations in more than fifty countries.

General Motors' Operations

General Motors North American Operation manufactures vehicles for the following nameplates: Chevrolet, Pontiac, Buick, Cadillac, GMC, and Saturn.

General Motors International Operations meet the demands of customers outside North America, with vehicles designed and manufactured for the following nameplates: Opel, Vauxhall, Holden, Isuzu, and Saab.

General Motors Acceptance Corporation (GMAC) provides a broad range of financial services, including consumer vehicle financing, full-service leasing and fleet leasing, dealer financing, car and truck extended-service contracts, residential and commercial mortgage services, and vehicle and homeowners insurance. GMAC's business spans thirty-three markets around the world.

General Motors Locomotive Group manufactures diesel-electric locomotives, medium-speed diesel engines, locomotive components, locomotive services, and light-armored vehicles to a global customer base. In 2003, the company sold its light-armored vehicles to General Dynamics so that it could devote its full attention to making cars and trucks.

Allison Transmission Division is the world's largest producer of heavy-duty automatic transmissions for commercial-duty trucks and buses, off-highway equipment, and military vehicles.

Shortcomings to Bear in Mind

- Efraim Levy, CFA, an analyst with *Standard & Poor's Stock Reports*, had this negative comment at the end of 2002. "We are not especially enthusiastic about the recent purchase of Daewoo Motor, as we believe it will be difficult to generate a reasonable return on investment at the troubled Korean automaker, but the terms and risks appear more favorable than we expected."

- "In the late 1900s, auto makers, their finance companies, and banks pumped up vehicle sales with great deals on leases," according to David Welch, writing for *BusinessWeek* in November of 2002. "In the past year, the industry kept sales roaring with 0 percent financing deals. Both schemes helped move plenty of metal, but they also caused a flood of trade-ins and off-lease cars to dealers' lots this year. The influx of cars—combined with a soft economy—has sent used-car prices tumbling 4 percent this year, to below the average of 2000.

  "That's bad news for car makers, for several reasons. First, the industry will be stuck with 3.3 million cars coming off lease this year, many of which the car makers and finance companies will have to sell at a loss. Second, manufacturers have to stick with profit-eating 0 percent financing and rebates to keep buyers from snapping up the good deals on used cars."

Reasons to Buy

- Writing for the *Detroit News* on January 22, 2003, Ed Garsten said, "Calling General Motors Corp.'s North American operations 'leaps and bounds ahead of Detroit peers,' UBS Warburg analyst Saul Rubin upgraded the automaker's stock Tuesday to 'buy' from 'neutral,' and raised his 2003 earnings projection to $4.75 a share from $4.50.

  "The report was important because Rubin is a longtime bear on the outlook for Detroit automakers. At the same time, Rubin made an initial 2004 earnings estimate of $5.30 a share for GM.

  "He pointed to GM's improvement in quality and productivity and its standing as the low variable cost producer among major Detroit automakers as prime reasons for his upgrade."

- According to a General Motors spokesman, "The car of tomorrow won't float in the air or rocket back in time as Hollywood sometimes predicts. But tomorrow's cars and trucks are likely to be radically different—powered by an abundant, renewable energy source that is more than twice as efficient as gasoline and much cleaner.

  "And while it's one thing to talk about futuristic vehicles, it's even more impressive to let people actually get behind the wheel. With that in mind, GM is taking its advanced vehicles around the country to give government officials, journalists, and other opinion leaders a hands-on preview of some of the most advanced vehicles ever developed.

  "Vehicles featured in GM's Technology Tour include a wide range of advanced technologies—some on the road today, some a few years off. One current vehicle on the tour is the new 2002 Saturn VUE equipped with the optional continuously viable transmission that provides the same fuel efficiency of a manual transmission. The program is also giving an early look at gasoline-electric hybrid-powered trucks that will hit the road in 2004.

  "The real stars of the Tech Tour are the fuel cell vehicles. These vehicles, such as GM's HydroGen1 minivan, convert hydrogen to electric power. The only thing that comes from the tailpipe is clean water vapor. GM plans to begin offering production fuel cell vehicles toward the end of this decade."

■ General Motors is no longer an also-ran. It is closing the gap with its rivals. For most of the 1990s, Ford dominated the market for big pickups and SUVs, while GM, busy investing cash to revamp its aging car line, remained a perennial laggard. But thanks to improved styling, the freshest products on the market, coupled with aggressive pricing, GM has already grabbed the lead in full-size SUVS and pickups. Thanks to its popular new Chevy Tahoe, General Motors is taking market share in full-size SUVs, where profits are $10,000 to $15,000 per vehicle. Now it's out to beat a suddenly vulnerable Ford in Detroit's largest market: midsize SUVs, long ruled by Ford's popular Explorer.

■ In March of 2002, GM reported that its bread-and-butter Chevrolet division outsold archrival Ford division for the first time in more than a decade.

■ For the first time in years, many Wall Street analysts are recommending General Motors stock in 2002. According to Scott Hill, an analyst with Sanford C. Bernstein, "GM is doing all the right things right now."

■ In the all-important truck market, General Motors has taken the lead from Ford, thanks to hot-selling SUVs like the Chevrolet TrailBlazer and Tahoe, which have dramatically upgraded engines and interiors.

■ Just a few years ago, Cadillac was the number one luxury car. By 1997, it had lost that distinction to Lincoln. Three years later, moreover, it had sagged even further to the number-three slot. General Motors, for its part, is determined to reverse the slide. The company has pledged to invest $4.3 billion over the next three or four years to get back into the winner's circle. That amounts to 15 percent of GM's capital budget, aimed at a division that brings in a paltry 4 percent of GM's revenues.

By 2004, there will be as many as nine models, up from five. Among them are the following: a car-based sport utility in 2002; the 2001 Cadillac version of the Chevy Avalanche SUV; and the all-new Catera sport utility sedan. While the old Catera was modeled on the stodgy European Opel Omega, the new Catera is being completely redesigned. The new Cadillacs will not only be sportier, but they will be equipped with more powerful engines, better handling, and the edgy styling of the Evoq concept car. The Evoq is Cadillac's new two-seat roadster that was introduced in 2002 under a yet-to-be-determined name. "This is the best strategy Cadillac has had in two decades," said Christopher W. Cedergren, an analyst at marketing firm Nextrend, Inc.

Total assets: $371 billion
Current ratio: 0.74
Common shares outstanding: 560 million
Return on 2002 shareholders' equity: 24.8%

		2002	2001	2000	1999	1998	1997	1996	1995
Revenues (millions)		186,763	177,268	175,332	76,558	161,315	153,782	164,069	168,829
Net income (millions)		1,689	502	4,452	6,002	2,956	6,698	4,668	6,932
Earnings per share		3.35	1.77	6.68	8.53	5.21	8.70	5.72	7.28
Dividends per share		2.00	2.00	2.00	2.00	2.00	2.00	1.60	1.10
Price	High	68.2	67.8	94.6	94.9	76.7	72.4	59.4	53.1
	Low	30.8	39.2	48.4	59.8	47.1	52.3	45.8	37.4

Genuine Parts Company

2999 Circle 75 Parkway □ Atlanta, Georgia 30339 □ (770) 612-2048 □ Direct dividend reinvestment plan available: (800)568-3476 □ Web site: www.genpt.com □ Listed: NYSE □ Ticker symbol: GPC □ S&P rating: A □ Value Line financial strength rating: A++

"There are approximately 200 million vehicles on the road in the United States," said Mario Gabelli, in an interview published in *Barron's* on January 20, 2003. Mr. Gabelli is chairman of Gabelli Asset Management, Rye, New York. "The average age of a passenger car is 9.3 years, up from 8.1 years at the beginning of the 1990s. Light trucks are getting older, too.

"When I was growing up in the Bronx, a car lasted for 50,000 miles. Fifteen or twenty years ago, it lasted 100,000. Today, a new car will last 170,000 miles. In addition, years ago you used to get a two- or three-year warranty. Now, it's five years. So cars between five and nine years old are the sweet spot for parts consumption. Between 1996 and 2001, cars in the sweet spot declined 2.2 percent, to 61 million units. In the next five years, they are going to grow 15 percent, to 70 million. This is good news for Genuine Parts."

Mr. Gabelli went on to say, "Genuine Parts is a purveyor of expendable auto components. The company is a leader in its market. If inflation picks up, parts prices will rise, and its growth will rise more."

Company Profile

Genuine Parts is a service organization engaged in the distribution of automotive replacement parts, industrial replacement parts, office products, and electrical/electronic materials. As of 2002, Genuine Parts operated sixty-one NAPA warehouse distribution centers in the United States, about 840 company-owned jobbing stores, six Rayloc auto parts rebuilding plants, four Belkamp distribution centers, and about twelve Johnson Industries facilities.

The automotive parts segment (52 percent of 2002 revenues and 54 percent of profits) serves some 5,700 NAPA Auto Parts jobbing stores, including more than 900 company-owned stores. These stores sell to garages, service stations, car and truck dealers, fleet operators, leasing companies, and bus and truck lines, among other customers.

Rebuilt parts are distributed under the Rayloc brand name. Majority-owned Belkamp distributes service and supply items to NAPA distribution centers. UAP, Inc., is Canada's leading automotive parts distributor.

The industrial parts segment (27 percent of revenues and 25 percent of earnings) distributes more than 200,000 parts and related supply items, including bearings, power transmission equipment replacement parts, hydraulic and pneumatic products, material-handling components, agricultural and irrigation equipment, and related items from locations in forty-eight states, seven Mexican cities, and nine Canadian provinces, with some 500 branches, twenty-seven service centers, seven distribution centers, and three redistribution centers.

The office products group, S.P. Richards Company, (17 percent of company sales and 20 percent of profits) distributes more than 30,000 office products, such as information-processing supplies and office furniture, machines, and supplies. This operation is handled through forty-four facilities in twenty-eight states and in western Canada.

The company's smallest operation (only 4 percent of revenues and 1 percent of profits) is EIS, Inc., a wholesale distributor of materials and supplies to the electrical and electronic industries.

Shortcomings to Bear in Mind

- The company doesn't have a very spectacular growth record—at least not in recent years. In the 1992-2002 period, earnings per share inched ahead from $1.28 to $3.10, a compound annual growth rate of only 5.1 percent. Similar, the dividends advanced from $.67 to $1.16, a growth rate of only 5.6 percent.

Reasons to Buy

- On a more positive note, the company boasts forty-seven consecutive years of dividend increases. And the dividend is well covered by earnings. That's a hard combination to beat. Even so, I have tagged this stock for income, rather than growth.
- In spite of the poor economic conditions in 2002, Genuine Parts had positive results. Automotive parts sales rose 2.3 percent, while industrial parts revenues rose a modest 0.1 percent, and office products sales increased 1 percent. However, the company's smallest unit, EIS electrical/electronics, suffered a decline of 18 percent. Even so, overall sales of the company advanced 0.5 percent. To be sure, that is not exactly a robust achievement, unless you compare it to the economy as a whole.
- In February of 2003, John Casesa, an analyst with Merrill Lynch, told *Barron's* that Genuine Parts' business is "benefiting from the rising number and increasing complexity of vehicles."
- "The company's balance sheet is solid," said Justin T. Sebastiano, an analyst with *Value Line Investment Survey*, on January 3, 2003. "At September 30th, the long-term debt-to-total debt capital ratio stood at 24 percent. This already small debt burden likely fell to about 20

percent at the close of calendar 2002. We believe that management will use excess cash flow to reduce borrowings even further in 2003, to about $550 million, which would lower long-term debt to about 17 percent of capital.

"The annual dividend should not be a casualty as a result of this aggressive debt-reduction plan. In fact, we expect Genuine Parts to steadily increase the dividend over the next several years, in order to maintain its 49 percent/50 percent dividend payout ratio."

- Efraim Levy, CFA, an analyst with *Standard & Poor's Stock Reports*, had this to say in February of 2003. "Long-term prospects for GPC's auto part segment are enhanced by a rising number and increasing complexity of vehicles. The average vehicle in the U.S. is currently more than eight years old. The company should benefit from expanding market share, as long-term industry consolidation drives out smaller participants. It will also likely use its distribution strength to leverage sales of acquired parts companies."
- In February of 2003, Larry Prince, chairman of the board of directors, said, "We would characterize the year 2002 as another challenging one, but with a number of positives to report for Genuine Parts Company. First, we can report that both sales and earnings, before an accounting change, increased for the year. The increase was modest but returned us to the pattern of improving our results as we have done consistently through the years. Secondly, we can report that we remain financially strong and with a balance sheet that will support our opportunities and activities for the future."

Mr. Prince went on to say, "Despite facing a difficult economy with no immediate signs of substantial improvement, we look ahead to 2003 with plans for continued growth in both sales and earnings. Most of our gains will come from organic growth and increased unit volume, as we do not anticipate material acquisitions in our businesses, and we expect only modest price increases. We are fortunate to be market leaders in each of our four business segments, and the markets we serve remain highly fragmented. Growth opportunities are there for us, and we are optimistic that we can achieve market share gains as we look ahead."

- At the end of 2002, Argus Research Company said, "A rebound in the broader economy will eventually trickle down to the business sector, which will ultimately help GPC's non-Automotive segments realize sales gains. This, coupled with an increasing number of NAPA stores, keeps our outlook for the company bullish and makes the shares a good value in that respect."

Total assets: $4,020 million
Current ratio: 3.12
Common shares outstanding: 175 million
Return on 2002 shareholders' equity: 15.7%

	2002	2001	2000	1999	1998	1997	1996	1995
Revenues (millions)	8,259	8,221	8,370	7,982	6,614	6,005	5,721	5,262
Net income (millions)	367	362	385	378	356	342	330	309
Earnings per share	2.10	2.08	2.20	2.11	1.98	1.90	1.82	1.68
Dividends per share	1.16	1.14	1.10	1.04	.99	.96	.89	.84
Price High	38.8	37.9	26.7	35.8	38.3	35.9	31.7	28.0
Low	27.1	23.9	18.3	22.3	28.3	28.7	26.7	23.7

AGGRESSIVE GROWTH

The Gillette Company

Prudential Tower Building □ Boston, Massachusetts 02199-8004 □ (617) 421-7968 □ Listed: NYSE □ Direct dividend reinvestment plan available: (888) 218-2841 □ Web site: www.gillette.com □ Ticker symbol: G □ S&P rating: A- □ Value Line Financial Strength A+

In recent years, Gillette—once a revered growth stock—has fallen from favor and has not been included in this book. Now, under the leadership of Jim Kilts, a sharp turnaround has investors aware that it's time to take another look at Gillette.

According to Katrina Brooker, writing for *Fortune* magazine in December of 2002, "When he took over Gillette in February 2001, Kilts inherited one of the biggest headaches in consumer products. The once high-flying company, the maker of Mach3 razors, Duracell batteries, and Oral-B toothbrushes, had missed its earnings for fourteen consecutive quarters. Neither sales nor earnings had grown in five years. Two-thirds of Gillette's products were losing share."

Ms. Brooker went on to say, "It was a problem tailor-made for Kilts. When it comes to turning around troubled businesses, few managers are as experienced or successful as he is. At fifty-four, he's been involved in more than a dozen turnarounds."

"It was a natural move," recalls Warren Buffett, a Gillette board member who controls 9 percent of its stock. He made up his mind about hiring Kilts—the first outside CEO Gillette has had in seventy years—after just one meeting.

Some months after talking the helm, Jim Kilts commented on what he has in mind to fix the business.

"We began our financial turnaround and business transformation by reintroducing reality into our business objectives. We calibrated realistic targets and moved ahead forcefully.

• We increased marketing support to stabilize shares.

• We stopped trade loading and related practices. (Note: Trade loading is a pernicious practice used by salesmen. To hit their numbers each quarter, they were willing to do anything—offer cut-rate deals, rearrange product packaging—whatever it took to make a deal.)

• We launched a wide-ranging attack on costs.

• We focused on improving productivity and asset management.

• And we started upgrading our processes and strengthening our organization."

Mr. Kilts went on to say, "While these efforts are still in their early stages, the initial results are very encouraging. The business transformation and financial turnaround are in gear. Our aggressive programs to stabilize—and then reverse declining market shares—are paying off.

"At the end of 2000, Gillette was losing share in categories representing 65 percent of our business; by the end of 2001, we were gaining share in 64 percent. Our initiative to eliminate excess trade inventories of blades and batteries was successful, hitting our targeted levels. Our inventories and our receivables were reduced to levels not seen in over twenty years."

Company Profile

Founded in 1901, the Gillette Company is the world leader in male grooming, a category that includes blades, razors, and shaving preparations. Gillette also holds the number one position worldwide in selected female grooming products, such as wet shaving products and hair depilation devices.

The company holds the number one position worldwide in manual and power toothbrushes and is the world leader in alkaline batteries.

According to the company, "Our focus is on placing resources behind Gillette's three core businesses: grooming, batteries, and oral care. Our core businesses account for nearly 80 percent of our sales and 90 percent of our profits. We are—in all three—the undisputed global leader.

"Some of our core brands include:
• Gillette Mach3
• Gillette for Women Venus
• Gillette Series
• Right Guard
• Duracell Copper Top
• Oral-B
• Braun Oral-B
• Braun"

Gillette manufacturing operations are conducted at thirty-four facilities in fifteen countries. Products are distributed through wholesalers, retailers, and agents in more than 200 countries and territories.

Shortcomings to Bear in Mind

■ In January 2003, Energizer Holdings, Inc., announced plans to expand beyond batteries and pay $930 million in cash for the Schick-Wilkinson Sword shaving business from Pfizer. Razors and batteries are often sold in the same retail chains, according to Energizer's CEO Pat Mulcahy. "Energizer and Schick are very compatible with common customers, and similar distribution channels, high-speed manufacturing, and product innovation capabilities, and corporate cultures."

In an article in the *Boston Globe* on January 22, 2003, Chris Reidy wrote, "The Energizer transaction 'means tougher competition' for Gillette, said

Fredric Russell of Fredric E. Russell Investment Management Co., which owns 50,000 Gillette shares."

- Kenneth A. Nugent, an analyst with *Value Line Investment Survey*, was less than enthusiastic about Gillette at the end of 2002. "Neutrally ranked Gillette shares are not an outstanding selection for the long haul. Although we have increased our sales and earnings projections through 2005–2007, the stock offers lackluster capital appreciation potential over that time frame."

Reasons to Buy

- At the end of 2002, Howard Choe, an analyst with *Standard & Poor's Stock Reports*, had these positive remarks: "The company continues to sustain sales growth through new product introductions and increased penetration in developing markets. Over the past year, the company has regained market share in razors and batteries, reduced inventory and receivables, cut costs, and improved return on capital. Although the battery business remains difficult, management has managed to raise margins on the business. With the company controlling some of the leading global consumer brands and maintaining the industry's highest margins, we believe the shares warrant a premium to peers."

- Although Gillette is often regarded as primarily a razor blade company, investors should not overlook its other interests, such as Braun. In 2002, Mr. Kilts had these comments on that operation. "One of the best illustrations of strategic redirection can be found with our Braun business. Early last year, the constant question was whether Braun belonged in the Gillette portfolio. Now, based on almost any metric, Braun has made a remarkable turnaround, driven by the change in strategy.

"In the past, Braun operated as a small appliance company, seeking to broaden its product line and extend its geographic reach. The new strategic governing statement gives Braun a narrowed charge. It will focus on dry shaving, ensure that each product line minimally returns greater than its cost of capital, and restrict distribution to profitable geographics.

"That strategic change has made all the difference. Profit from operations, operating margin, and return on assets each increased."

- The Braun Oral-B 3D Excel is a top-of-the-line power toothbrush featuring advanced technology that leaves teeth with "a remarkably clean, fresh feeling similar to that experienced after a professional cleaning," said a company spokesman. "The Braun Oral-B 3D Excel outperforms ordinary toothbrushes in the key areas of plaque removal, gingivitis reduction, and the reduction of gingival bleeding."

- Duracell, another troubled segment, has also responded to Mr. Kilts's magic touch. In 2002, he said, "Equally dramatic, was our strategic redirection of the battery business, which had been focused on a trade-up strategy in an effort to move consumers from the mainstream brand—Duracell Copper & Black—to the super-premium brand—Duracell Ultra. While trade-up works well in shaving, it lost Duracell nearly 7 share points in the U.S. since its introduction.

"Therefore, the strategic redirection for Duracell was to go back to basics by improving and focusing marketing efforts predominantly on Copper & Black, which was restaged as Copper Top. The results were dramatic. In the U.S., Duracell went from twenty-one consecutive months of market share declines to seven consecutive months of market share growth."

- For the category that is Gillette's largest, Blades & Razors, the new strategic governing statement, said Mr. Kilts, "aims to increase financial returns so they match the incredible marketplace successes. Gillette is the clear market leader in a very advantaged category. Gillette's value shares of the U.S. blade and razor market last year reached the highest levels in forty years." Mr. Kilts went on to say, "Driving this growth has been the exceptional marketplace performance of our premium shaving systems, Mach3 and Gillette for Women Venus."

In the spring of 2002, the company made the U.S. introduction of "an exceptional new product, the Mach3-Turbo, with thirty-five patents protecting its technologies and features, that we're confident will drive category growth and further increase our share."

- Every day, more than 1 billion people around the world use one or more Gillette products. From blades and razors to toothbrushes, from alkaline batteries to oral care appliances, Gillette is the world leader in nearly a dozen major consumer product categories.

According to a company spokesman, "And we are constantly challenging ourselves to develop new products. An example is Venus, our new shaving system for women. Gillette for Women Venus combines breakthrough design with easy storage to redefine women's shaving.

"In recent years, Gillette has introduced more than twenty new products annually. Among these new products were the Gillette Mach3 shaving system, the Duracell Ultra line of premium-performing alkaline batteries, the Braun Oral-B 3D Excel power toothbrush, and the premium Oral-B CrossAction manual toothbrush."

Total assets: $9,963 million
Current ratio: 0.94
Return on 2002 equity: 15.9%
Common shares outstanding: 1,058 million

	2002	2001	2000	1999	1998	1997	1996	1995
Revenues (millions)	8,453	8,084	9,295	9,898	10,056	10,062	9,698	6,795
Net income (millions)	1,216	1,045	1,251	1,260	1,428	1,427	1,232	824
Earnings per share	1.15	.86	1.18	1.15	1.27	1.28	1.11	.93
Dividends per share	.65	.65	.65	.59	.51	.43	.36	.30
Price High	37.3	36.4	43.0	64.4	62.7	53.2	38.9	27.7
Low	27.6	24.5	27.1	33.1	35.3	36.0	24.1	17.7

CONSERVATIVE GROWTH

W. W. Grainger, Inc.

100 Grainger Parkway □ Lake Forest Illinois 60045-5201 □ (847) 535-0881 □ Dividend reinvestment plan not available □ Web site: www.grainger.com □ Listed: NYSE □ Ticker symbol: GWW □ S&P rating: A- □ Value Line financial strength rating: A+

"When it is completed by the end of 2003, Grainger's new logistics network should generate considerable cost savings," said a spokesman for the company in 2002. "We will reduce redundant inventory and minimize the handling of products as we eliminate a distribution layer and consolidate shipping at the distribution centers.

"Also, greater automation at each facility will help our employees pick upwards of 50 percent more products per hour. As a result of these improvements, we will reduce headcount by approximately 1,000 jobs—half from the distribution centers, and half from the branches. These improvements will help return Grainger's operating margins to historic levels."

Company Profile

Dating back to 1928, W. W. Grainger is the leading North American distributor of products used by businesses and institutions to maintain, repair, and operate their facilities. The company offers a breadth of maintenance, repair, and operating (MRO) solutions by combining products, services, and information. It tailors its capabilities with a view toward providing the lowest total cost MRO solution to its customers.

Grainger helps customers get the job done by offering the broadest product selection in the industry. The ability to find the right products at competitive prices, backed by superior customer service and reliable information, makes customers turn to Grainger more than 100,000 times a day.

Customers can choose convenient ways to do business with Grainger: over the telephone, at the local Grainger's branch, or online at the company's Web site, www.grainger.com. Across all channels, there are more than 1,900 trained customer service associates available to assist customers. Once the order is placed, it is filled either at one of nearly 400 branches or shipped same day from one of nine distribution centers by a state-of-the-art logistics network.

The company also has internal business support functions that provide coordination and guidance in the areas of accounting, administrative services, business development, communications, compensation and benefits, employee development, enterprise systems, finance, human resources, industrial relations, investor relations, insurance and risk management, internal audit, international operations, legal, real estate and construction services, security and safety, taxes, and treasury services.

Grainger does not engage in basic or substantive product research and development activities. New items are added regularly to the company's product line on the basis of market information and by recommendations from its employees, customers, suppliers, as well as by other factors. However, the company's research and development efforts are focused on methods of serving customers and the product distribution process.

Grainger's supply chain has evolved since the company was launched in 1927. As the company has grown, its distribution network has kept up. With a tenfold increase in its product lines over the past two decades, Grainger has developed a sophisticated platform for receiving products, shipping to customers, and replenishing branches.

In 2002, Grainger entered the second year of its three-year distribution network redesign for a capital cost of more than $200 million. The multiyear project is expected to provide more than $20 million in annual cost savings to the company when completed. The five new and four redesigned facilities will take over most of the $1 billion in annual shipping currently processed through the branches. In addition, by removing a step in the logistics system, Grainger employees won't handle the same product multiple times, a change that will save time and money. The company estimates about a $100-million reduction in inventory as a result of eliminating the regional distribution layer.

Shortcomings to Bear in Mind

- Grainger is not immune to the vagaries of the business cycle. For instance, 2001 "was a challenging one for Grainger," according to CEO Richard L. Keyser.

"Sales progressively weakened throughout the year as the economy softened, and December (2001) was the weakest month in recent memory. In the second quarter, we made some difficult decisions about the direction of our business. We elected to discontinue operations of Material Logic, part of our e-commerce business that was taking too long to mature. We also wrote down other related investments. Instead, we are concentrating on Web sites central to our growth, particularly www.grainger.com. In total, we recorded charges of $37 million, or thirty-nine cents a share. Our reported results reflect these charges."

- At the beginning of 2003, Mr. Keyser was still cautious about the prospects for the year ahead. He said, "In spite of a drop-off in sales during the last half of December, we delivered increased sales and earnings for the fourth quarter. Looking forward, we are cautious, as recent industry trends indicate continued softness, and we are experiencing a difficult sales environment in January.

"Even with the slow start to the year, we are still committed to our strategic initiatives. Our major effort remains completing the transformation of our logistics network. We are investing heavily in the first quarter, but we don't expect to see the benefits until 2004. Improved sales, coupled with lower supply chain costs, should position Grainger well going forward."

Reasons to Buy

- With almost 400 branches across the United States, most of Grainger's customers are located within twenty minutes of a branch. Grainger's Canadian operation has 184 locations, and in 2001 the company opened three branches in Mexico.

Proximity is a big advantage, since customers' needs frequently are unplanned. To help customers find what they need in a hurry, Grainger is increasing its investment in local inventory, tailoring the product to the demand patterns seen in each area.

Grainger is also transitioning much of the telephone call volume to service centers and consolidating shipping in its distribution centers, helping branch personnel remain focused on attending to the needs of customers who stop by.

Branches range in size to meet a variety of customer needs. From the smallest facility (a 1,150-square-foot double-wide trailer at Denver International Airport, replenished twice a day by another nearby branch) to Cranford, New Jersey (57,750 square feet and boasting an extensive display area), Grainger's branch network offers customers a quick and convenient solution to the problems they face every day.

- The Grainger Web site has been the industry leader since 1995. By logging on to www.grainger.com, Grainger customers have fast and easy access to maintenance, repair and operating supplies, and repair parts. All orders placed over the Internet transfer seamlessly to one of Grainger's distribution centers for shipping or to branches for will call. An order over the Web offers Grainger a 200-basis-point cost advantage over a traditional order billed in a branch. (One hundred basis points equal 1 percent).

More than 4,000 customer locations are connected to the Grainger Web site through e-procurement systems. More than 200,000 customers have purchased via the Grainger Web site to date.

- Grainger is the only U.S. distributor in the facilities maintenance industry with its own repair parts business, a competitive edge for customers seeking to reduce their number of suppliers. Grainger Parts offers customers access to more than 2.5

million repair parts and accessories from more than 550 leading commercial and industrial original equipment manufacturers. Because parts are difficult to locate and because they represent a cost savings to customers, Grainger's service commands a premium.

Customers can purchase from Grainger Parts by telephone or online at *www.grainger.com*. The Internet channel increases customers' awareness of parts availability and selection. Trained technical representatives are also available to assist customers with product selection and availability, pricing, and order status twenty-four hours a day, seven days a week.

- Grainger Global Sourcing is a direct importer of more than 3,600 high-quality, competitively priced products sourced outside the United States. With procurement offices in Lake Forest, Illinois, and in Hong Kong, Grainger Global Sourcing ensures that all suppliers meet stringent quality requirements on all products.

- Sourcing is another of Grainger's competitive advantages. For customers who can't find what they are looking for in the Grainger catalog, Grainger offer FindMRO sourcing services. With access to thousands of brands and more than 5 million products, FindMRO sources hard-to-find maintenance, repair, and operating supplies for Grainger customers, providing them with a one-stop shopping experience.

FindMRO played a key role in Grainger's response to the terrorist attacks on September 11, 2001. FindMRO sourced nearly $1 million worth of critical products for the relief efforts, including hydraulic rescue tools, rebar cutters, tents, traffic barriers, and heat-resistant boots.

- Lab Safety Supply is a wholly owned subsidiary of Grainger and the leading business-to-business direct marketer of safety and other industrial products in North America. A Grainger business since 1992, Lab Safety Supply is tailored for customers who know the products they need, do not require face-to-face interaction, and prefer ordering through a catalog or online.

In 2001, Lab Safety Supply acquired The Ben Meadows Company, a $20-million business-to-business direct marketer of equipment for the natural resources and forestry management market. This relationship with Ben Meadows is expected to provide Lab Safety Supply with a leading position in the environmental and forestry markets, a $500-million industry.

Total assets: $2,417 million
Current ratio: 2.37
Common shares outstanding: 91 million
Return on 2002 shareholders' equity: 14%

	2002	2001	2000	1999	1998	1997	1996	1995
Revenues (millions)	4,643	4,754	4,977	4,534	4,341	4,137	3,537	3,277
Net income (millions)	235	211	175	181	238	232	208	187
Earnings per share	2.50	2.23	1.86	1.92	2.44	2.27	2.02	1.82
Dividends per share	.72	.70	.67	.63	.59	.53	.49	.45
Price High	59.4	49.0	56.9	58.1	54.7	49.9	40.8	33.8
Low	39.2	29.5	24.3	36.9	36.4	35.3	31.3	27.8

Harman International Industries, Inc.

1101 Pennsylvania Avenue, N.W. ▢ Suite 1010 ▢ Washington, D.C. 20004 ▢ (818) 893-8411 ▢ Dividend reinvestment plan not available ▢ Web site: www.harman.com ▢ Fiscal years end June 30 ▢ Listed: NYSE ▢ Ticker symbol: HAR ▢ S&P rating: B+ ▢ Value Line financial strength rating: B++

Harman Multimedia, a leading provider of audio products for the desktop, announced in early 2003 the JBL Invader audio system, the company's first 4.1 speaker system. JBL Invader is the direct result of customer requests for a high-performance surround-sound computer audio system combining high fidelity and innovative design worthy of the JBL brand.

The eighty-watt, 4.1 multichannel audio system includes four satellites and a powerful subwoofer to produce a high-performance sound experience for gaming, DVD playback, and music. JBL Invader can also function as a 2.1 system to create stunning stereo imaging for CDs and MP3s.

"After introducing the award-winning Soundsticks and Creature products, Harman Multimedia is now launching an innovative 4.1 system optimized for gamers and music aficionados," said James A. Druckrey, president of Harman Multimedia. "JBL Invader is the next step for consumers looking for a powerful surround-sound experience offering unsurpassed audio quality and product design."

The JBL Invader audio system uses simple interconnects that provide effortless control of volume, treble, and subwoofer levels with minimal desktop wiring. The powerful thirty-two-watt subwoofer incorporates a new proprietary port design and a MAGNUM transducer providing clean, strong bass. The four twelve-watt satellite speakers complement the subwoofer to provide the level of high sound quality consumers desire for games, DVDs, and music.

JBL Invader is compatible with all analog stereo and multichannel sound cards in desktop and laptop computers, as well as MP3 players and personal CD players. It is available online at *www.jblinvader.com* for a suggested retail price of $179.99 and at national retailers.

Company Profile

For more than five decades, Harman International has been a leader and innovator in creating loudspeakers and electronic audio products that deliver superior sound. The company designs, manufactures, and markets high-fidelity audio products and audio systems for consumer and professional use. What's more, Harman also has a stake in the manufacture of infotainment systems for many of the major automotive makers of the world. (Infotainment systems combine audio, video, navigation, telecoms, and Internet access.)

Harman International has developed, both internally and through a series of strategic acquisitions, a broad range of product offerings sold in its principal markets under renowned brand names (which are also expensive!). The company's development efforts aim to secure engineering, manufacturing, and marketing leadership and to strengthen its ability to provide total audio system solutions to its customers.

Harman serves two major audio markets: consumer and professional. The Consumer Systems market, which accounted for 77 percent of sales in fiscal 2002, makes loudspeakers, audio electronics, and infotainment systems for vehicles, as well as loudspeakers and electronics for home video, audio, and computer applications. These products are sold under such brand names as JBL, Infinity, Harman Kardon,

Lexicon, Becker, Mark Levinson, Proceed, Revel, and AudioAccess.

The Professional Group, which accounted for 23 percent of sales in 2002, manufactures products in all significant segments of the professional audio market. It offers complete system solutions to professional installations and users around the globe. The Professional Group includes JBL, Professional, Soundcraft, Crown, DOD, Digitech, dbx, AKG, BSS, and Studer. Sales to Daimler-Chrysler accounted for 21 percent of sales in fiscal 2002.

Shortcomings to Bear in Mind

- The CEO of the company is eighty-three-year-old Sidney Harman. He is a bit of a curmudgeon, according to an article in *The Economist*, a prestigious British publication. "Mr. Harman's customers do his marketing for him ('Lexus sells its cars as containers for our sound system. It's marvelous'). But he is in no hurry to enlighten Wall Street about the benefits this will bring to his margins. Let the analysts work it out in their own time, he says. Mr. Harman is 'not very damn interested' in public relations. His offices in Washington are within a stone's throw of the center of American political power, but he has never hired a lobbyist. He makes announcements, he says, when he has something to announce. He cares little that few have noticed his achievements. His products, quite literally, speak for themselves."

Reasons to Buy

- The company's management is convinced that a number of growth opportunities exist through the following channels:
  - Automotive original equipment manufacturer customers
  - Higher penetration levels within existing models
  - Increases in the number of models offering its audio systems
  - Supply agreements with additional automakers
  - Increases in per-vehicle content through the provision of integrated infotainment systems
  - New hardware and software licensing agreements.

- "Harman International should continue to reap gains from large auto-OEM (original equipment manufacturer) sales increases," said Damon Churchwell, an analyst with *Value Line Investment Survey*, on January 17, 2003. "Auto-OEM sales ought to continue to grow at a blistering pace, as Harman is rolling out its higher-margined 'infotainment' and navigation systems.

  "Demand for BMW 7 series vehicle has been solid, and several other European automobiles are being equipped with the products this year." The *Value Line* analyst also said, "Looking ahead, we expect Harman to penetrate the domestic auto market. In fiscal 2004, its largest OEM customer, Chrysler, will begin installing infotainment systems in many vehicles."

- "In fiscal 2002, we opened a state-of-the-art research facility in Farmington Hills, Michigan to create a U.S. counterpart to the extraordinary capability we have established in Europe," said Sidney Harman. "Today, Harman employs more than 1,200 engineers skilled in the digital world and motivated by the conviction that they are revolutionizing the automotive industry.

  "The revolution is chronicled virtually daily by automotive industry and general business publications and has led to a growing body of analysis and review. The Arthur D. Little Company produced a strategic study for the period November 2001 through March 2002, entitled 'How Electrics-Electronics Will

Change the Automotive Landscape.' Fifty-five companies contributed to the findings in the report which states, 'Growth projections from various sources all indicate the tremendous impact of E-E on the automotive industry. Over the next few years, in-vehicle infotainment is set to explode, connecting both driver and passenger to any available information and/or enter-tainment.'

"The study predicts that in the year 2010 no less than 50 percent of the elec-tric-electronic content of the car will be devoted to infotainment. Clearly, our work is becoming the centerpiece of the automobile."

■ Harman Professional audio systems serve Washington's John F. Kennedy Center, the home of the arts in the nation's capital. They serve the Amer-ican Airline Center in Dallas, home of the NBA Mavericks and NHL Stars; Ford Field in Detroit, home of the NFL Lions; Pro Player Stadium in Miami, home of the NFL Dolphins; and USTA Center, site of the U.S. Open Tennis Tournament in New York. Upcoming are the new Disney Concert Hall in Los Angeles and the new San Diego Padres major league baseball stadium.

Total assets: $1,480 million
Current ratio: 2.03
Common shares outstanding: 32 million
Return on 2002 shareholders' equity: 12.1%

	2002	2001	2000	1999	1998	1997	1996	1995
Revenues (millions)	1,826	1,717	1,678	1,500	1,513	1,474	1,362	1,170
Net income (millions)	63	58	73	58	54	55	52	41
Earnings per share	1.87	1.72	2.07	1.60	1.43	1.48	1.58	1.30
Dividends per share	.10	.10	.10	.10	.10	.10	.10	.09
Price High	65.3	46.6	50.3	28.1	23.4	28.5	28.3	24.9
Low	38.2	23.3	27.5	17.1	15.8	16.2	16.0	16.2

AGGRESSIVE GROWTH

Health Management Associates, Inc.

5811 Pelican Bay Boulevard □ Suite 500 □ Naples, Florida 34108-2710 □ (941) 598-3104 □ Dividend reinvestment plan not available □ Fiscal years end September 30 □ Listed: NYSE □ Web site: www.hma-corp.com □ Ticker symbol: HMA □ S&P rating: B+ □ Value Line financial strength rating: B+

Fiscal 2002 was once again notable for acquisitions for Health Management Asso-ciates, a leading manager of acute-care hos-pitals, operating in fourteen states. The company completed five transactions in 2002. This represented a total of 650 licensed beds and an expansion of its oper-ations into two new states, Tennessee and Texas. "HMA began fiscal 2002 with an objective of acquiring between two and four hospitals over the course of the year," said CEO Joseph V. Vumbacco in October

of 2002. "On May 1st, we exceeded that objective by acquiring the 172-bed Mesquite Community Hospital from Manor Care, Inc. HMA has already infused capital into needed areas, recruiting neces-sary physicians, and has reversed out-migration trends in these acquired hospi-tals. Without exception, these hospitals have exceeded our expectations and repre-sent tremendous opportunities for HMA to improve the access to and quality of the health care being delivered.

"With over 200 non-urban acquisition opportunities identified in just the fourteen states in which HMA already currently has operations, we believe that there are significant opportunities available to continue our growth rate for the foreseeable future."

Acquisitions, to be sure, are the company's primary route to expansion. However, new construction is also an option. On June 14, 2002, HMA received approval from the State of Florida's Agency for Health Care Administration to build a 100-bed hospital in Collier Country, Florida. "We are very excited about this wonderful opportunity to serve Collier County," said Mr. Vumbacco. "Naples and the Collier County area is the second-fastest-growing community in the United States, and we believe that there is a true need for this hospital, as shown by the overwhelming community support."

Company Profile

Health Management Associates is the premier operator of acute-care hospitals in the Southeast and Southwest regions of non-urban America. As of October 2002, the company operated forty-four hospitals in fourteen states, with a total of 5,987 licensed beds.

For the most part, the company seeks to acquire hospitals with 100 to 300 beds in high-growth, non-urban areas, with populations of 30,000 to 400,000, and with an established group of doctors. Many of these institutions are unprofitable at the time they are acquired.

"The company's acute-care hospitals offer a broad range of medical and surgical services," according to Phillip M. Seligman, an analyst with *Standard & Poor's Stock Reports*, "including inpatient care, intensive and cardiac care, diagnostic services, and emergency services that are physician-staffed twenty-four hours a day, seven days a week. HMA also provides outpatient services such as one-day surgery, laboratory, X-ray, respi-

ratory therapy, cardiology, and physical therapy. Some of the hospitals provide specialty services such as oncology, radiation therapy, CT scanning, MRI imaging, lithotripsy, and full-service obstetrics."

When HMA acquires a hospital, it immediately sets out to upgrade the quality of health care delivery and simultaneously expand its medical services so that except in rare instances, community residents no longer need to commute to major urban centers for specialty medical care. Apart from upgrading additional medical services, HMA upgrades the physical facility to today's technology. It also introduces a number of proven hospital management practices that greatly improve a patient's hospitalization experience, principally through decentralization management with centralized operating systems.

The company's strategy enables local physicians to refer more patients to the HMA community hospital than they could before. In addition, patients from outlying areas can now use the upgraded HMA health care centers—previously, they journeyed long distances to larger city hospitals. What's more, the strategy enables HMA to generate substantially more revenue per dollar of fixed cost than the same hospitals did before Health Management Associates acquired them.

Shortcomings to Bear in Mind

- One problem not soon to be solved is the critical shortage of registered nurses. It has plagued the entire hospital industry. To retain nurses and attract more to the company's hospitals will require, among other things, higher salaries.
- Although most people need hospital care from time to time, not everyone can afford to pay. In the final quarter of 2002, for instance, bad-debt expense was 7.8 percent, about the same as it was for the same quarter a year earlier. In order to alleviate the problem, management

believes "that opportunities exist at its most recent acquisitions to further improve these results." Mr. Vumbacco said, "Our primary focus in the business office is cash collections. From front-end collections and accurate billing, to financial assistance qualification and follow-up collection efforts to ensure accurate reimbursement, we are seeing the results."

Reasons to Buy

- In a recent report by *Standard & Poor's Stock Reports*, the analyst said, "HMA and its industry peers may see greater regulatory scrutiny regarding pricing and industry consolidation, following recent developments surrounding Tenet Healthcare (THC). We don't think the normal, annual increases in Medicare payments will end, but Medicare outlier payments may become more restricted. This should impact HMA little, as outlier payments account for a small fraction of its revenues. Although it's been investing in emergency room operations and new equipment, as well as physician recruitment to enhance and expand its services, it has neither the facilities nor specialists that normally handle high acuity cases that can result in outlier payments."

  In November of 2002, the company said that its outlier reimbursements were "in line" with the rest of the hospital industry. HMA's payments represented 4.1 percent of Medicare inpatient revenue is fiscal 2002, or 1.1 percent of Health Management's total sales, said Mr. Vumbacco. He made the comments as Tenet Healthcare Corporation, the nation's number-two hospital chain, faced a government audit of the so-called outlier payments, which Medicare makes for patients whose care costs far more than average.

- *Value Line Investment Survey* had a similar view of the company in the fall of 2002. The analyst, Erik M. Manning, had this to say, "This equity seems likely

to do well, relative to both the year-ahead market and over the three- to five-year pull. We project continued rapid growth in earnings, reflecting the company's ongoing advances in same-hospital revenues via larger amounts of surgeries and admissions. It's worth noting that this assumption does not take into account potential acquisitions that may take place in the future."

- Goldman Sachs, a leading brokerage firm, made some favorable comments in late 2002. "We continue to believe that HMA shares offer investors an attractive opportunity to buy a self-financing, mid-cap growth story with low execution risk and a company that generates among the highest returns on capital in our health-care facilities coverage universe."

- In the past ten years (1992–2002), earnings per share advanced every year, climbing from $.10 to $.97, a compound annual growth rate of 25.5 percent. That's why I have labeled this stock "aggressive growth." Nor was this performance halted in the most recent fiscal year, which ended September 30, 2002. In that span, earnings per share increased 21 percent, climbing to $.97, compared with $.80 in 2001.

- Total admissions for the twelve-month period ending September 30, 2002, increased 15.4 percent, reflecting the admission contribution from hospitals acquired during the period. HMA also reported total net patient service revenue for the twelve-month period of about $2.3 billion, an increase of 20 percent in the same period of the prior year.

- On November 6, 2001, *Standard & Poor's* added Health Management Associates to its S&P 500 Index. "This inclusion reflects our leading position in the acute-care hospital industry over a long period of time and marks a significant milestone in our history," said Mr. Vumbacco.

Total assets: $2,364 million
Current ratio: 2.42
Common shares outstanding: 242 million
Return on 2002 shareholders' equity: 18.3%

	2002	2001	2000	1999	1998	1997	1996	1995
Revenues (millions)	2,263	1,880	1,578	1,356	1,139	896	714	531
Net income (millions)	346	195	168	150	137	108	84	63
Earnings per share	.97	.80	.68	.59	.54	.43	.34	.26
Dividends per share	Nil	—	—	—	—	—	—	—
Price High	23.0	22.2	22.8	21.6	25.8	17.7	11.1	8.0
Low	16.2	13.4	9.6	7.0	14.9	9.5	7.4	4.6

CONSERVATIVE GROWTH

Hormel Foods Corporation

1 Hormel Place □ Austin, Minnesota 55912-3680 □ (507) 437-5007 □ Dividend reinvestment plan is available: (877) 536-3559 □ Fiscal years end on the last Saturday of October □ Listed: NYSE □ Web site: www.hormel.com □ Ticker symbol: HRL □ S&P rating: A □ Value Line financial strength rating: A

"Under the leadership of CEO Joel Johnson (a former Kraft executive), Hormel has become a leader in the pork industry by focusing on offering more convenient, value-added products. The company has grown sales and earnings primarily by expanding into higher-margin, value-added meat products. Between 1997 and 2001, sales and operating profit grew at a compound annual rate of 6.1 percent and 15.4 percent, respectively." This comment was made by an analyst with Goldman Sachs, a leading brokerage firm.

Published in 2002, the report also pointed out, "We believe Hormel has a number of key strengths that differentiate it from its competitors. These strengths include: 1) Above-average growth potential; 2) Improving product mix; 3) Less earnings volatility compared to other protein companies, and 4) Improving return on invested capital."

Company Profile

Founded by George A. Hormel in 1891 in Austin, Minnesota, Hormel Corporation is a multinational manufacturer of consumer-branded meat and food products, many of which are among the best-known and most trusted in the food industry. The company, according to management, "enjoys a strong reputation among consumers, retail grocers, and foodservice and industrial customers for products highly regarded for quality, taste, nutrition, convenience, and value."

The company's larger subsidiaries include Jennie-O Turkey Store, the nation's largest turkey processor; Vista International Packaging, Inc., a manufacturer of casings; and Hormel Foods International Corporation, which markets Hormel products throughout the world.

The company's business is reported in four segments: **Refrigerated Foods** (accounting for 52 percent of total Hormel Foods sales in 2002 and 23 percent of operating profits), **Grocery Products** (20 percent and 48 percent), **Jennie-O Turkey Store** (23 percent and 21 percent) and **All Other** (5 percent and 8 percent).

The company's products include hams, bacon, sausages, franks, canned luncheon meats, stews, chilies, hash, meat spreads, shelf-stable microwaveable entrees, salsas, and frozen processed meats.

These selections are sold to retail, foodservice, and wholesale operations under many well-established trademarks that include the following: Black Label, By George, Cure 81, Always Tender, Curemaster, Di Lusso, Dinty Moore, Dubuque, Fast 'n Easy, Homeland, Hormel, House of Tsang, Jennie-O-Kid's Kitchen, Layout Pack, Light & Lean 100, Little Sizzlers, May Kitchen, Old Smokehouse, Peloponnese, Range Brand, Rosa Grande, Sandwich Maker, Spam, and Wranglers.

These products are sold in all fifty states by a Hormel Foods sales force assigned to offices in major cities throughout the United States. Their efforts are supplemented by sales brokers and distributors.

The headquarters for Hormel Foods is in Austin, Minnesota, along with the company's Research and Development division and its flagship plant. Company facilities that manufacture meat and food products are situated in such states as Iowa, Georgia, Illinois, Wisconsin, Nebraska, Oklahoma, California, and Kansas. In addition, custom manufacturing of selected Hormel Foods products is performed by various companies that adhere to stringent corporate guidelines and quality standards.

Hormel Foods International Corporation (HFIC), a wholly owned subsidiary in Austin, has established a number of joint venture and licensing agreements in such countries as Australia, China, Colombia, Costa Rica, Denmark, England, Japan, Korea, Mexico, Panama, the Philippines, Poland, and Spain, among others. HFIC exports products to more than forty countries.

Highlights of Fiscal 2002

- Earnings per share advanced to $1.35, versus $1.30 in 2001.
- Record dollar sales were $3.9 billion, up 1 percent.
- Volume was up 2 percent, despite Hormel's decision to reduce processing of non-value-added products.
- The company maintained its strong financial position, with debt-to-capital ratio of 28 percent.
- Branded, value-added products climbed to 79 percent of dollar sales.
- Ethnic foods sales were up 7 percent.

Shortcomings to Bear in Mind

- In fiscal 2003, the company's Refrigerated Foods segment was hurt by the pressures related to the oversupply of protein inventories and higher grain prices. The oversupply, according to a company spokesman, "negatively pressured product pricing.

"Low hog markets caused the company's long-term pork procurement contracts to pay $81.1 million more in fiscal 2002 for hogs, compared to the open market price. These pressures caused operating profit to decline 7 percent for the year. Without the positive margin contributions from value-added products, fiscal 2002 operating profit would have been considerably lower."

Reasons to Buy

- Dollar sales in fiscal 2002 were $882 million for the Jennie-O Turkey Store, or 12 percent ahead of the prior year. According a report issued by Hormel, "In fiscal 2002, sales of items introduced within the past two years totaled $45 million, with major contributions from Jennie-O Turkey Store Marinated Tenders, Cajun Fried Turkey, So Easy entrees, and Oven Roasted Turkey Breast, Flavored Ground Turkey, Corn Dogs, and Flavored Deli-Style Chicken."
- Value-added products are also helping the Jennie-O Turkey Store. This segment now offers a broad selection of value-added branded products such as Thanksgiving Tonight oven-roasted turkey breast, which "delivers holiday flavor and everyday convenience."

Demand for value-added turkey

items, moreover, are growing faster than that for traditional products.

- Over the past ten years (1992–2002), earnings per share advanced from $0.62 to $1.35, a compound annual growth rate of 8.1 percent. In the same span, dividends climbed from $0.18 to $0.39, a growth rate of 8.0 percent. To be sure, these are not dazzling growth rates, but they are steady and consistent. Thus, I have put Hormel Foods into the conservative growth category. As further confirmation of this, the beta coefficient is incredibly low, at .55. That means you can expect this stock to hold up well when the stock market is weak, but you can also look for it to lag behind when investors are optimistic.

- Justin Hellman, an analyst with *Value Line Investment Survey*, had this to say about Hormel in late 2002: "The company is benefiting from a shift toward higher-margined, value-added products. In fact, Hormel's gross margin widened by nearly 3 percentage points in the third quarter of fiscal 2002 (year ended October 26th), as the company continued to introduce branded pork and turkey products. (Branded sales now account for about 70 percent of the top line, up from 60 percent a year ago.) The focus on branded products should reduce earnings volatility and limit Hormel's exposure to commodity prices."

- Developing new products takes some effort. For Hormel, it means asking customers "about features that make their lives better." A case in point is the award-winning kid-friendly plastic packaging "of our popular Kid's Kitchen brand of microwave-ready foods."

- The company's recent acquisition of Diamond Crystal Brands Nutritional Products and Cliffdale Farms further strengthened Hormel Foods' brand presence in the fast-growing managed health care foods business. Hormel Foods is among the top providers in this field, which has strong growth prospects. The population worldwide of people aged sixty and over is expected to double between 2000 and 2025.

Total assets: $2,220 million
Current ratio: 2.35
Common shares outstanding: 139 million
Return on 2002 shareholders' equity: 17.9%

		2002	2001	2000	1999	1998	1997	1996	1995
Revenues (millions)		3,910	4,124	3,675	3,358	3,261	3,257	3,099	3,046
Net income (millions)		189	182	170	160	122	106	88	120
Earnings per share		1.35	1.30	1.20	1.09	.81	.70	.58	.79
Dividends per share		.39	.37	.35	.33	.32	.31	.30	.29
Price	High	28.2	27.3	21.0	23.1	19.7	16.5	14.0	14.0
	Low	20.0	17.0	13.6	15.5	12.8	11.8	9.7	11.4

CONSERVATIVE GROWTH

Illinois Tool Works, Inc.

3600 West Lake Avenue □ Glenview, Illinois 60025-5811 □ (847) 657-4104 □ Dividend reinvestment plan is available: (888) 829-7424 □ Web site: www.itw.com □ Listed: NYSE □ Ticker symbol: ITW □ S&P rating: A+ □ Value Line financial strength rating: A

"We recently upgraded our opinion on the stock to accumulate from hold, based on valuation and the company's strong financial position," said James R. Sanders, an analyst with *Standard & Poor's Stock Reports*, on February 4, 2003. "Our cash flow models (which value ITW by adding the sum of cash earnings growing at a projected 8 percent to 10 percent annual rate over the next ten years, and 3.5 percent thereafter) indicates a fair range of $67 to $72 a share.

"In terms of the company's overall financial health, we believe long-term shareholders should continue to benefit from management's proven ability to control costs, maintain a healthy balance sheet, and generate strong free cash flow."

The report went on to say, "In short, we believe the chances are good that the company will be able to continue to generate healthy EPS (earnings per share) growth and ROE (return on equity)."

Company Profile

Illinois Tool Works is a multinational manufacturer of highly engineered fasteners, components, assemblies, and systems. ITW's businesses are small and focused, so they can work more effectively in a decentralized structure to add value to customers' products.

The company has subsidiaries and affiliates in forty countries on six continents. The more than 600 ITW operating units are divided into several business segments.

Premark International, Inc.

In 1999, Illinois Tool Works made its biggest purchase yet—Premark International, Inc.—a $2.7-billion conglomerate that makes everything from industrial food equipment to gym equipment to residential flooring and appliances.

The Street did not take kindly to this huge acquisition. The day after the announcement, the stock dropped 8 percent, closing at $73.69 on September 10,

1999. More than a year later, the stock was still under siege, as it sagged below $50. No one seemed to notice that 90 percent of Premark's revenue came from non-consumer goods, making it, at least in management's view, a good fit for ITW.

Engineered Products—North America

Businesses in this segment are located in North America. They manufacture short-lead-time components and fasteners, as well as specialty products such as adhesives, resealable packaging, and electronic component packaging.

Engineered Products—International

Businesses in this segment are located outside North America. They manufacture short-lead-time components and fasteners and specialty products, such as electronic component packaging and adhesives.

Specialty Systems—North America

Businesses in this segment operate in North America. They produce longer-lead-time machinery and related consumables, as well as specialty equipment for applications such as industrial spray coating, quality measurement, and static control.

Specialty Systems—International

Operations in this segment do business outside North America. They have stakes in longer-lead-time machinery and related consumables, as well as specialty equipment for industrial spray coating and other applications.

How Illinois Tool Works Got Started

Founded in 1912, Illinois Tool Works' earliest products included milling cutters and hobs, which were used to cut gears. Today ITW is a multinational manufacturer of highly engineered components and systems.

In 1923, the company developed the Shakeproof fastener, a patented twisted tooth-lock washer. This product's success enabled ITW to become the leader in a new industry segment—engineered metal fasteners.

Illinois Tool soon expanded the Shakeproof line to include thread-cutting screws, preassembled screws, and other metal fasteners.

By the late 1940s, the line had grown to include plastic and metal/plastic combination fasteners. Today, ITW units produce fasteners for appliance, automotive, construction, general industrial, and other applications.

After World War II, the company's expansion into electrical controls and instruments culminated in the formation of its Licon division in the late 1950s. Today, ITW units provide a wide range of switch components and panel assemblies used in appliance, electronic, and industrial markets.

In the early 1960s, the newly formed Hi-Cone operating unit developed the plastic multipack carrier that revolutionized the packaging industry. Hi-Cone multipacks today are used to package beverage and food products as well as a variety of other products.

Also in the 1960s, the company formed Buildex to market its Shakeproof fasteners and a line of masonry fasteners to the construction industry. Buildex today manufactures fasteners for drywall, general construction, and roofing applications.

In the mid-1980s, ITW acquired Ramset, Phillips Drill (Red Head), and SPIT, manufacturers of concrete anchoring, epoxy anchoring, and powder-actuated systems; and Paslode, maker of pneumatic and cordless nailers, staplers, and systems for wood construction applications. Today, the construction industry is the largest market that Illinois Tool Works serves.

In the 1970s, ITW purchased Devcon Corporation, a producer of adhesives, sealants, and related specialty chemicals.

Today the company's engineered polymers businesses offer a variety of products with home, construction, and industrial applications.

In 1986, Illinois Tool acquired Signode Packaging Systems, a multinational manufacturer of metal and plastic strapping stretch film, industrial tape, application equipment, and related products. Today, ITW offers a wide range of industrial packaging systems, including Dynatec hot-melt adhesive application equipment.

In 1989, Illinois Tool Works acquired Ransburg Corporation, a leading producer of finishing equipment.

ITW expanded its capabilities in industrial finishing with the purchase of DeVilbiss Industrial/Commercial division in 1990. Today, DeVilbiss and Ransburg manufacture conventional and liquid electrostatic equipment, while Gema Volstatic (acquired with the Ransburg and DeVilbiss purchases) produces electrostatic powder coating systems.

The company acquired the Miller Group in 1993. Miller is a leading manufacturer of arc welding equipment and related systems. Miller's emphasis on new product development and innovative design made a good fit with ITW's engineering and manufacturing strategies.

Shortcomings to Bear in Mind

- The stock has historically traded at a premium to the market, but based on its exceptional performance over the years, its price would appear to be warranted. With some 600 businesses, Illinois Tool offers investors wide diversification by product line, geographic region, and industry. This helps insulate the company from weakness in any one sector. Over the years, this has resulted in consistent performance despite the cyclical nature of the automotive and construction sectors.

Reasons to Buy

- Acquisitions are likely to remain a key component of the company's growth strategy. Illinois Tool Works has grown steadily over the years largely by taking underperforming businesses and turning them into solid performers.

  In most years, the company completes a dozen or two "bottom-up" acquisitions—companies that are directly related to or integrated into an existing product line or market. These transactions, typically representing more than $1 billion in combined revenues, are normally initiated by operating management for both North American and international businesses. According to management, "Looking ahead, our pipeline of potential acquisitions remains full."

  A second type of acquisition, which the company undertakes far less frequently, is a major, or "top-down," proposition. These transactions are identified by senior management and represent entirely new businesses for the company. Illinois Tool completed the largest transaction of this type in its history when it merged with Premark in 1999.

  This merger brought the company nearly eighty decentralized businesses with products marketed in more than 100 countries. Two principal lines of business—commercial food equipment and laminate product used in construction—represent about $2.5 billion in revenues. Their products have strong brand names, such as Hobart, Wilsonart, Traulsen, Vulcan, and Wittco. They also enjoy established market positions, good distribution channels, and benefit from value-added engineering—all the things Illinois Tool looks for in a successful acquisition.

- Illinois Tools' record of sustained quality earnings is the result of a very practical view of the world. The company relies on market penetration—rather than price increases—to fuel operating income growth. What's more, the company's conservative accounting practices serve as a reliable yardstick of financial performance. These results then generate the cash needed to fund ITW's growth—through both investing in core businesses and acquisitions.

- Illinois Tool Works has an impressive record of growth. In the 1992–2002 period, earnings per share climbed from $0.86 to $3.02, an annual compound growth rate of 13.4 percent. In the same ten-year stretch, dividends advanced from $0.23 to $0.92, for a growth rate of 14.9 percent.

Total assets: $10,623 million
Current ratio: 2.48
Common shares outstanding: 306 million
Return on 2002 shareholders' equity: 14%

		2002	2001	2000	1999	1998	1997	1996	1995
Revenues (millions)		9,468	9,293	9,984	9,333	5,648	5,220	4,997	4,152
Net income (millions)		932	806	958	841	810	587	486	388
Earnings per share		3.02	2.63	3.15	2.99	2.67	2.33	1.97	1.65
Dividends per share		.92	.82	.76	.63	.54	.46	.36	.31
Price	High	77.8	72.0	69.0	82.0	73.2	60.1	48.7	32.8
	Low	55.0	49.2	49.5	58.0	45.2	37.4	26.0	19.9

Intel Corporation

2200 Mission College Boulevard □ Santa Clara, California 95052-8119 □ (408) 765-1679 □ Dividend reinvestment plan available: (800) 298-0146 □ Web site: www.intc.com □ Listed: NASDAQ □ Ticker symbol: INTC □ S&P rating: A □ Value Line financial strength rating: A++

"Intel Corp. is stepping up efforts to use memory and manufacturing technology to break into high-end cellular phones, hoping to challenge market leader Texas Instruments, Inc.," according to an article in the *Wall Street Journal*, written by Don Clark and H. Asher Bolande.

At a technical conference in Taiwan in late 2002, Intel announced flash memory chips that consume less electric current and products that stack microprocessor chips on top of memory chips. "The developments are designed to help shrink the size of pocket phones while boosting computing power, data storage capacity, and battery life.

"Intel already is the number-one supplier of flash memory chips, which are popular in mobile phones because they retain data when electricity is switched off. But it lags far behind Texas Instruments in other chips that go into phones, which historically haven't required the sophisticated computing capabilities that are a hallmark of Intel's microprocessor chips.

"More advanced phones that can snap photographs and run software are becoming increasingly popular, however, and Intel is betting that a greater convergence between phones and computing will create an opening. 'This is a great untapped frontier for Intel,' said Alex Slawsby, an analyst at International Data Corp., a market-research firm in Framingham, Mass."

Company Profile

It has been three decades since Intel introduced the world's first microprocessor, making technology history. The computer revolution that this technology spawned has changed the world. Today, Intel supplies the computing industry with the chips, boards, systems, and software that are the "ingredients" of computer architecture. These products are used by industry members to create advanced computing systems.

Intel Architecture Platform Products

Microprocessors, also called central processing units (CPUs), or chips, are frequently described as the "brains" of a computer because they control the central processing of data in personal computers (PCs), servers, workstations, and other computers. Intel offers microprocessors optimized for each segment of the computing market. Chipsets perform essential logic functions surrounding the CPU in computers, and they support and extend the graphics, video, and other capabilities of many Intel processor-based systems. Motherboards combine Intel microprocessors and chipsets to form the basic subsystem of a PC or server.

Wireless Communications and Computing Products

Wireless products are component-level hardware and software. They focus on digital cellular communications and other applications that need both low-power processing and reprogrammable, retained memory capability (flash memory). These products are used in mobile phones, handheld devices, two-way pagers, and many other products.

Networking and Communications Products

System-level products consist of hardware, software, and support services for e-business data centers as well as building blocks for communications access solutions. These products include e-commerce infra-structure appliances; hubs, switches, and routers for Ethernet networks; and com-puter telephony components. Component-level products include communications silicon components and embedded control chips designed to perform specific functions in networking and communications applica-tions, such as telecommunications, hubs, routers, and wide-area networking. Embedded control chips are also used in laser printers, imaging, storage media, auto-motive systems, and other applications.

Solutions and Services

These products and services include e-commerce data center services as well as connected peripherals and security access software.

Major Customers

• Original equipment manufacturers of computer systems and peripherals

• PC users, who buy Intel's PC enhancements, business communications products, and networking products through reseller, retail, and OEM channels

• Other manufacturers, including makers of a wide range of industrial and telecommunications equipment.

Shortcomings to Bear in Mind

■ In March 2003, Intel introduced a set of chips, called Centrino, that promise to make wireless Internet access a standard feature on laptops and to untie com-puter users from power outlets and tele-phone jacks.

Not everyone agrees, however, that this is a positive development. "Intel Corp., the world's largest micro-processor maker, already dominates the market for laptop chips, and the com-pany's new Centrino system is supposed to lock in that dominant position for

years to come," said Hiawatha Bray on March 13, 2003, in the *Boston Globe*. "But not without a fight. As Intel was introducing Centrino to a roomful of industry analysts and journalists in Manhattan yesterday, rival chipmaker Advanced Micro Devices, Inc., was in Germany rolling out a dozen new laptop processors of its own. Even tiny com-petitor Transmeta Corp. announced a new processor earlier last week, aimed at the ultralight laptop market."

The *Boston Globe* writer went on to say, "At the heart of the Centrino is a new addition to the venerable Pentium processor line, the Pentium M, that is designed to use less electric power and run cooler. The Pentium M actually runs at a lower speed than its prede-cessor, the Pentium 4, which helps it use less power. But it's designed to carry out more operations, and Intel claims it performs better than the Pentium 4."

Reasons to Buy

■ Here's another view of the Centrino devel-opment, which was launched in March 2003: "Wielding $300 million in adver-tising cash and a new trio of computer components it calls Centrino, chipmaker Intel Corp. on Wednesday launched a huge effort to introduce the world to high-speed wireless Internet," said Jim Krane, a reporter for the Associated Press.

Mr. Krane went on to say, "The Cen-trino design bundles Intel's energy-efficient Pentium M processor with a high-speed wireless receiver and a set of other laptop-friendly chips. Intel believes Centrino's spread will trigger a wireless revolution, akin to the 1960s transforma-tion heralded by the transistor radio.

"That revolution gave folks 'freedom to use the radio anytime, anywhere, any-place,' Intel chief executive Craig Bar-rett said in a music-video-fueled spec-tacle in Manhattan's Hammerstein

Ballroom. 'That's what we intend to do with Centrino technology.'"

- "Looking at the fallout from failed online businesses over the past couple of years has led some naysayers to dismiss the importance of the Internet," said Intel Chairman Andy Grove in 2002. "But I believe that claims of the demise of the Internet, like Mark Twain said about news of his death, have been greatly exaggerated. While economics and other factors have currently slowed the deployment of the Internet infrastructure, data shows that Internet use has continued to accelerate. Our industry is poised for significant expansion in the future as the Internet evolves, and Intel is well positioned to be at the center of that evolution."

- In March of 2002, Intel said it had developed ultrasmall memory circuitry with an advanced production technology that will be ready for the market in 2003. The company said that it had fabricated a dime-sized test chip with 330 million transistors, or 50 percent more than its most complex design to date. The chip, known as SRAM (for static random access memory) can store 52 million bits of data, compared with 32 million for chips produced by its competitors. Data is stored in cells that are a mere 1 micron small, or half the size of previous circuitry. A micron is 1 millionth of a meter.

- In 2003, Intel built special security features into its microprocessor chips for the first time, a move designed to address problems such as computer viruses and tampering by malicious hackers. The technology, which the company calls LaGrande, could become a factor in a widening debate over how to prevent PC users from unauthorized copying of digital information, such as movies or music. Intel has often been critical of attempts by Hollywood to mandate content-protection technology.

On the other hand, its long-time partner, Microsoft, has been adding such features to its software.

Paul Otellini, Intel's president and chief operating officer, said the company doesn't plan to offer any copy protection as part of LaGrande. But he acknowledged that the technology could be a foundation for other companies to do so, possibly working with Microsoft. Initially, the LaGrande technology was included in Prescott, Intel's code name for a new extension of its Pentium chip line that came out in the second half of 2003.

- In a cost-cutting move, IBM stopped selling desktop PCs in the United States with Advanced Micro Devices (AMD) microprocessors and might also drop AMD processors from its computers sold in Asia. IBM's desktops will now carry only Intel's processors. "With the low margins on PCs, it doesn't make sense for us to invest in two sets of chip platforms," said a spokesman for IBM's PC division.

- For many years, Intel has had to fend off competitive thrusts from its weaker—but feisty—competitor, AMD. Of late, however, its snarl has been worse than its bite. "Many of AMD's travails appear self-inflicted," said Cliff Edwards, writing for *BusinessWeek* in late 2002. "Its current chips are too slow for the higher-margin desktops PC makers are now concentrating on to boost profits, while production glitches have delayed the next-generation PC chips. Worse, AMD is falling behind in its bid to crack the lucrative server market."

Mr. Edwards went on to say, "That's quite a reversal for a company that only two and a half years ago boasted the fasted microprocessors in the world. Now, with Intel Corp. preparing to roll out a souped-up three-gigahertz Pentium 4 processor in November (2002), and AMD is still struggling to make chips that pass the two-gigahertz mark."

Total assets: $44,224 million
Current ratio: 2.87
Common shares outstanding: 6,665 million
Return on 2002 shareholders equity: 8.8%

		2002	2001	2000	1999	1998	1997	1996	1995
Revenues (millions)		26,764	26,539	33,726	29,389	26,273	25,070	20,847	16,202
Net income (millions)		3,117	1,291	10,535	7,314	6,178	6,945	5,157	3,491
Earnings per share		.46	.19	1.51	1.17	.89	.97	.73	50
Dividends per share		.08	.08	.07	.05	.04	.03	.03	.02
Price	High	36.8	38.6	75.8	44.8	31.6	15.5	17.7	9.8
	Low	12.9	19.0	29.8	25.1	16.4	15.7	6.3	4.0

AGGRESSIVE GROWTH

International Business Machines Corporation (IBM)

New Orchard Road □ Armonk, New York 10504 □ (914) 499-7777 □ Direct dividend reinvestment plan is available: (888) IBM-6700 □ Web site: www.ibm.com □ Listed: NYSE □ Ticker symbol: IBM □ S&P rating: B □ Value Line financial strength rating: A++

At the end of 2002, in an effort to bolster its software operations, IBM acquired Rational Software Corporation. Rational helps programmers design and test software applications. The company paid $2.1 billion for Rational, its biggest acquisition since it snapped up Lotus Development Corporation seven years earlier.

Rational's tools enable developers to build models of their software applications before they actually write the code. Developers at IBM and another ninety-seven of the *Fortune* 100 companies have used the tools to build databases, design semiconductors, and write software applications for everything from medical devices to cell phones.

For software providers like IBM, building a strong tools business is critical. For one thing, it's too expensive to train developers to use multiple toolkits. That's why buyers typically stick with one and its family of products. That means toolkit providers that lock customers in can drive sales of other software. To be sure, IBM already makes its own basic toolkit, called Web Sphere Studio. However, it doesn't have the high-end software needed to build

the most sophisticated applications. IBM bought Rational Software to fill that hole.

It will help the high-tech giant better compete with Microsoft, said one analyst.

Most important, the market is huge: Some 600,000 developers use Rational's services and software development platform. The overall market for software development tools is expected to expand from $9 billion in 2002 to $15 billion in 2006.

Company Profile

Big Blue is the world's leading provider of computer hardware. IBM makes a broad range of computers, including PCs, notebooks, mainframes, and network servers. The company also develops software—it's number two in the market, behind Microsoft—and peripherals. IBM derives about one-third of its revenues from an ever-expanding service arm that is the largest in the world. IBM owns Lotus Development, the software pioneer that makes the Lotus Notes messaging system.

The company's subsidiary, Tivoli Systems, develops tools that manage corporate computer networks. Finally, in an effort to keep up with the times, IBM has been making a concerted effort to obtain a slice of Internet business.

Shortcomings to Bear in Mind

- In mid-2002, IBM put down a big bet on the semiconductor industry when it held a ribbon-cutting ceremony for a $3-billion chip-fabrication plant in East Fishkill, New York. The plant—IBM's costliest-ever capital investment—opened in the middle of a chip-industry slump. At the time, some investors feared that the plant wouldn't have enough business to cover its depreciation costs. Uncertainty about the giant plant's success makes predicting IBM's future earnings a "crapshoot," said Toni Sacconaghi, an analyst with Sanford C. Bernstein & Company.

  According to William M. Bulkeley, writing for the *Wall Street Journal*, "John Kelly, senior vice president in charge of IBM's semiconductor unit, said such fears are unwarranted. In an interview, Mr. Kelly said the plant has signed up enough customers to become profitable by the end of this year (2002). What's more, he said the new plant, combined with cost-cutting elsewhere, will enable the semiconductor unit to 'return to profitability in the second half (of 2002).'"

- The legendary Louis V. Gerstner had been at the helm of IBM for a span of eight years when he retired in favor of Samuel J. Palmisano, the CEO's right-hand man during that period. Although it may be too early to tell, it is likely that the company's style and image may be in for a transformation. People who have watched the two men say their management styles are very different. Mr. Gerstner is imposing and autocratic. His successor is regarded as gregarious and overtly competitive. "Mr. Palmisano has the potential to be a visible, charismatic leader," said Thomas Bittman, a former IBM manager. In view of the remarkable results turned in by Mr. Gerstner, however, it would be hard to believe that the new CEO will be able to match the performance of his mentor.

- In February 2003, Dell Computer ended a $16-billion purchasing contract with IBM and greatly pared back a $6-billion services partnership. Also, Dell will no longer work with IBM's consulting unit, Global Services, unless customers request its services. Dell had purchased hard disk drives, flat panel displays, and various chips from IBM since 1999.

Reasons to Buy

- IBM, which spent $5.29 billion, or 6.2 percent of its revenues, on research and development in 2001, is one of the nation's biggest-spending and most productive research operations. The vast bulk of that spending has gone for hard sciences, such as materials science, electrical engineering, software development, and pure mathematics.

- Although IBM is well-known as the titan of computer hardware, it is the Global Services division that is proving to be the company's star performer. While sales for the rest of Big Blue are barely inching ahead, the services division is averaging more than 10 percent sales growth a year. That has helped pull up overall growth at IBM to about 5 percent per year.

- In an aggressive move to build a dominant position in the $8-billion market for database software, IBM made a major acquisition in 2001. They acquired Informix Corporation's database-software business for $1 billion. The move gives IBM a significant lead in market share over Oracle Corporation, which in recent years has been a close rival of IBM in the database sphere.

  IBM has acquired an enterprise with about $800 million in annual revenue. It has some 100,000 customers, compared with IBM's database customer list of about 400,000. "We are buying a great database team and a great set of skills to win the database war," said Janet Perna, general manager of IBM's software data management solutions. "The company that's got the best talent and the most customers is going to win this."

- In 2001, IBM invested $1 billion in the Linux operating systems because it's the best answer to competing private standards and increasing demands on the Internet. With predictions of a thousandfold increase in Internet traffic in the next few years, the networked world will be "several orders of magnitude more complicated than anything we know today," said IBM's CEO at that time, Louis Gerstner. He went on to say that the proliferation of wireless devices, as well as demands on Web servers, amount to a prescription for meltdowns. "We're headed for a wall," he said. This means more viruses, hacker attacks, and security problems at a time when voice, data, dial tone, and switching are converging, he said. Mr. Gerstner said IBM decided to invest in Linux because it's growing faster than the mainstay operating system, Microsoft's Windows NT.

- Competing against everyone from Electronic Data Systems to Big Four accounting firms to boutique shops offering only Web services, IBM has emerged as the world's largest purveyor of technology services, according to *BusinessWeek*. It counsels customers on technology strategy, helps them prepare for mishaps, runs all their computer operations, develops their applications, procures their supplies, trains their employees and even gets them into the dot-com realm.

- IBM launched a security system that it expects will set the industry standard for protecting confidential documents such as those used in the growing sector of electronic commerce. Unlike previous security measures that rely on software "fireballs" that filter out unauthorized users of information, IBM has developed a security chip embedded within the computer hardware, which adds additional levels of security. "People from outside your organization can get at your software," said Anne Gardner, general manager of desktop systems for IBM. "People from the outside can't get to your hardware."

- "IBM is making life miserable for many of its rivals," said Spencer E. Ante, writing for *BusinessWeek* magazine in late 2002.

  "Thanks to its July 2001 acquisition of database maker Informix, IBM last year (2001) surpassed Oracle as leader in the market for programs that store and organize corporate data, snatching a 35 percent share vs. Oracle's 32 percent. It's hot on the trail of BEA Systems, a $1-billion San Jose (Calif.) maker of software that dishes up Web applications. And it's ramping up to challenge Microsoft for sales to midsize businesses."

- In mid-2002, IBM acquired the consulting arm of PricewaterhouseCoopers LLP (PWC) for $3.5 billion in cash and stock, continuing IBM's shift away from its computer roots and into the services and consulting business. Even before this move, consulting was already IBM's biggest business with about $35 billion in annual revenues. The PWC acquisition adds another $5 billion. It also cemented IBM's position as the world's largest technology services company. By comparison, the next-largest competitor, Electronic Data Systems Corporation, has annual sales of about $21 billion. Most important, the acquisition brings IBM hundreds of big new customers and the high-margin consulting skills it had lacked.

Total assets: $96,484 million
Current ratio: 1.21
Common shares outstanding: 1723 million
Return on 2002 shareholders' equity: 15.5%

		2002	2001	2000	1999	1998	1997	1996	1995
Revenues (millions)		81,186	83,067	88,396	87,548	81,667	78,508	75,947	71,940
Net income (millions)		3579	7495	8093	7712	6328	6093	5429	6334
Earnings per share		3.13	4.69	4.44	4.12	3.29	3.01	2.76	2.76
Dividends per share		.60	.55	.51	.47	.44	.39	.33	.25
Price	High	124.0	124.7	134.9	139.2	95.0	56.8	41.5	28.7
	Low	54.0	83.8	80.1	80.9	47.8	31.8	20.8	17.6

CONSERVATIVE GROWTH

Johnson & Johnson

One Johnson & Johnson Plaza □ New Brunswick, New Jersey 08933 □ (800) 950-5089 □ Dividend reinvestment plan is available: (800) 328-9033 □ Web site: www.jnj.com □ Listed: NYSE □ Ticker symbol: JNJ □ S&P rating: A+ □ Value Line financial strength rating: A++

Johnson & Johnson, the world's largest diversified health care company, had six products or franchises with annual sales exceeding $1 billion in 2002. What's more, the company obtains 70 percent of its sales from products that hold the number one or number two market share, such as these:

- Disposable contact lenses, number one
- Blood glucose monitoring, number two
- Orthopedics, number one
- Minimally invasive surgery, number one
- Surgical sutures, number one
- Blood screening and typing, number one
- Women's health procedures, number one
- Wound care, number one
- Over-the-counter pharmaceuticals, number one.

Company Profile

Johnson & Johnson is the largest and most comprehensive health care company in the world, with 2002 sales of $36 billion.

Johnson & Johnson offers a broad line of consumer products, ethical and over-the-counter drugs, and various other medical devices and diagnostic equipment.

The company has a stake in a wide variety of endeavors: anti-infectives, biotechnology, cardiology and circulatory diseases, the central nervous system, diagnostics, gastrointestinals, minimally invasive therapies, nutraceuticals, orthopaedics, pain management, skin care, vision care, women's health, and wound care.

Johnson & Johnson has more than 200 operating companies in fifty-four countries. All told, they sell some 50,000 products in more than 175 countries.

One of Johnson & Johnson's assets is its well-entrenched brand names, which are widely known in the United States and abroad. As a marketer, Johnson & Johnson's reputation has enabled it to build strong ties to health care providers.

Its international presence includes not only marketing, but also production and distribution capability in a vast array of regions outside the United States.

There is one major advantage to Johnson & Johnson's worldwide organization. Emerging markets, such as China, Latin America, and Africa, offer growth potential for mature product lines.

The company's well-known trade names include Band-Aid adhesive bandages; Tylenol; Stayfree, Carefree, and Sure & Natural feminine hygiene products; Mylanta and Pepcid AC; Neutrogena; Johnson's baby powder, shampoo, and oil; and Reach toothbrushes.

The company's professional items include ligatures and sutures, mechanical wound closure products, diagnostic products, medical equipment and devices, surgical dressings, surgical apparel and accessories, and disposable contact lenses.

Shortcomings to Bear in Mind

- Nancy Chow, an analyst with *Value Line Investment Survey*, had this to say in a report issued in late 2002: "The company faces several challenges during the next few years. Amgen's Aranesp, a long-acting version of J&J's Procrit/ Eprex franchise, has recently gained FDA approval for chemotherapy-induced anemia. We think Aranesp's more convenient dosing regimen will steal market share from J&J's product. (Procrit/Eprex accounted for $3.4 billion in sales last year [2001], or 10.4 percent of the company's top line.) However, at the moment, Aranesp's higher price point will likely hinder the rate at which Amgen will take market share from J&J. We estimate that Procrit treatment costs roughly half of Aranesp therapy."

- Because of its stunning record, Johnson & Johnson is priced rather generously, typically at thirty times earnings or more. It might pay to wait until someone says something nasty about the stock, pushing it down a notch or two before you buy.

Reasons to Buy

- Research is the name of the game for drug companies. Johnson & Johnson has been increasing its research outlays year by year. For instance, in 1991 it invested

$1.1 billion in R&D, or 8.9 percent of sales. In 2002, it allocated nearly $4 billion, or 10.9 percent of sales.

- Over the years, the company has made many acquisitions, some medium-sized, others quite large. In the past ten years, Johnson & Johnson has made fifty-two acquisitions.

Johnson & Johnson acquired Alza Corporation in 2001 for $10.5 billion. The deal will add about $700 million to the company's pharmaceutical business. Alza developed the bestselling time-release delivery of the NicoDerm anti-smoking patch, which is sold by Glaxo-SmithKline plc.

Alza also makes time-release capsules that enable patients to take pills less often, as well as systems that use electricity to push drugs through the skin. In addition, Alza will contribute to Johnson & Johnson's line with such products as Concerta, a once-a-day remedy for an attention-deficit-hyperactivity disorder drug; Ditropan XL for urinary incontinence; and the cancer drug Doxil.

The Alza products are expected to immediately benefit from Johnson & Johnson's deep pockets and worldwide marketing reach. These are likely to produce more revenue for the drugs than if they were sold by Alza on its own.

- In February 2003, Johnson & Johnson acquired Scios, Inc., for $2.4 billion, bolstering its pharmaceutical pipeline and adding to its position in biotechnology. Scios's major product is Natrecor, a heart-failure drug. However, what attracted Johnson & Johnson to Scios is an arthritis drug that is under investigation. Known as SCIO-469, it targets p38, an enzyme responsible for inflammation in rheumatoid arthritis and other afflictions. Now in its second round of tests, the drug could become a billion-dollar-a-year blockbuster, according to analysts.

"Natrecor is a young product with room to grow, and the arthritis drug candidate is risky but potentially rewarding," said Scott Hensley and Robin Sidel, in a February 2003 article in the *Wall Street Journal*. "Those prospects could aid J&J as sales growth of some of its most important products begins to slow and before an increased investment in internal drug discovery pays off."

- The Food and Drug Administration (FDA) approved Johnson & Johnson's new drug for Alzheimer's disease in 2001. Reminyl, which became available in May of 2001, was approved to treat mild to moderate Alzheimer's cases. The Alzheimer's Association estimates 4 million Americans suffer from progressive neurological disease. The association believes that if no cure is found, as many as 14 million will develop the Alzheimer's by the middle of the century. Reminyl was shown to be effective in improving or helping to stabilize patients' ability to think and perform daily tasks in studies involving more than 2,650 subjects.

  Initially, the company launched the sale of Reminyl in the United States, the United Kingdom, Denmark, and Sweden. Approval has also been granted by over a dozen other countries.

- Stents, the tiny metal scaffolds that transformed the care of heart patients in the 1990s, are on the threshold of a major advance that may put an end to one of cardiology's most baffling enigmas.

  Each year, about 700,000 patients in the United States undergo angioplasty, a procedure in which a balloon is used to clear an obstruction in a coronary artery. A stent is deployed to keep the artery open. Unfortunately, a high percentage of procedures—some 15 to 20 percent—develop serious problems within six months, as the stent develops restenosis (arterial scarring).

Now, heart researchers and stent makers are developing a new generation of stents that not only prop open the artery but deliver drugs to the site of the blockage in an effort to keep the vessel open. Research studies suggest that stents coated with a drug called rapamycin put a stop to restenosis. Rapamycin is an immune-system suppressant drug marketed by American Home Products. Johnson & Johnson has licensed the drug, which it calls Sirolimus for use with stents. It halts the replication of certain cells that, as part of the body's response to injury, are involved in the proliferation of scar tissue.

Johnson & Johnson is well along in the development of its "pharma stent," which is coated with rapamycin. The company is widely regarded as being well ahead of competitors in a race to bring similar coated devices to market.

In 1994, Johnson & Johnson initiated a new era in heart treatment with its first stent, which dominated the market for three years. But its days of glory were short-lived when rivals invaded its domain with better technology.

Now, however, the company is poised to make a comeback. Analysts and physicians are convinced that Johnson & Johnson's Cordis unit is about to reclaim much of its former market share for angioplasty devices. Among other recent accomplishments, Cordis received FDA approval for the Checkmate System for gamma radiation of in-stent restenosis. Even better, this benefit is coupled with the acquisition of Atrionix, which brings Johnson & Johnson a company with promising technology for treating atrial fibrillation—a condition for which, until now, there has been no effective treatment.

"We're predicting that J&J is going to be the leader in this field for a few years," said William O'Neill, director of cardiology at William Beaumont Hospital, Royal Oak, Michigan.

- H. B. Saftlas, an analyst with *Standard & Poor's Stock Reports*, had this to say about the company in a report issued in late 2002: "We expect revenues to rise 10 percent in 2003. The gain should be led by a projected 60 percent increase in sales at the Cordis division, driven largely by the new Cypher drug-coated stent. Introduced in Europe in April 2002, Cypher is expected to receive FDA approval in the spring of 2003. Cypher should also have an estimated six-month lead over anticipated rival stents from Guidant and Boston Scientific.

"Strong gains are also seen for glucose monitoring products. Drug sales should benefit from continued growth in Procrit treatment for anemia, Duragesic transdermal patch for chronic pain, and Remicade anti-inflammatory agent."

- Johnson & Johnson has an impressive record of growth—seventy years of consecutive sales increases; eighteen years of consecutive double-digit earnings increases; and forty years of consecutive dividend increases. Johnson & Johnson has thirty drugs with annual sales exceeding $50 million; twenty drugs with annual sales of more than $100 million; and more than 100 drugs that are sold in 150 countries.

Total assets: $40,556 million
Current ratio: 1.68
Common shares outstanding: 2,975 million
Return on 2002 shareholders' equity: 28.1%

		2002	2001	2000	1999	1998	1997	1996	1995
Revenues (millions)		36,298	32,317	29,139	27,471	23,657	22,629	21,620	18,842
Net income (millions)		6,651	5,668	4,800	4,167	3,669	3,303	2,887	2,403
Earnings per share		2.18	1.84	1.63	1.47	1.34	1.21	1.09	.93
Dividends per share		.82	.70	.62	.55	.49	.43	.37	.32
Price	High	65.9	61.0	53.0	53.5	44.9	33.7	27.0	23.1
	Low	41.4	40.3	33.1	38.5	31.7	24.3	20.8	13.4

CONSERVATIVE GROWTH

Johnson Controls, Inc.

Post Office Box 591 □ Milwaukee, Wisconsin 53201-0591 □ (414) 524-3155 □ Direct dividend reinvestment plan is available: (877) 602-7397 □ Fiscal years end September 30 □ Web site: www.johnsoncontrols.com □ Listed: NYSE □ Ticker symbol: JCI □ S&P rating: A+ □ Value Line financial strength rating: A

"As Wisconsin's largest public corporation, Johnson Controls is a rock of stability," said Thomas Content (a reporter for the *Milwaukee Journal Sentinel*) in the spring of 2002.

"Its roots stretch to 1885, before other corporate mainstays such as Harley-Davidson and Briggs & Stratton were born.

"It still operates in the business of climate control for commercial buildings, a venture launched when Warren Johnson

invented the electric room thermostat in 1883 while a professor at Whitewater State College.

"And Johnson Controls has consistently produced record earnings for more than a decade, and record sales for more than half a century—during times of recession or boom. This is a company that has embraced change, seizing on a dramatic shift in the auto industry to catapult itself into a dominant global player in the business of designing and building the interiors of cars and minivans."

Nor did the giant Wisconsin company disappoint investors in fiscal 2002 (ended September 30, 2002), as sales advanced 9.1 percent to $20.1 billion. Earnings per share, moreover, surged to $6.35, compared with $5.11 the prior year.

Commenting on this impressive showing during a period of recession and global tensions, CEO John M. Barth, said, "Both our automotive and controls businesses achieved record results for the year. Revenues rose as Johnson Controls' market shares increased, and we were able to supply more integrated systems and solutions to our customers. In addition, we continue to improve the quality and productivity of our products and processes, which increase customer satisfaction and enable us to reinvest in innovation and technology."

He went on to say that "free cash flow increased to $621 million for 2002, compared with $367 million last year due to the increase in net income and a decline in capital expenditures. Capital spending decreased to $496 million for 2002, from $621 million due to delays and spending efficiencies. The company's ratio of total debt to total capitalization declined to 36 percent at September 30, 2002, from 38 percent at the end of 2001."

Company Profile

Johnson Controls, Inc., is a global market leader in automotive systems and facility management and control. In the automotive market, it is a major supplier of seating and interior systems and batteries. For nonresidential facilities, Johnson Controls provides building control systems and services, energy management, and integrated facility management.

Automotive Systems Group
- Global market leader in seating and interior systems for light vehicles,

including passenger cars and light trucks.
- Systems supplied include seating, overhead, door, instrument panels, storage, electronics, and batteries.
- All systems are sold to the original equipment automotive market. However, the automotive replacement market is the major course of sales for batteries.
- Major customers include Auto-Zone, Costco, DaimlerChrysler, Fiat, Ford, General Motors, Honda, Interstate Battery Systems of America, John Deere, Mazda, Mitsubishi, Nissan, NUMMI, Peugeot, Renault, Sears, Toyota, Volkswagen, and Wal-Mart.
- Worldwide presence, with 275 locations.

Controls Group
- The Controls business is a leader in supplying systems to control heating, ventilating, and air conditioning (HVAC), as well as lighting, security, and fire management for buildings. Services include complete mechanical and electrical maintenance.
- World leader in integrated facility management, providing facility management and consulting services for many *Fortune* 500 companies. The company manages more than 1 billion square feet worldwide.
- Customers worldwide include education, health care, industrial, government, and office buildings.
- Worldwide presence, with 300 locations.

Shortcomings to Bear in Mind
- In the fall of 2002, Goldman Sachs, a leading brokerage firm, had some disturbing comments: "JCI hit some bumps in the fourth quarter of 2002, notably weak margins in Controls and Europe Automotive. Management is optimistic the factors are one-time, although shortfalls in Controls and Europe are recurring themes. Lower European margin

was driven by start-up costs; we note that's a recurring theme among suppliers. Lower Controls margin was driven by contract issues, integration and marketing costs; we note that Controls has had three disappointments in margin or revenue in the past quarter."

■ The company's large exposure to the automotive industry often worries investors. While it is difficult to argue that such concerns are unfounded, some analysts are convinced that they are overemphasized. For one thing, during periods of economic weakness, Johnson Controls's earnings have typically held up considerably better than those of most auto suppliers. On the other hand, there is no doubt that car sales are subject to sharp ups and downs.

Reasons to Buy

■ Over the past ten years, 1992–2002, the company's earnings per share increased without interruption, climbing from $1.37 to $6.35, an impressive annual compound growth rate of 16.6 percent. In the same ten-year span, dividends advanced from $.62 to $1.32, a more modest growth rate of 7.8 percent.

■ Integration of electronics into vehicle interiors is one of the company's specialties, ranging from global positioning systems to digital compasses and Homelink. The company, moreover, is continuously developing new products and holds more patents than any other automotive interior supplier.

■ The company's automotive business is expected to expand in the years ahead as automakers continue outsourcing seating and interior systems in North America and Europe, as well as in emerging global markets.

What's more, the company's development of innovative features and application of new technologies for the automotive interior will strengthen the company's leadership position, as Johnson Controls makes its customers' vehicles more comfortable, convenient, and safe.

■ Nearly every automotive system the company makes today includes electronics. New products such as the company's AutoVision, in-vehicle video system, and PSI tire-pressure sensing system are electronics-based. What's more, electronics are a part of its seats and other interior systems as well. Innovative use of electronics creates new features and functions for car interiors, as well as new ways for the company's automaker customers to differentiate their vehicles.

■ Industry studies estimate that 75 percent of all tires are improperly inflated. The company's PSI system uses a radio-frequency transmitter in each tire, which sends air pressure information to an in-vehicle electronic display.

■ The annual market for automotive electronics in North America will reach a total of $28 billion by 2004. To help meet this demand, according to management, "We're expanding and accelerating our electronics capabilities and creating new partnering programs with leading electronics firms."

■ According to a spokesman for the company, "With more than 110 years of experience in the controls industry, Johnson Controls understands buildings better than anyone else. That's why tens of thousands of commercial, institutional, and government building owner and managers around the world turn to Johnson Controls to improve the quality of buildings' indoor environments by maximizing comfort, productivity, safety, and energy efficiency."

■ The company engineers, manufactures, and installs control systems that automate a building's heating, ventilating, and air conditioning, as well as its lighting and fire-safety equipment. Its

Metasys Facility Management System automates a building's mechanical systems for optimal comfort levels while using the least amount of energy. In addition, it monitors fire sensors and building access, controls lights, tracks equipment maintenance, and helps building managers make better decisions.

- Building systems at some companies are critical to achieving their corporate missions. In the pharmaceutical industry, for example, the failure of a building's equipment or staff to maintain the proper laboratory conditions could mean the loss of years of new drug research and development. In a bank's data center, moreover, the failure of cooling equipment could shut down computer systems, delaying millions of dollars in transactions every minute.

- The company's Controls Group does business with more than 7,000 school districts, colleges, and universities, as well as more than 2,000 health care organizations. These customers benefit from performance contracting, a solution that lets them implement needed facility repairs and updates without up-front capital costs. Performance contracting uses a project's energy and operational cost savings to pay its costs over time. For instance, using a performance contract, Grady Health System in Atlanta was able to complete energy efficiency upgrades that will generate $20 million in savings over the next ten years.

Total assets: $10,914 million
Current ratio: 1.04
Common shares outstanding: 88 million
Return on 2002 shareholders' equity: 17%

	2002	2001	2000	1999	1998	1997	1996	1995
Revenues (millions)	20,103	18,427	17,155	16,139	12,587	11,145	10,009	8,330
Net income (millions)	601	542	472	387	303	265	235	196
Earnings per share	6.35	5.11	5.09	4.13	3.25	2.85	2.14	1.80
Dividends per share	1.32	1.24	1.12	1.00	.92	.86	.82	.78
Price High	93.2	82.7	65.1	76.7	61.9	51.0	42.7	34.9
Low	69.1	48.2	45.8	49.0	40.5	35.4	31.3	22.9

INCOME

Kimco Realty Corporation

3333 New Hyde Park Road □ Suite 100 □ New Hyde Park, New York 11042-0020 □ (516) 869-7288 □ Direct dividend reinvestment plan available: (866) 557-8695 □ Web site: www.kimcorealty.com □ Listed: NYSE □ Ticker symbol: KIM □ S&P rating: Not rated □ Value Line financial strength rating: B++

Kimco continues to have success leasing and disposing of vacancies that resulted from the Kmart bankruptcy. In the fourth quarter of 2002, for instance, the company executed eight leases and sold seven former Kmart sites. During the year, the company made significant progress repositioning twenty-nine of thirty-one leases rejected by Kmart.

What's more, management does not anticipate the recent store closing announcement by Kmart will have a material impact on the company's expected 2003 operating results.

Company Profile

Kimco Realty Corporation is the largest publicly traded real estate investment trust (REIT) that owns and operates a portfolio of neighborhood and community shopping centers (measured by gross leasable area). It has interests in 610 properties (up from 126 when it went public in 1991): 432 shopping centers, two regional malls, fifty-five retail store leases, and other projects totaling 81 million square feet of leasable area in forty-one states and in Canada.

Since incorporating in 1966, Kimco has specialized in the acquisition, development, and management of well-located centers with strong growth potential. Self-administered and self-managed, the company's focus is to increase the cash flow and enhance the value of its shopping center properties through strategic retenanting, redevelopment, renovation, and expansion. The company also aims to make selective acquisitions of neighborhood and community shopping centers that have below market-rate leases or other cash-flow growth potential.

A substantial portion of Kimco's income consists of rent received under long-term leases, most of which provide for the payment of fixed-base rents and a pro rata share of various expenses. Many of the leases also provide for the payment of additional rent as a percentage of gross sales.

Kimco's neighborhood and community shopping center properties are designed to attract local area customers and typically are anchored by a supermarket, discount department store, or drugstore, offering day-to-day necessities rather than high-priced luxury items. Among the company's major tenants are Kmart, Wal-Mart, Kohl's, and TJX Companies.

Kimco's core strategy is to acquire older shopping centers carrying below-market rents. This space is then re-leased at much higher rates.

Funds from Operations

REITs are not valued by earnings per share (EPS), but rather by funds from operations (FFO) per share. FFO is calcu-lated by adding net income and depreciation expense and then subtracting profits from the sale of assets. If a REIT pays out 90 percent or more of its taxable income in dividends, it is exempt from paying federal income taxes. FFO per share is in excess of net income because depreciation is added in. This means that a REIT such as Kimco pays out only about 66 percent of its FFO in dividends, with the balance of 34 percent available for acquisitions and improving existing properties.

If you want to check the Internet on REITS, here are some Web sites (some free, some not) that might be useful:

- *www.morningstar.com*
- *www.investinreits.com*
- *www.reitnet.com*
- *www.nareit.com*
- *www.realtystocks.com*

Shortcomings to Bear in Mind

■ Raymond Mathis, an analyst with *Standard & Poor's Stock Reports*, cast a negative vote on Kimco in a report issued in January of 2003. "We expect rental revenue to continue to decline in 2003, due to the bankruptcy of several tenants, including Kmart, KIM's largest tenant as a percentage of base revenues."

The S&P analyst also said, "Although retail REITs substantially outperformed the broader market in 2002, KIM provided only fractionally positive return. Of the retail REITs we cover, it has the highest exposure to tenant bankruptcies. KIM is probably the best prepared REIT to handle big-box vacancies, and it is the only landlord represented on Kmart's unsecured creditor committee. One of KIM's subsidiaries, Retail Property Solutions, is devoted to working out distressed property situations. Nevertheless, we believe the share price will be restricted by the impact of a second round of Kmart closures."

Reasons to Buy

- Kimco continued to expand in 2002 by acquiring interests in 107 shopping centers, with an aggregate cost of about $1.4 billion.
- In 2001, Milton Cooper, then age seventy-two, announced that he would step down as CEO of Kimco, a company he cofounded forty years before. However, he was replaced by an experienced executive, David B. Henry, who resigned his post at General Electric. He was chief investment officer and senior vice president at GE Capital Real Estate, as well as chairman of GE Capital Investment Advisors. David Henry, age fifty-one, joined Kimco as chief investment officer, with the expectation that he would become Kimco's CEO in one year.

  Mr. Cooper, who has known Mr. Henry for more than fifteen years, said, "Finding a person to entrust the future of my life's work was not easy, but I believe he is perfectly suited to lead Kimco. His impressive background and vast industry relationships will help Kimco expand its business platform and operating capabilities. He will lead our company to the next level." Although Mr. Cooper will no longer be CEO when Mr. David takes the reins, he will remain with Kimco as chairman.
- Kimco's customers include some of the strongest and most rapidly growing chains in the United States, such as Costco, Home Depot, Circuit City, Best Buy, Wal-Mart, Value City, Target, and Kohl's.
- Nearly all of the company's revenue is contractual. This means that even when a retailer's sales slump, it does-not change the rent they must pay to Kimco under the lease agreement or the value of the company's real estate.
- Knowledge of local markets and trends is crucial to success in the real-estate sector. Kimco's decentralized asset management staff—situated in such cities as New York, Los Angeles, Chicago, Philadelphia, Dallas, Phoenix, Tampa, Charlotte, and Dayton—provides knowledge of real estate developments that are analyzed by professionals on the scene.
- Kimco's success comes not by accident but as the careful product of business principles that have remained firmly in place since the company was founded in the 1950s. The company invests in properties that are undervalued assets, where management knows it will be able to capitalize on the margin between the price at which it can buy the property and the price at which it can lease it. The average rent on properties in Kimco's portfolio remains below the market, providing the company with significant upside potential.
- Management is clearly aligned with shareholders, as is indicated by their collective 21.2 percent ownership stake in the company.
- Kimco has had a knack for opportunistic buys. In 1998, it did a sale-leaseback to take control of some 10 million square feet of space of Venture Stores real estate. It seemed like a risky move because Venture Stores was tottering. When the retailer eventually went belly-up, Kimco quickly leased the Venture units to new tenants at even higher rates.

  In a more recent move into the bankruptcy realm, Kimco was awarded asset designation rights for thirty-four former Hechinger Stores and Builders Square locations at the end of 1999. The rights enable Kimco to direct the disposition of the positions held by the bankrupt estate. Separately, Kimco acquired fee title to seven Hechinger locations and one ground lease position.
- To continue growing its portfolio and income, the company has established

special-purpose ventures to acquire properties, such as the following:

- The Kimco Retail Opportunity Portfolio is a joint venture with GE Capital Real Estate.
- Kimco formed a joint venture with RioCan real estate investment trust, Canada's largest REIT.
- In 1999, the company launched the Kimco Income REIT, which currently consists of more than $1.2 billion in assets.
- Anticipating new opportunities when the REIT Modernization Act became effective on January 1, 2001, Kimco formed Kimco Developers, Inc. (KDI), which operates as a merchant developer. The new legislation allows

KDI to immediately sell properties and capture the developer's profit for future reinvestment. KDI generated income of $8.1 million in its first full year of operations.

- In 2002, Kimco, in a joint venture with Prometheus Southeast Retail Trust, reached an agreement to acquire Konover Property Trust. The transaction was valued at about $280 million. Konover Property Trust is a REIT engaged in the management, leasing, and development of neighborhood and community shopping centers. The company owns thirty-seven shopping centers in seven states, totaling about 4.8 million square feet.

Total assets: $3,757 million
Current ratio: NA
Return on 2002 equity: 12.9%
Common shares outstanding: 105 million

	2002	2001	2000	1999	1998	1997	1996	1995
Rental income (millions)	451	450	459	434	339	199	168	143
Net income (millions)	246	237	205	177	122	86	74	52
Earnings per share	2.16	2.16	1.91	1.64	1.35	1.19	1.07	.89
Funds from operations	3.03	2.99	2.69	2.41	2.02	1.75	1.58	1.44
Dividends per share	2.10	1.96	1.83	1.62	1.31	1.15	1.04	.96
Price High	33.9	34.1	29.8	27.2	27.8	24.1	23.3	18.8
Low	25.0	27.2	21.8	20.6	22.3	20.2	16.8	15.7

GROWTH AND INCOME

Lancaster Colony Corporation

37 West Broad Street □ Columbus, Ohio 43215 □ (614) 224-7141 □ Dividend reinvestment plan is available: (800) 278-4353 □ Web site: www.lancastercolony.com □ Fiscal years end June 30 □ Listed: NASDAQ □ Ticker symbol: LANC □ Standard & Poor's rating: A+ □ Value Line financial strength rating: A

Since its original acquisition of T. Marzetti in 1970, the Specialty Foods Group of Lancaster Colony has been a stellar performer. What's more, its performance in fiscal 2002 (ended June 30, 2002) was no exception: The group reported its thirty-second consecutive year of record sales.

For the fifth consecutive year, the Specialty Foods Group was recognized by

Frozen Food Age magazine with the 10 & 10 Club Award, which is earned by brands with at least $10 million in sales and 10 percent growth. The New York Brand, Mamma Bella, and Sister Schubert's brands each received this award, making Lancaster Colony the only company with three award-winning brands.

The Specialty Foods Group, which achieved a 12 percent increase in sales and a 7.6 percent increase in operating income in 2002, now accounts for 51 percent of Lancaster Colony's net sales and 85 percent of total operating income. Contributing to the success of this key group in 2002 were such developments as the following:

• Exceptional growth of the Sister Schubert's brand via new distribution channels and market expansion.

• The introduction of several specialty dressing flavors in the retail salad dressing business, including Balsamic Basil and Shiitake Chardonnay under the Girard's label, along with Vintage White Wine, Poppyseed with Shallots, and Kalamata Olive with Romano Cheese under the Cardini's label.

• Significant gains in the company's produce dip categories, spearheaded by new Marzetti branded products, expanded distribution and increased merchandising. In addition, the company added two new single-serve multipack items—Salsa and Blue Cheese—to the veggie dip business, and successfully introduced Apple Crisp as an extension of its Apple Dip business, with sales topping "our original estimate by more than 50 percent," said the company in its 2002 annual report.

Company Profile

Lancaster Colony is a diversified manufacturer of consumer products, including Specialty Foods for the retail and foodservice markets; Glassware and Candles for the retail, industrial, floral and foodservice markets; and Automotive products for the original equipment market and aftermarket.

Specialty Foods

This segment's focus is on the supermarket produce department, supplying T. Marzetti's salad dressings, vegetable dips, and Chatham Village croutons. Well-known retail brand products include Car-

dini's dressings and marinades; Marzetti, Girard's, and Pfeiffer dressings; New York Brand, Sister Schubert's, and Mamma Bella frozen breads and rolls; Reames frozen noodles and pastas; Inn Maid premium dry egg noodles; Mountain Top premium frozen pies; Texas Best barbecue and grilling sauces; and Romanoff caviar.

In fiscal 2002, this segment had sales of $579.9 million, up from $517.7 million the prior year. Operating income climbed to $113.7 million from $105.7 million.

Glassware and Candles

The group's Candle-lite division is the top producer of candles for the mass market and is also a leading marketer of potpourri. In one of the world's most automated manufacturing facilities, Candle-lite produces candles in all popular sizes, shapes, colors, and scents. Glassware lines include Indian Glass everyday drinkware and tabletop items; upscale Colony giftware; and Brody floral containers.

In fiscal 2002, this operation had revenues of $314.6 million, down from $336.3 million. Operating income, however, decreased sharply to $10.5 million from $47.2 million in 2001.

Automotive

As one of the country's largest producers of automotive floormats, the group manufactures products for both the original equipment manufacturer (OEM) market and the retail aftermarket. Aftermarket floor mats are sold under the Rubber Queen brand name.

This group also offers a variety of aluminum accessories for the light-truck market under the Dee Zee brand name. Other product offerings in the automotive family include Koneta heavy-duty truck and trailer splash guards, Protecta pickup truck bed mats, and Rubber Queen plastic accessories.

In fiscal 2002, Automotive had sales of $235.2 million, off modestly from the prior year's $238.6 million. But operating earnings bounced back impressively to $15.2 million, compared with $ .67 million in 2001 and $7.45 million in 2000. These results came about because of the faster-than-expected turnaround of the floor mat portion of the company's Automotive Group.

Shortcomings to Bear in Mind

- The troubles at Kmart hurt Lancaster Colony in 2002. The big retailer's Chapter 11 filing resulted in an $8.8 million after-tax charge in Lancaster's second quarter.
- According to the company's CEO, John B. Gerlach, Jr., "Our biggest challenge—which remains an issue in the current year (2003)—was achieving sustained growth in all of our businesses. A sluggish economy, coupled with an extremely competitive marketplace, affected our segments somewhat differently."

    Mr. Gerlach was particularly disturbed by the Glassware and Candles Group, which declined 6.5 percent in fiscal 2002. "Candle category growth rates have slowed significantly," he said, "a situation that was magnified for us by the midyear loss of a key mass-market customer. Meanwhile, the weak candle market and generally sluggish retail sales hurt glassware volume. Enhanced marketing strategies and product line development will be important for this group's future growth."

Reasons to Buy

- In the most recent ten-year period (1992–2002), earnings per share climbed from $.71 to $2.49 (with only one dip along the way), a compound annual growth rate of 13.4 percent. In the same stretch, dividends per share advanced from $.22 to $.71, a growth rate of 12.4 percent.
- The company has no long-term debt. And its ratio of current assets to current liabilities is a most impressive 4.10. By

contrast, most companies are lucky to have a 2.0 ratio. It's no wonder that *Standard & Poor's* gives Lancaster Colony an A+ rating, while *Value Line* awards the company an A for financial strength. What's more, it has no pension liability. Despite the company's solid financial status and excellent record of growth, the stock normally sells at a modest P/E ratio.

- In a report issued late in 2002, an analyst with *Value Line Investment Survey*, Jerome H. Kaplan, spoke favorably about Lancaster Colony.

    "Specialty foods are leading the way at Lancaster. Last year (2002), they accounted for 51 percent of revenues and 81 percent of operating income. This unit gets 52 percent of its business from retail stores and has the number one or two position in eleven of its twelve categories. The laggard, rated number three, is a fast-growing acquisition. The remaining 48 percent of sales come from the food-service industry, where the company is also growing faster than its peers."

- In the Automotive Group, the floor mat operation showed significant improvement in 2002. According to management, "Top-line, we received new floor mat orders or increased volume commitments from several OEMs, including Honda, Toyota, and General Motors. A portion of this new volume is the result of an innovative program for an internally developed sound-absorbing floor mat with a patent-pending design. We will also begin to benefit from a new all-rubber floor mat program for a major OEM that commenced in June 2002.

    "In fiscal 2003, we will introduce a new four-piece carpet set for our aftermarket customers. We are also developing a new all-season floor mat with an updated design for the retail market. Although low-priced import mats have increased the competitive nature of the aftermarket, we're pleased to report our high-level customer service allowed us to win back an aftermarket customer that had made an interim switch to an imported mat supplier."

Total assets: $619 million
Current ratio: 4.10
Common shares outstanding: 37 million
Return on 2002 shareholders' equity: 18.3%

	2002	2001	2000	1999	1998	1997	1996	1995
Revenues (millions)	1,130	1,099	1,104	1,046	1,009	923	856	795
Net income (millions)	92	90	102	95	96	99	76	71
Earnings per share	2.49	2.40	2.59	2.28	2.22	2.01	1.71	1.57
Dividends per share	.71	.67	.64	.59	.54	.48	.44	.37
Price High	47.2	37.4	34.8	37.0	45.4	38.5	30.7	25.3
Low	31.6	25.0	18.5	24.7	24.1	26.2	22.0	19.2

GROWTH AND INCOME

La-Z-Boy, Inc.

1284 North Telegraph Road ▢ Monroe, Michigan 48162-3390 ▢ (734) 241-4414 ▢ Web site: www.lazboy.com ▢ ▢ Dividend reinvestment plan is available: (800) 937-5449 ▢ Fiscal years end April 30 ▢ Listed: NYSE ▢ Ticker symbol: LZB ▢ Standard & Poor's rating: A ▢ Value Line financial strength rating: B++

According to the U.S. Department of Commerce, there are now more than 500 residential furniture manufacturers in the United States. This proliferation of manufacturers and brands often leads to a high degree of confusion among consumers. For this reason, a brand name that consumers know and trust is a prized asset for a furniture manufacturer.

In this regard, La-Z-Boy has the clear advantage. As the best-known domestic furniture brand, and according to the 2001 *HFN* Magazine Brand Survey, the fifth best-known household consumer brand overall, La-Z-Boy enjoys a favorable competitive position in the marketplace.

According to Gerald L. Kiser, the company's CEO, "Another major marketing edge for La-Z-Boy is its large and growing proprietary distribution system. In addition to stand-alone La-Z-Boy Furniture Galleries stores and La-Z-Boy In-Store Gallery partnerships, other La-Z-Boy, Inc., companies are aggressively seeking to leverage the power of 'the name,' while pursuing their own unique, proprietary distribution strategies. An example of this is our La-Z-Boy Youth Collection by Lea that has met with great success in a pilot program and is being selectively expanded to more of our dealers."

Company Profile

Dating back seventy-five years, La-Z-Boy is one of the leading residential furniture makers in the world. What's more, it is by far the best-known furniture brand among U.S. consumers. With more than $2 billion in annual sales, the company has a nearly 10 percent overall market share among domestic furniture makers and about a 16 percent share in upholstery.

The La-Z-Boy family of companies produces and markets a broad range of furniture for every room of the home and for the office. These products are sold through traditional retail outlets, including independent furniture stores, regional and national chain stores, and independent stores. Sales are supported by way of a strong proprietary distribution network, consisting of independently owned, stand-alone retail stores and in-store galleries. About 40 percent of corporate sales are derived from these proprietary outlets. La-Z-Boy is also a leading provider of furniture for the hospitality, assisted-living, health care, and government markets.

The Upholstery Group

The Upholstery group, which accounted for 72 percent of revenues in fiscal 2002, manufactures upholstered furniture. The segment's major operating groups are the following: Bauhaus, Centurion, Clayton Marcus, England, Hickory-Mark, La-Z-Boy Residential, La-Z-Boy Contract Furniture Group, and Sam Moore. Products include recliners and motion furniture, sofas, love seats, chairs, ottomans, and sleeper sofas.

The Casegoods Group

The Casegoods group (28 percent of sales) sells manufactured or imported hardwood or hardwood veneer furniture to furniture retailers and the hospitality industry. The segment's operating divisions are Alexvale, American Drew, American of Martinsville, Hammary, Kincaid, Lea, and Pennsylvania House. Products include tables, entertainment centers, headboards, and dressers.

According to Amrit Tewary, an analyst with *Standard & Poor's Stock Reports*, "LZB sells to more than 9,000 customers, with no customer accounting for more than 3 percent of fiscal 2002 sales in either the upholstery group or the casegoods group. The customer mix consisted of 38 percent proprietary, 13 percent major dealers (including Federated, the May Company, and Nebraska Furniture Mart), and 49 percent general dealers. The company owns twenty-six proprietary stores and has agreements with independent dealers for 274 stand-alone stores and in-store galleries, all

dedicated entirely to its products and accessory products that it approves.

"In fiscal 2002, the company imported finished casegoods accounting for 6 percent of total sales. It plans to improve its purchasing, logistics, and warehousing of imports across its divisions, as this part of its business continues to grow."

La-Z-Boy was founded in Monroe, Michigan, in 1927 as Floral City Furniture, a tiny producer of the La-Z-Boy slat-back reclining chair. The company formally changed its name to La-Z-Boy in 1996.

The company has paid continuous quarterly dividends since its 1972 listing on the New York Stock Exchange and has offered its shareholders a dividend reinvestment and stock-purchase plan since 1978.

Shortcomings to Bear in Mind

- Although the company has a solid record of growth, it is clearly not immune to the vagaries of the economy. Earnings per share declined from $1.60 in 2000 to $1.13 in 2001, and they slipped even further in 2002, to $1.01. At the same time, return on shareholders' equity declined from 16.3 percent in 2000 to only 8.8 percent in 2002.

- One reason that earnings were hurt during these years is the nature of the furniture industry. Unlike food, drugs, mortgage payments, and electricity, furniture purchases can be postponed for months or years. That's why this industry is classed under the "consumer discretion" category.

- According to Michael P. Gorman, an analyst writing for *Value Line Investment Survey*, "Domestic furniture producers are facing increased competition from overseas, particularly China. However, most of the pressure is in wood furniture, partially insulating the upholstery segment. And the company is currently taking steps to increase it competitiveness. Management expects that 30 percent of its casegoods business will be imported this year, with that number reaching 40–50 percent in the future."

Reasons to Buy

- The company paid down $74 million in debt in 2002 and ended the year with a 16.6 percent debt-to-capitalization ratio. According to Mr. Kiser, "This balance sheet strength provides La-Z-Boy with yet another competitive advantage: financial flexibility. Aided by a strengthening economy and improving consumer confidence, we anticipate substantially improved sales and profitability in fiscal 2003."

- In 2002, in a significant international marketing move, La-Z-Boy and the Steinhoff Group joined forces to create La-Z-Boy Europe, a new joint venture company that designs, manufactures, markets, and distributes motion furniture overseas. According to management, "It is a powerful combination that brings together the superb manufacturing and distribution capabilities of Steinhoff and the marketing savvy and powerful brand name of La-Z-Boy, all in one organization."

- In the words of a company spokesman, "To strengthen our already powerful brand name, La-Z-Boy continues to engage in a strong, targeted marketing campaign. It is an effort that goes back two years to the launch of our 'New Look of Comfort' campaign, an initiative that sought to showcase La-Z-Boy products within cleverly written, bright and modern design concepts. In fact, this campaign has proven so successful that some customers have carried the actual ads into stores and ordered merchandise exactly as depicted."

- Several of the La-Z-Boy companies, in addition to marketing their products under their own trade names, have negotiated mutually beneficial licensing arrangements with well-known personalities to enhance consumer recognition of specific product lines. These successful licensing programs have featured celebrities in a wide variety of professions, ranging from athletics, to art, to fashion design.

- According to the company's 2002 annual report, "The verdict is in: Customers love the new La-Z-Boy Furniture Galleries stores! In fact, several new stores have posted sales of more than $1 million in their opening months. It is performance that is setting new records, delivering substantially higher sales per square foot across the board, outpacing industry averages, and exceeding expectations.

  "It is a result that comes after several years of extensive study and preparation. In late summer 2001, all that work came to fruition with the opening of the first new format, 16,000-plus square-foot La-Z-Boy Furniture Galleries store in Virginia. The ambitious design featured a striking, centrally positioned Design Center with a fourteen-foot-high ceiling and four distinct product gallery sections.

  "Eleven of the new generation stores were operating at the end of fiscal 2002. By the end of fiscal 2003, another twenty-five to thirty new stores are expected to be operating. In addition, approximately twenty-five older format La-Z-Boy Furniture Galleries stores are scheduled to be remodeled to the new format during fiscal 2003. Moving forward, the new generation La-Z-Boy Furniture Galleries store program will become the standard for our retail presence."

- La-Z-Boy gets nearly three-quarters of its sales from upholstered furniture, such as couches, easy chairs, and ottomans. That distinguishes it from competitors, such as Ethan Allen Interiors, that focus on more expensive wooden furniture, such as dining-room sets. This focus helps in a weak economy, since people usually replace upholstered furniture every six or seven years, said Mr. Kiser. "Customers will go out and spend $999 on a sofa for a

living room/great room more quickly than they'll go out and spend, say, $5,000 on a bedroom suite."

Total assets: $1,161 million
Current ratio: 2.96
Common shares outstanding: 60 million
Return on 2002 shareholders' equity: 8.8%

	2002	2001	2000	1999	1998	1997	1996	1995
Revenues (millions)	2,154	2,256	1,717	1,288	1,108	1,006	947	805
Net income (millions)	61.8	68.3	87.6	66.1	49.9	45.3	39.2	36.3
Earnings per share	1.01	1.13	1.60	1.24	0.93	0.83	0.71	0.67
Dividends per share	0.35	0.32	0.32	0.30	0.28	0.26	0.25	0.23
Price High	30.9	23.3	17.8	24.6	22.6	15.0	11.3	11.2
Low	19.2	14.7	13.0	15.4	14.1	9.9	9.0	8.5

CONSERVATIVE GROWTH

Leggett & Platt, Inc.

No. 1 Leggett Road □ Carthage, Missouri 64836 □ (417) 358-8131 □ Dividend reinvestment plan not available □ Web site: www.leggett.com □ Listed: NYSE □ Ticker symbol: LEG □ S&P rating: A- □ Value Line financial strength rating: A

To an extent, Leggett & Platt's business is tied to home-buying and new housing starts. The two years after a home is purchased are normally years of heavy furniture purchases.

According to a U.S. Department of Labor Study, the age group that spends the most amount on furniture is the 45-to 54-year-old bracket. The second-highest amount is spent by those 35 to 44. The Census Bureau says the number of consumers in the 45-to-54 age group expanded 14.1 percent in a recent five-year period. The 35-to-44 age group advanced 7.3 percent. At the same time, the general population increased only 4.7 percent.

There are a number of reasons why middle-aged people spend more money on furniture:

• Their income is high during this span of their lives.

• They are more likely to be home-owners than are younger people.

• These more mature couples have sold their starter homes. Their new homes, moreover, are larger and may need a whole new set of more expensive furniture.

In 1993, the average home had 2,100 square feet of living space, up 5 percent from 1988. According to surveys, the average home has now increased to 2,200 square feet. Larger homes require much more furniture than smaller ones. For instance, a home with 3,000 square feet needs 2.5 times more furniture than one with 2,000 square feet.

Company Profile

Founded in 1883, Leggett & Platt is a diversified manufacturer that designs and produces a variety of components and products for customers worldwide.

Leggett & Platt is North America's leading independent manufacturer of the following: retail store fixtures and point-of-purchase displays; components for residential furniture and bedding; components for office furniture; non-automotive aluminum die castings; drawn steel wire; automotive seat support and lumbar systems; and bedding industry machinery for wire forming, sewing, and quilting.

A member of the *Fortune* 500, the company is composed of 29 business units, 31,000 employees, and more than 300 facilities in 18 countries.

The company has grown at an average of 15 percent annually since going public in 1967, with about one-third of the growth coming from internal expansion and market share gains. Leggett & Platt augments internal growth with an active acquisition program. The company has completed more than 100 acquisitions over the last six years, with the average acquisition adding $15 to $20 million to annual sales.

Standard & Poor's added Leggett & Platt to the S&P 500 Index in October of 1999. The S&P 500 is widely regarded as one of the most important standards for measuring performance in the U.S. stock market. The index includes a cross-section of large-capitalization companies in a host of industries. As a component of the S&P 500, Leggett should gain increasing recognition throughout the investment community.

The following sections provide an overview of Leggett's businesses.

Residential Furnishings

Leggett & Platt is the world's leading supplier of a broad line of components that go into bedding and residential furniture. Many of these products are proprietary. Manufacturers of mattresses and box springs can buy almost all of their component requirements from Leggett. Product lines have been expanded to include a wide range of components for stationary and motion upholstered furniture as well.

In addition, the company designs and produces select lines of finished home furnishings and consumer products. Cus-

tomers include manufacturers, retailers, distributors, and institutions.

Residential Furnishings is by far the company's largest segment. In 2002, its sales increased 4.1 percent, totaling $2.2 billion.

Commercial Fixturing and Components

Leggett's rapidly expanding lines of commercial fixturing include creatively designed store fixtures, point-of-purchase displays, and storage and material handling systems. A multitude of retailers, brand-name packagers of consumer products, and companies in the foodservice, health care, and other industries are increasingly looking to Leggett as a one-stop/one-shop resource. Manufacturers of office and institutional furnishings and additional commercial products also can buy Leggett components designed and produced to meet their requirements. The company's components add significant value, comfort, and distinctive features to chairs and other office furniture.

Commercial Fixturing, Leggett's second-largest segment, experienced a revenue decrease of 4.9 percent in 2002, to $898.6 million.

Aluminum Products

The Leggett companies in its aluminum group are North America's leading independent suppliers of aluminum die castings, primarily for non-automotive applications. Major customers include manufacturers of consumer products, telecommunications, and electrical equipment, plus other industrial products that incorporate aluminum and zinc die cast components. Leggett's aluminum smelting and refining operations produce raw materials for internal use in die-casting plants, and for sale to other manufacturers of aluminum products.

Aluminum Products fared well in 2002, as total sales increased by 6.0 percent, to $487.3 million.

Industrial Materials

Several Leggett companies produce industrial materials for a wide range of customers, including other Leggett operations. Drawn steel wire and welded steel tubing are produced in various strategic locations. Additional operations produce specialty wire products, such as rolled, flattened, and shaped wire, proprietary bale ties, tying heads, and other parts for automatic baling equipment.

Industrial Materials, also enhanced by acquisitions, had a revenue growth in 2002 of 15.9 percent, to $611.2 million. However, without the acquisitions, sales would have risen only 2.5 percent.

Specialized Products

Two smaller units are engaged in manufacturing specialized products. One concentrates on manufacturing components destined primarily for automotive applications. The other business unit designs, builds, and sells specialized machinery and equipment. In the automotive segment, Leggett manufactures seating suspension, lumbar support, and control cable systems. In the machinery sector, the company manufactures highly automated quilting machines for fabrics used to cover mattresses and other home furnishings. It also has a stake in the implements that are used to fabricate springs of various types, industrial sewing machines, and other equipment designed primarily for the assembly of bedding.

Specialized Products turned in satisfactory results in 2002, with revenues inching up 4.3 percent to reach $407.2 million.

Shortcomings to Bear in Mind

- Leggett & Platt does best when new housing is booming, as it has been in the past two years. Some analysts believe that this strength will not continue.

Reasons to Buy

- Leggett & Platt boasts a solid record of growth. In the 1992–2002 period—despite dips in EPS in 2000 and 2001—earnings per share climbed from $0.41 to $1.17, a compound annual rate of 11.1 percent. In the same ten-year stretch, dividends per share expanded from $0.11 to $0.50, a growth rate of 16.3 percent. What's more, Leggett & Platt has increased its dividend for thirty-two consecutive years.

- Since 1967, acquisitions have been a key part of Leggett's growth strategy. Traditionally, the company pursues friendly acquisitions—those that fit with existing operations, either in marketing, technology, or both.

    Normally, Leggett's acquisitions broaden the company's product lines, providing entry into additional markets or secure sources of select raw materials. The company uses cash, stock, or combinations of the two in making acquisitions.

    On average, each acquired company accounted for $21 million in annual revenue. As a result of the relatively small size of each individual acquisition, the company lessens its exposure to blunders. This strategy, while difficult to execute, has been and will continue to be the backbone of Leggett & Platt's future growth.

- Leggett's commitment to research and development has kept pace with company growth. The company has R&D facilities at both centralized and divisional locations. At those locations, engineers and technicians design and build new and improved products in all major lines and machinery. They also perform extensive tests for durability and function. Leggett's experience and accumulation of data in this highly specialized area of R&D is unmatched.

- Participation in such diverse furnishings categories as bedding and residential, office, and contract furniture gives Leggett & Platt the opportunity to spread new product developments into several sectors at all price points, while limiting its exposure to any one sector.

- On January 6, 2003, Leggett & Platt again was selected for *Forbes* magazine's Platinum List of the best big companies in America.

**Total assets: $3,531 million
Current ratio: 2.37
Common shares outstanding: 195 million
Return on 2002 shareholders' equity: 12.2%**

	2002	2001	2000	1999	1998	1997	1996	1995
Revenues (millions)	4,272	4,114	4,276	3,779	3,370	2,909	2,466	2,110
Net income (millions)	233	188	264	290	248	208	153	135
Earnings per share	1.17	.94	1.32	1.45	1.24	1.08	.93	.80
Dividends per share	.50	.48	.42	.35	.32	.27	.23	.19
Price High	27.4	24.5	22.6	28.3	28.8	23.9	17.4	13.4
Low	18.6	16.8	14.2	18.6	16.9	15.8	10.3	8.5

AGGRESSIVE GROWTH

Lennar Corporation

700 Northwest 107th Avenue □ Miami, Florida 33172 □ (305) 485-2092 □ Web site: www.lennar.com □ Dividend reinvestment plan not available □ Fiscal years end November 30 □ Listed: NYSE □ Ticker symbol: LEN □ S&P rating: A- □ Value Line financial strength B+

Lennar Corporation, a leading home-builder, has been on the acquisition trail in recent years. Since 1997, the company has added eleven companies, highlighted by the acquisition of U.S. Home in 2000. Also included in the group was Patriot Homes in Baltimore and, more recently, Don Galloway Homes and Sunstar Communities in the Carolinas.

According to the company's chief executive officer, Stuart Miller, "These acquisitions have uniquely positioned us as one of the most diverse builders in the marketplace. Our product offerings now range from homes for first-time buyers to homes for the active adult. Our product offerings now range from under $100,000 entry-level homes to over $1-million ocean view homes.

"Our dual marketing strategy of both Design Studio and Everything's Included provides us a vehicle for internal growth, faster and more efficient use of our net assets, and a larger market share capture. Our geographic diversification now finds us in sixteen states and forty-four metropolitan areas from the east coast to the west coast."

Company Profile

Lennar Corporation, founded in 1954, is headquartered in Miami, Florida. The company has homebuilding operations in sixteen states and is one of the nation's leading builders of quality homes. Lennar builds affordable, move-up, and retirement homes.

Under the Lennar Family of Builders banner, the company includes the following brand names: Lennar Homes, U.S. Home, Greystone Homes, Village Builders, Renaissance Homes, Orrin Thompson Homes, Lundgren Brothers, Winncrest Homes, Sunstar Communities, Don Galloway Homes, Patriot Homes, Rutenberg Homes, and NuHome. The company's active adult communities are primarily marketed under the Heritage and Greenbriar brand names.

Lennar's Financial Services Division provides residential mortgage services, title, and closing services. Its Strategic Technologies Division provides high-speed Internet access, cable television, and alarm-monitoring services for both Lennar home buyers and other customers.

In 2000, the company acquired U.S. Home (with $1.8 billion in 1999 revenues) for $510 million in cash and common stock, plus the assumption of $650 million in debt. Prior to this move, Lennar was the leading homebuilder in Florida. The company also has extensive operations in California, Texas, Arizona, and Nevada. U.S. Home also had a strong presence in Florida, Texas, and Arizona, and it added to Lennar's geographic presence with big positions in Denver, Minneapolis, and the Eastern Seaboard.

Lennar subsequently entered the North Carolina and South Carolina markets through the acquisition of certain properties of Fortress Group in December 2001. The following year, Lennar purchased the Arizona operations of Fortress.

Shortcomings to Bear in Mind

- Low interest rates are a spur to housing. However, as the economy strengthens, rates are likely to begin rising, which makes it more difficult for home buyers to afford new homes.
- According to the company's 10-K report, "The housing industry is highly competitive. In our activities, we compete with numerous developers and builders of various sizes, both national and local, who are building homes in and near the areas where our communities are located. Competition is on the basis of location, design, quality, amenities, price, service, and reputation. Sales of existing homes also provide competition.

Some of our principal national competitors include Centex Corporation, D. R. Horton, Inc., KB Home, and Pulte Homes, Inc."

- The company's 10-K report also points out some problems with regulation. "In recent years, several cities and counties in which we have developments have submitted to voters "slow growth" initiatives and other ballot measures which could impact the affordability and availability of homes and land within these localities. Although many of these initiatives have been defeated, we believe that if similar initiatives were approved, residential construction by us and others within certain cities or counties could be seriously impacted."

Reasons to Buy

- Inventories of completed homes are at record lows, and the availability of new homes is constrained because of the difficulty of entitling land. What's more, America's used housing stock is aging, and new homes are more attractive than ever.
- On the demand side, interest rates remain low, keeping homes affordable and home ownership rising. Household formations are projected to continue to grow steadily, fueled by immigration.
- The company has 128,000 home sites owned or under its control.

  With the highest level of capital liquidity in its history, the company is, according to Mr. Miller, "positioned to continue the growth of our company."
- In the words of William G. Ferguson, an analyst with *Value Line Investment Survey*, "The company's national purchasing program has resulted in a savings of about $1,000 per home so far in fiscal 2002. Based on the latest results and our belief that Lennar's business is well positioned to deliver strong results, we have raised our fiscal 2002 estimate

by \$.30, to \$6.55. Fiscal 2003 should be another good year."

According to the company's 10-K report, "We supervise and control the development and building of our residential communities. We employ subcontractors for site improvements and virtually all of the work involved in the construction of homes. In almost all instances, the arrangements with our subcontractors commit the subcontractors to complete specified work in accordance with written prices schedules. These price schedules normally change to meet changes in labor force and material costs.

"We do not own heavy construction equipment and only have a relatively small labor force used to supervise development and construction and perform routine maintenance and minor amounts of other work. We generally finance construction and land development activities with cash generated from operations as well as from borrowings under our working capital lines and issuance of public debt."

■ Lennar Corporation has a solid record of growth. In the 1992–2002 period, earn-

ings per share advanced from \$1.11 to \$7.72, a compound annual growth rate of 21.4 percent. What's more, during that ten-year span, earnings declined only once (in 1997).

■ According to Bruce Gross, Lennar's chief financial officer, "Lennar's strong balance sheet has positioned us for strong growth and has minimized our downside risk. We view cycles as our ally, not an adversary, since weaker economic times present buying opportunities, and our strong balance sheet positions us to seize opportunities when they exist.

"With our strong cash position of \$824 million at the end of the year, we are in a position to pursue additional opportunities. Finally, our strong balance sheet allows Lennar to do well in good times and capitalize on market inefficiencies in slower times."

Mr. Gross also said, "By far the strongest in the industry, our balance sheet reflected an almost 20 percent return on net capital which greatly exceeded our 10 percent cost of capital."

Total assets: \$5,756 million
Current ratio: 2.80
Common shares outstanding: 64 million
Return on 2002 shareholders' equity: 24.5%

	2002	2001	2000	1999	1998	1997	1996	1995
Revenues (millions)	7,320	6,029	4,707	3,118	2,417	1,209	1,092	805
Net income (millions)	545	418	229	173	144	68	88	70
Earnings per share	7.72	6.01	3.64	2.74	2.49	1.79	2.44	1.95
Dividends per share	.05	.05	.05	.05	.05	.09	.10	.10
Price High	64.0	49.9	39.4	27.9	36.2	44.7	27.3	25.5
Low	43.2	31.0	15.3	13.1	14.9	15.8	21.6	15.3

AGGRESSIVE GROWTH

Eli Lilly and Company

Lilly Corporate Center □ Indianapolis, Indiana 46285 □ (317) 276-2506 □ Direct dividend reinvestment plan is available: (800)833-8699 □ Web site: www.lilly.com □ Listed: NYSE □ Ticker symbol: LLY □ S&P rating: B+ □ Value Line financial strength rating: A++

"The worst is undoubtedly over for Eli Lilly," said George Rho, an analyst with *Value Line Investment Survey* late in 2002.

"In the second quarter of 2001, Prozac accounted for 23 percent of the company's total revenues. Generic copies of the antidepressant became available soon thereafter, exerting devastating pressure on the price. Consequently, Lilly's one-time flagship represented only 7 percent of aggregate sales in 2002's June period. Its top-line contribution was down a whopping 72 percent (to $195 million), and year-over-year share-net comparisons were negative for the fourth successive quarter. "Results from the just-concluded September period will have some remnants of Prozac's descent, but we still expect a positive earnings match-up. That's because sales of the company's newer, so-called GAZE (Gemzar, Actos, Zyprexa, and Evista) drugs continue to expand at robust double-digit rates."

Company Profile

Eli Lilly is one of the world's foremost health care companies. With a solid dedication to research and development, Lilly is a leader in the development of ethical drugs—those available on prescription.

The company is well known for making such drugs as Prozac, which treats depression; a number of antibiotics, such as Ceclor, Vancocin, Keflex, and Lorabid; and insulin and other diabetic care items. Some of its other important drugs include Gemzar (to treat cancer of the lung and pancreas); Evista (to treat and prevent osteoporosis); ReoPro (a drug used to prevent adverse side effects from angioplasty procedures); Zyprexa (a breakthrough treatment for schizophrenia and bipolar disorder); Dobutrex (for congestive heart failure); Axid (a medication that reduces excess stomach acid); and Sarafem (for the treatment of premenstrual dysphoric disorder).

Lilly also has a stake in animal health and agricultural products.

Like most drug companies, Lilly is active abroad and does business in 120 countries.

Here's how the company's ten largest products have fared:

ANNUAL SALES IN MILLIONS OF DOLLARS		
	2002	2001
Zyprexa	$3,688.9	$3,086.6
Humulin	1,004.0	1,060.6
Gemzar	874.6	722.9
Humalog	834.2	627.8
Evista	821.9	644.8
Prozac, Prozac Weekly, and Sarafem	733.7	1,990.0
Actos	391.7	360.6
ReoPro	384.0	431.4
Humatrope	329.3	312.7

Shortcomings to Bear in Mind

- Zyprexa is facing new competition and has come up against concerns about whether it and other relatively new schizophrenia drugs may promote diabetes in some patients. Despite this negative, sales have been increasing at a 20 percent rate.
- The Food & Drug Administration (FDA) began itemizing manufacturing and record-keeping shortcomings at Lilly's Indianapolis facilities in January of 2001, particularly at a plant called Building 105 used for injectable pharmaceuticals. The FDA also discovered that Lilly was deficient in record-keeping at the plant, and it found some manufacturing flaws, including some that led to a recall by the company. Lilly recalled thirty-seven lots of products, ranging from older drugs (antibiotics and the heart medicine dobutamine) to Gemzar, a newer drug for pancreatic and lung cancer.

In July of 2002, Lilly said it had overhauled its quality-assurance division, but that it wouldn't be ready for a reinspection of Building 105 until early 2003.

That means that Lilly's new-drug pipeline—among the best in the industry—will be hampered, notably for such important drugs as Zyprexa, the company's leading product and the world's number one product for the treatment of psychosis and schizophrenia. It is growing at rate of 23 percent a year.

Reasons to Buy

- Mr. Taurel vowed not to be painted into a corner again: "The situation we had in the mid-1990s, of having 35 percent of our sales dependent on Prozac, won't repeat itself." Eight new drugs are in the pipeline for introduction in the 2002–2004 period. According to an article in *BusinessWeek*, "Lilly has the financial muscle to pay the $1 billion it can take to bring out a new drug. Lilly also has an 11,500-member sales force to push new pharmaceuticals." Sales are important, to be sure, but research is the real key. Again, according to *BusinessWeek*, Mr. Taurel "furiously ramped up new-drug development after becoming CEO and chairman in 1998. He increased the research and development budget about 30 percent, to more than $2.2 billion, hired 700 scientists in the last year alone, and in a search for the next blockbuster, ordered Lilly's 6,900 researchers not to bother with any drug unlikely to top $500 million in annual sales. The payoff is that Lilly now has a medicine cabinet stocked full of promising new drugs, including treatments for schizophrenia and for sepsis—a potentially fatal form of bacterial infection."
- As the developer of the first insulin product and one of the world's major suppliers of insulin, Lilly has long been a global leader in the field. But diabetes, which affects more than 100 million people worldwide, continues to cause severe long-term complications, suffering, lost productivity, and death.

For many patients with this disease, diabetes is also inconvenient. Diabetics have to check their blood glucose several times a day. They may have to give themselves one or more shots of insulin or risk severe complications.

Lilly believes that it has an answer that gives patients with diabetes a better quality of life—and a good deal more convenience. Humalog acts faster than traditional insulin to control blood glucose levels. Patients take it right before a meal, compared with the thirty to forty-five minutes they were required to wait using current products. Humalog provides them with more freedom, better health, and fewer complications.

- In late 2002, Lilly paid $325 million to Amylin Pharmaceuticals, a biotechnology company, for the rights to a potentially promising treatment for diabetes. The drug, a synthetic version of a compound found in the venom of a poisonous lizard, known as the Gila monster, could become an alternative to insulin for some people with type 2, or adult-onset, diabetes, which accounts for most of the 17 million cases of diabetes in the United States.

There is some evidence that the drug can reduce the risk of low blood sugar, which can cause a diabetic to lose consciousness. The Amylin drug, known as AC2993, is less likely to cause weight gain that can be caused by insulin. The drug is in the final stages of testing and could reach the market in 2005.

- "We expect revenues to advance about 10 percent in 2003," said a report issued by *Standard & Poor's Stock Reports* at the end of 2002. H. B. Saftlas said, "Continued strength is forecast for key established lines such as Zyprexa for schizophrenia, Gemzar anticancer therapy, Humalog rapid-acting human insulin, Xigris for sepsis, and Evista for osteoporosis. Volume should also be augmented by recently approved Forteo for severe osteoporosis and Strattera for attention deficit hyperactivity disorder (ADHD). Contributions are also likely from Cymbalta antidepressant and Cialis for erectile dysfunction (pending FDA clearance)."

The S&P report also said, "We recently upgraded our opinion on Lilly to buy, from hold, based on our belief that LLY's lineup of potentially best-in-class new drugs should fuel superior EPS growth over the coming years."

■ Two new drugs are expected to begin competing with Viagra in the second half of 2003. Viagra has had the market to itself since it was introduced by Pfizer in 1998. As of late March 2003, these two drugs (Cialis and Levitra) were already on sale in Europe and were taking market share from Viagra. Their attributes are quicker action and longer duration. Lilly's Cialis, according to Vanessa Fuhrmans, writing for the *Wall Street Journal*, "snapped up 28 percent of Viagra's market share," in its seventh week on the market.

Ms. Fuhrmans went on to say, "For all of its popularity, the little blue pill has a spotty record with many patients. Doctors say about half of the men who take it don't refill their prescriptions within a year, either because they give up after a few failed attempts or because of side effects.

"In clinical trials, men who took Cialis or Levitra were able to have sex within thirty minutes, often achieving an erection within fifteen to twenty minutes. With Viagra, doctors say it can take an hour before men are able to have sex."

■ The first new drug for ADHD in decades, Strattera is regarded as a potentially important drug because most of the existing treatments for the condition—such as Ritalin, generic methylphenidate, Adderall, and Concerta—are stimulants and can interfere with sleep and appetite. What's more, they are controlled substances under federal law. This means that access to them is restricted, and that their sales are monitored by the Federal Drug Enforcement Administration.

ADHD, which can be a subjective diagnosis, is believed to be widely overdiagnosed and yet quite prevalent. It is estimated that as many as 5 percent to 10 percent of school-age children have the affliction. ADHD involves compulsive behavior, great difficulty concentrating, and often a learning disability. Finally, the condition tends to be inherited and can continue into adulthood.

■ One of Lilly's new drugs, Cymbalta, is superior to Prozac in that it affects two neurotransmitters involved in depression (serotonin and norepinephrine). Other antidepressants, including Prozac, affect only serotonin. Scientists believe an imbalance of the two transmitters may explain the physical and emotional symptoms that depressed patients often endure.

Total assets: $19,042 million
Current ratio: 1.54
Common shares outstanding: 1,123 million
Return on 2002 shareholders' equity: 35.2%

	2002	2001	2000	1999	1998	1997	1996	1995
Revenues (millions)	11,077	11,543	10,953	10,003	9,237	8,518	7,346	6,764
Net income (millions)	2,763	3,014	2,905	2,721	2,098	1,774	1,524	1,307
Earnings per share	2.55	2.76	2.65	2.28	1.94	1.57	1.33	1.15
Dividends per share	1.24	1.12	1.04	.92	.80	.74	.69	.66
Price High	81.1	95.0	109.0	97.8	91.3	70.4	40.2	28.5
Low	43.8	70.0	54.0	60.6	57.7	35.6	24.7	15.6

Lockheed Martin Corporation

6801 Rockledge Drive □ Bethesda, Maryland 20817 □ (301) 897-6584 □ Dividend reinvestment plan not available □ Web site: www.lockheedmartin.com □ Listed: NYSE □ Ticker symbol: LMT □ S&P rating: B- □ Value Line financial strength rating: B+

"Poland today named U.S. Lockheed Martin Corp.'s Fighting Falcon the winner of a three-way tender to supply forty-eight combat jets in a $3.5-billion deal, eastern Europe's largest defense order," according to an article prepared by Reuters News Service at the end of 2002.

Lockheed, with its Block 52 F-16 C/D model, powered by F-100-229 engines from United Technologies' Pratt and Whitney unit, beat French and Anglo-Swedish rivals to land its first major defense order in the region. Competing against the Lockheed craft were the F-16 Dassault Aviation Mirage 2000-5 Mk 2 and the Anglo-Swedish Jas-39 Gripen, built by BAE Systems and Saab.

The deal marks a triumph for a lobbying drive led by President Bush. It dealt a blow to Europe's aerospace industry just two weeks after the European Economic Union invited Poland and nine other countries to join the EEU in 2004.

Poland has been a member of NATO since 1999. However, when Poland awarded this contract to Lockheed Martin, there was still an undercurrent of grumbling that Poland had buckled under pressure from the United States. In response to this, the country's defense minister, Jerzy Szmajdzinski, said, "Poland based its decision on merit, not politics. This deal guarantees our ability to participate in NATO operations and increase our security."

The F-16s will be delivered between 2006 and 2008, enabling ex–Warsaw Pact member Poland to scrap its obsolete Soviet-era plans, some of which have been in the air since 1960.

Company Profile

Lockheed Martin was created in 1995 when Lockheed Corporation merged with Martin Marietta. The new stock began trading on March 16, 1995. Lockheed Martin has a stake in the operation of advanced technology systems, products, and services. Its products and services range from aircraft, spacecraft, and launch vehicles to missiles, electronics, information systems, and telecommunications.

Areas of concentration include space and missile systems, electronics, aeronautics, and information systems. Among the company's well-known products are the following: the F-16, F-22, and F-117A aircraft; Trident ballistic missile systems; the C-130 military transport; and Titan launch vehicles. The company operates in five principal business segments, as described in the following sections.

Systems Integration

Systems Integration has a stake in the design, development, and integration of complex systems for global defense, civil government, and commercial markets. Core operations include undersea warfare, surface warfare, and land surveillance systems; tactical missiles, air defense systems, and fire-control and sensor systems; information superiority systems; simulation and training systems; air-traffic management systems; aerospace systems and platform integration; business system solutions; and distribution technologies. The latter includes automated material handling solutions for postal systems and commercial customers.

Space Systems

Space Systems designs, develops, engineers, and produces civil, commercial, and military space systems. Major products include spacecraft, space launch vehicles, and human space systems, and their supporting ground systems and services, as well as strategic fleet ballistic missiles.

Aeronautics

This segment is engaged in the design, research, development, and production of combat aircraft, surveillance/command systems, reconnaissance systems, and platform systems. Major products include the F-16 fighter, the F-22 fighter, and the C-130J tactical airlift aircraft.

Technology Services

This unit provides a wide variety of management, engineering, scientific, logistic, and information services to federal agencies and other customers.

Global Telecommunications

Global Telecommunications has a stake in communications services and advanced technology solutions through three lines of business. Enterprise Solutions provides telecommunications services, managed networks, and information technology solutions in the United States and international markets. Satellite Services provides global fixed and mobile satellite services.

Finally, Systems and Technology designs, builds, and integrates satellite gateways. It also provides systems integration services for telecommunications networks.

Shortcomings to Bear in Mind

- *Standard & Poor's Stock Reports* has some doubts about the future of Lockheed Martin. In early 2003, Robert E. Friedman, CPA, said, "EPS should rise about 10 percent in 2003, to $2.39, primarily driven by increased sales of LMT's less profitable developmental F-22s, satellite, and payload-carrying rockets and information systems and should keep operating and net profit margins below 8 percent and 4 percent, respectively.

"Consequently, we believe LMT will only be able to post debt-adjusted return on equity (ROE) of 8 percent-plus for 2003, far below our 15 percent minimum threshold for a recommendation. As a result, we're projecting that growth in LMT's per-share net worth (an important intrinsic value proxy) may expand a middling 5 percent to 10 percent rate in 2003. Our long-term outlook is not much more sanguine."

Reasons to Buy

- In 2003, a Lockheed Martin Titan II launch vehicle successfully placed the Coriolis mission into orbit for the U.S. Air Force and the U.S. Navy. The Coriolis mission comprises two payloads: the Navy Windsat Radiometer and the Air Force Solar Mass Ejection Imager. Both payloads were successfully placed in a low Earth/Sun synchronous orbit of 516 miles.

- In 2003, Lockheed Martin completed the ahead-of-schedule nationwide rollout of a critical computer upgrade at twenty-three air-traffic control facilities, helping the Federal Aviation Administration continue its modernization of the core en route airspace system.

- In 2002, a U.S. Air Force Milstar II military communications satellite lifted off from Cape Canaveral Air Station, Florida, aboard a Titan IVB launch vehicle. The satellite and launch vehicle were built by Lockheed Martin Space Systems Company. The satellite, designated Milstar II, is the defense department's most technologically advanced telecommunications satellite. It is only the second satellite to carry the Medium

Data Rate (MDR) payload, which can process data at speeds of 1.5 megabits per second. The U.S. Air Force transitioned to the Block II configuration with an earlier successful launch of the first Milstar II satellite. The Milstar Block II system offers a variety of enhanced communications features for the U.S. military, including added security through the use of specially designed antennas and faster data-rate transitions for users.

- In 2002, Lockheed Martin and Boeing were chosen to team up to create a multibillion-dollar U.S. drive to build missile shields. As comanagers of the so-called national team being shaped by the Pentagon, the two companies—the two largest domestic military contractors—will have key roles in meshing more effectively the dozen or so existing missile defense programs.

  Boeing will take the lead in defining the architecture of a planned multilayered shield that could involve systems based on land, ships, in space, and on modified Boeing 747 aircraft. A second group, led by Lockheed Martin, will put the overlapping systems to work through integrated battle-management and command-control software.

  In 2002, President Bush signed into law a defense funding bill that includes $8 billion for missile defense development to meet what he called a growing threat of intercontinental ballistic missile attack from such "rogue" states as North Korea and Iran.

- In 2002, the federal government tapped Lockheed Martin to train the recently federalized work force of airport screeners. Under the contract, valued at over $100 million, the company has the task of training about 30,000 people to screen passengers and their carry-on luggage.

Capping a four-year, $1-billion Concept Demonstration Program, the defense department selected Lockheed Martin (along with its subcontractors) over Boeing to receive up to $200 billion to build a fleet of Joint Strike Force fighters. Over the next twenty-five years, Lockheed Martin will design and build nearly 3,000 Joint Strike Fighters (JSF), a single-engine, supersonic, multirole stealth aircraft, which will be known as the F-35. Announced in October of 2001, the contract was the largest the Pentagon had ever awarded.

The new contract positions Lockheed Martin to dominate the domestic and foreign jet fighter markets for decades to come. Scheduled to enter service in 2008, the new F-35 will replace a number of older jets, including the F-14 and F-16 fighters, the A-10, the AV-8 Harrier, and the F/A-18. To save the costs of developing more specialized planes, each of the services will receive different versions of the JSF. For instance, a U.S. Navy model will be able to operate from an aircraft carrier, while one developed for the U.S. Marines will be able to take off vertically. What's more, Lockheed will also produce a version of the F-35 for the U.K. Royal Air Force and the Royal Navy.

All variants will be supersonic and stealthy (radar-evading), and equipped with cutting-edge avionics designed to enhance the pilot's situational awareness. Range and payload will be markedly greater than those of today's fighters. Finally, the Joint Strike Fighter is designed to require significantly less maintenance and support, cutting long-term ownership costs by half.

Total assets: $28,919 million
Current ratio: 1.16
Common shares outstanding: 456 million
Return on 2002 shareholders' equity: 6.9%

		2002	2001	2000	1999	1998	1997	1996	1995
Revenues (millions)		26,578	23,990	25,329	25,530	26,266	28,069	26,875	22,853
Net income (millions)		533	79	432	575	1,184	1,300	1,205	1,118
Earnings per share		2.58	0.18	1.07	1.41	3.11	3.05	2.70	2.50
Dividends per share		.44	.44	.44	.88	.82	.80	.80	.67
Price	High	71.5	53.0	37.6	46.0	58.9	56.7	48.3	39.8
	Low	45.8	31.0	16.5	16.4	41.0	39.1	36.5	25.0

CONSERVATIVE GROWTH

Lowe's Companies, Inc.

1605 Curtis Bridge Road □ Post Office Box 1111 □ Wilkesboro, North Carolina 28656 □ (336) 658-5239 □ Direct dividend reinvestment plan is available: (877) 282-1174 □ Web site: www.lowes.com □ Fiscal years end Friday closest to January 31 of following year □ Listed: NYSE □ Ticker symbol: LOW □ S&P rating: A+ □ Value Line financial strength rating: A+

"The difference between a Lowe's store and a Home Depot has been fairly clear-cut up to now," said the author of an article in *BusinessWeek* in mid-2002. "Presentation counts at Lowe's. Its warehouse-style stores are laid out so that two shopping carts can pass in comfort—a feature that has helped Lowe's appeal to women shoppers. It has made a conscious decision to target women because, as Executive Vice-President for Merchandise Dale C. Pond says, '80 percent of home projects are initiated by females.'

"That effort is paying off. In the late 1980s, only 13 percent of Lowe's shoppers were women, and many such customers were turned off by buying things 'in lumber shops,' said CEO Robert Tillman, age fifty-nine (who has worked at Lowe's for forty years). Today, half of Lowe's clientele is female, and the chain is attracting more and more non-professional home-improvement shoppers."

Company Profile

Lowe's is the second-largest domestic retailer of home-improvement products serving the do-it-yourself and commercial business customers. (Home Depot is number one.) Capitalizing on a growing number of U.S. households (about 100 million) the company has expanded from fifteen stores in 1962 and now operates 840 stores in forty-three states. Lowe's competes in the highly fragmented, $300-billion, home-improvement industry.

The company sells more than 40,000 home-improvement products, including plumbing and electrical products, tools, building materials, hardware, outdoor hard lines, appliances, lumber, nursery and gardening products, millwork, paint, sundries, and cabinets and furniture. Lowe's has often been listed as one of the "100 Best Companies to Work for in America."

The company obtains its products from about 6,500 merchandise vendors from around the globe. In most instances, Lowe's deals directly with foreign manufacturers, rather than third-party importers.

In order to maintain appropriate inventory levels in stores and to enhance efficiency and distribution, Lowe's operates six highly automated, efficient, state-of-the-art regional distribution centers (RDCs). RDCs are strategically situated in

North Carolina, Georgia, Ohio, Indiana, Pennsylvania, Washington, and Texas.

In 2000, the company broke ground in Findlay, Ohio, on an $80-million regional distribution center. Completed in October of 2001, the 1.25-million-square-foot facility employs 500 people and supplies products to some 100 stores throughout the lower Great Lakes region.

Lowe's serves both retail and commercial business customers. Retail customers are primarily do-it-yourself homeowners and others buying for personal and family use. Commercial business customers include building contractors, repair and remodeling contractors, electricians, landscapers, painters, plumbers, and commercial building maintenance professionals.

During 1999, Lowe's acquired Eagle Hardware & Garden, a thirty-six-store chain of home-improvement and garden centers in the West. The acquisition accelerated the company's West Coast expansion and provided a stepping-stone for Lowes into ten new states and a number of key metropolitan markets.

In recent years, the company has been transforming its store base from a chain of small stores into a chain of home-improvement warehouses. The current prototype store (the largest in the industry) has 150,000 square feet of sales floor and another 35,000 dedicated to lawn and garden products. The company is in the midst of its most aggressive expansion in company history. Lowe's is investing $2 billion a year and opening more than one store each week.

Shortcomings to Bear in Mind

- Interest rates have been low, which has been a spur to home ownership and home improvement projects, which helps Lowe's. If interest rates start to climb and mortgage rates follow suit, however, that ball game may come to an end.

- According to Alan Rifkin, an analyst with Lehman Brothers, a leading brokerage firm, in November of 2002, "We've asked an awful lot of the consumer in the last few years, and they're showing signs of fatigue." He cautioned that lagging consumer confidence is creeping into home-improvement spending.

Reasons to Buy

- Lowe's finished 2002 (ended January 31, 2003) with a flourish. Dan Morse, writing for the *Wall Street Journal* (February 25, 2003) said: "Lowe's Co.'s fiscal fourth quarter earnings jumped 46 percent on solid gains in sales, further indicating the home-improvement retailer is grabbing customers from larger rival Home Depot Inc."

- The company is optimistic about 2003. Management had this to say on February 24, 2003:
  - "The company expects to open 130 stores in 2003, reflecting total square footage growth of 15 to 16 percent.
  - Total sales are expected to increase approximately 16 to 17 percent for the year.
  - The company expects to report a comparable store sales of approximately 4 to 5 percent.
  - Operating margin (defined as gross margin less SG&A and depreciation) is expected to increase approximately 20 basis points. (There are 100 basis points in 1 percent.)
  - Store opening costs are expected to be approximately $140 million.
  - Diluted earnings per share of $2.16 to $2.20 are expected for the fiscal year ending January 30, 2004."

- In a report issued in late 2002, *Value Line Investment Survey* had some favorable comments. Its analyst, Carrie Galeotafiore, had this to say: "Despite uncertainties with regard to the state of the overall U.S. economy, the housing industry has proven to be quite resilient, helped by low mortgage rates. And, at these low rates, many homeowners have been refinancing. Homebuilding materials suppliers, such as Lowe's, should continue to benefit from this trend, as about one-third of homeowners tend to use equity taken out of their home (via refinancing) on home improvement projects. Indeed, others who use refinancing only to lower their mortgage payment, and opt not to take out cash, will generally use a portion of the added disposable income to fund home improvement spending."

- "The trend is likely to continue," according to Lucy Stoeva, writing for *Ticker* magazine in 2002. "New households, baby boomers buying a second home, career women with good incomes, and immigrants are expected to continue boosting home sales. Economy.com, a market researcher in West Chester, Pennsylvania, estimates that 1.23 million new households will be formed each year for the next ten years."

- Lowe's has broken into the *Fortune* 100 top list of corporations. Ranked at 108 in the 2001 listings, Lowe's jumped fourteen places to rank at number 94 for 2002. This ranking is based on corporate revenue.

- *BusinessWeek* magazine ranked Lowe's at number eight in their annual *BusinessWeek* 50 edition. The listings are based on corporate sales growth, earnings growth, and total shareholder return. The results are tallied for one- and three-year periods to gauge staying power.

- *Forbes* magazine ranked Lowe's at number 77 on the *Forbes* Super 500 List. Inclusion on this list is based on the individual rankings of the 824 firms that made one or more of the sales, profits, assets, and market value lists.

- To enhance its extensive line of national brands, such as DeWalt, Armstrong, American Standard, Olympic, Owens

Corning, Sylvania, Harbor Breeze, and Delta, the company is teaming up with vendors to offer preferred brands exclusive to Lowe's. These include Laura Ashley, Sta-Green, Troy-Bilt, and Alexander Julian, among others.

In categories in which preferred brands are not available, Lowe's has created its own brands, including Kobalt tools, Reliabilt doors and windows, and Top Choice lumber.

- Lowe's advanced to the number two spot in domestic appliance sales in 2000. However, the company is the number one seller of appliances among home-improvement centers. In its stores, Lowe's features such leading brands as Whirlpool, KitchenAid, Frigidaire, Maytag, Jenn-Air, and General Electric.

- In the spring of 2002, Waverly, one of the premier home furnishing brands, became exclusively available at Lowe's stores. "Waverly Home Classics" consist of a variety of classic Waverly designs in wall covering, with complementary window treatments and drapery hardware. "Our customers are looking for coordinated solutions for their home-decorating projects," said Melissa Birdsong, Lowe's director of trend forecasting and design. "The Waverly brand is among the most recognized in home decor and is an outstanding addition to Lowe's assortment of exclusive premier brands."

- "Home Depot, with 1,500 stores to Lowe's 840, still generates more sales and operating profit per square foot ($368 and $37, respectively, compared to $293 and $27 for Lowe's), but Lowe's is narrowing the gap," said Bruce Upbin, writing for *Forbes* magazine in January of 2003. "Its new stores are bigger— 121,000 square feet on average, compared with 109,000 for Home Depot— and its older stores do better repeat business."

Mr. Upbin went on to say, "'Bob Tillman is one of the most under-rated leaders in American business,' says Joseph Galli, Jr., chief executive of

Newell Rubbermaid. 'He has a remarkable ability to visualize, aisle by aisle, how a store should be.'"

Total assets: $16,109 million
Current ratio: 1.56
Common shares outstanding: 780 million
Return on 2002 shareholders' equity: 20.1%

	2002	2001	2000	1999	1998	1997	1996	1995
Revenues (millions)	26,491	22,111	18,779	15,905	12,245	10,137	8,600	7,075
Net income (millions)	1,471	1,023	810	673	482	357	292	226
Earnings per share	1.85	1.30	1.06	.90	.68	.51	.43	.34
Dividends per share	.08	.075	.07	.06	.06	.06	.05	.05
Price High	50.0	48.9	33.6	33.2	26.1	12.3	10.9	9.7
Low	32.5	21.9	17.1	21.5	10.8	7.9	7.2	6.5

CONSERVATIVE GROWTH

McCormick & Company, Inc.

18 Loveton Circle □ Post Office Box 6000 □ Sparks, Maryland 21152-6000 □ (410) 771-7244 □ Direct dividend reinvestment plan is available: (800)401-1957 □ Web site: www.mccormick.com □ Fiscal years end November 30 □ Listed: NYSE □ Ticker symbol: MKC □ S&P rating: A- □ Value Line financial strength rating: B++

In February of 2003, Richard Joy, an analyst with *Standard & Poor's Stock Reports*, had this to say about McCormick: "We continue our accumulate recommendation on the shares, reflecting anticipated long-term annual EPS (earnings per share) growth of 10 percent to 11 percent and solid growth for the company's consumer and industrial businesses."

The S&P report (one of my favorite sources of stock information) went on to say, "MKC's financial strength continues to improve, and free cash flow generation is rising. Internal volume trends remain solid, with volume gains exceeding category growth for several core product lines. Long-term growth prospects remain bright, reflecting the company's dominant and expanding U.S. spice market share (over 45 percent), as well as its leading share of the European consumer market (over 20 percent)."

Company Profile

McCormick, the world's foremost maker of spices and seasonings, is committed to the development of tasty, easy-to-use new products to satisfy consumer demand.

When investors hear the name McCormick, they think of the spices they use every day. Indeed, McCormick is the world's largest spice company. Yet the company is also the leader in the manufacture, marketing, and distribution of such products as seasonings and flavors for the entire food industry. These customers include foodservice and food-processing businesses, as well as retail outlets. This industrial segment was responsible for 45 percent of sales and 36 percent of operating profits in 2002. A majority of the top 100 food companies are McCormick customers.

McCormick also has a stake in packaging (7 percent of sales and 6 percent of operating profits). This group manufactures specialty plastic bottles and tubes for food, personal care, and for other industries.

Founded in 1889, McCormick distributes its products in about 100 countries.

McCormick's U.S. Consumer business (47 percent and 58 percent), its oldest and largest, is dedicated to the manufacture and sale of consumer spices, herbs, extracts, proprietary seasoning blends, sauces, and marinades. They are sold under such brand names as McCormick, Schilling, Produce Partners, Golden Dipt, Old Bay, and Mojave.

Many of the spices and herbs purchased by the company are imported into the United States from the company of origin. However, significant quantities of some materials, such as paprika, dehydrated vegetables, onion, and garlic, as well as food ingredients other than spices and herbs originate in the United States.

McCormick is a direct importer of certain raw materials, mainly black pepper, vanilla beans, cinnamon, herbs, and seeds from the countries of origin.

The raw materials most important to the company are onion, garlic, and capsicums (paprika and chili peppers), which are produced in the United States; black pepper, most of which originates in India, Indonesia, Malaysia, and Brazil; and vanilla beans, a large portion of which the company obtains from the Malagasy Republic and Indonesia.

Historical Highlights
- 1889: Founding of McCormick & Co., Inc.
- 1932: Multiple Management business philosophy established.
- 1947: Acquired Schilling, gaining coast-to-coast distribution in the United States.
- 1956: Joint venture in Mexico formed.
- 1960s: Acquired Canada's largest spice firm. Expansion into Australia, industrial business, real-estate business, cake decorating, and packaging business.

- 1980s: Acquired leading brand of spices and seasonings in the United Kingdom. Established business in China. Expanded industrial business with acquisition of Stange and packaging business with acquisition of Setco. Sold real-estate business.
- 1990s: Expanded consumer business through acquisitions, including Golden Dipt in the United States, Keen's in Australia, and Butty in Switzerland. Fierce competitor impacted financial results in the mid-1990s, but led to rejuvenation of McCormick's business and improved sales and profits by 1998.
- 2000: Leading position in Europe gained through acquisition of Ducros S.A.
- 2001: Including company's share of joint venture revenues, worldwide sales reached $ 2.5 billion.

Shortcomings to Bear in Mind

- The company purchases certain raw materials that are subject to price volatility caused by weather and other unpredictable factors. While future movements of raw material costs are uncertain, a variety of programs, including periodic raw material purchases and customer price adjustments, help McCormick address this risk. Generally, the company does not use derivatives to manage the volatility related to this risk.

- The company does not have a strong balance sheet, since only 56 percent of capitalization is in common equity. On the other hand, this is a definite improvement over the prior year, when it was only 48 percent.

Reasons to Buy

- "One of the ways we improve margins is by focusing marketing support and development resources on value-added, higher-margin products," said CEO Robert J. Lawless early in 2003. "Today, value-added products account for 65 percent of sales, with the other 35 percent coming from ingredients. Our B2K program, with a strong emphasis on optimizing the management of our supply chain, creates a global platform for future profit improvement, more efficient working capital, and enhanced relationships with our trading partners. We have identified more than 100 distinct opportunities to reduce costs in our supply chain. These opportunities include the global procurement of ingredients and packaging, more efficient logistics, and streamlined, lower-cost operations."

Mr. Lawless also said, "We are investing in our business to drive sales. Research and development expenditures have nearly doubled in the last five years. In 2002, for example, a new sensory center was opened in order to increase our ability to explore and determine preferences in taste. The center is one of many ways we are maintaining our competitive edge in supplying the grocery industry, food processors, and the restaurant industry with consumer-preferred flavors. New products developed in the last three years accounted for 10 percent of 2002 sales."

- The market environment for McCormick's consumer products—such as spices, herbs, extracts, propriety seasoning blends, sauces, and marinades—varies worldwide. In the United States, for instance, usage is up, and consumers are seeking new and bolder tastes.

Although many people use prepared foods and eat out, a *Parade* magazine survey reports that 75 percent of families polled eat dinner together at least four nights a week. A study conducted by National Panel Diary indicates that 70 percent of all meals are prepared at home, and a Canned Food Association Survey reports that 51 percent of women aged eighteen to sixty-four actually "scratch-cook" meals six times a week.

- In the company's industrial business, said Mr. Lawless, "Our customers are constantly seeking new flavors for their products. In this environment, the ability to identify, develop, and market winning flavors is essential. We flavor all kinds of products—spaghetti sauce, snack chips, frozen entrees, yogurt, a pack of chewing gum. In restaurants, we provide seasonings for a gourmet meal, salad dressings at a casual dining chain, and coating and sauce for a quick-service chicken sandwich.

"To anticipate and respond to changing tastes in markets worldwide, we are investing in research and development staff, equipment, instrumentation, and facilities. These investments enable us not only to create innovative products but also to use sensory skills to make sure that the flavors we deliver are winners in the marketplace."

- McCormick has paid dividends every year since 1925, and dividends have been raised in each of the past fifteen years. In the 1992–2002 period, dividends climbed from $.19 to $.42, a compound annual growth rate of 8.2 percent. In the same ten-year stretch, earnings per share advanced from $.57 to $1.26, a growth rate of 8.2 percent.

- In 2002, gross profit margins continued to improve, reaching 36.9 percent, up from 35.9 percent the prior year. This improvement reflects increasing sales of higher-margin, value-added products; reduced costs from customer and product segmentation; lower-cost procurement of materials and services on a global basis; use of trading exchanges in areas such as logistics; and improved expense containment.

- Worldwide, the retail grocery industry continues to consolidate, creating larger customers. What's more, in many of McCormick's markets, the company has multiyear contracts with customers to secure the shelf space for its products.

McCormick's capabilities in category management and electronic data interchange, along with its high-quality products and service, also forge a link to its increasingly larger customers.

- The company's past successes and future potential are rooted in the strength of the McCormick name. As a consequence, the company is now experiencing a 95 percent brand-awareness rating in the United States. This leadership role in the food industry ensures that consumers will enjoy a McCormick product at nearly every eating occasion. Grocery store aisles present more than 700 well-known products from major processors that rely on McCormick for seasoning or flavor.

Total assets: $1,931 million
Current ratio: 2.08
Common shares outstanding: 16 million voting, 124 million non-voting
Return on 2002 shareholders' equity: 34.1%

	2002	2001	2000	1999	1998	1997	1996	1995
Revenues (millions)	2,320	2,372	2,124	2,007	1,881	1,801	1,732	1,859
Net income (millions)	180	147	138	122	106	998	83	98
Earnings per share	1.26	1.05	1.00	.85	.72	.65	.52	.60
Dividends per share	.42	.40	.38	.34	.32	.30	.28	.26
Price High	27.3	23.3	18.9	17.3	18.2	14.2	12.7	13.3
Low	20.7	17.0	11.9	13.3	13.6	11.3	9.5	9.1

CONSERVATIVE GROWTH

The McGraw-Hill Companies, Inc.

1221 Avenue of the Americas □ New York, New York 10020 □ (212) 512-4321 □ Direct dividend reinvestment program available: (888) 201-5538 □ Web site: www.mcgraw-hill.com □ Listed: NYSE □ Ticker symbol: MHP □ S&P rating: not rated □ Value Line financial strength rating: A+

William H. Donald, an analyst with *Standard & Poor's Stock Reports*, had these encouraging comments on McGraw-Hill in a report issued in February 2003. "The longer-term operating outlook for MHP appears to be favorable. Demand for educational materials remains healthy, bolstered by projections of rising enrollments and increased federal spending.

"Strong growth prospects worldwide, new products and services, and a favorable interest rate environment favor operations at S&P (*Standard & Poor's*). The long-term outlook for advertising-supported business is also favorable. In addition to these considerations, a healthy balance sheet, strong and rising cash flow, and returns on equity above 20 percent should help support the stock."

Company Profile

The McGraw-Hill Companies is a multimedia information provider. The company publishes textbooks, technical and popular books, and periodicals (*BusinessWeek, Aviation Week, ENR,* and others). McGraw-Hill holds leadership positions in each of the markets it serves.

Financial Services

- *Standard & Poor's Ratings Services* is the number one rating service in the world. It is applying its leadership to rating and evaluating a growing array of nontraditional financial instrument.

- *Standard & Poor's Indexes,* led by the S&P 500, are the world's benchmark measures of equity market performance.

- *Standard & Poor's Compustat* is the leading source of financial databases and advanced PC-based software for financial analysis.
- *Standard & Poor's MMS* supplies the world with real-time fundamental and technical analysis in the global money, bond, foreign exchange, and equity markets.
- *Standard & Poor's Platt's* is the key provider of price assessments with the petroleum, petrochemical, and power markets.
- *Standard & Poor's J. J. Kenny* produces the most comprehensive evaluating pricing information for the fixed-income investment community.
- *Standard & Poor's DRI* is the leading supplier of economics-driven information to corporate and government clients.

Educational and Professional Publishing
- The McGraw-Hill School Division stands at number one in providing educational materials to elementary schools.
- Glencoe/McGraw-Hill tops the grade six-to-twelve segment.
- CTB/McGraw-Hill is the pre-eminent publisher of nationally standardized tests for the U.S. K–12 market.
- Irwin/McGraw-Hill is the premier publisher of higher-education materials in business, economics, and information technology.
- The Professional Book Group is the leading publisher of business, computing, and reference books serving the needs of professionals and consumer worldwide.

Information and Media Services
- BusinessWeek is the world's most widely read business publication, with a global audience of 6.3 million.
- F. W. Dodge is the leading provider of information to construction professionals.

- Sweet's Group is the premier supplier of building products information, in print and electronically.
- *Architectural Record* stands atop its industry as the official publication of the American Institute of Architects.
- *Aviation Week & Space Technology* is the world's most authoritative aerospace magazine.
- Tower Group International is the leading provider of customs brokerage and freight forwarding services.

Shortcomings to Bear in Mind
- Steven Barlow, an analyst with Prudential Financial (in the process of becoming part of Wachovia Securities), had this to say in January 2003: "We believe each of MHP's businesses is challenged to some extent by the overall economic climate in 2003. BusinessWeek and its television stations are dependent on the return of advertising which is beginning to happen, but is unpredictable as the pace of the advertising recovery is hard to call at this point.

"In education, the usual variables of the uncertainty of state education budgets loom, but may be offset with money from the federal government. Much can happen between now and the critical third quarter.

"In Financial Services, we think the low double-digit revenue growth rate seen in 2002 is at risk, owing to the uncertain geopolitical environment and tough comparisons. Some areas of debt issuance should grow, such as municipals, and others should fall, and we feel business in Europe may not be as solid as 2002, but Asia could pick up the slack."

Reasons to Buy
- At the end of January 2003, CEO Harold McGraw, III, made this comment, "We are poised for another very good year in 2003. With double-digit

growth in Financial Services, an advantageous position in the Pre-K-to-16 education market, and improvement in advertising, we expect this year to produce a 7–9 percent increase in earnings per share, which includes a five-cent impact for a non-recurring, non-cash change in our pension accounting assumptions."

- In mid-December 2002, Kevin Calabrese, an analyst with *Argus Company Report*, made these comments: "MHP has been very successful in rolling out youth-oriented product offerings that target and capture a growing interest in early childhood education in this country. We expect this focus to be a large boost to company profitability over the coming decade, as schooling begins earlier and with greater focus across the nation. The current informal pre-kindergarten programs are likely to be adopted into the standard elementary school curriculum within the next five years. This will provide an opportunity for MHP to provide materials to this segment.

  "Also, the national testing system that is being implemented in education provides opportunities for the company to sell both course and test preparation materials. This new testing for grades 3–8 should nearly double the market opportunity for test materials to $1.5 billion by 2007."

- Jennifer Ablan, writing for *Barron's* on February 24, 2003, had these comments: "Edward Atorino, a veteran media analyst at Blaylock & Partners, says while there are many challenges facing McGraw-Hill, the company is 'well-positioned' to dominate in higher education and to show renewed growth at *BusinessWeek* and in broadcasting.

  "Advertising pages were up 6 percent at *BusinessWeek* in the fourth quarter (of 2002), while the broadcasting group's revenue surged 18 percent amid an adverting upturn."

- S&P Indexes are the foundation for a growing array of investment funds and exchange-traded products that continue to generate new revenue. The company receives fees based on assets and trading activity. In addition, the recent volatility of the stock market has increased the revenue stream. Currently, more than $700 billion is invested in mutual funds tied to the S&P indexes.

- Europe's contribution of almost half of McGraw-Hill's international revenue is growing at a double-digit rate. With a push from the new Monetary Union, the European market will be a springboard for growth in many of the company's key businesses. Here are some expectations:
  - European companies that once financed their growth mainly by borrowing from banks are shifting to the issuance of corporate bonds instead, while nontraditional financial instruments also boom. Those are both large opportunities for *Standard & Poor's Rating Services*, which has built the world's largest network of ratings professionals.
  - Increases in investments by Europeans building retirement funds—the result of a transition to privately funded pension plans—will accelerate demand for global financial information. These are pluses for *Standard & Poor's Financial Information Services*.
  - English continues to be used more and more in business communications and as a second language in everyday use. These trends will benefit the company's educational products and the European edition of *BusinessWeek*.
  - The promise of the global economy depends on educational training. This is a plus for McGraw-Hill's global publishing activities—most notably the company's business, finance, engineering, information technology, and English instruction products.

- In the construction industry, The McGraw-Hill Construction Information Group (MH-CIG) is the foremost source of information crucial to new construction projects and planning. MH-CIG has increasingly turned to the Internet and other electronic tools as a means of gathering and distributing information.

Dodge Plans is the latest of several MH-CIG electronic products stemming from print media. It provides access—online or by CD-ROM twice weekly—to the plans, specifications, and bidding requirements for more than 60,000 new construction and renovation projects.

- The McGraw-Hill Professional Book Group publishes nearly 800 titles per year in the computing, business, science, technical, medical, and reference markets. The group continues to expand by creating publishing alliances with partners such as Oracle and Global Knowledge and by transforming key reference titles into Internet-based services. In addition, the Professional Book Group offers electronic products, ranging from Internet subscription services to CD-ROMs, and is building its capabilities in on-demand publishing.

- In 2001, Stephen B. Shepard, editor-in-chief of McGraw-Hill's *BusinessWeek*, received the highest honor awarded by the magazine industry, the Henry Johnson Fisher Award. Under Mr. Shepard's leadership, *BusinessWeek* helped set the national agenda for business and economic issues, pioneered coverage of the New Economy, exposed the Mob on Wall Street, and broke the story of prison labor in China. What's more, circulation has expanded by 40 percent since Mr. Shepard became editor-in-chief of McGraw-Hill's flagship business publication in 1984.

During those years, moreover, *BusinessWeek* has been a National Magazine Award finalist eighteen times, winning four times. The publication also won numerous Overseas Press Club Awards and three Gerald Loeb Awards for distinguished business and financial journalism, among others.

Total assets: $5,296 million
Current ratio: 1.03
Common shares outstanding: 194 million
Return on 2002 shareholders' equity: 27.5%

	2002	2001	2000	1999	1998	1997	1996	1995
Revenues (millions)	4,788	4,646	4,308	3,992	3,729	3,534	3,075	2,935
Net income (millions)	577	380	481	402	342	291	250	227
Earnings per share	2.96	2.45	2.41	2.02	1.71	1.46	1.25	1.14
Dividends per share	1.02	.98	.94	.86	.78	.72	.66	.60
Price High	69.7	70.9	67.7	63.1	51.7	37.7	24.6	21.9
Low	50.7	48.7	41.9	47.1	34.3	22.4	18.6	15.9

GROWTH AND INCOME

MDU Resources Group, Inc.

Schuchart Building □ Post Office Box 5650 □ Bismarck, North Dakota 58506-5650 □ (800) 437-8000 □ Direct dividend reinvestment plan is available: (800) 813-3324 □ Web site: www.mdu.com □ Listed: NYSE □ Ticker symbol: MDU □ S&P rating: A □ Value Line financial strength rating: A+

"Overall, I am pleased with our 2002 results," said Martin A. White, chief executive officer of MDU Resources, in January of 2003. "Our pipeline and energy services segment set new records in both pipeline and gathering throughput. Both natural gas and oil production and reserves increased at our natural gas and oil production segment. The construction materials and mining segment had record annual earnings, and our natural gas distribution business earnings returned to a more normal level."

Mr. White also said, "The strategic direction of our company is proving to be beneficial with the slower economy the United States is currently experiencing. The fact that the products and services our company provides are essential to the nation's infrastructure has helped us succeed. In addition, the reserves we have in natural gas, oil, and aggregates will prove beneficial as the economy improves. The hard assets we have in power plants and pipelines are invaluable. I remain bullish on our company and its ability to provide earnings growth well into the future."

Company Profile

MDU Resources Group, Inc., is a natural resource company. The company's diversified operations, such as oil and gas and construction materials, should help MDU Resources grow at a better rate than electric utilities that depend entirely on their electric business. MDU Resources Group has a number of operations.

Electric Distribution

Montana-Dakota Utilities Company generates, transmits, and distributes electricity, and provided related value-added products and services in the Northern Great Plains. In 2002, the electric segment earnings totaled $15.8 million, compared with earnings of $18.7 million the prior year. The decrease was largely the result of average realized wholesale electric prices that were 34 percent lower than in 2001, due primarily to a weaker demand in the wholesale spot markets. However, increased retail rates somewhat offset this decrease.

Natural Gas Distribution

Montana-Dakota Utilities Company and Great Plains Natural Gas Company distribute natural gas and provide related value-added products and services in the Northern Great Plains. In 2002, the natural gas distribution segment increased earnings to $3.6 million, a $2.9-million increase over 2001. The increase was largely due to increased retail sales as a result of weather that was 9 percent colder than the prior year, combined with retail rate increases in Minnesota, Montana, and North Dakota.

Utility Services

Operating throughout most of the United States, Utility Services, Inc., is a diversified infrastructure construction company specializing in electric, natural gas, and telecommunication utility construction, as well as interior industrial electrical, exterior lighting, and traffic stabilization.

Earnings from the company's utility services segment were $6.4 million for 2002, compared with $12.9 million the prior year. The decrease was due primarily to a slowdown in telecommunications, inside electrical, and engineering service work. The slowdown was brought about by a slowdown in these industries, which resulted in lower construction revenues and margins.

Independent Power Production

Earnings at the company's new independent power production segment totaled $.9 million. The majority of these earnings came from the newly acquired 213-megawatt natural gas–fired electric generating facilities in Colorado. The Brazilian operations also contributed to the gain.

Pipeline and Energy Services

WBI Holdings, Inc., provides natural gas transportation, underground storage, and gathering services through regulated and non-regulated pipeline systems. The business also provides energy marketing and management throughout the United States. Operations are situated primarily in the Rocky Mountain, Midwest, Southern, and Central regions of the United States.

Pipeline and energy services segment earnings for 2002 totaled $19.1 million, compared with $16.4 million for 2001. The pipeline and gathering operations produced higher earnings as a result of higher volumes transported and gathered at higher average rates, as well as higher storage revenues.

Oil and Natural Gas Production

Fidelity Exploration & Production Company is engaged in oil and natural gas acquisition, exploration, and production throughout the United States and in the Gulf of Mexico.

Earnings at the natural gas and oil production segment were $53.2 million, compared with $63.2 million in 2001. The company's combined natural gas and oil production increased 14 percent, largely as a result of increased natural gas production at the company-operated properties in the Rocky Mountain region, which posted an impressive 55 percent growth. Also contributing to 2002 results was the one-time effect of a compromise agreement resulting in a $16.6-million after-tax non-recurring gain realized in the first quarter of 2002. However, these increases were more than offset by realized natural gas prices that were 28 percent lower, as well as oil prices that were 7 percent lower than 2001.

Construction Materials and Mining

Knife River Corporation mines and markets aggregates and related value-added construction materials, products, and services in the western United States,

including Alaska and Hawaii. It also operates lignite and coal mines in Montana and North Dakota.

Record earnings of $48.7 million were recorded at the construction materials and mining segment, an increase of $11.7 million over 2001. Increased earnings were the result of increased aggregate, asphalt, and cement sales volumes. Construction revenues also increased substantially because of several big projects, mainly in California and Oregon.

Shortcomings to Bear in Mind

- Paul E. Debbas, CFA, an analyst with *Value Line Investment Survey*, said in a report in November 2002: "The utility is heavily involved in rate cases. In some cases, base tariffs hadn't been raised since the mid- to late-1980s. But MDU can only go so long without rate relief. The Montana commission recently granted the company an interim rate hike of $2.1 million. Gas rate filings totaling $5 million are pending in North Dakota, Wyoming, and Minnesota. On the down side, the North Dakota commission cut MDU's electric rates by $4.3 million. The company has implemented only $800,000 of the reduction, pending a court decision. The remaining $3.5 million is being collected from customers, subject to refund."

Reasons to Buy

- In 2002, the company increased its dividend by more than 4 percent, making it the twelfth consecutive year of increased dividends. What's more, MDU has an unbroken record of paying quarterly dividends that dates back to 1937.
- MDU Resources has an established position in the coal-bed natural gas fields in the Powder River Basin of Wyoming and Montana. This region provides the company's natural gas and oil production segment with additional reserve potential of low-cost coal bed natural gas.

In addition, MDU continues enhancing production from its existing gas fields in Colorado and Montana. The company's strong reserve position, both onshore and offshore in the Gulf of Mexico, provides this group a large geographic base upon which to expand.

- In 2002, MDU Resources was named to *Fortune*'s list of the "100 Fastest-Growing Companies." The magazine ranks domestic publicly traded companies on a variety of factors, including earnings per share growth of at least 25 percent for three straight years and total returns to investors. The company was also named to *Forbes* magazine's "Platinum List of America's 400 Best Big Companies" for the third consecutive year.

- In February 2003, the company announced the formation of Centennial Energy Resources, LLC. It was created in response to the success of MDU Resources' independent power production ventures. "We have moved into the independent power production arena, both domestically and internationally," said Mr. White. "Our independent power production activities have grown rapidly and are at the point where they are significant enterprises that must be managed separately."

The independent power production business segment includes Centennial Power and Centennial Energy Resources International, formerly known as MDU Resources International. So far, MDU Resources' independent power-produc-

tion projects include one international development project and three domestic acquisitions:

- In July 2002, MDU Resources International and its partners began commercial operation of a 200-megawatt natural gas–fired power plant in the Brazilian state of Ceara.

- In February 2002, Centennial Power, Inc., acquired Rocky Mountain Power, Inc., and the rights to construct a 113-megawatt, coal-fired electric generation facility.

- In November 2002, Centennial Power acquired Brush Power, LLC, a 213-megawatt electric generating facility in Brush, Colorado.

- In December 2002, Centennial Power agreed to purchase the Mountain View project, a 66.6-megawatt wind farm northwest of Palm Springs, California.

- In February 2003, Craig K. Shere, CFA, an analyst with *Standard & Poor's Stock Reports*, made these comments: "During 2003, we see total revenues rising almost 10 percent, driven by more rapid growth in the new independent power production (IPP) segment and in natural gas and oil production. Revenue and earnings for the IPP unit should benefit from new power plants, while production operations should benefit from higher volumes and commodity prices. Utility services earnings should jump in the absence of about $5.2 million of one-time expenses in 2002."

Total assets: $2,870 million
Current ratio: 1.75
Common shares outstanding: 71 million
Return on 2002 shareholders' equity: 12.4%

	2002	2001	2000	1999	1998	1997	1996	1995
Revenues (millions)	2,032	2,224	1,874	1,280	897	608	515	464
Net income (millions)	148	156	110	83	74	55	46	42
Earnings per share	2.07	2.29	1.80	1.52	1.44	1.24	1.05	.95
Dividends per share	.94	.90	.86	.82	.78	.75	.73	.72
Price High	33.4	40.4	33.0	27.2	28.9	22.3	15.7	15.4
Low	18.0	22.4	17.6	18.8	18.8	14.0	13.3	11.5

AGGRESSIVE GROWTH

Medtronic, Inc.

710 Medtronic Parkway N. E. □ **Minneapolis, Minnesota 55432-5604** □ **Listed: NYSE** □ **(763) 505-2692** □
Dividend reinvestment plan is available: (888) 648-8154 □ **Web site: www.medtronic.com** □ **Ticker symbol: MDT**
□ **Fiscal years end April 30** □ **S&P rating: A-** □ **Value Line financial strength rating: A+**

Medtronic has a pipeline filled with treatments for a number of profitable (but uncrowded) markets. Its Activa, for example, which uses electronic stimulation to alleviate many of the symptoms associated with Parkinson's disease, received approval in 2002 from the U.S. Food & Drug Administration (FDA).

Parkinson's disease impacts the lives of an estimated 1 million people in the United States and 2 million worldwide. Activa, according to the company, "utilizing our brain pacemaker, can significantly reduce shaking, slowness, and stiffness for patients who live with this debilitating disease. The dramatic benefits of this therapy were vividly demonstrated during an extensive media campaign that followed USFDA approval, including a report that aired on CBS Television's *60 Minutes* in February 2002."

In another realm, Medtronic's InSync ICD system is one of the only treatments for heart failure that does not rely on the use of drugs. Heart failure, the progressive deterioration of the heart's pumping capability, afflicts more than 22 million people worldwide and over 5 million in the United States. According to management, the company's InSync and InSync ICD cardiac devices address "one of the largest and fastest-growing new market opportunities. As reported in the *New England Journal of Medicine*, it is estimated that more than 3 million heart failure patients around the world can experience improved quality of life from this new biventricular pacing therapy.

"Sudden Cardiac Arrest strikes one American every two minutes and is the leading cause of death in the U.S. Research data reported in the *New England Journal of Medicine* shows dramatically reduced mortality from sudden cardiac arrest in the heart attack survivors who receive implantable cardioverter defibrillators (ICDs). This expanded indication for ICDs approximately doubles the market potential to more than 600,000 patients a year in the U.S. alone."

Company Profile

Medtronic is the world's leading medical-technology company.

Over the past half-century, Medtronic has pioneered in the development of sophisticated instruments that help restore health, extend life, and alleviate pain.

Medtronic's devices help regulate erratic heartbeats, tremors, and incontinence. About half of the company's revenues come from the sale of defibrillators and pacing devices, including products for slow, irregular, and rapid heartbeats.

Medtronic also has a stake in spinal implant devices, mechanical and tissue heart valves, and implantable neurostimulation and drug-delivery systems, catheters, stents, and guide wires used in angioplasties.

Shortcomings to Bear in Mind

- Like most great growth companies, Medtronic typically sells at a lofty P/E ratio.
- Medtronic lags behind Johnson & Johnson in the race to produce a drug-coated stent, which is expected to all but replace today's stents (devices used to prop open weak arteries).

Reasons to Buy

- Medtronic has an impressive record of growth. In the 1992–2002 period, earnings per share climbed from $.17 to $1.21, a compound annual growth rate of 21.7 percent. In the same ten-year span, dividends per share advanced from $.03 to $.23, a growth rate of 22.6 percent.

- Medtronic is a pioneer in the emerging field of medicine that promises to restore normal brain function and chemistry to millions of patients with central nervous system disorders. The company's implantable neurostimulation and infusion systems treat disorders by modulating the nervous system. Electrical stimulation, chemicals, and biological agents are delivered in precise amounts to specific sites in the brain and spinal cord.

  The company is awaiting FDA approval of its Activa neurostimulator for the treatment of Parkinson's disease, and exploring new treatments for other diseases, including epilepsy, obsessive-compulsive disorder (OCD), depression, and movement disorders.

- At the end of 2001, Medtronic acquired Endonetics, Inc., a developer of technologies for the diagnosis and treatment of gastroesophageal reflux disease (GERD). GERD, a common disorder characterized by serious heartburn, is caused when the lower esophageal sphincter muscle becomes weak and ineffective, allowing bitter digestive acids to back up into the esophagus.

  More than 60 million American adults experience GERD and heartburn at least once a month, and about 25 million suffer every day from heartburn. "We expect Endonetics's products to set the gold standard for patient-friendly, minimally invasive, and therapeutic techniques for the treatment of GERD," said Art Collins, Medtronic president and CEO.

- In 2001, Medtronic continued to broaden its portfolio of medical devices by agreeing to pay $3.7 billion for MiniMed, Inc., a manufacturer of insulin pumps and wearable glucose monitors, and Medical Research Group, Inc., a related closely held company. MiniMed is the leading insulin-pump manufacturer, with an estimated 80 percent market share in the United States. The main product of MiniMed is an external pump, worn on a patient's belt, to administer insulin continuously to people with type 1 diabetes. Type 1 affects people who are born without the ability to make insulin, whereas type 2 patients (who are far more numerous) develop the affliction late in life, usually after the age of fifty.

- Since its origin, Medtronic has held a clear market leadership in cardiac pacing, chiefly with pacemakers designed to treat bradycardia (hearts that beat irregularly or too slow) and more recently, tachyarrhythmia (hearts that beat too fast or quiver uncontrollably, called tachycardia and fibrillation). Today, more than half the cardiac rhythm devices and leads implanted throughout the world come from Medtronic.

- The worldwide coronary vascular market is estimated at $4 billion and is expected to grow because it serves significant, unmet medical needs. Medtronic's coronary vascular products include several types of catheters used to unblock coronary arteries; stents that support the walls of an artery and prevent more blockage; and products used in minimally invasive vascular procedures for coronary heart disease, the chief cause of heart attack and angina.

- Medtronic's cardiac surgery group offers superior products to support cardiac surgeons, including tissue heart valves that are best represented by the Freestyle stentless valve, the Mosaic stented tissue valve, and the Hall mechanical valve. In addition, the company is expanding its leadership in cardiac cannulae, which are used to connect a patient's circulatory system to external perfusion systems used in conventional and minimally invasive surgeries.

The acquisition of Avecor adds to Medtronic's well-established line of perfusion systems designed to sustain patients during open-heart surgery. These systems include market-leading oxygenators, blood pumps, arterial filters, and autotransfusion and monitoring products that are used to circulate and oxygenate the blood and regulate body temperature during procedures when the heart must be stopped while repairs are made.

Finally, Medtronic is leading the way in developing products to make cardiac surgery less invasive and, ultimately, to reduce pain, patient recovery time, and medical costs. One new product that addresses these needs is the Octopus2 tissue-stabilization system that allows the cardiac surgeon to repair blocked blood vessels while the heart is still beating.

■ At the end of 2001, the U.S. Food and Drug Administration approved the Medtronic Kappa 900 series of cardiac pacemakers. This series features new atrial monitoring and diagnostic functions to help physicians make more precise patient-management decisions. This pacemaker represents the next generation of the Medtronic Kappa family, the world's most prescribed pacemaker. The Kappa family provides therapies that treat patients with chronic heart problems, in which the heart beats too slowly to adequately support the body's circulatory needs.

In addition, the Kappa 900 now offers expanded monitoring information of the atria (upper chamber) and ventricles (lower chambers) that is easy to interpret and enables doctors to more efficiently assess atrial rhythm control and ventricular control. The new diagnostic information can result in more confident patient-management decisions on the part of physicians and shorter follow-up visits for patients.

A genetically engineered bone-growth developed by Medtronic has proven effective in a clinical study of back surgery. This advance—which was announced in late 2001—may sidestep the need for patients to undergo painful hip surgery in order to transplant the bone needed to rebuild the spine.

Total assets: $10,905 million
Current ratio: 0.88
Common shares outstanding: 1,215 million
Return on 2002 shareholders' equity: 16.5%

	2002	2001	2000	1999	1998	1997	1996	1995
Revenues (millions)	6,411	5,552	5,015	4,134	2,605	2,438	2,169	1,742
Net income (millions)	984	1,282	1,111	905	595	530	438	294
Earnings per share	1.21	1.05	.90	.75	.61	.53	.46	.30
Dividends per share	.23	.20	.16	.13	.11	.10	.07	.05
Price High	49.7	62.0	62.0	44.6	38.4	26.4	17.5	15.0
Low	32.5	36.6	32.8	29.9	22.7	14.4	11.1	6.5

GROWTH AND INCOME

Merck & Co., Inc.

One Merck Drive □ P. O. Box 100 □ Whitehouse Station, New Jersey 08889-0100 □ (908) 423-5881 □ Direct dividend reinvestment plan available: (800) 613-2104 □ Web site: www.merck.com □ Listed: NYSE □ Ticker symbol: MRK □ S&P rating: A+ □ Value Line Financial Rating: A++

Efforts to convince the public that drug companies are charging too much are getting a great deal of publicity. This information drive is particularly meant to benefit people on Social Security—an influential and vocal group of voters. In Vermont, for instance, people are crossing the nearby border to Montreal, where prescription drugs are far cheaper, apparently due to their subsidization by the Canadian government. The drug companies are described as greedy monsters, with little regard for those who depend on their medicines for the relief of their ailments.

To be sure, most pharmaceutical companies are doing well. However, there are other factors to bear in mind. For one thing, companies such as Merck, Bristol-Myers Squibb, and Eli Lilly are suffering because some of their most lucrative drugs are losing patent protection. When that happens, firms that make generic versions jump in like hungry vultures, and drug prices are cut drastically. After all, the generic manufacturers haven't invested million of dollars in research. Understandably, this new horde of competitors wreaks havoc with the price of the drug that is being copied.

The best way for the drug companies to battle back is to bring out new and more effective drugs, which they are doing. But the cost of finding a new drug is staggering. In a study done by Tufts University, the cost of bringing out a new drug has spiraled to $802 million. What's more, that's two-and-half times the cost in 1987, when it was a mere $231 million. Part of the problem revolves around the number of patients who have to use the drug during the test period. This number has increased to 4,000, up from 1,300 in the early 1980s.

That's the bad news. The good news is that the stock prices of such companies as Merck, Lilly, Pfizer, and Bristol-Myers came tumbling down in 2001 and 2002. Drug stocks are noted for selling at high P/E ratios. Now they are available at multiples

that take some of the bad news into account. You may find this to be a good time to add a drug company to your portfolio. In fact, two or three companies might be even better.

Company Profile

Merck is a leading research-driven pharmaceutical products and services company. Directly and through its joint ventures, the company discovers, develops, manufactures, and markets a broad range of innovative products to improve human and animal health. Merck also provides pharmaceutical and benefit services through Merck-Medco Managed Care. In April 2003, the company announced it would spin off Medco to shareholders.

Human Health Products

Human health products include therapeutic and preventative drugs, generally sold by prescription, for the treatment of human disorders. Among these are elevated-cholesterol products, which include Zocor and Mevacor; hypertensive/heart failure products, including Vasotec, the largest-selling product among this group; Cozaar, Hyzaar, Prinivil, and Vaseretic; antiulcerants, of which Pepcid is the largest-selling; and antibiotics, of which Primaxin and Noroxin are the largest-selling. Among the ophthalmologicals that Merck produces, Timoptic, Timoptic-XE, and Trusopt are the largest-selling. Merck also produces a wide range of vaccines/biologicals, among which the following are the largest selling: Recombivax HB, a hepatitis B vaccine recombinant; M-M-R II, a pediatric vaccine for measles, mumps, and rubella; and Varivax, a live virus vaccine for the prevention of chickenpox. Merck makes a treatment for HIV: Comprised of Crixivan, a protease inhibitor for the treatment of human immunodeficiency viral infection in adults, it was launched in the United States in 1996. The company's osteoporosis medication, which includes Fosamax, is designed for the treatment and prevention of osteoporosis in postmenopausal women.

Animal Health Products

Animal health products include medicinals used to control and alleviate disease in livestock, small animals, and poultry. Crop protection includes products for the control of crop pests and fungal disease.

Merck-Medco

Merck-Medco primarily includes Merck-Medco sales of both non-Merck products and Merck-Medco pharmaceutical benefit services, primarily managed prescription drug programs, and programs to manage health and drug utilization.

Shortcomings to Bear in Mind

- Merck and Pharmacia have been locked in one of the fiercest marketing battles in drug-industry history, with both companies selling rival pain pills called Cox-2 inhibitors. Celebrex, a huge seller for Pharmacia (now part of Pfizer), was the first company to obtain FDA approval for its Cox-2 inhibitor (in 1999). Merck followed several months later with Vioxx. Pharmacia teamed up with Pfizer as a comarketer, and the two launched Bextra, a similar drug, in April of 2002. So far, Pharmacia and Pfizer have been winning the battle.

- The markets in which the company's business is conducted are highly competitive and highly regulated in many ways. Global efforts toward health care cost containment continue to exert pressure on product pricing.

  In the United States, government efforts to slow the increase of health care costs and the demand for price discounts from managed-care groups have limited Merck's ability to mitigate the effect of inflation on costs and expenses through pricing.

  Outside of the United States, government-mandated cost-containment programs have required the company to similarly limit selling prices. Additionally, government actions have significantly reduced the sales growth of certain products by decreasing the patient-reimbursement cost of the drug, restricting the volume of drugs that physicians can prescribe, and increasing the use of generic products. It is anticipated that the worldwide trend for cost containment and competitive pricing will continue and result in continued pricing pressures.

- George Rho, an analyst with *Value Line Investment Survey*, had a negative comment in a report issued in late 2002: "The company has a couple of exciting new-drug prospects, but given its size, we're not confident that its pipeline is sufficient to generate better-than-average earnings and share-price gains over the three-to-five-year haul."

Reasons to Buy

- "Zocor, Merck's largest-selling medicine and one of the most prescribed cholesterol-modifying medicines in the world, currently is experiencing growth in Europe because of the results of Oxford University's Heart Protection Study (HPS), the largest study ever using a cholesterol-modifying medicine," said Merck's CEO, Raymond V. Gilmartin, in December of 2002. "HPS found that Zocor 40 mg saved lives by significantly reducing the risk of heart attack and stroke in a broad range of high-risk patients."

- Merck expanded its cholesterol-modifying franchise in October of 2002 with the approval of Zetia, a cholesterol absorption inhibitor from Merck/Schering-Plough Pharmaceuticals. What's more, the partnership anticipates filing a New Drug Application (NDA) with the U.S. Food & Drug Administration (FDA) for a Zetia/Zocor combination tablet in late 2003.

Zetia is the first new approach to lowering cholesterol in fifteen years. Zetia offers a new treatment paradigm lowering cholesterol by a different, but complementary, action to Zocor and other statins. Clinical studies have found that Zetia, when added to a statin, has demonstrated superior efficacy in comparison with a statin alone in helping patients reach their cholesterol goals. Zetia was launched in November of 2002 in the United States and in Germany, where it is marketed under the trade name Ezetrol.

- Vioxx, Merck's once-a-day Cox-2 selective medicine, is the number one prescribed arthritis pain medication in many countries around the world. Vioxx offers powerful relief with once-a-day dosing. It is the only coxib proven to reduce the risk of clinically important gastrointestinal (GI) side effects, compared to naproxen (another leading medication for arthritis pain). Vioxx has achieved exclusive formulary status that covers an additional 15 million lives since the GI outcome-data from the landmark 8,000-patient Vioxx Gastrointestinal Outcomes Research (VIGOR) study were added to its label.

- Arcoxia has been launched in nineteen countries throughout the world, including the United Kingdom, Sweden, Ireland, Mexico, Peru, Brazil, Ecuador, Singapore, and New Zealand. Arcoxia is currently in development for a wide range of indications, including osteoarthritis, rheumatoid arthritis, chronic pain, acute pain, menstrual pain, acute gouty arthritis, and ankylosing spondylitis.

- In 2001, Merck purchased Rosetta Inpharmatics, Inc., a company that makes equipment and software used to speed development of gene-based drugs. Merck has long been known for its dedication to its own research prowess. But in recent years, the company has made a determined effort to bolster its ties with academics and to bring new technologies developed elsewhere into its laboratories.

"This is a longer-term purchase that will augment their research and leave them better-positioned," said Leonard Yaffe, an analyst at Banc of America Securities. "Over the next twenty years, genomics is going to become a lot more influential, so it makes sense."

- John Simons, writing for *Fortune* magazine, said in a 2002 article, "What's odd about Merck's predicament is that its scientists have been demonstrably more innovative than the competition. Since 1996, Merck researchers have patented 1,933 new compounds, 400 more than second-place Pharmacia. Certainly not all newly discovered compounds lead to viable products, but patents are a prime indicator of research productivity. Even more impressive, Merck's scientists do more with less. Their discoveries cost an average of $6 million per patent, the lowest in the industry. Competitors like Pfizer, Eli Lilly, and Pharmacia plow about 20 percent of drug revenues back into R&D, while Merck reinvests just 12 percent."

Total assets: $47,561 million
Current ratio: 1.07
Common shares outstanding: 2,277 million
Return on 2002 equity: 41.7%

		2002	2001	2000	1999	1998	1997	1996	1995
Revenues (millions)		51,790	47,716	40,363	32,714	26,898	23,637	19,829	16,681
Net income (millions)		7,150	7,281	6,822	5,890	5,248	4,614	3,881	3,335
Earnings per share		3.14	3.14	2.90	2.45	2.15	1.92	1.60	1.35
Dividends per share		1.44	1.37	1.21	1.10	.95	.85	.71	.62
Price	High	64.5	95.3	79.0	87.4	80.9	54.1	42.1	33.6
	Low	38.5	56.8	52.0	60.9	50.7	39.0	28.3	18.2

Meredith Corporation

1716 Locust Street □ Des Moines, Iowa 50309 □ (515) 284-2205 □ Dividend reinvestment plan not available □ Fiscal years end June 30 □ Listed: NYSE □ Web site: www.meredith.com □ Ticker symbol: MDP □ S&P rating: A- □ Value Line financial strength rating: B+

In November of 2002, Meredith Corporation, a leading magazine publisher and television-broadcasting enterprise, announced that it had reached an agreement with Primedia, Inc., to acquire *American Baby* magazine and its related properties for $115 million. Meredith said that the transaction could help earnings as early as fiscal 2003.

"The acquisition of *American Baby* builds on our strategy to extend our leadership position across a culturally diverse and younger demographic spectrum of the family marketplace," said Steve Lacy, president of Meredith Publishing Group. "We believe this multi-tier franchise will help us reach young families who are just beginning to build their homes and family lives. It's a great fit to the 'family side' of our existing home and family titles," which include such well-known titles as *Better Homes and Gardens*, *Ladies' Home Journal*, *Country Home*, *Traditional Home*, and *MORE*, among others.

Mr. Lacy noted that the *American Baby* is a well-established large-scale brand with a strong array of products that reaches "younger women and the Hispanic market—two areas that we believe will enhance our already strong presence in the home and family arena."

The cornerstone of the group is *American Baby* magazine, which was launched in 1938. It is currently published monthly and has a circulation of 2 million. According to the Publishers Information Bureau, *American Baby* experienced a 28 percent increase in advertising revenues and 23 percent increase in advertising pages for the period from January to September of 2002, compared against the same period the prior year.

Company Profile

Meredith Corporation is one of America's leading media and marketing companies. Its business centers on magazine and book publishing, television broadcasting, interactive media, and integrated marketing. The company's roots go back to 1902, when it was an agricultural publisher.

The Meredith Publishing Group is the country's foremost home and family publisher. The group creates and markets magazines, including *Better Homes and Gardens*, *Ladies' Home Journal*, *Country Home*, *Creative Home*, *Midwest Living*, *Traditional Home*, *WOOD*, *Hometown Cooking*, *Successful Farming*, *MORE*, *Renovation Style*, *Country Gardens*, *American Patchwork & Quilting*, *Garden Shed*, *Do It Yourself Garden*, *Deck and Landscape*, *Decorating*, and more than 140 issues of special-interest publications.

The Publishing Group also creates custom marketing programs through Meredith Integrated Marketing, licenses the *Better Homes and Gardens* brand, and publishes books created and sold under Meredith and Ortho trademarks. Meredith has nearly 300 books in print and has established marketing relationships with some of America's leading companies, including Home Depot, Daimler-Chrysler, and Carnival Cruise Lines. Meredith's most popular book is the familiar red-plaid *Better Homes and Gardens New Cook Book*.

The Meredith Broadcasting Group includes eleven television stations in locations across the continental United States, in such cities as Atlanta, Georgia; Phoenix, Arizona; Portland, Oregon; Hartford-New Haven, Connecticut; Kansas City, Missouri; Nashville, Tennessee; Greenville-Spartanburg-Anderson, South Carolina; Asheville, North Carolina; Las Vegas, Nevada; Flint-Saginaw, Michigan; and Bend, Oregon. The network affiliations include CBS (five affiliates), NBC (one), UPN (one), and FOX (four).

Meredith's consumer database contains more than 60 million names, making it one of the largest domestic databases among media companies. These databases enable magazine and television advertisers to precisely target marketing campaigns. In addition, the company has an extensive Internet presence, including branded anchor tenant positions on America Online.

Shortcomings to Bear in Mind

- The company's profits depend heavily on advertising revenues. The recession in the early part of the current decade was particularly hard on advertising, which can be a volatile factor. When a company's are hurting, they often lay off employees and pare back advertising.
- The company has a somewhat leveraged balance sheet, with only 52 percent of capitalization in common equity. With this much debt, it is more difficult for a company to make acquisitions, and it is more vulnerable during a period of tough times.

Reasons to Buy

- In the fall of 2002, William H. Donald, an analyst with *Standard & Poor's Stock Reports*, had this comment: "We still believe that with demographic trends strongly in its favor, MDP should continue to benefit in the long term from its position as the largest publisher of shelter magazines."
- In late November of 2002, *Value Line Investment Survey*'s analyst, Stuart

Plesser, had this to say: "Meredith's fiscal 2003, that began July 1, 2002, is off to a strong start. Publishing revenues grew 3 percent on a comparable basis, despite difficult year-over-year comparisons. Most impressively, the company's flagship magazine—*Better Homes and Gardens* (the largest in the field)—retained an 11 percentage-point market-share lead over its nearest competitor.

"On the broadcast side, recent management changes appear to be paying off, as revenues for the unit advanced roughly 14 percent, to $64.2 million in the September period, versus last year. Too, the company's recently revamped newscasts have led to higher ratings, which should help boost advertising revenues in the coming quarters."

- In the 1992–2002 period, earnings per share advanced from $.27 to $1.79, a compound annual growth rate of 20.8 percent. In the same ten-year span, however, dividends per share expanded less impressively, from $.16 to $.35, a growth rate of 8.1 percent.
- "Americans are coming home," said a company spokesman. "Research shows they are devoting more time to their homes and their families, and the Meredith Publishing Group is ideally positioned to serve them. Through our century-long commitment to quality service journalism, we have built a reputation as a trusted source of information. Our subscription magazines, special interest publications, book, Web sites, and other materials are respected resources for Americans seeking to enrich their homes through remodeling, decorating, gardening, and cooking."
- In the face of a difficult economy, Meredith increased its market share for its magazines, beginning with its two largest titles, *Better Homes and Gardens* and *Ladies' Home Journal*.

In fiscal 2002, these two publications

grew their combined share of the women's service field advertising revenues by 2.5 percentage points, to 40 percent, as measured by the Publishers Information Bureau. The July issue of *Better Homes and Gardens* alone achieved a 30 percent share of advertising revenues in the women's service field, or more than any of the company's competitors two-magazine combinations.

■ Commenting on results in fiscal 2002, CEO William T. Kerr said, "Fiscal 2002 was a challenging year for the entire media industry and for Meredith. A deep advertising recession, compounded by the effects of the September 11th tragedies, created the worst economic environment for the media industry in sixty years."

Mr. Kerr went on to say, "Excluding special items, our earnings per share were $1.11, compared with $1.55 for fiscal 2001. These results are not typical for our company. But we take solace in the fact that we out-performed both industries in which we compete. In our publishing business, magazine adver-

tising pages in our Publishers Information Bureau–measured titles rose nearly 5 percent in fiscal 2002, compared to a decline of nearly 12 percent for the publishing industry as a whole. On the broadcasting front, Meredith advertising revenue declined 6 percent, compared to nearly 8 percent for the industry."

Mr. Kerr also commented in more detail on the broadcasting operation. "In our Broadcasting group, we made significant progress at improving performance and rebuilding margins. Revitalizing leadership, increasing advertising revenues, and improving news programming were priorities in fiscal 2002.

"We hired Kevin O'Brien—a thirty-three-year television industry veteran with a strong track record—to lead the group. Immediately, Kevin began to change the culture at our stations, insisting on a stronger focus on sales and customer service. He rebuilt much of our management team, replacing five general managers, six news directors, and six general sales managers."

Total assets: $1,460 million
Current ratio: 0.92
Common shares outstanding: 50 million
Return on 2002 shareholders' equity: 19.1%

	2002	2001	2000	1999	1998	1997	1996	1995
Revenues (millions)	988	1,053	1,097	1,036	1,010	855	867	885
Net income (millions)	91.4	71.3	71.0	89.7	79.9	67.6	54.7	39.8
Earnings per share	1.79	1.39	1.35	1.67	1.46	1.22	.97	.72
Dividends per share	.35	.33	.31	.29	.27	.24	.21	.19
Price High	47.8	39.0	41.0	42.0	48.5	36.9	26.9	21.3
Low	33.4	26.5	22.4	30.6	26.7	22.1	19.6	11.3

AGGRESSIVE GROWTH

Microsoft Corporation

One Microsoft Way □ Redmond, Washington 98052-6399 □ (425) 706-3703 □ Dividend reinvestment plan not available □ Web site: www.microsoft.com □ Listed: NASDAQ □ Fiscal year ends June 30 □ □ Ticker symbol: MSFT □ S&P rating: B+ □ Value Line financial strength rating: A++

"Fiscal 2002 was a year of solid growth, significant product releases, and a continued focus on developing new technologies that position Microsoft for the future," said Bill Gates, Chairman and Chief Software Architect of the company. "Despite a challenging economic climate, revenues for the year increased by $3.07 billion, to $28.37 billion and operating income grew by $190 million, to $11.91 billion.

"Strong demand for Windows XP and other desktop software contributed to our positive performance. Revenue from enterprise software outpaced the highly competitive server market by a wide margin. And our consumer business saw a dramatic rise in sales, with the launch of the Xbox video game system and strong growth in MSN subscription income.

"During the coming year, Microsoft will launch several important new products, including Windows XP Tablet PC Edition and Windows.NET Servers, and we plan to increase spending on research and development by 20 percent, to $5.2 billion."

Mr. Gates went on to say, "A highlight of the past year was the overwhelming market acceptance that greeted the launch of Windows XP, which brings enhanced reliability, security, and performance to PC users at home and work. The year also saw sustained momentum for Office XP, with more than 60 million licenses sold in the twelve months after its launch in May 2001. A new version of Office, scheduled for release in 2003, will enable users to communicate and collaborate in new ways with even greater ease."

Company Profile

Microsoft is the dominant player in the PC software market. It climbed to prominence on the popularity of its operating-systems software and now rules the business-applications software market. Microsoft, moreover, has set its sights on becoming the leading provider of software services for the Internet.

By virtue of it size, market positioning, and financial strength, Microsoft is a formidable competitor in any market it seeks to enter. Earnings have shown explosive growth in recent years, enhanced by a strong PC market in general, along with new product introductions and market-share gains. Of course, the last couple of years have seen the PC market sag, along with most everything else. But better times should return.

Microsoft is best known for its operating-systems software programs, which run on close to 90 percent of the PCs currently in use. Its original DOS operating system, of course, gave way to Windows, a graphical user interface program run in conjunction with DOS, which made using a PC easier.

The company entered the business-applications market in the early 1990s via a lineup of strong offerings, combined with aggressive and innovative marketing and sales strategies. The company's Office 97 suite, which includes the popular Word (word processing), Excel (spreadsheet), and PowerPoint (graphics) software programs, is now by far the best-selling applications software package.

Shortcomings to Bear in Mind

- Microsoft may be one of the world's greatest stocks, but apparently the big shots who work there are not convinced. In a recent nine-month period, insiders such as executives and board members were selling the stock with great abandon. There were thirty-two separate sales during this span—and only one lone purchase.

- *Value Line Investment Survey* seems to side with these bearish insiders. Its analyst, George A. Niemond, had this to say in mid-2002: "But there is little investment appeal here. Microsoft shares are ranked to move with the market during the next six to twelve months. And the current price (then $52.38) already appears to discount a good portion of the earnings gains we expect by 2005–2007."

Reasons to Buy

- On the other hand, Jonathan Rudy, CFA, an analyst with *Standard & Poor's Stock Reports*, wrote a favorable assessment in November of 2002. "We recently upgraded the shares to buy, from accumulate, following recent approval by a federal judge of the 2001 favorable tentative settlement reached with the Justice Department.

  "Aside from civil litigation, we believe investors can now focus on MSFT's strong fundamentals. PC sales should begin to accelerate modestly in 2003, driven in part by interest in Windows XP. The company has also successfully diversified its revenue stream into new areas, enabling MSFT to produce solid growth and profitability while many competitors have been decimated."

- Despite the recession, Microsoft has managed to make a profit every year during this turbulent period. In 2002, for instance, earnings per share actually advanced. Not too many companies can say the same. In the past ten years (1992–2002), earnings per share climbed from $.15 to $1.41, for a compound annual growth rate of 25.1 percent. That's a tough act to follow.

- With more than 250 million unique users worldwide each month, MSN is now one of the most popular destinations on the Internet. And with the launch of the newest version of MSN in 2002, the momentum continues. This latest offering includes a new home page design, improved performance, and several updates to help users better communicate and enjoy digital media. It also provides fast and reliable Internet access in the United States with the new MSN Broadband service.

- Xbox is Microsoft's future-generation video game system that gives the game players experiences they have yet to imagine. With a built-in hard disk drive, Xbox delivers much richer game worlds. And with Dolby Digital 5.1 sound, gamers will actually feel what's happening. Xbox is the only system designed to enable players to compete or collaborate with other players around the world through broadband online gaming.

- Microsoft's push into consumers' living rooms took a big step forward in fiscal 2002 when the company announced that Charter Communications, Inc., the nation's fourth-largest cable company, would deploy Microsoft's interactive-television software in a million homes.

  The deal was a major boost for Microsoft's interactive-television business, which had suffered several setbacks over the prior year. AT&T, for instance, announced earlier that year that it was scaling back plans to deploy Microsoft's advanced television software. What's more, AT&T also invited a rival software firm, Liberate Technologies, Inc., of San Carlos, California, to compete for some of its business.

  That move by AT&T was devastating news to Microsoft, which had invested $5 billion in AT&T to get its technology into the cable boxes that sit on top of televisions in customers' homes.

  Fortunately, Charter, a St. Louis company with nearly 7 million customers, is now giving the same Microsoft advanced-television software new life. Charter now uses Microsoft's technology to offer customers a premium service package, with cable television and new types of entertainment and information services, including video on demand, digital video clips to go with news and sports services, as well as high-speed Web access.

Microsoft, in its battle with market leader Palm, Inc.—with an 80 percent share—unveiled a new version of the Pocket PC handheld computer in fiscal 2002. The device is powered by Microsoft software that boasts improved links to other Microsoft products. At a festive launch event in San Francisco, Steve Ballmer, CEO of MSFT, dubbed the new pocket computer a "connectivity machine."

Those connections to products such as Microsoft's Exchange server, which runs the popular Outlook e-mail and calendar software, and the company's SQL Server database are expected to help Microsoft gain market share, particularly among corporate users. Most companies' employees already use programs such as Microsoft Office at work.

Microsoft's Pocket PCs have more features than Palm's devices and are nearly as easy to use. In addition to the usual selection of address books, calendars, memo pads, and calculators, Microsoft handheld computers come with Windows Media Player for music

and a broad assortment of software, including Microsoft Money, Pocket Word, and Pocket Excel (all of which synchronize with the full desktop version); the Pocket Streets map suite; and Microsoft Reader for e-books.

- Here's an excerpt from an article that appeared in *Money* magazine in December of 2002: "Even if Microsoft is tied to the fortunes of the slumping PC industry (some 90 percent of all computers run its Windows software), its $40-billion cash hoard and 48 percent operating profit margins provide enough ballast and ammunition for it to outlast competitors in old and new markets.

"Its installed base of users ensures that Microsoft does great repeat business. And thanks to its loyal following, its new software products like Windows. Net gain an instant market presence. Plus the company has the wherewithal and patience to develop many non-PC businesses, such as video games with Xbox, server software with Windows NT, or an Internet portal business with MSN."

Total assets: $67,646 million
Current ratio: 3.81
Common shares outstanding: 10,830 million
Return on 2002 shareholders' equity: 15.7%

	2002	2001	2000	1999	1998	1997	1996	1995
Revenues (millions)	28,365	25,296	22,956	19,747	14,484	11,358	8,671	5,937
Net income (millions)	7,829	7,785	9,421	7,625	4,786	3,454	2,176	1,453
Earnings per share	.70	.69	.85	.70	.45	.36	.22	.15
Dividends per share	.08	Nil	—	—	—	—	—	—
Price High	35.3	38.1	58.6	60.0	36.0	18.9	10.8	6.9
Low	20.7	21.3	20.2	34.0	15.6	10.1	5.0	3.7

GROWTH AND INCOME

National City Corporation

Post Office Box 5756, Dept. 2101 □ Cleveland, Ohio 44101-0756 □ (800) 622-4204 □ Dividend reinvestment plan is available: (800) 622-6757 □ Web site: www.nationalcity.com □ Listed: NYSE □ Ticker symbol: NCC □ S&P rating: A □ Value Line financial strength rating: A

"National City achieved a record performance in 2002, with revenue, net income, and earnings per share reaching the highest levels in our 158-year history," said CEO David A. Daberko in early 2003.

"Net income of $1.6 billion, or $2.59 per share, was up 15 percent over 2001. Return on assets was 1.54 percent, and return on equity was 19.9 percent, both at superior levels, relative to the industry. The dividend was increased once again, the seventeenth time in the last ten years.

"The strong earnings performance was most evident in the consumer lending and mortgage-related businesses, which were well-positioned to benefit from the low interest rate environment that prevailed throughout the year. Mortgage-related lending, including conventional mortgages, home-equity lines and loans, and nonconforming mortgages, all posted record origination volumes."

To be sure, 2002 had some weaknesses, according to Mr. Daberko. "The high performance in these areas overcame weaker results in corporate banking and asset management, which have been adversely affected by a soft economy and poor equity markets.

"Credit costs rose in 2002 from 2001; however, the loan portfolios are in good shape, and nonperforming assets appear to have peaked. At the same time, we have built loan loss reserves in recognition of greater uncertainty about the economy."

Company Profile

National City, founded in 1845, is the tenth-largest domestic bank holding company. National City provides broad-based banking and financial Services to about 8.5 million consumers in Ohio, Pennsylvania, Kentucky, Michigan, Illinois, and Indiana. Services are delivered through more than 1,100 branch offices and more than 1,600 ATMs. A growing number of customers choose the convenience of National City's online

banking service at *www.nationalcity.com*. Enhancements completed in 2000 have increased the Web site's versatility, functionality, ease of use, and interconnectivity.

Since David A. Daberko was named chairman and CEO of National City Corporation in 1995, the company, once known only to Ohioans, has more than doubled in size through acquisitions.

National City subsidiaries provide financial services that meet a wide range of customer needs, including commercial and retail banking, trust and investment services, item processing, mortgage banking, and credit card processing.

Retail Banking

The retail banking business includes the deposit-gathering branch franchise, along with lending to individuals and small businesses. Lending activities include residential mortgages, indirect and direct consumer installment loans, leasing, credit cards, and student lending.

Fee-Based Businesses

The fee-based businesses include institutional trust, mortgage banking, and item processing:

- Institutional trust includes employee benefit administration, mutual fund management, charitable and endowment services, and custodial services.
- Mortgage banking includes the origination of mortgages through retail offices, broker networks, and mortgage servicing.
- Item processing is conducted by National City's majority-owned subsidiary, National Processing, Inc. (NYSE:NAP), and includes merchant credit card processing, airline ticket processing, check guarantee services, and receivables and payables processing services.

Customer Needs and Preferences

To gain insight into customer preferences, National City has been making substantial investments in data warehouse technology to more effectively capture and manage customer information. This capability has already resulted in more effective cross-selling and has given the bank tools to better understand and predict customer needs and preferences.

The bank is well aware that customer demand for financial services transcends traditional time-and-place limitations. To that end, the company initiated a multi-year plan to reconfigure its branch delivery system—reducing traditional, full-service branches, while expanding nontraditional alternatives. This reconfiguration includes in-store locations, limited-service facilities, and off-site ATMs—which, along with better call-center capability, makes it easier and more convenient for customers to do business with National City.

Shortcomings to Bear in Mind

- Stephen R. Biggar, an analyst with *Standard & Poor's Stock Reports*, had this to say in January 2003: "The company's mortgage business, which was particularly strong in 2002, is expected to experience slower growth in 2003." He also said, "Following strong 2002 earnings, thanks to a thriving mortgage market, we see more difficult comparisons in 2003."

- In recent years, banks have been finding it increasingly difficult to expand revenues. Those with the broadest product mix are more likely to have an easier time registering top-line growth. In addition, savings from cost-cutting efforts, which have propelled earnings for many large banks in recent years, are becoming more difficult to come by, placing greater emphasis on top-line growth. Loan growth also remains a regional phenomenon, with strength in areas of the Southeast and Midwest, where economies continue to grow at a rate above the national average.

Reasons to Buy

- National City has a solid record of growth. In the 1992–2002 period, earnings per share expanded from $1.05 to $2.59, a compound annual growth rate of 9.4 percent. In the same ten-year span, dividends per share equaled EPS growth, climbing from $.47 cents to $1.20, a growth rate of 9.8 percent.

- In corporate banking, National City's second-largest business, the bank has worked hard to retain its position as the number one middle-market lender in its region. The bank's markets have been economically vibrant, as evidenced over the past several years by low rates of unemployment and significant growth in small and medium-sized businesses. The bank's decentralized system of credit approval permits quick responsiveness to customer needs. At the same time, the company's product capability is second to none. For example, NCC introduced an innovative lending product, Corporate Select, that uses built-in interest-rate protection options inside a conventional loan. This helps companies manage risk in a seamless, straightforward manner. Corporate Select offers a competitive advantage in winning and strengthening customer relationships. There is no comparable product currently available in the market. Through initiatives such as these and a strong team of relationship managers, National City has been able to maintain or increase market share in virtually all of its markets. What's more, the company has been particularly successful in western Pennsylvania, an area it entered through the merger with Integra Financial Corporation.

- National City is finding that fee-based businesses are growing at a healthy clip, compared with more conventional banking operations.

National Processing, for example, is

enjoying a substantial momentum as a leading processor of merchant card transactions, as it continues to expand from its strong base of national accounts into midsize and smaller merchants.

■ National City is the sixth-largest small business lender in the country and the number one SBA lender in the bank's six-state region.

■ In 2002, *BtoB* magazine ranked National City's corporate Web site among the top-rated sites operated by a bank.

■ Gomez Advisors ranked *www.national-city.com* at tenth place in its biannual scorecard ranking, an improvement from fifty-ninth just three years ago.

■ NCC's stock transfer group received the number one rating in customer satisfaction, in their category, for the fifth consecutive year, from an annual independent study of the securities industry. What's more, National City is the only company to have earned this rating so often.

■ Theresa Brophy, an analyst with *Value Line Investment Survey*, had some favorable comments in December 2002. "The more aggressive customer acquisition and retention efforts of the past year, which included new deposit products, should pay off in faster growth in consumer banking profits by the latter half of 2003.

"Economic activity and stock market valuations will eventually improve, supporting stronger corporate banking and asset management profits. Also, write-downs of auto lease residual values, as cars come off lease, should become smaller and less frequent, as the auto lease portfolio shrinks in size."

Total assets: $118,258 million
Return on average Assets in 2002: 1.54%
Common shares outstanding: 612 million
Return on 2002 shareholders' equity: 19.9%

	2002	2001	2000	1999	1998	1997	1996	1995
Loans (millions)	72,135	68,041	65,604	60,204	58,011	39,573	35,830	25,732
Net income (millions)	1,594	1,388	1,302	1,404	1,333	807	733	465
Earnings per share	2.59	2.27	2.13	2.22	2.00	1.83	1.64	1.48
Dividends per share	1.20	1.16	1.14	1.09	.97	.86	.94	.65
Price High	33.8	32.7	29.8	37.8	38.8	33.8	23.6	16.9
Low	24.6	23.7	16.0	22.1	28.5	21.3	15.3	12.6

CONSERVATIVE GROWTH

The New York Times Company

229 West 43rd Street □ New York, New York 10036 □ Investor Contact: (212) 556-1981 □ Dividend reinvestment plan is available: (800) 317-4445 □ Web site: www.nytco.com □ Listed: NYSE □ Ticker symbol: NYT □ S&P rating: B+ □ Value Line financial strength rating: B++

"*The New York Times* continues to capture market share, mainly at the expense of the *Wall Street Journal, BusinessWeek,* and *Fortune,*" said Stuart Plesser, an analyst with *Value Line Investment Survey,* in a report issued November 22, 2002.

"The success of the paper, we believe, is due to the high quality of its journalism, which has enabled it to rapidly expand on a national basis. Indeed, *New York Times* home delivery is now available in 228 markets across the country—up from 206 just a year ago and only sixty-two markets five years ago.

"Moreover, the paper is now number one in nineteen of thirty-five advertising categories. As such, effective October 1st, 2002, the company increased the rate for non-contract advertisers by 10 percent (except for recruitment advertising)."

Company Profile

Dating back to 1851, the New York Times Company is a diversified media company. Its segments consist of three groups: newspapers, broadcasting, and New York Times Digital segments.

The Newspaper Group is comprised of the following operating segments: the *New York Times* (which is circulated in all fifty states, in U.S. territories, and around the world). The *Times* has an average daily circulation of 1,130,000. On Sundays, circulation jumps to 1,681,100. About 60 percent of the Monday-through-Friday circulation is sold in the thirty-one counties that make up the greater New York City area, which includes New York City, Westchester, and parts of upstate New York, Connecticut, and New Jersey; the remaining 40 percent of the papers are sold elsewhere. On Sundays, however, 56 percent of circulation is sold in the greater New York City area and 44 percent go elsewhere.

Since 1993, the company has owned the *Boston Globe*, New England's largest newspaper. Launched in 1872, the *Globe* has a weekday circulation of 465,800, which shoots up to 716,500 on Sundays.

The New York Times Company also has a stake in twenty-two regional newspapers with total daily circulation during the week of 736,800, which moves up modestly to 787,600 on Sundays. Among these newspapers are such names as the *Gadsden Times*, the *Tuscaloosa News*, *Times Daily*, *Santa Barbara News-Press*, the *Press Democrat*, and the *Sarasota Herald-Tribune*.

The company also owns newspaper distributors, a news service, a features syndicate, TimesFax, licensing operations of the *New York Times* databases and microfilm, and Internet-related operations.

The Broadcast Group, based in Memphis, includes television stations WREG-TV in Memphis, Tennessee; WTKR-TV in Norfolk, Virginia; KFOR-TV in Oklahoma City, Oklahoma; WNEP-TV in Scranton, Pennsylvania; WHO-TV in Des Moines, Iowa; WHNT-TV in Huntsville, Alabama; WQAD-TV in Moline, Illinois; and KFSM-TV in Fort Smith, Arkansas. The company's radio stations are WQXR (FM) and WQEW (AM) in New York City.

The company's Internet sites are consolidated under a separate division, **New York Times Digital**. The sites, which total more than forty, include *www.nytimes.com*, *www.boston.com*, *www.nytoday.com*, and *www.abuzz.com*.

In 2001, newspaper publishing represented 93 percent of revenues and 92 percent of operating profits. Television broadcasting accounted for 3 percent and 8 percent, respectively. New York Times Digital represented 2 percent of revenues and incurred $7.3 million of operating losses.

Shortcomings to Bear in Mind

- Newspapers are not immune to the vagaries of the economy. Advertising is always a place that companies can retrench when they are having trouble coping with a slump in revenues. The vulnerability to a dip in advertising can be seen if you examine the company's revenue sources. The Newspaper Group's major source of revenues is advertising, not circulation.
- There is always the threat of fewer readers, as younger people view the news on television or the Internet.

Reasons to Buy

- "The year had a strong finish, with earnings improving significantly in the fourth quarter as a result of robust revenue growth across all of our four business divisions," said CEO Russell T. Lewis on January 28, 2003. "Advertising revenues, which rose 10.1 percent, continued to strengthen during the quarter, as they have since the beginning of 2002.

"Circulation revenue growth remained strong at our Newspaper Group, while our Broadcasting stations saw a record level of political advertising. New York Times Digital, the company's Internet and business information division, showed a year-over-year improvement in operating income of nearly $16 million, making 2002 its first full year of operating profitability.

"Our fourth-quarter results reflect the company's continued success in executing its long-term strategy, which is to operate the leading news and advertising media in each of the markets we serve, both national and local," Mr. Lewis said. "With regard to the national, and increasingly global, part of our strategy, in January we completed the purchase of the *International Herald Tribune*, which provides us with a strong print voice outside the United States."

Mr. Lewis went on to say, "With our company's proven growth strategy, our strong focus on cost containment and a better economy, we believe our earnings will continue to improve in 2003. We continue to believe that an improving ad market will enable us to achieve an EPS growth rate from the mid-single digits to low double digits."

- Enhancing the company's future is the continuing transformation of the *Times* from a New York City into a national newspaper. According to an official of the company, "Our ad revenue base at the *Times* is now broader and more diverse than that of any other newspaper in the country. That makes us less vulnerable to a softening in any particular category. At the same time, our ongoing national expansion effort supports the aggressive advertising rate increase that we've made in such areas as color premiums."

- In a move to widen its distribution over the Web, the Internet unit of the *New York Times* signed a deal in 2001 to provide some of its articles to Internet media giant Yahoo!

Under the pact, the *Times* provides Yahoo's News section with articles each day from the national, politics, business, international, technology, and arts sections of the *Times*, as well as local news from *www.nytoday.com* and *www.boston.com*.

"We're pleased to be working with Yahoo! in this important syndication agreement," said Catherine Levene, vice president of strategy and business development for New York Times Digital. While the *New York Times* has been syndicating its content over the Internet for years, it has been mostly in the form of headlines or abstracts.

According to Robert Hertzberg, an analyst with Jupiter Media Metrix, "You can describe their syndication strategy up to now as a tease. This is really giving away a lot of the goods, and I expect it will be good for the *Times*, through subscription to print publication and building traffic at the *New York Times* site."

- In the fall of 2002, William H. Donald, an analyst with *Standard & Poor's Stock Reports*, said, "Despite some lingering economic softness in its markets, we believe NYT is an attractive vehicle for long-term capital gains. Investors recognize the company's leading position in the New York metropolitan market and its strength in national advertising sales. NYT's attractive mix of media businesses also contributes to the stock's appeal."

- The *New York Times* has always said that it publishes "All the news that's fit to print." There are ample reasons why. The paper has reporters in every corner of the world. In addition to about 100 reporters in New York City, eight news bureaus report to the metropolitan desk. Outside of New York, the largest news bureau of the *Times* is in Washington, where about thirty reporters and seven editors cover news not only for the national desk but for other sections as well, including foreign, business, and metropolitan.

The *Times* has about thirty domestic reporters stationed around the United States, outside of Washington and the New York region. Twenty of them are national correspondents based in news bureaus in eleven cities, while the remainder work for the business news and cultural news departments.

The foreign desk is responsible for gathering and reporting news from outside the United States. The foreign desk has over forty staff correspondents, numerous contributors, and twenty-six news bureaus around the world.

Total assets: $3,509 million
Current ratio: .61
Common shares outstanding: 151 million
Return on 2002 shareholders' equity: 23.8%

		2002	2001	2000	1999	1998	1997	1996	1995
Revenues (millions)		3,079	3,016	3,489	3,131	2,937	2,866	2,615	2,409
Net income (millions)		300	202	360	310	287	262	84	136
Earnings per share		1.94	1.26	2.10	1.73	1.49	1.33	0.43	0.70
Dividends per share		.54	.50	.45	.41	.37	.32	.28	.28
Price	High	53.0	48.0	49.9	49.8	40.6	33.2	20.0	15.5
	Low	38.6	35.5	32.6	26.5	20.5	18.2	12.8	10.1

AGGRESSIVE GROWTH

Newell Rubbermaid, Inc.

29 East Stephenson Street □ Freeport, Illinois 61032 □ (815) 381-8150 □ Direct dividend reinvestment plan available: (888) 565-6553 □ Web site: www.newellco.com □ Listed: NYSE □ Ticker symbol: NWL □ S&P rating: A- □ Value Line Financial Strength B+

An important ingredient in the recent success of Newell Rubbermaid is CEO Joseph Galli, Jr., age forty-three, according to a December 2002 article in *Fortune* magazine. The author, Matthew Boyle, said, "By the time Galli arrived in January 2001, the situation was indeed dire. Lowe's had summarily removed Rubbermaid storage containers from a Pottsville, Pa., distribution center that served 110 stores and replaced them with plastic products from rival supplier Sterilite. Wal-Mart had pulled $75 million of Rubbermaid home products off its shelves. 'This was not a rosy picture,' says Galli. In 2000, Newell Rubbermaid's sales at Home Depot and Lowe's combined were down 3 percent, and sales at Wal-Mart were flat—and this at a time when those retailers were growing at a 15 percent to 20 percent clip.

"The first act was to purge upper management, bringing in a slew of his trusted Black & Decker cronies to head key divisions and customer accounts." In addition, said Mr. Boyle, "Borrowing from a program he had successfully run at Black & Decker, Galli's recruiting team scoured 120 college campuses and hired 451 students, offering them $37,000 a year and a chance to prove themselves. He wasn't looking for Ivy League MBAs. Rather, he sent recruiters to state schools to track down personable jocks and ambitious sorority presidents. Galli, who was a wrestling champion at the University of North Carolina, says he looks for 'achievers, and more often than not, that's outside the classroom.'"

Mr. Boyle also said, "Like other CEOs these days, Galli is closing plants and laying people off. After all, he needs to make Newell profitable. But he also knows that if he ignores the job of molding the next generation of managers, he can't truly succeed."

Company Profile

Newell Rubbermaid, Inc., is a global manufacturer and marketer of consumer products with revenues in excess of $7 billion in 2002. It has a powerful brand family including Sharpie, Paper Mate, Waterman, Colorific, Rubbermaid, Stain Shield, Blue Ice, TakeAlongs, Roughneck, Calphalon, Little Tikes, Graco, Levolor, Kirsch, Shur-Line, BernzOmatic, Goody, Vise-Grip, Quick-Grip, and Irwin.

Products are distributed through volume purchasers, including discount stores and warehouse clubs, home centers, hardware stores, office superstores, and contract stationers.

Office products consist of Sanford and Berol markers, Eberhard Faber pencils and rolling ball pens; Stuart Hall school and office supplies; Newell Office Products; and Rogers & Keene desktop office and computer accessories.

The infant/juvenile care and play business is made up of the Little Tikes and Graco/Century divisions. These businesses design and manufacture products such as toys, highchairs, infant seats, ride-ons, and outdoor activity play equipment.

The food preparation, cooking, and serving businesses are made up of the Mirro, Panex, and Calphalon cookware and bakeware divisions, as well as the Anchor Hocking and Newell Europe glasswares divisions.

The hardware and tools operation is made up of Amerock, EZ Paintr, BernzOmatic, Lee Rowan, and Newell Hardware Europe. The divisions produce cabinet and window hardware, paint applicators, torches, and storage and closet products.

Shortcomings to Bear in Mind

- The company's balance sheet is not up to my standards, with common equity representing only 42 percent of total capital. Coverage of bond interest is also too low, at only 4.5 times. These weaknesses are reflected in *Value Line*'s below-average Financial Strength rating of B+.

Reasons to Buy

- Charles W. Noh, an analyst with *Value Line Investment Survey*, had this positive observation in late 2002: "The company has gained an important new client, Kohl's. That specialty department-store chain plans to open a store within a store featuring Newell's Calphalon cookware, one of its more profitable businesses. Growth prospects for this high-end product line, which is currently sold in Bed Bath and Beyond and in Sears, Roebuck, are particularly bright."

- "Another reason why I'm so optimistic is the strong support that our approach has elicited from our most important trade accounts, which collectively represent the 'sweet spot' of the retail sector," said CEO Joseph Galli, Jr., in 2002. "The fact is, Newell Rubbermaid is among the most important suppliers to many of the biggest, brightest, and fastest-growing names in retail today—companies like Wal-Mart (our single largest customer), The Home Depot, Lowe's, Target, Toys "R" Us, Office Depot, Kohl's, Bed Bath and Beyond, Walgreens, Menard's, Canadian Tire, and Carrefour.

"And I can tell you that these companies are not only rooting for us to succeed, but giving us every opportunity to do so. Why? Because our products offer retailers extremely attractive profit margins, and we now support our brand portfolio with the kind of marketing and merchandising that builds store traffic, increases inventory turns, and generates impulse sales."

- Since Mr. Galli, age forty-three, took the reins of leadership in January of 2001, he has made some bold moves. He plans to make more. "We're driving major productivity gains across all of our businesses, with a commitment to reduce our cost of goods sold by 5 percent annually," he said in 2002.

  "Our goal is to be the low-cost supplier in every business in which we compete. To accomplish this, we're optimizing the balance between products that we manufacture ourselves and those we source from third parties. We're pursuing lower-cost manufacturing opportunities in places like Mexico, China, Poland, and Hungary. We're also starting to leverage the company's combined purchasing power. Resin, corrugated, and transportation are all good examples of how buying as one entity is much more effective than the division-by-division purchasing we've historically done. Our perpetual productivity obsession will help fuel gross margin expansion for years to come."

- New products are also a key area for the company, said Mr. Galli. "We're creating marketplace excitement through a steady stream of innovative, value-added, and fashion-forward new products. Newell Rubbermaid intends to be an unrivaled leader in this arena. To do this, we're augmented our existing product development capability with more than fifty world-class product designers and engineers; we've upgraded

our research and development facilities with state-of-the-art technology; and we've begun to significantly shorten product development lead times in order to be quicker and more agile in response to customers' desires.

"In 2001 alone, we launched such exciting and successful new entries as Rubbermaid's Tool Tower and the Wrap 'n Craft storage container, Calphalon's tri-ply stainless steel cookware, the Sharpie Chisel Tip marker, the Little Tikes' Cozy Coupe convertible, and Levolor's faux wood blinds."

- In 2001, a consumer survey by a leading trade publication, *HFN*, named Rubbermaid number one among the 100 most powerful brands in the home products industry.

- In late 2002, Howard Choe, an analyst with *Standard & Poor's Stock Reports*, had some favorable comments on Newell Rubbermaid. "Sales in 2003 should benefit from the May acquisition of American Tool and the proposed December acquisition of American Saw & Manufacturing. We expect sales to improve across the board, but expect the most significant increase from the Levolor/hardware division.

  "We expect modest growth from the Rubbermaid, cookware, and writing instrument divisions. Gross margins should continue to widen, on higher volume, productivity efforts, and a mix shift toward higher margin products. Operating profitability should advance, despite slightly higher marketing expenses."

  The S&P report also said, "NWL's efforts to improve customer relationships and increased marketing efforts are paying off as sales have increased markedly since the beginning of the year."

Total assets: $7,389 million
Current ratio: 1.18
Return on 2002 equity: 20.5%
Common shares outstanding: 267 million

	2002	2001	2000	1999	1998	1997	1996	1995
Revenues (millions)	7,454	6,909	6,935	6,413	3,720	3,234	2,873	2,498
Net income (millions)	423	320	454	320	290	256	222	196
Earnings per share	1.58	1.20	1.71	1.65	1.94	1.82	1.62	1.41
Dividends per share	.84	.84	.84	.80	.72	.64	.56	.46
Price High	36.7	29.5	31.9	52.0	55.2	43.8	33.8	27.3
Low	26.1	20.5	18.3	25.3	35.7	30.1	25.0	20.3

AGGRESSIVE GROWTH

Oshkosh Truck Corporation

2307 Oregon Street □ Post Office Box 2566 □ Oshkosh, Wisconsin 54903 □ (920)233-9332 □ Web site: www.oshkoshtruck.com □ Dividend reinvestment plan not available □ Fiscal years end September 30 □ Listed: NYSE □ Ticker symbol: OSK □ S&P rating: B+ □ Value Line financial strength rating: no rating

"Oshkosh Truck Corporation, which has enjoyed a remarkable turnaround from purely a defense contractor to a manufacturer of heavy trucks for a variety of uses, has won a top award in the annual state Manufacturer of the Year competition," said Thomas Content, a reporter for the Milwaukee Journal Sentinel, on Feb. 27, 2003.

"Oshkosh Truck, which saw sales decline for two straight years in the mid-1990s, has rebounded through acquisitions that added fire trucks, ambulances, and concrete placement trucks to a lineup of military and garbage trucks.

"Sales have since quadrupled, from $439 million in 1996 to $1.74 billion. In the three past years, when the U.S. economy dipped into recession and the long 1990s bull market ended painfully for investors, Oshkosh Truck's net income has topped $49 million each year. For investors, Oshkosh is one of just six Wisconsin firms whose stock doubled from 2000 to 2002."

Mr. Content went on to say, "Recent years have seen Oshkosh focus intensely on expanding the commercial side of its business, but the company is now focused on beefing up its military contracts. Earlier this year, Oshkosh was named the preferred bidder for a $250 million contract from the United Kingdom."

Company Profile

Oshkosh Truck is a manufacturer of a broad range of specialty commercial, fire, emergency, and military trucks and truck bodies. It sells mostly to customers in domestic and European markets. The company sells trucks under the Oshkosh and Pierce trademarks; truck bodies under the McNeilus, MTM, Medtec, Geesink, and Norba trademarks; and mobile and stationary compactors under the Geesink Kiggen trademark.

Oshkosh began business in 1917 and was among the early pioneers of four-wheel-drive technology.

The company's commercial truck lines include refuse truck bodies, rear and front-discharge concrete mixers, and all-wheel-drive truck chassis. Its custom and commercial fire apparatus and emergency vehicles include pumpers; aerial and ladder trucks; tankers; light-, medium-, and heavy-duty rescue vehicles; wildland and rough-terrain response vehicles; aircraft rescue and firefighting vehicles and ambulances; and snow-removal vehicles.

As a manufacturer of severe-duty, heavy-tactical trucks for the U.S. Department of Defense, Oshkosh Truck manufactures vehicles that perform a variety of demanding tasks, such as hauling tanks, missile systems, ammunition, fuel, and cargo for combat units.

In fiscal 2002, the company's commercial segment contributed about 39 percent of revenues and 42 percent of operating profits. Oshkosh's fire and emergency segment accounted for 27 percent of sales and 44 percent of operating profits. Finally, the company's defense truck segment was responsible for 34 percent of revenues and 37 percent of operating profits.

Shortcomings to Bear in Mind

- "Because of the costs associated with both winning and maintaining government contracts and the cyclical nature of its commercial end markets, we believe that OSK's profitability and cash earnings growth rate will continue to be erratic," said James R. Sanders, an analyst with *Standard & Poor's Stock Reports*, at the end of November of 2002. "As a result, we anticipate that the company's average long-term ROE (return on equity) will hover around 10 percent to 12 percent."

Reasons to Buy

- At the end of fiscal 2002 (which ended September 30, 2002), CEO Robert G. Bohn said, "In the wake of another weak year for U.S. and European commercial markets, Oshkosh delivered a solid financial performance in fiscal 2002. Revenues reached $1.74 billion, a 20.6 percent increase over fiscal 2001, while net income grew 17.2 percent, to $59.6 million, aided by the elimination of goodwill amortization. As a result, earnings per share were $3.45, compared to $2.98 last year.

   "In these difficult economic conditions, cash is paramount. We paid down $209.3 million of debt by year-end, eliminating Geesink Norba acquisition debt in less than one year and bringing our debt-to-capital ratio down to 26.8 percent. Throughout the year, we focused on de-leveraging our balance sheet to create the financial flexibility to continue our diversification strategy."

- Mr. Bohn made these comments on the company's attention to research and development: "Leadership in technology and product development has been a main driver of our past success and continues to be a vital foundation for our future.

   "In fiscal 2002, investments in research and development rose 24.8 percent, to $17.9 million corporate-wide. Most notably, we introduced the Revolution composite concrete mixer drum, a new StreetForce line of refuse bodies, and a new wildland fire truck, the Hawk Extreme, that contribute to our leadership position in those markets.

- "The Revolution mixer is integral to our long-term growth strategy. By the end of fiscal 2003, Oshkosh plans to have a U.S. plant operational at high rate production for sales beginning in fiscal 2004. In fiscal 2005 and 2006, we expect to introduce this technology to Europe and Asia."

   In an industry where efficiency and productivity go directly to the bottom line, the working payload of concrete mixers is a primary concern. Understanding this, McNeilus and its partner invested more than $10 million over the past four years in exhaustive research, engineering, prototype building, and testing to develop a composite drum that is lighter, quieter, and carries more concrete than a typical drum.

   McNeilus worked with Geiger Ready Mix in Kansas City, Kansas, to field test the drum. Geiger is a long-time McNeilus customer, and a company always looking for better ways of doing business.

In its first six months of service, Geiger reported the Revolution outperformed all expectations. The composite material that it makes is easier to load and unload than concrete. It does not require the kind of dirty, difficult cleaning that steel drums need, and it keeps the concrete cooler, giving the operator more time to pour a load.

- The launch of the new StreetForce refuse bodies from McNeilus is a "remarkable example of how Oshkosh Truck capitalized on its core capabilities to build a line of trucks that customers needed and no one else in the industry could deliver," said a company official.

"In the summer of 2001, Western Disposal Services, Inc., of Boulder, Colorado, came to McNeilus with a challenge. Western needed an automated refuse hauler with a rear-loading mechanism, a lower rear-loading height, the ability to handle all forms of trash, and one that reduced spillage and noise.

"To create the StreetForce line, McNeilus engineers complemented their expertise with designs and technology from the Geesink Norba Group and Oshkosh."

- "The Hawk Extreme is a high-mobility water tender, specifically designed for the wildland segment of the fire service," said a company spokesman. "It is built on an Oshkosh MTVR chassis, originally developed for the U.S. Marines, with all-wheel drive, TAK-4 independent suspension, central tire inflation, a seven-ton off-road payload, and unmatched off-road capabilities. To that chassis, Pierce added a fire-fighting system, including a 2,500-gallon water tank, sixty-gallon foam tank, front-mounted water turret, scene lighting, and more.

"Pierce Manufacturing is already the leader in custom fire apparatus for the municipal market. By tapping into Oshkosh technology, Pierce has expanded its wildland product line with a vehicle that allows fire fighters to fight wildland blazes more efficiently. This truck goes where others simply can't.

"In the past, water tenders would stay on the perimeter of a fire and 'nurse' four-wheel-drive pickup trucks equipped with 100-gallon water tanks. The smaller vehicles would then tackle the tough terrain to fight the fire. The Hawk Extreme is able to traverse extremely rugged terrain, allowing the fire fighters to bring large amounts of water directly to the fire, saving time in critical situations.

"The Hawk Extreme was put to the test this summer in South Dakota. This truck was on hand when a large wild fire raged near the town of Spearfish. Its performance was so impressive, the governor of South Dakota approved special funding to purchase two Hawk Extremes for the protection of the western half of the state."

- The development of the ProPulse hybrid electric drive systems exemplifies Oshkosh Truck's ability to deliver new technologies to meet the changing demands of all Oshkosh business segments. ProPulse alternative-drive technology increases fuel economy up to 40 percent and generates 400 kilowatts of electricity onboard, enough to power an airport, hospital, command center, or an entire city block.

According to a company executive, "Oshkosh was the first company to apply hybrid technology to severe-duty vehicles. With some of the most experienced engineers in the industry working on the project, the Oshkosh team developed many breakthrough technologies for the ProPulse project. Oshkosh has patents pending for many of the technologies incorporated into the ProPulse system.

"The ProPulse technology has applications well beyond the military use, including refuse trucks, fire apparatus, snow removal, and other commercial vehicles. In fact, Oshkosh is already adapting the ProPulse technology to a refuse-hauling vehicle."

Total assets: $1,024 million
Current ratio: 1.09
Common shares outstanding: 17 million
Return on 2002 shareholders' equity: 15.8%

		2002	2001	2000	1999	1998	1997	1996	1995
Revenues (millions)		1,744	1,445	1,324	1,165	903	683	413	438
Net income (millions)		59.6	50.9	48.5	31.2	16.3	10.0	-0.24	11.6
Earnings per share		3.45	2.98	2.96	2.39	1.27	0.79	-0.02	.88
Dividends per share		.35	.35	.35	.34	.33	.33	.33	.33
Price	High	65.4	49.8	44.0	38.5	23.3	14.2	10.5	10.5
	Low	46.1	31.9	21.6	19.3	11.6	6.8	6.8	7.2

AGGRESSIVE GROWTH

Patterson Dental Company

1031 Mendota Heights Road □ St. Paul, Minnesota 55120-1419 □ (651) 686-1600 □ Dividend reinvestment not plan available □ Web site: www.pattersondental.com □ Fiscal years end last Saturday in April □ Listed: NASDAQ □ Ticker symbol: PDCO □ Standard & Poor's rating: B+ □ Value Line financial strength rating: A

The CEO of Patterson Dental Company, Peter L. Frechette, believes "the North American dental supply market is growing at an estimated 7 percent to 9 percent annual rate, and due to a number of factors, we believe growth at this pace will be sustainable for some time to come. For example, demand for dental services is growing faster than the available number of dentists."

Mr. Frechette went on to say, "This market imbalance is due partly to the aging of the general North American population, since growing numbers of older individuals require more dental procedures than any other age group. The growth of the dental market also is benefiting from the introduction of new therapeutic technologies that are enabling dentists to treat more patients, while improving clinical outcomes. As a result, dentists are converting to such new-generation, productivity-enhancing dental equipment as digital radiography and the CEREC 3 restoration system.

"In addition, consumer demand is growing for cosmetic dentistry and other specialized procedures that are augmenting the income steams of dental practices. Dental insurance also is enabling more people to regularly visit their dentists."

Company Profile

In 1877, two brothers, John and Myron Patterson, opened a drugstore in Milwaukee, Wisconsin. Patterson's Drug Store sold dental and surgical instruments and supplies. The brothers soon realized that the dental business offered more opportunities than the surgical field, and with the Western expansion in full swing, they also understood that the future of the dental business lay in the West.

The brothers decided to divide their holdings, with Myron, or "M.F.," keeping the drugstore. He eventually sold the drugstore and moved to St. Paul, Minnesota, where he opened the M. F. Patterson Dental Supply Company in 1891.

Today, Patterson Dental Company is a distributor serving North American dental supply and companion-pet (such as dogs and cats) veterinary supply markets. Its divisions include Patterson Dental Supply Company and Webster Veterinary Supply.

Patterson Dental Supply Company

As Patterson's largest business, Patterson Dental Supply provides a virtually complete range of consumable dental products, clinical and laboratory equipment, and value-added services to dentists, dental laboratories, institutions, and other health care providers throughout North America.

Consumable dental and printed products accounted for 64 percent of net sales in fiscal 2002. The company offers both its own private label line of anesthetics, instruments, and preventative and restorative products, as well as brand-name supplies including x-ray film, protective clothing, toothbrushes, and other dental accessories.

Printed products, sold through both a dedicated sales force and catalogs, include insurance and billing forms, stationery, appointment books, and other stock office-supply products.

The company offers a wide range of dental equipment, which accounted for 28 percent of net sales in fiscal 2002. The product line includes x-ray machines, sterilizers, dental chairs, dental lights, and diagnostic equipment. Patterson also distributes newer technology equipment that provides customers with the tools to improve productivity and patient satisfaction. Examples include the CEREC product family (a chair-side restoration system) and air abrasion systems.

The remaining 8 percent of sales came from software services, equipment installation, repair and maintenance, dental office design, and equipment financing.

Patterson Dental Supply, which is growing significantly faster than its market, has the largest direct sales force in the industry, totaling more than 1,200 sales representatives, equipment specialists, and technology representatives serving the United States and Canada.

Webster Veterinary Supply

Webster is the leading distributor of veterinary supplies to companion-pet veterinary clinics in the eastern United States and the third-largest nationally. One of the most respected names in the veterinary supply industry, Webster is a value-added, full-service distributor of consumable supplies, equipment, diagnostic products, biologicals (vaccines), and pharmaceuticals.

Shortcomings to Bear in Mind

- As noted in the next section, Patterson Dental has a most impressive record of consistent growth. It is not surprising that the stock normally sells at a lofty P/E ratio.
- During 2002, insiders (such as executives and board members) were net sellers of the stock. There were no buyers.

Reasons to Buy

- In fiscal 2002, sales of Patterson's dental operations increased 11.4 percent, and by more than 18 percent in the fourth quarter, reflecting strong sales of consumer supplies, core equipment, and the CEREC 3 dental restorative system.

Late in the fourth quarter of 2002, the company acquired Thompson Dental Company of Columbia, South Carolina. A leading value-added distributor of dental supplies, equipment, and services in the mid-Atlantic and southeastern United States, Thompson ranked among the ten largest dental distributors in the country.

In 2002, the Webster Veterinary Supply unit exceeded estimates, with a sales increase of 9 percent. Although solidly profitable, the contribution to the company's earnings per share was only

$0.04. Clearly, the dental business is the key to this company's future.

- In the 1993–2002 period, earnings per share climbed—without interruption—from $0.21 to $1.40, a compound annual growth rate of 23.5 percent, which makes this an aggressive-growth stock.
- In the fall of 2002, Alex Hudson, writing for *Value Line Investment Survey*, said, "These shares are ranked to outpace the year-ahead market. Supporting this equity's above-average ranking are a steady stream of favorable quarterly earnings comparisons, as well as a positive near-term outlook. We see no end in sight to this impressive trend, and estimate solid double-digit share-net growth over the next few years."
- The CEREC 3 dental restorative system is a clear example of new-generation equipment that benefits both the patient and the dentist. In addition to providing certain clinical advantages in comparison to traditional restoration techniques, the CEREC 3 increases office productivity by eliminating the need for a second office visit to complete a tooth restoration. As a result, CEREC 3 enables a dentist to treat additional patients, thus creating a revenue-generating opportunity.

  The CEREC 3 also increases the profitability of restoration procedures by eliminating outside lab work. In 2002, the company extended its exclusive distribution agreement with Sirona Dental Systems GmbH through September 2004 for the CEREC 3 and the new CEREC inLab system, which is designed for restoration processes performed in dental labs.
- Because of the fragmented nature of the North American dental-supply market and Patterson's strong financial condition, the company has historically been able to augment its internal growth with strategic acquisitions. Over the past five years, Patterson has made twelve acquisitions, each of which has been accretive to the company's consolidated profitability. Management is convinced that additional acquisition opportunities exist and "Patterson is committed to seeking transactions that make good business sense and economic sense," said Mr. Frechette.

- In the Webster Veterinary Supply sector, according to Mr. Frechette, Webster "is planning to expand its marketing of veterinary equipment. This is a largely untapped opportunity, since little veterinary equipment is currently sold through companion-pet distributors. However, veterinary equipment, including digital X-ray systems, clinical and practice management software, sterilizers, and surgical instruments, represents a significant opportunity.

  "As the leading distributor of dental equipment, Patterson's experience with equipment marketing, financing, and technical service will be of considerable value to Webster as it pursues this growth opportunity."
- Webster Veterinary Supply serves the $2.2-billion domestic companion-pet veterinary-supply market, which the company believes to be growing at a 6 percent to 7 percent rate. Small-animal or companion-pet veterinarians are the largest and fastest-growing segment of the overall veterinary market.

  A variety of factors are driving the growth of this segment, including rising pet ownership. It is currently estimated that about 31 million U.S. households own dogs, while 27 million own cats. Consistent with the growth of pet ownership, annual consumer spending on veterinary care is far higher today than it was a decade ago. The willingness of owners to spend more on their pets is related in part to the advent of new procedures and drugs that significantly improve clinical outcomes.
- The companion-pet veterinary supply market, like the dental supply market, is

highly fragmented. The top three distributors nationally, including Webster, account for about 40 percent of the market. Another 70 percent or so local and regional distributors account for the remaining 60 percent of the national marketplace. In addition, the companion-pet veterinary-supply market is made up of about 21,000 office practices; Webster now serves 8,200 of those in the eastern part of the nation.

The average practice, consisting of two veterinarians and limited support staff, purchases an estimated $80,000 to $120,000 of supplies each year.

The distributor's sales representative tends to be viewed as a consultant, providing veterinary customers with news of industry developments, information on new products and technologies, and general assessments of what is working and not working for other practices.

Total assets: $718 million
Current ratio: 2.97
Common shares outstanding: 68 million
Return on 2002 shareholders' equity: 20.7%

	2002	2001	2000	1999	1998	1997	1996	1995
Revenues (millions)	1,416	1,156	1,040	879	778	662	582	533
Net income (millions)	95.3	76.5	64.5	49.9	40.8	32.4	28.7	24.2
Earnings per share	1.40	1.13	0.96	0.74	0.61	0.50	0.44	0.37
Dividends per share	Nil	—	—	—	—	—	—	—
Price High	55.1	42.1	34.5	25.1	23.2	15.3	12.3	9.8
Low	38.1	27.5	16.3	16.6	14.1	8.9	6.7	6.7

CONSERVATIVE GROWTH

PepsiCo, Inc.

700 Anderson Hill Road □ Purchase, New York 10577-1444 □ (914) 253-2711 □ Dividend reinvestment plan is available: (800) 226-0083 □ Web site: www.pepsico.com □ Listed: NYSE □ Ticker symbol: PEP □ S&P rating: A □ Value Line financial strength rating: A+

When the economy is weak, and the stock market is not rewarding investors, beverage companies are often a good place to invest. PepsiCo proved this rule in 2002, when earnings per share climbed to $1.85, an increase of 26 percent over the prior year.

In February of 2003, CEO Reinemund said: "In 2002 our portfolio of businesses complemented each other and performed very well overall. We're pleased to report very strong operating profit and earnings per share growth. Our margins expanded as a result of synergies from our merger with Quaker, as well as strong productivity across our divisions. We increased our market share across our key U.S. businesses, and our cash flow was extremely robust.

"Our businesses are fundamentally very healthy. We're focused on driving top-line growth through innovation and by leveraging our strong brands and go-to-market systems. At the same time we are driving productivity improvements that will allow us to re-invest in the top line and continue to expand our margins. Looking forward, over the long run we believe that we can sustainably grow volume and net revenues in the mid-single digits and earnings per share in the low double-digits."

Company Profile

The company consists of the snack businesses of Frito-Lay North America and

Frito-Lay International; the beverage businesses of Pepsi-Cola North America, Gatorade/Tropicana North America, and PepsiCo Beverages International; and Quaker Foods North America, manufacturer and marketer of ready-to-eat cereals and other food products. PepsiCo brands are available in nearly 200 countries and territories.

Many of PepsiCo's brand names are more than 100 years old, but the corporation is relatively young. PepsiCo was founded in 1965 through the merger of Pepsi-Cola and Frito-Lay. Tropicana was acquired in 1998, and PepsiCo merged with the Quaker Oats Company, which included Gatorade, in 2001.

Frito-Lay North America and Frito-Lay International

PepsiCo's snack food operations had their start in 1932 when two separate events took place. In San Antonio, Texas, Elmer Doolin bought the recipe for an unknown food product—a corn chip—and started an entirely new industry. The product was Fritos brand corn chips, and his firm became the Frito Company.

That same year in Nashville, Tennessee, Herman W. Lay started his own business distributing potato chips. Mr. Lay later bought the company that supplied him with product and changed its name to H. W. Lay Company. The Frito Company and H. W. Lay Company merged in 1961 to become Frito-Lay, Inc.

Today, Frito-Lay brands account for more than half of the U.S. snack chip industry.

PepsiCo began its international snack food operations in 1966. Today, with operations in more than forty countries, it is the leading multinational snack chip company, accounting for more than one-quarter of international retail snack chip sales. Products are available in some 120 countries. Frito-Lay North America

includes Canada and the United States. Major Frito-Lay International markets include Australia, Brazil, Mexico, the Netherlands, South Africa, the United Kingdom, and Spain.

Often Frito-Lay products are known by local names. These names include Matutano in Spain, Sabritas and Gamesa in Mexico, Elma Chips in Brazil, and Walkers in the United Kingdom. The company markets Frito-Lay brands on a global level, and introduces unique products for local tastes.

Major Frito-Lay products include Ruffles, Lay's, and Doritos brands snack chips. Other major brands include Cheetos cheese-flavored snacks, Tostitos tortilla chips, Santitas tortilla chips, Rold Gold pretzels, and SunChips multigrain snacks. Frito-Lay also sells a variety of snack dips and cookies, nuts, and crackers.

Pepsi-Cola North America and PepsiCo Beverages International

PepsiCo's beverage business was founded at the turn of the century by Caleb Bradham, a New Bern, North Carolina druggist, who first formulated Pepsi-Cola. Today consumers spend about $33 billion on Pepsi-Cola beverages. Brand Pepsi and other Pepsi-Cola products—including Diet Pepsi, Pepsi-One, Mountain Dew, Slice, Sierra Mist, and Mug brands—account for nearly one-third of total soft-drink sales in the United States, a consumer market totaling about $60 billion.

Pepsi-Cola also offers a variety of non-carbonated beverages, including Aquafina bottled water, Fruitworks, and All Sport.

In 1992 Pepsi-Cola formed a partnership with Thomas J. Lipton, Co. Today Lipton is the biggest-selling ready-to-drink tea brand in the United States. Pepsi-Cola also markets Frappuccino ready-to-drink coffee through a partnership with Starbucks.

In 2001 SoBe became a part of Pepsi-Cola. SoBe manufactures and markets an innovative line of beverages, including fruit blends, energy drinks, dairy-based drinks, exotic teas, and other beverages with herbal ingredients.

Outside the United States, Pepsi-Cola soft-drink operations include the business of Seven-Up International. Pepsi-Cola beverages are available in about 160 countries and territories.

Gatorade/Tropicana North America

Tropicana was founded in 1947 by Anthony Rossi as a Florida fruit-packaging business. The company entered the concentrate orange juice business in 1949, registering Tropicana as a trademark.

In 1954, Rossi pioneered a pasteurization process for orange juice. For the first time, consumers could enjoy the fresh taste of pure not-from-concentrate 100 percent Florida orange juice in a ready-to-serve package. The juice, Tropicana Pure Premium, became the company's flagship product.

In 1957 the name of the company was changed to Tropicana Products, headquartered in Bradenton, Florida. The company went public in 1957, was purchased by Beatrice Foods Co. in 1978, acquired by Kohlberg Kravis & Roberts in 1986, and sold to the Seagram Company, Ltd., in 1988. Seagram purchased the Dole global juice business in 1995. PepsiCo acquired Tropicana, including the Dole juice business, in August 1998.

Today the Tropicana brand is available in sixty-three countries. Principal brands in North America are Tropicana Pure Premium, Tropicana Season's Best, Dole Juices, and Tropicana Twister. Internationally, principal brands include Tropicana Pure Premium and Dole juices along with Frui'Vita, Lo'za, and Copella. Tropicana Pure Premium is the third-largest brand of all food products sold in grocery stores in the United States.

Gatorade sports drinks was acquired by the Quaker Oats Company in 1983 and became a part of PepsiCo with the merger in 2001. Gatorade is the first isotonic sports drink. Created in 1965 by researchers at the University of Florida for the school's football team—The Gators—Gatorade is now the world's leading sport's drink.

Quaker Foods North America

The Quaker Oats Company was formed in 1901 when several American pioneers in oat milling came together to incorporate. In Ravenna, Ohio, Henry D. Seymour and William Heston established the Quaker Mill Company and registered the now-famous trademark.

The first major acquisition of the company was Aunt Jemina Mills Company in 1926, which is today the leading manufacturer of pancake mixes and syrup.

In 1986, the Quaker Oats Company acquired the Golden Grain Company, producers of Rice-A-Roni.

PepsiCo merged with the Quaker Oats Company in 2001. Its products still have the eminence of wholesome, good-for-you food, as envisioned by the company over a century ago.

Shortcomings to Bear in Mind

- The acquisition of Quaker Oats has its negative aspects. Acquiring Quaker's food business came at a time when consumers are becoming increasingly impatient with sit-down meals. About 11 percent of the Pepsi's business is now in an ailing food business, ranging from pasta to cereal, that grows at a snail's pace of 2 percent a year. On the other hand, there is some speculation that the company may sell the food business in the next year or two. Under current accounting rules, the company must wait two years following an acquisition. In any event, Steven S. Reinemund, PepsiCo's new CEO, says there are no immediate plans to shed this line. "We haven't bought a collection of cats and dogs here," said Mr. Reinemund. "These are great brands. We intend to grow all of it."

Reasons to Buy

- The sports drink Gatorade was the big prize in the company's recent purchase of Quaker Oats. However, management is salivating over the possibilities that Quaker brings for boosting its sales of snacks and fruit drinks. According to Roger A. Enrico, vice chairman of PepsiCo, Quaker's clout in the non-carbonated beverage aisle could also pay dividends by getting retailers to provide shelf space for its Tropicana division's growing line of fruit drinks, such as Tropicana Twisters. The market for non-carbonated drinks is about $16 billion, compared with $58 billion for carbonated drinks, but is growing much faster, according to the industry trade publication *Beverage Digest*. Enrico also says that Quaker's granola bars, rice cakes, and fruit bars are complementary to the Frito-Lay division's industry-leading lineup of salty snacks such as Tostitos corn chips and Lay's potato chips.

- Carbonated drinks, such as Pepsi and Mountain Dew, are still the mainstay of the company's business. However, sales of non-carbonated beverages, such as Aquafina bottled water and SoBe drinks, are expanding at a rapid pace, as consumer's tastes become more diverse.

- With the acquisition of Quaker Oats, Pepsi now has an immense stable of strong brands, thus boosting its clout among retailers. This provides the company with greater advantage in the tussle among beverage companies for hard-to-get space in convenience-store coolers. "When the PepsiCo guy walks into 7-Eleven, they're going to have to pay a lot more attention to him than they do to Coke," one Pepsi bottler said. "He'll have Pepsi, Gatorade, SoBe, and Tropicana. He owns the refrigerator door."

Total assets: $23,474 million
Current ratio: 1.17
Common shares outstanding: 1,789 million
Return on 2002 shareholders' equity: 36.9%

		2002	2001	2000	1999	1998	1997	1996	1995
Revenues (millions)		25,112	23,512	25,480	20,367	22,348	20,917	31,645	30,421
Net income (millions)		3,313	2,660	2,540	1,845	1,760	1,730	1,865	1,990
Earnings per share		1.85	1.47	1.42	1.23	1.16	1.10	1.17	1.24
Dividends per share		.60	.58	.56	.54	.52	.49	.45	.39
Price	High	53.5	50.5	49.9	42.6	44.8	41.3	35.9	29.4
	Low	34.0	40.3	29.7	30.1	27.6	28.3	27.3	16.9

AGGRESSIVE GROWTH

Pfizer, Inc.

235 East 42nd Street □ New York, New York 10017-5755 □ (212) 573-2323 □ Direct dividend reinvestment plan is available: (800) 733-9393 □ Web site: www.pfizer.com □ Listed: NYSE □ Ticker symbol: PFE □ S&P rating: A+ □ Value Line financial strength rating: A+

According to a report written by H. B. Saftlas for the *Standard & Poor's Stock Reports* in October 2002, the acquisition of Pharmacia at the end of 2002 gives Pfizer "a commanding lead in the global drug arena, with prescription drug sales of

$39 billion (over 10 percent of the world-wide market)." What's more, the merger gives Pfizer "the lead in most major therapeutic classifications, and enables it to dominate in the research and development arena, with over $7 billion spent annually on some 120 new chemical entities and a wide range of other compounds."

Company Profile

Pfizer traces its history back to 1849 when it was founded by Charles Pfizer and Charles Erhart. In those early days, Pfizer was a chemical firm. Today, it is a leading global pharmaceutical manufacturer, creating and marketing a wide range of prescription drugs.

In the prescription drug realm, Pfizer has some of the world's bestselling drugs. Principal cardiovascular drugs include Lipitor, the world's largest-selling cholesterol-lowering agent, and antihypertensives such as Norvasc, Cardura, and Accupril. Infectious disease drugs consist of Zithromax, a broad-spectrum quinolone antibiotic. Key central nervous system medicines are Zoloft, an antidepressant, and Neurontin, an anticonvulsant.

Nor is that all. Pfizer's prescription drugs also include Viagra for male erectile dysfunction, the antihistamine Zyrtec, and Glucotrol XL for type 2 diabetes.

In the over-the-counter sector, the company's consumer products include such well-known brands as Ben-Gay, Desitin, Sudafed, Benadryl, Listerine, Trident, Dentyne, Certs, Halls cough drops, and Schick shaving products. In 2003, Schick was sold to Energizer for $930 million.

Pfizer also has an important stake in hospital and animal health products.

Pfizer's growth over the past half century was paced by strategic acquisitions, new drug discoveries, and vigorous foreign expansion. Its most recent move involved the giant acquisition of Warner-Lambert in 2000, making the new firm the largest pharmaceutical company in the world—and even larger when it acquired Pharmacia Corporation in December of 2002.

Shortcomings to Bear in Mind

- "Celebrex has become one of the nation's top-selling drugs largely because of claims by the drug's marketers that it is gentle on the stomach," said Gardiner Harris, writing for the *Wall Street Journal* on June 10, 2002, "but federal drug regulators have concluded Celebrex is just as likely to cause ulcers as older, cheaper medicines like ibuprofen.

  "Nor is Celebrex any better at curing pain or inflammation than ibuprofen, regulators concluded. Indeed, a new label approved Friday for the blockbuster drug gives Celebrex, sold for about $2.50 a pill, no clear advantage over ibuprofen or another older pain pill, diclofenac, which are sold for about 10 cents per pill. Celebrex is co-marketed by Pharmacia Inc. and Pfizer Inc.

  "Managed-care companies have been complaining for years that Celebrex and a rival pill from Merck & Co., Vioxx, aren't worth their lofty price tags. Now, they say, they have proof about Celebrex."
- Like most stocks with bright prospects, Pfizer often sells at an elevated P/E ratio.
- Most drug companies, including Pfizer, are suffering from a lack of new discoveries. The last blockbuster drug to come out of Pfizer's laboratories, which now spend more on research than any other pharmaceutical company, was Viagra, approved in 1998. Some observers say that Pfizer is not leading the way in hiring the best research scientists. John Archer, an executive recruiter at Russell Reynolds Associates, said scientists have recently been drawn to Abbott Laboratories, where research is led by Dr. Jeff Leiden, and to Eli Lilly, where Dr. Steven M. Paulis is the director of research.

Reasons to Buy

- According to an article that appeared in the *Boston Globe* in mid-2002, "Pfizer's all-stock offer for Pharmacia was widely viewed as an admission that its research laboratories aren't generating enough new drugs to sustain its ambitious growth targets."

  In response to this allegation, Pfizer said "the acquisition would enable its earnings per share to grow to 19 percent for the next three years, compared to 16 percent without the Pharmacia acquisition. Growth in annual revenues for the combined firm would dip slightly, to 10 percent, from 11 percent for Pfizer alone."

- "In all my thirty-five years on Wall Street, I have never seen such a clear separation from the pack," said David Saks of the Saks MedScience Fund at Ladenburg Thalmann. "Pfizer demonstrated a confidence and crispness that is not had by anybody else in the industry. It is top-notch in terms of management, business model, execution and results."

- Each day, 20,000 people around the world go to work promoting Pfizer products to the medical profession. They fill their "detail" bags with free samples of popular drugs such as Viagra and Zithromax, and they quote favorable conclusions from scientific studies (often company-sponsored) that show how Lipitor is the most potent way to control cholesterol and should be used instead of Merck's Zocor. By nearly all counts, Pfizer is the industry's largest, and most effective, sales force.

  According to Henry A. McKinnell, Ph.D., who became the company's CEO in 2001, "Pfizer has never been stronger and today possesses strengths and capabilities unequaled in the pharmaceutical industry. Our U.S. sales force, for example, was recently ranked as best in class in a survey of physicians, the sixth year in a row for this honor."

- Pfizer's Animal Health Group (AHG) is not only one of the largest in the world, but is also noteworthy for the breadth of its product lines and its geographic coverage. Innovative marketing has become an AHG hallmark in its efforts to succeed in a highly competitive market. An independent survey of U.S. veterinarians, for example, named the Pfizer sales force the best in the industry.

- In a report issued by *Value Line Investment Survey* late in 2002, analyst George Rho said, "Pfizer is currently in the process of rolling out six new medicines—Bextra, Spiriva, Vfend, Geodon, Relpax, and Rebif. That's not all, it has a pipeline that's chock full of prospects, as well as a massive R&D budget (5.2 billion in 2002). Share-net comparisons will also be aided by an aggressive share-repurchase program; 93 million shares were bought back just in the third quarter." Bextra is a COX2 inhibitor for the treatment of arthritis and pain; Spiriva for pulmonary disease; Vfend is an antifungal; Geodon is for schizophrenia; Relpax is for the treatment of migraine; and Rebif is used in the treatment of multiple sclerosis.

- Pfizer regularly makes use of partnerships and licensing agreements to extend its reach. Although the company must share the profits from any products developed with a partner, the deals take some pressure off Pfizer's research arm. Given its marketing expertise and reputation for successful collaborations, many smaller drug companies are reported to view Pfizer as their first choice as a partner. A recent example is Aricept, a drug developed by Eisai Company of Japan. It was copromoted by Pfizer and quickly became the leading treatment for Alzheimer's disease in the United States.

- In 2002, the company had ten products that Pfizer markets or copromotes that had annual revenues of $1 billion or more: Lipitor, Norvasc, Zoloft, Neurontin, Viagra, Zithromax, Celebrex, Zyrtec, Diflucan, and Aricept. Leading the pack was Lipitor, the world's leading cholesterol-lowering medicine and the largest-selling pharmaceutical of any kind, with revenues in 2002 of $7.972 billion, an industry record.

Total assets: $39,153 million
Current ratio: 1.37
Common shares outstanding: 6,190 million
Return on 2002 shareholders' equity: 47.5%

	2002	2001	2000	1999	1998	1997	1996	1995
Revenues (millions)	32,373	32,259	29,574	16,204	13,544	12,504	11,306	10,021
Net income (millions)	9,126	7,788	6,495	3,360	2,627	2,213	1,929	1,554
Earnings per share	1.59	1.31	1.02	.87	.67	.57	.50	.41
Dividends per share	.52	.44	.36	.31	.25	.23	.20	.17
Price High	42.5	46.8	49.3	50.0	43.0	26.7	15.2	11.1
Low	25.1	34.0	30.0	31.5	23.7	13.4	10.0	6.2

INCOME

Piedmont Natural Gas Company, Inc.

Post Office Box 33068 ◻ Charlotte, North Carolina 28233 ◻ (704) 731-4438 ◻ Dividend reinvestment program is available (800) 937-5449 ◻ Fiscal years end October 31 ◻ Listed: NYSE ◻ Web site: www.piedmontng.com ◻ Ticker symbol: PNY ◻ S&P rating: A- ◻ Value Line financial strength rating: B++

"The company's marketing and sales strengths remained evident in 2002, despite less-than-favorable economic conditions during the year," said a company spokesman in 2003.

"The economic diversity of our markets and a focus on profitable customer additions and customer satisfaction resulted in the company adding more than 28,000 new customers to our distribution system during the year. Representing a growth rate of nearly 4 percent, the company's market growth continues to place it in the upper tier of local distribution companies nationwide.

"In the residential market, the company added 25,000 customers. Of this total, 20,700 were the result of new home construction, a market segment in which the company enjoys a market share in excess of 90 percent in the areas it serves. The other 4,900 residential additions were from existing home owners converting their primary energy source to natural gas.

"Significantly, nearly 80 percent of all residential customers added, utilize natural gas water heating, in addition to gas heating. The addition of water heating load increases the company's profitability by enhancing the efficient utilization of capital resources used to serve customers. At the same time, natural gas water heating reduces the customer's overall energy bill through efficiency and operating advantages, compared with the electric alternative."

Company Profile

Incorporated in 1950, Piedmont Natural Gas is an energy services company, primarily engaged in the transportation, distribution, and sale of natural gas and the sale of propane to residential, commercial, and industrial customers in North Carolina, South Carolina, and Tennessee.

The company is the second-largest natural gas utility in the Southeast, serving more than 740,000 natural gas customers.

Piedmont Natural Gas and its non-utility subsidiaries and divisions are also engaged in acquiring, marketing, transporting, and storing natural gas for large-volume customers, in retailing residential and commercial gas appliances and the sale of propane to more than 480,000 customers in twenty-eight states.

An unregulated subsidiary of the company is an equity participant in a venture that is marketing natural gas to an additional 476,000 customers in Georgia, the first state in the venture's eight-state Southeastern market to open to retail competition for natural gas.

Other business interests in which the company is engaged that are not subject to state utility regulation include the sale of propane. The company is invested in a natural gas pipeline and an interstate LNG (liquefied natural gas) storage facility, and it also markets natural gas and other energy products and services to deregulated markets.

Shortcomings to Bear in Mind

- The company has benefited from extraordinary growth in its service territory. However, customer growth can be a double-edged sword, as it is expensive to continuously expand an underground pipe system to keep up with new construction. On the other hand, Piedmont has effectively lowered its cost to connect a customer to about $1,800, a significant decline over prior years. Analysts, moreover, expect this cost to continue to decline, which would contribute to future earnings growth.

Reasons to Buy

- Piedmont Natural gas has increased its dividend for twenty-four consecutive years. In the 1992–2002 period, dividends expanded from $0.91 per share to $1.60, a compound annual growth rate of 5.8 percent, or well ahead of the pace of inflation.

- In fiscal 2002, Piedmont Natural Gas announced that it would build, own, and operate a natural gas pipeline that will deliver supplies to a 640-megawatt power plant in Cherokee County, South Carolina. The Mill Creek Plant, owned by Duke Energy Company, is scheduled to go into operation by June 2003. The eight simple-cycle combustion turbines at the Mill Creek plant are designed to operate as a "peaking" facility, providing power primarily during periods when customer use is at it greatest—during the hottest or coldest days of the year.

The agreement marks the fifth contract for power generation–related pipeline investments by Piedmont for the Carolinas, and this is its second such project with Duke Power, a subsidiary of Duke Energy. Piedmont already serves Duke Power's Lincoln County plant in North Carolina. Through these five agreements, Piedmont will have invested over $10 million to deliver natural gas to more than 4,500 megawatts of generating capacity in the Carolinas by 2003.

- The company continues to seek profitable utility growth opportunities beyond its existing distribution operations, consistent with its core business strategies. In 2002, Piedmont added 14,000 customers from the purchase of NUI's gas distribution in Reidsville, North Carolina, which brought the company's total fiscal 2002 gross customer additions to 42,000. NUI is a natural gas utility serving New Jersey and Florida.

- The company's non-utility investment subsidiaries include Piedmont Interstate Pipeline, Piedmont Energy, Piedmont Intrastate Pipeline, Piedmont Propane, and Piedmont Greenbrier Pipeline. These investments contributed $11.2 million to net income in 2002.

Piedmont Interstate Pipeline is a 35 percent member of Pine Needle LNG

Company, L.L.C., which owns and operates an LNG (liquid natural gas) facility located in Guilford County, North Carolina. The 4.14 million dekatherm interstate storage facility is one of the largest of its kind in the nation, with liquefaction capacity of 21,000 dekatherms per day and vaporization capacity of 414,000 dekatherms per day. (A dekatherm is equal to 1 million British thermal units, or BTUs.) Pine Needle provides cost-effective storage peaking service to customers on the Williams-Transco pipeline system in the Southeastern gas markets and is fully subscribed under long-term contracts.

Piedmont Energy has a 30 percent interest in SouthStar Energy Services, L.L.C. SouthStar markets unregulated natural gas to residential, commercial, and industrial customers in the Southeast. As of November 2002, SouthStar, operating as Georgia Natural Gas Services, was selling natural gas to more than 550,000 customers in Georgia, representing a 38 percent market share, the largest in the state. SouthStar also sells natural gas to industrial customers in Georgia, North Carolina, South Carolina, and Tennessee.

■ Piedmont Natural Gas enjoys an economically robust and diverse service area that is among the fastest growing in the nation. The company's three-state service area consists of the Piedmont region of the Carolinas—Charlotte, Salisbury, Greensboro, Winston-Salem, High Point, Burlington, and Hickory in North Carolina and Anderson, Greenville, and Spartanburg in South Carolina—and the metropolitan area of Nashville, Tennessee. Both *Plant Sites* and *Parks and Site Selection* magazines continue to rank the Carolinas and Tennessee among the best in the nation for business relocation and expansion and business climate.

The center of the Piedmont Carolinas area is the Greater Charlotte urban region—sixth largest in the nation—with more than 6 million people within a 100-mile radius. Charlotte is the nation's second-largest financial center. It is the headquarters city for Bank of America, the nation's largest bank, and for First Union National bank, the sixth largest. Wachovia Corporation, the nation's sixteenth-largest bank, is headquartered in Winston-Salem.

Charlotte/Douglas International Airport, with more than 500 flights per day and 23 million passengers annually, is US Airways' largest hub and the twentieth busiest airport in the world.

The Nashville region is a diverse center of a retail trading area of over 2 million people, where health care is the largest industry. It is also home to major transportation, publishing, printing, financial, insurance, and communications companies, as well as twenty colleges and universities.

■ An important factor in analyzing any public utility is the region's regulatory environment. In Piedmont's states, regulators have generally been supportive of the company's regulatory needs over the past few years. In the opinion of Daniel M. Fidell and Tracey W. McMillin, analysts with A. G. Edwards, "Our conclusion is based on several factors, such as purchased gas and weather normalization mechanisms in rates that serve to smooth the impact of changes in gas prices and abnormal weather conditions. In addition, PNY has benefited from fair and timely rate relief in the past to recover costs associated with extensive system growth."

Total assets: $1,445 million
Current ratio: 0.86
Common shares outstanding: 33 million
Return on 2002 shareholders' equity: 10.6%

	2002	2001	2000	1999	1998	1997	1996	1995
Revenues (millions)	832	1,108	830	686	765	776	685	505
Net income (millions)	62	65	64	58	60	55	49	40
Earnings per share	1.89	2.02	2.01	1.86	1.96	1.85	1.67	1.45
Dividends per share	1.60	1.52	1.44	1.36	1.28	1.21	1.15	1.09
Price High	38.0	38.0	39.4	36.6	36.1	36.4	25.8	24.9
Low	27.4	29.2	28.6	27.9	22.0	20.5	18.3	18.0

GROWTH AND INCOME

Pitney Bowes, Inc.

1 Elmcroft Road □ Stamford, Connecticut 06926-0700 □ (203) 351-6349 □ Dividend reinvestment plan is available: (800) 648-8170 □ Web site: www.pitneybowes.com □ Listed: NYSE □ Ticker symbol: PBI □ S&P rating: A □ Value Line financial strength rating: A

"With the economy expected to pick up in 2003, the overall mailing category should improve as well," according to a report issued by S&P late in 2002. "We expect revenues to increase about 6 percent in 2003, following an anticipated 7 percent rise in 2002. Results are likely to be aided by the benefits of an ongoing migration to electronic and digital meters, as well as by acquisition activity. Margins should widen, reflecting a more favorable product mix and lower manufacturing expenses. Interest charges should continue to decline, as a portion of free cash flow is used for debt reduction. EPS comparisons should also benefit from the company's ongoing repurchases of common stock," said Richard N. STICE, CFA.

Company Profile

A pioneer and world leader in mailing systems, Pitney Bowes is a multinational manufacturing and marketing company that provides mailing, shipping, dictating, copying, and facsimile systems; item identification and tracking systems and supplies; mailroom, reprographics, and related management services; and product financing.

The key to Pitney Bowes will probably continue to be consistency rather than spectacular growth, in view of the maturity of its highly profitable postage-meter rental business and the moderate growth of some of its other annuity revenues, such as service.

On the other hand, analysts believe that the stock has limited downside risk; it should appeal largely to long-term investors.

Pitney Bowes is best known as the worldwide leader in mailing systems. It markets a full line of mailing systems, shipping and weighing systems, addressing systems, production mail systems, folding and inserting systems, and mailing software.

Pitney Bowes Software Systems, a division of Mailing Systems located in Illinois, offers a full range of advanced software and services for business communications as well as marketing and mailing applications to *Fortune* 1000 companies.

Shipping and Weighing Systems (SWS) provides parcel and freight information and automation systems for the shipping and transportation management functions of the logistics market.

SWS's products are marketed through Mailing Systems' worldwide distribution channels, with particular emphasis on

North America. Service is provided by specially trained service representatives and a National Remote Diagnostic Center.

Pitney Bowes Transportation Software, a division of Pitney Bowes located in Minnesota, markets and develops logistics management solutions and provides consulting services.

Other Businesses of Pitney Bowes

The company's other businesses are also important. A brief description of each follows.

Pitney Bowes Management Services (PBMS) is a leading provider of facilities management services for the business support functions of creating, processing, storage, retrieval, distribution, and tracking of information, messages, documents, and packages.

Using the latest available technology, PBMS manages mail centers, copy and reprographic centers, facsimile services, electronic printing and imaging services, and records management services for customers across the United States, as well as in Canada and the United Kingdom.

Pitney Bowes Facsimile Systems is a leading supplier of high-quality facsimile equipment to the business market. It is the only facsimile system supplier in the United States that markets solely through its own direct sales force nationwide.

Pitney Bowes Copier Systems concentrates on serving larger corporations with multi-unit installations of its full line of equipment.

Pitney Bowes Financial Services provides lease financing programs for customers who use products marketed by Pitney Bowes companies.

Shortcomings to Bear in Mind

- Pitney Bowes has a very leveraged balance sheet, with long-term debt accounting for the greater part of total capitalization.

Reasons to Buy

- In early 2002, CEO Michael J. Critelli said, "During the fourth quarter, we successfully completed the spin-off of Imagistics International, Inc., to shareholders and also completed the acquisition of Secap SA, a leading provider of digital mailing and paper-handling systems in France. Both of these transactions enhance our strategy of delivering shareholder value by providing leading-edge global, integrated mail, and document-management solutions to organizations of all sizes."

- Some observers are concerned that the volume of mail may be declining, as people rely more on the telephone and their connection with the Internet.

  Mr. Critelli, responded to this concern, "Outside experts confirm our internal findings that mail volumes worldwide will continue to increase for the next ten years. Lots of paper-based communication is going away, but it is more than being offset by growth engines."

  According to Mr. Critelli, there is explosive growth in direct-mail marketing. To be sure, individual mailings are falling a couple of percent each year. On the other hand, direct mail is climbing at a far faster pace, between 6 and 8 percent a year. As a result, says the Pitney CEO, the overall volume of mail is going up each year. What's more, the same trend is visible in other developed markets. In the developing world, moreover, the growth of mail is even more explosive. China, for example, is registering increases of 25 percent a year.

- Pitney Bowes has a consistent record of earnings growth. In the 1992–2002 period, earnings per share advanced from $0.98 to $2.37, an annual compound growth rate of 9.2 percent. In the same ten-year stretch, dividends per share climbed from $0.39 to $1.18, a growth rate of 11.7 percent. What's more, the dividend was raised every year.

- As the largest business unit of Pitney Bowes, Mailing Systems is the world leader in helping customers manage their messages through mailing solutions. These systems are marketed to businesses of all sizes—from the smallest office to *Fortune* 500 companies. With more than 2 million customers worldwide, Pitney Bowes Mailing Systems is focused on keeping business messages moving and its customers ahead of the curve.

  With products such as the DocuMatch Integrated Mail System, Paragon II Mail Processor, and the AddressRight System, large mailers are provided the tools they need to drive their businesses and enhance competitiveness. The Galaxy Mailing System and Series 3 Folder and Inserter address similar needs in midsize organizations. With DirectNet, a hybrid mailing service, the company is able to assist customers of all sizes with value-added capabilities to improve the efficiency and impact of their messaging applications.

- Pitney Bowes has a number of businesses that lag behind the economic cycle, but they should also resist a downturn. About two-thirds of total revenues comes from annuity sources such as postage meter rentals, rentals of other mailing and business equipment, facilities management, rental, finance, service, and supply revenues.

- Patents and other intellectual property will be more valuable than ever in the Internet era. For more than a decade, Pitney Bowes has been one of the 200 top companies in terms of numbers of domestic patents issued. The company holds more than 3,500 active patents worldwide—more than 200 on Internet concepts alone.

- In 2001, Pitney Bowes acquired Danka Services International (DSI), a wholly owned subsidiary of Danka Business Systems PLC, for $290 million. It is now part of Pitney Bowes Management Services, a leading provider of facilities management services for the business support functions of creating, processing, storage, retrieval, distribution, and tracking of information, messages, documents, and packages.

"Acquiring DSI is in accord with our mission to provide leading-edge, global, integrated mail, and document-management solutions," said Michael J. Critelli, CEO of Pitney Bowes. "More than ever, today's corporations see their documents as strategic assets and understand that information sharing, through efficient document imaging, distribution, and management, can 'unlock' this value and build distinct competitive advantage.

"From outgoing and incoming mail and messaging management, document creation production, to distribution, archiving and retrieval, Pitney Bowes Management Services provides a variety of ways to input, access, and manage documents, giving customers tools to match their tasks, processes, and their individual work habits," said Critelli.

Beginning operations in 1991 as Kodak Imaging Services (a division of Eastman Kodak), it was acquired by Danka in 1996 and became Danka Services International. Today, DSI has about 330 customer operations and employs about 3,400 people in the United States, Canada, the United Kingdom, Ireland, France, Italy, Denmark, Sweden, Germany, Norway, the Netherlands, and Belgium.

Pitney Bowes Management Services today represents more than 15 percent of Pitney Bowes' consolidated revenue. It is among the fastest-growing components of the business. Combined, Pitney Bowes Management Services and DSI will produce nearly $1 billion in annualized revenue, making it one of the largest players in the market.

"DSI has a solid track record of providing customers with leading-edge technology, process management expertise, and turn-key people-friendly solutions," said Randy Miller, who will remain with the combined companies as president.

Total assets: $8,318 million
Current ratio: 0.80
Common shares outstanding: 237 million
Return on 2002 shareholders' equity: 57%

	2002	2001	2000	1999	1998	1997	1996	1995
Revenues (millions)	4,410	4,122	3,881	3,812	4,221	4,100	3,859	3,555
Net income (millions)	572	514	563	533	568	526	469	408
Earnings per share	2.37	2.26	2.19	1.96	2.03	1.80	1.56	1.34
Dividends per share	1.18	1.16	1.14	1.02	.90	.80	.69	.60
Price High	44.4	44.7	54.1	73.3	66.4	45.8	30.7	24.1
Low	28.5	32.0	24.0	40.9	42.2	26.8	20.9	15.0

CONSERVATIVE GROWTH

Praxair, Inc.

39 Old Ridgebury Road □ Danbury, Connecticut 06810-5113 □ (203) 837-2354 □ Dividend reinvestment plan is available: (800) 432-0140 □ Web site: www.praxair.com □ Listed: NYSE □ Ticker symbol: PX □ S&P rating: A □ Value Line financial strength rating: B++

In January of 2003, Praxair reached an agreement with GE Aircraft Engines to significantly expand an existing production agreement for electron beam physical vapor deposition (EBPVD) coatings for gas turbine airfoils. The new agreement will increase production by nearly 70 percent and add a new in-house platinum aluminide coating capability for the company's subsidiary, Praxair Surface Technologies.

EBPVD coatings are applied in the production and refurbishment of turbine blades and vanes used in commercial and military jet engines, as well as industrial turbines, to enable them to withstand extreme temperatures while minimizing corrosion and wear.

Praxair will also boost production at its existing EBPVD facility in Indianapolis, with the addition of a second EBPVD coating unit. "Our new platinum aluminide coatings capability will enable us to offer to both the aero engine and industrial engine markets the full range of airfoil coatings in use today," said Dr. Martin Holdsworth, global director, Technology, for Praxair's Surface Technologies.

Company Profile

Praxair, Inc., is a global *Fortune* 500 company that supplies atmospheric, process, and specialty gases, high-performance coatings, and related services and technologies. Praxair, which was spun off to Union Carbide shareholders in June 1992, is the largest producer of industrial gases in North and South America; it is the third-largest company of its kind in the world.

Praxair's primary products are the following: atmospheric gases (oxygen, nitrogen, argon); rare gases (produced when air is purified, compressed, cooled, distilled, and condensed); and process and specialty gases, such as carbon dioxide, helium, hydrogen, semiconductor process gases, and acetylene (produced as by-products of chemical production or recovered from natural gas).

The company also designs, engineers, and constructs cryogenic and non-cryogenic supply systems. Praxair Surface Technologies is a subsidiary that applies metallic and ceramic coatings and powders to metal surfaces in order to resist wear, high temperatures, and corrosion. Aircraft engines are its primary market, but it serves others, including the printing, textile, chemical, and primary-metals markets. The company also provides aircraft engine and airframe component overhaul services. Praxair adopted its name in 1992, from the Greek word *praxis*, or practical application, and "air," the company's primary raw material. Praxair was originally founded in 1907 when it was the first company to commercialize cryogenically separated oxygen. Over the near century of its existence, Praxair has remained a leader in the development of processes and technologies that have revolutionized the industrial gases industry. The company introduced the first distribution system for liquid gas in 1917, and it developed on-site gas supply by the end of World War II. In the 1960s, Praxair introduced non-cryogenic means of air separation, and since then it has continued to introduce innovative applications technologies for various industries. The company holds almost 3,000 patents. Praxair serves a wide range of industries: food and beverages, health care, semiconductors, chemicals, refining, primary metals, metal fabrication, and other areas of general industry.

Shortcomings to Bear in Mind

- "Praxair's Surface Technologies division remains burdened by a lackluster aircraft industry, which has crimped demand for worldwide coatings," said Edward Plank, an analyst with *Value Line Investment Survey*, on December 20, 2002. "The positive side is that once the aerospace industry recovers, Praxair should be in a position to reap good gains." Mr. Plank also said, "What's more, the stock's three- to five-year appreciation potential is limited, given our earnings forecast over that period."

Reasons to Buy

- The company had relatively good results in 2002. In January of 2003, CEO Dennis H. Reilley said, "Weak global economic conditions posed challenges for all of our businesses throughout the year. However, we achieved record operating results in 2002 due to our intense customer focus, which allowed us to gain new business in many markets."

  Mr. Reilley went on to say, "We are committed to grow earnings without much help from the economy. Our focus in the short term will be to drive our growth programs in health care, refinery hydrogen, electronics, technology licensing, and China. These programs, combined with our relentless focus on productivity and capital discipline, will deliver superior results in 2003."

- In early 2003, Praxair opened its new metal fabrication laboratory in Tonawanda, New York. The facility provides a full range of research and development capabilities, including manual, automated, and robotic welding systems; new technology power supplies; shielding gas development; and laser application technology.

  "Our development work, product evaluations, and training help our customers better understand their welding costs and determine the optimum shielding gas, wire, and process combinations for improved productivity, better quality welds, and lower costs," said Kevin Lyttle, Praxair's manager of the metal fabrication lab. "We also do comparative work using new and existing welding processes and process variations to evaluate potential new consumables."

- At the end of 2001, Nestle USA, Inc., selected Praxair to provide engineering services in the design and installation of a carbon dioxide (CO2) mechanical refrigeration-based food-freezing system for Nestle's new state-of-the-art frozen foods plant in Jonesboro, Arkansas. The refrigeration system will employ Praxair's patented CO2 Mechanical Refrigeration technology, which allows food processors to operate their freezing systems at temperatures below those that traditional ammonia-based refrigeration systems can reach, while also eliminating the presence of ammonia in the processing rooms.

According to Michael Sinicropi, director of Praxair Food Technologies, "Our patented technology is another new offering in Praxair's portfolio of low-temperature freezing and chilling systems for the food industry. These offerings help to increase productivity while enabling processors to more easily comply with safety and environmental regulations."

- Hydrogen is part of a comprehensive portfolio of bulk and specialty gases, technologies, and services Praxair provides to its refining and chemical customers worldwide. For example, Praxair supplies more than fifty refineries and petrochemical plants from its 280 miles of pipeline along the Texas and Louisiana Gulf Coast. Other Praxair pipeline enclaves serving these industries are situated in Ecorse, Michigan; Edmonton, Alberta, Canada; Salvador, Brazil; Antwerp, Belgium; and Beijing, China.

- In addition to helium for fiber optics, Praxair's $400-million electronics portfolio includes semiconductor materials and services, electronic assembly applications, and specialty materials being developed by Praxair Surface Technologies. One of the fastest-growing businesses, Praxair Semiconductor Materials builds and manages advanced gas systems in Asia, Europe, and North America, helping chip manufacturers

lower the cost of ownership, reduce environmental impact, and improve productivity.

- Beyond its longstanding supply of pure oxygen and bulk storage equipment to hospitals and other medical facilities worldwide, Praxair delivers respiratory therapy gases and equipment and a host of on-site gas-management services, including asset, inventory, transaction, and distribution management. Praxair's home oxygen services, moreover, provide respiratory patients with life support, as well as therapies to help with sleep disorders or other illnesses in the home environment.

- The addition of carbon dioxide to Praxair's portfolio opens up new avenues for growth in the relatively noncyclical markets of food preservation, beverage carbonation, and water treatment. Looking ahead, increased demand for beverage carbonation and water treatment, particularly in emerging South American and Asian markets, promises to generate continued growth. Supplying global beverage-carbonation customers also leads to opportunities in new markets for other Praxair products and technology. Use of carbon dioxide in new food-preservation markets, such as bakery goods and dairy products, also is on the verge of rapid growth.

- The company sees opportunities to differentiate its offering in the food and beverage segment, based on the need for higher standards of food safety. Praxair is bringing the potential to save 15 billion or more gallons of water and $70 million each year to the U.S. poultry-processing industry through a water-recycling system that helps increase production and reduce water consumption without compromising food safety.

- The sparkle in soft drinks, the freshness of pastries, the crunch in an apple— chances are, Praxair carbon dioxide or nitrogen had something to do with it. At Praxair's Food Technology Laboratory— the only one of its kind in the industry—technologies and equipment are developed and tested to assist bakers, meat processors, and specialty-foods producers deliver products that retain their taste and freshness.

Total assets: $7,401 million
Current ratio: 1.17
Common shares outstanding: 162 million
Return on 2002 shareholders' equity: 17.0%

	2002	2001	2000	1999	1998	1997	1996	1995
Revenues (millions)	5,128	5,158	5,043	4,639	4,833	4,735	4,449	3,146
Net income (millions)	548	432	432	441	425	416	335	262
Earnings per share	3.33	2.64	2.98	2.72	2.60	2.53	2.11	1.82
Dividends per share	.76	.68	.62	.56	.50	.44	.38	.32
Price High	61.1	55.8	54.9	58.1	53.9	58.0	50.1	34.1
Low	44.6	36.5	30.3	32.0	30.7	39.3	31.5	19.8

CONSERVATIVE GROWTH

The Procter & Gamble Company

Post Office Box 599 □ Cincinnati, Ohio 45201-0599 □ (513) 983-2414 □ Direct dividend reinvestment plan is available: (800) 764-7483 □ Web site: www.pg.com □ Listed: NYSE □ Fiscal years end June 30 □ Ticker symbol: PG □ S&P rating: A □ Value Line financial strength rating: A++

While most stocks have been a huge disappointment since the market hit a peak on March 24, 2000, Procter & Gamble has made an impressive comeback. Much of its recent success can be attributed to its CEO, Alan G. Lafley. Lafley took the reins of the company in June of 2000, when it was "the sort of ink-stained mess you'd find in a Tide commercial," according to Katrina Brooker, writing for *Fortune* magazine in the fall of 2002.

In the words of Ms. Brooker, "Since he's been P&G's chief, Lafley has managed to pull off what neither of his two predecessors could—turn around the global behemoth. And he did it in the midst of a world economic slowdown to boot."

Ms. Brooker also points out that Mr. Lafley "is a listener, not a storyteller. He's likable but not awe-inspiring. He's the type of guy who gets excited in the mop aisle of a grocery store. His plan to fix P&G isn't anything ground-breaking, but rather a straightforward, back-to-the-basics

tack. And so far it's worked. He has rallied his troops not with big speeches and dazzling promises, but by hearing them out (practically) one at a time. It's a little dull, perhaps. Workaday dull."

In another part of the *Fortune* article, Katrina Brooker said, "Lafley, who got his start at P&G a quarter-century ago as a brand assistant for Joy dishwashing liquid, wouldn't be all that interesting to watch— were it not for the fact that he's so darn good at his job."

Company Profile

Procter & Gamble dates back to 1837, when William Procter and James Gamble began making soap and candles in Cincinnati. The company's first major product introduction took place in 1879, when it launched Ivory soap. Since then, P&G has traditionally created a host of blockbuster products that have made the company a cash-generating machine.

Procter & Gamble is a uniquely diversified consumer-products company with a strong global presence. P&G today markets its broad line of products to nearly 5 billion consumers in more than 160 countries.

Procter & Gamble is a recognized leader in the development, manufacturing, and marketing of superior-quality laundry, cleaning, paper, personal care, food, beverage, and health care products, including prescription pharmaceuticals.

Among the company's nearly 300 brands are Tide, Always, Whisper, Didronel, Pro-V, Oil of Olay, Pringles, Ariel, Crest, Pampers, Pantene, Vicks, Bold, Dawn, Head & Shoulders, Cascade, Iams, Zest, Bounty, Comet, Scope, Old Spice, Folgers, Charmin, Tampax, Downy, Cheer, and Prell.

Procter & Gamble is a huge company, with 2002 sales of over $40 billion. In the same fiscal year (which ended June 30, 2002), earnings per share advanced from $2.07 to $3.09. Dividends also climbed—as they have for many years—from $1.40 to $1.52. The company has nearly 102,000 employees working in almost eighty countries.

Shortcomings to Bear in Mind

- "Retailers are sometimes competitors as well as partners," said Mr. Lafley. "Their own brands are growing as the retailers, themselves, grow. Private labels, or store brands, strive to match innovation quickly and try to present a compelling value alternative in many categories. This is healthy, in my opinion. It requires that we continue to lead innovation and price P&G products competitively. Further, the growing strength of store brands underscores the importance of always being the number-one or number-two brand in any category. Brands that can't maintain this leadership stature will find it difficult to compete effectively with the best store brands. Based on our internal global share measures, we have the number-one or number-two brand in seventeen of our nineteen key global categories—categories that account for about 70 percent of sales and earnings. P&G is in a strong position, and ready to become an even better retail partner."

- Argus Research Corporation had some negative comments on Procter & Gamble in mid-2002. "As impressive as P&G's innovative new products have been, a closer look at the company's return from R&D should raise investors' eyebrows. P&G now employs 8,000 researchers and devotes 4.5 percent of revenues ($1.8 billion) to new product development each year. This scale of effort nearly guarantees the company its high share of top-performing products each year, but the overall payoff is not so high. Among seven household products firms with market capitalizations above the $500-million mark (P&G, Gillette, Kimberly-Clark, Colgate-Palmolive, Estee Lauder, Avon Products, and Alberto-Culver), the intensity of P&G research effort dwarfs all others.

  "Gillette, for example, devotes just 2.1 percent of revenues to R&D. Colgate-Palmolive and Kimberly-Clark allocate just 2 percent. P&G's R&D expenditures used to be even more lavish—they were $1.9 billion per year when current CEO A. G. Lafley took over in June 2000—but they have not corresponded to healthy revenue growth over the last five years. In that period, P&G's annual revenue growth rate has been just 2.15 percent, in the middle of the seven-member pack. Net income growth is at the bottom of the pile, at -0.8 percent per year. Thus, while we re-emphasize the real possibility that P&G's teams will revolutionize hair care with radical new anti-gray agents, we also remind investors of the risks P&G is taking with its bloated R&D budgets."

Reasons to Buy

- According to Mr. Lafley, "Cash generation is a key indicator of a company's underlying health, and P&G's management is focused on creating leadership, sustained cash flow growth in each of our business units. Free cash flow—operating cash after capital spending—was $6.1 billion in 2002, up 83 percent from last year and more than triple the free cash flow generated two years ago. Capital spending improvement has been a key driver. Our objective was to reduce capital spending to 6 percent of sales by fiscal 2004, and we've exceeded that goal two years ahead of schedule. We are now resetting our capital spending target to below 5 percent of sales, and continue to look for opportunities to improve asset efficiencies."

- The company got off to a solid start in the first quarter of fiscal 2003, as earnings shot up 33 percent, bolstered by a strong performance in P&G's beauty and health care operations. Beauty care sales bounded ahead 27 percent, led by the Clairol brands and new Olay skin creams. Sales in health care were helped by Crest and a new once-a-week dose of Actonel, an osteoporosis drug.

  P&G is also benefiting from a restructuring plan put in motion about three years ago. The plan called for lower operating costs and a greater emphasis on key brands such as Tide laundry detergents, Olay skin care products, and Crest toothpaste. What's more, the company is allocating the $2 billion saved from cost cutting to cranking up advertising, particularly for such higher-priced products as Olay anti-aging creams.

- In a recent U.S. survey by Cannondale Associates, retailers were asked to rank manufacturers on a number of competencies. P&G was ranked number one in virtually every category, including the following:

  - Clearest company strategy
  - Brands most important to retailers
  - Best brand marketers overall
  - Most innovative marketing programs

- P&G made the biggest deal in its history in March 2003 with the purchase of a controlling interest in the German hair care company, Wella AG, strengthening its position in the fast-growing global hair care business. The deal exceeds the 2001 purchase of Clairol for $4.95 billion. In this transaction, Procter & Gamble paid $5.75 billion for a 77.6 percent interest in Wella. Professional salon hair care sales are $10 billion a year worldwide. Wella estimates that it has a 22 percent global share—number two behind L'Oréal (a French company regarded as a model of best practices in the sector), which is P&G's biggest competitor. Overall, retail hair care is a $34-billion industry worldwide.

  Mr. Lafley says that Procter won't disturb Wella's salon business, the company's crown jewel. Unlike the purchase of Clairol, this transaction puts Procter & Gamble in the business of serving a new type of customer: professional hairdressers. Wella generated half of its $3.6 billion sales in 2002 selling its products in salons. Meanwhile, P&G will do what it knows best—plow Wella's shampoo, conditioner, and styling brands through mass-market retailers such as Wal-Mart.

  Finally, Mr. Lafley intends to incorporate Wella's fragrance brands, which include Gucci, Rochas, and Escada, into its own fragrance business, where it licenses brands like Hugo Boss and Lacoste. This strategy will enhance the geographic reach of Wella's brands.

- Procter & Gamble in known for product innovation. More than 8,000 scientists and researchers are accelerating the pace of new products. The company has a global network of eighteen technical centers in nine countries on four continents.

What's more, P&G holds more than 27,000 patents and applies for 3,000 more each year. Not surprisingly, the company is among the top ten patent-producing companies in the world—well ahead of any other consumer-products manufacturer.

■ Writing for the *Wall Street Journal*, Emily Nelson said in mid-2002, "The Cincinnati consumer-products maker is benefiting from new products and new advertising for its major brands, including Tide, Pantene, Folgers, and Pampers. Each generates $1 billion or more in annual sales. Another driver is Clairol, the hair-care line it purchased last year."

Ms. Nelson went on to say, "Much of P&G's recent success is due to the basic, ages-old strategy of adding a small new feature to an old product, backed by new marketing, to pique the interest of shoppers. Tide laundry detergent, which P&G

has made since 1946, recently introduced a new scent, Tide Clean Breeze. A television ad shows a woman loading her laundry basket on the roof of her car and driving from the city to a green grassy field to air out her clean clothes. Instead, she can now use Tide Clean Breeze for that fresh-air scent, the ad states."

■ Procter & Gamble believes in product quality. One of the reasons given for the company's problems in 2000 was its refusal to get into the lower-quality, lower-cost private-label business. That just goes against the grain.

P&G believes that the consumer will reward even minor product advantages, and it will not launch a brand if it does not have a competitive advantage. Then it will continually improve its products and make every effort to maintain that advantage. Tide, for example, has been improved more than seventy times over the years.

Total assets: $40,776 million
Current ratio: 0.83
Common shares outstanding: 1,299 million
Return on 2002 shareholders' equity: 31.8%

	2002	2001	2000	1999	1998	1997	1996	1995
Revenues (millions)	40,238	39,244	39,951	38,125	37,154	35,764	35,284	33,434
Net income (millions)	4,352	2,922	4,230	4,148	3,780	3,415	3,046	2,645
Earnings per share	3.09	2.07	2.95	2.85	2.56	2.28	2.15	1.86
Dividends per share	1.52	1.40	1.28	1.14	1.01	.90	.80	.70
Price High	94.8	81.72	118.4	115.6	94.8	83.4	55.5	44.8
Low	74.1	55.96	52.8	82.0	65.1	51.8	39.7	30.3

CONSERVATIVE GROWTH

The Reynolds & Reynolds Company

115 South Ludlow Street □ Dayton, Ohio 45402 □ (937) 485-8111 □ Dividend reinvestment plan is available: (800) 842-7629 □ Web site: www.reyrey.com □ Fiscal years end September 30 □ Listed: NYSE □ Ticker symbol: REY □ S&P rating: A □ Value Line financial strength rating: B++

The Reynolds & Reynolds Company announced in February 2003 that it had set an industry record, as its 10,000th active customer adopted Reynolds' systems to run its dealership. The announcement

was made at the National Automobile Dealers Association (NADA) convention in San Francisco.

Reynolds installed the record-setting system at Brighton Ford-Mercury in

Brighton, Michigan. Brighton Ford-Mercury has deployed the Reynolds Generations Series family of automotive retailing solutions, including Reynolds' Contact Management and Electronic Document Management tools.

The Reynolds Generations Series was introduced one year earlier. It incorporates advanced CRM (customer-relationship management) solutions and reporting tools that provide new customer insights and information when and where automotive retailers and car companies need it. Built on application service provider-based modules, these solutions are supported by a full complement of Reynolds' award-winning professional services, support, and education.

Sixteen years ago at NADA, Reynolds introduced a dealer management system named ERA. The system represented the next generation of technology and software for automotive retailers. The Reynolds Generations Series is easily integrated into a dealership's existing technology—including ERA systems—so that customers making a technology investment can build upon it for the future.

"ERA systems rapidly won acceptance in the marketplace when they were introduced in 1987 and have remained a mainstay of dealer management systems for automotive retailers large and small," said Scott M. Schafer, senior vice present of Sales, Marketing, and Services for Reynolds. "Today, we are also installing the Reynolds Generations Series as the new foundation on which automotive retailers can grow and enhance the profitability of their businesses."

Mr. Schafer said that the 10,000-system milestone is equivalent to installing a dozen systems every week of every year for sixteen years. "That's a phenomenal track record of innovation, dependability, and performance in the industry—and a large reason why the Reynolds name is as respected as it is and why we are leaders in the market."

Company Profile

Founded in 1866, Reynolds is the leading North American provider of integrated solutions that help automotive retailers grow, manage change, and improve their profitability. It enables car companies and automotive retailers to work together to build the lifetime value of their customers. The company's focus is clear: equipping car companies and retailers with the tools and training they need to create a positive purchase experience for the consumer, while getting closer to their customers and improving profits.

The company's businesses are segregated into four segments. The **Software Solutions** segment consists of the Software Solutions and Info-Structure Services units. These units provide integrated information management solutions and consulting services to the automotive retailing marketplace.

The **Documents** segment manufactures and distributes printed business forms to automotive retailers.

The **Transformation Solutions** segment provides specialized training, Web services, and customer relationship–management products and services.

The **Financial Services** segment provides financing for the company's computer systems products through wholly owned Reyna Capital Corporation.

Today, Reynolds is a billion-dollar company with over seventy years of experience in the automotive retailing industry and operations in twenty countries. Using this deep market knowledge, Reynolds & Reynolds has created the broadest portfolio of innovative, customer-driven products and services available to the worldwide automotive retailing marketplace.

Backing up Reynolds' solutions is the largest customer-facing organization in the industry. Almost 2,000 of its 5,000 associates work on-site every day with automotive dealerships, delivering service, support, training, and consulting.

Over the years, the company's ability to consistently deliver leading-edge solutions and the highest customer satisfaction in the industry has made Reynolds the undisputed market leader. Here's the evidence:

• Reynolds & Reynolds has a presence in more than 90 percent of North America's automotive retailers.

• Nearly half of all cars sold in North America are sold through Reynolds & Reynolds systems.

• The company has business relationships with nearly every car company on the planet.

• The company's market share for core systems surpasses that of its two nearest competitors combined.

• Reynolds & Reynolds has honed this competitive position through a widely recognized obsession with customer satisfaction and a demonstrable commitment to deliver value, not merely new technology.

Shortcomings to Bear in Mind

■ Over the past ten years (1992–2002), earnings per share climbed nicely, from $0.41 to $1.58, a compound annual growth rate of 14.4 percent. Similarly, dividends per share increased from $0.11 to $0.44, a growth rate of 14.9 percent.

On a more negative note, annual revenues have not fared nearly as well. In that ten-year span, revenues advanced from $644.8 million to $992.4 million, a compound growth rate of only 4.1 percent.

Reasons to Buy

■ "Reynolds and Reynolds is the market leader, providing information technology, software, and professional services to automotive retailers," said CEO Lloyd G. "Buzz" Waterhouse. "During 2002, we increased our overall market share at the same time that we gained significantly in newer areas of the market, such as Customer Relationship

Management and Web services, to name only two."

Mr. Waterhouse went on to say, "In the midst of a weak market for corporate spending on information technology, revenues at Reynolds were off only slightly from 2001 levels. Yet revenues in 2002 delivered more profit. Operating income increased; operating margins improved; and earnings per share from continuing operations reached $1.58.

"Our conversion of sales to profit was more efficient due largely to new products introduced during the year, improved product mix, smart cost management, and more disciplined supply chain management across our business. We expect these factors to continue during 2003."

■ "Over the past several years, REY focused its strategies and efforts on the rapidly transforming automotive retailing technology marketplace," said W. H. Donald, an analyst with *Standard & Poor's Stock Reports*, on January 22, 2003. "A significant element of its strategy was the August 2000 sale of the company's document services business, the Information Solutions Group, for $360 million. REY also embarked on a multi-faceted plan to expand the scope of its solutions and augment existing offerings. As part of the plan, it joined with other industry leaders to form ChoiceParts LLC, an independent business-to-business company that provides an online parts exchange that enables buyers and sellers in the parts supply chain to instantly locate, order, and sell repair parts. REY has also acquired a number of leading providers of learning, customer relationship management, and e-business services to automotive retailers and manufacturers, including HAC Group, LLC, DealerKid, and MSN Autos' Dealerpoint business.

"The initiatives have paid off in several ways," said the S&P report.

"During fiscal 2001 and 2002, REY increased market share in core systems, adding more than 300 new customers in 2001 alone. It introduced forty-two new services over the course of two years, including a number of industry-leading Distance Learning solutions, as well as retail, customer, and procurement management services for auto dealers."

- "Reynolds has solid earnings growth prospects through 2005–2007," said David R. Cohen, an analyst with *Value Line Investment Survey*, on January 17, 2003. "Maintenance and service fees should continue to increase at low double-digit percentage rates over this period. (Recurring billings now account for 80 percent of Reynolds' revenues, compared to 60 percent three years ago.) Also, we expect losses at Transformation

Solutions (marketing services and training) to be soon reversed. Finally, an ongoing share-repurchase program ought to enhance earnings gains."

- In December 2002, Reynolds acquired Networkcar, a company that provides proprietary wireless technology for collecting and delivering real-time automotive diagnostic data. Through a small, wireless device installed in the vehicle, performance data from the engine's computer is collected and delivered to the car owner as usable information on a personalized, secure Web site. The consumer's dealership service department also receives information about the vehicle's operation and potential trouble spots. Beyond remote diagnostics, the device also can be used to locate a stolen or stalled vehicle.

Total assets: $1,137 million
Current ratio: 2.03
Common shares outstanding: 69 million
Return on 2002 shareholders' equity: 17.0%

		2002	2001	2000	1999	1998	1997	1996	1995
Revenues (millions)		992	1,004	924	1,563	1,486	1,386	1,100	911
Net income (millions)		116	100	112	123	114	94	94	79
Earnings per share		1.58	1.33	1.41	1.53	1.40	1.11	1.10	.93
Dividends per share		.44	.44	.44	.40	.36	.32	.25	.20
Price	High	31.5	26.0	33.0	25.3	24.0	30.6	28.3	19.8
	Low	19.7	18.2	15.9	17.3	12.6	14.4	18.2	11.4

GROWTH AND INCOME

RPM International, Inc.

Post Office Box 777 □ Medina, Ohio 44258 □ (330) 273-5090 □ Dividend reinvestment plan is available: (800) 776-4488 □ Web site: www.rpminc.com □ Listed: NYSE □ Fiscal years end May 31 □ Ticker symbol: RPM □ S&P rating: A □ Value Line financial strength rating: B

"We are pleased that RPM's long-term efforts to communicate with individual investors were recognized this past March, when *Investor Relations* magazine, in association with *Barron's*, cited RPM for 'Best Communications in the Retail Market,'" said CEO Thomas C. Sullivan.

"The distinction was determined through a survey of more than 1,800 U.S. portfolio managers, security analysts, and retail investors. RPM's recognition of the importance of individual investors began more than a quarter century ago, when we first began our long-term association with the National Association of Investors Corporation (NAIC). Our latest effort aimed at this group is RPM's award-winning investor Web site (*www.rpminc.com*), which contains in-depth, user-friendly information for professional and retail investors alike."

Company Profile

RPM International, Inc. (formerly RPM, Inc.), is a world leader in specialty coatings, with products that typically command the number one or two position in the markets they serve. About 53 percent of RPM's revenues in fiscal 2002 were generated by industrial waterproofing, corrosion control, polymer flooring, and specialty chemical products. The remaining 47 percent of sales were of consumer products used by professionals, do-it-yourselfers, and hobbyists for home, automotive, and boat maintenance.

Leading industrial brands from RPM include Day-Glo fluorescent pigments, Tremco roofing systems, Carboline corrosion coatings, Stonhard flooring systems, Euro concrete additives, and Kop-Coat wood treatments. Major brands include Rust-Oleum rust-preventative and general purpose paints, DAP caulks and sealants, Zinsser primer-sealers and wall covering products, Flecto interior stains and finishes, and Wolman deck coverings.

Founded in 1947 as Republic Powdered Metals, RPM sells its products in some 130 countries, with 19 percent of its revenues coming from abroad.

At the board of directors meeting on October 11, 2002, Thomas C. Sullivan and James A. Karman stepped down as executive officers of RPM, following some four decades of service to the company and more than three decades as its leaders. Both have remained on the board of directors.

Frank C. Sullivan, who became CEO, has served RPM for more than fifteen years in positions of increasing responsibility, including his former positions as RPM's

president and chief operating officer. Frank Sullivan was instrumental in the recent restructuring program and was responsible for the corporate reorganization.

In addition, Frank Sullivan had been involved in all of the company's major acquisitions of the previous ten years. He served as lead negotiator in the highly successful Tremco acquisition in 1997. During his six years as chief financial officer, Mr. Sullivan became closely involved with the operating planning process. He led the financing activities related to major acquisitions, maintained RPM's commercial and investment banking relationships, and established close working relationships with operating company management.

Highlights of Fiscal 2002

- Net income grew 61 percent, to $101.6 million, from the $63 million earned in fiscal 2001. Earnings per diluted share increased 56 percent, to $0.97, from $0.62 a year earlier. "For fifty-four of our fifty-five years in business," said Tom Sullivan, "RPM has reported higher earnings than the previous year." Cash from operations increased 157 percent, to $191.4 million, from $74.5 million the prior year.
- Mr. Sullivan said, "The earnings improvement resulted from the positive impact of our restructuring program; lower interest costs due to both lower rates and reduced borrowings; and adoption of Statement of Financial Accounting Standards number 142, accounting for goodwill, at the beginning of the fiscal year to the consolidated financial statements."
- Mr. Sullivan also said, "As expected, net sales declined slightly, to $1.99 billion, from $2.01 billion in fiscal 2001, due in large part to the divestiture in March 2001 of DAP's $30-million commercial unit, and to weak market conditions affecting our industrial businesses. Excluding the

effect of the divestiture, consumer segment net sales increased 6 percent, to $932.5 million. Industrial segment net sales of $1.05 billion declined 3 percent, adjusted for foreign exchange differences. We believe that this decline is a result of customer postponement of major projects due to economic uncertainty and not due to loss of market share. In fact, as the economy rebounds, we expect industrial segment sales to improve markedly due to pent-up demand."

Shortcomings to Bear in Mind

- "One risk is that asbestos claims have been rising, and insurance coverage may dwindle in the coming years," said Noah Goldner, an analyst with *Value Line Investment Survey.* "Current indications are that RPM would be able to cover these costs from cash flow, however."

Reasons to Buy

- "The past three years have not been easy," said Tom Sullivan in mid-2002. "While it is likely that RPM could have continued its earnings records beyond the fifty-two consecutive record years achieved, we felt it important to make tough decisions to improve the structure of the business and to give the incoming management team a fresh start.

  "During this period, we reorganized the business into six focused growth platforms under the direction of seasoned operating company executives. We completed our first-ever restructuring program, consolidating seventeen manufacturing facilities and reducing the work force by approximately 10 percent.

  "Then, just as these moves were completed, we faced overall economic uncertainty further clouded by the tragic events of September 11, 2001. RPM's resumption of earnings growth in this difficult environment is testimony to the fact that these programs are working. Moreover, the company's new management team, which played a pivotal role in accomplishing our turnaround, has proven to be up to the task of continuing RPM's growth."

- In fiscal 2002, cash dividends increased for the twenty-eighth consecutive year.

- "With our renewed financial flexibility, we have resumed our acquisition program, which has long been an RPM strength," said Mr. Sullivan. "Over the past ten years, RPM has made more fifty acquisitions and has a strong, established reputation as an industry consolidator. In our acquisition program, we pursue three distinct types of opportunities:

  - Synergistic, or 'bolt-on' product line acquisitions. In these, we look primarily for established consumer brands that can augment one of our existing lines and be sold within our existing distribution channels. As a result, these acquisitions are expected to be immediately accretive to earnings.

  - Acquisitions of entrepreneurial niche market leaders. We want to continue RPM's position as the best home for entrepreneurial companies in the markets we serve. Our RPM II growth platform provides such a home and focuses on companies with sales of between $10 million and $100 million whose entrepreneurial owners will stay with RPM and continue to grow their businesses as part of a larger enterprise.

  - Strategic acquisitions involving companies with substantial sales volume. These can enhance RPM's presence in the specialty coatings industry through addition of a major new product line or product category that complements our existing operations."

Total assets: $2,036 million
Current ratio: 2.44
Common shares outstanding: 115 million
Return on 2002 shareholders' equity: 13.6%

	2002	2001	2000	1999	1998	1997	1996	1995
Revenues (millions)	1,986	2,008	1,954	1,712	1,615	1,350	1,136	1,017
Net income (millions)	101.6	63.0	78.6	94.5	87.8	78.3	68.9	61.1
Earnings per share	.97	.62	.73	.86	.84	.76	.69	.65
Dividends per share	.50	.50	.49	.46	.44	.41	.38	.35
Price High	17.9	15.0	11.3	16.5	18.0	16.8	14.9	13.8
Low	11.6	7.9	7.8	9.9	12.8	12.5	11.5	11.4

CONSERVATIVE GROWTH

Ruby Tuesday, Inc.

150 West Church Avenue □ Maryville, Tennessee 37801 □ (865) 379-5700 □ Web site: www.ruby-tuesday.com □ Dividend reinvestment plan not available □ Fiscal years end first Tuesday after May 30 □ Listed: NYSE □ Ticker symbol: RI □ Standard & Poor's rating: B+ □ Value Line financial strength rating: B++

Growth in the casual-dining category of food service, in which Ruby Tuesday is a major national player, has outpaced the entire restaurant industry and is projected to continue to do so. The bar-and-grill segment, where Ruby Tuesday is one of the four leading brands, represents about half of all casual dining sales. According to CEO Sandy Beall, "This segment is projected to continue to grow an annual compound rate of 9 percent, compared to a projected rate of 6 percent for the overall casual-dining category, with the majority of new units coming from large national chains—like ours. And while the total number of casual-dining units has remained basically flat in recent years, unit growth by major chains has continued growing, and the number of independents and small chains has declined.

"Casual-dining chains currently have a 30 percent market share, and we believe their share in the coming years will mirror that of the fast-food category, where chains now represent 66 percent of total outlets.

"With continued opportunity for significant growth, our developing strategy includes a focus on opening low-risk, high-return company-owned restaurants in markets in the eastern United States where we have current units that are proven successes."

Mr. Beall went on to say, "Every potential new site is visited and approved or rejected by the CEO, and each new restaurant is led by a managing partner who invests in the potential and the performance of his or her unit. We currently have more than 400 company-owned restaurants and expect to open approximately fifty company-owned units each year in the next three to five years. We believe there is potential for several thousand additional Ruby Tuesdays across the U.S."

Company Profile

Ruby Tuesday, Inc., owns and operates Ruby Tuesday casual dining restaurants. The company also franchises the Ruby Tuesday concept in selected domestic and international markets. At the end of fiscal 2002, the company owned and operated 397 Ruby Tuesday restaurants, situated in twenty-five states and the District of Columbia. It also had 183 domestic franchise restaurants in nineteen states and sixteen international franchise units situated in the Asia Pacific region, India, Puerto Rico, Iceland, and in Central and South America.

The first Ruby Tuesday restaurant opened in 1972 in Knoxville, Tennessee. The Ruby Tuesday concept, which consisted of sixteen units, was acquired by Morrison Restaurants, Inc., in 1982.

During the following years, Morrison added other casual dining concepts, including the internally developed American Café. In 1995, Morrison completed the acquisition of Tias, Inc., a chain of Tex-Mex restaurants. In a spin-off transaction that took place in March 1996, shareholders of Morrison approved the distribution of two separate businesses of Morrison to its shareholders. In conjunction with the spin-off, Morrison was reincorporated in the state of Georgia and changed its name to Ruby Tuesday, Inc.

Ruby Tuesday restaurants are casual, full-service restaurants with warm woods, whimsical artifacts, and classic Tiffany-style lamps, which create a comfortable, nostalgic look and feel. The menu is based on variety, with something for just about everyone. Some of Ruby Tuesday's most popular entree items, which are prepared fresh daily, are the following: fajitas, ribs, chicken, steak, seafood, pasta, burgers, soups, sandwiches, the company's signature salad bar, and signature Tallcake desserts in strawberry and chocolate varieties. Entrées range in price from $6.29 to $16.99.

Shortcomings to Bear in Mind

- During 2002, several insiders sold shares in Ruby Tuesday. All together, there were eighteen sales and only two purchases by these executives or board members.

Reasons to Buy

- Amy M. Greene, an analyst with Avondale Partners, LLC, said in mid-2002,

"While many of the company's competitors in the casual dining group rely heavily on media advertising and/or couponing to drive quarterly same-store sales, Ruby Tuesday has repeatedly shown that it can grow and increase profitability without a dependence on the 'latest, greatest program or ad.'" She went on to say, "We continue to believe that this consistent growth in same-store sales points to the loyalty of the company's core customer base and the strength of the RI concept."

- In the same report, Ms. Greene said, "We continue to be impressed with the evolution of the RI concept, units, and menu. Most casual dining companies neglect to adapt their units and their menus to the ever-evolving consumer taste and preferences.

"In a move which we think differentiates RI from some of its competitors, it has several different unit sizes, layouts, menu formats, etc., which it can use as would best fit a given market."

- In July of 2002, the company said it would eliminate its synthetic lease program within the following two or three months. According to a report issued by Morgan Keegan & Company, Inc., the move was made to "mute the negative perception of overly aggressive accounting practices. We applaud this move and expect little if any cash flow impact from this conversion. Generally, synthetic leases are financing arrangements used by many public companies to finance the cost of acquiring property. Under such leases, a company places property in a special purpose entity (SPE) and leases it back. As long as the SPE can attract an outside investor to hold a 3 percent stake in the investment, the lease remains off the company's financial statements. The company records the payment as rent expense, but for tax purposes is allowed to take tax deductions for interest and depreciation as if they owned the property. Though the debt remains off the company's financial statements, a potential liability remains for the lessee who has guaranteed the value of the property at the end of the lease. Ruby's will now convert its $209 million of synthetic leases to bank debt, reflect the assets and liabilities on its balance sheet, and record both depreciation and interest expense on its P&L, versus only rent expense previously."

What this accounting change amounts to is this: the elimination of synthetic leases will lower rent expenses by $10 million, increase interest expenses by $10 million, and add $5.5 million of annual depreciation, thus creating a $.05 dilution to earnings per share.

This may seem like a negative, but getting rid of this aggressive—some analysts say "cloudy"—accounting is a move in the right direction, particularly in an age of accounting flimflam and other irregularities and downright illegal mischief. According to analysts writing for Raymond James & Associates, "We believe RI will remain the fastest-growing casual dining company with system-wide sales in excess of $1 billion per year."

■ Ruby Tuesday is currently pursing an expansion strategy that should enable it to boost annual revenues by 10 percent or more for the next several years. The company looks to open at least fifty company-owned units and some twenty franchised restaurants in fiscal 2003.

According to Dennis Milton, an analyst with *Standard & Poor's Stock Reports*, "We expect system-wide sales to grow 15 percent during the year, primarily due to store openings and average unit volume growth of 3 percent. Revenues should increase nearly 13 percent. Results should benefit from tame food and labor costs, and from leverage over the increased sales base."

Total assets: $520 million
Current ratio: 0.95
Common shares outstanding: 64 million
Return on 2002 shareholders' equity: 18.8%

	2002	2001	2000	1999	1998	1997	1996	1995
Revenues (millions)	833	790	798	722	711	655	620	*
Net income (millions)	76	59	46	36	29	25	19	
Earnings per share	1.15	.91	.72	.54	.42	.35	.28	
Dividends per share	.05	.05	.05	.05	.02	Nil	—	
Price High	27.2	21.7	16.6	11.0	10.6	7.2	5.8	
Low	14.2	13.3	7.8	8.2	6.0	4.2	3.8	

* The company was part of Morrison Restaurants prior to early 1996.

AGGRESSIVE GROWTH

Scholastic Corporation

557 Broadway □ New York, New York 10012 □ (212) 343-6741 □ Dividend reinvestment program is not available □ Fiscal years end May 31 □ Web site: www.scholastic.com □ Listed: NASDAQ □ Ticker symbol: SCHL □ S&P rating: B □ Value Line financial strength rating: B

"The release of the fifth hardcover Harry Potter title, although tentatively rescheduled for the early spring of calendar 2003, may be published too late to provide a meaningful boost to fiscal 2003 (ended May 30, 2003) revenues and earnings," said William H. Donald, an analyst writing for *Standard & Poor's Stock Reports* in October 2002.

"However, even without the effect of the Harry Potter release in fiscal 2003, we project a nearly 10 percent rise in total revenues for the year. Revenues are benefiting from the popular supplemental reading programs, new products and services, and strength in SCHL's trade series."

Company Profile

Founded eighty-two years ago, Scholastic Corporation is a global children's publishing and media company. Scholastic believes that it is the world's largest publisher and distributor of children's books. The company creates educational, entertaining materials and products for use in school and at home, including children's books, textbooks, magazines, technology-based products, teacher materials, television programming, videos, and toys.

Scholastic distributes its products and services through a variety of channels, including school-based book clubs, school-based book fairs, school-based and direct-to-home continuity programs, retail stores, schools, libraries, television networks, and the Internet.

The company's Web site, *www.scholastic.com*, is a leading site for teachers, classrooms, and parents and an award-winning destination for children. With the 2000 acquisition of Grolier, Inc., for $400 million in cash, the company became the leading domestic operator of direct-to-home book clubs, primarily serving children age five and under. At the same time, Scholastic became the leading print and online publisher of children's

reference and non-fiction products sold primarily to U.S. school libraries.

Internationally, Scholastic has long-established operations in Canada, the United Kingdom, Australia, and New Zealand, with newer operations in Argentina, Hong Kong, India, Ireland, and Mexico.

The company categorizes its businesses into four operating segments:

• Children's Book Publishing and Distributions, with revenues in fiscal 2002 of $1,168.6 million, or 61 percent of the corporate total. The company believes it's the largest publisher and distributor of children's books and is the largest operator of school-based book clubs and school-based book fares in the United States.

• Educational Publishing, with 2002 revenues of $315.5 million, or 16.6 percent of all corporate sales. This segment of Scholastic includes the publication and distribution to schools and libraries of curriculum materials, classroom magazines, and print and online reference and non-fiction products for grades K–12 in the United States.

• Media, Licensing, and Advertising includes the production and/or distribution in the United States of software and Internet services and production and/or distribution of programing and consumer products (such as children's television programming, videos, software, feature films, promotional activities, and non-book merchandising). This segment was responsible for 6.8 percent of sales in 2002.

• International, 15.7 percent of annual revenues, includes publication and distribution of products and services outside the United States. With the acquisition of Grolier, the company expanded into the direct-to-home book club business primarily serving children aged five and under in Canada, the United Kingdom, and Australia.

Scholastic Canada, founded in 1957, is a leading publisher of English- and French-language children's books. It is the largest school-based book club and is one of the leading suppliers of original and licensed children's books to the Canadian trade market.

Scholastic UK, founded in 1964, is a leading children's publisher in the United Kingdom, where its trade books appear frequently on children's bestseller lists. Scholastic UK's bestselling original book series, Horrible Histories, has been adapted for television.

Shortcomings to Bear in Mind

- Scholastic's balance sheet is somewhat leveraged, with only 59 percent of capitalization in equity. My preference is for 75 percent.

- The company is the publisher of the Harry Potter books in the United States. In Britain, the series is published by Bloomsbury Publishing, which before Harry Potter was an obscure literary publisher. According to an article in the *Wall Street Journal* (November of 2002) by Charles Goldsmith, "But giving birth to a superstar such as Harry Potter can be a mixed blessing. For one thing, financial analysts have been questioning whether Bloomsbury is a one-trick pony. There is still life in the series, with number five out of seven expected next year (2003). But the two-year-plus interlude between numbers four and five has unnerved investors."

The fourth title of this runaway bestseller brought in $190 million for Scholastic (or 10 percent of total sales) in fiscal 2001. The absence of a new Harry Potter book in 2002 kept revenues from an increase—they declined 2 percent.

Reasons to Buy

- *Value Line Investment Survey* commented favorably on Scholastic in the

fall of 2002. Terese S. Fabian, its analyst, said, "Scholastic is building a unique niche in children's book publishing and distribution. The company regularly introduces new authors, titles, and products to its already broad base. Scholastic is also the undisputed leader in sales through school-based book clubs and book fairs (104,000 fairs at 65,000 schools last year). And it is seeing good momentum in sales of reading intervention materials. Additionally, international operations are being expanded with some good results."

- The company had a solid record of earnings increases. In the 1992–2002 period, earnings per share advanced from $.82 to $2.47, a compound annual growth rate of 11.7 percent.

- Through its largest operation, the Children's Book Publishing and Distribution segment, Scholastic helps millions of parents, teachers and booksellers guide children to quality books. Through proprietary school-based clubs and fairs, continuities, and Internet sites—as well as traditional retail outlets—"we are the market leader, distributing more than 320 million books in fiscal 2002," said the 2002 annual report. "Our strategy is to continue to strengthen our existing channels, while expanding distribution directly to the home through mass and specialty retail.

"In fiscal 2003, our new line-up includes more of what kids love, like Clifford and Captain Underpants, as well as the new series *Outernet*, *McGrowl*, and *Deltora Shadowlands*. A long-awaited sequel by Don and Audrey Wood, *Merry Christmas Big Hungry Bear* tops our list of picture books, along with *David Gets in Trouble* by bestselling author David Shannon and *How Do Dinosaurs Get Well Soon?* from Jane Yolen and Mark Teague."

- In 2002, more than 1 million teachers

sponsored Scholastic Book Clubs, generating more than 10 million orders. More than 65,000 schools held over 100,000 Scholastic Book Fairs.

■ Scholastic is a leader in creating engaging print and technology materials that support teachers and help students become successful readers. In 2002, said the company, "Our comprehensive reading-intervention program, Read 180, had a strong year, establishing Scholastic as a leader in reading improvement. New research further validated its effectiveness, and we recently launched a high school edition. We also positioned Scholastic Read XL as a leading middle school intervention program, launched Scholastic Summer School for grades 1–8, and developed new products such as the Scholastic Early Childhood Program."

Total assets: $1,637 million
Current ratio: 1.92
Common shares outstanding: 38.9 million
Return on 2002 shareholders' equity: 16.3%

	2002	2001	2000	1999	1998	1997	1996	1995
Revenues (millions)	1,917	1,962	1,402	1,155	1,058	966	929	750
Net income (millions)	99	81	57	37	24	.4	47	39
Earnings per share	2.47	2.24	1.51	1.11	.73	.01	1.42	1.19
Dividends per share	Nil	—	—	—	—	—	—	—
Price High	56.8	50.7	48.5	32.1	28.5	33.4	39.4	39.1
Low	33.1	34.1	21.8	19.5	14.4	10.4	29.5	23.9

AGGRESSIVE GROWTH

E. W. Scripps Company

Post Office Box 5380 □ 312 Walnut Street, Suite 2800 □ Cincinnati, Ohio 45201 □ (513) 977-3825 □ Dividend reinvestment plan not available □ Web site: www.scripps.com □ Listed: NYSE □ Ticker symbol: SSP □ S&P rating: B+ □ Value Line financial strength rating: B+

The advertising industry was a major casualty during the recent recession. And, of course, newspapers and magazines depend heavily on advertising revenues. Despite this, E. W. Scripps fared well in 2002. Here's how its operating groups performed:

● Newspapers: Total revenues increased 2.3 percent, to $756 million. Operating cash flow increased 14 percent, to $270 million. Operating income at the *Rocky Mountain News* was $8.9 million, compared with a $14.4-million loss in 2001.

● Broadcast television: Revenues increased 9.9 percent, to $305 million. Operating cash flow increased 23 percent, to $98.1 million. Political advertising revenues for the year were $23.7 million, compared with 2.4 million the prior year.

● Scripps Networks (the company's cable television networks and its fastest-growing division): Home & Garden Television revenues increased 15 percent, to $246 million; operating cash flow increased 35 percent, to $111 million. Food Network revenues increased 34 percent, to $158 million; operating cash flow was $52.6 million, compared with $16.2 million in 2001. However, start-up losses to establish DIY and Fine Living brands were $38 million, compared with $22.1 million in 2001.

● Shop At Home Network: On a pro forma basis (as if the company had owned the business for the full year in 2001 and 2002), revenues increased 16 percent, to $213 million.

- Licensing and other media: Total revenues were up 1.7 percent, to $90.3 million; operating cash flow increased 16 percent, to $17.3 million.

Company Profile

Now having celebrated its 125th anniversary, The E. W. Scripps Company is a diverse media concern with interests in newspaper publishing, broadcast television, national television networks, and interactive media and television retailing. Scripps operates twenty-one daily newspapers, ten broadcast television stations, four cable and satellite television programming services, and a home shopping network. All of the company's media businesses provide content and advertising services via the Internet.

Today, twenty-one daily Scripps newspapers are read by nearly 1.4 million Americans, making the company the ninth-largest newspaper publisher in the nation. The company emerged as a broadcast pioneer in the 1930s, launching some of the earliest radio and television stations. Today, the company operates ten television stations, all of which are in the nation's fifty largest metropolitan areas. Scripps television stations serve nearly 10 million American households as local affiliates of the NBC and ABC television networks.

Scripps Networks brands include Home & Garden Television, Food Network, DIY—Do It Yourself Network—and Fine Living. Home & Garden and Food Network each can be seen on television in about 80 million U.S. households. Scripps Networks is home to three of the Internet's most popular Web sites—*www.foodtv.com*, *www.hgtv.com*, and *www.diynet.com*. Scripps Networks programming can be seen in twenty-five countries.

The company's home-shopping subsidiary, the Shop At Home Network, markets a growing range of consumer goods directly to television viewers and visitors to the Shop At Home Web site, *www.shopathometv.com*. Shop At Home reaches about 46 million full-time equivalent U.S. households.

Scripps also operates Scripps Howard News Service and United Media, which is the worldwide licensing and syndication home of Peanuts and Dilbert (both leading newspaper comic strips).

Shortcomings to Bear in Mind

- Scripps's success has not gone unnoticed. Thus, its P/E ratio is quite often higher than stocks in general.
- Value Line *Investment Survey* is lukewarm on the stock. Near the end of 2002, its analyst, Stuart Plesser, said, "The stock is a timely selection for year-ahead price appreciation. Led by the strength of the Scripps Network, the company will likely advance earnings by roughly 55 percent this year (2002). Still, at its current quotation (it was $77 at the time), even factoring in double-digit earnings growth out to mid-decade, the stock offers below-average capital-appreciation potential to 2005–2007."
- The company's affiliation with ABC television has been a thorn in Scripps's side. Commenting on this situation, Rich Boehne, Scripps's executive vice president, said, "Our success in attracting new business also has helped us mitigate to some extent our station group's exposure to ABC's ratings woes. Although we're somewhat encouraged by ABC's improvement during the November sweeps, we think the network still has a long way to go, especially in strengthening programming that leads into late news."

Reasons to Buy

- At a meeting sponsored by UBS Warburg at the end of 2002, CEO Ken Lowe said, "One of the nice things about coming to New York every year in

December is that it gives us a chance to showcase any new holiday shopping offerings. This year it's the new book by Scott Adams, *Dilbert and The Way of the Weasel*. This is Scott's fifth hardcover book, and it just hit the bookstores a few weeks ago. The cover, as you can see, reflects the main theme—that being Scott's theory that there's a little weasel in all of us, especially in the workplace. I'm sure this group can relate.

"For those of you who might not be totally familiar with Scripps, Dilbert is one of the many world-famous characters and comic strips that are licensed and syndicated by our United Media subsidiary. United Media also is the licensing and syndication home for Peanuts, For Better or For Worse, and the Precious Moments characters, just to name a few."

■ At the same meeting, Rich Boehne, the company's executive vice president, made some comments on Scripps Networks, which consists of a portfolio of four distinct national programming services, each designed to target the passions and interests of viewers in specific consumer categories.

Mr. Boehne said, "These are categories that—until we came along—were under-served on the television screen. We've built a valuable business by following a simple, yet very effective model. It starts by identifying what our viewers want. Then, we match those wants with quality, original programming that's both entertaining and informative—programming that, in turn, provides valuable, targeted platforms for advertisers who want to efficiently reach highly motivated consumers. Today, our flagship networks—Home & Garden Television and Food Network—have grown into widely distributed, nationally known brands that literally are woven into the fabric of America's media landscape.

"Our newer networks, Do It Yourself and Fine Living, are in development, but definitely gaining traction. DIY, by design a digital tier programming service, is in 12 million homes and, as Ken pointed out, we inked a big carriage deal that boosted Fine Living's reach to 13 million homes just a few weeks ago."

■ Mr. Boehne also discussed some new services. "Specifically, we continue to move toward rolling out programming that appeals to Hispanic audiences, and we're working with cable operators to develop video on demand and subscription video on demand services using our rich archives of evergreen lifestyle and how-to programming.

"Our Hispanic programming strategy targets one of the country's fastest-growing markets. We're exploring a service that would be concentrated geographically in markets that have the highest percentages of Spanish-speaking viewers. Our early market analysis indicates that interest in Hispanic lifestyle programming is very strong."

■ Mr. Boehne made some comments on the company's string of twenty-one newspapers. "In all of the markets where we do business, our newspapers capture the largest share of advertising. We've been successful at strengthening the dominant market share position of most of our newspapers by introducing new print and online products that generate new revenue streams.

"Our newspapers have fared well in a very difficult environment this year (2002), with modest top line growth that outperformed our peer group. Our relatively better performance is in large part a function of geography. By design, we've concentrated our newspapers in solid, mid-size markets that tend to be shielded from business cycle extremes. For example, most of our newspapers had less exposure to the extreme fall-off in help wanted advertising that many of the larger metropolitan newspapers experienced in the past eighteen months.

"One thought on Denver. We think it's important to point out that we've successfully restored profitability without compromising our commitment to quality journalism. In our opinion, *The Rocky Mountain News* remains the best daily newspaper in Colorado."

Switching to another topic, Mr. Boehne commented on the company's broadcasting segment. "Our key sta-tions—we call them our 'Core 4'—contribute 80 percent of the group's total cash flow. These are the Scripps stations that have long held number one or two positions in their markets. Two of them—WEWS in Cleveland and WCPO in Cincinnati—have been Scripps stations since they went on the air in the late '40s. As expected, our sta-tion group has had a good year. Revenues were up 8 percent, and operating cash flow was up a healthy 14 percent through September (2002)."

Total assets: $2,662 million
Current ratio: 1.22
Common shares outstanding: 80 million
Return on 2002 shareholders' equity: 12.8%

	2002	2001	2000	1999	1998	1997	1996	1995
Revenues (millions)	1,780	1,613	1,719	1,571	1,455	1,242	1,122	1,030
Net income (millions)	188	138	163	147	131	133	113	94
Earnings per share	2.34	1.73	2.06	1.86	1.62	1.93	1.62	1.17
Dividends per share	.60	.60	.56	.56	.54	.52	.52	.50
Price High	87.5	71.7	63.3	53.0	58.5	48.9	52.4	40.6
Low	65.1	54.7	42.4	40.5	38.5	32.3	32.8	26.9

AGGRESSIVE GROWTH

Staples, Inc.

500 Staples Drive □ Framingham, Massachusetts 01702 □ (800) 468-7751 □ Web site: www.staples.com □ Dividend reinvestment plan not available □ Fiscal years end Saturday closest to January 31 □ Listed: NASDAQ and ASE □ Ticker symbol: SPLS □ S&P rating: B+ □ Value Line financial strength rating: A

"As Ronald Sargent was about to assume the chief executive post at Staples, Inc., a little over a year ago, he called a staff meeting to discuss a radical idea: elimi-nating more than 800 items from the chain's shelves," said Joseph Pereira, in an article that appeared in the *Wall Street Journal* March 5, 2003.

"The nixed items were aimed at casual shoppers, and included cheap printers, cartoon-themed notepads, and novelty pens adorned with feathers or edible candies.

"Mr. Sargent argued that the com-pany needed to shift focus, de-emphasizing occasional shoppers looking for discounts in favor of bigger-spending small busi-nesses and 'power users.' Although a group of Staples sales and merchandising executives balked, arguing that the com-pany couldn't afford to alienate any poten-tial customers in the midst of the post-Sept. 11 downturn, Mr. Sargent prevailed."

In the year that ended February 1, 2003, it was clear that the new strategy was working. Sales and profits were well ahead of the prior year. "Mr. Sargent theo-rizes that despite a poor economy, small businesses are sprouting, as large compa-nies continue to lay off employees and many former dot-comers seek out new ventures."

Company Profile

Staples, Inc., launched the office supplies superstore industry with the opening of its first store in Brighton (near Boston) Massachusetts in May 1986. Its goal was simple: to provide small business owners the same low prices on office supplies that had previously been enjoyed only by large corporations. Staples is now an $11-billion retailer of office supplies, business services, furniture, and technology. Its customers include consumers and businesses—from home-based businesses to *Fortune* 500 companies in the United States, Canada, the United Kingdom, France, Italy, Spain, Belgium, Germany, the Netherlands, and Portugal. Customers can shop with Staples however they choose, either by walking in, calling in, or logging on.

Staples is the largest operator of office superstores in the world, serving customers in some 1,500 office superstores, mail-order catalogs, e-commerce, and a contract business.

The company operates three business segments: North American Retail, North American Delivery, and European operations.

The company's North American Retail segment consists of the company's U.S. and Canadian business units that sell office products, supplies, and services.

The Staples North American Delivery segment consists of the company's U.S. and Canadian contract, catalog, and Internet business units that sell and deliver office products, supplies, and services directly to customers.

The Staples European Operations segment consists of the company's business units, which operate 188 retail stores in the United Kingdom, Germany, the Netherlands, and Portugal. The company also sells and delivers office products and supplies directly to businesses throughout the United Kingdom and Germany. The company's delivery operations comprise the catalog business (Staples Direct and Quill Corporation), the contract stationer business (Staples National Advantage and Staples Business Advantage), and the Internet e-commerce business (*www.staples.com*). Quill, acquired in 1998, is a direct-mail catalog business, serving more than 1 million medium-sized businesses in the United States.

In mid-2002, for $383 million, Staples acquired Medical Arts Press, a leading provider of specialized printed products and supplies for medical offices. In October 2002, the company acquired Guilbert's European mail order business for about $788 million.

At the retail level, stores operate under the names Staples—the Office Superstore and Staples Express. The prototype superstore has about 24,000 square feet of sales space, which the company plans to reduce to 20,000 in fiscal 2003. Stores carry about 8,500 stock items.

Express stores are much smaller, with between 6,000 square feet and 10,000 square feet of sales space. They also handle fewer items, generally about 6,000, and are situated in downtown business sectors. By contrast, the larger units tend to be situated in the suburbs.

Sales by product are as follows: office supplies and services, 40.8 percent; business machines and telecommunications services, 29.8 percent; computers and related products, 22.3 percent; and office furniture, 7.1 percent.

Shortcomings to Bear in Mind

- In a recent nine-month period, insiders such as executives and board members sold a great deal of stock. In that period, there were thirty-four sales—and no purchases!
- If you are looking for a conservative stock, you had better avoid Staples. It

has a beta coefficient of 1.45, which means it is very volatile. In other words, if the stock market rises or falls a certain percentage, Staples will rise or fall 45 percent more.

Reasons to Buy

- Staples announced on March 5, 2003, the results for the fiscal year that ended February 1, 2003. The company achieved a record performance with net income excluding special items of $417 million for the full year, or $.88 per share on a diluted basis. "Staples had a phenomenal year that reflects the power of people unified behind a winning strategy," said CEO Ron Sargent. "The outstanding performance by Staples associates drove record results and advanced our ability to truly make buying office products easy. We now look to build on our momentum, capitalize on the investments we made this past year, and deliver sustainable results going forward."

- Mr. Sargent went on to say that the improved results were due to better performance and remodeled stores that appealed to customers, even though spending was somewhat subdued in a flat economy. "I don't think the economy is helping us a bit. It's been a very tough environment out there. I think it's a function of the basics, of focusing."

- Highlights of the year ended February 1, 2003, included the following:
  - Shifted the customer mix by selling more to small businesses and power users and reduced reliance on less profitable casual consumers.
  - Increased the focus on selling Staples branded products to enhance customer loyalty and increase sales margins.
  - Acquired two Delivery businesses with better margin characteristics to increase the overall margin profile of the company.

- Developed a differentiated store format and remodeled a large percentage of stores to the new, customer-centric "Dover" model.
- Shifted the channel mix by growing the Delivery business faster than the Retail business, with benefits of higher margins and returns.
- Transitioned from a primarily North American entity to a much more global presence with the acquisition of the European catalog business, giving Staples access to four new countries.
- Shifted the Staples culture from one based on tasks and transitioned to one based on customers, driven by the Back to Brighton service initiative, and a new brand promise of making it easy to buy office products at Staples.

- Staples has a solid balance sheet, with 77 percent of its capitalization in shareholders' equity. Total interest coverage, moreover, is impressive, at 15.8 times.

- Staples has an outstanding record of growth. In the past ten years (1992–2002) earnings per share climbed steadily, with only one dip (in 2000, EPS declined to $.58, from $.67 the prior year). In that span, EPS zoomed from $.07 to $.88, a compound annual growth rate of 28.8 percent.

- "Earnings may well advance by 15 percent to 18 percent in each of the three to five years following fiscal 2002," said David R. Cohen, an analyst with *Value Line Investment Survey*, on January 17, 2003. "In addition to likely strength at the two aforementioned divisions, we expect profits at North American Retail to increase by about 10 percent per annum, on average. The rollout of a new, smaller format, recent customer-service innovations, and ongoing expansion of the private-label program are key factors behind our projections. Also,

Office Depot's and OfficeMax's domestic expansion plans will likely remain subdued for a while."

■ "We believe Staples is best-positioned to succeed and gain share in the intensifying, competitive environment," said a Bear Stearns analyst, Dana Telsey, in a report issued in February 2003.

■ While retail comparable sales declined 3 percent in the fourth quarter of 2002 (hurt by weak performance in Germany), store operations in the United Kingdom, the Netherlands, and Portugal performed well, with improved prof-itability and sales for 2002. Staples opened three new stores in Europe in the fourth quarter and fourteen for the year, bringing the total to 188 stores in the four countries where the company operates retail outlets.

■ In March 2003, Staples rolled out a new advertising campaign with the tag line, "That was easy," replacing "Yeah, we've got that." Management said research indicated customers expected good prices and selection, but they were most interested in a convenient shopping experience.

Total assets: $5,721 million
Current ratio: 1.25
Common shares outstanding: 471 million
Return on 2002 shareholders' equity: 17.7%

		2002	2001	2000	1999	1998	1997	1996	1995
Revenues (millions)		11,596	10,744	10,674	8,937	7,132	5,181	3,968	3,068
Net income (millions)		417	307	264	315	238	149	106	74
Earnings per share		.88	.66	.58	.67	.53	.39	.28	.20
Dividends per share		Nil	—	—	—	—	—	—	—
Price	High	22.5	19.5	28.8	35.9	30.8	13.4	10.1	8.6
	Low	11.7	11.0	10.3	16.4	10.6	7.6	5.6	4.2

AGGRESSIVE GROWTH

Stryker Corporation

Post Office Box 4085 □ Kalamazoo, Michigan 49003-4085 □ (616) 385-2600 □ Web site: www.strykercorp.com □ Listed: NYSE □ Dividend reinvestment plan not available □ Ticker symbol: SYK □ S&P rating: B+ □ Value Line financial strength rating: A

In January of 2003, Stryker Corporation announced that one of its divisions, Stryker Howmedica Osteonics, a leading provider of orthopaedic implants, had launched an online Joint Replacement Resource Center. The sponsored Resource Center, aimed at educating patients on joint replacement therapies for hips, knees, and shoulders, provides content that is developed by Stryker Howmedica Osteonics and that is hosted by WebMD at *www.joints.webmd.com*.

With increasing numbers of consumers undergoing various joint replace-ment procedures, the site is designed to help patients, potential patients, and caregivers make better-informed medical decisions as they work with their orthopedic surgeons to consider joint replacement. The Joint Replacement Resource Center is a virtual center where visitors can learn about joint replacement and receive support for the various steps in considering joint replacement. Visitors can take an interactive self-test related to joint replacement, find tools to help them prepare for a visit with their orthopedic surgeon, and access educational information on joint replacement from medical experts and other patients.

"Advances in technology and medicine have made joint replacement therapies more effective and beneficial than ever before," said Ned Lipes, Group President of Stryker Howmedica Osteonics. "As more consumers pursue these therapies, the need for responsible information about the benefits, risks, and opportunities has also risen. We believe this new resource will provide patients with the information they need to get the best care and make the most informed decisions."

Stryker Howmedica Osteonics offers an extensive orthopaedic product portfolio including hip, knee, and upper-extremity reconstructive devices, bone cement, trauma implants, bone substitutes, and spine systems.

Company Profile

Stryker Corporation was founded in 1941 by Dr. Homer H. Stryker, a leading orthopedic surgeon and the inventor of several orthopedic products. The company now ranks as a dominant player in a $12-billion global orthopedics industry. Stryker has a significant market share in such sectors as artificial hips, prosthetic knees, and trauma products.

Stryker develops, manufactures, and markets specialty surgical and medical products worldwide. These products include orthopedic implants, trauma systems, powered surgical instruments, endoscopic systems, and patient care and handling equipment.

Through a network of 302 centers in twenty-six states, Stryker's Physiotherapy Associates division provides physical, occupational, and speech therapy to orthopedic and neurology patients. The physical therapy business represents a solid complementary business for Stryker, in view of the high number of its surgeon customers who prescribe physical therapy following orthopedic surgery.

A major component of Stryker's success is the optimal use of resources in manufacturing and distribution. Taking advantage of both information technology and leading-edge workflow management practices, the company monitors quality and service levels at its sixteen plants throughout North America and Europe for continuous improvement. This attention to operations has resulted in the inclusion of Stryker facilities in the elite *Industry-Week* "Best Plants" list two times in the last three years. The Stryker Instruments plant in Kalamazoo, Michigan, was named one of the Best Plants in 2000, and the Howmedica Osteonics facility in Allendale, New Jersey, was honored in 1998.

Shortcomings to Bear in Mind

- In the past ten years (1992–2002), Stryker's earnings per share advanced without a dip, from $0.25 to $1.70, a compound annual growth rate of 21.1 percent. It's hard to find a company growing at this pace that you can buy for a reasonable P/E ratio. Nor can you invest in Stryker at a bargain-basement share price. It is nearly always selling at a premium to the market. Let's hope it continues to be worth it.

  Robert M. Gold, an analyst with *Standard & Poor's Stock Reports*, believes that Stryker is worth its premium price tag. "We believe the premium is warranted by the company's historic earnings growth consistency and the positive underlying fundamentals evident throughout the orthopedics group. Thus, we believe the stock can appreciate in line with its earnings growth rate."

Reasons to Buy

- Stryker Spine entered the cervical-fixation market in 2001 with the Reflex system, which generated excellent customer acceptance here at home as well as in Europe. This innovative product addresses the increasing demand for fixation products for the upper part of the spine. The Reflex system features Stryker's proprietary TMZF advanced alloy material, a one-step locking system, and simple-to-use instrument technology.

- Stryker Trauma's T2 nailing system, launched in 2001 in the United States, Europe, and Japan, provides a wide range of fracture repair options for long bones, using a common set of instruments. The expertise of the same engineering team and manufacturing personnel who created the well-established best-in-class Gamma family of nails for hip fractures was leveraged to facilitate rapid development of the T2.

According to a company spokesman, "It earned immediate favorable response from our customers. In addition, Stryker Trauma further specialized its three production plants in Switzerland and Germany, fine-tuned inventory control, and initiated a dedicated sales force in Japan's largest cities."

- In hip and knee implants, Stryker offers comprehensive lines to fill every need, from early intervention to revision. By using the same geometrics and instrumentation throughout the line, "we offer the surgeon both ease of use and greater intra-operative choice. In 2001— its first full year on the market—our Scorpio TS revision knee system achieved stellar sales growth."

The Scorpio TX is designed to work with the Modular Rotating Hinge (MRH)—also introduced in 2001—and the Modular Revision System (MRS). Using a single set of bone cuts, the surgeon can begin the procedure and then choose the most appropriate of these three implants, depending on the amount of bone remaining.

According to a company spokesman, "We have taken a similar approach to addressing regional needs, particularly in Japan, which has different size, range-of-motion, and flexion requirements than the United States and Europe. In 2000, we adapted our Scorpio knee for Japan, branding it Superflex, and in 2001, we did the same with our Eon and Secur-fit hips, known as Super Eon and Super Secur-fit in their Japanese versions."

- Analysts believe that industry trends are setting the stage for continued growth for Stryker in the years ahead. Virtually all market dynamics point in that direction. These are the key factors:
  - The population as a whole is aging. In fact, the target population for orthopedic implants for knees and hips is expected to increase 68 percent in the next nine years, according to a report issued by Gerard Klauer Mattison & Company, Inc., a brokerage firm headquartered in New York City.
  - Mild inflation in average selling prices for orthopedic implants in the United States compares favorably to the declining price environment of the past decade.
  - Consolidation among orthopedic implant and device manufacturers over the past few years has greatly decreased the number of competitors in sectors such as orthopedic implants, spinal devices, arthroscopy products, and other orthopedic products. This serves to consolidate market share and also mitigates price competition.
  - Advances in orthopedic technology— much of which has taken place in the past decade—have markedly decreased operating and recovery times. These advances have decreased the amount of time a surgeon must spend with each patient, thus giving the surgeon more time to perform more operations in a period. Consequently, according to the Gerard Klauer Mattison report,

"we believe that procedural volume will increase."

For its part, Stryker has set itself up to benefit from these microeconomic dynamics, according to the report issued by this same brokerage house. "For example, Stryker has strategically used acquisitions over the past few years to broaden and deepen its product portfolio. Furthermore, innovation in orthopedic implants and instrumentation has provided the company with certain competitive advantages that should be important ingredients for gaining market share in the coming years."

- In 2001, Stryker achieved a goal it has been seeking for twenty years. The company received marketing approval for OP-1 (osteogenic protein-1), its proprietary bone-growth factor, in three key regions of the world: the United States, Australia, and the European Union.

These approvals were the first for a bone morphogenic protein in each of the three jurisdictions, and they led to Stryker's creation of the Biotech, Spine, and Trauma Group. This group has a global focus in product development and manufacturing. More than 60 percent of its products are sold abroad. According to CEO John W. Brown, "We expect that this new structure will further accelerate the fast-growing spine and trauma divisions of the company, and that it will enable us to enhance future opportunities for synergy between spine and trauma products and OP-1."

Each of the three specific approval indications for OP-1 involves nonunion—or difficult-to-heal—fractures of long bones. The OP-1 is mixed with a collagen carrier and wetted to form a paste that is surgically implanted into the fracture gap.

Total assets: $2,815 million
Current ratio: 1.63
Common shares outstanding: 198 million
Return on 2002 shareholder's equity: 24%

	2002	2001	2000	1999	1998	1997	1996	1995
Revenues (millions)	3,012	2,602	2,289	2,104	1,103	980	910	872
Net income (millions)	346	272	221	161	150	125	101	87
Earnings per share	1.70	1.34	1.10	.81	.77	.64	.52	.45
Dividends per share	.10	.08	.07	.07	.06	.06	.05	.02
Price High	69.0	63.2	57.8	36.6	27.9	22.7	16.1	14.6
Low	43.8	43.3	43.3	22.2	15.5	12.1	9.9	9.0

CONSERVATIVE GROWTH

Sysco Corporation

1390 Enclave Parkway □ Houston, Texas 77077-2099 □ (281) 584-1308 □ Web site: www.sysco.com □ Dividend reinvestment plan is available: (800) 730-4001 □ Fiscal years end the Saturday closest to June 30 □ Listed: NYSE □ Ticker symbol: SYY □ Standard & Poor's rating: A+ □ Value Line financial strength rating: A++

With the advent of two household incomes, with both husband and wife working outside the home, it is not surprising that no one wants to come home after eight hours at the office and still have to face cooking supper— not to mention cleaning up after the repast.

Today, about half of Americans' food dollars are spent on meals prepared away from home. That figure far surpasses the 37 percent that was spent on away-from-home meals in 1972. It reveals how heavily our society now depends on foodservice operations to satisfy consumers' nutritional needs by providing a variety of quality meals at affordable prices.

Benefiting from this trend is Sysco's chain restaurant distribution arm, the SYGMA Network, Inc. It serves customers from thirteen facilities strategically located across the United States. SYGMA enjoyed a successful year in fiscal 2002 (ended June 30, 2002), as sales increased to $2.7 billion, up a healthy 10.6 percent above the prior year.

Company Profile

As they go about their lives, many people encounter the familiar Sysco trucks, bearing their giant blue lettering, delivering products to customers. Few are aware, however, of Sysco's far-reaching influence on meals served daily throughout North America. As the continent's largest marketer and distributor of foodservice products, Sysco operates 142 distribution facilities, serving more than 400,000 restaurants, hotels, schools, hospitals, retirement homes, and other locations where food is prepared to be eaten on the premises or taken away and enjoyed in the comfort of the diner's chosen environment.

Sysco is by far the largest company in the foodservice distribution industry. In sales, Sysco dwarfs its two chief competitors, US Foodservice and Performance Food Group.

The company's operations break down as follows: restaurants (65 percent sales); hospitals and nursing homes (10 percent); schools and colleges (6 percent); hotels and motels (5 percent); other (14 percent).

With annual sales in 2002 of $23.4 billion, Sysco distributes a wide variety of fresh and frozen meats, seafood, poultry, fruits and vegetables, plus bakery products, canned and dry foods, paper and disposables, sanitation items, dairy foods, beverages, kitchen and tabletop equipment, as well as medical and surgical supplies.

Sysco's innovations in food technology, packaging, and transportation provide customers with quality products that are delivered on time, in excellent condition, and at reasonable prices.

Shortcomings to Bear in Mind

- During a recession, it's possible that more food will be prepared at home, and restaurants will see some empty tables. In response to this idea, Mark Husson, a food retail analyst with Merrill Lynch said, "I don't think the economy will take a shuddering downward turn, but if it does, we can't rely on people's collective memory of how to cook. People think it's their God-given right to eat in restaurants."

Reasons to Buy

- George A. Niemond, an analyst with *Value Line Investment Survey*, had this to say in the fall of 2002: "We think the company will maintain its string of earnings advances through our three- to five-year investment horizon. For starters, foodservice industry trends are favorable, since people are consuming more meals that are prepared away from home.

  "And the company aims to capture more of the business. Sysco is using a 'foldout' strategy to expand its distribution system. It opens a facility on the outskirts of a region served by an older distribution center that is nearing capacity, and then transfers customers and workers to the new facility to give it a ready customer base and experienced staff."
- Whether dining in an upscale restaurant or picking up pasta as the entrée for a meal at home, people spend less time on food preparation than ever before. They want variety and flavor in the foods they choose to eat, yet their time to prepare meals is constantly in competition with work and leisure activities. More than ever, people are turning to meals pre-

pared away from home for greater convenience, quality and, most of all, choice.

This is a trend that started in World War II, as women began to work outside the home. Business cafeterias, coffee shops, school lunchrooms, and restaurants broadened the range of dining choices for people who were used to much simpler fare. Twenty-five years ago, not many consumers could identify a kiwi fruit. During the past three decades, foodservice offerings have moved from fruit cocktail with a cherry on top to kiwi and other exotic fare; from steak and potatoes to fajitas with all the trimmings.

- As the largest distributor of foodservice products in North America, Sysco assists customers in creating a vast array of dining choices. Menus have greatly improved since a French chef named Boulanger offered a choice of soups, or "restorative," to patrons who paused at his inn to refresh themselves as they traveled during the 1700s. The sign in French read "restaurant," and his establishment may have been the first to offer a menu.

Today's diverse menu choices could not have been imagined then: raspberries from Australia served fresh in Wisconsin in January; gourmet pesto sauce rich with garlic, fresh basil, and pine nuts delivered to a Vancouver chef's doorstep; or artfully prepared hearts of lettuce served in an Arizona college's cafeterias each day. Providing choices from soup to nuts, and everything in between, Sysco leads the way in helping chefs in restaurants, schools, business cafeterias, health care locations, lodging, and other facilities increase the variety and quality of food choices in North America.

- In January of 2001, Sysco announced the signing of a multiyear contract with the Ross Products Division of Abbott Laboratories, one of the nation's leading pharmaceutical companies. The agree-

ment provided Sysco an exclusive access to Abbott's Nutra-Balance brand name for use in marketing and sales of nutritional products that Sysco distributes to hospitals, nursing homes, and other medical and extended-care facilities.

"Sysco's market share in the foodservice long-term health-care segment is experiencing continued growth," said Richard J. Schnieders, the company's president and chief operating officer. "This joint marketing strategy will further enhance our 'one-stop-shopping' concept and provide additional efficiencies to our valued health-care customers."

- Unlike some of its competitors, who order all their products from headquarters, Mr. Cotros encourages his seventy-eight branches to reach their own decisions about which products to carry and how to price them. Sysco's 6,500 sales representatives carry laptop computers that can instantly place orders and confirm inventory. By contract, smaller distributors still take orders with pads and pencils and are often unsure which items are on the warehouse shelf.

- Sysco keeps margins high by selling products under its own label, a strategy it began a year after its founding. It saves on national advertising and passes some of the savings along to its customers. Its private-label business carries an estimated 24 percent gross margin, or 10 percent more than it earns on national brands.

- Sysco has an exceptional record of growth. In the past ten years (1992–2002), earnings per share advanced from $0.23 to $1.01 (with no dips along the way), a compound annual growth rate of 15.9 percent. In the same decade, dividends per share climbed from $0.05 to $0.36, a growth rate of 21.8 percent. Sysco has increased its quarterly cash dividend thirty-three times in its thirty-two years as a public company.

■ Many of Sysco's operations have been the result of acquisitions. For instance, the March 2002 acquisition of SERCA Foodservice, Inc., a division of Sobeys, Inc., significantly expanded the company's presence coast-to-coast in the $9-billion Canadian foodservice distribution market, completing Sysco's strategy of broadening its geographic reach. Foodservices, Inc., now operates from seventeen locations in eight provinces of Canada, providing products and services to 65,000 customers.

Two additional acquisitions were completed during fiscal 2002. Fulton Provision Company of Portland, Oregon, a custom-cut beef distributor with annual sales of about $25 million in calendar 2000, joined the company's specialty meat company family. Also, Guest Supply acquired Franklin Supply Company located in Louisburg, North Carolina. This specialty distributor to the lodging industry generated $19 million in sales for its fiscal year ended February 28, 2001. This acquisition enables Guest Supply to expand product depth and increase offerings to customers in the southeastern United States hospitality market.

■ Each day, the drivers of Sysco's 5,800 delivery vehicles crisscross the cities and counties of North America to deliver more than 2 million cases of product. From the back-alley door of a small deli in Los Angeles to the loading dock of a major hospital in St. Louis, Sysco distributes a range of 275,000 products system-wide that have been transported by rail, trucked, or flown from points near and far around the globe to Sysco warehouses. That foods are shipped so reliably and accurately every day is possible only because of advances in computer technology, transportation, refrigeration, and warehousing.

In the 1970s, the typical fleet unit was a twelve- to sixteen-foot truck with modest refrigeration capabilities. Frozen and dry goods were the primary commodities of the foodservice industry. Today's twenty-eight- to thirty-six-foot, single-axle trucks typically have three separate food storage compartments with the most reliable mechanical refrigeration systems available.

Total assets: $5,990 million
Current ratio: 1.42
Common shares outstanding: 663 million
Return on 2002 shareholders' equity: 32.1%

	2002	2001	2000	1999	1998	1997	1996	1995
Revenues (millions)	23,351	21,784	19,303	17,423	15,328	14,455	13,395	12,118
Net income (millions)	680	597	454	362	325	302	277	252
Earnings per share	1.01	.88	.68	.54	.48	.43	.38	.34
Dividends per share	.36	.28	.22	.19	.16	.15	.12	.10
Price High	32.6	30.1	30.4	20.6	14.4	11.8	9.0	8.2
Low	21.2	21.8	13.1	12.5	10.0	7.3	6.9	6.2

AGGRESSIVE GROWTH

Target Corporation

1000 Nicollet Mall □ Minneapolis, Minnesota 55403 □ (612) 761-6735 □ Direct dividend reinvestment plan is available: (888) 268-0203 □ Web site: www.target.com □ Fiscal years end Saturday closest to January 31 of following year □ Listed: NYSE □ Ticker symbol: TGT □ S&P rating: A □ Value Line financial strength rating: A

Among the 1,147 Target units are about 100 larger stores called SuperTargets, which started appearing on the scene in 2000. These 175,000-square-foot facilities devote 30,000 square feet to high-quality groceries. The number of these SuperTargets is on track to reach 125 by the end of fiscal 2003. Thanks to the conversion of twenty-five former Montgomery Ward units, space increased by 12 percent in 2002.

According to CEO Robert J. Ulrich, "SuperTarget supplements the tremendous growth opportunities provided by our traditional discount stores and raises the potential to strengthen our brand in key markets. By combining a high-quality, full-line grocery assortment with our general merchandise offering, SuperTarget creates a convenient one-stop shopping experience for our guests. Like Target, SuperTarget strives to set itself apart from competitors and be preferred by guests. Our merchandising is innovative and differentiated and is focused on delivering fashion and freshness.

"Our assortment includes natural and organic products, Choice beef and top-grade produce, as well as premium brands, such as Krispy Kreme doughnuts, Starbucks coffee, Fannie May chocolates, Philippe Starck organic foods, and La Brea breads.

In addition, our expanding private-label line of Archer Farms items provides a high-quality, low-priced alternative to similar, nationally branded grocery products."

Company Profile

Target Corporation (formerly Dayton Hudson Corporation) was formed in 1969 through the merger of two old-line department store companies, Dayton Corporation and J. L. Hudson Company. In 1990, Target acquired another venerable retailer, Marshall Field & Company. The department stores (once run separately, but now under the Marshall Field umbrella) have since been eclipsed by the company's fast-growing Target division, which accounts for the bulk of revenues and profits.

Target is the nation's fourth-largest general merchandise retailer. The stores specialize in large-store formats, including discount stores, moderate-priced promotional stores, and traditional department stores. The company operates Target stores, Marshall Field's, and Mervyn's stores.

At the end of fiscal 2002 (February 1, 2003), the company operated 1,147 Target discount stores (accounting for 83 percent of retail sales). The Target operation is the company's strongest retail franchise and is its growth vehicle for the future. Most of the remaining units operate under Mervyn's banner. These 264 outlets handle soft goods (10 percent of sales). Finally, the department store segment consists mostly of sixty-four Marshall Field's department stores and four home-furnishing units (7 percent of annual sales).

Target stores are situated largely in such states as California, Texas, Florida, and the upper Midwest. Mervyn's are clustered largely in California and Texas.

In 2000, the company formed target.direct, the direct merchandising and electronic retailing organization. The business combines the e-commerce team of Target with its direct merchandising unit into one integrated organization. The target.direct organization operates seven Web sites, which support the store and catalog brands in an online environment and produce six retail catalogs.

Shortcomings to Bear in Mind

- Because Target has a greater proportion of trendy, discretionary merchandise and has been rapidly increasing its credit card business, analysts consider it more sensitive to economic swings than its chief rival Wal-Mart. "Of any company we follow, Target is probably the most cyclical," said Deborah Weinswig, a retail analyst with Salomon Smith Barney.

- In the year ended February 1, 2003, the expense rate, excluding credit card operations, was unfavorable compared with the prior year, principally because of slower-than-expected same-store sales growth. This effect was only partially offset by the benefit of overall growth at Target, the company's lowest expense rate division. (Expense rate represents selling, general, and administrative expenses as a percentage of sales. It includes buying and occupancy, advertising, start-up, and other expenses. However, it excludes depreciation and expenses associated with credit card operations.)
- The retail business is always subject to competitive pressures from such outstanding companies as Bed Bath & Beyond, Wal-Mart, Costco, Lowe's, and Home Depot.

Reasons to Buy

- Unlike many companies, 2002 was a good year for Target. Earnings per share advanced 20.7 percent, to $1.81, and revenues rose to $42.7 billion, for a gain of 9.2 percent over the prior year. More of the same is in store for 2003, said CEO Bob Ulrich. "In 2003, we will continue to focus on delivering even greater value to our guests and achieving profitable market share growth. We remain confident that we will continue to generate average annual earnings per share growth of 15 percent or more over time."
- Target has an outstanding record of growth. In the last ten years (1992–2002), earnings per share climbed from $0.40 to $1.81, a compound annual growth rate of 16.3 percent. In the same period, dividends advanced from $0.13 to $0.24, a growth rate of only 6.3 percent. Although not exactly impressive, the small dividend is indicative of a growth stock.
- The company's primary growth comes from new store expansion within the Target Stores division. Through a combination of new discount stores and new SuperTarget stores, the company plans to continue adding an average of 8 to 10 percent retail square footage annually. In the words of CEO Bob Ulrich, "We continue to build out less penetrated markets, such as Boston, New York, and Philadelphia, that provide substantial growth opportunities because of the dense population and the favorable demographics of potential guests.

  "We also continue to introduce Target into entirely new markets, such as our entry into Portland, Maine, in the fall of 2001. But increasingly, Target is expanding its store density in more mature markets, such as Atlanta, Phoenix, and Dallas/Fort Worth, reflecting our growing recognition and strength of the Target brand in major metropolitan areas across the U.S."
- Store expansion is only part of the whole story, according to Mr. Ulrich. "In addition to store expansion, the growth of our Target stores division is propelled by our ability to protect and enhance our distinctive brand character. We strive to provide our guests with a stopping experience that is consistently better than, and different from, their experiences at our competitors' stores.

  "By offering innovative, well-designed merchandise, compelling prices, and clean, attractive stores, we deliver the excitement and value that our guests expect and demand. In 2000, we introduced Philips Kitchen Appliances, Martex domestics, and Liz Claiborne fashions, among other brands. And in 2001, our assortment of new, exclusive products included Mossimo apparel, Waverly home furnishings, and Eddie Bauer camping gear."
- The credit card business has been a major plus factor. In the year ended February 1, 2003, the contribution from the company's credit card operations

increased 19.6 percent, to $532 million, from $445 million in 2001. At year-end, gross receivables were $5.964 billion, compared with $4.092 billion at the end of 2001. These result were due to continued growth in issuance and usage of the Target Visa card.

The provision for bad debt expense exceeded net write-offs by $138 million for the year, as a result of the company's consistent practice of providing for projected future write-offs as receivables are created.

Total assets: $28,603 million
Current ratio: 1.59
Common shares outstanding: 908 million
Return on 2002 shareholders' equity: 19.1%

	2002	2001	2000	1999	1998	1997	1996	1995
Revenues (millions)	42,722	39,888	36,903	33,702	30,662	27,487	25,371	23,516
Net income (millions)	1,654	1,368	1,264	1,185	962	775	555	311
Earnings per share	1.81	1.50	1.38	1.27	1.02	.82	.59	.32
Dividends per share	.24	.22	.21	.20	.18	.17	.16	.15
Price High	46.2	41.7	39.2	38.5	27.1	18.5	10.2	6.7
Low	24.9	26.0	21.6	25.0	15.7	9.0	5.8	5.3

AGGRESSIVE GROWTH

Toll Brothers, Inc.

3103 Philmont Avenue □ Huntington Valley, Pennsylvania 19006 □ (215) 938-8045 □ Dividend reinvestment plan not available □ Web site: www.tollbrothers.com □ Fiscal years end on October 31 □ Ticker symbol: TOL □ Listed: NYSE □ S&P rating: B+ □ Value Line financial strength rating: B+

Toll Brothers is not without its problems. For one thing, municipalities continue to create new rules and requirements for securing final approvals that delay the start of construction and the opening of new communities.

"In the short run, these regulations can hamper our results," said Robert I. Toll, chief executive officer of Toll Brothers, a leading home builder that prefers to do business with the "carriage trade." The company's houses sell for an average of $500,000.

"But in the long run, they create barriers to entry and further restrict the supply of available home sites. This environment favors Toll Brothers and other large builders with the capital and expertise to prevail through arduous approval processes. With control of 41,000 home sites in many of the nation's most affluent

markets, we will continue to gain market share from our smaller, less well-capitalized luxury market competitors."

For thirty-five years in the home building business and sixteen as a public company, said Mr. Toll, "We have survived and flourished through many economic cycles. The steps we've taken in the past decade to increase our capital base, diversify our product mix, and expand geographically should help us to remain strong through downturns and capitalize on our strength as the economy rebounds."

Looking ahead to the coming year, Mr. Toll said, "We enter fiscal 2003 with 170 selling communities, the most in our industry, and our largest year-end backlog ever. At $1.87 billion, our backlog equals 82 percent of FY 2002's home building revenues and offers nine months of revenue visibility. We believe this pipeline, totaling nearly 3,400 homes, positions us to produce record revenues of approximately $2.6 billion (5,000 home deliveries) in 2003. And with a projected community count of approximately 185 by fiscal year end 2003, we believe we can produce revenues of approximately $3 billion (6,000 home deliveries) in 2004, assuming current demand."

Company Profile

Founded in 1967, Toll Brothers is the eighth-largest domestic home builder, based on revenues. The company designs, builds, and markets single-family detached and attached homes in middle-income and high-income residential communities catering to move-up buyers (those who have previously owned a home), and empty-nesters (buyers aged fifty or older, without children) in twenty-two states. The communities are typically situated on land the company has either developed or acquired fully developed. Toll Brothers operates its own land-development, architectural, engineering, mortgage, title, security-monitoring, landscape, cable television, broadband Internet access, lumber distribution, house component assembly, and manufacturing operations.

The company builds the majority of its homes in Pennsylvania and New Jersey, but it has been diversifying into new regions to take advantage of differing regional economic cycles. Since 1994, it has expanded into California, Arizona, Texas, Florida, and North Carolina, all forecast to continue high population growth. More recently, Toll Brothers expanded into Rhode Island (in 2000), New Hampshire (2000), Colorado (2001), and South Carolina (2002). The company prefers to set up shop in communities in affluent areas near highways, with access to major cities.

The company's homes break down into three groups.

Luxury Move-Up

The move-up market (previous home owners) has been the core of its business for thirty-five years. In this sector, Toll Brothers builds homes ranging in size from 2,000 to over 6,000 square feet, and in price from the low $200,000s to over $1 million.

With the largest group of baby boomers—the more than 4 million people who were born annually between 1954 and 1964—now entering their peak earning years and move-up home-buying years, "we anticipate strong demand for move-up homes throughout the decade," said a company spokesman. "Our move-up buyers are typically growing families. They love our homes for their spacious, flexible living environments, state-of-the-art technology, and elegance—key features that enhance their achievement-oriented lifestyles."

Luxury Empty-Nester

Since entering the empty-nester market in the early 1990s, Toll Brothers has expanded this segment to more than 30 percent of its home sales. Empty-nesters are generally over fifty and have no children living at home. According to the company, "Some buy our smaller jewel box homes loaded with the latest amenities and luxuries. Others buy our larger homes with first-floor master suites, multiple home offices, and gorgeous entertainment areas. Some buy more than one home from us: a primary residence in a northern locale and a second home in a Sun Belt market. Empty-nesters are particularly drawn to our recreation-oriented communities with golf courses, pool complexes, walking trails, tennis courts, and country clubs."

Luxury Active Adult

Active adults are pre-retirees and retirees seeking age-qualified (fifty-five or older), recreational lifestyle communities. The company opened its first luxury active-adult community in 1999 and now has five selling communities, with another twelve in development. "Most active adults want to remain near family and friends," said a company spokesman. "Therefore, we locate most of our communities in areas not typically associated with adult-active living, such as the Northeast, Midwest, and Mid-Atlantic states. With over 6,000 home sites for active-adult communities in our pipeline, we envision this business generating up to 15 percent of our home sales in the next few years."

Shortcomings to Bear in Mind

Michael W. Jaffe, an analyst writing for *Standard & Poor's Stock Reports* in late 2002, had some reservations about the company's future. "We expect TOL's order trends for the coming year to be aided by ongoing low mortgage rates, and we also see the company's business assisted by the demographics of its upper-end housing markets, as baby boomers entering their peak earnings years seek move-up homes. Despite our positive sales outlook, we see margins narrowing in fiscal 2003, limited by the costs of setting up new communities under TOL's planned expansion program."

Reasons to Buy

- At the end of fiscal 2002, Mr. Toll said, "In the last five years, without any major acquisitions, we have doubled our revenues, tripled our earnings, and grown each year through a period which has included rising interest rates (in 1999 and 2000), a stock market crash, a recession, the tragedies of September 11, and several international financial crises. Our results speak to the strength of our industry, its lack of cyclicality, and our own company's ability to grow in difficult economic times."

Mr. Toll also said, "Experts project that the combination of new household formations, demand for new second homes, and the need to replace obsolete housing stock will propel demand for new homes to 1.7 million units per year during this decade. Due to ongoing no-growth supply constraints, we believe home prices likely will continue to rise and the large home building companies who can win approvals will continue to gain market share. We now own or control nearly 41,000 home sites and have demonstrated our ability to gain approvals, to open new communities, to diversify geographically, and to expand our move-up, empty-nester, and active-adult products lines."

- The company's success has not gone unrecognized. In 1996, Toll was named "America's Best Builder" by the National Association of Home Builders. In 1995, the same organization awarded the company the National Housing Quality Award. And in 1988, it was declared Builder of the Year by *Professional Builder*.

- Toll Brothers serves forty-one affluent markets with more than 6 million households earning $100,000 and above. What's more, two dozen potential expansion markets contain another 2.5 million affluent households. Finally, the company sells from 155 communities, up 55 percent in the last five year.

- The company boasts ten consecutive years of record earnings and revenues. Stockholders equity, moreover, has grown at a compound annual pace of 23 percent in the past ten years. In addition, Toll Brothers has the highest net profit and operating profit margins among the *Fortune* 1000 home builders.

Total assets: $2,895 million
Current ratio: Not available
Common shares outstanding: 36 million
Return on 2002 shareholders' equity: 25.8%

		2002	2001	2000	1999	1998	1997	1996	1995
Revenues (millions)		2,280	2,208	1,802	1,464	1,206	972	761	646
Net income (millions)		220	214	146	103	86	68	54	50
Earnings per share		2.91	2.76	1.95	1.38	1.13	.97	.78	.73
Dividends per share		Nil	—	—	—	—	—	—	—
Price	High	31.8	22.9	21.4	12.2	15.8	13.7	11.8	11.5
	Low	17.8	12.9	8.0	7.8	8.7	8.7	7.3	5.9

CONSERVATIVE GROWTH

Tractor Supply Company

320 Plus Park Boulevard □ Nashville, Tennessee 37217 □ (615) 366-4600 □ Web site: www.tractorsupplyco.com □ Dividend reinvestment plan not available □ Listed: NASDAQ □ Ticker symbol: TSCO □ S&P rating: B+ □ Value Line financial strength rating: Not rated

"Perhaps you recall the old joke about the farmer who won a million dollars. When asked what he would do with the cash, the farmer replied: 'I guess I'll just keep on farming until all the money is gone.'"

Those are the words of Jonathan Heller, a writer with the magazine, *On Investing*, a Charles Schwab publication. "The joke contains more than a bit of truth about the fragile state of agriculture, which makes you wonder why any company connected with farming would be a winner," said Mr. Heller in the February 2003 issue.

"One explanation is that Tractor Supply doesn't specialize in sales to the big combines. 'Tractor Supply has done an excellent job in defining its target market, mostly consisting of hobby farmers, part-time farmers, and non-farm consumers in rural areas. Full-time farmers represent just 8 percent of customers,' says David Cumberland, an analyst with Baird."

Company Profile
In 1938, Charles E. Schmidt, Sr., of Chicago, Illinois, established a mail order tractor parts business. By 1939, it had grown into a successful retail store in Minot, North Dakota.

Today, Tractor Supply Company is the largest operator of retail farm and ranch stores in the United States. Its 433 stores in thirty states focus on supplying the lifestyle needs of those who enjoy the rural lifestyle. The company looks for its business to emanate from hobby, part-time, and full-time farmers and ranchers, as well as contractors, tradesmen, and rural customers. Stores are situated in towns outlying major metropolitan markets and in rural communities.

The company offers the following comprehensive selection of merchandise:
- Livestock and pet products, including everything necessary for their health, care, growth, and containment, such as specialty feeds, supplements, equine supplies, medicines, veterinary supplies, fencing and livestock feeders, and maintenance products for agricultural and rural use.
- Hardware and tool products, such as air compressors, welders, generators, pumps, plumbing, and hand tools.
- Truck, trailer, and towing products, including truck toolboxes, trailers, towing accessories, tires, lubricants, and batteries.

- Seasonal products, such as riding mowers, tillers, lawn and garden supplies, and heaters.
- Agricultural products, including tractor parts and accessories, agricultural spraying equipment, and tillage parts.
- Clothing and footwear for the entire family.

The company's stores carry a consistent merchandise mix, and they stock an average of 12,000 to 14,000 products, including a wide selection of quality, nationally recognized brand names. In addition, Tractor Supply markets private-label merchandise. The average store has about 13,000 square feet of inside selling space and at least 12,000 square feet of outside space.

Shortcomings to Bear in Mind

- The company's business tends to be seasonal. In the past, its sales and profits have been highest in the second and fourth quarters of the year. Typically, Tractor Supply suffers from red ink in the first quarter of each year. Unseasonable weather is also a negative, including too much rain, not enough rain, and early or late frosts. On the plus side, the company's broad geographic reach tends to mitigate these seasonal factors.
- The company does not pay a dividend. In a weak market, non-dividend-paying stocks often perform worse than the market. On the other hand, in a strong market, such stocks tend to act better than the market.

Reasons to Buy

- In order to further lessen the impact of foul weather in one or more regions of the country, the company has been steadily adding more stores and tapping new states. In the 1994–2001 period, the company opened 177 new stores and relocated fifteen.

In another move, the company purchased certain assets from its largest competitor, Quality Stores, Inc., following the bankruptcy of that company in 2002. Tractor Supply acquired the property of twenty-four stores and the lease rights to seventy-six stores, for about $35 million. Also included was the furniture and fixtures from 100 Quality Stores.

- The company had one of its best years in 2002, with net sales up 42.4 percent. What's more, same-store sales for the full year increased 9.6 percent, and gross margin improved 140 basis points (or 1.4 percent), to 28.3 percent. Net income increased 40.5 percent.

Commenting on these results, CEO Joe Scarlett said, "We have just concluded an outstanding year for Tractor Supply Company, and this is particularly gratifying as the exceptional performance was in the midst of one of the most challenging market environments in recent memory. Despite the difficult external conditions, throughout the fourth-quarter sales at both new and existing stores remained above plan due to strong sales at our differentiated product offering. We continue to supply the strong demand for basic maintenance needs to our target customers, and the team's execution of our business strategy has been extraordinary."

Mr. Scarlett went on to say, "We have made tremendous strides improving management of our inventory. We operated the entire year with a minimum of 97 percent in-stock rate at stores on the 450 'driver items.' At the same time, average inventory per store during the year declined 3 percent. Our merchandising initiatives have generated the additional gross margins we planned, and the lower inventory has reduced our borrowings and related interest expense.

"In addition, last year we successfully opened 113 new stores, including two in the fourth quarter. Our consistently strong results demonstrate the strength of our market niche as well as the growing recognition and popularity of our unique retail concept, extensive, and distinctive merchandise selection, and premier customer service."

■ "Based on consistently improving operational results, we have grown increasingly positive about TSCO's outlook," said Markos N. Kaminis, an analyst with *Standard & Poor's Stock Reports*, in January 2003. "Efforts to strengthen operations are achieving success; same-store sales grew 9.6 percent in 2002.

"The company originally targeted twenty-five new openings for 2002, but added a total of 112 stores, including the Quality Stores acquisition. For 2003, TSCO is targeting twenty-five new locations, with 8 percent to 10 percent unit growth to follow, including eventual expansion west of the Rocky Mountains. Growth in 2002 posed a threat of straining management resources, but management's continued solid execution has earned our confidence."

■ At the end of 2002, Tractor Supply announced that it would break ground on a new 305,000-square-foot Waco Distribution Center in January 2003. The new

Texas center will have a workforce of 170 within thirty-six months. "We're delighted to make this announcement during a year of extraordinary growth for our company," said Mr. Scarlett. "We're experienced a lot of success in this region, and we believe Waco is the ideal site for our new distribution center." The new center in Waco, Texas, replaces one less than one-third its size, a 100,000-square-foot facility.

The new center is scheduled to open in late summer of 2003, said Mr. Scarlett. The company's other distribution facilities are situated in Pendleton, Indiana; Omaha, Nebraska; and Rural Hall, North Carolina.

■ Tractor Supply has an outstanding record of growth. In the 1993–2002 period, earnings per share advanced from $.50 to $1.97, a compound annual growth rate of 16.5 percent. During those years, EPS declined twice (from $1.01 in 1999 to $.94 in 2000, and from $.75 in 1996 to $.62 the following year).

■ Tractor Supply has a solid balance sheet, with only a modest of amount of long-term debt. This balance sheet strength makes it easier for the company to finance acquisitions, since it has good borrowing power.

Total assets: $458 million
Current ratio: 1.76
Common shares outstanding: 18 million
Return on 2002 shareholders' equity: 19.0%

	2002	2001	2000	1999	1998	1997	1996	1995
Revenues (millions)	1,210	850	759	688	601	509	449	384
Net income (millions)	38.8	25.8	16.4	17.9	14.8	11.8	13.2	12.5
Earnings per share	1.97	1.43	.94	1.01	.84	.62	.75	.70
Dividends per share	Nil	—	—	—	—	—	—	—
Price High	45.5	17.5	11.0	15.2	13.5	11.0	13.7	12.2
Low	16.8	4.25	3.2	6.4	6.7	6.9	9.8	7.3

UnitedHealth Group, Inc.

9900 Bren Road East □ Minneapolis, Minnesota 55343 □ Listed: NYSE □ (952) 936-7265 □ Dividend reinvestment plan is not available □ Web site: www.unitedhealthgroup.com □ Ticker symbol: UNH □ S&P rating: A □ Value Line financial strength rating: A

In 2002, UnitedHealth acquired Ameri-Choice, a health care benefits and services provider for Medicaid beneficiaries. The company said it plans to combine the Medicaid-services businesses of the companies into one unit "working exclusively with selected states to address the needs of their medically vulnerable populations under their Medicaid programs."

Wall Street analysts said the purchase is a sensible move for UnitedHealth, the nation's largest health insurer, because it provides a strong management team and infrastructure for what is already a $1 billion business. UnitedHealth had 655,000 Medicaid members in fifteen states at the time of the acquisition in mid-2002. Buying AmeriChoice boosted its membership to 1 million in seventeen states. AmeriChoice serves Medicaid beneficiaries in New York, New Jersey, and Pennsylvania.

Company Profile

UnitedHealth Group is a U.S. leader in health care management, providing a broad range of health care products and services, including health maintenance organizations (HMOs), point of service (POS) plans, preferred provider organizations (PPOs), and managed fee for service programs. It also offers managed behavioral health services, utilization management, workers' compensation, and disability management services, specialized provider networks, and third-party administration services. The following sections describe its four segments.

UnitedHealthcare coordinates network-based health and well-being services on behalf of local employers and consumers in six broad regional markets, including commercial, Medicare, and Medicaid products and services.

Ovations offers health and well-being services for Americans age fifty and older and their families, including Medicare supplement insurance, hospital indemnity coverage, and pharmacy services for members of the health insurance program of AARP. Ovations also provides health and well-being services for elderly, vulnerable, and chronically ill populations through Evercare.

Uniprise provides network-based health and well-being services, business-to-business infrastructure services, consumer connectivity and service, and technology support services for large employers and health plans.

Specialized Care Services offers a comprehensive array of specialized benefits, networks, services and resources to help consumers improve their health and well-being, including employee assistance/counseling programs, mental health/substance abuse services, solid organ transplant programs and related services, twenty-four-hour health and well-being information services and publications, dental benefits, vision care benefits, life, accident and critical illness benefits, and chiropractic, physical therapy, and complementary medicine benefits.

Ingenix serves providers, payers, employers, governments, and pharmaceutical companies, as well as medical device manufacturers, academic, and other research institutions through two divisions. Ingenix Health Intelligence offers business-to-business publications and data and software analytic products. Ingenix Pharmaceutical Services is a global drug development and marketing services organization offering clinical trial management services, consulting services, medical education, and epidemiological and economic research.

Time Line of Selected Highlights and Innovations

- 1974: Charter Med, Inc., is founded by a group of physicians and other health care professionals.
- 1977: United HealthCare Corporation is created and acquires Charter Med, Inc.
- 1979: United HealthCare Corporation introduces the first network-based health plan for seniors and participates in the earliest experiments with the possibilities of offering a private-market alternatives for Medicare.
- 1984: United HealthCare Corporation becomes a publicly traded company.
- 1989: William W. McGuire, M.D., assumes leadership of the company. Annual revenues are just over $400 million. Today they are over $26 billion.
- 1995: The company acquires The MetraHealth Companies, Inc., for $1.65 billion. MetraHealth is a privately held company that was formed by combining the group health-care operations of the Travelers Insurance Company and Metropolitan Life Insurance Company.
- 1996: The company patents artificial intelligence system AdjudiPro, which is entered into the permanent research collection of the Smithsonian Institution and awarded the CIO Enterprise Value Award.
- 1998: United HealthCare Corporation becomes known as UnitedHealth Group and launches a strategic realignment into independent but strategically linked business segments—UnitedHealthcare, Ovations, Uniprise, Specialized Care Services, and Ingenix.
- 1998: The first release of Clinical Profiles takes place. Clinical Profiles, pro-

duced by Ingenix, provides network physicians with data comparing their clinical practices to nationally accepted benchmarks for care.

- 2001: UnitedHealthcare uses Web-enabled technology to simplify and improve service for physicians, enabling them to check benefit eligibility for patients and submit and review claims. The company also launches a Web-based distribution portal to serve small business brokers.
- 2002: Ingenix continues to introduce new knowledge and information products—including Parallax i iCES and Galaxy clinical and financial insights and improve the quality of health care delivery and administration. (Parallax I iCES aggregates health data from multiple systems, enabling users to identify and analyze multifaceted benefit issues.)

Shortcomings to Bear in Mind

- During a nine-month period in 2002, several insiders, such as officers and board members, sold stock in the company. All told, there were fifteen sales and no purchases.

Reasons to Buy

- I'm not the only person who likes UnitedHealth Group. Here are some of their recent awards:
  - *Fortune* magazine (April 16, 2001) ranked UnitedHealth Group number 91 in the 2001 rankings of the 500 largest U.S. corporations, based on 2000 revenues. *Fortune* also ranked UnitedHealth Group number two in the health care industry (based on 2000 revenues).
  - UnitedHealth Group Chairman and CEO Bill McGuire was ranked number 26 on *Worth* magazine's Top 50 CEO list (May 2001). The magazine selected business leaders based on their foresight, judgment, and competitive edge.

- The company was ranked number 12 on *Barron's* 500 (April 23, 2001), a report card that grades company's overall performance for investors.
- *Fortune* magazine has ranked United-Health Group the first or second most admired health care company in America every year since 1995.
- For the second consecutive year, Care-Data, the health care division of J. D. Power and Associates (September 19, 2000), ranked UnitedHealthcare the number one–managed health care organization in a member satisfaction survey of leading national health plans.
- *Computerworld* magazine (June 4, 2001) listed UnitedHealth Group in its annual list of the 100 Best Places to Work in IT for the eighth consecutive year.

■ In the past ten years (1992–2002) earnings per share advanced sharply, from $0.21 to $2.13, a compound annual growth rate of 26.3 percent. The only exception was 1996, when earning fell from $0.53 to $0.44.

■ Since its inception, UnitedHealth Group and its affiliated companies have led the marketplace by introducing key innovations that make health care services more accessible and affordable for customers, improving the quality and coordination of health care services, and that help individuals and their physicians make more informed health care decisions.

■ "UNH shows strong, consistent performance and has a robust operating outlook," said Phillip M. Seligman, an analyst with *Standard & Poor's Stock Reports*, in January of 2003. "The Health Care Services unit continues to produce solid results. Rapid growth underway at most of the high-margin, fee-based non-health-care units provides a significant portion of earnings growth. The company bought back 22.3 million shares in 2002, and in light of healthy free cash flow, we would not be surprised if at least as many shares were repurchased in 2003."

■ In December of 2002, an analyst with *Value Line Investment Survey*, George Rho, also had some kind words to say, "We look for earnings to continue surging in 2003. Management recently indicated that overall revenues would approximate $29 billion, with all of the company's businesses contributing to organic growth of some 13 percent. It further suggested that per-share profits would rise by at least 20 percent, supported to incremental gains in operating margin and the continuation of an aggressive share-buyback program."

Total assets: $14,164 million
Current ratio: .62
Common shares outstanding: 304 million
Return on 2002 shareholders' equity: 32.5%

		2002	2001	2000	1999	1998	1997	1996	1995
Revenues (millions)		25,020	23,454	21,122	19,562	17,355	11,794	10,074	5,671
Net income (millions)		1,352	913	705	563	509	460	356	383
Earnings per share		2.13	1.40	1.05	.80	.66	.44	.53	.45
Dividends per share		.015	.015	.01	.01	.01	.01	.01	.01
Price	High	50.5	36.4	31.7	17.5	18.5	15.1	17.3	16.4
	Low	34.0	25.3	11.6	9.9	7.4	10.6	7.5	8.6

United Parcel Service, Inc.

55 Glenlake Parkway N. E. □ Atlanta, Georgia 30328 □ (404) 828-6977 □ Dividend reinvestment plan not available □ Web site: www.ups.com □ Listed: NYSE □ Ticker symbol: UPS □ S&P rating: Not rated □ Value Line financial strength rating: A+

United Parcel Service—popularly known as UPS—introduced UPS World Ease in early 2003. UPS World Ease combines the speed and tracking of express delivery with the efficiency and cost savings of consolidated customs clearance, a service that allows customers to ship multiple packages to many destinations in the same country as one consolidated shipment. This allows goods to move directly through customs as a single unit, reducing the need for warehousing, inventory, and shipping.

"This means that UPS's transportation network becomes a sort of 'in-transit warehouse' for us, eliminating our added expense of warehouse inventory," said Anil Agrawal, chief operating officer of EcoQuest International. Tennessee-based EcoQuest, a UPS customer that manufactures and markets air and water purification systems, already projects a world of difference using World Ease. "Because our shipments clear customs all at once, we can get our systems to international customers within days, instead of weeks. Adding World Ease will save at least $1 million in supply chain costs over the next five years."

UPS World Ease is a contract service that works through the UPS small-package network. Once the shipment clears customs, it is separated back into smaller shipments for final destination delivery throughout a country by UPS. UPS World Ease is available in sixty-one countries, in combination with delivery services UPS Worldwide Express, UPS Worldwide Expedited, and UPS Standard services.

Company Profile

United Parcel—known as Big Brown—is one of the largest employee-owned companies in the nation. With a fleet of 88,000 vehicles and 600 aircraft, UPS delivers 13.5 million packages and documents each day, or well over 3 billion a year.

The company's primary business is the delivery of packages and documents throughout the United States and to more than 200 other countries and territories. In addition, UPS provides logistic services, including comprehensive management of supply chains, for major companies worldwide.

United Parcel has built a strong brand equity by being a leader in quality service and product innovation in its industry. UPS has been rated the second-strongest business-to-business brand in the United States in a recent Image Power survey and has been *Fortune* magazine's Most Admired Transportation Company in the mail, package, and freight category for sixteen consecutive years.

UPS entered the international arena in 1975. It now handles more than 1.2 million international shipments each day. What's more, its international package-delivery service (14 percent of revenues) is growing faster than its domestic business, and this trend is likely to continue. The company is also moving to expand its presence in Asia. In 2001, the Department of Transportation awarded UPS the right to fly directly from the U.S. to China.

Non-package businesses, although only 8 percent of revenues, comprise the company's fastest-growing segment. These operations include UPS Logistics Group and UPS Capital Corporation. A truck-leasing business was sold in 2000. The logistics business provides global supply chain management, service parts logistics, and transportation and technology services. UPS Capital, launched in 1998, provides services to expedite the flow of funds through the supply chain.

The company has been active on the acquisition front. In 2001, for instance, UPS completed twelve acquisitions, the largest of which was Fritz Companies, a global freight-forwarding, customs brokerage, and logistics company. Another major purchase was Mail Boxes Etc., a franchiser of shipping centers.

The UPS shares sold in late 1999 represent about 10 percent of the company's total ownership. The rest is still owned by about 125,000 of its managers, supervisors, hourly workers, retirees, foundations, and descendants of the company's early leaders. The company sold only Class B shares to the public. Each share has one vote, compared with the Class A stock, which has ten votes per share.

Shortcomings to Bear in Mind

- UPS is being affected by "continued sluggishness in the domestic economy, as well as slower-than-expected recovery of business that was lost to competitors in May and June (2002), the time UPS and the Teamsters were negotiating a new labor contract," said Deborah Y. Fung, an analyst with *Value Line Investment Survey*, in a report issued in December 2002. "About half of the customers that had diverted freight during this period have come back to UPS, but, we believe that the remaining 50 percent will be harder to win back, since they are larger customers who are less likely to make major changes in their supply chain."

Reasons to Buy

- At the end of 2002, the company's business had improved, particularly overseas, according to Scott Davis, the company's chief financial officer. On January 28, 2003, he said, "While we have not seen signs of an economic rebound in the United States, our international business is showing strong growth, and our non-package initiatives are paying off. Within the U.S., the holiday peak season started slowly and then surged at the end, providing a test that our new UPS Worldport air hub passed with flying colors.

  "On the international front, the fourth quarter was our second consecutive record quarter. Our expanded network in Asia, coupled with increased service through more than 100 additional Asian flights during the West Coast dock disruption, contributed substantially. In addition, the European export market continued to demonstrate significant double-digit growth."

  Mr. Davis went on to say, "In the United States, the timing of the economic recovery is definitely the biggest unknown. Outside the U.S., we expect to see continued strong export growth, particularly in Asia and Europe, and an increase in international profitability of 20 percent or more."

- The company's former CEO, James P. Kelly, has repositioned the UPS delivery folks as foot soldiers of the dot-com revolution. "We're a ninety-two-year-old company that's reinvented itself several times, and we're doing it again," he said. Kelly has lived through many of these reinventions since he started as a UPS relief driver for the 1963 holiday season. Working his way through night school at Rutgers University, Kelly decided to become a full-time driver when he realized it paid double what he was making as an accountant. From there, he climbed up the management ladder, handling labor relations and other divisions before becoming CEO in 1997.

The recast United Parcel is more than just a cargo hauler. Kelly has organized the company to manage an array of logistics systems for its dot-com customers, from managing inventory to performing customer service functions. Some six years ago, Kelly saw the power of the Internet as a sales channel and made it a key focus. Kelly's big bets are paying off. Already UPS handles 55 percent of all Internet purchases. By contrast, the U.S. Postal Service accounts for 32 percent, with 10 percent left for Federal Express.

- At the end of January 2003, the company's UPS Supply Chain Solutions operation announced that its ocean freight forwarding unit, UPS Ocean Freight Services, had received certification from the United States Customs Service to submit advance cargo manifest information via the Automated Manifest System (AMS).

    "By providing Customs with the appropriate information, we ensure our customers that their shipments won't face penalties, unnecessary delays, and disruption to their supply chain," said Michael Gargaro, vice president, UPS Supply Chain Solutions, ocean freight services. "Indeed, we actually streamline the process because we can file manifest information directly to Customs instead of going through ocean carriers."

    UPS Supply Chain Solutions, a unit of UPS, provides distribution and logistics, international trade, transportation, and freight services.

- The company acquired Fritz Companies, Inc., in 2001. Fritz is one of the world's leading freight-forwarding, customs-brokerage, and logistics concerns, with $1.6 billion in gross revenues in the most recent fiscal year. The company owns and operates 400 facilities in more than 120 countries.

    "This acquisition enhances UPS's strategy by providing comprehensive solutions across the supply chain at any point our customers desire, moving goods of any size, by any mode, anywhere in the world," said Joe Pyne, UPS's senior vice president for corporate development. "This expands our flexibility to offer a broader portfolio of services including air, ground, and ocean freight, to our global customer base."

- UPS has had its share of honors and awards. In the fall of 2002, for instance, *Frontline Solutions* magazine named UPS the category leader for Logistics in its *Frontline Solutions* Top 25.

    UPS was also named best logistics company in *Global Finance* magazine's "World's Best Companies."

    In August of 2002, UPS was named "Corporation of the Year" by the Georgia Minority Supplier Development Council, Georgia's leading organization dedicated to expanding business opportunities between corporations and minority-owned companies. *World Trade* magazine ranked UPS Freight Services as the number one Best Freight Forwarder in August 2002.

- UPS obtains the vast majority of its revenue from small-package deliveries here at home. On the other hand, overseas shipments, finance and supply-chain management are growing at a fast clip— and that's where the company believes its future is headed.

Total assets: $25,442 million
Current ratio: 1.35
Common shares outstanding: 1,117 million
Return on 2002 shareholders' equity: 31.8%

	2002	2001	2000	1999	1998	1997	1996	1995
Revenues (millions)	31,272	30,321	29,771	27,052	24,788	22,458	*	
Net income (millions)	3,254	2,425	2,795	2,325	1,741	909		
Earnings per share	2.84	2.10	2.38	2.04	1.57			
Dividends per share	.76	.76	.68	.58	.43			
Price High	67.1	62.5	69.8	76.9				
Low	54.3	46.2	49.5	61.0				

* United Parcel was a private company prior to 1999, and thus no additional statistics are available.

CONSERVATIVE GROWTH

United Technologies Corporation

One Financial Plaza ▫ Hartford, Connecticut 06103 ▫ (860) 728-7575 ▫ Listed: NYSE ▫ Dividend reinvestment plan is available: (800) 519-3111 ▫ Web site: www.utc.com ▫ Listed: NYSE ▫ Ticker symbol: UTX ▫ S&P rating: A- ▫ Value Line Financial Strength A++

The Comanche is a new helicopter under development for the U.S. Army by the Boeing-Sikorsky team. This sophisticated piece of hardware will more accurately and effectively relay critical information from the battlefield to the command center than any other system in place today. Sikorsky is part of United Technologies' Flight Systems, one of the company's four segments.

While it has the ability to carry out light attack missions, the Comanche will mainly serve as a reconnaissance aircraft that will coordinate the many aircraft and ground forces involved in a combat mission. For this reason the U.S. Army has called the Comanche critical to the twenty-first-century Objective Force.

The Comanche is designed, manufactured, and tested by the Boeing-Sikorsky team, with help from over fifteen leading aerospace manufacturers. In addition to Sikorsky, another one of United Technologies' subsidiaries, Hamilton Sundstrand, will provide the electrical power generating system and the environmental control system for the Comanche.

The battlefield of the twenty-first century will be almost entirely digitalized. As such, the Comanche, which carries highly advanced electronic equipment, will be essential for receiving and processing intelligence and sending it on to other assets. This aircraft can visually detect and classify targets seven times quicker than any other U.S. Army surveillance device today, and it can hand off precise coordinates to shooters within seconds. What's more, it can operate at any time of the day and in all weather conditions. The Comanche has been undergoing rigorous testing for almost ten years. Initial deployment is scheduled for the end of the decade.

Company Profile

United Technologies provides high-technology products to the aerospace and building systems industries throughout the world. Its companies are industry leaders and include Pratt & Whitney, Carrier, Otis, Sikorsky, International Fuel Cells, and Hamilton Sundstrand. Sikorsky and Hamilton Sundstrand make up the Flight Systems segment.

Pratt & Whitney

Products and services include large and small commercial and military jet engines, spare parts and product support, specialized engine maintenance and overhaul and repair services for airlines, air forces and corporate fleets; rocket engines and space propulsion systems; and industrial gas turbines.

In 2002, Pratt & Whitney's revenues were essentially unchanged from the previous year, at $7,645 million. Similarly, operating profits slipped only slightly, at $1,282 million.

Primary customers include commercial airlines and aircraft-leasing companies; commercial and corporate aircraft manufacturers; the U.S. government, including NASA and the military services; and regional and commuter airlines.

Carrier

Products and services include heating, ventilating, and air conditioning (HVAC) equipment for commercial, industrial, and residential buildings; HVAC replacement parts and services; building controls; commercial, industrial and transport refrigeration equipment.

Carrier emphasizes energy-efficient, quiet operation and environmental stewardship in its new residential and commercial products. The new WeatherMaker residential air conditioner using Puron, a non-ozone-depleting refrigerant, provides the domestic market with low operating costs and sound levels—about the same as a refrigerator's. The Puron unit gives Carrier a healthy lead over competitors, as chlorine-free refrigerants become the standard.

In 2002, Carrier's revenues slipped a modest 1.4 percent, to $8,773 million. Operating profit, however, advanced 32 percent, to $779 million.

Primary customers include mechanical and building contractors; homeowners, building owners, developers and retailers;

architects and building consultants; transportation and refrigeration companies; and shipping operations.

Otis

Products and services include elevators, escalators, moving walks and shuttle systems, and related installation, maintenance, and repair services; and modernization products and service for elevators and escalators.

In 2002, Otis revenues advanced 7.5 percent, to $6,811 million. Similarly, operating profit surged 24.8 percent, to $1.057 million.

Primary customers include mechanical and building contractors; building owners and developers; home owners; architects and building consultants.

Flight Systems

Products and services include aircraft electrical and power distribution systems; engine and flight controls; propulsion systems; environmental controls for aircraft, spacecraft, and submarines; auxiliary power units; space life-support systems; industrial products including mechanical power transmissions, compressors, metering devices, and fluid-handling equipment; military and commercial helicopters, spare parts, civil helicopter operations; and maintenance services for helicopters and fixed-wing aircraft.

In 2002, Flight Systems rose 5.3 percent, to $5,571 million. Operating profit rose from $670 million to $741 million, an increase of 10.6 percent.

Primary customers include the U.S. government, including NASA, FAA, and the military services; non-U.S. governments; aerospace and defense prime contractors; commercial airlines; aircraft and jet engine manufacturers; oil and gas exploration companies; mining and water companies; construction companies; hospitals and charters.

Shortcomings to Bear in Mind

- Robert E. Friedman, CPA, an analyst writing for *Standard & Poor's Stock Reports*, had some negative comments in the fall of 2002. "Big cuts expected in Boeing and Airbus commercial aircraft production could materially reduce near-term demand for UTX's Pratt & Whitney jet engines. Softening construction spending should cool demand for Carrier air conditioners and Otis Elevators."

- Brett Nelson, writing for *Forbes* magazine on March 3, 2003, had this negative comment: "Until the next Honeywell comes along, David [CEO George David] is pushing his engineers to pry open new markets. Problem is, David is a bit of a cheapskate on R&D spending, preferring instead to use excess cash to make acquisitions, buy back UTC stock or boost the dividend. Last year, aerospace companies spent an average 6 percent of revenues on R&D, according to *R&D* magazine. UTC spent 4.2 percent—down from 5.4 percent in 1999."

  On a more positive note, "'It's a bit of a concern that R&D has come down,' says Thomas Leritz, capital goods analyst at Bank of America. (UTC's research budget, however, was boosted by an extra $1.2 billion from government grants.)"

Reasons to Buy

- Through internal growth and acquisition, Carrier's commercial refrigeration business has become a leader in the highly fragmented $17-billion global industry. Carrier's acquisition of Electrolux Commercial Refrigeration will broaden its offerings to supermarkets, convenience stores, and food and beverage markets, particularly in Europe. A new transport refrigeration unit, the Vector, can cool a trailer from 30 to minus 20 degrees Celsius twice as fast as a conventional unit can.

- In 2002, Hawaiian Airlines signed a twenty-year agreement with Pratt & Whitney to provide a fleet-management program for the airline's PW4060-powered 767-300ER aircraft. The agreement covers thirty-six engines and has an estimated value of $325 million.

  The full-scale overhaul and maintenance work will be performed at Pratt & Whitney's Cheshire Engine Center in Connecticut. The center is currently capable of overhauling JT9D, PW2000, PW4000, F117, and V2500 engine models. Pratt & Whitney Aftermarket Services offers overhaul and repair services at nearly thirty locations around the world.

- Pratt & Whitney scored a major coup by being chosen by the Pentagon as the lead engine supplier on both versions of the Joint Strike Fighter, as well as the F-22 fighter, two of the military's highest-profile new programs. Pratt is also tapping into markets it once chose to leave to others, aggressively seeking commercial-engine overhaul and maintenance business that could be valued at more than $1 billion a year. What's more, the company also has seized on an opportunity provided by the nation's power woes: It expects to sell fifty-four modified JT8D engines for industrial electric generation for major power companies in need of cheap and quickly obtainable electric power.

- United Technologies ranks as the "most admired" company in its industry in both the United States and the world, according to separate lists published by *Fortune* magazine in March 2002. This is the second straight year that United Technologies was named the most admired U.S. aerospace/defense company and the first time it was named the most admired in the world in that category.

- Otis Elevator Company won the contract to supply elevators and escalators for

Beijing's biggest public transit project, a new facility under construction in preparation for the Olympic Summer Games in Beijing in 2008. Otis will supply and install eleven elevators and thirty-eight escalators for the Transit Center.

- In the fall of 2002, Sears, Roebuck selected a unit of Carrier to be the exclusive original equipment manufacturer of Kenmore brand residential, central heating, and cooling equipment. Kenmore, which has been on the scene for seventy-five years, is America's most popular brand of appliances, used in one out of every two homes today.

- George David, chairman and CEO of United Technologies, was named 2002 CEO of the Year by IndustryWeek magazine in its January 2003 issue. A cover story, entitled "UTC's Master of Principle," outlined the "disciplined management style" of David, who "thrives on competition, winning and the rule of reason." IndustryWeek applauded David and United Technologies for delivering solid financial results in 2002, despite a downturn in the aerospace business and a slow recovery in the broader economy from the 2001 recession.

Total assets: $29.1 billion
Current ratio: 1.49
Return on 2002 equity: 26.8%
Common shares outstanding: 473 million

		2002	2001	2000	1999	1998	1997	1996	1995
Revenues (millions)		28,212	27,897	26,583	24,127	25,715	24,713	23,512	22,802
Net income (millions)		2,236	1,938	1,808	841	1,255	1,072	906	750
Earnings per share		4.42	3.83	3.55	1.65	2.53	2.11	1.73	1.43
Dividends per share		.96	.90	.83	.76	.70	.62	.55	.52
Price	High	77.8	87.5	79.8	78.0	56.2	44.5	35.2	24.5
	Low	48.8	40.1	46.5	51.6	33.5	32.6	22.7	15.6

AGGRESSIVE GROWTH

Varian Medical Systems, Inc.

3100 Hansen Way, M/S E290 □ Palo Alto, California 94304-1038 □ (650) 424-5782 □ Dividend reinvestment plan not available □ Web site: www.varian.com □ Fiscal years end on Friday nearest September 30 □ Ticker symbol: VAR □ Listed: NYSE □ S&P rating: B+ □ Value Line financial strength rating: B++

In fiscal 2003, Varian Medical Systems, the leading maker of integrated cancer-care systems, announced that it had received clearance from the U.S. Food and Drug Administration (FDA) for Acuity, a new medical imaging product that for the first time integrates planning, simulation, and verification software for treating cancer with radiation therapy.

The new product is intended to accelerate adoption of IMRT (intensity modulated radiation therapy), an advanced technique for treating cancer. It is uniquely designed to support ultra-precise radiotherapy by dynamically tracking tumor motion during the simulation and verification process.

According to Tim Guertin, president of Varian's Oncology Systems business, Acuity "will make the implementation of modern radiation therapy treatments simpler, cheaper, and faster for cancer treatment centers. It will improve both the efficiency and efficacy of advanced and routine treatments, and will allow clinics to treat more patients in less time."

Company Profile

Varian Medical Systems is the world's leading manufacturer of integrated radiotherapy systems for treating cancer and other diseases; it is also a leading supplier of x-ray tubes for imaging in medical, scientific, and industrial applications. Established in 1948, the company has manufacturing sites in North America and Europe and forty sales and support offices worldwide.

In 1999, the company (formerly Varian Associates, Inc.) reorganized itself into three separate publicly traded companies by spinning off two of its businesses to stockholders via a tax-free distribution.

Since then, the company has significantly broadened its product and business offerings, acquired new businesses, and set records for sales and net orders. More importantly, Varian put itself at the forefront of a radiotherapy revolution that is making a dramatic difference in the struggle against cancer.

About three out of every ten people will be afflicted with some form of cancer. The good news is that their chances of surviving, of beating cancer, have greatly improved, thanks to recent advances in radiation therapy—many of which have been led by Varian Medical Systems.

The company has three segments.

Varian Oncology Systems

Varian Oncology Systems is the world's leading supplier of radiotherapy systems for treating cancer. Its integrated medical systems include linear accelerators and accessories, as well as a broad range of interconnected software tools for planning and delivering the sophisticated radiation treatments available to cancer patients. Thousands of patients all over the world are treated daily on Varian systems. Oncology Systems works closely with health care professionals in community clinics, hospitals, and universities to improve cancer outcomes. The business unit also supplies linear accelerators for industrial inspection applications.

Varian X-Ray Products

Varian X-Ray Products is the world's premier independent supplier of x-ray tubes, serving manufacturers of radiology equipment and industrial inspection equipment, as well as distributors of replacement tubes. This business provides the industry's broadest selection of x-ray tubes expressly designed for the most advanced diagnostic applications, including CT scanning, radiography, and mammography. These products meet evolving requirements for improved resolution, faster patient throughput, longer tube life, smaller dimensions, and greater cost efficiency. X-Ray Products also supplies a new line of amorphous silicon flat-panel x-ray detectors for medical and industrial applications.

Ginzton Technology Center

The Ginzton Technology Center acts as Varian Medical Systems' research and development facility for breakthrough technologies and operates a growing brachytherapy business for the delivery of internal radiation to treat cancer and cardiovascular disease. In addition to brachytherapy, current efforts are focused on next-generation imaging systems and advanced targeting technologies for radiotherapy. The center is also investigating the combination of radiotherapy with other treatment modalities, such as bioengineered gene delivery systems.

Shortcomings to Bear in Mind

- Investors are well aware that Varian Medical has a bright future—they have pushed the price-earnings ratio of Varian to lofty levels. You might want to wait for a sinking spell before you buy shares in this strong growth company.

Reasons to Buy

■ In the year 2002, more than 6 million people worldwide succumbed to cancer. Nearly twice as many others were diagnosed with the disease. In some countries, cancer is a leading cause of death among children. Mostly though, it is a disease primarily of aging, with people fifty-five or older—the "baby boomers"—now accounting for nearly 80 percent of diagnosed cases. In the United States, the chances that you'll eventually develop cancer are one in three if you are female, one in two if you are male. In a very real sense, cancer victimizes not only patients, but also their families and friends, colleagues and neighbors. Ultimately, the disease affects us all. The social and economic costs are staggering.

The fact is that half of U.S. patients receive radiotherapy as part of their treatment. Now, thanks to the new technology that Varian Medical Systems has helped to develop, radiotherapy is poised to play an even stronger role in cancer treatment, and many more patients could be cured by it. It's technology that is being implemented in all corners of the world.

■ With certain cancers, the odds of surviving are improving markedly, thanks to the growing use of a radiotherapy advance called intensity modulated radiation therapy, or IMRT. IMRT is being used to treat head and neck, breast, prostate, pancreatic, lung, liver, and central nervous system cancers. IMRT makes it possible for a larger and more effective dose of radiation to be delivered directly to the tumor, greatly sparing surrounding, healthy tissues. This is expected to result in a higher likelihood of cure with lower complication rates.

The clinical outcomes using IMRT are extremely promising. A study of early-stage prostate cancer has shown that the higher radiation doses possible with IMRT have the potential to double the rate of tumor control to more than 95 percent. Using IMRT, clinicians were able to deliver high doses while reducing the rate of normal tissue complications from 10 percent to 2 percent. Similar results have been reported by doctors using IMRT to treat cancers of the head and neck.

Varian Medical Systems has joined forces with GE Medical Systems to combine the latest in diagnostic imaging results with advanced radiotherapy technologies in what are called See & Treat Cancer Care imaging and treatment tools. This approach enables physicians to see the distribution of malignant cells more clearly and treat them more effectively with precisely targeted radiation doses using IMRT.

■ Varian Medical Systems has long been the world's leading supplier of radiotherapy equipment. Now, the company's SmartBeam IMRT system, the culmination of twelve years and $300 million of development effort, is already making a difference for thousands of patients.

Today, a little more than 500 of the world's 5,700 radiotherapy centers for cancer treatment have acquired a set of integrated tools for SmartBeam IMRT from Varian Medical Systems.

Almost one-fifth of them are now offering it to their patients, and many others are close behind.

In addition to promising outcomes and public demand for better care, new Medicare and Medicaid reimbursement rates are expected to help accelerate the rapid adoption of IMRT by both hospitals and freestanding cancer centers in the United States. In international markets, public health systems are under pressure to reduce patients' waiting periods by updating systems with more effective treatment technology that can treat more patients.

In a report issued by *Standard & Poor's Stock Reports* in late 2002, Robert M. Gold said, "IMRT is rapidly emerging as the new standard of care, enabling the delivery of higher, and thus more potent, doses of radiation to target tumors, while concurrently reducing the amount of radiation absorbed by surrounding normal healthy tissue. Gross margins are seen at 39 percent, and we see room for some operating margin growth."

Total assets: $910 million
Current ratio: 1.82
Common shares outstanding: 68 million
Return on 2002 shareholders' equity: 20.3%

	2002	2001	2000	1999	1998	1997	1996	1995
Revenues (millions)	873	774	690	590	1,422	1,426	1,599	1,576
Net income (millions)	94	68	53	8	74	82	122	106
Earnings per share	1.33	1.05	.82	.14	1.22	1.83	1.91	1.51
Dividends per share	Nil	Nil	Nil	.05	.20	.18	.15	.17
Price High	51.7	38.6	35.5	21.5	29.2	33.5	31.4	28.7
Low	31.6	27.0	14.2	8.1	15.8	22.9	20.3	17.3

AGGRESSIVE GROWTH

Walgreen Company

200 Wilmot Road □ Mailstop #2261 □ Deerfield, Illinois 60015 □ (847) 914-2972 □ Direct dividend reinvestment program is available (888) 290-7264 □ Fiscal years end August 31 □ Web site: www.walgreens.com □ Listed: NYSE □ Ticker symbol: WAG □ S&P rating: A+ □ Value Line financial strength rating: A+

"We're the only major drugstore chain expanding its store base," said Dan Jorndt, chairman of Walgreens. The company is expanding its store base faster than its top three competitors combined. In 2002, Walgreens opened 363 new stores (including store closings and relocations), as contrasted with a net loss of 276 stores for the next three largest chains combined.

What's more, Walgreens' growth plans for fiscal 2003 remain on schedule, with the company opening more than 450 new units (for a net increase after closings and relocations of about 360 stores), adding more than 10,000 new jobs and budgeting $1 billion in capital investments.

The company's expansion emphasizes the southern half of the country. "We'll concentrate our heaviest growth in Florida, Texas, California, Nevada, and Georgia, where demographics and growing popula-tions provide the most opportunity," said CEO David Bernauer. Under the company's current expansion plans, Walgreens will operate more than 7,000 stores by 2010—up from 3,883 at the end of fiscal 2002.

Since 1991, prescriptions filled in the United States have increased more than 50 percent. Even so, the number of pharmacies has declined by nearly 2,000. During those same years, Walgreens increased its store base by more than 2,200 (or 136 percent) and its yearly prescription volume by more than 250 million (or 228 percent).

Company Profile

Walgreens, one of the fastest-growing retailers in the United States, leads the chain drugstore industry in sales and profits. Sales for 2002 reached $28.7 billion, produced by 3,883 stores in forty-three states and Puerto Rico.

Founded in 1901, Walgreens today has 130,000 employees. The company's drugstores serve more than 3 million customers daily and average $6.8 million in annual sales per unit. That's $628 per square foot, among the highest in the industry. Walgreens has paid dividends in every quarter since 1933 and has raised the dividend in each of the past twenty-five years.

Stand-Alone Stores

Competition from the supermarkets has convinced Walgreens that the best strategy is to build stand-alone stores. Since the rise of managed care, many pharmacy customers now make only minimal copayments for prescriptions. That leaves convenience as the major factor in choosing a pharmacy. The freestanding format makes room for drive-thru windows, which provide a speedy way for drugstore customers to pick up or drop off prescriptions.

On the other hand, the company's stand-alone strategy is more expensive. Walgreen insists on building its units on corner lots near an intersection with a traffic light. Such leases normally cost more than a site in a strip mall.

More Than a Pharmacy

Home meal replacement has become a $100-billion business industry-wide. In the company's food section, Walgreens carries staples as well as frozen dinners, desserts, and pizzas. In some stores, expanded food sections carry such items as fruit and ready-to-eat salads.

In the photo department, the company builds loyalty through a wide selection of products and the service of trained technicians. Walgreens experimented with one-hour photo service as early as 1982, but it was in the mid-1990s before, according to CEO Dan Jorndt, "We really figured it out." Since 1998, one-hour processing has been available chain-wide, made profitable by "our high volume of business. We've introduced several digital photo products that are selling well and are evaluating the long-term impact of digital on the mass market."

Shortcomings to Bear in Mind

- Often, Walgreen chooses a freestanding location on the site of an existing strip center—for instance, a piece of the mall parking lot. For the property's owners, this usually means an opportunity to charge more for the stand-alone space while renting out the old strip center space. Increasingly, however, supermarkets and other big retailers are starting to put exclusionary provisions in their leases, prohibiting a drugstore from occupying freestanding space on shopping center properties they anchor. Walgreen management says it has encountered such provisions but insists that they aren't yet "a real problem."

- Although the company is still outperforming most of corporate America, there is some concern over its prescription departments, which contribute the bulk of company sales and profits. In several states, Medicaid health insurance programs for the poor are cutting what they pay pharmacists to dispense drugs. Private insurers as well are slashing what they pay pharmacists and drugstore chains as a way to cut rapidly rising health care costs. Walgreens executives, however, have a plan to deal with such pressures. "Our goal is to offset any margin declines by lowering selling, general, and administration expenses at a faster rate," said Rick Hans, the company's finance director.

- The stock has performed so well in recent years that its P/E multiple is well above average, sometimes as high as 35 times earnings.

Reasons to Buy

- Favorable demographics include 77 million aging baby boomers (forty-five to sixty-four years old) and their estimated increased usage. For instance, the typical forty-year-old takes six-plus prescriptions annually; at age fifty, the number goes up to eight; at sixty, the annual rate is eleven; and at seventy, the number of prescriptions reaches fifteen.

- Some investors are concerned that the company is diluting sales by putting stores so close together, and just cannibalizing itself. To that concern, Mr. Bernauer replied, "I haven't gone to a party in two years where that question hasn't come up. The answer is yes—when we open a store very near another one, the old store usually sees a drop in sales. But in virtually every case, it builds back to its original volume and beyond. Here's the scenario: As you add stores, overall sales in the market increase, while expenses are spread over a larger base. Bottom line, profitability increases. Our most profitable markets are the ones where we've built the strongest market share."

- Investors are also wondering about e-commerce. They ask, "Is there a long-term future?" To this concern, Mr. Bernauer said, "Though there's a lot of carnage on the early e-commerce road, we definitely see a future for Walgreens.com. That's not, however, in delivered-to-your-door merchandise. Frankly, we never thought there would be a big demand for prescriptions by mail, and we were correct—well over 90 percent of prescription orders placed through our Web site are for store pickup. It's not convenient, when you need a prescription or a few drugstore items to wait three days for it to show up.

  "What does excite us is using the Internet to provide better service and information. We're already communicating by e-mail with nearly 20,000 prescription customers per day."

- The company's new pharmacy system, Intercom Plus, is now up and running in all Walgreens stores across the country. This system—costing over $150 million—has raised Walgreens service and productivity to a new level. While providing increased patient access to Walgreen's pharmacists, it also substantially raises the number of prescriptions each store can efficiently dispense.

- Walgreen's management is heartened by the increase in prescription usage in the United States, due to the dramatic aging of the population. Between 1995 and 2005, the number of people aged fifty-five or older in the United States will grow at a compound rate of 3.8 percent—double the rate of the rest of the population. The good news for Walgreens is that these graying Americans need twice as many prescriptions per year as the rest of the population.

- A high number of drugs are coming off patent over the next few years, which means more generic drugs will come to market and will become a bigger percentage of prescriptions. To be sure, generics have a much lower price, but the drug store can add on a bigger profit.

- Food departments are another example. Recently, a major grocery chain cited drugstores as a reason behind disappointing sales gains: "Fill-in shopping needs," said the grocery CEO, "are increasingly being satisfied in convenience and drug stores." Walgreens, with its highly convenient, on-the-way-home locations, is on the receiving end of this trend.

- According to the company's annual report, "As baby boomers retire, they'll migrate to states like Arizona, Florida, Georgia, Texas, and the Carolinas. Walgreens will be ready for them. At the end of 2002, we'll have 1,617 stores in the Sunbelt, with plans for continued expansion. And as the number of people sixty-five years and older skyrockets, dollars spent on prescriptions will also swell—rising almost 40 percent by 2006. Just since 1996, prescriptions have jumped from 45 percent of Walgreens total sales to nearly 58 percent.

"But the challenge for everyone in the business is the number of pharmacists, which will increase only 5.4 percent in the same time period. That means that by 2006 our pharmacists will be filling 40 percent more prescriptions than they do today.

"To handle this jump, we'll continue to improve our technology, training systems, and physical work environments, already recognized as superior within the industry. By being more efficient, we plan to increase the average number of

prescriptions filled per store from 300 to more than 400 per day in the next five years.

"Other boosts to the prescription business are the influx of new drugs and the generic availability of highly prescribed drugs like Prozac. As branded drugs go generic, prices for customers are lowered significantly, and both managed-care companies and retailers benefit as well."

- With stores in forty-three states and Puerto Rico, Walgreens has a base of customers that covers more of the United States than any other drugstore chain. The company's national coverage is a major advantage in negotiations with managed-care pharmacy companies.

Total assets: $9,456 million
Current ratio: 1.73
Common shares outstanding: 1,024 million
Return on 2002 shareholders' equity: 16.5%

		2002	2001	2000	1999	1998	1997	1996	1995
Revenues (millions)		28,681	24,623	21,207	17,839	15,307	13,363	11,778	10,395
Net income (millions)		1,019	886	756	624	514	436	372	321
Earnings per share		.99	.86	.74	.62	.51	.44	.38	.33
Dividends per share		.15	.14	.14	.13	.13	.12	.11	.10
Price	High	40.7	45.3	45.8	33.9	30.2	16.8	10.9	7.8
	Low	27.7	28.7	22.1	22.7	14.8	9.6	7.3	5.4

AGGRESSIVE GROWTH

Wal-Mart Stores, Inc.

702 Southwest Eighth Street □ Post Office Box 116 □ Bentonville, Arkansas 72716-8611 □ (479) 273-8446 □ Direct dividend reinvestment plan is available: (800) 438-6278 □ Web site: www.wal-mart.com □ Listed: NYSE □ Fiscal years end January 31 □ Ticker symbol: WMT □ S&P rating: A+ □ Value Line financial strength rating: A++

Wal-Mart did not appear to be a corporate colossus in 1962. That was the year that Sam Walton opened his first store in Rogers, Arkansas, with a sign saying "Wal-Mart Discount City. We sell for less." In the decades since, Wal-Mart has evolved into a $244-billion-a-year empire by selling—at a discount, of course—prodigious quantities of all manner of items, from clothing, food, hardware, and eye glasses to Kleenex, tooth brushes, pots and pans, and pharmaceuticals.

An essential key to Wal-Mart's success, says H. Lee Scott, Jr., the company's CEO, is "driving unnecessary costs out of businesses."

To keep prices at rock bottom, the company insists that its 65,000 suppliers become leaner machines that examine every farthing they spend. This ruthless drive to whittle away fat has clearly reshaped the practices of businesses that deal with Wal-Mart, as well as those that compete against them. Wal-Mart's strategies for holding costs in check—the use of cutting-edge technology, innovative logistics, reliance on imported goods, and a nonunion work force—are becoming industry standards.

Company Profile

Wal-Mart is the world's number one retailer—larger than Sears, Kmart, and J. C. Penney combined. The company operates nearly 3,500 facilities in the United States and more than 1,100 units in the following countries: Mexico (551), Puerto Rico (17), Canada (196), Argentina (11), Brazil (23), China (19), Korea (9), Germany (95), and the United Kingdom (250). More than 100 million customers per week visit Wal-Mart Stores.

Wal-Mart operates four different retail concepts:

• *Wal-Mart Discount Stores.* Since founder Sam Walton opened his first store in 1962, Wal-Mart has built more than 1,600 discount stores in the United States. The stores range in size from 40,000 to 125,000 square feet and carry 80,000 different items, including family apparel, automotive products, health and beauty aids, home furnishings, electronics, hardware, toys, sporting goods, lawn and garden items, pet supplies, jewelry, and housewares.

• *Wal-Mart Supercenters.* Developed in 1988 to meet the growing demand for one-stop family shopping, Wal-Mart supercenters today number more than 1,050 nationwide and are open twenty-four hours a day. Supercenters save customers time and money by combining full grocery lines and general merchandise under one roof. These units range in size from 109,000 to 230,000 square feet and carry 100,000 different items, 30,000 of which are grocery products.

• *Wal-Mart Neighborhood Markets.* These stores offer groceries, pharmaceuticals, and general merchandise. Generally,

these units are situated in markets with Wal-Mart Supercenters, supplementing a strong food distribution network and providing added convenience while maintaining Wal-Mart's everyday low prices. First opened in 1998, Neighborhood Markets range from 42,000 to 55,000 square feet and feature a wide variety of products, including fresh produce, deli foods, fresh meat and dairy items, health and beauty aids, one-hour photo, and drive-through pharmacies, to name a few.

• *Sam's Clubs.* The nation's leading members-only warehouse club offers a broad selection of general merchandise and large-volume items at value prices. Since 1983, Sam's Club has been the preferred choice for small businesses, families, or anyone looking for great prices on name-brand products. Ranging in size from 110,000 to 130,000 square feet, the 500 Sam's Clubs nationwide offer merchandise for both office and personal use, bulk paper products, furniture, computer hardware and software, groceries, television sets, and clothing. A nominal membership fee ($30 per year for businesses and $35 for individuals) helps defray operating costs and keeps prices exceptionally low.

Shortcomings to Bear in Mind

■ At 192,000 square feet, Wal-Mart Supercenters are about the size of four football fields. Wal-Mart quickly found that some customers have trouble navigating them. According to one shopper, "The stores are too big. It takes too long to get around." On the other hand, the store's "really good prices" keep them coming back, but the shopper warns, "We've just about decided we'll go somewhere else and pay more not to have to go through all the hassle."

■ Wal-Mart, whose trademark policy is "Everyday low prices," has been pricing its merchandise more aggressively in response to heavier discounting from

Kmart, Target, and other competitors. As an offset, it's looking to pare expenses, speed up deliveries, and strengthen its clothing lines. "We are paranoid," said CEO Lee Scott, who, along with other executives, shops competitors once a week. "Everyone is getting better." Mr. Scott, a twenty-two-year Wal-Mart veteran, rose through the ranks to become CEO in January of 2000.

- In the fourth quarter of fiscal 2003 (actually 2002, since only January 2003 is not in 2002), Wal-Mart's Sam's Club division continued to lag behind the rest of the company, posting a fourth-quarter same-store sales gain of only 0.4 percent and a revenue increase of 5.2 percent.

However, results for all of Wal-Mart were most impressive, as revenues for all of 2002 climbed 12.3 percent, and earnings per share shot up 21.5 percent.

Reasons to Buy

- Wal-Mart's success is no secret. The company was named "Retailer of the Century" by *Discount Store News*; made *Fortune* magazine's lists of the "Most Admired Companies in America" and the "100 Best Companies to Work For," and was ranked on the *Financial Times* "Most Respected in the World" list.
- In March of 2002, the company made its first foray into the $3.9-trillion Japanese economy by buying a minority interest in a Japanese retailer, Seiyu, Ltd. Wal-Mart invested $46.5 million to acquire 6.1 percent of Seiyu, the nation's fifth-largest supermarket chain, with $8.5 billion in annual sales.

However, this is just the beginning. Wal-Mart could eventually raise its stake to 66.7 percent. "The retail industry has been in a very difficult state for the last few years," said Masao Kiuchi, president of the Japanese company. "We have been restructuring and making dramatic changes, but we thought it was necessary to find a strong business partner like Wal-Mart."

- Wal-Mart makes a concerted effort to find out precisely what its customers want. To do this, the company relies on information technology. It does this by collecting and analyzing internally developed information, which it calls "data-mining." It has been doing this since 1990.

The result, by now, is an enormous database of purchasing information that enables management to place the right item in the right store at the right time. The company's computer system receives 8.4 million updates every minute on the items that customers take home—and the relationship between the items in each basket.

Many retailers talk a good game when it comes to mining data at cash registers as a way to build sales. Wal-Mart, since it has been doing this for the past dozen years, is sitting on an information trove so vast and detailed that it far exceeds what many manufacturers know about their own products. What's more, Wal-Mart's database is second in size only to that of the U.S. government, says one analyst. Wal-Mart also collects "market-basket data" from customer receipts at all of its stores, so it knows what products are likely to be purchased together. The company receives about 100,000 queries a week from suppliers and its own buyers looking for purchase patterns or checking a product.

Wal-Mart plans to use the data in its new Neighborhood Markets. Equipped with a drive-through pharmacy and selling both dry goods and perishables, the stores are a little smaller than typical suburban supermarkets. They are much smaller than Wal-Mart's Supercenters, the massive grocery-discount store combinations that Wal-Mart began opening in 1987.

This kind of information has significant value in and of itself. According to management, "Consider Wal-Mart's ability to keep the shelves stocked with exactly what customers want most, but still be able to keep inventories under tight control. Consider the common banana—so common, in fact, that the grocery carts of America contain bananas more often than any other single item. So why not make it easy for a shopper to remember bananas? In Wal-Mart grocery departments, bananas can be found not just in the produce section, but in the cereal and dairy aisles too."

- Wal-Mart has learned some painful lessons about consumers, regulators, and suppliers around the world. Through trial and error, the company has quietly built a powerful force outside the United States. It's now the biggest retailer in Canada and Mexico.

- The bankruptcy of Kmart creates fresh opportunities for Wal-Mart to lure to its aisle price-conscious shoppers.

Total assets: $94,552 million
Current ratio: 0.90
Common shares outstanding: 4,423 million
Return on 2002 shareholders' equity: 20.5%

		2002	2001	2000	1999	1998	1997	1996	1995
Revenues (millions)		244,524	217,799	191,329	165,013	137,634	117,958	104,859	93,627
Net income (millions)		8,039	6,671	6,295	5,377	4,430	3,526	3,056	2,740
Earnings per share		1.81	1.49	1.40	1.28	0.99	0.78	0.67	0.60
Dividends per share		.30	.28	.24	.20	0.16	0.14	0.11	0.10
Price	High	63.9	58.8	68.9	70.3	41.4	21.0	14.2	13.8
	Low	43.7	41.5	41.4	38.7	18.8	11.0	9.6	10.2

INCOME

Washington Real Estate Investment Trust

6110 Executive Boulevard □ Suite 800 □ Rockville, Maryland 20852 □ (301) 984-9400 □ Listed: NYSE □ Direct dividend reinvestment plan is available: (877) 386-8123 □ Web site: www.writ.com □ Ticker symbol: WRE □ S&P rating: Not rated □ Value Line Financial Strength B++

In January of 2003, Washington Real Estate Investment Trust (WRIT) announced that it had acquired Fullerton Industrial Center for $10.55 million. The Fullerton property is a three-building industrial holding in Springfield, Virginia.

Fullerton contains 137,405 rentable square feet and is 100 percent leased to sixteen tenants. The complex is situated in the fully completed Fullerton Industrial Park, which contains about 1.7 million square feet in forty-eight buildings, with a very attractive 1.5 percent vacancy rate.

Washington has significant industrial property holdings nearby, including Fullerton Business Center (103,692 square feet), Alban Business Center (86,684 square feet), and Northern Virginia Industrial Park (820,225 square feet). The company now owns twenty-one industrial buildings in the Springfield/Newington submarket, containing more than 1 million square feet. These properties, which are 94.2 percent leased, give Washington Real Estate Investment Trust significant synergistic leasing opportunities to accommodate the changing needs of the more than 120 tenants located at these properties.

Company Profile

Washington Real Estate Investment Trust, founded in 1960, invests in a diversified range of income-producing properties. Management's purpose is to acquire and manage real-estate investments in markets it knows well and to protect the company's assets from the risk of owning a single property-type, such as apartments, office buildings, industrial parks, or shopping centers.

The trust achieves its objectives by owning properties in four different categories. Its properties are primarily situated within a two-hour radius of Washington, D.C., that stretches from Philadelphia in the north to Richmond, Virginia, in the south. Its diversified portfolio at the end of 2002 consisted of 60 properties: 24 office buildings, 11 retail shopping centers, 9 multifamily properties, and 16 industrial properties.

Shortcomings to Bear in Mind

- Although Washington is well diversified by type of property, it is not diversified geographically, since all of its holdings are within a two-hour radius of Washington, D.C. In the event of a serious disaster in that region, Washington Real Estate Investment Trust might have problems. By contrast, many REITS have scores of properties across the United States, thus shielding them from hard times or natural disasters in any one location.

Reasons to Buy

- Not surprisingly, 2002 was not a great year for most companies, including Washington Real Estate Investment Trust. CEO Edmund B. Cronin, Jr., summed up the year: "We are proud to announce our thirtieth consecutive year of increased FFO per share. In this economy, our geographic focus, diversified real estate portfolio, and conservative balance sheet are serving us well.

Our office and industrial properties have been adversely affected by the soft economy, while the apartment and retail properties are performing well. Furthermore, WRIT's dividend remains secure."

- Mr. Cronin is convinced that Washington Real Estate Investment Trust has lower risk than most investments. "One aspect of this lower risk profile is that the greater Washington-Baltimore technology sector achieves 38 percent of its sales to the federal government, as compared to 5 percent in Silicon Valley. That, along with the fact that federal government spending will continue to grow, provides a platform for a soft landing in this region."

- The economy of greater Washington, D.C., is a unique blend of "old economy" service companies and "new economy" high-technology growth companies, anchored by the very significant federal government presence. The following opportunities are on the growth side:

  - Washington Dulles International Airport and Baltimore-Washington International Airport were ranked number one and two in passenger growth in 1999, the most recent year for which data are available.

  - The greater-D.C. region ranks first in the United States in high-tech and bio-tech employment.

  - George Mason University Center for Regional Analysis (GMU) projects economic growth in the region of 4.1 percent in 2001, which is substantially higher than is projected for the nation as a whole.

  - Federal spending in this region has increased every year for twenty-one consecutive years, even in years when federal spending has decreased nationally. GMU projects that federal spending in the region will grow by 3 percent per year.

While growth is very important, from an investment perspective, economic stability is equally important. In this context, no other region in the country can compete with the greater-D.C. region.

- Federal government spending accounts for 31 percent of the area's gross regional product.
- The greater-D.C. region is not exposed to new or old economy manufacturing fluctuations.
- Washington, D.C., and the surrounding region are home to thirty-two colleges and universities, several of which have world-class reputations at both the undergraduate and graduate levels.

■ MAE East, situated in Tysons Corner, Virginia, is one of only two Internet convergence centers in the United States. The presence of MAE East and the thousands of high-tech firms in the area has spawned a concentration of data centers in the region where large Internet and other high-tech firms process tremendous amounts of data. As a result, it is estimated that up to 60 percent of the world's Internet traffic flows through Northern Virginia.

This concentration of high-tech companies has served to attract even more high-tech firms. Amazon.com, Cisco Systems, and Global Crossing have all set up shop in the Washington-Baltimore market.

The region's real-estate markets are the beneficiary of this growth. Vacancies are extremely low, and rental rate growth is very strong.

■ Prior to acquiring a property, Washington Real Estate Investment Trust performs extensive inspections, tests, and financial analyses to gain confidence about the property's future operating performance, to learn about any required near-term improvements, and

to forecast long-term capital expenditures. Upon completion of this evaluation, the company develops well-informed operating projections for the property. Accordingly, when the company announces an acquisition and its anticipated return on investment, it is confident that the property will meet or exceed its projections.

■ Washington Real Estate Investment Trust has always recognized the value of capital improvements to remain competitive, increase revenues, reduce operating costs, and maintain and increase the value of its properties.

■ A common REIT industry performance measure is core portfolio net-operating income (NOI) growth or same-store NOI growth. NOI represents real-estate portfolio income before interest expense, depreciation, and corporate general and administrative expenses.

Core portfolio NOI growth excludes income attributable to new acquisitions and developments and is therefore a good measure of how a company's existing portfolio performed in the most recent period, as compared to the prior period. WRIT's core portfolio NOI growth is among the highest in the industry and dramatically higher than the REIT industry overall. Using this measure, Washington Real Estate had average annual growth of 8.5 percent in the past three years, compared with the industry's 5.6 percent.

■ The company has a long history of dividend increases. It has paid 165 consecutive quarterly dividends at equal or increasing rates. What's more, WRIT dividends have increased every year for thirty-two consecutive years. During these thirty-two years, the company's dividends have increased thirty-seven times, a record unmatched by any other publicly traded real estate investment trust.

■ "High, and likely growing, federal expenditures in the Washington, D.C., region should keep it healthy for real estate," said Sigourney B. Romaine, an analyst with *Value Line Investment Survey*, on January 24, 2003. "Since the 1990s, the capital region has always had less unemployment than the national average, and the present is no exception. We think the federal presence will continue to insulate the region's economy from the business cycle. And its high technology industries will probably start to add to, rather than subtract from, real estate demand by sometime next year."

Total assets: $756 million
Current ratio: not relevant
Return on 2002 equity: 15%
Common shares outstanding: 39 million

	2002	2001	2000	1999	1998	1997	1996	1995
Revenues (millions)	153	148	135	119	104	79	66	53
Net income (millions)	52	52	45	44	41	30	28	26
Funds from operations	1.97	1.96	1.79	1.57	1.39	1.23	1.13	1.05
Earnings per share	1.32	1.38	1.16	1.02	.96	.90	.88	.88
Dividends per share	1.39	1.31	1.23	1.16	1.11	1.07	1.03	.99
Price High	30.2	25.5	25.0	18.8	18.8	19.6	17.5	16.6
Low	20.4	20.8	14.3	13.8	15.1	15.5	15.3	13.9

INCOME

Weingarten Realty Investors

2600 Citadel Plaza Drive □ Post Office Box 924133 □ Houston, Texas 77292-4133 □ (713) 866-6050 □ Direct dividend reinvestment program available: (888) 887-2966 □ Web site: www.weingarten.com □ Listed: NYSE □ Ticker symbol: WRI □ S&P rating: not rated □ Value Line financial strength rating: B++

"Through the successful execution of our longstanding strategy of enhancing our existing properties and growing the portfolio through selective acquisitions and new developments, we have once again increased the dividend to our common shareholders, something we have accomplished each of the seventeen years we have been a public company," said Weingarten's CEO Drew Alexander in February of 2003. "Additionally, Weingarten provided a total return for the year (stock price appreciation and dividends paid) of 22.1 percent for our shareholders."

Mr. Alexander also noted that the company made a significant expansion in the Raleigh, North Carolina, market with the acquisition of eight supermarket-anchored shopping centers. Weingarten also purchased four properties in Florida, and one each in the Dallas, Texas; Denver, Colorado; and Los Angeles, California markets. All of these acquisitions were supermarket-anchored properties, which Mr. Alexander commented is consistent with the growth strategy of the company. Total acquisitions for 2002 aggregated 2.5-million square feet and represent a total investment of $247.7 million, with a projected stabilized return of more than 9.7 percent.

Company Profile

Weingarten Realty Investors is an equity-based real estate investment trust (REIT). The company focuses primarily on the development, acquisition, and long-term ownership of anchored neighborhood and community shopping centers and, to a lesser degree, industrial properties.

At the end of 2002, the Weingarten portfolio included 303 income-producing properties in eighteen states that spanned the southern half of the United States, from coast to coast. Included in the portfolio are 245 neighborhood and community shopping centers, fifty-seven industrial properties, and one office building aggregating 38.4 million square feet.

Founded in 1948, Weingarten restructured itself into a real estate investment trust and was listed on the New York Stock Exchange in 1985. Its performance as a public company has been among the best in the industry. This is a product of fifty years of real-estate experience (in both growth and recessionary cycles), combined with a seasoned management team focused on specific segments of real estate. In addition to developing and acquiring properties, Weingarten adds value to them through consistent, high-quality operations that incorporate renovation, retailer recycling, and ongoing asset management.

Company History

Weingarten Realty Investors was founded in 1948 with two part-time employees, $60,000 in cash, and a portfolio of supermarket buildings totaling 51,000 square feet. The company was created to develop freestanding stores for J. Weingarten, Inc., a fast-growing grocery chain that was owned by the Weingarten family.

In addition to developing the stores, the company was charged with the responsibility of acquiring raw land for future development and expansion. As a result, management was in an ideal position to take advantage of the trend to develop "clusters of stores" as the evolution of the "shopping center" concept began to take shape in the early 1950s.

As Weingarten began its new course, it focused on the neighborhood and community shopping center that ranged in size from 100,000 to 400,000 square feet and was "anchored" primarily by supermarkets. This practice is still continued today, with the company also focusing on certain industrial properties as well.

In 1980, the J. Weingarten supermarket chain was sold, and the realty company began to diversify and expand its relationships with other grocers and general retailers throughout the United States. Today, it boasts a diversified tenant roster of more than 2,900 different tenants, many with multiple locations. During the fifty-three years of Weingarten's existence, the company has emerged as one of the largest REITs listed on the NYSE. Its portfolio has expanded from those original four properties to a total of 303 at year-end 2002. The company's square footage has increased from 51,000 to nearly 38.4 million, and the company has expanded its holdings from one city and one state to fifty-seven cities in eighteen states. Likewise, Weingarten's revenue, funds from operations, and dividends have increased significantly over its fifteen years of being a REIT.

Funds from Operations—A Definition

Investors in common stock use "net income" as a key measure of profitability. However, in measuring a REIT, most investors prefer the term "funds from operations," or FFO. This is because earnings and expenses of a real estate investment trust must be looked at differently.

The Securities and Exchange Commission has a blanket requirement that all publicly traded companies file audited financial statements. On a financial statement, the term "net income" has a meaning clearly defined under generally accepted accounting principles. Since a REIT falls under the classification of a publicly traded company, net income therefore appears on a REIT's audited financial statement.

For a REIT, on the other hand, this figure is less meaningful as a measure of operating success than it is for other types of corporations. The reason is that, in accounting, real-estate "depreciation" is always treated as an expense. In the real world, most well-maintained quality properties have retained their value over the years. This is because of rising land values. In other words, it is because of steadily rising rental income, property upgrades, or higher costs for new construction for competing properties. Whatever the reason, a REIT's net income, since it suffers from a large depreciation expense, is a less-than-meaningful measure of how a REIT's operations have actually fared. It is because of this reasoning that FFO is often a better way to judge a real estate investment trust than traditional net income. You will note that I have used this alternative term in the table at the end of the article.

Shortcomings to Bear in Mind

- Weingarten Realty Investors is primarily an income stock, which often yields 6 percent or more. In terms of growth, however, it is not exciting. In the 1992–2002 period, funds from operations advanced from $1.57 to $3.28, a compound annual growth rate of only 7.6 percent. Similarly, dividends during this ten-year span advanced from $1.36 to $2.22, a growth rate of 5.0 percent.
- There is no way to avoid risk completely. Real-estate ownership and management, like any other business, is subject to all sorts of risks. Mall REITs, for instance, are subject to the changing tastes and lifestyles of consumers.

Reasons to Buy

- "The shares continue to perform well in a difficult market environment, due to heightened investor interest in the stability of grocery-anchored strip center returns," said Raymond Mathis, an analyst with *Standard & Poor's Stock Reports*, in October of 2002. "However, this enthusiasm has been tempered by the high profile bankruptcies of some major retailers. While the shares of some peers have been pressured, WRI's low exposure to Kmart has helped its stock outperform.

"Although the 5.9 percent dividend yield is lower than the REIT industry average, a robust growth rate compensates for this. The dividend was raised 5.4 percent with the March 2002 payment, and a three-for-two stock split was effected in April. We expect 2003 EPS growth to enhance the security of the dividend and allow for future dividend increases. We view the shares, trading at a discount to peer earnings multiples and to our dividend discount valuation, as attractive for total return."

- Similarly, the analyst with *Value Line Investment Survey*, Milton Schlein, had a favorable comment in January of 2003. "Many investors will find merit in Weingarten stock. Those who stress current income will be impressed with the issue's yield. Based on our expectations of a 5 percent rise in the payout in March (2003), the yield is far above that of most income vehicles. And, unlike bonds, and other fixed-payment instruments, the dividend will likely continue to rise annually, following a pattern that goes back many years."

- With respect to new development, Weingarten had twenty shopping centers in various stages of development. These properties will add 1.9 million square feet to the portfolio and will represent a total investment upon completion of $269.2 million, with a projected stabilized return in excess of 10 percent. The company anticipates that these developments will come online by the end of 2003.

- In early 2003, Mr. Alexander noted that

the company's portfolio of neighborhood and community shopping centers remain quite stable due to the tenant base "of our retailers that provide basic everyday necessities for the consumer."

Occupancy rates were 91.7 percent, down slightly from 92.2 percent at the end of 2001, but up from the third quarter 2002 occupancy rate of 91.4 percent. The company also reported the completion of 1,301 new leases or renewals for the year, totaling 5.1 million square feet. Rental rates increased an average of 8.2 percent on a same-space basis. Net of capital costs, the average increase was 5.6 percent.

Total assets: $2,424 million
Current ratio: NM*
Common shares outstanding: 52 million
Return on 2002 shareholders' equity: 14.2%

	2002	2001	2000	1999	1998	1997	1996	1995
Rental income (millions)	365	309	243	223	195	169	145	125
Net income(millions)	131.9	108.5	79.0	96.3	61.8	55.0	53.9	44.8
Funds from operations	3.28	3.05	2.83	2.62	2.40	2.21	2.06	1.88
Dividends per share	2.22	2.11	2.00	1.89	1.79	1.71	1.65	1.60
Price High	39.2	33.8	30.0	30.4	31.3	30.4	27.2	25.7
Low	29.3	25.9	23.1	24.7	23.9	25.9	22.9	22.3

* Not meaningful

Index of Stocks by Category

Aggressive Growth
Alcoa
Automatic Data
AutoZone
Baxter International
Biomet, Inc.
Boeing
Brinker International
Cardinal Health
Cintas
Costco Wholesale
Craftmade
DeVry
Ecolab
Ethan Allen
Family Dollar Stores
FedEx Corporation
Gillette
Harman International
Health Mgt. Assoc.
Intel
Int'l Business Machines
  (IBM)
Lennar Corporation
Lilly, Eli
Lockheed Martin
Medtronic
Microsoft
Newell Rubbermaid
Oshkosh Truck
Patterson Dental
Pfizer
Scholastic Corp.
Scripps, E. W.
Staples
Stryker
Target
Toll Brothers
United Parcel Service (UPS)
Varian Medical
Walgreen
Wal-Mart

Conservative Growth
Abbott Laboratories
Air Products
Alberto-Culver
Anheuser-Busch
Avery Dennison
Bard, C.R.
Becton, Dickinson
Bemis Company
Block, H&R
Brown-Forman
Coca-Cola
Colgate-Palmolive
Darden Restaurants
Donaldson
Gannett
Grainger, W. W.
Hormel Foods
Illinois Tool Works
Johnson Controls
Johnson & Johnson
Leggett & Platt
Lowe's Companies
McCormick & Co.
McGraw-Hill
Meredith
The New York Times
PepsiCo
Praxair
Procter & Gamble
Reynolds & Reynolds
Ruby Tuesday
Sysco Corporation
Tractor Supply
UnitedHealth
United Technologies

Growth & Income
3M Company
Banta
Caterpillar
Clorox
Emerson Electric
Fortune Brands
General Electric
General Motors
Lancaster Colony
La-Z-Boy
Merck
MDU Resources
National City
Pitney Bowes
RPM International

Income
Boston Properties
Cedar Fair
ConAgra
Dominion Resources
Equity Office Properties
Genuine Parts
Kimco Realty
Piedmont Natural Gas
Washington Real Estate
Weingarten Realty

About the Author

John Slatter has a varied investment background and has served as a stock broker, securities analyst, and portfolio strategist. He is now a consultant with Prim Asset Management, a firm in Cleveland, Ohio, that manages investment portfolios on a fee basis.

Mr. Slatter has written hundreds of articles for such publications as *Barron's, Physician's Management, Ophthalmology Times,* and *Better Investing,* as well as for brokerage firms he has worked for, including Hugh Johnson & Company and Wachovia Securities. His books include: *Safe Investing, Straight Talk About Stock Investing,* and seven prior editions of *The 100 Best Stocks You Can Buy.*

Mr. Slatter has also been quoted in such periodicals as the *Cleveland Plain Dealer,* the *New York Times,* the *Gannett News Service,* the *Burlington Free Press,* the *Wall Street Journal,* the *Cincinnati Enquirer,* the *Toledo Blade,* the *Christian Science Monitor, Money* magazine, the *Dayton Daily News,* and the *Buffalo News.* He has been quoted in a number of books, including *The Dividend Investor* and *Stocks for the Long Run,* and he has also been interviewed by a number of radio stations, as well as by the daily television program, CNBC (Today's Business).

In August of 1988, John Slatter was featured in the *Wall Street Journal* concerning his innovative investment strategy that calls for investing in the ten highest-yielding stocks in the Dow Jones Industrial Average. This approach to stock selection is sometimes referred as *The Dogs of the Dow,* a pejorative reference that Mr. Slatter does *not* believe is justified, since the stocks with high yields have, in the past, included such blue chips as Merck, IBM, 3M, General Electric, AT&T, Caterpillar, DuPont, ExxonMobil, J. P. Morgan Chase, and Altria Group.

John Slatter may be reached by calling (802) 879-4154 (during business hours only) or by writing him at 70 Beech Street, Essex Junction, Vermont 05452. His e-mail address is *john.slatter@verizon.net* and his fax number is (802) 878-1171.